THE

PUBLICATIONS

OF THE

SURTEES SOCIETY

ESTABLISHED IN THE YEAR

M.DCCC.XXXIV.

VOL. XXXVI.

FOR THE YEAR M.DCCC.LIX.

LONDON:
J. B. NICHOLS AND SONS, PRINTERS,
25, PARLIAMENT STREET.

THE VISITATION OF THE COUNTY OF YORKE,

BEGUN IN

A° DÑI MDCLXV.

AND FINISHED

A° DÑI MDCLXVI.

BY WILLIAM DUGDALE, ESQ^R,

NORROY KING OF ARMES.

Published for the Society

BY GEORGE ANDREWS, DURHAM;

WHITTAKER & Co. 13, AVE MARIA LANE; T. & W. BOONE,

29, NEW BOND STREET, LONDON;

BLACKWOOD AND SONS, EDINBURGH.

AT a MEETING of the COUNCIL of the SURTEES SOCIETY, held in the Castle of Durham on the 11th of March, 1858,

"IT WAS ORDERED, That DUGDALE'S VISITATION of YORKSHIRE should form one of the publications of the SOCIETY for 1859, and that it should be edited by Mr. DAVIES of York."

And at a similar MEETING on the 25th of February, 1859,

"IT WAS ORDERED, That a volume of HERALDIC VISITATIONS should be the only publication of the SOCIETY for the current year."

JAMES RAINE, *Secretary.*

PREFACE.

THE volume presented this year to the Surtees Society contains "The heraldic visitation of the county of York," made by Sir William Dugdale, then Norroy King of Arms, in the years 1665 and 1666. This valuable genealogical record is now for the first time printed entire from a copy in the handwriting of the late Dr. Raine, collated by the editor with Dugdale's original copy which has been for many years the property of Miss Currer of Eshton Hall, who has most kindly and liberally allowed the Society the use of it for this purpose.

Miss Currer's "noble" MS., as it has been justly designated by a high authority,* was stated in the proposals issued by a late accomplished genealogist † for publishing "Dugdale's Heraldic Visitation of Yorkshire with additions," to be the "only perfect copy out of the Heralds' College." It forms a large folio volume, consisting of nearly 300 leaves of paper, and containing the pedigrees of 472 families, a pen-

* Sir Charles George Young, Garter.

† William Radclyffe, Esq.

and-ink drawing in trick of the armorial bearings of each family being placed at the head of the pedigree.

A small part of the contents of the volume is believed to be in the handwriting of Sir William Dugdale himself, but the greater number of the pedigrees, and of the shields of arms which are executed with much artistic spirit and elegance, are undoubtedly the work of Gregory King, afterwards Lancaster Herald, who was in Dugdale's service and accompanied him in all his visitations of the Northern counties. Sir William Dugdale appears to have retained possession of the MS. until he was created Garter King of Arms in April 1677. A few days after his promotion he presented the volume to Sir Henry St.George, his successor in the office of Norroy, who was at a later period advanced to the rank of Garter, and died in the year 1715. It was probably upon his death that the MS. passed into the possession of Robert Dale, who at that time was Blanch Lyon Pursuivant and Deputy Registrar of the College of Arms, and, it is said, had accompanied Sir Henry St.George when Clarencieux in some of his visitations.

A few months before his death, which happened in April 1722, Robert Dale was created Richmond Herald, and a son of his appears to have been the next possessor of the MS. The Dales sprang from a Yorkshire family of the agricultural class settled at Great Smeaton, a parish on the banks of the Tees, a few miles distant from Darlington, and this fact may perhaps diminish our surprise upon finding that during the latter part of the last century the volume had passed into the hands of a person in humble circumstances residing at Darlington, by whom it was offered for sale to the late George Allan, Esquire, the well known antiquary. Mr. Allan declined purchasing the MS., but took the opportunity of making a copy of it for his own use, and of this copy, which is now in the Library of the Dean and Chapter of Durham, he subsequently permitted several transcripts to be taken, one of which was made by the late Rev. James Raine, D.C.L., whose loss the Surtees Society has so much reason to deplore.

In the year 1797 the MS. was bought by the late Sir Mark Masterman Sykes, Baronet, of a Mr. W. Prince of York; and in the year 1824, when Sir M. M. Sykes's collections were dispersed by public auction, it was added to the treasures of Miss Currer's splendid library.

In transcribing and collating the present volume for the press, the Editor has been anxious that it should contain a faithful reproduction of Dugdale's MS. The peculiarities of the orthography, and especially the irregularities in the spelling of the names of persons and places, are scrupulously retained. A few errors of fact which have crept into some of the pedigrees are so obvious and unimportant that it seemed unnecessary to attempt any correction of them.

To those members of the Surtees Society who are acquainted with the localities it may not be uninteresting to trace the route taken by the illustrious herald in his Visitation of the great county of York nearly two centuries ago. On the 1st of August, 1665, Sir William Dugdale commenced his sittings at Doncaster, and during the former half of the month he held courts at Barnsley, Pontefract, Leeds, Knaresborough, and Skipton. From Skipton he crossed the mountainous country which divides the West and North Ridings, and on the 18th of August he arrived at Richmond, where he was occupied three or four days. Thence he passed to Thirsk, Stokesley, and Malton. Leaving Malton on the 30th of August he entered upon his Visitation of the East Riding at a small market town in the heart of the wolds called Kilham, where his court was attended by the heads of nearly twenty families then flourishing in the surrounding district, a few of which are still among the most distinguished of the gentry of that part of Yorkshire—the Boyntons, the Grimstones, the Legards, the Osbaldestons.

Besides Kilham, the only East Riding towns visited by Dugdale in this journey were Hull and Pocklington. On the 9th of September he commenced his sittings at York,* and remained there several days, his courts being attended by the gentry of the city and the immediate neighbourhood, and by many from more distant parts of the county. On the 14th of September he again sat at Doncaster, and from thence

* At the George Inn in Coney Street.

paid a second visit to Barnsley. On the 16th of September he sat at Rotherham, where he concluded the Visitation of this year.

In the spring of the following year Sir William Dugdale resumed his Visitation of Yorkshire. On the 14th of March, 1665-6, he set out from his own house, Blythe Hall in Warwickshire, and proceeded straight to York, where, on the 19th, he commenced his sittings, and was occupied several days in recording the genealogies of nearly forty families whose representatives attended his summonses from all parts of the county. From York he went to Ripon, where it does not appear that he transacted any business, and thence to Skipton. The pedigrees of the two families of Currer of Skipton and Currer of Kildwick seem to be the only results of his sitting at Skipton on this occasion. Whilst he was in this district he passed a few days with his friend and brother-antiquary Charles Fairfax esquire at his house at Menston near Otley; and on the 1st of April he was at Halifax, a town he had not previously visited. Thence he went to Leeds, Wakefield, Pontefract, Doncaster, and Sheffield. From Sheffield he returned home.

In the month of August Dugdale entered upon his Visitation of the counties of Durham and Northumberland; and on his way through Yorkshire he sat a few days at York. In September he returned into Yorkshire. On the 8th he was at Stokesley, and on the 10th at Malton. Thence he crossed the East

Riding wolds to Beverley, resting a night at the "Golden Gryphon," at Kilham. After he left Beverley a few pedigrees appear to have been taken at Hull and Malton, but it may be inferred that Norroy himself went from Beverley to visit Lord Fairfax at Nun-Appleton,* where he arrived on the 17th of September. On the 21st he was again at his own residence in Warwickshire.

When Sir William Dugdale undertook his Heraldic Visitation of the Northern Counties he had passed the sixtieth year of his age. Yet all his journeys—and he must have traversed many a wild moor and rugged valley—were performed on horseback. His only companions were his two clerks, one of whom was Gregory King, then a youth of seventeen or eighteen years, but already remarkable for his skill in the transcribing of pedigrees, and the tricking and depicting of armorial bearings.†

It is evident that in the earlier years of the Restoration the pride of family was not universally prevalent in the county of York. Nearly one-third of the whole number of gentry whom the herald called upon to appear before him with proofs of their arms and pedigrees treated his summonses with neglect. The following precept, which was not issued by Dugdale until two years after he had concluded his Visitation

* He notes in his Diary that at this time he "borrowed of my Lord Fairfax 18 manuscript bookes which were Mr. Dodsworth's, whereof 15 are in folio and 3 in 4to."—Hamper's Life, p. 124.

† See the life of Gregory King, in Dallaway's Heraldry, p. xxix.

of Yorkshire, gives us a list of the persons who were contumacious.

To the High Sheriff of the County of York.

Whereas the King's most excellent Majesty, being desireous that the Nobility of this his Realm should be preserved in each degree as well in hon[r] as in worship, and that every person and persons, bodies politic and corporate, and others, should be known in their states and mysteries without confusion and disorder, hath authorised me, William Dugdale, Esq[re], Norroy King of Armes of the North East and West parts of this his Realm of England, not only to visit all the said province, and to peruse, take knowledge and . . . . . of all manner of Arms, Cognizances, Crests, and other like devices, with the notes of the Descents, Pedigrees, and Marriages of all the Gentry therein contained, but also to reprove, control, and make infamous by Proclamation all such as unlawfully and without just authority, vocation, or due calling do, or have done, or shall usurp or take upon him or them any name or title of honour or dignity, as Esquire, Gentleman, or other, forbidding also and straitly comanding all his Shireves, Commissioners, Archdeacons, Officials, Scriveners, Clerks, Writers, or other whatsoever they be, to call, name, or write in any Assize, Sessions Court, or other open place or places, or to use in any writing the addition of Esquire or Gentleman to any person or persons within this my province abovementioned, unless they be able to stand unto and justify the same by Law of Arms of this his Realm, or else be ascertained thereof by advertizement in writing from me the said Norroy King of Arms, my Deputy or Deputies, Attorney or Attornies, in that behalf, as by his said Majesties Commision, under the Great Seale of England, more fully doth appear.

Know ye therefore that I, the said Norroy, in pursuance and accomplishment of his said Majesties desire, and furtherance of his service herein, having in my last visit within this County of York, by due summons, required the persons whose names are hereunto annext, to shew unto me by what right they do use and bear any such Arms, Cognizances, and Crests as above . . . . . . and take upon them those titles and dignities of Esq[re] or Gentleman, and having received no sufficient proof of such their right thereunto, and my own justifycation for allowance thereof according to the trust reposed in me by his said Majesty in that behalf, but that they have presumptuously usurped the same without any good ground or authority, contrary to all right, and to the ancient and laudable custome of this Realm and usage of the Law of Arms, do hereby declare that from henceforth they are not to use those Arms and Titles, upon such further pain and peril as by the Earl Marshal of England, or his Majesties most Hon[ble] Commissioners for the executing of that office, may be inflicted upon them; wherefore (in pursuance of his Majesties further pleasure signified in his Commission) I have thought fit hereby to advertize you and all other his Majesties good and loyall subjects of this County, that as you and they tender his said Majesties pleasure herein, from henceforth you forbear in any writing or otherwise to attribute unto them those additions of Esquire or Gentleman, until the said persons so assuming those titles shall stand to or justifye the same by the Law of Arms of this his Majesties Realm, or that you be ascertained thereof in writing by advertisement from me the said Norroy King of Arms, or my lawful Deputy or Deputies, Attorney or Attorneys in that behalf. Given at the Office of Arms, &c. this 24th day of November, 20th Charles 2[d] (1668).

WILLM. DUGDALE,
Norroy King of Arms.

LIST.

Wapentakes.	Residence.	Persons' Names
	EAST RIDING.	
Baynton Beacon	Beverley	Mr. Tho. Johnson.
"	"	Mr. Rob[t] Bethell.
"	"	Mr. Blunt.
"	Emswall	John Best.
"	Hugett	Mr. Catterell.
"	Middleton	Mr. Crouche.
"	North Dalton	Mr. Ramsden.
Buckrose	Bugthorpe	Paler Wolfe.
Dickering	Besonby cum Eston	Rich[d] Staveley.
"	Frasthorpe	Nich. Woodhouse.
"	Nassenton	Mr. Lukins.
"	Thwing	Mr. Rob[t] Stafford sleighted the Summons.

Wapentakes.	Residence.	Persons' Names.
Hunsley Beacon . .	Hotham	Mr. Gill.
Wilton Beacon . . .	South Cave	John Belton.
North Bayliwick of Holderness	Skypsey	Leon^d Aclam.
D^o Middle Bayliwick .	Hinton cum Etherwick	Marke Greene.
Ouse and Darwent .	South Duffeild . . .	Willm Hadlersey.
,,	Hemingbrough . . .	John Bacon.
,,	Kexby	Fran. Forbusher.
South Bayliwick of Holderness	Skefling	Edwd Bee.
,,	Easington	Willm Overton.
	West Riding.	
Claro	Azerley	Willm Dawson.
,,	Aldfeild	Char. Elsley.
,,	Kirk Dighton . . .	Abra. Thornton.
,,	Green Hamerton . .	John Weedall.
,,	Kirkby	Mr. Gale.
,,	,,	Mr. Dodson.
,,	,,	Fra. Steele.
,,	Kirkby Malsard . .	Benj. Brown.
,,	,,	Timo. Horsman.
,,	Kirkby Hall . . .	Tho. Dickenson.
,,	Knaresborough . . .	Simon Warrener.
,,	,,	John Scot.
,,	,,	Richd Rhodes.
,,	Nun Monkton . . .	John Tindall.
,,	Newhall in Chifton .	Will'm Hardesty.
,,	Wetherby	John Wood.
,,	,,	John Catherall.
Staincross	Ardesley	Richd Mawde.
,,	Barnsley	Robt Daniell.
,,	,,	Richd Taylor.
,,	Bentley	John Allot.
,,	Brearley	Geo. Holgate.
,,	Dodworth	Mr. Senior.
,,	,,	Mr. Brook.

Wapentakes.	Residence.	Persons' Names.
Staincross	Hunsworth	Tho. Ramsden.
"	"	Mr. Wrightson.
"	Gunthwayt	Mr. Sedasone.
"	Peniston	Josiah Wordsworth.
"	Wolley	Edw. Prince.
"	Clayton	Thos Clayton.
"	"	Richd Allot.
"	Monk Bretton . . .	John Crooke.
"	"	Robt Wood.
"	"	Geo. Cooper.
Staincliff & Ewcross .	Appletreewick . . .	John Winterburne.
"	Coniston	Tho. Warde.
"	Coniston Cold . . .	Josiah Warde.
"	East Halton	Robt Glover.
"	Ingleton	Antho. Booth.
"	Gisburne	Henry Marsden.
"	Kildwick	John Coates.
"	Steeton	Willm Garford.
"	Slaidburne	John Marsden.
Strafford & Tickhill .	Attercliff	Nich. Shircliff.
"	Doncaster	Mr. Webster.
"	Darfeild	Mr. Dixson.
"	Barnshall	Benjn Watts.
"	Eccleshall	Hen. Bright.
"	Hansworth	Mr. Frippet.
"	Maltby	Thos Marshall.
"	Truslow	Mr. Burrows.
"	Tickhill	John Hyman.
"	Thorne	Mr. Forster.
"	Warmesworth . . .	Mr. Childers.
Osgodcross	Croule	Geo. Empson
"	Hundell	Geo. Abbot.
"	Kellington	Mr. Heyworth.
"	Norton Priory . . .	John Rowe.
"	Pollington	John Crathorne.
"	Pontefract	Robt Tatham, ald.
"	"	Tho. Fulwood.

Wapentakes.	Residence.	Persons' Names.
Osgodcross	Pontefract	Mr. Athendon.
"	"	Tho Jackson, ald.
"	"	Geo. Shilito, ald.
"	"	Willm Oates.
"	Upton	Fra. Day.
"	Whitgift	John Stevenson.
"	"	Mr. Poutler.
Barkstone Ash . . .	Bramham cum Oglethorpe	Hen. Drewell.
"	Burton Salmon . . .	Thos Norman.
"	Cawood	Willm Smith.
"	"	Will'm Rowden.
"	"	Mr. Richardson.
"	Fairborne	Mr. Spinke.
"	Hambleton	Mr. Woodall.
"	Lotherton & Aberforth	Mr. Plant.
"	"	Mr. Lekringall.
"	"	Geo. Rodes.
"	Selby	Mr. Dawtrey.
"	"	Mr. Morrwood.
"	"	Mr. Frith.
"	"	Mr. Curlew.
"	Tadcaster	Willm Marshall.
"	Wistow	Thos Bate.
Skyrack	Adell cum Ecup . .	Fran. Wood.
"	Bingley	Abra. Binns.
"	Collingham	Willm Chambers.
"	Garforth	Mr. Brook.
"	Horsforth	Antho. Saxton.
"	Morkton	James Morgateride.
"	Rawden	Francis Rawden.
"	Newsome	Jam. Dawson.
Aggbrigg & Morley .	Croston	Tho. Potter.
"	Emley	John Allot.
"	Elland cum Greteland	Mr. Ramsden.
"	"	Tho. Crosley.
"	"	John Clay.

Wapentakes.	Residence.	Persons' Names.
Agbrigg & Morley	Hallifax	Jonathan Mawde.
,,	,,	Antho. Foxcroft.
,,	Horbury	John Langley.
,,	Huthersfield . . .	Math. Wilkinson.
,,	Hipperholme cum Brigghouse	Steph. Ellis.
,,	,,	Richd Langley.
,,	,,	Nath. Whitley.
,,	Methley	John Shan.
,,	,,	Peter Colling.
,,	Pudsey	Robt Milner.
,,	Rasbick	Richd Law.
,,	Stanley	Gervase Hatfield.
,,	,,	Dan. Mawde.
,,	Sowerby	Isaac Naylor.
,,	Thornhill	Tho. Squire.
,,	Wakefield	Joshua Mawde.
,,	,,	Geo. Ratcliffe.
,,	Wareley	James Morgateride.

NORTH RIDING.

Wapentakes.	Residence.	Persons' Names.
Bulmer	Boswell	Willm Clement.
,,	Easingwould . . .	Fran. Driffield.
,,	Crake	Willm Fryer.
,,	Hutton upon Darw^t .	John Heslarton.
,,	Raskelfe	Geo. Kitchingman.
,,	Stillington	Tho. Wayte.
,,	,,	Mr. Faceby.
Rydale	Kirkby Moreside . .	Robt Otterburne.
,,	Old Malton	Geo. Parker.
,,	,,	Mr. Watson.
,,	Normanby	John Hill.
,,	Bagby	John Martin.
,,	Murton	Willm Spinke.
,,	Marderby	Willm Trueman.
,,	Sandhutton	Richd Warde.
,,	Sutton	Roger Baynes.

Wapentakes.	Residence.	Persons' Names.
Rydale	Topcliffe	John Kittlewell.
,,	Upsall	Mr. Baxter.
Whitby Strand	Egton	John Burdet.
,,	,,	Thos Smith.
,,	Whitby Strand	Willm Wiggoner.
,,	Hawsker	Robt Norrison.
,,	Ruswarp	John Geffarson.
,,	Stokesley	Henry Cockerell
,,	Whitby	Giles Wiggoner.
,,	Harkness	Willm Chapman.
Pickering Lithe	Ayton	Chris. Beckwith.
,,	Cayton	John Hebden.
,,	Pickering	Antho. Colcote.
,,	Newhouse	Tho. Garforth.
,,	Throstonby	Tho. Keld.
,,	Wickham	John Chapman.
,,	,,	Willm Bower.
Langbargh	Acklam	Willm Hustler.
,,	Stanesby	Edw. Westrope.
,,	Tanton	Willm Stooper.
Allertonshire	Holme cum Homgrave	John Brown.
,,	Hornby	Tho. Hall.
,,	Knaton and Brawith	Tho. Jackson.
,,	Lasonby	Jam. Cleseby.
Gilling West	Carleton	John Caterick.
,,	Gillingwest	Willm Smith.
,,	Lartington	Fra. Appleby.
,,	Marrick	Giles Blackburne.
,,	Mickleton	Tho. Tothall.
,,	Melsonby	John Phillipson.
,,	Ravensworth cum Washton	Ninian Collings.
,,	Rookesby	Humphr. Harvey.
Gilling East	Maunby	Willm Smith.
,,	Kirkbywisk	Mr. Wood.
,,	wton	Math. Taylor.
,,	Newby Wiske	Robt Wittye.

Wapentakes.	Residence.	Persons' Names.
Gilling East . . .	Reedham	Rich[d] Metrick.
,,	Sapleton	Geo. Blakeston.
,,	South Cowton . . .	Mr. Pepper.
,,	Scorton	John Burton.
,,	Smeaton	Fran. Wilkinson.
Hangwest	Bardin	Mr. Spence.
,,	Coverham	Will. Holdesworth.
,,	Downham cum Waybron	Will[m] Frankland.
,,	Middleton	Tho. Holdesworth.
,,	Preston	Phil. Forster.
,,	Wensley	Leon[d] Calvert.
,,	,,	Ralph Atkinson.
Hang East	Patrick Brompton . .	Tho[s] Lowden.
,,	Screwton	Mark Robinson.
,,	Scotton	Hen. Tennant.
Hallikeld	Aysonby	Will[m] Blythe.
,,	Disforth	Peter Norton.
,,	Gatonby	John Warcup.
,,	Leekby	Tho. Walters.
,,	Melmorby	W[m] Elsley.
,,	Pickhall	Will[m] Tindall.
,,	Ranton	John Ramsforth.
The Citty of Yorke .	St. John Baptist's Parish	Mr. Leonard Thompson.
,,	,,	Mr. Cressy Burnet.
,,	Trinity in Micklegate	Mr. Chris[r] Topham.
,,	St. Martin's and St. Gregories	Mr. Rich. Hewet.
,,	,,	Will[m] Barwick.
,,	,,	Andrew Taylor.
,,	,,	Rich. Metcalfe.
,,	,,	Ambrose Spenser.
,,	Bishophill	Geo Ramsden.
,,	Christ's Parish . . .	John Taylor.
,,	,,	Francis Elcock.
,,	,,	Timothy Squire.
,,	St. John Delpick's Parish	Dr. Broome.

Wapentakes.	Residence.	Persons' Names.
The City of Yorke .	St. Saviour's . . .	John Slynger.
"	St. Michael's Parish in Walmgate Warde	Bryan Dawson. Joseph Scott.
"	All Saints in the Pavement	George Lamplugh.
"	St. Michaell's Belfrey Parish	Mr. Richardson.
"	"	Anthony Walker.
"	"	Francis Swayne.
"	"	Humphr. Harwood.
"	St. Helen's in Stonegate	Mr. Arnold.
"	St. Martin's in Coney Street	Mr. Fox.
"	"	. . . . . . Croft, heir of Ald. Croft.
"	"	Mr. Arnold, a Phisitian.
The Aynesty in ye County of ye Citty of Yorke	Askham Bryan . .	Willm Camplesham.
"	Rufforth	Robt. Gale.
"	"	Peter Calvert.
The Borough of Leeds	. . . .	John Ross.
"	. . . .	Mr. Albyn.
"	. . . .	Mich. Hutchenson.
"	. . . .	Thos Dixson.
"	. . . .	Geo. Marshall.
"	Potter Newton . . .	Tho. Hardwick.
The Borough and Liberty of Ripon	Arzmonderby cum Broadgate	John Atkinson. Hen. Thompson.
"	Bishop Thornton . .	Tho. Barney.
"	"	Will. Wextley.
"	Felix Kirke . . .	Willm Trueman.
"	Fountaines Abbey . .	John Messenger.
"	Fountaines Park . .	Steph. Wilkes.
"	Markinton cum Wallowthwayte	Willm Markenfield. John Barney.
"	Whitcliffe cum Thorpe	Tho. Readshaw.

Wapentakes.	Residence.	Persons' Names.
The Borough and Liberty of Ripon	Skelgate	Geo. Redshaw.
"	Allhallowgate . . .	Hen. Redshaw.
"	. . . .	Tho. Thompson.

In this list may be recognised a few of the well-known antient gentry of the county, besides many heads of families whose descendants at this day would have rejoiced had they then placed their pedigrees upon record. But the majority of the names were probably then of little note, and are now wholly lost sight of.

Some light is thrown upon the circumstances which caused this inattention on the part of the gentry of Yorkshire, by the following passage of a letter addressed to Sir William Dugdale by his friend Charles Fairfax, in the month of June 1666 :—"I received your letter, wherein I have (so far as I could) observed your commands. Some gentlemen will attend you at the next assizes to whom I gave notice; but many (not sensible of the honour of their families) I find remiss, yet hope (upon their better thought) they will do right to posterity and give their attendance. Your too short stay in your several circuits (and their coincident appearances upon summonses before the Deputy Lieutenants) they alledge for excuse they could not wait on you." *

We must necessarily lament the absence of the pedigrees of so many families from that which was destined to be the last of the heraldic visitations of

* Hamper's Life of Dugdale, p. 364.

the great county of York; yet without them it contains a rich mine of genealogical and heraldic evidence, from whence all future labourers in those vast fields of Yorkshire history and topography which have been hitherto unexplored and uncultivated cannot fail to derive information and assistance of the highest value and importance.

The Council of the Surtees Society were desirous of appending to the present volume Sir William Dugdale's Visitation of the County Palatine of Durham. The only copy, however, of this record that they could obtain has been found to be so inaccurate and incomplete that they have resolved not to lay it before the Members of the Society.

R. D.

York, December 31st, 1859.

VISITATION OF YORKSHIRE,

BY SIR WILLIAM DUGDALE,

A.D. 1665 AND 1666.

STRAFFORTH AND TIKHILL WAPENTAKE. *Doncaster*, 3 *Aug.* 1665.

GREENE OF THUNDERCLIFFE.

ARMS.—Azure, three demi-lions rampant erased erminois.
CREST.—Out of a mural coronet gules, a demi-lion rampant erminois.

Thomas Greene, of Cawthorne in com. Eborum, to whom Richard St. George Esq. Norroy K. of Armes, granted the coate and crest here exprest, 6 Oct. 1612. = Alice, daughter of James Dyson of Westwood in com. ....

3. James Greene of Thundercliffe Grange, 3d son. = Anne, daughter of Nicholas Shercliffe of Ecclesfield in com. Eborum.

Robert Greene, of Thundercliffe Grange, æt. 52 ann. 3° Aug. 1665. = Alice, daughter of Edward Fawcett of Rufford in com. Eborū.

2. Robert.
3. James.
4. Matthew.
5. Benjamin.
6. Joseph.

1. William Greene, æt. 28 ann. 3° Aug. a° 1665. = Mary, daughter of Nicholas Stones of Norton in com. Derb.

1. Alice, wife to Francis Kellam of Pomfret in com. Eborum.

2. Sarah.
3. Mary.
4. Mabell.

William, æt. 2 an. et amplius 3 Aug. a° 1665. Alice.

STAINECROSSE WAPENTAKE. *Barnesley*, 5 *Aug*. 1665.

KERESFORTH OF PUELL-HILL.

ARMS.—Quarterly: 1 and 4, Azure, two mill-rinds fesseways in pale argent; 2 and 3, Argent, a fess embattled sable between three butterflies gules.

John Keresforth, of Keresforth Hill in com. Eborū. = ... daughter of .... Bosvile, of Ardesley, in com. Eborum.

2. John Keresforth, of Wombwell in com. Eborum. = ... daughter of .... Barker, of Dore in com. Derb.

1. Richard Keresforth. = ...

Robert Keresforth of Ardesley in co. Eborum. = ... daughter of .... Warde, of Barnesley in com. Ebor.

Gabraell Keresforth, of Keresforth Hill, died in a° 1641. = Katherine, daughter of .... Hall, of Bolton-upon-Derne in co. Ebor.

1. Jane, wife of Edmund Barrowclough of Barnesley in co. Ebor.

2. Grace, wife of = Robert Bower of Barnesley in co. Ebor.

Cotton Keresforth, died unmarried.

Thos. Keresforth, of Puell-Hill in co. Ebor. æt. 67 ann. 5° Aug. a° 1665. = Elizabeth, daughter of Humphry Clyncard of Abyngton in com. Berks.

Robert Bower, of Barnesley, died in a° 1659. = ...

1. Nathaniell Bower, ætatis 18 ann. 5 Aug. a° 1665.

2. Joshua.

STAINECROSSE WAPENTAKE. *Barnesley*, 5 *Aug*. 1665.

BURDET OF BIRTHWAYT.

ARMS.—Paly of six argent and sable, on a bend gules three martlets of the first; a crescent for difference.

CREST.—On a tower argent a martlet with wings displayed or.

Jane, dau. of Ranulph Barton of Smithells in co. Lanc. Esq. 2. wife. = Francis Burdet, of Birthwayt, died in a° .... = Catherine, dau. of Edward Boughton of Causton in com. Warr. Esq. 1. wife.

Amor Burdet, of Swawell in com. Ebor.

Francis Burdet, of Birthwayt in com. Ebor. died in a° 1644. = ... daughter of Sr Ferdinando Lee of Middleton in com. Ebor. Kt.

Francis Burdet, of Birthwayt Esq. æt. 22 ann. 5° Aug. a° 1665.

1. Magdalen.

2. Elizabeth.

OSGODCROSSE WAPENTAKE. *Pomfret*, 1° *Aug.* 1665.

FRANKE OF POMFRET.

ARMS.—Vert, a saltire engrailed or.

John Franke, of Pomfret, died in a° 1624 vel circ. = Dorothy, daughter of .... Bawne of Bawne Towne in com. Eboru.

4. Matthew, died unmarried.

3. Charles Franke of ...... = ... daughter of ...... Keeling.
- Martha.
- John.

2. Robert Franke of Pomfret, died in a° 1663. = Eliz. daugh. of Richard Abbot, of Preston Jacklin, in com. Lanc.

1. Richard Franke of Pomfret, of whom noe issue male is remayn^g.

1. Jane, wife unto John Gale.
2. Isabell, wife unto Willm Otes of Pomfret.
3. Alice, wife of Nathaniell Eyre of Bramley in co. Eborum.
4. Elizabeth, y^e wife unto Will. Wood of the Lanes in com. Eborum.
5. Anne, the wife of William Wakefield of Pomfret.
6. Rosamund, y^e wife of John Booth of Glossop in com. Derbiæ.

Children of Robert Franke and Eliz. Abbot:

Robert.

John Franke, of Pomfret, æt. 32 ann. 7 Aug. 1665. = Mary, daughter and coheir of Wm Harbred of Wistow in co. Ebor.
- Robert, æt. 5 an. 7 Aug. 1665.
- Mary.

Dorothy.
Elizabeth.
Debora.

STRAFFORD AND TICKHILL WAPENTAKE. *Doncaster*, 4 *Aug.* 1665.

WENTWORTH OF BROADSWORTH.

ARMS.—Quarterly of six; a crescent for difference:
1. Sable, a chevron between three leopard's faces or.
2. Paly of four argent and sable, on a bend gules three mullets or.
3. Gules, three fleurs-de-lis argent.
4. Vert, two lions passant guardant argent.
5. Gules, on a bend argent three escallops azure.
6. Azure, a chevron between three birds argent.

Thomas Wentworth, of Elmeshall in com. Ebor. Esqr. = Elizabeth, daughter of Rich. Gooderick of Ribston in co. Ebor. Esq.

4. John Wentworth, died without issue.

3. William Wentworth, died without issue.

2. Darcy Wentworth, of Broadsworth in com. Ebor. æt. 73 ann. 4° Aug. a° 1665. Gentleman Huisher of the Black Rod to Thomas late Earle of Strafford, Ld Lieutenant of Ireland. = Elizab. daughter of Sr Edw. Warren, of Poynton in com. Cestr. K^t.

1. Sir Thomas Wentworth, of Elmeshall, K^t died in a° 1651.

1. Catherine, wife to Sr Rowland Wandsford, K^t, Attorney of y^e Court of Wards.
2. Anne, the wife of Sr Richard Hawkesworth of Hawkesworth in co. Ebor. K^t.

Barkeston Ashe. *Pomfret*, 8 *Aug.* 1665.

BEILBY OF MICKLETHWAYT-GRANGE.

Arms.—Sable, a saltire or.

Crest.—A leopard's head guardant erased at the neck argent, pellettée.

Thomas Beilby, of Micklethwayt Grange and of Killerby in com. Ebor. died in a° 1639, or thereabouts. = Thomasine, daughter of Thomas Thwenge of Heworth in comitatu Eborum.

- 3. Isabel, married to Francis Shan of Medley in com. Eboru.
- 2. Anne, wife of Roger Wyvell of Osgodby in com. Eborum.
- 1. Frances, wife of Samuell Lacy, of Orton in com. Eborum.
- William Beilby, of Micklethwayt Grange, died 27 May, a° 1665. = Susan, dau. of Richard Sunderland of Coley Hall in co. Ebor. Esq.

Children of William Beilby and Susan:

- 2. John Beilby, of Micklethwayte Grange, Esqr, now one of his Maties Justices of Peace and Quorum in this county of Yorke. Æt. 31 an. 8 Aug. a° 1665. = Barbara, daughter unto Sr John Lowther of Lowther in co. Westmerland, Bart.
- 1. Richard, Beilby, died in a° 1650. = Dorothy, daughter of Lawr. Sayre of Worsell in com. Eborum.
- 1. Anne, wife of John Mompesson of Thorn Parke in com. Eborum.
- 2. Frances, first married to Jonas Tomson of Kilham in com. Ebor. secondly to Francis Dodsworth of Watlas; thirdly to Cuthbert Wade of Kilsey Esq.
- 3. Susanna, wife unto Francis Wilkinson of Thorpe in com. Ebor.
- 4. Thomasine, wife unto Walter Laycock of Copmanthorpe in co. Ebor.

Children of John Beilby and Barbara:

- 1. John, died an infant.
- 2. Mary, æt. 2 ann. et dim. 8 Aug. 1665.

Children of Richard Beilby and Dorothy:

- William, died a child.
- 1. Elizabeth.
- 2. Susan.

Stainecrosse Wapentake. *Hickleton*, 5 *Aug.* 1665.

CUTLER OF STAINEBROUGH.

Arms.—Azure, three dragon's heads erased within a bordure or.

Crest.—A dragon's head erased or, ducally gorged azure.

Thomas Cutler, of Staineburgh in co. Eborum. = Ellen, daughter to Roger Rayney of Smethley in com. Eborum.

Elizabeth, daugh. and coheire of Sr John Bentley, of .... in co. Derb. K^t^. 1 wife. = Sr Gervase Cutler, K^t^, died in Pontefract Castle at the time of the siege, a° 1645, or thereabouts. = Magdalen, daughter to the Right Ho^ble^ John Earle of Bridgwater. 2 wife.

By the first wife:

- Mary, wife to Sr Edward Moseley of Hough in co. Lanc. Bart.

By the second wife:

- 3. Elizabeth.
- 4. Eleanor.
- 5. Penelope.
- 1. Frances.
- 2. Magdalen, wife unto Henry Lewes.
- 1. Sr Gervase Cutler of Staineborough K^t^, æt. 24 an. 5 Aug. 1665.
- 2. Thomas Cutler.

JACKSON OF HICKLETON.

ARMS.— Quarterly of six:

1. Gules, a fess between three shovellers argent, a crescent for difference.
2. Azure, a chevron checky argent and gules.
3. Argent, on a bend sable three owls of the first, a mullet for difference.
4. Sable, a cross pattée or.
5. Argent, a bend sable between an eagle displayed vert in chief and a cross fleury of the second in base.
6. Argent, a cross moline sable.

CREST.—A shoveller proper.

John Jackson, of Edderthorp in com. Ebor. died in Febr. aº 1590. = Helen, daughter of John Wilkinson of Bolton-upon-Dearn in com. Eborum.

Jane, daughter to Richard Garth of Morden in Surry, first wife. = Sr John Savile, Kt. one of the Barons of the Exchequer. = Elizabeth, daughter of Thomas Wentworth of Elmeshall in com. Eborum. 2 wife.

7. Helen, wife of Thomas Darley of Brereley in co. Ebor.

6. Anne, died unmarried.

5. Margaret, ye wife of Rob. Ramsden of Hemsworth in co. Ebor.

4. Margt, died young.

3. Edith, ye wife of Williã Elvish of Bolton in co. Ebor.

2. Elizabeth, wife of . . . . . Turven of Tickhill in co. Ebor.

1. Catherine, wife unto Raphe Elliot of Goldthorp in co. Ebor.

4. Roger, 5. Francis, 6. William, 7. Benjamin, citizens of London.

3. Richard Jackson, citizen of Lond.

2. Thomas Jackson, of Knottingley, in co. Eborum.

1. Sr John Jackson, of Edderthorp, Kt, one of the councell at Yorke, and the King's Attorney there. = 1. Elizabeth, eldest daughter of Sr John Savile, Kt, one of the Barons of the Exchequer.

2. . . . . wife of Sir Henry Goodrick, of Ribston, in com. Ebor, Kt.

Sir Henry Savile, of Medley, in co. Eboru. ob. s. prole.

John Savile. = ⅄

Elizabeth, daughter of Sir Francis Thorney of Fenton in co. Nott. Kt, 1st wife. = Sir John Jackson, of Edderthorpe Knt, died in aº 1638, or thereabouts. = Fienes, daughter to Sr Thomas Waller Kt. Governour of Dover Castle, 2d wife.

Henry Jackson, died without issue.

Francis Jackson, of Hooton-Paynell in com. Eborum.

Jane, wife of Sr Francis Thorney of Fenton in co. Nott. Kt.

Elizabeth, first married to . . . . Williamson of Walkringham in com. Nott. afterwards to Sr Richard Hutton of Hooton-Paynell in co. Ebor. Kt.

Lucie, wife of Henry Tindall of Brotherton in com. Ebor.

Sir John Jackson, of Hickleton in com. Ebor. Bart. æt. 34 ann. 4º Aug. aº 1665. = Katherine, daughter of William Boothe, son and heire apparent to Sir George Boothe of Dunham in com. Cestr. Kt & Bart.

Rowland Jackson, died unmarrd.

Margaret.

Jane, died unmarried.

Katherine. Vere. Fienes. John, æt. 11 ann. 4º Aug. 1665.

OSGODCROSSE WAPENTAKE. *Pontfract*, 7 *Aug.* 1665.

JOHNSTON OF POMFRET.

ARMS.—Argent, a saltire sable, on a chief gules two cushions or; an escutcheon of pretence, Sable, a chevron ermine between three maiden's heads couped below the shoulders proper.

CREST.—On a mound a castle in ruins, all proper.

Gawen Johnston, commonly called Gawen of the Wood = ...

Archibald Johnston = ...

Gawyn Johnston, seised of Elsi-sheilds by the grant of Gawen his grandfather, a° 1486. = ...

Katherine Kirk-patrick, first wife. = Wilkin Johnston, seized of Elsi-sheilds, a° 1520. = ... daughter to the Lord Totholock, 2 wife.

.... Johnston of Triplo & Redhall near Dumfreeze in Scotl. = ...

John Johnston, of Elsi-sheilds, a° 1560. = .. daughter to .... Macknath.

James Johnston, of Kellowbanke, a° 1556. = Margaret, daugh. of.... Crage, sister to Dr Crage, phisician to K. James.

Wilkin Johnston, a° 1581. = ..

John Johnston, Advocate, Lairde of Castle-Milke, Abbot of Halliwood, and Commendator of Sautlet, a° 1610. = Barbara, daughter of Nicholas Udwart, Merchant Burgesse of Edenburgh.

JamesJohnston, of Elsi-sheilds, a° 1606, died without issue.

Archibald, brother, and heire of Elsi-sheilds, a° 1629.

1. Thomas Johnston, Lairde of Castle-Milke, died without issue.

3. Alexander Johnston, Advocate in Edenburgh. = Sophia, daugh. of Wilkin Johnston.

2. John Johnston, Rector of Sutton-upon Darwent, died a° 1657. = Elizabeth, daughter of Henry Hobson of Usflete in com. Eborum.

1. Jennet, wife of Arthur Naysmith, Steward to Esme, Duke of Lenox.

2. Helen, wife to Samuell Hunter of Edenburgh.

3. Alexander, died at Mittau in Poland.

4. Samuel.

5. Joseph.

6. Benjamin.

7. Henry.

2. John Johnston, of Pomfret, æt. 36 ann. 7 Aug. 1665. = Frances, daughter of .... Longbotham, widow of Malachy Doyle.

1. Nathaniell Johnston, of Pomfret, in com. Ebor. Dr. in Phisick, ætatis 38 an. 7° Aug. 1665. = Anne, daugh. and co-heire of Rich. Cudworth, of Eastfield in Yorksh.

Sarah.

1. Cudworth, borne 21 Sept. 1654.

2. Charles.

3. Nathaniel.

4. John.

Anne.

OSGODCROSSE WAPENTAKE. *Pontefract*, 7 *Aug*. 1665.

PERCY OF STUBBS-WALDEN.

ARMS.—Per fess argent and gules, a lion rampant per fess sable and argent.

Francis Percy, of Scotton in com. Ebor. died in aº 1634, vel circa. = Frances, daughter of Raufe Vavasour, a younger brother to John Vavasour of Haslewood in co. Ebor. Esq.

1. Eleanor, wife unto Henry Oglethorpe of Beghall, vulgarly called Beale, in com. Ebor.
2. Jane, wife to Brian Haworth of Parr in co. Lanc. gent.
3. Mary, a nunne at Gant in Flanders.
4. Theodosia, wife of Rich. Shercliffe of Ecclesfield parish in co. Eborum.
5. Elizabeth, wife of Rowland Revell of Stannington in co. Ebor.
6. Lucye.

1. John Percy, of Stubbs-Walden in co. Eboru. Esqr æt. 81 ann. 7º Aug. 1665. = Frances, dau. of Andrew Yonge and sister and co-heire of Sr Andrew Yonge of Beorn in com. Eborum, Kn[t].

2. Bartholomew.
3. Thomas.
4. Robert.
5. Josselyne.
} died without issue remayning.

2. John Percy, slayne in the fight at Willoughby, in com. Nott. aº 1648, fighting on the King's part.

1. Thomas Percy, son and heire, ætatis 38 ann. 7º Aug. 1665. = Cecelie, daughter of Robert Shawe of Metley in co. Eborum, and coheire.

1. Dorothy, wife of John Bretton of Bretton in com. Eborum.

2. Frances, wife of Sr Willm. Langdale of Lanthrope in Holdernesse in com. Eborum.

3. Ursula.

4. Elizabeth, wife of Thomas Ingleby of Thornton Woods in com. Ebor.

Mary. 1. John, æt. 15 ann. 7 Aug. 1665. 2. Robert. 3. Thomas 4. Francis 5. William. 6. Philip. 7. Charles.

OSGODCROSSE WAPENTAKE. *Pontfract*, 7 *Aug.* 1665.

BRADLEY OF ACWORTH.

ARMS.—Or, a fess azure between three buckles gules.

He refers himselfe to ye Visitation of Berksh. for proofe of ye armes.

John Bradley, of ...... in com. Ebor. an ensigne in King Henry the Eight's army upon his expedition to Bulloigne in France. = ...

Issue:

- Henry Bradley, of Okehingham in com. Berks, died in aº 1645. = Barbara, daughter of Walter Lane of Reding in com. Berks.
- 1. Richard. 3. Abel. died without issue.

Issue of Henry and Barbara:

- 1. John Bradley of Miles near Okingham in Berkshire. = Susan, daughter of John Feilder of .... in com. Southton.
  - Henry Bradley, of Richmund in Surry.
- 2. Thomas Bradley, dr in divinity and chaplein to K. Charles the First, now prebend in the cathedral church of York and rector of Ackworth, in com. Ebor. æt. 67 an. 7º Aug. aº 1665. = Frances, daughter unto John Lord Savile, of Pomfret in com. Eborum.
  - 3. Francis Bradley.
  - 2. Savile Bradley, Fellow of Magdalen Coledge in Oxford.
  - 1. Thomas Bradley, a merchant in Virginia, æt. 32 an. 7º Aug. 1665.
  - Barbara, wife of Daniell Godfrey of Muffield in com. Oxon. =
    - 1. Daniel. 2. Charles.

BARKESTON ASHE WAPENTAKE. *Pontefract*, 8 *Aug.* 1665.

FAIRFAX OF OGLETHORPE.

ARMS.—Quarterly of eight, a crescent for difference:

1. Argent, three bars gemelles gules surmounted by a lion rampant sable.
2. Argent, a bend sable and a chief indented gules.
3. Checky or and azure, on a canton sable an etoile argent.
4. Argent, a chevron between three hind's heads erased gules.
5. Barry argent and gules, on a canton sable a cross flory or.
6. Or, a bend sable.
7. Or, a bend azure.
8. Argent, on a fess sable, between three fleurs-de-lis gules, as many annulets or.

CREST.—A lion's head erased sable, a crescent for difference.

Sr Thomas Fairfax, of Denton, Kt, created Visc. Fairfax of Cameron, 3 Caroli primi. Died 1º May, 1640. = Eleanor, daughter of Robert Aske of Aughton in com. Ebor. Died 23 Aug. aº 1620.

Issue:

- 2. Henry Fairfax, of Oglethorpe in com. Ebor. died in Aprill, 1665. = Mary, daughter to SrHenry Chorley of Roxby in com. Ebor.
  - Bryan.
  - Henry Fairfax of Oglethorpe Esqr æt. 33 an. 8 Aug. aº 1665. = Frances, sole daughter to Sr Robert Barwick of Tolston in co.Ebor.Kt, Recorder of Yorke.
    - 3. Bryan.
    - 2. Henry æt. 6 ann.
    - 1. Thomas, æt. 8 an. 8 Aug. aº 1665.
    - 1. Dorothy, æt. 9 an. 1665.
    - 2. Ursula.
    - 3. Frances.
- Mary, daughter to Edm. Earle of Mulgrave. 1st wife. = 1. Ferdinando Ld Fairfax. Died in aº 1647. = Rhoda, daughter and heire to Thomas Chapman Esqr, widow to Sr .... Hussey, Bart, 2d wife.
  - Thomas Ld Fairfax, now living, aº 1665.

THE BURROUGH OF LEEDES. *Leedes*, 11° *Aug.* 1665.

SIMPSON OF LEEDES.

ARMS.—Per bend or and sable, a lion rampant counterchanged.

Richard Simpson, of Leedes in com. Eborum. = ...

Richard Simpson, of Leedes. = ...

3. Thomas. 4. George. died unmarried.

2. Anthony Simpson, of Leedes, died in a° 1628, or thereabouts. = Jane, daughter of John Wilson of Fryton in co. Eborum.

1. William Simpson, died without issue.

1. Elizabeth, wife unto Hugh Booth, merchant of Leeds.

2. Frances, wife unto George Fletcher of Retford in com. Nott.

Mary.

John Simpson, of Leedes, æt. 56 an. 11° Aug. 1665. = Elizabeth, daughter of Gervase Shaw of Chesterfield in com. Derb.

Elizabeth, wife of Samuell Sykes, a merchant in Leedes.

STAINCROSSE WAPENTAKE. *Barnsley*, 5 *Aug.* 1665.

EDMUNDS OF WORSBROUGH.

ARMS.—Per chevron or and sable, three fleurs-de-lis counterchanged.
CREST.—A ship in full sail upon the sea, all proper.

Concessa per Will'm Dugdale, Norroy Armorum R.

Thomas Edmonds, of Wosbrough in com. Eboru. died in January, a° 1662. = Anne, daughter of Henry Cookeson, of .... in com. Eboru.

Henry Edmonds, of Wosbrough Esqr, now one of his Majesties Justices of the Peace for the county of Yorke, æt. 37 ann. 5 Aug. 1665. = Jane, daughter of Richard Robinson of Thicket in co. Eborum.

Anne, died young.

STAINCROSSE WAPENTAKE. *Barnesley*, 5 *Aug.* 1665.

WENTWORTH OF WOLLEY.

ARMS—Quarterly: 1 and 4, Wentworth: Sable, a chevron between three leopard's faces or; a crescent for difference.
2, Whitley: Azure, on a bend or three torteaux.
3, Downes of Herefordshire: Argent, three palets wavy gules.

Michaell Wentworth, of Wolley in com. Eborum Esq. died in a° 1641. = Frances, daughter and sole heire to George Downes of Pawnton in com. Heref.

5. John Wentworth, of Wolley, Esq. æt. 59 ann. 5 Aug. a° 1665. = Elizabeth, daughter of Arthur Aldburgh of Aldburgh in com. Ebor. Esq.

4. Matthew, died without issue.

Anne, daughter to Thomas Ld Fairfax, of Camron, first wife. = 3. Sir George Wentworth, Knight. = Averell, daugh. of Christopher Maltby, Alderman, of Yorke, 2d wife.

2. Michael, died unmarried.

1. Thomas, died unmarried.

1. Dorothy, wife of John Wood of Copmanthorpe in co. Ebor.

2. Elizabeth, first married to Thomas Oldfield of Wadlands in com. Ebor.; secondly, to Richard Beaumont of Murfield in com. Ebor. Esq.

3. Alice, died unmarried.

4. Mary, wife of Richard Langley, of Millington, in co. Ebor.

5. Rosamund, first married to Bertram Reveley of Throple in com. Northumbr.; secondly, to Roger Widdrington of Cartington in com. Northumbr. Esq.

6. Margaret, wife of William Wombwell of Wombwell in com. Ebor. Esq.

Children of John Wentworth and Elizabeth:

1. Michael, æt. 11 an. 5 Aug. a° 1665.

2. John, died in his infancy.

1. Elizabeth, 2. Frances, died young.

Children of Sir George Wentworth:

2. William, died young.

1. Michael Wentworth. = Katherine, daughter of Sr William St Quintin, Bart.

Michaell, died in his infancy.

1. Everilda, wife of John Thornhill of Fixby in co. Ebor. Esq.

2. Frances, wife of Thomas Grantham of Meaux Abby in Holdernes, Esq.

3. Anne, wife of Will'm Osbaldeston of Hunmanby in co. Ebor. Esq.

1. Christopher, 2. George, died infants.

OSGODCROSSE WAPENTAKE. *Pontfract*, 7° *Aug*. 1665.

STABLES OF TANSHELFE.

ARMS.—Argent, on a saltire gules five acorns slipped or, on a chief of the second three mullets of the first.

Qu. for proofe of these armes ?

William Stables, mayor of ye burrough of Pomfret, a° 1593. = ...

Thomas Stables, mayor of Pomfret in a° 1606.

William Stables of Pomfret. = Elizabeth, daughter of .... Copeland.

Nicholas Stables. = Elizabeth, daughter of William Wilkinson of Pomfret.

Richard Stables, of Tanshelfe juxta Pomfret, died circa ann. 1656. = Isabell, daughter of William Bywater, alderman of Pomfret.

4. Leonard Stables, alderman of Pomfret. = Dorothy, daughter to John Stevenson of Swynfleet in co. Linc. heire to ... Stevenson, her brother.

2. Richard.
3. John.
died unmarried.

1. William Stables, of Tanshelfe, æt. 44 an. 7 Aug. a° 1665, Lieutenant of horse in the army of King Charles ye First. = Jane, daughter and coheir to Gervase Hamerton of Aukborow in co. Linc. gent. of the house of Monkerode.

1. Thomasin, wife unto George Shillito of Pomfret in co. Eborum.
2. Elizabeth, wife unto Edward Atkinson alderman of Leedes.
3. Susan.
4. Isabell, the wife unto Richard Austwicke, now mayor of Pomfret, a° 1665.

1. William. 2. Richard.

STRAFFORD AND TICKHILL WAPENTAKE. *Doncaster*, 4 *Aug.* 1665.

SPENSER OF ATTERCLIFFE.

ARMS.—Azure, a fess ermine between six sea-mew's heads erased argent.

Thomas Spenser, of Sheffield in com. Ebor = ... daughter of .... Hatfield.

William Spenser, of Bramley Grange, died in the yeare 1622, or thereabout. = Anne, daughter of .... Staniforth, of Tindesley in com. Ebor.

3. Thomas Spenser, of Hooton on the Hill in com. Eborum.

2. George Spenser, of Newell Grange, in com. Eborum.

1. William Spenser, of Attercliffe in co. Ebor. Gent. died in April, 1649. = Alice, daughter of James Mitchell of Morthing in com. Eborum.

3. John Spenser of Attercliffe in co. Ebor.

2. Michael Spenser, a merchant in London. = Elizabeth, daughter of .... Taylor of Chesterfield in Derbysh.

Elizabeth, daughter of Leonard Gill of Norton in co. Derb. 1 wife. = 1. William Spenser, of Attercliffe Esqr. now one of his Maties Justices of the Peace, in com. Ebor. æt. 53 ann. 4° Aug. a° 1665. = Sarah, dau. of George Westby of Gilfit, in the parish of Whiston in co. Ebor. 2^d wife.

1. Anne, wife unto James Bright of Sheffeild in co. Ebor.; after of John Dawson of Misterton in co. Nott.
2. Margaret, wife unto Raphe Freschevill of Helleby in com. Ebor.
3. Mary, wife of Andrew Morewood of Dronfield in co. Derb.

3. Samuell.

2. John.

1. William; æt. 23 ann. 4. Aug. a° 1665.

1. Sarah, wife of John Wadsworth of Swathe Hall in com. Ebor.

2. Faythe, wife of Samuel Childe of Leedes in com. Ebor.

STRAFFORTH AND TICKHILL WAPENTAKE. *Doncaster*, 4 *Aug.* 1665.

EYRE OF BRAMLEY.

ARMS.—Argent, on a pile sable three quatrefoils or.

CREST.—A leg in armour, couped at the thigh, quarterly argent and sable, spurred or, charged with a quatrefoil quarterly or and argent.

William Eyre, of Bramley in com. Ebor. = Alice, daughter of Roger Fretwell of Hellowby in com. Ebor.

William Eyre, of Bramley, died in a° 1601, vel circa. = Edith, daughter and co-heire of Robert Marsh of Darton in com. Eborum.

1. Mary, wife of Leonard Stanley of Mixbrough in co. Ebor.
2. Martha, wife of Thomas Raysin of Doncaster.
3. Sarah wife of Thomas Shirle of Wikersley in co. Ebor.
4. Judith, wife of James Bothomley of Cawthorn in co. Ebor.
5. Edith, wife of Thomas Bone of Rampton in co. Nott.

1. Nathaniell Eyre, of Bramley, died in August a° 1659. = Alice, dau. of John Franke of Pontefract in co. Ebor.

2. Reresby Eyre, of Darton in com. Eborum. = Mary, daughter of .... Batt of Okewell in com. Eborum.

3. Alice, wife of Nathaniell Revell of Brampton-le-Morthing in com. Eborum.

2. Edith, wife of Christopher Balme of Mansfield in com. Nott.

1. Isabell, wife of William Wood, son and heire of Robert Wood of Burton Abby in com. Eboru.

1. Henry Eyre, of Bramley, D[r] of Phisick, ætatis 40 an. 4° Aug. 1665.

2. John Eyre, a Hamborough merchant.

BARKESTON ASHE WAPENTAKE. *Pomfret*, 8° *Aug.* 1665.

WALMESLEY OF STAYNER-HALL.

ARMS.—Quarterly of six :
1. Gules, on a chief ermine two hurts, a crescent or for difference.
2. Argent, three weaver's shuttles in pale sable, tipped and quilled or.
3. Sable, two bars vairée, argent and vert.
4. Sable, on a bend cotised a lion passant between two mullets argent.
5. Argent, an eagle displayed and double-headed purpure ; a crescent for difference.
6. Argent, a chevron between three hedgehogs sable.

CREST.—A lion statant guardant ermine, ducally crowned gules, charged on the breast with a crescent azure.

Thomas Walmisley, died in a° 26° Reginæ Eliz. = Margaret, daughter of . . . . . Livesay.

Children:

- William. Nicholas. Merchants of London.
- Edward Walmisley, of Banaster Hall.
- Robert Walmisley, of Coldcotes.
- Richard Walmisley, of Sholay.
- Sir Tho. Walmisley Knt, one of the Justices of the Court of Common Pleas, died 10 Jac. Regis. = Anne, sole dau. and heire of Robert Shotleworth of Hacking in co. Lanc. Esq. & of Jane his wife, sister and coheire of Richard Browne.
- Alice, wife of . . . . Hothersall of Hothersall.
- Elizabeth, ye wife of . . . . Nowell of Meareley.

Eleanor, daughter of Sr John Danvers and sister of Henry Lord Danvers of Dantsey, first wife. = Thomas Walmisley, Esq. superstes a° 1617. = Mary, sister of Sr Richard Houghton, of Houghton Tower in com. Lanc. Bart. second wife.

Charles Walmsley, of Stayner-Hall near Selby in com. Ebor. Esqr. ætatis 57 ann. 8 Aug. a° 1665. = Mary, daughter of Thomas Charnock of Astley in com. Lanc. Esq.

OSGODCROSSE WAPENTAKE. *Pontefract*, 8° *Aug*. 1665.

HIPPON OF NEWHALL.

ARMS.—Azure, three fleurs-de-lis and as many keys erect or.

George Hippon, of Newall in com. Ebor. died in a° 1627, vel circa. = Elizabeth, daughter to Edwd Rolleston of Toynton in co. Linc.

2. Francis Hippon, died in Ireland, unmarried. 3. John Hippon.	1. Thomas Hippon, of Newhall in Fetherston, æt. 52 an. 8 Aug. a° 1665. =	Anne, daughter and heire to John Horncastle of Fetherston.	1. Anne, wife to Francis Corker of Hessell in com. Ebor.	2. Barbara, wife of Raphe Oglethorpe.	3. Margaret, wife unto George Thimelby.	4. Alice. 5. Bridget, wife of Richard Scolah.

Children of Thomas Hippon and Anne:

1. Elizabeth. 2. Hannah. 3. Alice.	1. George Hippon, æt. 29 ann. 8° Aug. a° 1665.	2. Edward. 3. Francis. 4. Robert.

BARKESTON ASHE WAPENTAKE. *Pontfract*, 8 *Aug*. 1665.

POCKLEY OF THORPE-WILLOUGHBY.

ARMS.—Gules, a bend argent cotised or between two covered cups of the second.
CREST.—A dove, wings displayed, argent, in her beak an oak-branch slipped vert.

No proofe made of these armes.

Lancelot Pockley, of Burton Agnes in the county of Yorke. = ...

Lancelot Pockley, of Burton Agnes, died circa annum 1645. = Jane, daughter of John Pearson of .... near Kirkby Moreside in com. Ebor.

3. Mathew Pockley.	2. Richard Pockley.	1. John Pockley, of Burton Agnes, died in a° 1657. vel circa. =	Helen, daughter of Robert Taylor of Creme in co. Ebor.	1. Jane, wife of Peter Rudston of Carnaby in com. Ebor.	2. Margaret, wife unto Mathew Taylor.

Children of John Pockley and Helen:

John Pockley, of Thorpe-Willoughby in co. Ebor. æt. 40 an. 8 Aug. 1665.	1. Anne, wife of Sr Jeremy Smith of Hemingbrough in com. Ebor. Kt.	2. Ellen, wife of Edward Thorpe of Colton in com. Eborum.	3. Alice, wife of Henry Mese of Skerne in com. Ebor.

BARKESTON ASHE WAPENTAKE. *Pontfract*, 9 *Aug.* 1665.

TAYLOR OF TEMPLE-HURST.

ARMS.—Ermine, on a chief sable three escallops argent.

CREST.—Out of a ducal coronet or a dexter arm embowed in armour proper, the hand grasping a sword argent, pommelled and flamed of the first.

He refers to the Visit. of Shropshire, but there is nothing there.

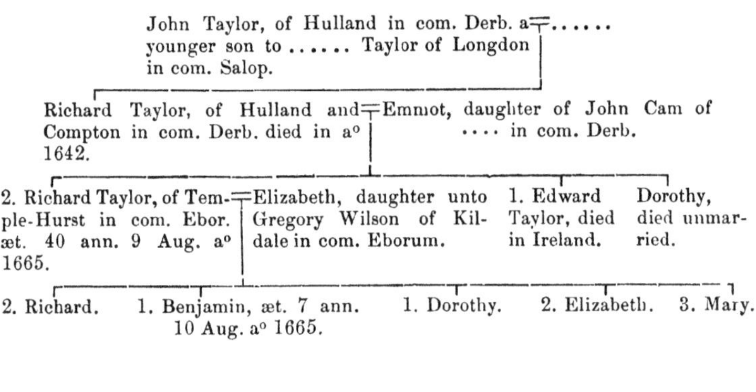

John Taylor, of Hulland in com. Derb. a younger son to ..... Taylor of Longdon in com. Salop. = ...

Richard Taylor, of Hulland and Compton in com. Derb. died in a° 1642. = Emmot, daughter of John Cam of .... in com. Derb.

2. Richard Taylor, of Temple-Hurst in com. Ebor. æt. 40 ann. 9 Aug. a° 1665. = Elizabeth, daughter unto Gregory Wilson of Kildale in com. Eborum.

1. Edward Taylor, died in Ireland.

Dorothy, died unmarried.

2. Richard.

1. Benjamin, æt. 7 ann. 10 Aug. a° 1665.

1. Dorothy.

2. Elizabeth.

3. Mary.

OSGODCROSSE WAPENTAKE. *Pontefract*, 7 *Aug.* 1665.

LAKE OF CASTLEFORD.

ARMS.—Sable, a bend between six crosses botonée fitchée argent.

CREST.—A sea-horse's head couped argent gorged with two bars gules, in the nostrils an annulet of the first.

Hugh Lake, of Castleford in com. Ebor. died a° 44 Eliz. = Jane, daughter to .... Pilkinton of Stanley in com. Ebor.

Thomas Lake, of Castleford, a° 44 Eliz. = Anne, daughter to Thomas Shilittoe of Whitwood in co. Ebor.

Thomas Lake, died in a° 1660. = Margaret, daughter of William Hustler of Kennington in com. Ebor.

John Lake, of Castleford, ætatis 29 an. 7 Aug. 1665. = Margaret, daughter to Peter Swyfte of Pontefract in com. Eborum.

Thomas, died in the lifetime of his father.

John, æt. 3 ann. 7 Aug. 1665.

Peter, æt. 3 mens.

OSGODCROSSE WAPENTAKE. *Pontefract*, 7 *Aug.* 1665.

ADAMS OF EAST-HARDWICK.

ARMS.—Gules, a lion rampant between three escallops or, on a chief argent as many palets engrailed of the first.

CREST.—A demi-griffin segreant erminois, winged and beaked azure, holding an escallop argent.

William Adams of East-Hardwick in com. Eborum. = Elizabeth, daughter of .... Tinley of Wath in com. Ebor.

Lawrence Adams of East-Hardwick, æt. 70 ann. 7° Aug. a° 1665. = Elizabeth, dau. of Mathew Heather of Sharlston in com. Eborum.

William Adams, ætat. 41 an. 7 Aug. 1665. = Elizabeth, daughter of William Kellum of Pomfret, widow of Richard Otes.

1. Elizabeth, wife of Henry Aikroyd, a mercht in Yorke.

2. Mary, wife of George Abbot of Hundale in co. Ebor.

William, æt. 2 ann. et amplius 7 Aug. 1665.

Elizabeth, æt. septem mensium.

OSGODCROSSE WAPENTAKE. *Pontefract*, 7 *Aug.* 1665.

BOOTHE OF CRIDLYNG-PARKE.

ARMS.—Argent, three boar's heads erect and erased within a bordure sable.
CREST.—A lion statant . . . ducally gorged . . . Qy the coloures?

Sir Raphe Boothe of Barton in co. Lanc. Kt. = Catherine, daughter to .... Stanley.

2. Charles Boothe. = ... daughter of John Towneley of Glossop in co. Derb. Esqr.

1. Ralph Boothe. =

Robert Boothe of Glossop in com. Derb. = Jane, daughter of ..... Bramhall.

3. Raphe Boothe of .... in Glossopdale in com. Derb.

2. Nicholas Boothe of Pontfract in co. Ebor.

1. George Boothe of Glossop died in a° 1636. = Dorothy, daughter of Alan Austwicke of Pontfract in co. Eborum.

John Boothe of Glossop in com. Derb. died in his father's lifetime. = Rosamund, daughter of John Franke of Pomfrett in co. Ebor.

1. Mary, wife of Thomas Wheatley of Whitecrosse in co. Ebor.

2. Elizabeth, wife of Samuell Cryer, minister of Castleton in co. Eborum.

George Boothe of Crydling Parke in com. Ebor. æt. 30 an. 7 Aug. 1665. = Dorothy, daughter of Arthur Ingram of Knottingley in com. Ebor.

Dorothy, wife of Edward Harrison, a planter in the Barbadoes.

2. William. 1. John, æt. 6 ann. 7° Aug. 1665. 1. Katherine. 2. Hester. 3. Mary.

BARKESTON ASHE. *Pontfract*, 8 *Aug*. 1665.

ROBINSON OF RITHER.

ARMS.—Vert, on a chevron between three bucks trippant or as many cinquefoils gules, in chief a trefoil slipped argent.

CREST.—A buck trippant or, pellettée and gorged with a chaplet vert.

Elizabeth, daughter of Sr Richard Rogers of Brianston in co. Dorset, Kt. 1st wife. = Sr John Robinson of Rither in com. Ebor. Esqr. = Susan, daughter of Sr Edward Holmden, Kt, alderman of the citty of London. 2d wife.

2. Henry Robinson, died unmarried.

1. John Robinson of Rither, Esqr, died in ao 1647, or thereabouts. = Rachael, daughter of ... Wadeson, citizen of London.

1. Mary, wife of John Savile of Medley in co. Ebor.

2. Susan, wife of Thomas Newarke of Akum in co. Ebor.

Elizabeth, wife unto John Rouse of Tamworth in co. Warr.

Elizabeth, daughter of Sr Roger Jaques of Elvington in co. Ebor. Kt. 1st wife. = Bridget, daughter to Sr Willm Fleetwood of Woodstoke in com. Oxon. Kt. 2d wife. = 1. John Robinson, of Rither, Esqre, æt. 32 ann. 8o Aug. 1665. = Margaret, daughter of Sr Matthew Boynton of Barmston in com. Ebor. Bart. 3d wife.

2. William.
3. Humfry Robinson, married .... daughter of .... Needham.

2. Charles, æt. 9 an. 8 Aug. ao 1665.

1. John, æt. 10 an. 8 Aug. 1665.

1. Elizabeth.

2. Catherine.

3. Mary.

OSGODCROSSE WAPENTAKE. *Pontfract*, 8 *Aug*. 1665.

HITCHING OF CARLETON.

ARMS.—.... a chevron between three pelicans ......

No proofe made of these armes.

Thomas Hitching of Hitching in co. Hartf. = ...

3. Mark.
2. Henry.

Anne, daughter of ...... Chapman. 1 wife. = 1. Thomas Hitching of Pomfret in co. Ebor. died in ao 1644, vel circa. = Elizabeth, sole daughter and heire of John Skipton of Pomfret. 2 wife.

1. Thomas Hitching, of Pontfract, died in ao 1652 (vel circa). =

2. John Hitching of Carleton juxta Pontfract, æt. 31 ann. 8 Aug. ao 1665. = Fayth, daughter of Will'm Wakefield of Pontfract.

1. Sarah.
2. Dorothy.

Elizabeth, wife of ... Nicholls, of Normanton in com. Ebor.

Thomas, æt. 5 an. 8 Aug. ao 1665.

1. Elizabeth.
2. Fayth.
3. Anne.

OSGODCROSSE WAPENTAKE. *Pomfret*, 8 *Aug.* 1665.

EMPSON OF GOWLE.

ARMS.—Azure, a chevron between three crosses formée argent.

No proofe made of these armes.

Richard Empson of Gowle in com. Ebor. gent. = ... daughter of .... Gathorne.

George Empson of Gowle, ætatis 46 ann. 8 Aug. aº 1665. = Elizabeth daughter of John Anby of Sherwood in com. Ebor.

BARKESTONE ASHE WAPENTAKE. *Pontfract*, 8 *Aug.* 1665.

FLETCHER OF TOWTON.

ARMS.—Argent, a chevron between three mullets sable, a crescent for difference.

Bartholmew Fletcher of Campsall, died in aº 1631 (vel circa). = Jane, daughter of Tho. Ricard of Hatfield in co. Eborū.

2. Anthony Fletcher of Yorke, a merchant of Dordreicht and deputy to the company of English merchants there, æt. 64 ann. 8º Aug. 1665. = Joane, ye daughter of Edw. Missenden of Hackney in com. Midd.

1. Thomas Fletcher of St Edmondsbury in Suffolk, serjeant-at-law, died in aº 1659, or thereabouts. = ... daughter of ...... Wood.

1. Elizabeth, wife of Gervase Hamond of Scardingwell in com. Ebor. Esqr.
2. Jane, wife of .... Wildebore of Balne in com. Ebor.

Children of Anthony and Joane:

1. Elizabeth.
2. Mary.

1. Edward Fletcher æt. 33 ann. 8 Aug. aº 1665.
2. Anthony Fletcher of Towton in com. Ebor. æt. 25 ann. 8 Aug. 1665.
3. Christopher.
4. Gervase.
5. Marke.
6. Samuell.

Children of Thomas:

1. Thomas, now living, aº 1665.
2. Anthony.

1. Anne, wife of Sr Robt Sewster of Raveley in com. Hunt. Kt.
2. Elizabeth.
3. Frances.
4. Jane.
5. Alice.

THE BURROUGH OF LEEDES. *Leedes*, 11 *Aug*. 1665.

SPENSER OF LEEDS.

ARMS.—Argent, two bars gemelles between three sea-mews displayed sable.

It appeares that the grant of the armes was to Sr John Spencer, Ld Mayor, and his descendants: therefore these have no right to them.

William Spenser of .... neer Stanford in com. Linc. cosen german to Sr John Spenser, late Ld Mayor of London. = ...

3. Oliver Spenser of Enfield in com. Midd.

2. John Spenser of Enfield in com. Midd.

1. Robert Spenser, citizen and wax chandler of London, now living, 11° Aug. a° 1665. = Elizabeth, daughter of Edward Pitt of Houghton in com. Heref.

Ralph Spenser, a merchant in Leedes, æt. 33 an. 11° Aug. a° 1665. = Mary, daughter of Edmund Ogden of Rochedale in com. Lanc. draper.

Robert, æt. 2 an. 11 Aug. a° 1665.

SKYRACK WAPENTAKE. *Leedes*, 11 *Aug*. 1665.

KILLINGBECK OF CHAPELL-ALLERTON.

ARMS.—Argent, on a chevron sable between three unicorn's heads couped azure as many annulets or.

Robert Killingbeck of Chapell Allerton in co. Ebor. a°. 1566. = Jane, daughter of Robt. Cockson of Allerton Gleadow in co. Ebor.

William Killingbeck of Chapell Allerton, died in a° 1525. = Frances, daughter of Richard Grimshaw of Mearehills in co. Lanc.

2. William Killingbeck of Chapell-Allerton, died a° 1650, vel circa. = Elizabeth, daughter of Peter Brame of Leedes in com. Ebor.

1. Robert Killingbeck of Chapell-Allerton. = Frances, daughter of Alexander Palmer of Linley in com. Ebor.

Thomas Killingbeck of Chapell-Allerton, æt. 49 ann. 11 Aug. a° 1665. = Mary, daughter of Richard Wilkinson of Manningham in com. Eborum.

1. Ursula, wife of John Stopper of Kettlewell in com. Ebor.

2. Anne.

3. Thomasine, wife of John Lathom of Whitekirke in com. Ebor.

William, died in ye lifetime of his father.

2. Thomas.

1. William, æt. 17 an. 11° Aug. a° 1665.

1. Jane.

2. Mary.

3. Elizabeth.

SKYRACK WAPENTAKE. *Leedes*, 11° *Aug*. 1665.

SUNDERLAND OF HARDEN.

ARMS.— ...... three lions passant ...... a crescent for difference.
CREST.—An antelope's head erased ......
Qu. for the colours and better proofe for ye bearinge.

Richard Sunderland of Sunderland in com. Ebor.=....

Richard Sunderland, of Sunderland.=....

2. Richard Sunderland, of Sunderland, died in a° 1634.=Mary, daughter of Sr Rich. Saltonstall, late Ld. Mayor of Lond.

1. Abraham, died without issue.

2. Mary, wife of Edw. Parker of Brous-holme in co. Ebor. Esq.

1. Susan, wife of William Beilby of Mickle-thwayt Grange in com. Ebor.

1. Abraham Sunderland of Sunderland, died in Pontfract Castle, in the time of the late siege.

2. Samuell Sunderland of Harden in com. Ebor. æt. 67 ann. 11° Aug. 1665.=Anne, daughter of Edward Waterhouse of Preistley in com. Ebor.

3. Peter Sunderland of Fair-weather-Greene near Bradford in co. Ebor.=

THE BURROUGH OF LEEDES. *Leedes*, 11 *Aug*. 1665.

SKELTON OF OSMUNDTHORPE.

ARMS.—Quarterly, 1 and 4, Azure, a fess between three fleurs-de-lis or ; 2 and 3, ... three crescents ......

Seth Skelton of Osmondthorpe in com. Ebor. died circa an. 1646.=Mary, daughter of Israell Forde of Hadley.

2. Henry Skelton of Osmundthorpe, in the parish of Leedes, and now Mayor of Leedes, æt. 45 an. 11° Aug. a° 1665.=Helen, daughter of Willm. Marshall of Moretowne in the parish of Leedes in com. Ebor.

1. William Skelton, died unmarried.

1. Anne, wife of William Hopkinson of ...... in co. Eborū.

2. Elizabeth, wife of William Southwell.

3. Jane, wife of Samuell Burdet.

2. John, æt. 3 ann.

1. Seth Skelton, æt. 15 ann. 11° Aug. 1665.

Anne.

In a° 1664, upon taking up of a large and thick marble stone, lying in the midst of the Church of BEVERLEY, neare ye Entrance into the Quire, there was found under it—

A Vault of squared freestone, five foot in length, two foot in breadth at ye head, and one foot and an halfe at the foot.

In which Vault there was—

A Sheet of Lead foure foot in length, contayning the Dust of ST. JOHN of BEVERLEY; as also six beades, whereof three were of Cornelian, the other crumbled to dust: there were also in it three great brasse pins, and foure iron nayles.

Upon this Sheet of Lead was fixed—

A Plate of Lead, whereon was this following inscription—

Also,

A Box of Lead, about seven inches in length, six inches broad, and five in heighth, lying athwert the plate of Lead.

In this Box were—

Divers peices of Bones, mixt with dust, yeilding a sweet smell.

All which were reinterred, by direction of the present Archbysshop of Yorke.

The inscription.

✠ ANNO AB INCARNATIŌE D̄NI M°C°LXXX°VIII CŌBVSTA FUIT HEC ECCL̄IA IN M̄SE SEPTĒBRI IN SEQ̄NTI NOCTE POST FESTV̄ S̄CI MATH̄ AP̄LI: ET IN ANNO M°C°XCVII VI IDVS MARTII F̄CA FUIT INQ̄SITIO RELIQ̄AR̄ B̄ATI JOH̄IS IN HOC LOCO ET INVENTA S̄T H̄ OSSA IN ORIENTAL̄I PARTE SEPVLCHRI ET HIC RECŌDITA ET PVLVIS CEM̄TO MIXT̄ IBIDEM INVENT̄ EST ET RECONDITUS.

OSGODCROSSE WAPENTAKE. *Pontfract*, 8 *Aug*. 1665.

AUSTWICK OF PONTFRACT.

ARMS.—Sable, a chevron engrailed between three cross-crosslets fitchée argent.

Thomas Austwick, Bayliff of Pontfract = ... tempore Edw. 3.

.... = ...

John Austwick = Joane ......

Robert Austwick, mayor of Pontfract a° 5° Henr. 7. = Catherine, daughter of Dionis Leventhorpe, a widow a° 20 H. 7.

Dennis Austwick, mayor of Pontfract a° 1508. = ...

Walter.

Thomas Austwick, mayor of Pontfract in a° 1542 et 1559. = ...

Alan Austwick, mayor of Pontfract in a° 1589 and 1594, to whom Edw. Talbot, Esq[r] (afterwards Earle of Shrewsbury), gave the mace. = ...

Thomas Austwick, mayor of Pontfret in a° 1621 et 1640. Died in March 1648. = Sarah, daughter of Edward Morehouse of Simondley in co. Derb.

Dorothy, wife of George Boothe of Glossop in co. Derb.

Elizabeth, wife unto George Ethrington.

Jane.

Sarah, y[e] wife of John Sale of Darton in com. Ebor.

Thomas, died without issue.

Alan Austwick, lieutenant of horse in the service of K. Charles the First, and one of the persons excepted for life upon the render of Pontfract Castle, 21 Martij 1648. Died unmarried a° 1655. Buried at Standon in Wiltshire.

Richard Austwick, now mayor of Pontfract, æt. 35 ann. et amplius 8° Aug. 1665. = Isabell, daughter of Rich. Stable of Tanshelfe in co. Eborum.

Alan, died an infant.

Richard, died an infant.

Thomas, æt. 4 an. 8 Aug. 1665.

1. Sarah.

2. Elizabeth.

SKYRACK WAPENTAKE. *Leedes*, 10 *Aug.* 1665.

MORE OF AUSTROP.

ARMS.—Quarterly of seven:
1. Argent, a chevron and in chief a pile between three fleurs-de-lis sable. More of Austrop.
2. Argent, a fess between two greyhounds courant sable. Hall of Austrop.
3. ...... on a chevron between three fleurs-de-lis as many mullets. ...... Wayte.
4. .... Otterburne.
5. Or, a fess dancettée sable, a mullet for difference. Vavasour of Austrop.
6. Gules, six lions rampant argent. Heslarton.
7. Argent, a fess dancettée paly of four sable and gules between three mullets of the second. More of Hornesey.

An escutcheon of pretence: Argent, on a fess gules between three church-bells azure as many crosses formée of the field. Oxley.

Nicholas More of Austrop in com. Ebor. died circa annum 1653. = Jane, daughter of Robt Portington of Barneby super Dun in co. Ebor.

2. Nicholas More of Maltby in com. Linc. = Susan, daughter and coheir of John Priscot of Maltby, in com. Linc.

1. Richard Moore of Austrop, Esq[r], died in his father's lifetime. = Mary, daughter and sole heire of Rob[t] More of Hornesey in com. Ebor. Esq[r].

1. Susan, wife to Robert Franke of Allwoodley in co. Ebor.
2. Sarah, wife of .... Lawrence, clerke.
3. Anne, wife of John Barret.
4. Elizabeth, wife of Miles Douglas of Austrop-Hall neer Ledes in com. Ebor.

Children of Nicholas More of Maltby:
1. John.
2. Nicholas.
3. Ingram.
4. Richard.
Anne.

Children of Richard Moore:

Mary, wife of Edmund Clough, of Skipton-bridge, in com. Ebor. gent.

1. Nicholas More of Austrop, Esqr, æt. 35 ann. 10 Aug. 1665. = Mary, daugh. and sole heire of John Oxley of Yorke.

2. John More, æt. 34 an. 10 Aug. 1665. = Mary, 5th daughter of John Constable of Catfosse in co. Ebor. Esq.

Children of Nicholas More:
1. John, æt. 9° an. 10 Aug. 1665.
2. Richard, æt. 7 an. 10 Aug. 1665.
3. Thomas, æt. 2 an. 10° Aug. 1665.
4. Nicholas, died young.
1. Anne, died young.
2. Rebecca, ætatis sex septim. 10 Aug. a° 1665.

Children of John More:
1. Richard. 2. John.

STAINECROSSE WAPENTAKE. *Leedes*, 10 *Aug.* 1665.

ARMITAGE OF KERESFORTH-HILL.

ARMS.—Gules, a lion's head erased between three crosses botonnée argent, a mullet for difference.

Qu. To the Visitation of Linc. for proofe of these Armes.

John Armitage of Kirklees in com. Ebor. (Descended from the Armitages of Golberkirk, in co. Linc.) = Emme, dau. of John Gregory of Kingston-upon-Hull. 1st. wife.

- 3. Edward Armitage of Keresforth Hill in com. Ebor. died in Aug. 1643. = Elizabeth, sole daugh. and heire of Edw. Hanson of Little Royde in com. Ebor.
- 2. Gregory, Armitage of Netherton in co. Eborum. =
- 1. John Armitage of Kirklees in com. Ebor. = Winifride, daughter of Henry Knight of Knighthill and Brockhull

Children of Edward Armitage and Elizabeth:

- 2. Elizabeth. 3. Mary. died unmarried.
- 1. Anne, wife of William Gamble of Blacker in com. Ebor.
- Mary, sole daughter and heire of Mathew Whitley of Shelfe juxta Halifax in com. Ebor. 1 wife. = 1. John Armitage of Keresforth Hill, died 7° May 1664. = Elizabeth, daughter of John Dranfield of Eland in com. Eborum, 2d wife.
- 2. Edmund, died unmarried.

Children of John Armitage and Mary (1 wife):

- Mary, wife unto Henry Crowther of Eland in co. Eborum.
- 1. Edward Armitage of Keresforth Hill, æt. 29 ann. 10 Aug. 1665.

Children of John Armitage and Elizabeth (2d wife):

- 2. John, æt. 19 ann. 10 Aug. 1665.
- 3. William. 4. George. 5. Gervase.
- Elizabeth.

BURROUGH OF LEEDES. *Leedes*, 11 *Aug.* 1665.

SCUDAMORE OF LEEDES.

ARMS.—Gules, three stirrups leathered and buckled or, a canton argent.

CREST.—Out of a ducal coronet or, a lion's gamb erect sable charged with a trefoil slipped of the first.

Thomas Scudamore of Overton neere Yorke, died in a° 1621. = Mary, eldest daughter of John Jenkins of Yorke, Esq.

- 4. Hugh Scudamore of Holtby in co. Ebor, Clerke, died in May, a° 1665. = Alice, dau. of ...... Watkinson of Ilkley, in com. Ebor.
- 3. Francis Scudamoro, died unmarried.
- 2. John Scudamore. =
- 1. William Scudamore of Shipton in co. Ebor. =
- 1. Jane. 2. Elizabeth.

Children of Hugh Scudamore and Alice:

- 1. Thomas Scudamore of Leedes, æt. 35 ann. 11° Aug. 1665. = Barbara, daughter of Edward Ashton, of Clubcliffe Hall in com. Ebor.
- 2. Joseph Scudamore. 3. John Scudamore.
- 1. Elizabeth, died unmarried.
- 2. Dorothy, wife of Thomas Lasenby of Durham.
- 3. Alice.

Children of Thomas Scudamore and Barbara:

- Thomas, æt. 5. ann. 11° Aug. a° 1665.
- 1. Mary.
- 2. Alice.
- 3. Elizabeth.
- 4. Eleanor.

THE BURROUGH OF LEEDES. *Leedes*, 11° *Aug.* 1665.

BEAVOT OF LEEDES.

ARMS.—Sable, a chevron engrailed ermine between three wolf's heads erased argent.

CREST.—Out of a ducal coronet azure a wolf's head erased ermine, in the mouth a gilliflower proper.

Raphe Beavot of Wakefield in com. Ebor.=Margaret daughter of Henry Bentley.

1. Edward=........ Beavot of Kirkby.

2. Bryan Beavot=.... daughter of ..... Tattershall. of Wakefield in com. Ebor.

3. William Beavot of Wakefield in com. Ebor.=..

Robert Beavot of Kirkby in com. Eborum.=Elizabeth, daughter of Edward Goodrick of Eastkirk in com. Linc. Esq.

Thomas Beavot.=..

William Beavot of Leedes in com. Ebor. died in Aug. a°. 1660.=Susan, daughter of James Brokesbanke of Thorns neere Wakefield, in com Ebor.

Elizabeth, wife of Gilbert Dobson of Wodlesforth in com. Ebor.

Richard, now living, a°1665, unmarried.

Mary.

1. Edward Beavot, ob. s. prole.

2. Robert Beavot, ob. s. prole.

Richard Beavot, died a° 1655. vel circa.=..

Two daughters.

Richard Beavot, of Leedes, æt. 26 ann. 11° Aug. 1665.

CLARO WAPENTAKE. *Knaresborough*, 14 *Aug.* 1665.

BRANDLING OF LEATHLEY.

ARMS.—Gules, a cross flory argent, in the dexter chief point an escallop or, a crescent for difference.

CREST.—The trunk of an oak erased per pale or and vert, from the sinister two sprigs, leaves vert, fructed or, from the top flames issuing proper.

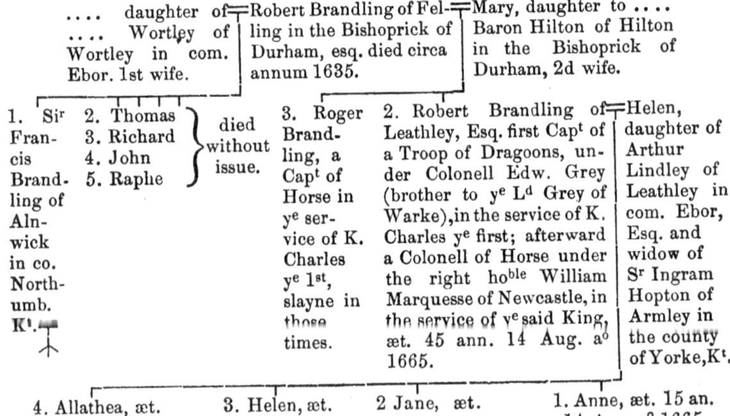

.... daughter of .... Wortley of Wortley in com. Ebor. 1st wife.=Robert Brandling of Felling in the Bishoprick of Durham, esq. died circa annum 1635.=Mary, daughter to .... Baron Hilton of Hilton in the Bishoprick of Durham, 2d wife.

1. Sir Francis Brandling of Alnwick in co. Northumb. Kt.

2. Thomas, 3. Richard, 4. John, 5. Raphe — died without issue.

3. Roger Brandling, a Capt of Horse in ye service of K. Charles ye 1st, slayne in those times.

2. Robert Brandling of Leathley, Esq. first Capt of a Troop of Dragoons, under Colonell Edw. Grey (brother to ye Ld Grey of Warke), in the service of K. Charles ye first; afterward a Colonell of Horse under the right hoble William Marquesse of Newcastle, in the service of ye said King, æt. 45 ann. 14 Aug. a° 1665.=Helen, daughter of Arthur Lindley of Leathley in com. Ebor, Esq. and widow of Sr Ingram Hopton of Armley in the county of Yorke, Kt.

4. Allathea, æt. 9 ann. 1665.

3. Helen, æt. 11 ann.

2 Jane, æt. 13 ann.

1. Anne, æt. 15 an. 14 Aug. a° 1665.

CLARO WAPENTAKE. *Knaresborough*, 14 *Aug.* 1665.

BURGOINE OF ADDLETHORPE.

ARMS.—Azure, a talbot passant argent.
CREST.—An heraldic antelope sejant argent, attired sable.

Thomas Burgoine of Long-Stanton in co. Cantabrigiæ. = Catherine, daughter to the Ld Chidiok Paulet, a younger son to the right hoble Will'm Earle of Wiltshire and first Ld Marquesse of Winchester.

Katherine, ye wife of ...... Blackshaw, citizen of London.
Frances, wife of .... Walton, afterwards of ....
Mary, wife of .... Darcy of ...., brother to Conyers Ld Darcy.

George Burgoigne of Spoford in com. Ebor. died ao 1657. = Elizabeth, daughter, of William Cheney of Kirkby-Overblows in com. Ebor.

2. William.
3. Francis.
died unmarried.

1. Peter Burgoigne of Addlethorpe in the parish of Spoford in co. Ebor. æt. 45 ann. 14o Aug. 1665. = Margaret, daugh. of Robert Menill of .... in Cleveland.

1. Thomas Burgoigne, died without issue.

Elizabeth, died young.

1. Elizabeth, died young.
2. Catherine, died young.
3. Margaret, æt. 3 ann. et dimidiu' 14 Aug. ao 1665.

CLARO WAPENTAKE. *Knaresborough*, 15 *Aug.* 1665.

FERRAND OF WESTHALL.

ARMS.—Argent, on a chief gules two crosses fleury vair, in the fess point a trefoil azure.
CREST.—A cubit-arm erect vested vair, the hand argent grasping a battle-axe proper.

William Ferrand of Skipton in Craven in com. Ebor. = Elizabeth, daughter of Tho. Blenkensop of Helbeck in com. Westmerl.

2. William Ferrand of Westhall in co. Ebor. died ao 1650 or thereabouts. = Anne, da. of Anth. Tomlinson of Gargrave in co. Ebor.

1. Thomas Ferrand of Carleton in Craven in com. Ebor. =

Thomas Ferrand of Westhall, æt. 63 ann. 15 Aug. 1665. = Agnes, daughter of Martin Flathers of Leathley in com. Ebor.

3. John, æt. 21 ann. 1665.
2. Thomas, æt. 27 ann. ao 1665.
1. William Ferrand, æt. 30 ann. 15 Aug. 1665. = Eleanor, daugh. of Joscelin Percy of Beverley in com. Ebor.
1. Anne, wife of Francis Swayne, a barrister-at-law, now residing at Yorke.
2. Frances.
3. Eleanor.

STAINECLIFFE WAPENTAKE. *Skipton*, 17 *Aug*. 1665.

PARKER OF BROUSHOLME.

ARMS.—Vert, a chevron between three buck's heads cabossed or.
CREST.—A stag trippant proper.

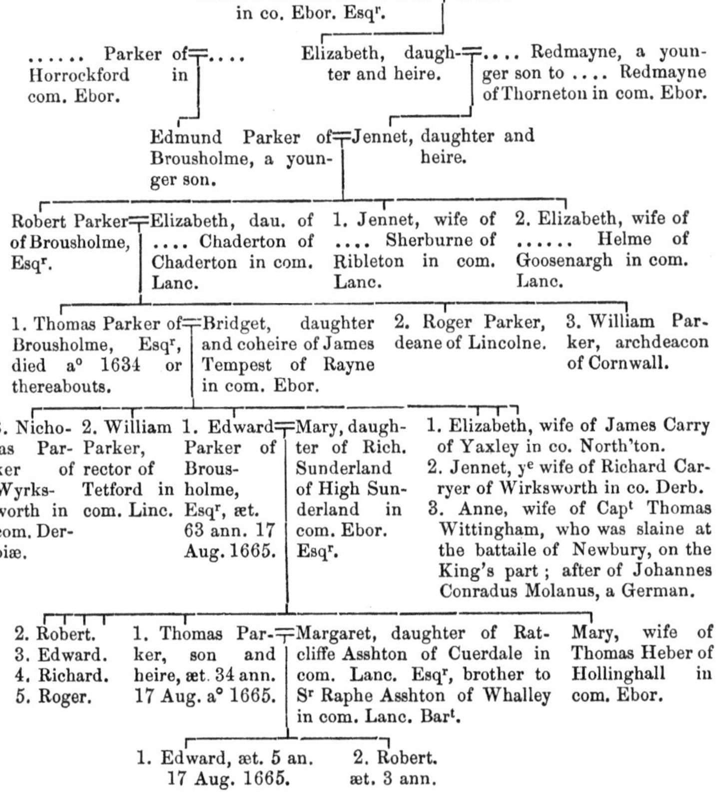

GILLING WEST WAPENTAKE. *Richmund*, 21 *Aug.* 1665.

PUDSEY OF LAWFEILD.

ARMS.—Vert, a chevron between three mullets or, a canton argent.

Thomas Pudsey of Barford in com. Ebor. died 34 H. 8. = Elizabeth, daughter to .... Lord Scroope of Bolton.

- 3. Ambrose Pudsey of High Close in S[t] John's parish in com. Ebor. died in a° 1624 or thereabouts. = ... daughter of .... Plaice of Dinsdale in com. Palat. Dunelm. widow of .... Dent. 1 wife. = Jane, daughter of Edward Wilkinson of North Allerton in com. Ebor. 2[d] wife.
  - (by the 1st wife) Elizabeth.
  - (by the 2nd wife) Michaell Pudsey of Lawfield in com. Ebor. æt. 46 ann. 21° Aug. a° 1665. = Mary, daughter to Gerard Salvein of Croxdale in co. Dunelm.
    - Thomas, æt. 11 ann. 21° Aug. 1665.
    - 1. Mary, æt. 22 an. 21 Aug. 1665.
    - 2. Elizabeth.
    - 3. Anne.
    - 4. Margaret.
  - 1. Margaret, wife unto Philip Anne of Frickley in co. Ebor.
  - 2. Catherine, wife unto Rob. Plaice of Dinsdale in co. Durham.
- 2. Henry, obijt sine prole.
- 1. William Pudsey of Bolton. =

CLARO WAPENTAKE. *Knaresborough*, 14 *Aug.* 1665.

FAWKES OF WOODHALL.

ARMS.—Ermine, a mascle sable.

Marmaduke Fawkes of South Duffeild in com. Ebor. living a° 1584. = Joane, daughter and heire of James Blanchard of Bowthorp in com. Ebor.

- Katherine, daughter of Peter Newarke of Acham in com. Ebor. Esq. 1st wife. Obijt s. prole. = Jane, daughter of ...... Arthington of Arthington in co. Ebor. Esq[r]. 2d wife. Obiit s. prole. = 3. Michaell Fawkes of Woodhall, South Duffeild, and Farneley in com. Ebor. Esqr, died a° 1647. = Mary, eldest da. of Sir John Molineux of Teversall in co. Nott. Bart. 3 wife.
  - 2. Martha.
  - 1. Anne, wife of Henry, son and heire of Henry Procter of Newhall in co. Ebor.
  - Thomas Fawkes of Farneley in com. Ebor. Esqr, æt. 25 ann. 14° Aug. 1665.
- 1. William.
- 2. Marmaduke.

  (William and Marmaduke) died unmarried.

CLARO WAPENTAKE. *Knaresborough*, 14 *Aug*. 1665.

INGLEBY OF RIPLEY.

ARMS.—Quarterly of nine:
1. Sable, an etoile of six points argent, on a canton the badge of Baronet of England. Ingleby.
2. Gules, a lion rampant argent within a bordure engrailed or. Moubray of Calton.
3. Argent, a chevron counter-embattled between three bird's heads erased sable. Chaumont of Colton.
4. Argent, a chevron between three lion's heads erased gules. Roucliffe of Roucliffe.
5. Argent, a saltire gules, on a chief of the second three escallops of the first. Talboys.
6. ...., on a bend three cinquefoils ....
7. Gules, two bendlets argent. Gant.
8. Gules, a cinquefoil within an orle of eight cross-crosslets fleury or. Humfreville.
9. ...., a chevron between ten cross-crosslets .... Kyme.

CREST.—A boar's head couped and erect argent, tusked or.

Sir William Ingleby of Ripley, Knt, Treasurer of the Towne of Barwick.=Anne, daughter of William Malory, of Studley in com. Ebor.

Their children:

- 6. John Ingleby, married Anne, daughter of ...... Babthorpe.
- 5. Sampson Ingleby, Steward to ye Earle of Northumberld, and resided at Spoford manour in co. Ebor.=Jane, daughter of .... Lambert of Killinghall in com Ebor.
- 3. John. 4. Francis. died without issue.
- 2. David Ingleby.=Anne, daughter of Charles Nevill Earle of Westmerland.
  - Mary, sole daughter and heire, wife to Sr Peter Middleton of Stockell in co. Ebor, Kt.
- Anne, sole daughter and heire of Thomas Thwaytes of Marston in co. Ebor. died without issue, 1 wife.=Sir Willm. Ingleby of Ripley, Kt, died without issue, 5 Jan. 1617.=Catherine, sole daughter and heire of Anthony Smith, alias Smetheley, of Brantingham in co. Ebor. died without issue, second wife.

Children of Sampson Ingleby and Jane:

- 2. Thomas Ingleby, died without issue.
- 1. Sr William Ingleby of Ripley, Kt and Bart. Cosyn and next heire to his Uncle Sir Willm. died 22° Jan. a° 1652.=Anne, daughter of Sr James Bellingham of Levens in com. Westmerland, Knt.
- Katherine, died unmarried.
- Mary, wife of Francis Appleby of Lartington in com. Ebor.
- Anne, wife of Francis Swale of Stainley in com. Ebor. Esqr.
- Elizabeth, a Nunne at Gant in Flanders.
- Jane, died unmarried.

Children of Sr William Ingleby and Anne:

- Agnes, died young
- 1. John. 2. Sampson. died young.
- 3. Sr Willm. Ingleby of Ripley, Bart. æt. 44 ann. 14 Aug. a° 1665.=Margaret, daughter of John Savile of Medley in com. Ebor. Esqr.
- 4. Henry Ingleby of Harrowgate in com. Ebor. died unmarried.

Children of Sr Willm. Ingleby and Margaret:

- Margaret, æt. 2 ann. et 6 mens. 14° Aug. a° 1665.
- John Ingleby, ætatis 9 mens. 14° Aug. 1665.

GILLING WEST WAPENTAKE. *Richmund*, 21 *Aug*. 1665.

TUNSTALL OF SCARGILL.

ARMS.—Quarterly, 1 and 4, Sable, three combs argent; 2. Argent, a chevron between three cross-crosslets sable; 3. Argent, on a chevron sable three buck's heads cabossed of the field.

Marmaduke Tunstall of Scargill in com. Ebor. Esqr. died in a° 1657. = Catherine, daughter and co-heire of William Wicliffe of Wicliffe in com. Ebor. Esqr.

2. Francis Tunstall of Ovington in com. Ebor. æt. 42 ann. 21 Aug. 1665.	= Anne, daughter of Sr Tho. Ridell of Fenham in in com. Northumbr. Kn^t.	1. William Tunstall of Scargill, Esqr. æt. 52 ann. 21 Aug. 1665.	= Mary, eldest da. to Sr Edw. Radcliffe of Dilston in com. Northumb. Bart.	1. Elizabeth, y^e wife of George Markham of Ollerton in com. Nott. Esqr.	2. Catherine, y^e wife of Thomas Cholmeley of Bransby in co. Ebor. Esqr.

Children of Francis and Anne: 1. Catherine. 2. Barbara. 3. Mary. 1. Marmaduke, ætatis 6 ann. 21 Aug. 1665. 2. Willm. æt. 5 ann. 3. Thomas, ætatis 3 ann.

Children of William and Mary: 2. Thomas, æt. 25 ann. 1. Francis Tunstall, æt. 28 ann. 21 Aug. 1665. = Cecelie, daughter of John Viscount Dunbar (*nunc gravida*). 1. Mary, wife of Henry Liddell of Farnacres in Episc. Dunelm. ar. 2. Christian. 3. Margaret. 4. Elizabeth. 5. Anne.

STAINECLIFFE WAPENTAKE. *Skipton*, 17 *Aug*. 1665.

FERRAND OF FLASBY.

ARMS.—Argent, on a chief gules two crosses fleury vair, a crescent for difference.
CREST.—A cubit-arm erect vested vair, the hand grasping a battle-axe proper.

Mary, daughter of Edmund Dudley of Yenwith in com. Westmerland, 1st wife. = Thomas Farrand of Carleton in Com. Ebor. died a° 1627. = Blanch, daughter of Edmund Towneley of Royle in com. Lanc. 2d wife.

By 1st wife: Edmund Ferrand. = ⊥

By 2d wife:

2. Brian Ferrand of Flasby in Craven in co. Ebor. æt. 42 ann. 17 Aug. a° 1665.	= Jane, daughter of Thomas Wayte of Bernoldswick in co. Ebor.	1. William Ferrand, died an infant.	1. Elizabeth, y^e wife of John Foufeld of Bolton in y^e Moores in com. Lanc.	2. Mary, wife of George Martinscroft of Manchester in co. Lanc.	3. Blanch, wife unto Hugh Currer of Kildwick in com. Ebor.

Children of Brian and Jane: Thomas, æt. 11 ann. 17 Aug. 1665. Catherine.

STAINECLIFFE WAPENTAKE. *Skipton*, 17 *Aug.* 1665.

LYSTER OF ARNOLDS BIGGIN.

ARMS.—Quarterly:

1. Ermine, on a fess sable three mullets or.
2. Azure, a chevron argent between three mullets gules, on the dexter and sinister chief points two arrows in pale or.
3. Argent, a water-bouget between four fleurs-de-lis sable.
4. Or, on a bend sable three roses of the field.

CREST.—A stag's head erased, per fess proper and or, a crescent for difference.

Thomas Lyster of Westby in co. Ebor. Esq. = Jane, daughter of Tho. Heber of Marton in com. Ebor. Esqr.

Thomas Lyster of Westby, Esqr, died in a^o 1642. = Catherine, daughter of Sr Rich. Fletcher of Hutton, in co. Cumb^r K^t.

2. John Lyster of Arnolds Biggin in co. Ebor. Esqr, æt. 24 ann. 17 Aug. a^o 1665. = Mary, daughter of Will'm Lodge, a merchant in Leeds in com. Ebor.

1. Thomas Lyster of Arnolds Biggin, Esqr, died in Oct. a^o 1660. = Mary, daughter of ...... Deane of Ovenden Wood in com. Ebor.

Barbara, wife of Will'm Nowell of Merclay in co. Lanc.

Catherine, æt. 4 ann. 17 Aug. a^o 1665.

STAINECLIFFE WAPENTAKE. *Skipton*, 17 *Aug.* 1665.

WADE OF KILNSAY.

ARMS.—Azure, a saltire between four escallops or.
CREST.—A rhinoceros argent.

No proofe made of these armes.

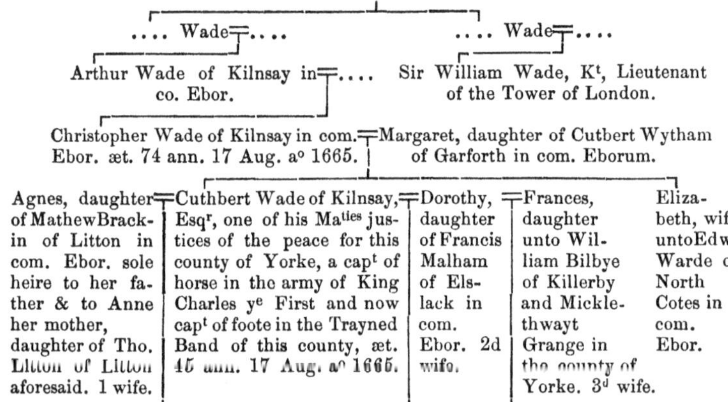

.... = ...

.... Wade = ...

.... Wade = ...

Arthur Wade of Kilnsay in co. Ebor. = ...

Sir William Wade, K^t, Lieutenant of the Tower of London.

Christopher Wade of Kilnsay in com. Ebor. æt. 74 ann. 17 Aug. a^o 1665. = Margaret, daughter of Cutbert Wytham of Garforth in com. Eborum.

Agnes, daughter of Mathew Brackin of Litton in com. Ebor. sole heire to her father & to Anne her mother, daughter of Tho. Litton of Litton aforesaid. 1 wife. = Cuthbert Wade of Kilnsay, Esqr, one of his Maties justices of the peace for this county of Yorke, a capt^t of horse in the army of King Charles y^e First and now cap^t of foote in the Trayned Band of this county, æt. 45 ann. 17 Aug. a^o 1665. = Dorothy, daughter of Francis Malham of Elslack in com. Ebor. 2d wife. = Frances, daughter unto William Bilbye of Killerby and Micklethwayt Grange in the county of Yorke. 3^d wife.

Elizabeth, wife unto Edw. Warde of North Cotes in com. Ebor.

1. Christopher, died in his father's lifetime unmarried.
2. Cutbert, died unmarried.

1. Margaret.
2. Elizabeth.
3. Anne.
4. Mary.

Francis, died young.
Hesther, died young.

Cutbert, æt. 2 an. 17 Aug. 1665.

Frances, ætatis 1 anni.

STAINECLIFFE WAPENTAKE. *Skipton*, 16 *Aug.* 1665.

CRAVEN OF APPLETREEWICK.

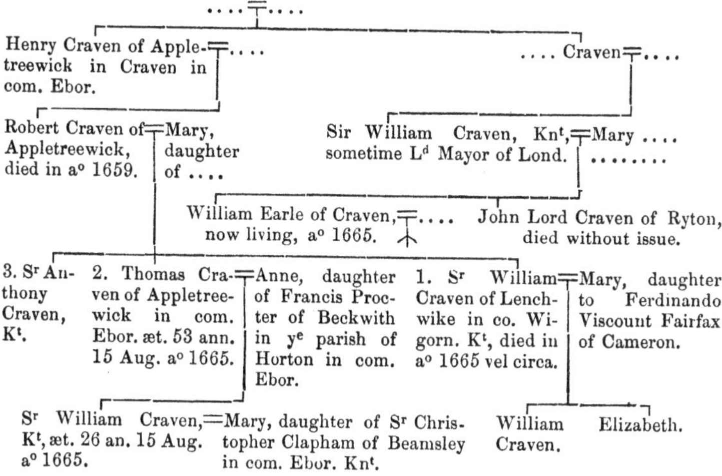

The Deeds of Charitie done by Sir Wm Craven, Kn^t, sometime Lord Mayor of London :

1. He founded a freeschoole in Burnesall in com. Ebor. and endowed it with Lands of xx^{li} per an. to the Head Master and x^{li} per annum to the Usher.
2. He gave x^{li} per ann. lands for repairs of bridges and highwayes in the same parish.
3. He built three stone bridges, one over the river Barbon, another over the river Wherfe, and the third over the river Hogill, all in or near Burnesall, and paved the highwayes betwixt Burnesall and Appletreewick.
4. He new seated the church of Burnesall, repaired it well, and gave xl^s per ann. for the perpetuall repaire of it.

The Deedes of Charitie of Mary, wife of the aforesaid Sir William Craven, K^t:
She gave c^{li} for a stock for the poore of Burnesall parish aforesaid.

The Deeds of Charitie done by John Ld Craven of Ryton, 2d sonne of the aforesaid Sr William Craven, K^t:

1. He gave c^{li}, the one halfe for the putting of poore children apprentices of the parish of Burnesall, and the other halfe for a stock for the poore of that parish.
2. He gave cc^{li} to the poore of Skipton in Craven for a stock.
3. He gave cc^{li} to the poore of Rippon for a stock.
4. He gave cc^{li} to the poore of Ripley.
5. He gave cc^{li} to the poore of Knaresborough.
6. He gave cc^{li} to the poore of Burroughbrigg.

STAINECLIFFE WAPENTAKE. *Skipton*, 17 *Aug.* 1665.

HEBER OF STAINTON.

ARMS.—Per fess azure and gules, a lion rampant or, in the dexter chief point a cinquefoil argent.

CREST.—Out of a ducal coronet or, a woman's head and shoulders in profile proper, crined or.

Mary, daughter of . . . . Wicliffe, 2 wife. = Thomas Heber of Marton in com. Ebor, Esqr. = Eleanor, daughter of . . . . Ferrand of Carleton in Craven in co. Ebor. 1 wife.

3. Thomas Heber of Marton, Esqr. died in a^{o} 1659 or thereabout. = Anne, daughter of William Lowther of Ingleton in com. Ebor. Esq.

2. Josias.

1. Francis.

Thomas Heber of Staynton and Marton in com. Ebor. Esqr. ætat. 44 ann. 17 Aug. 1665. = Bridget, daughter of Will'm Pennington of Moncaster in com. Cumbr. Esqr.

Jane, wife of Thomas Lyster of Westby, afterwards of Ric. Aske.

4. Ambrose.

3. Pennington, æt. 5 ann.

2. Reginald, æt. 10 ann.

1. Thomas, æt. 18 an. 17° Aug. 1665.

1. Anne.

2. Catherine.

3. Eleanor.

GILLINGWEST WAPENTAKE. *Richmund*, 19 *Aug.* 1665.

ROBINSON OF ROKESBY.

ARMS.—Vert, on a chevron or between three bucks trippant of the second, pellettée, as many quatrefoils gules.

CREST.—A buck, as in the arms.

Respite for proofe of these arms.

William Robynson, a Merchant in London, first resided at Rokesby in com. Ebor. died a^{o} 1643. = ...

2. John Robinson, Vicar of Burneston in co. Ebor. =

1. Thomas Robinson, an utter-barrister of Grayes Inne, died in his father's lifetime. = Frances, daughter of Leonard Smelt of Kirkby Fletham in co. Richmund.

Catherine, wife of Percevall Philips of Wensley in com. Ebor. afterward of Rich. Smith of Cottingham, in co. Ebor.

3. Leonard Robinson, Merch^{t} of London.

2. Mathew Robinson of Burneston in co. Ebor. D^{r} of Phisick.

1. William Robinson of Rokesby, Esqr. now one of his Maties justices of peace in this county, æt. 40 ann. 19 Aug. 1665. = Mary, daughter of Francis Layton of Rawden in com. Ebor. Esqr.

1. Mary, wife of Christopher Blenco of Blenco in co. Cumbr. Esqr.

2. Frances, wife of George Gray of Sudwick in the bishoprick of Durham.

Thomas Robinson, æt. 13 an. 19 Aug. 1665.

1. Frances.

2. Anne.

HANGWEST WAPENTAKE. *Richmund*, 19 *Aug*. 1665.

WAYTE OF LAYBURNE.

Respit given for inserting the armes.

James Wayte of Layborne in co. Ebor. ╤ Anne, daughter of Gilbert Metcalfe of Hude in com. Ebor.

Their children:

- 2. James Wayte, died unmarried.
- 1. George Wayte of Layborne, died 9° Martij a° 1664. ╤ Agnes, daughter of John Towneley of Hurstwood in com. Lanc.
- Helen, died young.

Children of George Wayte and Agnes:

- 5. Frances, wife of Francis Thorneborough of Selshead in co. Westmerl.
- 4. Jane, ye wife of John Lambert of Askrigg in co. Ebor.
- 3. Elizabeth, wife of Robt Rennison of Layburne in com. Eborum.
- 2. Anne, wife of John Adamson of Thornton in co. Ebor.
- 1. Helen.
- 1. James Wayte, æt. 48 ann. 19 Aug. 1665.
- 2. George Wayte of Layburne, æt. 40 ann. 19 Aug. 1665. ╤ Mary, daughter of Abraham Langton of the Lowe in com. Lanc. Esqr.

Children of George Wayte and Mary:

- George, æt. 3 septim. 19 Aug. 1665.
- Mary.

HANGWEST WAPENTAKE. *Richmund*, 19° *Aug*. 1665.

BEVERLEY OF GREAT-SMETON.

ARMS.—Ermine, a chevron sable, on a chief of the second three bull's heads cabossed argent.
CREST.—A bull's head erased sable.

Thomas Beverley of Selbye in com. Ebor. Esqr. ╤ Eleanor, daughter and coheire of Marmaduke Vincent of Great Smeton in com. Ebor. 2d wife.

Their children:

- 2. John Beverley of Gainsted. ╤ (issue shown by a descent mark)
- 1. Vincent Beverley of Great Smeton, Esqr. died a° 1634, or thereabouts. ╤ Mary, daughter of George Twisleton of Barlow in com. Ebor.

Children of Vincent Beverley and Mary:

- John Beverley of great Smeton in co. Ebor. Esqr. æt. 47 ann. 19 Aug. 1665.
  - married first: Elizabeth, dau. of Rich. Beaumont of Whitley in co. Ebor. Esqr. first wife, ob. s. prole.
  - married second: ╤ Mary, daughter of John Dalton of Hawkeswell in com. Ebor. Esqr. 2d wife.
- Jane, wife of John Robinson of ...... in com. Ebor.

Children of John Beverley and Mary:

- 2. Thomas.
- 1. John, æt. 9 an. 19 Aug. 1665.
- 1. Dorothy, æt. 11 an. a° 1665.
- 2. Elizabeth.
- 3. Mary.
- 4. Anne.

HANGWEST WAPENTAKE. *Richmond*, 19º *Aug.* 1665.

SCROOPE OF DANBY.

ARMS.—Quarterly of twelve:

1. Azure, a bend or.
2. ...... a fess between three leopard's faces ......
3. Azure, a chief gules, over all a lion rampant or.
4. Argent, on a bend gules three pairs of wings conjoined and inverted of the field.
5. Argent, a saltire engrailed gules.
6. Argent, a fess double-cotised gules.
7. Azure, a bend or, over all a label of three points argent, a crescent for difference.
8. Argent, a chevron and in the dexter chief point an annulet sable.
9. Or, three chevrons gules, over all a label of three points ......
10. ...... a manche ......
11. ...... a lion rampant ......
12. ...... three covered cups or.

CREST.—Out of a ducal coronet or a plume of ostrich's feathers azure.

Henry Lᵈ Scroope of Bolton ═ Elizabeth, daughter of Henry Percy Earle of Northumberland.

Their issue:

- 1. Henry Lᵈ Scroope of Bolton ═ (1) .... daughter to the Lᵈ Scroope of Upsall. 1 wife; ═ (2) Alice, sole daughter and heire to Thomas Lᵈ Dacres of Gilsland. 2d wife.
    - By the 1st wife: Alice, died without issue.
    - By the 2d wife: John Lᵈ Scroope of Bolton ═ Catherine, daugh. to Henry Earle of Cumberland.
        - Henry Lᵈ Scroope, Kᵗ of the most noble order of the Garter and Warden of the West Marches towards Scotland ═ (1) Mary, daughter of .. Lord North. 1 wife; ═ (2) Margaret, sister to Tho. Duke of Norffolke. 2d wife.
            - Thomas Lord Scroope ═ Philadelpha, daughter to Henry Lord Hunsden.
                - Emanuell Lᵈ Scrope Earle of Sunderland, died without issue legitimate.
- 2. John Scroope of Spenithorn in co. Ebor. ═ .... daughter unto Thomas Rokesby.
    - 1. Henry Scroope of Spenithorne, in co. Ebor. Esqʳ. ═ Margaret, daughter of Symon Conyers of Danby in com. Ebor. Esqʳ.
        - 1. Francis Scroope of Danby, Esqʳ, died without issue. ═ ..
        - 2. Henry, obiit sine prole.
        - 3. Christopher Scroope of Spenithorne, died in aº 1637. ═ Margaret, daughter of .... Beesley.
            - 1. Henry Scroope, died in aº 1642. ═ Anne, da. of Sʳ Edw. Plompton of Plompton in co. Ebor. Kᵗ.
                - Anne, wife of Thomas Tempest, brother to Sʳ Stephen Tempest.
            - 2. Francis. 3. John. ob. s. p.
            - 4. Symon Scroope of Danby, Esqʳ, æt. 50 an. 19 Aug. 1665. ═ Mary, da. of Michaell Wharton of Beverley in co. Ebor. Esqʳ
                - Catherine, æt. 1 anni et 9 mens. 19 Aug. aº 1665.
            - 5. Christopher.
            - 6. Thomas Scroope. ═ Margaret, daugh. of John Wray of .... in com. Ebor.
                - Christopher, æt. 11 ann. 19 Aug. aº 1665.
            - Anne yᵉ wife of Edward Topham of Aglethorpe in com. Eboru.
            - Bridget.
            - Mary, wife of Frederick Windsor.
        - 4. John Scroope. ═ .... da. of .... Thersby.
        - .... wife of .. Hyndemersh.
        - .... wife of .. Conyers.
    - 2. Raphe Scroope. ═ .... the Lady Windsor.

HANGWEST WAPENTAKE. *Richmund*, 19 *Aug*. 1665.

WYVELL OF BELLARBY.

ARMS.—Quarterly:
1. Gules, three chevronels braced in base vair, a chief or.
2. Argent, three pickaxes sable, a crescent for difference,
3. Sable, a chief indented argent.
4. Azure, a bend or, over all a label of three points argent.

CREST.—A wyvern with wings endorsed......

Sir Marmaduke Wyvell of Constable Burton in com. Ebor. K^t^ & Bar^t^. = Magdalen, daughter of Sr Christopher Danby of Thorneley in com. Ebor. K^t^.

Francis Wyvell, Rector of the Church of Spenithorne in com. Ebor. the third son from whom any issue remaynes, died in a° 1649. = Helen, daughter of Thomas Norton of Burnby in co. Ebor.

3. Rowland.

Elizabeth, daughter of Peter Norton of Dishford in com. Ebor. 2 wife. = 2. Edward Wyvell. = Elizabeth, da. of Henry Pearson of Richmond, first wife.

1. Thomas Wyvell of Bellerby in co. Ebor. æt. 45 ann. 19 Aug. 1665. = Mary, daugh. of Christoph^r^ Place of Dinsdale in Episcopatu Dunelmensi.

Helen, wife of Thomas Crosfeild, of ...... in co. Westmerl. afterwards of Edw. Preston, citizen of Yorke.

Francis, æt. septē mens. 19 Aug. a°. 1665.

Edward, æt. 8 an. 19 Aug. 1665.

Margaret, ætatis 6 ann. 1665.

Mary, æt. 7 ann. 19 Aug. 1665.

ALLERTONSHIRE WAPENTAKE. *Threske*, 23 *Aug.* 1665.

TALBOT OF THORNETON-LE-STREETE.

ARMS.—Quarterly:

1. Argent, three lions rampant purpure.
2. Per pale ...... and ...... a lion rampant ......
3. ...... three cross-crosslets fitchée and a chief ......
4. Quarterly ...... and ......, a bend ......

Another shield, quarterly of twelve:

1. Argent, three lions rampant purpure.
2. Quarterly or and gules.
3. Or, an escarbuncle sable.
4. Vairée or and gules, a bordure argent semée of lozenges sable.
5. Gules, two lions passant in pale argent, on a canton sable a fret or.
6. Per pale gules and sable, a lion rampant gardant argent ducally crowned or.
7. Azure, three mascles or, a crescent for difference.
8. Argent, two bars azure, in chief as many escallops gules.
9. Gules, three cross-crosslets fitchée and a chief or.
10. Or, a chevron gules between three martlets sable.
11. Argent, on a bend between six martlets gules three bezants.
12. Azure, three crescents argent.

John Talbot of Thornton in com. Ebor. Esqr. died in a^o 1645 or thereabout. = Frances, daughter to John Crosland of Hemsley in com. Ebor.

- 2. Charles, died unmarried.
- 1. John Talbot of Thorneton in le Streete, Esqr. died in a^o 1659. = Jane, daughter of Roger Southaby of Pocklington in co. Ebor.
- 1. Mary, wife of Christopher Fauconbridge of South Ottrington in co. Ebor.
- 2. Jane, died unmarried.

Children of John Talbot and Jane:

- John Talbot.
- 1. Roger Talbot of Thorneton in the Streete, Esqr. æt. 46 an. 23 Aug. 1665. = Eliz. daugh. of Ambrose Pudsey of Bolton in Craven in co. Ebor. Esqr.
- 1. Jane, died unmarried.
- 2. Isabell, wife of Rich. Meynill, a younger son to Tho. Meynill of Kilvington in com. Ebor.
- 3. Cath. wife of Rowland Hurwood, batchelour of law.
- 4. Mary, wife of Timothy Cliburne of Cliburne in co. Westmerl.
- 5. Elizabeth.

Children of Roger Talbot and Eliz.:

- 1. Bridget.
- 2. Jane.
- 3. Elizabeth.
- 4. Anne.
- 5. Catherine.
- 6. Florentia
- 1. Roger, æt. 6 ann. 23 Aug. 1665.
- 2. Ambrose.

CLARO WAPENTAKE. *Knaresborough*, 14° *Aug.* 1665.

SIMPSON OF WETHERBY.

Respit given for exhibiting the armes, but nothing done.

Robert Simpson of Great Edston in com. Ebor. = Elizabeth, daughter of Will. Wivill of Osgodby in co. Ebor. 2d wife.

1. Roger. 2. Willm. 3. Thomas. 4. George. died without issue.	John Simpson of Wetherby in com. Ebor. æt. 60 ann. 14 Aug. a° 1665, a cap[t] of foote in the army of King Charles the First in the regiment of Sr Will'm Pennyman, Bart.	= Anne, daughter to .... Penvaux of ...... in Wales, widow to George Hall of Wetherby in the county of Yorke.	1. Frances, wife of George Tildesley of Killerby in co. Ebor.	2. Elizabeth, wife unto Rob. Kirke of Kirkby-Moreside in com. Ebor.	3. Mary, wife of Francis Jackson of Sinnington in com. Ebor.

GILLING EST WAPENTAKE. *Richmund*, 21° *Aug.* 1665.

SMITHSON OF MOULTON.

ARMS.—Sable, three horseshoes or, in chief a label of three points ermine.
CREST.—A horse's head couped sable, bit and reins or.

Leonard Smithson of Moulton in com. Eborū = ...

4. Nicholas Smithson.	3. John Smithson.	2. Cutbert Smithson, died unmarried.	1. Christopher Smithson of Moulton, died in a° 1650.	= Dorothy, daughter of Leonard Calvert of Kipling in com. Ebor.	Jane, wife of John Pattison of Dobsole in com. Ebor.

Children of Christopher Smithson and Dorothy:

5. Grace, wife of Nich. Conyers of Cleasby in com. Eborum.	4. Helen, wife of Matthew Wastell of Ellerton-super-Swale in co. Ebor.	3. Elizabeth, wife unto John Meryton of Moulton in com. Eborum.	2. Mary, wife unto John Slingar of Danby Whisk in co. Ebor.	1. Frances, wife of John Burnet of Hurworth in episc. Dunelm.	1. George Smithson of Moulton, Esq. æt. 45 an. 21 Aug. 1665, now one of the justices of the peace for this county.	= Eleanor, da. of Col. Chas. Fairfax, a younger son of Tho. late Ld Fairfax of Cameron.	2. Thomas Smithson of Moulton, æt. 40 ann. 21° Aug. a° 1665.

Children of George Smithson and Eleanor:

2. William. 3. Charles. 4. Thomas.	George, æt. 12 an. 21° Aug. 1665.	1. Eleanor. 2. Mary. 3. Dorothy.

CLARO WAPENTAKE. *Knaresborough*, 15 *Aug.* 1665.

NORTON OF SAWLEY.

ARMS.—Azure, a maunche ermine, over all a bend gules.

Richard Norton of Norton in com. Ebor. Esqr, attainted in Qu. Eliz. time. = Susan, daughter unto Richard Lord Latimer.

3. Edmund Norton. = Cecelie, da. of .... Boynton & sister to Sr Thomas Boynton of Hanaby in co. Ebor. K^t.

2. John, died without issue male.

1. Francis Norton = Albreda, sister of Tho. Wimbish of .... in com. Linc.

Robert Norton of Swinton in co. Ebor. = ... daughter and coheire of ...... Staveley.

William Norton. = Margaret, sole da. and heire of Will'm Welbury of Newton in Cleveland.

Francis, a naturall son (of Francis Norton) =

John, died young.

Henry Norton of Burrowbrig. = Catherine, y^e daughter of Will. Tankard of Branton in com. Ebor.

Mauger Norton of Richmund in co. Ebor.

William Norton of Sawley, in co. Eborum. = Anne, eldest daughter and coheire of Sr Will'm Hilliard of Bishop-Wilton in co. Ebor. died circa an. 1645.

John, now 67 yeares & unmarr.

1. Theophilus.
2. Basill.
} died unmarried.

2. John.
3. Will'm.
4. Robert.

1. Welbury Norton of Sawley in com. Ebor. Esqr, now one of the justices of peace for this county, æt. 33 ann. 15° Aug. a° 1665. = Catherine, da. unto Thomas Norton of Langthorne in com. Ebor.

Anne.

2. Thomas, æt. 7 ann. 1665.

1. William, æt. 8 an. 15 Aug. 1665.

1. Catherine.
2. Mary.
3. Anne.
4. Helen.

CLARO WAPENTAKE. *Knaresborough*, 15° *Aug.* 1665.

GRAHAM OF NORTON-CONYERS.

ARMS.—Quarterly:

1. Or, on a chief sable three escallops of the field, all within a bordure engrailed azure, a crescent for difference.

2 and 3. Or, a fess checky argent and azure, in chief a chevron gules, all within a bordure engrailed of the third.

4. Azure, six annulets or, three, two, and one. Musgrave.

CREST.—Two wings addorsed or, charged with a crescent gules.

Sir Richard Graham of Netherby in com. Cumbr. Kt and Bart, died 28 Jan. a° 1650. = Catherine, daughter and co-heire of Thomas Musgrave of Comcatch in co. Cumbr. Esqr.

- 2. Sir Richard Graham of Norton-Conyers in com. Ebor. Bart, ætat. 28 ann. 15 Aug. a° 1665. = Elizabeth, daughter of Chichester Fortescue, son and heire to Sr Faythfull Fortescue of Tremiskin in the realme of Ireland, Knt.
  - 2. Chichester Graham, æt. 2 ann. 15 Aug. 1665.
  - 1. Richard, æt. 4 an. 15 Aug. a° 1665.
  - 1. Elizabeth, æt. 3 an. 15 Aug. a° 1665.
  - 2. Susan, ætatis 1 anni 15 Aug. a° 1665.
- 1. Sr George Graham of Netherby, Bart. = (issue)

SWALE OF SOUTH STAINLEY.

ARMS.—Quarterly of twelve: on an inescutcheon the badge of baronet of England.

1. Azure, a bend nebulée argent.
2. Sable, three buck's heads cabossed argent.
3. Sable, treillissée, the batunes interlaced, or, a canton gules.
4. Argent, on a fess cotised between three mullets pierced gules a greyhound courant or.
5. Argent, a friar habited sable, crined of the first, his hands proper conjoined and holding a cross pattée fitchée elevated in bend, and another pendent from a chaplet of beads, all or.
6. Azure, a chevron between three owls argent.
7. Paly of six argent and sable, on a bend gules three mullets or.
8. Or, a chief indented azure.
9. Azure, a bend or, over all a label of three points gules.
10. Argent, a lion rampant azure between three cross-crosslets gules.
11. Azure, on a bend or between six fusils sable, each charged with an escallop of the second, three escallops of the third.
12. As the first.

CREST.—A cross of the passion argent.

Francis Swale of South Stainley in com. Ebor. Esqr, died 26 Dec. 1629. = Anne, daughter of Sampson Ingilby of Ripley in com. Ebor. a younger son of Sr Will'm Ingleby of Ripley, K^t.

Issue:

- 13. Robert Swale, a capt of horse in the army of K. Charles the first and likewise of K. Charles ye 2d. = Mary, daugh. of ... Hawes, 1st wife. = ... 2d wife.
  - John.
  - John Swale.
  - Catherine.
- 5. Francis. 6. William. 7. Peter. 8. Francis. 9. Sampson. 10. George. 11. Henry. 12. Sampson. — all died young.
- 4. Charles Swale, a major in ye army of K. Charles 1st in the garrison of Oxford, and after the render thereof died a commander in France.
- Sarah, da. of Will'm Wilson of .... in com. Suff. gent. 1 wife. = 3. John Swale, capt of a foote company in ye army of King Charles ye First. = Eliza-beth, da. of ...... Hawes. 2d wife. = ... 3d wife.
  - 7. Alured.
  - 6. Godfrey, died young.
  - 5. Solomon.
  - 4. Robert.
- 2. Thomas, died unmarried.
- Mary, daughter of Robert Porey of Poryes in com. Norff. gent. 1 wife. = 1. Sr Solomon Swale of Swale Hall and South Stainley in com. Ebor. Bar^t, ætatis 55 ann. 14 Aug. 1665. = Anne, daughter of Charles Tankard of Whixley in co. Ebor. Esqr.
  - 3. Henry Swale, Esqr, æt. 26 ann. 14 Aug. 1665. = Dorothy, da. of Raphe Crathorne of Crathorne in co. Ebor. Esqr.
  - 1. John. 2. Will'm. — died unmarried.
  - 1. Mary, died young.
  - 2. Anne.
  - 3. Mary, died young.
- 1. Anne, died young.
- 2. Elizab. wife unto William Pinkney =
  - 1. Solomon.
  - 2. William.
  - Elizabeth.
- 3. Anne. 4. Jane. 5. Frances. — died unmarried.

Knaresborough, 15 *Aug*. 1665.

CLAPHAM OF BEAMSLEY.

ARMS.—Quarterly of six:

1. Argent, on a bend azure six fleurs-de-lis or, two, two, and two.
2. Argent, on a bend sable three covered cups or.
3. Gules, on a tower or a heron argent.
4. Gules, a cock standing on an escallop or.
5. Argent, three greyhounds in pale courant sable, collared or.
6. Sable, a cross between four maiden-heads couped at the shoulders argent, habited of the second, crined or.

CREST.—A lion rampant sable holding a sword argent, hilt and pomel or.

Catherine, daughter of Wm Thwayts of Londe in co. .... 1st wife. ═ George Clapham of Beamsley in com. Ebor. Esqr. ═ Eliz. daughter of .... Morgan of .... in com. Heref. 2d wife.

2. William. 3. Charles.

1. Gresham Clapham of Beamsley in co. Ebor. Esqr. died aº 1602. ═ Anne, daughter of Capt Will. Fisher, son of John Fisher of Packington in co. Warr.

Elizabeth.

Sr Sheffield Clapham, Kt, Major Generall at Stoad in Germany. ═ ...., daughter of .... Brabant.

George Clapham of Beamsley, Esqr, died in aº .... ═ Martha, daugh. of Reginald Heber of Marton in com. Ebor.

...... wife to ...... Asshton, son to Sr Raphe Assheton of Whalley in com. Lanc.

3. Anne, wife of Thomas Morley of Winnington in co. Lanc. Esqr.

2. Jane, wife of Robert Godsonne of Waterfouforth neere unto Yorke.

1. Elizabeth, wife to Richard Dawson of Heworth in co. Ebor.

6. William Clapham, a Canary Merchant.

5. Thomas Clapham, slayne at Preston fight in Lancash. aº 16.., in the service of K. Charles ye 1st.

4. Richard Clapham, capt of a foote company under Sr Richard Biron.

3. George Clapham, capt of a troope of horse for K. Charles the First under Sr Tho. Glemham, Kt. He died when the Scotts entred England at Sunderland, aº 1639.

2. Josias Clapham, Citizen of Yorke.

Mary, daughter of John Lowden of Wrenthorpe juxta Wakefield in com. Ebor. Esqr, 1 wife. ═ 1. Sr Christopher Clapham of Beamsley, Kt, æt. 57 ann. 15 Aug. 1665. ═ Margaret, daughter of Anth. Oldfeild of Spalding in com. Linc. Esqr, widow of Robert Moyle, Esq. one of the prothonotaryes of the court of Common Pleas, 2d wife.

1. Sheffeild Clapham, Esq. æt. 36 ann. 15 Aug. 1665. ═ Elizabeth, daughter of Sr Benjamin Thornbury, son to Dr Thornbury, late Bisshop of Worcester.

1. Mary, wife of .... Pitman, citizen of London.

2. Margaret, wife of Sr Willm. Craven of Appletreewick in co. Ebor.

3. Elizabeth.

2. Christopher. 9. Anthony.

George. Geffrey. } died young.

Martha. Anne. } died young.

3. Willm. æt. 4 ann.

2. Richard, æt. 5 an. 1665.

1. Christopher, æt. 8 ann. 15 Aug 1665.

1. Elizabeth, æt. 14 an. 1665.

2. Anne, æt. 10 ann.

3. Mary, æt. 2 ann. 1665.

GILLING WEST. *Richmund*, 21 *Aug.* 1665.

BRUNSKELL OF BOWES.

ARMS.—Or, a chevron sable, on a canton of the second an escallop of the field.
CREST.—A cubit-arm erect vested proper, the hand holding an escallop.

No proofe made of these armes.

Philip Brunskell of Bowes in com. Ebor. = ...

3. William of Brunskell, merchant of London.
2. Ambrose Brunskell of Northall, in co. Hertf.
1. Philip Brunskell of Bowes, æt. 50 an. 21 Aug. 1665. = Mary, daughter of Percevall Philips of Brignell in com. Eborum.

3. Francis. 2. Percevall. 1. Philip, æt. 21 an. 21 Aug 1665. Mary.

EWECROSSE WAPENTAKE. *Skipton*, 17 *Aug.* 1665.

BAYNES OF MEWITH-HEAD.

ARMS.—........ a thigh bone in fess surmounted of another in pale.

The proofe respited, but nothing done.

...... = ...

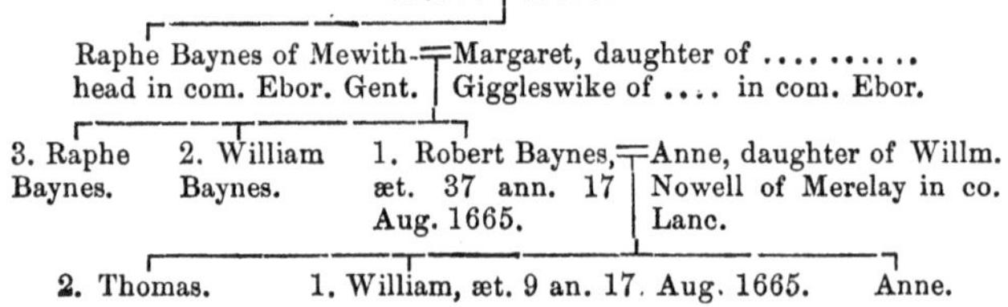

Raphe Baynes of Mewith-head in com. Ebor. Gent. = Margaret, daughter of .... Giggleswike of .... in com. Ebor.

3. Raphe Baynes.
2. William Baynes.
1. Robert Baynes, æt. 37 ann. 17 Aug. 1665. = Anne, daughter of Willm. Nowell of Merelay in co. Lanc.

2. Thomas. 1. William, æt. 9 an. 17. Aug. 1665. Anne.

EWECROSSE WAPENTAKE. *Skipton*, 17 *Aug*. 1665.

MARES OF SEDBRIDGE.

ARMS.—......, a ship with three masts in full sail.

The proofe of the coate respited, but nothing done.

John Mares of Sedbridge in com. Ebor.=......

Daniel Mares of Sedbridge in com. Ebor. died aº 1646 vel circa.=Catherine.

3. Thomas Mares, now in Ireland.

2. Daniell Mares, a capt of horse in the army of K. Charles the First, died unmarried.

1. John Mares of Sedbridge, commissary to ye Archdeacon of Richmund, ætatis 45 an. 17 Aug. 1665.=Margaret, da. of John Cowper of Sedbridge in co. Ebor.

Catherine, wife unto.... Burneley of .... in com. Ebor.

Daniell, æt. 10 an. 17 Aug. 1665.

STAINECLIFFE WAPENTAKE. *Skipton*, 17 *Aug*. 1665.

PERKINSON OF CARLETON.

ARMS—Or, a fess between three greyhounds courant sable.

CREST.—On a mount vert a stag lodged proper.

No proofe made of these armes.

William Parkinson of Eastburne in co. Ebor. aº 37 H. 6.

John Parkinson of Eastburne, 8 H. 7.

John Parkinson of Eastburne, 1 H. 8.=......

2. Edward.

1. William Parkinson, son and heire, 1 H. 8.=Elizabeth, daughter of John Stansfeild.

Will'm Perkinson=......

Dennis Perkinson, died in aº 1624 vel circa.=Elizabeth, daugh. of .... Hill of Winterburne in com. Ebor.

John Perkinson=.... daughter of .... Hyde of Winterburne in com. Ebor.

Rose, sole da. and heire, wife of Henry Jackson of Staveley in com. Derb.

4. Peter Perkinson of Denton in co. Ebor.

3. William Perkinson of Winterburne.

2. Thomas Perkinson of Carleton in Craven in co. Ebor. æt. 58 ann. 17 Aug. aº 1665.=Anne, daughter of Thomas Ellys of Bradley in co. Ebor.

1. John Perkinson of Estburne, æt. 70 an. 17 Aug. aº 1665.=Mary, daughter of .. Bradley of Connondley in com. Ebor.

1. Stephen
2. Nathaniell } died in their father's lifetime unmar.

1. Anna.
2. Mary.

1. William, ætat. 42 ann. 17 Aug. aº 1665.
2. Jonathan.

Elizabeth, wife of Stephen Morehouse of Eastburne in com. Ebor.

EWECROSSE WAPENTAKE. *Skipton*, 17 *Aug*. 1665.

INGLEBY OF LAWKELAND.

ARMS.—Quarterly:
1. Sable, an etoile argent, a canton or.
2. Gules, a lion rampant argent within a bordure engrailed or.
3. Argent, a chevron counter-embattled between three bird's heads erased sable.
4. Argent, a chevron between three lion's heads erased gules.

CREST.—A boar's head erect couped argent, tusked or.

Will'm Ingleby of Ripley in co. Ebor. Esqr = Cecelye, daughter to Sir George Talboys of Kime in com. Linc. K^{t}, and afterwards coheire.

2. John Ingleby, Governour of Leeth in Scotland temp. Edw. 6. = Anne, daughter of Will'm Clapham of Beamesley in co. Ebor.

1. Sr William Ingleby of Ripley in co. Ebor. K^{t}. =

1. Anne.
2. Margaret.
3. Elizabeth.
4. Joane.

Thomas Ingleby of Lawkeland in com. Ebor. Esqr, died circa an. 1615. = ... daughter of Sr Raphe Lawson of Brough in co. Ebor. K^{t}.

3. Francis, died unmarried.
2. William Ingleby of Palithorp in co. Ebor.

Isabell, da. of Nich. Towneley of Royle in co. Lanc. Esqr, 1 wife. = John Ingleby of Lawkeland in co. Ebor. Esq. died 29 Nov. a° 1648. = Mary, da. of Sr Tho. Lake of Cannons in co. Midd. K^{t}, 2 wife.

1. Anne, wife of William Charnock of Leyland in co. Lanc.
2. Cath. wife of .... Kay of Cleveland in co. Ebor.
3. Mary, wife of William Watson of Austwick in com. Ebor.

1. Isabell, wife of Richard Sherburne of Stanihurst in co. Lanc. Esqr.
2. Catherine, died unmarried.

1. Mary.
2. Eliz.

1. Thomas, died unmarried.

2. Arthur Ingleby of Lawkeland, Esqr, æt. 32 an. 17 Aug. 1665. = Margery, daughter of William Ferrington of Werdon in co. Lanc. Esqr.

4. Columbus.
5. Charles.
3. John.

GILLING-EAST WAPENTAKE. *Richmund*, 19 *Aug*. 1665.

DALTON OF HAWKESWELL.

ARMS.—Azure, semée of cross-croslets or, a lion rampant gardant argent, a chief barry nebulée of three of the last and sable.

CREST.—A dragon's head with wings displayed vert, the outside of the wings or, gorged with a collar nebulée of the last.

Thomas Dalton of Sutton in Holdernes in com. Ebor. = Anne, 2d daughter of Sr Robert Tirwhit of Kettleby in co. Linc. Kt.

Thomas, obijt sine prole.	Sir Willm. Dalton of the citty of Yorke, and one of ye King's Councell in his court there for ye Northern parts, died in a° 1649. = ... daughter of .... Boothe of Killingholme, in com. Linc. widow of .... Agard.	Robert Dalton of Swyne in Holdernes.	

John Dalton of Hawkeswell in com. Ebor. Esqr. died in a° 1646. = Dorothy, daughter of Conyers Ld Darcy and Conyers of Hornby Castle in com. Ebor.	Anne, wife of .... Grimston of Grymston-garth in Holderness.	Mary, died unmarried.

2. Barbara, ye wife of Charles Tankard of Arden in co. Ebor. Esqr.	1. Mary, ye wife of John Beverley of Smeton in com. Ebor. Esqr.	1. Sr Willm. Dalton, of Hawkeswell, Kt, æt. 36 ann. 19 Aug. 1665. = Elizabeth, daughter of Sr Marmaduke Wyvill of Constable Burton in com. Ebor. Kt and Bart.	2. Thomas Dalton of Yorke. = Anne, daugh. of Sr Marmaduke Wyvill of Constable-Burton in co. Ebor. Kt. and Bart.	3. Marmaduke.

3. Charles, æt. 5 ann. 1665.	2. Christopher æt. 7 ann. 1665.	1. Marmaduke, æt. 10 ann. 19 Aug. 1665.	1. Isabell, æt. 8 ann.	2. Dorothy.	3. Elizabeth.	4. Ursula.

HANGWEST WAPENTAKE. *Richmund*, 19 *Aug*. 1665.

COLBYE OF BOWBRIDGE.

Respite given for inserting ye armes and proving them.

Francis Colbye of Layston in Suffolke. = ... daughter of .... Jennings of .... in Suffolke.

John Colbye of Nappa in com. Ebor. died a° 1616. = Mary, daughter of Walter Calverley of Calverley in com. Ebor.

John Colbye of Bowbridge in com. Ebor. æt. 51 an. 19 Aug. 1665. = Jane, daughter of Alexander Moore of Grantham in com. Linc.

2. Christopher.	1. Alexander, æt. 25 an. 19 Aug. 1665. = Jane, daughter unto Christopher Tod of Midleham in co. Ebor.	1. Anne.	2. Margaret.	3. Jane.

THE BOROUGH OF LEEDES. *Leedes*, 12 *Aug*. 1665.

FOXCROFT OF WEETWOOD.

ARMS.—Azure, a chevron or between three fox's heads erased proper.
The proofe of the coate respited, but nothing done.

Daniel Foxcroft of Weetwood in the parish of Leedes and com. Ebor. = Grace, ye daughter of . . . . . . Platts.

Samuel Foxcroft = Mary, daughter of . . . . Hurst.

Daniel Foxcroft of Weetwood, died circa ann. 1640. = Abigall, daughter of . . . . Biron.

Daniell Foxcroft of Weetwood, æt. 34 ann. 12° Aug. 1665. = Martha, daughter of Francis Layton of Rawdon in co. Ebor. Esqr. | Samuell Foxcroft, died unmarried. | Susan.

2. Martha. | 1. Jane. | 1. Samuell, æt. 11 ann. 12 Aug. 1665. | 2. Daniell. | 3. Francis. | 4. Robert. | 5. James.

SKYRACK WAPENTAKE. *Leedes*, 11 *Aug*. 1665.

FERRAND OF HARDEN-BECK.

ARMS.—Argent, on a chief gules two crosses fleury vair, in the fess point a cinquefoil azure.
CREST.—A cubit-arm erect, vested vair, charged with a cinquefoil as in the arms, the hand grasping a battle-axe proper.

To expect a certificate from Mr. Ferrand of Carleton that this gentleman is of his family.

Christopher Ferrand of Bingley in com. Ebor. = ...

Richard Ferrand of Bingley, died circa ann. 1643. = Margaret, daughter of Henry Atkinson of Bolton in Boland in com. Eborum.

4. Stephen Ferrand. = | 2. Edmund Ferrand. = | 1. George Ferrand of Bingley. = | 3. Robert Ferrand of Harden Grange, æt. 68 ann. 11° Aug. 1665. = Anne, daughter of Tho. Newton of Daventre in co. North'ton. | 1. Agnes, wife unto John Beane of Gilsted in com. Ebor. | 2. Mary, wife to Samuell Holeride of Bingley in co. Ebor. | 3. Alice, wife of Will. Wiley, citizen and chirurgeon of London. | 4. Anne, wife of William Crawshaw of Wilsden in co. Ebor.

Benjamin Ferrand of Harden Beck, æt. 41 ann. 11 Aug. a° 1665. = Martha, daughter of Edward Brokesbanke of Wilsden in com. Eborum. | 1. Dorothy, wife of Ambrose Metcalfe, a merchᵗ in Hull. | 2. Anne, wife unto Robᵗ Milner of Pudsey in com. Ebor. Esq.

1. Robert, æt. 18 ann. 11 Aug. 1665. | 2. Edward. | 3. David. | 4. Samuell. | 1. Anne. | 2. Lydia. | 3. Mary.

SKYRAKE WAPENTAKE. *Leedes*, 11° *Aug*. 1665.

GREENE OF HORSFORTH.

ARMS.—Argent, a cross engrailed gules.

Gabraell Greene of Horsforth, living a° 1585. = Alice, daughter of Thomas Lyster of Westby, in com. Ebor.

John Greene of Horsforth died in a° 1637, or thereabout. = Beatrice, daughter of Thomas Wentworth of Mendham Priory in Suffolke.

Michaell Greene of Horsforth, æt. 80 an. 11 Aug. a° 1665. =	Margaret, daughter of Laurence Habergham of Habergham in co. Lanc.	1. Alice, wife of Samuell Burdet of More-Grange in co. Ebor.	2. . . . . . wife of Robt Killingbeck of Deane-Grange in com. Ebor.	3. Margaret, wife unto William Stevenson of	4. Anne, wife of Thomas Shaw of Horsforth in com. Ebor.	5. . . . . . . wife of . . . . . . Midsley of Hellwood in co. Ebor.

2. Laurence Greene, citizen of Lond.	1. John Greene of Horsforth and Bramley in com. Ebor. æt. 53 an. 11° Aug. 1665. =	Anne, daughter of Gervase Smith, of . . . . in com. Linc.	1. Mary, first mar. to . . . . . . afterward to . . . . Austin.	2. Beatrice, wife of	3. Anne, wife of Jeremy Butler of Deane-Grange in co. Ebor.

1. George, æt. 8 ann. 11 Aug. a° 1665.	2. John.	3. Gabraell.

AGBRIGG AND MORLEY WAPENTAKE. *Leedes*, 11° *Aug.* 1665.

RICHARDSON OF NORTH BIERLEY.

ARMS.—Sable, on a chief argent three lion's heads erased ermines.

Margaret, daughter of John Midgley of Clayton in Broadfordale in com. Ebor. 1 wife. = Nicholas Richardson, borne in the county palatine of Durham, came into Yorkesh. and setled at Tonge a° 1551, 3° Eliz. = Anne, y^e daughter of Lionell Goodall, 2 wife.

Children of Nicholas and Margaret:

- 2. Ellen, wife of Richard Cordingley of Holme in Tonge in co. Ebor.
- 1. Margaret, wife unto Michaell Jenkinson of Pudsey in co. Ebor.
- Richard Richardson, of North Bierley neer Bradford in co. Ebor. = Anne, daughter and heire of William Pollard of North Biersley.

Children of Nicholas and Anne:

- Henry, died unmarried.
- Anne, wife of Christopher Cave of Otley.

Children of Richard Richardson and Anne Pollard:

- 3. Thomas.
- 1. William Richardson, died without issue in his father's lifetime. = Elizabeth, eldest daughter of George Hopkinson of Lofthouse.
- 2. Richard Richardson of North Bierley, died a°. 1654. = Jane, 2d daughter of George Hopkinson of Lofthouse.
- 1. Anne, wife of Thomas Langley of Horbury.
- 2. Alice, wife unto Thomas Senior.
- 3. Sarah, wife of Rich. Jenkinson.
- 4. Beatrice, wife of ...... Sayle of Pudsey.

Children of Richard Richardson and Jane Hopkinson:

- 2. Richard.
- 3. John.
- 4. George.
- 5. Samuell.
- 6. Joseph.
- 1. William Richardson, æt. 28 ann. 11° Aug. 1665. = Susan, daughter of Gilbert Savile of Greetland near Halifax, co. Ebor.
- 1. Elizabeth, wife unto William Pollard.
- 2. Anne, wife of Willm Brooke.
- 3. Judith, wife of John Thornton.
- 4. Sarah, wife of Willm Denison.
- 5. Judith.
- 6. Jane.

  (5 and 6) died young.

Children of William Richardson and Susan Savile:

- Richard, ætatis 18 mensium 11° Aug. a° 1665.
- Jane.

AGBRIDGE AND MORLEY WAPENTAKE. *Leedes*, 11 *Aug*. 1665.

HOPKINSON OF LOFTUS.

ARMS.—Vert, three pillows ermine.

William Hopkinson came out of Lincolnshire into Yorkeshire and settled at Folby. = Jane, daughter of John Foster of Folby in ye county of Yorke.

Children:
- Thomas Hopkinson of Folby, died in aº 1589, vel circa. = Isabella, daughter of George Moody of Winterset in com. Ebor.
- Alice, wife of John Crosland.

Children of Thomas and Isabella:
- Francis, died unmarried.
- Elizabeth, daughter and coheire of John Walker of Lofthouse, 1 wife. = George Hopkinson of Loftus in co. Ebor. died circa 1650. = Judith, da. unto John Langley of Horbury, 2 wife.
- Elizabeth, wife unto John Otley.
- Isabell, wife unto John Herst.

Children of George Hopkinson and Elizabeth (1 wife):
- Elizabeth, wife to William Richardson.
- George, died young.

Children of George Hopkinson and Judith (2 wife):
- 1. William, died young.
- 2. John Hopkinson of Loftus, æt. 54 ann. 11º Aug. 1665.
- 3. Richard. 4. Thomas. } died young.
- 5. George Hopkinson of Loftus. = Isabell, daugh. of Robt Abbot.
- 1. Judith, died young.
- 2. Jane, wife of Richard Richardson of North Bierley in com. Ebor.
- 3. Mary, wife of Will. Rookes.

Children of George Hopkinson and Isabell:
- 3. William.
- 2. George.
- 1. John, æt. 11 an. 11º Aug. aº 1665.
- 1. Anne.
- 2. Isabell.

OSGODCROSSE WAPENTAKE. *Pomfret*, 8 *Aug.* 1665.

WILKINSON OF PONTFRACT.

ARMS.—Gules, a fess vair, in chief a unicorn passant or, all within a bordure engrailed of the last pellettèe.

CREST.—A fox's head erased, per pale wavy vert and or, in the mouth a wing argent.

William Wilkinson of Doncaster, Mayor of Pontfract in a° 1619. Died in a° 1635 vel circa, æt. 75 ann. = Mary, daughter of Robt Warde of Pomfret, gen^t.

2. John Wilkinson, Mayor of Pontfract in a° 1642. = Elizabeth, daughter of George Lodge.

Elizabeth, wife unto Nicholas Stable, Alderman of Pontfract.

Susanna, da. of William Morehouse of Symondley in com. Derb. gent. 1 wife. = 1. Thomas Wilkinson, Mayor of Pontfract 15 Caroli Primi, a° 1639, slaine in Pontfract Castle, Colonell Lowther then being Governour for the King, a° 1644. = Susanna, daughter of William Ramsden of Hill Topp in the parish of Hudersfeild in com. Ebor. 2 wife.

Thomas, died an infant.

William Wilkinson, Alderman of Pontfract, Master of the Chancery in the Dutchy Court at Westm^r, and Mayor of Pomfret a° 1663, æt. 39 ann. 8 Aug. 1665. = Anne, daughter of Abraham Kenchley of West Ham in co. Sussex, gent.

Elizabeth, wife unto James Rossington of Sandall in co. Ebor.

Matthew Wilkinson, an attorney at y^e law, now residing at Yorke, a° 1665. = Judith, daughter unto Laurence Teyle, Register to y^e Deane & Chapter of Yorke.

Margaret, wife unto John Dixon, Towne Clarke of Pontfract.

Thomas, æt. decem mens. 8 Aug. 1665.

BARKESTON ASHE WAPENTAKE. *Pontfract*, 8° *Aug.* 1665.

FOLJAMBE OF STEVETON.

ARMS.—Sable, a bend between six escallops or.

CREST.—A leg in armour, couped at the thigh, quarterly or and sable.

This family have for many ages used their armes wth supporters; vizt. an antilope quarterly sable and or, and a tyger ar.

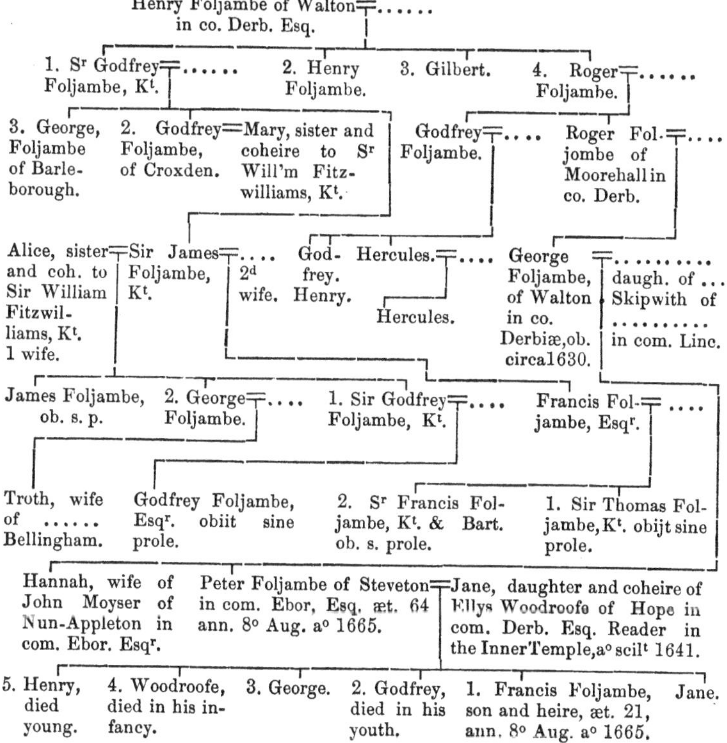

SKYRACK WAPENTAKE. *Leedes*, 11° *Aug*. 1665.

HEBER OF HOLLINGHALL.

ARMS.—Per fess azure and gules, a lion rampant or, a mullet for difference.

CREST.—Out of a ducal coronet or a woman's head and shoulders in profile proper, crined or.

Thomas Heber of Marton in com. Ebor. = Jane, daughter of Henry Colthurst of Edesforth in co. Ebor.

- 1. Thomas Heber of Marton. = ...
- 3. Reginald Heber of Hollinghall in com. Ebor. 3d son. = Anne, daughter of ...... Swindlehurst of the Hill in co. Ebor.
  - 3. Reginald Heber of Ilkley in co. Ebor.
  - 2. Christopher, died unmarried.
  - 1. John Heber of Hollinghall in com. Ebor. died circa annum 1654. = Jane, daughter of Willm. Willis, citizen of London.
    - Thomas Heber of Hollinghall in com. Ebor. æt. 25 ann. 11° Aug. a° 1665. = Mary, daughter of Edward Parker of Broxholme in com. Eborum.
      - John, æt. 18 mens. 11° Aug. 1665.
      - Bridget.
  - 1. Anne, wife of Henry Constantine of Conyston in com. Ebor.
  - 2. Martha,
  - 3. Lettice, died unmarried.

STAINECLIFFE WAPENTAKE. *Skipton*, 17 *Aug*. 1665.

MOORE OF LOWER HARROP.

ARMS.—Or, a chevron engrailed ermine between three moor's heads in profile couped sable, banded round the temples with a ribbon knotted behind argent and azure.

CREST.—A wolf's head erased gules, langued azure, collared and ringed or.

See the Visitation of Suff. for this descent and armes, there being no proofe made.

Richard Moore of St Edmundsbury, in com. Suff. = ...

- Richard Moore of St Edmundsbury in com. Suff. died circa annum 1619. = Anne, daughter of .... Baldwyn of Castle Heveningham in com. Suff.
  - 3. James Moore of Lower Harrop in com. Ebor. æt. 61 ann. 17 Aug. 1665. = Catherine, daughter of William Haughton, 2d brother to Sr Richard Haughton of Haughton Tower in com. Lanc. Bart.
    - James Moore, æt. 15 ann. 17 Aug. a° 1665.
    - 1. Grace, wife of Thomas Clayton of Lentworth in co. Lanc.
    - 2. Elizabeth, wife unto Edward Chewe of Potterford in co. Lanc.
    - 3. Catherine.
  - 1. John,
  - 2. Richard, died without issue surviving.
  - 1. Elizabeth, wife of John Brookes, son of Dr Brookes of Yorke.
  - 2. Anne, wife of John Lewes, vicar of Preston in Amundernesse in co. Lanc. and chaplein unto James Earle of Derby.

 Skipton, 17 *Aug*. 1665.

SLINGAR OF CATLOW.

Respit given for entring the armes.

Henry Slingar of Little Hutton in com. Ebor. = ... daughter of ...... Wrangham, of Wrangham in com. palat. Dunelm.

4. Peter, died unmarried.

3. Francis Slingar of Little Hutton in com. Ebor.

2. Tempest Slingar of Catlow in co. Ebor. died a° 1661. = Isabell, da. of Abraham Coulthurst of Burneley in co. Lanc.

1. Henry Slingar of Little Hutton in com. Eborum. = Elizabeth, daughter of Thomas Parker of Brousholme in com. Ebor. Esqr.

1. Isabell, y^e wife of Marmaduke Wawne of Alborough in co. Ebor.

2. Margaret, wife of ....

3. Catherine, wife of .... Lightfoot of Gilling, com. Eborum.

4. Elizabeth.

Children of Tempest Slingar and Isabell:

3. Henry Slingar. = Jane, da. of Rich. Ratcliffe of Berks in com. Ebor. widow of William Baynes of Mewyth co. Ebor.

2. Nicholas, died unmarried.

1. Tempest Slingar of Catlow in co. Ebor. now one of y^e justices of y^e peace, æt. 42 an. 17 Aug. 1665. = Milicent, daughter of John Bradhill of Portfield in co. Lanc. Esqr.

1. Margaret, first married unto Robert Fothergill of Ireby in com. Lanc. afterward to Robert Glover of Haughton East in com. Eborum.

2. Elizabeth, wife of Thomas Mytton of Sledburne in com. Eborum.

3. Alice, wife of Edward Hopkinson of Boseden in com. Ebor.

4. Anne, wife of William Foster of Barleybanke in co. Lanc.

5. Isabell, wife of John Hide of Sledburne in com. Ebor.

6. Mary, wife of Thomas Coze of Grange in co. Ebor.

Children of Tempest Slingar and Milicent:

Isabell, æt. 2 ann. 1665.

Margaret, died young.

1. Nicholas, æt. 13 an. 17 Aug. a° 1665.

2. Tempest, æt. 12 ann. 17° Aug. a° 1665.

3. John, æt. 10 an. 17 Aug. 1665.

Roger, æt. 7 ann. 1665.

TANKARD OF WHIXLEY.

ARMS.—Argent, a chevron between three escallops gules, a crescent or for difference.

CREST.—An olive tree vert, a crescent for difference.

Thomas Tankard, of Boroughbrigg in com. Ebor. Esqr. living in a° 1585. = Jane, daughter of Bernard Pever of Micklethwayt in com. Ebor. and one of his heires.

Their issue:

- 6. Charles Tankard of Whixley in co. Ebor. Esqr, 6th son, died in a° 1644. = Barbara, daughter of William Wyvell of Osgarby in co. Ebor.
- 2. James. 3. Thomas. 4. Richard. 5. Edmund. — died without any issue male.
- 1. William Tankard, son & heire, from whom Sr William Tankard, now of Branton in com. Ebor. B^t is descended.

Issue of Charles and Barbara:

- Mary, da. to Francis Nevill of Chevet in com. Ebor. Esqr, 1 wife. = 1. Sr Richard Tankard of Whixley, K^t æt. 58, ann. 14 Aug. a° 1665. = Anne, daughter of John Robinson of Hackforth in co. Ebor. widow of John Wastell of Scorton in com. Ebor. Counceller at Law, 2^d wife.
- 2. Henry Tankard of Killinghall, first married .... da. of .... Fletcher of Killinghall, and 2dly Dorothy, da. of Rich. Atkinson of Whixley, by whom he hath issue.
- 1. Helen, first married to Wm Barton of Cawton in co. Ebor. 2dly to .... Herbert a merchant of Yorke.
- 2. Mary, wife of Edward Calvert, citizen of Yorke.
- 3. Lucye, wife of John Coghill of Coghill Hall in Knaresbrough.
- 4. Anne, first married to Sr William Allanson of Yorke, K^t. after to Sr Solomon Swale of Swale Hall and Staineley in co. Ebor. B^t.

Issue of Sr Richard and Mary:

- Mary, died young.
- Charles Tankard, Esqr. æt. 28 ann. 14 Aug. 1665. = Dorothy, eldest daugh. of Sr Christopher Wyvill of Constable Burton in co. Ebor. B^t.
- 2. Nevill Tankard, died young.
- 3. Richard.
- 4. William, died young.
- 5. Henry, died young.
- 6. Thomas.
- 7. Francis.

Issue of Charles and Dorothy:

- 2. Richard, died young.
- 1. Christopher, æt. 5 ann. 14 Aug. 1665.
- 1. Ursula.
- 2. Mary.
- 3. Dorothy, died young.
- 4. Anne.

CLARO WAPENTAKE. *Knaresborough*, 15 *Aug.* 1665.

MIDDLETON OF STOCKHELD.

ARMS.—Quarterly of nine:
1. Argent, frettée sable, a canton of the second.
2. Argent, three greyhounds courant in pale sable.
3. Sable, an etoile argent.
4. Gules, a lion rampant argent within a bordure engrailed or.
5. Argent, a chevron embattled between three birds sable.
6. Argent, a chevron between three lion's heads erased gules.
7. Argent, a saltire gules, on a chief of the second three escallops of the field.
8. Argent, three cinquefoils sable.
9. Gules, semée of cross-crosslets or, a cinquefoil of the second.

CREST:—A garb or between two wings erect sable.

Marie, daughter of Edmund Eltofts of Farnhill in com. Ebor. 1 wife. = William Middleton of Stokeld in com. Ebor. Esqr, died in a° 1609 vel circa. = Anna, daughter of John Towneley of Towneley in com. Lanc. Esqr. 2 wife.

Sr Peter Middleton of Stockheld, Kn^t, died in a° 1645. = Mary, daughter and coheire of David Ingleby, a younger son of the house of Ripley.

William Middleton of Thurntofte in com. Ebor. = Anne, daughter of Thomas Walmsley of Dunkenhalgh in com. Lanc. Esqr.

1. Ursula, wife of Henry Farmer of Somerton in co. Oxon. Esqr.
2. Mary, first married to Edw. Topham of Coverham in Wensedale in com. Ebor. after to Thomas Thornton of Olsted in Yorksh.
3. Anne, a Nunne at Gant in Flanders.

1. William Middleton, of Stockeld, Esqr. died 22 Dec. a° 1658. = Kath. daughter of John Vicount Dunbar.

2. Sr John Middleton, K^t. = Anne, da. of .... Markham of ...... widow of .... Waterton of Walton in com. Ebor.

3. Robert, died unmarried.
4. Matthew.
5. Thomas, died unmarried.
6. Christopher, died young.

3. William, ætatis 9 ann.

2. Peter, æt. 11 ann.

1. John Middleton of Stockeld, Esqr, æt. 13 ann. 15 Aug. 1665.

1. Mary, wife of Ralphe Clavering of Calliley, in com. Northumbr.
2. Catherine, wife of Thomas Witham, 3d son of William Witham of Sledwick in Ep'atu Dunelm.

3. Margaret.
4. Anne.
5. Elizabeth.

RIPPON LIBERTIE. *Knaresborough*, 15 *Aug*. 1665.

JENNINGS OF RIPPON.

ARMS.—Quarterly :—
1 and 4, Argent, a chevron gules between three plummets sable.
2 and 3 ....

CREST.—A demi-griffin with wings addorsed or, from the beak a plummet pendent sable.

Peter Jennings of Silsden in com. Eboru. died 1° Sept. a° 1651. = Anne, daughter of .... Baldwyn of ...... in com. Ebor.

Children:

- Peter, died unmarried.
- Jonathan Jennings of Rippon, died 24 Aug. a° 1649. = Elizabeth, daughter and co-heir of Giles Parker of Newby in com. Ebor.
- Edmund, died unmarried.

Children of Jonathan and Elizabeth:

- 2. Jonathan Jennings. = Anne, da. of Sr Edw. Barkham of Totnam Highcrosse in com. Midd. Kt and Bart.
  - Margaret.
- 1. Sr Edmund Jennings of Rippon, Knt, æt. 38 ann. 15 Aug. a° 1665. = Margaret, da. of Sr Edward Barkham of Totnam Highcrosse in com. Midd. Kt & Bart.
  - 3. Marye, died an infant.
  - 1. Anne.
  - 2. Elizabeth.
  - 1. Jonathan, æt. 10 an. 15Aug. a° 1665.
  - 2. William, æt. 7 an. 1665.
  - 3. Edmund, æt. 6 an. 1665.
  - 4. Peter, æt. 1 anni.
- Elizabeth, first married to Christopher Hodgson of Beeston in com. Ebor. afterward to Henry Watkinson Dr of Law now residing in Yorke.

CLARO WAPENTAKE. *Knaresborough*, 15 *Aug*. 1665.

STOCKDALE OF BILTON-PARKE.

ARMS.—Ermine, on a bend sable three pheons argent, in the sinister chief an escallop gules; a crescent for difference.

Alice, daughter of Thomas Hallum of West-Hallum in co. Derb. 1st wife. = William Stockdale of Greene-Hamerton, living a° 1586. = Dorothy, daughter of Thomas Mill of ...... in the Bishoprick of Durham, 2d wife.

Children:

- 1. Tobias.
- 2. Gilbert.
- 3. Richard.
- 4. William.
- 5. Joseph.
- 6. Jerome.
- 7. Thomas.
- 1. Sarah, wife of Sr Nicholas Mordant Knt.
- 2. Elizabeth, wife of William Fenwick of .... in com. Northumb.

Next generation:

- 1. Thomas Stockdale of Bilton-Parke, died in a° 1657, or thereabouts. = Margt, da. of Sr Willm. Parsons, Kt and Bt, Mr of ye Wardes, and one of the Lds Justices of Ireland a° 1640.
- 2. Sampson.
- 3. Francis.
  (died without issue.)
- 4. John Stokdale of Green Hamerton. = (issue)
- 1. Anne.
- 2. Frances.
- 3. Eleanor.
  (died without issue.)
- 4. Dorothy, wife of Francis Jennings.
- 5. Jane, wife of ye Lord Boid of Scotland.

Children of Thomas and Margaret:

- William Stockdale of Bilton-Parke, æt. 29 ann 15 Aug. 1665.
- 1. Lettice, wife of Robert Waters of Cundall in co. Ebor.
- 2. Elizabeth.

DRAKE OF RIPPON.

Arms.—Argent, a wivern with wings displayed gules.
No proofe made of these armes to belong to this family.

.... Drake of Halley Greene in com. Ebor.=....

1. Gilbert Drake of Halley Greene in the parish of Halifax in co. Ebor.=....

4. William Drake of Lee in the parish of Halifax in co. Ebor.=...... daughter of ...... Broadley of Hipperholme in com. Ebor.

Humphrey Drake of Halifax, died in a° 1632.=Hester, da. of Will'm Drake of the Lee in ye parish of Halifax.

1. Joseph Drake.

2. Nathan Drake of Godley in the parish of Halifax in com. Ebor.=Eliz. da. of Francis Higgen of Hardwick in com. Ebor.

3. Jeremy.
4. Timothy.

1. Susan, ye wife of Samuell Lister of Shibden Hall in ye parish of Halifax.
2. Hesther, wife of Humph. Drake of Halifax.
3. Phœbe, wife of Edw. Hemenway of Northowrome Mill in co. Ebor.
4. Grace, wife of John Whitley of the Rookes in co. Ebor.
5 Judith, wife of Isaac Dickson of Carleton in com. Ebor.

1. Nathaniell, died unmarried.

John Drake, Subdeane of the Collegiate Church of Rippon, æt. 46 ann. 15° Aug. a° 1665.=Grace, daughter of James Foxcroft of Shipden Hall in co. Ebor.

2. Gilbert.
1. Humphrey. æt. 4 ann. 15 Aug. a° 1665.
1. Hesther.
2. Frances.
3. Susan.

Samuell Drake, Dr of Divinity, Vicar of Pomfret, æt. 42 an. 15° Aug. a° 1665.=Jane, daughter of Robert Abbot of Whitwood in com. Ebor.

2. Samuel.
3. Nathan.
4. John.
1. Francis, æt. 7 an. 15 Aug. 1665.
1. Anne.
2. Elizabeth.
3. Jane.

BIRDFORTH WAPONTAKE. *Threske*, 23 *Aug.* 1665.

CROSTON OF THRESKE.

ARMS.—Azure, a cross pattée fitchée at the foot or, on a chief of the second three fleurs-de-lis of the field.

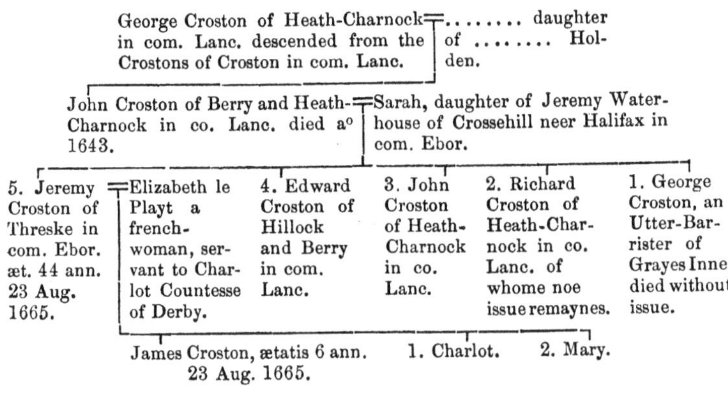

GILLING WEST WAPENTAKE. *Richmund*, 21 *Aug.* 1665.

FEILDING OF STARFORD.

ARMS.—Quarterly:—
1 and 4. Argent, on a fess azure three lozenges or, a crescent for difference.
2 and 3. Azure, six annulets or, three, two, and one, a crescent for difference.

Basill Feilding of Newnham in co. Warr. Esqr. = Godith, daughter & coheire of Willm. Willington of Barcheston, Esqr.

Everard Feilding, 2d son. = ...

2. William Feilding, Secretary to the Lord Scrope when he was Ld Warden of ye West Marches. = Anne, daughter of James Thwaytes of Marston in co. Ebor.

1. Basill Feilding of Copston in com. Warr.

Israell Feilding of Starford in com. Ebor. died in aº 1644. = Frances, daughter and coheire of Simon Musgrave of Plumpton in co. Cumbr. fourth wife.

2. Israell.
3. Basill.
4. Philip.

1. Willm. Feilding of Starford, æt. 40 ann. 21 Aug. aº 1665. = Susan, daughter of Sr Roger Feilding of Barnacle in co. Warr. Knt.

1. Catherine.
2. Anne.

3. Frances, wife of Willm. Feilding, a younger son to Sr Roger Feilding of Barnacle in co. Warr. Kt.

Israell, æt. 10 an. 21 Aug. 1665.

1. Frances.
2. Elizabeth.
3. Susanna.
4. Catherine.
5. Godith.
6. Bridget.

GILLING EAST WAPENTAKE. *Richmund*, 21 *Aug.* 1665.

CALVERLEY OF ERIHOLME.

ARMS.—Sable, an inescutcheon within an orle of owls argent, a crescent for difference.

Sr Will'm Calverley of Calverley, near Leeds, in com. Ebor. Kn[t]. = Elizabeth, daughter of S[r] Will'm Middleton of Stockheld in com. Ebor. K[t], 1 wife.

1. Walter Calverley, Esq[r]. =

2. Thomas Calverley of Littleburne in Episc. Dunelm. = Isabell, daughter of .... Anderson, sister to S[r] Henry Anderson of Couton in com. Ebor. K[t].

Anne, daughter of Mathew Hutton, Archbisshop of Yorke, 1st wife. = S[r] John Calverley of Littleburne, K[t], died in a[o] 1634 or thereabouts. = ... daughter of S[r] Timothy Whittingham of .... in co. Dunelm. 2 wife. = Elizabeth, daughter of .... Frevill of Walworth in Episc. Dunelm. 3 wife.

Barbara, wife of Rowland Tempest of Old Durham.

2. Tymothy.

1. John Calverley of Eryholme in co. Ebor. Esq[r]. died in a[o] 1660. = Margaret, da. of Tho. Jenison of Irchester in com, North[ton].

.... wife of .... Riddell of Newcastle.
.... wife of .... Conyers of .... in Episc. Dunelm.
.... wife of Clement Fulthorp of Tunstall in Episcopat. Dunelm.
.... wife of Percivall Potts.
.... wife of William Barnes of Darlinton in Episc. Dunelm.
.... wife unto .... Riddell of Newcastle.

2. Henry, æt. 24 ann.

1. John Calverley, of Eryholme, Esqr, æt. 25 ann. 21 Aug. a[o] 1665.

1. Anne, wife of Philip Prince of Yorke.

2. Margaret.

RYDALE WAPENTAKE. *Malton*, 28 *Aug*. 1665.

WORSLEY OF HOVINGHAM.

ARMS.—Quarterly of eight:
1. Argent, a chief gules.
2. Or, on a chief indented azure three plates.
3. Quarterly argent and gules, in the first a mullet sable.
4. Argent, on a bend sable three covered cups of the field.
5. Argent, a fess gules between three popinjays vert.
6. Argent, a squirrel sejant gules cracking a nut.
7. Argent, a fess sable.
8. As the first.

CREST.—A wivern with wings addorsed azure.

Thomas Worseley of Boothes in com. Lanc. Esqr, died in ao 1658. = Catherine, daughter and coheire of Henry Kighley of Kighley in com. Ebor. Esqr.

3. Edmund, died unmarried.

2. John Worseley of Crippleyate in com. Lanc. = Eliz. daugh. of Rob. Heywood of Heywood in co. Lanc. Esqr.

1. Thomas Worseley of Beeston in com. Ebor. died in his father's life time. = Eliz. eldest daugh. of Sr John Wood of Beeston in co. Ebor. Kt.

1. Elizabeth, died unmarried.
2. Jane, wife of Willm. Lascells of ...... in co. Ebor.

Alice, daughter of John Holcroft of Holcroft in com. Lanc. Esqr, 1 wife. = Thomas Worseley of Hovingham in com. Ebor. Esqr, died 3o Nov. ao 1664. = Penelope, daughter of Peter Egerton of Shaw in co. Lanc. Esqr, 2 wife.

Margaret.

1. Thomas Worseley of Hovingham in com. Ebor. Esqr, æt. 16 an. 28 Aug. ao 1665.

2. John, æt. 14 ann.

3. Charles Worseley, borne after his father's death, vizt 30 March 1665.

DENTON OF NAWTON.

ARMS.—Or, two bars gules, in chief three martlets of the second, a canton azure.

John Denton of Cardieu in com. Cumbr. Esqr. = Elizabeth, daughter of Thomas Gant of Stonehow in co. Essex, Esqr.

2. Lancelot Denton of Kirby Moreside in com. Ebor. = Anne, daughter of .... Jackson, alderman of the city of Yorke.

1. James Denton of Cardieu =

2. William Denton of Kirby-Moreside.
3. John Denton, citizen of Yorke.
4. Peter Denton of Stobaleigh in episc. Dunelm.
5. Robert Denton, citizen of York.

1. Thomas Denton of Nawton in co. Ebor. died in a° 1637. = Barbara, da. of Nicholas Assheton of Leven in Holdernesse.

1. Elizabeth, wife unto John Compton, citizen of London.
2. Anne, wife of Tho. Scarfe of Steathes in co. Ebor.
3. Mary, wife of Robt Collingwood of .... in com. Northumbriæ.

2. Lancelot Denton of Pickering in co. Ebor.

Anne, daugh. of Wm Maw of the Marishes in the parish of Pickering in co. Ebor. first wife. = 1. Robert Denton of Nawton in com. Ebor. æt. 50 ann. 28 Aug. 1665. = Frances, da. of Francis Johnson of Kirby Over-Carr in com. Ebor. 2 wife.

1. Grace wife of William Herst of Barugh in com. Ebor.
2. Mary, wife of William Nesse of Malton in com. Ebor.
3. Cath. wife of Thomas Wilson of Hornby parish in com. Ebor.

Children of the first wife:

- 2. Robert, died unmarried.
- 1. Thomas, died in his youth, unmarried.
- 1. Anne, wife of Will'm Ottterburne of Kirby-Moreside in com. Ebor.
- 2. Dorothy.

Children of the second wife:

- 1. Christopher, æt. 14 ann. 28 Aug. a° 1665.
- 2. Hierome, æt. 12 an. 1665.
- 3. Thomas, æt. 8 ann. 1665.
- 4. Charles, æt. 5 ann.
- Frances, æt. 2 ann. filia.

DICKERING WAPENTAKE. *Kilham*, 31° *Aug.* 1665.

GRYMSTON OF FRASTHORPE.

ARMS.—Argent, on a fess sable three mullets or pierced gules, a canton of the last.

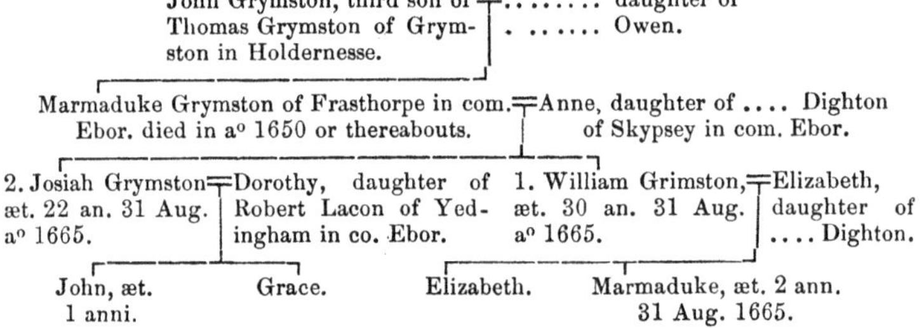

John Grymston, third son of Thomas Grymston of Grymston in Holdernesse. = ... daughter of . . . . Owen.

Marmaduke Grymston of Frasthorpe in com. Ebor. died in a° 1650 or thereabouts. = Anne, daughter of . . . . Dighton of Skypsey in com. Ebor.

2. Josiah Grymston, æt. 22 an. 31 Aug. a° 1665. = Dorothy, daughter of Robert Lacon of Yedingham in co. Ebor.

1. William Grimston, æt. 30 an. 31 Aug. a° 1665. = Elizabeth, daughter of . . . . Dighton.

John, æt. 1 anni. Grace.

Elizabeth. Marmaduke, æt. 2 ann. 31 Aug. 1665.

Malton, 28 *Aug*. 1665.

ROBYNSON OF THORNETON-RISEBOROUGH.

ARMS.—Vert, on a chevron between three bucks trippant or as many cinquefoils gules.

CREST.—A buck trippant or pellettée and gorged with a chaplet vert.

John Robynson, late citizen of London and merchant of the Staple, descended from the family of Robinson sometime of Drayton Basset in co. Staff. died in Febr. a° 1599. = Christian, eldest daughter of Thomas Anderson, citizen and grocer of London.

Children:

- Elizabeth, daughter of William Walthall, Alderman of the citty of London, first wife. = 3. Sr Arthur Robinson of Dighton in com. Ebor. K^t. died a° 1642, having been High Shireeve of Yorkeshire 8 Car. 1. = Jane, daughter of Sr John Garret, K^t. Alderman of the citty of London, second wife.
- 2. Henry Robinson of Buckton in com. Ebor. =
- 1. John Robinson of Rither in com. Ebor. =

Children of Sr Arthur Robinson (by first wife):

- 1. Elizabeth, died unmarried.
- 2. Margaret, wife of Robert Jegon of Buxton in com. Norff. Esqr.
- Frances. da. of Phineas Hodgson, D^r in Divinity & Chancelour of y^e Cathedrall of Yorke, 1 wife. = 1. Luke Robynson of Thornton Riseborough in com. Ebor. Esqr. æt. 55 ann. 28 Aug. a° 1665. = Mary, daugh. of Edward Pennell of Woodhall in com. Wigorn, Esqr, 2 wife. = Judith, daughter of Sr John Reade of Wrangle in co. Linc. Kn^t 3^d wife.

Children of Sr Arthur Robinson (by second wife):

- 2. John Robynson, died in a°1643. = Elizabeth, daughter of Sr Thomas Hutton of Poppleton in com. Ebor. K^t.
- 3. Arthur, Robinson of Dighton in co. Ebor. = Elizabeth, daughter of Raphe Rymer late of Broferton in co. Ebor.
- 3. Jane, wife of Henry Fotherby of Beverley in com. Ebor.

Children of Luke Robynson by first wife:

- Jane, wife of Thomas Strangways of Pickering in com. Ebor. Esqr.

Children of Luke Robynson by second wife:

- Arthur, died young.
- Cath. } died young.
- Martha. } died young.

Children of Luke Robynson by third wife:

- 1. Luke Robinson, æt. 14 an. 28 Aug. 1665.
- 2. Arthur, æt. 11 ann. 1665.
- 3. John, æt. 10 ann.
- Judith.

Children of John Robynson:

- Arthur died an infant.
- 1. Elizabeth, wife of Sutton Oglethorpe, son and heire of Sutton Oglethorpe, late of Oglethorpe in co. Ebor. Esqr.
- 2. Anne, wife of Sr Roger Burgoigne of Wroxhall in co. Warr. K^t & Bar^t.

Children of Arthur Robinson:

- Arthur.
- Elizabeth.

RYDALE WAPENTAKE. *Malton,* 28 *Aug.* 1665.

CARRINGTON OF SPAUNTON.

ARMS.—Sable, on a bend argent three lozenges of the field.
CREST.—Out of a ducal coronet or a unicorn's head argent.

William Carrington of Spawnton in com. Ebor. Esqr, living a[o] 1612. = Anne, daughter of John Bonvile of ...... in com. ......

2. John Carrington of Spawnton, æt. 72 an. 28 Aug. a[o] 1665. = Elizabeth, daughter of Henry Sympson of Edston in com. Ebor.

1. William Carrington of Spawnton. = ...

Children of John Carrington and Elizabeth: 2. Ralphe. 3. Francis. 1. James Carrington, æt. 30 ann. 28 Aug. a[o] 1665. = Judith, daughter of John Garforth of Ryton in com. Ebor. Elizabeth.

Child of William Carrington: Anne, wife of Willm. Medd of Lestingham in com. Ebor. sole daughter and heire.

Children of James Carrington and Judith: 1. Samuell, æt. 4 ann. 28 Aug. a[o] 1665. 2. Henry.

WHITBY STRAND. *Malton,* 28 *Aug.* 1665.

THOMLINSON OF WHITBY.

ARMS.—Sable, a fess between three falcons rising or.
No proofe made of these armes.

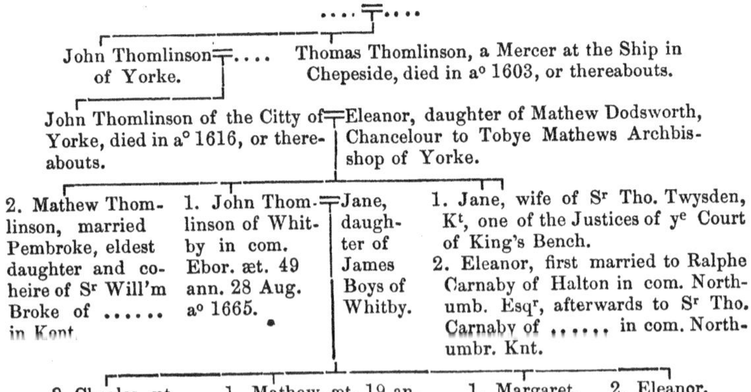

.... = ...

John Thomlinson of Yorke. = ...

Thomas Thomlinson, a Mercer at the Ship in Chepeside, died in a[o] 1603, or thereabouts.

John Thomlinson of the City of Yorke, died in a[o] 1616, or thereabouts. = Eleanor, daughter of Mathew Dodsworth, Chancelour to Tobye Mathews Archbisshop of Yorke.

2. Mathew Thomlinson, married Pembroke, eldest daughter and coheire of Sr Will'm Broke of ...... in Kent.

1. John Thomlinson of Whitby in com. Ebor. æt. 49 ann. 28 Aug. a[o] 1665. = Jane, daughter of James Boys of Whitby.

1. Jane, wife of Sr Tho. Twysden, K[t], one of the Justices of y[e] Court of King's Bench.

2. Eleanor, first married to Ralphe Carnaby of Halton in com. Northumb. Esqr, afterwards to Sr Tho. Carnaby of ...... in com. Northumbr. Knt.

Children of John Thomlinson and Jane: 2. Charles, æt. 16 ann. 1. Mathew, æt. 19 an. 28 Aug. 1665. 1. Margaret. 2. Eleanor.

RYDALE WAPENTAKE. *Malton*, 28 *Aug*. 1665.

THORNETON OF EAST-NEWTON.

ARMS.—Argent, a chevron sable between three hawthorn-trees proper.
CREST.—A lion's head erased purpure, ducally gorged or.

Dorothy, daughter of Thomas Metham of Metham in co. Ebor. Esqr, first wife. ═ Robert Thornton of East-Newton in co. Ebor. Esqr, died 17 May, a° 1637. ═ Elizabeth, daughter of Sr Richard Darley of Buttercrambe in com. Ebor. K^t, second wife.

1. Ursula, wife of Marmaduke Cholmeley of Brandsby in co. Ebor. Esqr.
2. Margaret, wife of Raphe Crathorne of Crathorne in com. Ebor. Esqr.
3. Anne, wife of Philip Langdale of Lanthorpe in com. Ebor. Esqr.

2. Richard, died unmarried.
3. Thomas.
4. John.

1. William Thornton of East-Newton in com. Ebor. Esqr, æt. 41 an. 28 Aug. a° 1665. ═ Alice, daugh. of Christoph^r Wandesford of Kirtlington in co. Ebor. Esqr, M^r of ye Rolls & Lord Deputie of Ireland.

1. Elizabeth, wife of John Denton of Manningham in com. Ebor. gent.
2. Mary, died unmarried.
3. Frances, wife of Timothy Portington of Malton, gent.

2. Robert, æt. 3 ann. 1. Willm. died young. 1. Alice. 2. Catherine.

WHITBY STRAND. *Malton*, 28 *Aug*. 1665.

NEWTON OF BAGDALE-HALL.

ARMS.—Sable, three pairs of shin-bones argent, each pair in saltire, the sinister surmounted of the dexter, a martlet or for difference.
No proofe made of these armes.

George Newton of Ruswarpe in Whitby Strand in com. Ebor. ═ ....

Christopher Newton of Ruswarpe, died a° 1645 (vel circa). ═ ....

2. John Newton.

1. Isaac Newton of Ruswarpe, died circa an. 1650. ═ Hesther, daughter of Nicholas Bushell of Ruswarpe.

2. John.

1. Isaac Newton of Bagdale-Hall in Ruswarpe in com. Ebor. æt. 32 ann. 28 Aug. a° 1665. ═ Elizabeth, daughter of Gyles Wiggener of Wevenho in Essex.

1. Elizabeth, wife of Nicholas Fenay of Fenay in com. Ebor.

2. Adeline.

Henry, æt. 2 dierum 28 Aug. a° 1665.

Elizabeth, æt. 1 anni et 9 mens. 28 Aug. a° 1665.

BUCKROSE WAPENTAKE. *Malton*, 28 *Aug*. 1665.

HARDY OF WETWANG.

ARMS.—Argent, a cross engrailed azure between four boars passant sable.

CREST.—A demi-eagle argent, wings displayed gules, charged on the breast with two bendlets sable, in the beak a rose-branch stalked and leaved vert, flower argent and gules.

No proofe made of these armes.

Michaell Hardy of Wetwang in com. Ebor. descended from .... Hardy, sometime Lord Mayor of London. = Alison, daughter of ...... Skelton of ...... in com. Eborum.

- 2. Michaell Hardy of Southbourne in co. Ebor.
- 3. Richard Hardy of Hunslow Beacon in com. Eborum.
- 1. John Hardy of Wetwang, died in a° 1641, vel circa. = Margaret, da. of John Newlove of Wetwang, widd. of George Hynesley of Wartre in co. Ebor.
- 1. Helen, wife of ...... Kirby of Hugget in co. Ebor.
- 2. Anne, wife of Christophr Crosse of Hugget in co. Eborū.
- 3. Eliz. wife of Marmaduke Taylor of Langtofte in co. Ebor.

Children of John Hardy and Margaret:

- 2. Michael.
- 3. John.
- 1. Willm. Hardy of Wetwang, æt. 55 ann. 28 Aug. a° 1665. = Emme, daughter of John Nicholson of Swinkell in co. Ebor.
- 1. Anne, wife of Thomas Moreton of Yorke.
- 2. Jane, wife of John Hudson of Tibthorpe in com. Ebor.
- 3. Mary, wife of William Hewetson, Citizen of Yorke.
- 4. Drusilla, wife of Tho. Bransby of Rippon in co. Ebor.

Children of Willm. Hardy and Emme:

- John, æt. 22 ann. 28 Aug. 1665.
- 1. Emme, æt. 24 ann.
- 2. Judith.
- 3. Ruthe.

DICKERING WAPENTAKE. *Kilham*, 31 *Aug.* 1665.

BUCK OF CARNABY.

William Buck of Holmeton a° 13 H. 8.

Thomas Bucke of Holmeton a° 31 H. 8.

Thomas Buck of Holmeton in com. Ebor. a° 13 Eliz. R. = ...

Mary, daughter of Robt Lightfoot of Carnaby in com. Ebor. = William Bucke of Holmeton. = ... daughter of .... Lutton of Knapton in com. Ebor.

Samuell Bucke of Holmeton, died in a° 1630, or thereabouts. = Alice, daughter of Thomas Pearson of Harpham in com. Ebor. gent.

3. Jane, wife of George Langkagle, a Merchant in Prusia at Elvin.
4. Anne, wife of Will. Holliday of Gardholme in co. Ebor.

Thomas Bucke of Carnaby in com. Ebor. æt. 53 ann. 31 Aug. a° 1665. = Mary, daughter of John Pearson of Multhorpe in com. Ebor.

1. Catherine, wife of Will'm Johnson of Cherri-Burton in com. Ebor.
2. Susan, wife of Tho. Tenant of Whitwell in Richmundshire.

2. John.
3. Will'm.

1. Samuel Bucke, æt. 26 an. 31 Aug. a° 1665. = Elizabeth, daughter of Will'm Pearson of Besingby in co. Ebor.

1. Mary, wife of Daniell Forde of Scarborough in com. Ebor.
2. Elizabeth.
3. Anne.

Thomas, æt. unius anni et 10 mens. 31 Aug. 1665.

Mathew, æt. unius septimanæ.

PICKERING LYTHE. *Malton*, 29° *Aug.* 1665.

ROBINSON OF FARMANBY.

No proofe made of the armes.

Henry Robinson of Farmanby in co. Ebor. = ... daughter of .... Greaves, sometime Ld Mayor of Yorke.

2 William Robinson, Citizen of Yorke.

1. John Robinson of Farmanby, died in a° 1659. = Jane, daughter of .... Ives of Gilling in co. Ebor. second wife.

Samuell Robinson of Farmanby æt. 38 ann. 29 Aug. 1665. = Helen, daughter of Bethell Hunter of Thornton in com. Ebor.

1. Jane, wife of Will'm Blanchard, Citizen of Yorke.

2. Margaret, wife of Will'm Nevill, Citizen of Yorke.

John, æt. 6 an. 29 Aug. a° 1665. 1. Jane. 2. Magdalen. 3. Helen.

DICKERING WAPENTAKE. *Kilham*, 31 *Aug*. 1665.

BUCK OF FLOTMANBY.

ARMS,—Lozengy or and azure, a canton ermine.
CREST.—A portcullis azure, garnished and chained or.

Sr John Buck of Hanby Grange in co. Linc. Kt. = Eleanor, daughter and heire of .... Wymarke of .... in com. Linc.

Sr John Buck of Hanby Grange, Kt, and afterward of Filey in co. Ebor. died in aº 1648. = Elizabeth, daughter and heire of Willm. Green of Filey in com. Ebor.

2. Robert Buck of Flotmanby in com. Ebor. æt. 34 ann. 31 Aug. aº 1665. = Mary, daughter of Edward Skipwith of Grantham in com. Linc.

1. Sr John Buck of Hanby-grange in co. Linc. Bart. =

2. William, æt. 2 an. 1665.
1. John, æt. 7 ann. 31 Aug. 1665.
1. Elizabeth.
2. Fayth.
3. Anne.
4. Mary.

DICKERING WAPENTAKE. *Kilham*, 31º *Aug*. 1665.

NOELL OF HAYHOLME.

ARMS.—Or, fretty gules, a canton ermine, a crescent for difference.

Sr Andrew Nowell of Dalby in com. Leic. Knt. = Mabell, daughter of Sr James Harrington of Exton in com. Rutl. Knt.

2. Arthur Noell of Hayholme in Holdernesse, æt. 69 an. 31 Aug 1665. = Bridget, daughter of Everard Carter of Stonesby in com. Leic.

1. Edward Viscount Cambden. =

2. Arthur.
3. William.
4. Cornelius.
5. Edward.
1. George Nowell, ætatis 26 an. 31 Aug. 1665.
1. Mary, wife of Samuell Lawson of ye citty of Lincolne.
2. Anne.
3. Penelope.
4. Elizabeth.

LANGBARGH WAPENTAKE. *Stokesley*, 25° *Aug.* 1665.

FORSTER OF STOKESLEY.

ARMS.—Argent, a chevron vert between three bugle-horns sable, on an inescutcheon the badge of a baronet of England.

CREST.—A buck trippant proper, attired or.

Will'm Foster of Erdswyke in com. Ebor. descended from the Forsters of Etherston in com. Northumbr. = ... daughter of .... Longley of ...... in the Bisshoprick of Durham, Esq[r].

Seth Forster, died unmarried.

S[r] Richard Forster of Stokesley in com. Ebor. K[t] and Bar[t]. Treasurer to Qu. Mary and likewise to K. Charles the 2[d] during their abode in France before his now Ma[ties] happy restoration. Created Baronet by K. Charles the 2[d] by his Patent bearing date at S[t] Germains in Lay the 18 Sept. in the first yere of his raigne a° scil[t] 1649. He died in France 17° Jan. a° 1661. = Joane, daughter of ...... Middleton of Leighton in com. Lanc. Esq[r].

2. S[r] Richard Forster of Stokesley, Bart. æt. 42 ann. 25 Aug. a° 1665. = Clare, daughter of Anthony Meynill of Kilvington in co. Ebor. Esqr.

1. Henry Forster, died in his father's lifetime. = Martha, daugh. of .... Anne of Frickley in com. Eborum.

Of whom there is now noe issue remayning.

Anne, Lady Abbesse of Pontoise in France.

Richard, æt. 7 annorum 25° Aug. 1665.

1. Mary, æt. 6 ann.

2. Clare, æt. 5 ann.

PICKERING LITHE. *Malton*, 29° *Aug.* 1665.

EGERTON OF ALLARSTON.

ARMS.—Argent, a lion rampant gules between three pheons sable.

Sr Richard Egerton of Ridley in co. Cestr. Knt. = ...

2. Thomas Egerton of Allarston in Pickering Lithe, Esqr. æt. 58 ann. 28° Aug. a° 1665. = Catherine, daughter of .... Dodson of .... in the Isle of Wight, widd. of Mich. Barbour, Citizen of Lond.

1. Richard Egerton, son and heire, ob. sine prole Jan. 1663. = Margaret, da. of Sr Will. Brereton, of Honford in com. Cestr. Bar[t].

1. Elizabeth, wife of ...... Warburton of ...... in Chesh.

2. Mary, wife of Sr Will'm Blakeston of Newton in com. Dunelm. Kn[t].

3. Jane, wife of George Boothe of Allarston in com. Ebor. gent.

Ralphe, æt. 4 ann. 29 Aug. 1665.

WHITBY STRAND. *Malton*, 28 *Aug*. 1665.

COMYN OF WHITBY.

ARMS.—Azure, a chevron erminois between three garbs or.

CREST.—Two arms embowed, vested erminois, cuffed argent, the hands proper holding a garb or.

Symon Comyn of the Citty of Durham, unto whom Rich. St George, Esqr granted the Crest here expressed unto the Armes antiently belonging to this family, 20 Aug. ao 1615 (13 Jacobi). = ...

Timothy Comyn of Durham, died in ao 1626, vel circa. = ... daughter of Sr Henry Cholmeley of Whitby-Abby in com. Ebor.

Francis Comyn of Whitby, æt. 34 an. 28 Aug. 1665. = Hannah, daughter of Willm. Wiggener of Whitby in com. Ebor. widow of Luke Bagwith of Whitby.

Mary, wife of Rich. Cholmley, of ..... in com. Linc.

1. Margaret, æt. 4 ann. 28o Aug. 1665.

2. Catherine, æt. 2 ann 1665.

LANGBARGH WAPENTAKE. *Stokesley*, 25 *Aug*. 1665.

LEVINGSTOUN OF DANBY-FOREST.

ARMS.—.......... three cinquefoils within a double tressure fleury ....
Qu. ? the coloures, and then to assigne a fit difference.

Robert Levingstoun of Skerling in Scotld, Clerke, descended of the house of Levingston of Wemes in the county of Fyfe in Scotland, died in ao 1658. = Mary, ye daughter of ...... Hebburne.

3. Samuell Levingstoun of Danby Forest in com. Ebor. æt 52 an. 25 Aug. ao 1665. = Margaret, daughter of John Ratcliffe of Stathes in com. Ebor.

2. Robert Levingston of Liberton in ye county of Clidesdale in Scotland.

1. George Levingstoun of Ingleby in co. Ebor.

1. Mary, wife of John Geare of Greet Broughton in com. Ebor.

2. Martha, wife of George Greeneside of Greet Broughton in co. Ebor.

GILLING-WEST WAPENTAKE. *Richmund*, 21 *Aug*. 1665.

SHUTTLEWORTH OF FORCET.

ARMS.—Argent, three weaver's shuttles sable tipped and quilled or, a crescent for difference.

Thomas Shuttleworth of Gawthropp in com. Lanc. Esqr. = ...

Nicholas Shuttleworth of Forcet in com. Ebor. æt 77 an. 21 Aug. 1665.

1. Richard Shuttleworth of Gawthrope in com. Lanc. Esqr. =

GILLING-WEST. *Richmund*, 21 *Aug*. 1665.

ROKEBY OF MORETON.

ARMS.—Quarterly, in the fess point a trefoil slipped gules:
1 and 4, Argent, a chevron sable between three rooks russet, legged azure.
2 and 3, Argent, three chevronels braced in base sable, on a chief of the second as many mullets of the first.

John Rokeby, living a° 1584. ═ Anne, daughter of .... Thwenge of Heslerton in com. Ebor.

Thomas Rokeby of Moreton, died a° 1629 vel circa. ═ Margaret, daughter of Sr Raphe Lawson of Brough in com. Ebor. Kn^t.

4. Anthony.
5. John.
6. Christoph^r.
died unmarr.

3. Francis Rokeby of Moreton in com. Ebor. Esqr, died in Febr. a° 1644. ═ Susanna, da. of James Fawcet, Citizen of London.

1. Will'm.
2. Raphe.
died unmarried.

1. Mary.
2. Alice, wife of Roger Alderson of Bowes in com. Ebor.
3. Margaret, died unmarried.

2. Raphe, died unmarried.

1. Thomas Rokeby, of Moreton, Esqr, æt. 25 ann. 21° Aug. 1665. ═ Margaret, daughter of John Wycliffe of Gales in com. Ebor. Esqr.

1. Frances, wife of Pelham Jackson of Haselrigg in co. Northumbr. gent. afterwards of Daniell Orde of Barwick upon Tweede; 3dly of Will'm Astley of .... in com. Warr. gent.
2. Susanna, wife of Gilb^t Swynnow of Barrington in co. Dunelm. Esqr.
3. Margaret.

1. Mary, æt. 3 ann. 21 Aug. 1665.
2. Susanna, died an infant.

RYDALE WAPENTAKE. *Malton*, 28 *Aug*. 1665.

GIBSON OF WELBORNE.

ARMS.—Barry of six ermine and sable, a lion rampant or.
CREST.—A stork argent, in the beak a plane-tree branch vert.

Sr John Gibson of Welborne in com. Ebor. K^t, died in a° 1638. ═ Anne, daughter of Sr John Allet of ...... widow of .... Dodershall of ...... in com. Buck.

Sr John Gibson of Welborne, K^t, died in June a° 1665. ═ Penelope, daughter of William Woodhall, Register of the Prerogative Office to the Archbisshop of Canterbury.

John Gibson of Welborne, Esqr, æt. 35 ann. 28 Aug. 1665. ═ Joane, daughter of James Pennyman of Ormesby in co. Ebor. Esqr.

4. Charles, æt. 5 ann.
3. Edward, ætat. 8 ann.
2. James, æt. 10 ann.
1. John, æt. 13 an. 28 Aug. 1665.
1. Joane, æt. 12 ann.
2. Penelope, ætatis 20 mensium.

 Malton, 28 *Aug*. 1665.

CHOLMELEY OF WEST-NEWTON.

ARMS.—Quarterly, a martlet for difference:
1 and 4. Gules, in chief a fleur-de-lis or upon a crescent ermine between two helmets argent, in base a garb of the second.
2 and 3. Argent, on a fess gules three plates.

CREST.—On a royal helmet argent a garb or charged with a crescent.

Susan, daughter of ..... Legard, a Merchant of London, first wife. = Sr Richard Cholmeley of Whitby in com. Ebor. Kt, died circa ann. 1625. = Margaret, daughter of ...... Cob, a Merchant in London, second wife.

1. Sir Hugh Cholmeley of Whitby, Kt and Bart, died 30 Nov. aº 1657. = Elizabeth, daughter of Sr William Twysden of Est-Peckham in Kent, Bart.

2. Sr Henry Cholmeley of West-Newton-Grange in co. Ebor. Kt, æt. 56 ann. 28 Aug. 1665. = Catherine, daughter of Henry Stapleton of Wighill in com. Ebor. Esqr.

1. Margaret, wife of Sr William Strickland of Boynton in com. Ebor. Kt and Bart.

2. Ursula, wife of George Trotter of Skelton in com. Ebor. Esqr.

3. Sr Richard Cholmeley of Grosmont in co. Ebor, Knt, slayne neer Axminster in com. Devon, in ye service of King Charles the First, being then Governr of that Towne for ye said King. = Margaret, daughter of John Lord Pawlet of Hinton St George in com. Somerset.

Children of Sir Hugh Cholmeley and Elizabeth:

1. Sir Willm. Cholmeley of Whitby, Bart, died in aº 1663. = Katherine, daughter of John Savile of Medley in com. Ebor. Esqr.

2. Sr Hugh Cholmeley, Bart, now at Tangier (scilt, 28 Aug. aº 1665).

1. Anne, wife of Rich. Stephen of Estington in com. Glouc. Esqr.
2. Elizabeth.

Children of Sr Henry Cholmeley and Catherine:

Hugh Cholmeley, æt. 23 ann. 28 Aug. 1665. = Margaret, daughter of Gregory Crake of Martin in co. Ebor. Esqr.

Henrietta, wife of Sr John Tempest of Tonge in com. Ebor. Bart.

Children of Sr Richard Cholmeley and Margaret:

1. Margaret.
2. Ursula.

Children of Sir Willm. Cholmeley and Katherine:

Sr Hugh Cholmeley, Bart. died in June aº 1665, in his childhood.

1. Elizabeth, æt. 6 an. 28 Aug. aº 1665.

2. Katherine, æt. 3 ann. aº 1665.

DICKERING WAPENTAKE. *Kilham*, 31 *Aug.* 1665.

LAMONT OF NORTH-BURTON.

ARMS.—Argent, a lion rampant vert.

Alan Lamont of Sconie in y[e] countie of Fife in Scotland. = Jennet, daughter of James Cockburn of Treton in Fyfe.

Andrew Lamont, D[r] in Divinity, and Rector of the mediety of Thwinge in co. Ebor. died a° 1662. = Margaret, daughter of Dr Robert Hovie, Regius Professor in the University of St. Andrew's in Scotland.

2. Andrew Lamont, D[r] in Divin. Rector of Beesley in com. Surr.
3. James Lamont.

1. Alan Lamont, of North Burton, in com. Ebor. ætatis 38 ann. 31° Aug. a° 1665. = Isabell, daugh. of Robert Knowsley, of Northburton, in co. Ebor. widow of Robert Ellis of Rudston, in com. Ebor.

1. Jennet, wife of Robt. Constable of Emthorpe in com. Ebor. Vicar of Muston in com. Ebor.

2. Agnes.
3. Margaret.

Alan, æt. 15 an. 31 Aug. a° 1665. 1. Margaret. 2. Isabell. 3. Anne. 4. Susanna.

BULMER WAPENTAKE. *Malton*, 28 *Aug.* 1665.

HASSELL OF HUTTON UPON DARWENT.

ARMS.—Vert, three adders erect argent.

CREST.—A dexter arm erect vested gules cuffed argent, the hand proper holding a branch of laurel.

Thomas Hassell, citizen of London. = Agnes, daughter of Mons[r] la Motte, a Frenchman, and Governour of Graveling.

Thomas Hassell of Connisthorpe in co. Ebor. = Juliana, daughter of Lancelot Mansfield of .... in com. Cumbr. Esq[r].

2. Thomas.
3. Raphe.
4. Mansfield.
5. Jerimie.

1. Samuell Hassell of Hutton upon Darwent in com. Ebor. died in a° 1655. = Mary, daughter of Richard Conyers of Horden in Episc. Dunelm. Esqr.

Anne, wife of John Harrison of Rudston in com. Eborum.

2. Samuell.
3. Raphe.

1. Thomas Hassell of Hutton upon Darwent, an Utter Barister of Grayes Inne, æt. 38 an. 28 Aug. 1665. = Elizabeth, daughter of Barney Wood of Thorpe, in the parish of Rudstone in com. Ebor.

Mary, wife of Francis Constable of Troutesdale in com. Ebor.

3. Raphe, æt. 4 ann. Thomas, æt. 7 an. 1665. 1. Samuell, æt. 10 an. 28 Aug. 1665. 1. Elizabeth. 2. Anne. 3. Mary. 4. Margaret.

PICKERING LYTHE. *Malton*, 29 *Aug*. 1665.

GATES OF THORNE-PARKE.

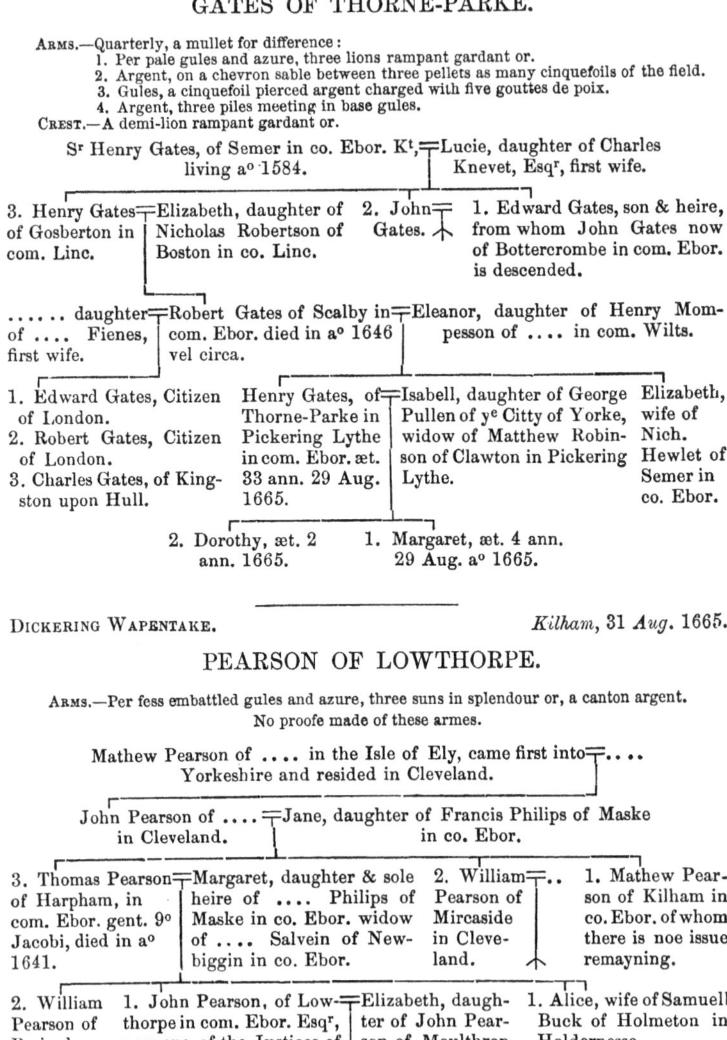

ARMS.—Quarterly, a mullet for difference:
1. Per pale gules and azure, three lions rampant gardant or.
2. Argent, on a chevron sable between three pellets as many cinquefoils of the field.
3. Gules, a cinquefoil pierced argent charged with five gouttes de poix.
4. Argent, three piles meeting in base gules.

CREST.—A demi-lion rampant gardant or.

Sr Henry Gates, of Semer in co. Ebor. Kt, living ao 1584. = Lucie, daughter of Charles Knevet, Esqr, first wife.

3. Henry Gates of Gosberton in com. Linc. = Elizabeth, daughter of Nicholas Robertson of Boston in co. Linc.

2. John Gates.

1. Edward Gates, son & heire, from whom John Gates now of Bottercrombe in com. Ebor. is descended.

...... daughter of .... Fienes, first wife. = Robert Gates of Scalby in com. Ebor. died in ao 1646 vel circa. = Eleanor, daughter of Henry Mompesson of .... in com. Wilts.

1. Edward Gates, Citizen of London.
2. Robert Gates, Citizen of London.
3. Charles Gates, of Kingston upon Hull.

Henry Gates, of Thorne-Parke in Pickering Lythe in com. Ebor. æt. 33 ann. 29 Aug. 1665. = Isabell, daughter of George Pullen of ye Citty of Yorke, widow of Matthew Robinson of Clawton in Pickering Lythe.

Elizabeth, wife of Nich. Hewlet of Semer in co. Ebor.

2. Dorothy, æt. 2 ann. 1665.

1. Margaret, æt. 4 ann. 29 Aug. ao 1665.

DICKERING WAPENTAKE. *Kilham*, 31 *Aug*. 1665.

PEARSON OF LOWTHORPE.

ARMS.—Per fess embattled gules and azure, three suns in splendour or, a canton argent. No proofe made of these armes.

Mathew Pearson of .... in the Isle of Ely, came first into Yorkeshire and resided in Cleveland. = ...

John Pearson of .... in Cleveland. = Jane, daughter of Francis Philips of Maske in co. Ebor.

3. Thomas Pearson of Harpham, in com. Ebor. gent. 9o Jacobi, died in ao 1641. = Margaret, daughter & sole heire of .... Philips of Maske in co. Ebor. widow of .... Salvein of Newbiggin in co. Ebor.

2. William Pearson of Mircaside in Cleveland. = ..

1. Mathew Pearson of Kilham in co. Ebor. of whom there is noe issue remayning.

2. William Pearson of Besingby in co. Ebor.

1. John Pearson, of Lowthorpe in com. Ebor. Esqr, now one of the Justices of Peace in this county, æt. 76 an. 31 Aug. ao 1665. = Elizabeth, daughter of John Pearson of Moulthrop in com. Ebor.

1. Alice, wife of Samuell Buck of Holmeton in Holdernesse.
2. Catherine, died unmarried.

3. William, æt. 5 ann.

2. John, æt. 11 ann. 1665.

1. Mathew Pearson, ætatis 14 ann. 31 Aug. 1665.

1. Sarah.
2. Frances.
3. Anne.

LUTTON OF KNAPTON.

ARMS—Gules, a chevron argent between three crosses pattée or.
CREST.—On the stump of a tree erased or a peacock close proper.

¶ Thomas Lutton of West-Lutton, Kt. = ...

John Lutton son and heire, 28 E. 1.

¶ Willm. Lutton of Lutton, Esqr, 18 H. 6.

¶ William Lutton of Knapton, Esqr, 22 H. 7.

¶ Thomas Lutton of Knapton in com. Ebor. Esqr. 18 Febr. ao 37 H. 8.

¶ Raphe Lutton, Esqr, dead in ao 1o Eliz. = ...

2. Philip Lutton, Esqr, brother and heire of Francis, 1o Apr. 3o Jac. = ...

1. Francis Lutton, son and heire, 10 Aug. ao 1o Eliz. died without issue.

1. Mary, wife of Raphe Eldrington of Egton in com. Ebor.
2. Elizabeth, wife of Roger Hunter of Mareshes in com. Ebor. gent.
3. ...... wife of John Bawne of Skerne in com. Eborum.
4. Anne, wife of Francis Proude, clerke.
5. Philippa, ye wife of ...... Harding, clerke.

2. Henry Lutton of Knapton.

Margaret, daughter of Robert Dakins of Lynton in com. Ebor. first wife. = Raphe Lutton of Knapton in co. Ebor. Esqr, died in ao 1657. = Barbara, daughter of .... Rosse of Hurstthwayte in com. Ebor. widow of Evers Fairfax, 2d wife.

1. Jane, wife of Thomas Warde, a merchant in Yorke.
2. Eliz. wife of Henry Sympson of Edston in co. Ebor.
3. Anne, wife of Roger Camplesham of Catton in co. Ebor.

2. Raphe Lutton, marr. Isabell, daughter of Robert Morley of Yorke, widow of Philip Wheath of Hinderwell in com. Ebor.

1. William Lutton of Knapton, Esqr, æt. 46 ann. 28 Aug. ao 1665. = Anne, daughter of Sr John Lyster of Kingston-super-Hull in com. Ebor.

4. Samuell Lutton, citizen of London.
5. Sidney Lutton, citizen of London.
6. Thomas.
7. John.

Mary, dau. of John Carvile of Catton in co. Ebor. ob. s. prole, 1 wife. = 3. Philip Lutton of Yedingham in com. Ebor. = Eliz. daugh. of William Blytheman of New Lathes in co. Ebor.

1. Barbara.
2. Debora, wife of .... Dobson of Heslarton, clerke.
3. Margaret.
4. Ruthe.

Philip, æt. 3 an. 28 Aug. 1665.

Mary.

Dickering Wapentake. *Kilham*, 31° *Aug.* 1665

WOOD OF THORPE.

Arms.—Sable, on a bend argent three fleurs-de-lis of the field.

Crest.—A wolf's head erased sable, collared and ringed or.

Thomas Wood of Thorpe in com. Ebor. died about the yeare 1632. = Margaret, daughter of Nicholas Richardson of Barnby in com. Ebor.

- 2. Thomas, died without issue.
- 1. Bernard Wood of Thorpe, died in a° 1665 or thereabouts. = Elizabeth Jewetson, daughter of Gilbert Jewetson of Nafferton in com. Ebor.
- Anne, died unmarried.

Issue of Bernard Wood and Elizabeth Jewetson:

- Thomas Wood of Thorpe, æt. 34 an. 31° Aug. 1665. = Anne, daughter of Marmaduke Norcliffe of Oswald-church in co. Ebor.
  - Anne, æt. 5 ann. 31 Aug. 1665.
- 1. Margaret, wife of Will. St Quintin, a younger son to Sr Will. St Quintin, Bart.
- 2. Elizabeth, wife of Thomas Hassell of Hutton upon Darwent in com. Ebor.
- 3. Anne, wife of Thomas St Quintin of Flamborough Esqr.

Birdforth Wapentake. *Threske*, 23 *Aug.* 1665.

FRANKLAND OF THIRKELBY.

Arms.—Azure, a dolphin naiant embowed or, on a chief of the second two saltires gules.

Crest.—A dolphin haurient or, entwined round an anchor erect azure, stock of the first.

Qu. How this family is descended from Hugh Frankland of Nelling in co. Ebor. to whom these armes were granted by W. Flower, Norroy.

William Frankland of Thirkelby in co. Ebor. came first into Yorkshire out of Hartfordshire. = Lucie, daughter of Sr Henry Butler of Woodhall in com. Hertford, Knt.

- 6. Mathew, Frankland, now living and unmarried.
- 7. Thomas.
- 4. William Frankland, died in Ireland. = (issue)
- 3. Charles. 5. Richard. died unmarried.
- 2. John, died unmarried.
- 1. Sr Henry Frankland of Thirkelby in com. Ebor. Kt, æt. 56 ann. 23 Aug. a° 1665. = Anne, daughter of Sr Arthur Harris of Crekesey in co. Essex, Kt.
- Frances, w[ife] of Sr H[…] Bethell of Ellerton i[n] com. Ebor Knt.

Sr William Frankland, Bart. æt. 25 ann. 23° Aug. a° 1665. = Arabella, daughter of Henry Bellasses, Esqr. son and heire apparent to Thomas Visc. Fauconbridge.

- Anne, æt. 3 ann. 23 Aug. 1665.

GILLING EAST WAPENTAKE. *Richmund*, 21 *Aug*. 1665.

FRANKE OF KNIGHTON.

ARMS.—Vert, a saltire engrailed or.
CREST.—A falcon close argent, beaked and belled or.

Sr Leonard Franke of Knighton in co. Ebor. Kt. = ... daughter of Thomas de Grantore of Flaseby in Craven in co. Ebor. Esqr.

Marmaduke Franke of Knighton, Esqr. = ... daughter and heire of ...... Danby of Leake.

Leonard Franke of Knighton in co. Ebor. Esqr. = Alice, daughter of Sr James Metcalfe of Nappa in com. Ebor. Kt.

Henry Franke of Knighton, Esqr. = Margaret, daughter of John Butler of Nunnington in com. Ebor. Esqr.

3. Christopher, setled in Sussex. 2. Thomas, died unmarried. 1. George Franke of Knighton, Esqr. died in ao 1607 vel circa. = Elizabeth, eldest daughter and coheire of William Beckwith of Clynt in com. Ebor. Esqr. Joane.

2. Thomas Franke. Catherine, daughter of John Ingleby, youngest brother to Sr Will'm Ingleby of Ripley in co. Ebor. Kt. 1 wife. = 1. Marmaduke Franke of Knighton, Esqr. ætatis 68 annorum 21o Aug. ao 1665. = Sarah, daughter and coheire of Robert Teasdale of Marsham in com. Eborum, 2 wife. = Mary, daughter of Francis Scargill of Tunstall in com. Ebor. Esqr. 3 wife.

2. Prisca. 1. Elizabeth, wife unto Nicholas Salkeld.

LANGBARGH WAPENTAKE. *Stokesley*, 25° *Aug*. 1665.

BATE OF ESEBY.

ARMS.—Sable, a fess engrailed argent between three dexter hands bendways couped at the wrist and open or.

CREST.—A stag's head erased argent, attired or, pierced through the neck with an arrow of the last.

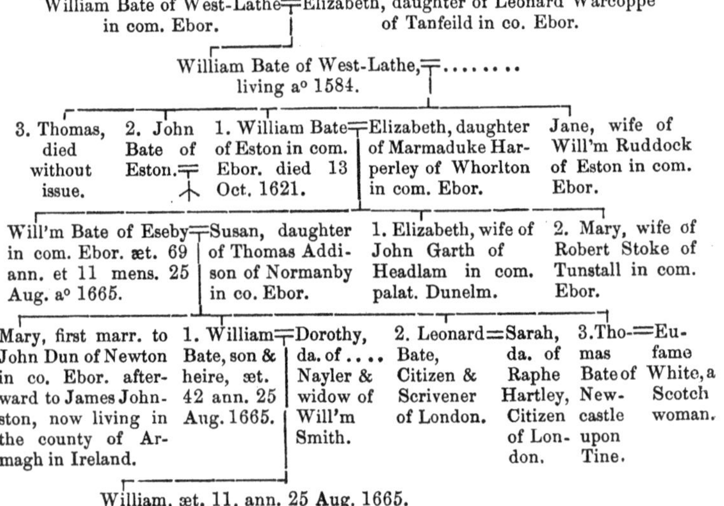

William Bate of West-Lathe in com. Ebor. = Elizabeth, daughter of Leonard Warcoppe of Tanfeild in co. Ebor.

William Bate of West-Lathe, living a° 1584. = ...

3. Thomas, died without issue. | 2. John Bate of Eston. = | 1. William Bate of Eston in com. Ebor. died 13 Oct. 1621. = Elizabeth, daughter of Marmaduke Harperley of Whorlton in com. Ebor. | Jane, wife of Will'm Ruddock of Eston in com. Ebor.

Will'm Bate of Eseby in com. Ebor. æt. 69 ann. et 11 mens. 25 Aug. a° 1665. = Susan, daughter of Thomas Addison of Normanby in co. Ebor. | 1. Elizabeth, wife of John Garth of Headlam in com. palat. Dunelm. | 2. Mary, wife of Robert Stoke of Tunstall in com. Ebor.

Mary, first marr. to John Dun of Newton in co. Ebor. afterward to James Johnston, now living in the county of Armagh in Ireland. | 1. William Bate, son & heire, æt. 42 ann. 25 Aug. 1665. = Dorothy, da. of .... Nayler & widow of Will'm Smith. | 2. Leonard Bate, Citizen & Scrivener of London. = Sarah, da. of Raphe Hartley, Citizen of London. | 3. Thomas Bate of Newcastle upon Tine. = Eufame White, a Scotch woman.

William, æt. 11. ann. 25 Aug. 1665.

GERE OF GREAT-BARUGH.

GERE OF GREAT BROUGHTON.

ARMS.—Gules, two bars or, each charged with three mascles azure, on a canton of the second a leopard's face of the third.

¶ Walter Gere of Havitree in com. Ebor. unto whom these Armes belonged.

¶ Robert Gere of Baynton upon the Would in com. Ebor. descended from Walter Gere of Havitre in com. Devon. as appeareth by a certificate from George Owen, Yorke Herauld, dated 7° Febr. 1651. = Anne, da. of .... Jackson, alias Lascells, of Eriholme in com. Ebor.

1. Stephen Gere, died without issue.

2. Robert Gere of Great Barugh in com. Ebor. died in a° 1643, vel circa. = Elizabeth, daughter of John Scarfe of Elloughton in com. Ebor.

3. Thomas Gere of .... in com. Linc. =

4. John Gere of Great Broughton in com. Ebor. died a° 1626, vel circa. = Susan, daughter of Henry Parkinson of Burneston in com. Ebor.

2. Dennis.
3. Thomas.
4. Stephen.
5. Edward.
died w[th]out issue.

Susanna, daughter of John Harbert of Skipwyth in co. Ebor. Esq[r], 1 wife. = 1. Robert Gere of Great Barugh, æt. 62 an. 28 Aug. 1665. = Frances, daughter of Isaac Mountaine of Westow in com. Ebor. Esq[r], 2[d] wife.

1. Elizabeth, wife of Joseph Heslarton of Hutton upon Darwent in co. Ebor. Gent.
2. Mary, wife of Thomas Lotherington of ...... in com. Ebor.

William Gere, of Great Broughton in co. Ebor. æt. 64 ann. 28° Aug. a° 1665. = Elizabeth, daughter of Willm. Watson of Knaton in com. Ebor.

Mary, wife of James Wilkinson of Sneaton Thorpe, in com. Ebor.

Susanna, wife of Tho. a younger son of Sr Henry Vaughan of Whitwell in com. Ebor. Knight. After of Christopher Percehay, a younger son of Christoph[r] Percehay of Ryton in com. Ebor. Esqr. =

Mary Vaughan, æt. 9 ann. 1665.

2. Isaac.
3. John.
4. Willm.

1. Thomas Gere, æt. 29 ann. 28 Aug. 1665. = Mary, daughter of Raphe Hassell of Thornton in com. Ebor. Gent.

1. Elizabeth, wife of Wm Dawson of Heworth in co. Ebor. Esqr.
2. Melior.

3. Anne, wife of Joseph Thorneton of Kirkby Moreside in co. Ebor.
4. Isabell.
5. Frances.
6. Penelope.
7. Theophila.

2. Robert.
3. William.

1. John Gere, æt. 31 ann. 28 Aug. a° 1665. = Mary, daughter of Samuell Levingstoun of Danby in com. Ebor.

1. Elizabeth, wife of Anth. Hill of Ugthorpe in com. Ebor.
2. Jane.
3. Susanna.
4. Margaret.

1. Sarah, æt. 4 an. 28 Aug. 1665. 2. Elizabeth, æt. 3 an. 1665. 3. Susanna, æt. 3 mens.

PICKERING LYTHE. *Malton*, 28 *Aug*. 1665.

LANGDALE OF SNAINTON.

ARMS.—Quarterly, a mullet azure for difference:
1 and 4. Or, a chevron between three mullets sable.
2 and 3. Gules, two chevrons or.

Raphe Langdale of Snainton in com. Ebor. living a° 1612. = Catherine, daughter of Thomas Jerome of Old Malton in co. Ebor.

6. Mary, wife of Richard Fisshe of Beverley in com. Ebor.
7. Catherine, wife of Edward Davy of Beverley.
8. Elizabeth.
9. Frances.

2. Ursula.
4. Barbara.
5. Susan.
died unmarried.

1. Isabell, wife of Will. Chapman.
3. Isabell, wife of Richard Dickenson.

1. Jeremie Langdale, of Snainton, died a° 1658. = Marg^t^, da. of Thomas Etherington of Eberston in co. Ebor.

2. Thomas, died unmarried.

2. Stephen Langdale, married Eliz. da. of Tho. Marshall of Beverley in co. Ebor.
3. Raphe.

1. Thomas Langdale of Snainton, æt. 26 ann. 29 Aug. 1665. = Jane, daughter of Henry Rosse of Preston in Holdernesse.

Anne.

WHITBY STRAND. *Malton*, 28 *Aug*. 1665.

BUSHELL OF WHITBY.

ARMS.—...... on a chevron ...... between three water bougets ...... as many roundlets.
No proofe made of these armes.

Robert Bushell of Whitby in com. Ebor. = ...

Leonard Bushell of Whitby, died in a° 1608, vel circa. = Jane, daughter of .... Lambe of Newcastle upon Tine.

2. Leonard Bushell of Limehouse in co. Middlesex.
3. Henry Bushell of Limehouse in co. Middlesex.
4. Samuell Bushell of Whitby in co. Eborū.
5. Daniell Bushell of Middleton in com. Ebor.

1. Richard Bushell of Whitby, died a° 1644. = Isabell, daughter of Robert Ellys of Rudston in com. Eborum.

1. Elizabeth, wife unto William Barnard of Kingston upon Hull.
2. Jane, wife of George Porter of Warthall in com. Ebor.
3. Ruthe, wife of Will'm Boyse in Virginia.

Robert Bushell of Whitby, ætat. 39 ann. 28 Aug. a° 1665. = Isabell, daughter of William Wigginer of Whitby in com. Ebor.

1. Eufemia, wife of Will. Wood of Galloway in Ireland.

2. Isabell, wife of Robert Winge of Skiplam in com. Eborū.

3. Jane, y^e^ wife of John Rymer of Whitby.

Leonard, æt. 10 ann. 28 Aug. 1665.

PICKERING LYTHE. *Malton*, 29 *Aug*. 1665.

HUTCHENSON OF WICKHAM.

ARMS.—Per pale gules and azure, semée of cross-crosslets or, a lion rampant argent.
CREST.—Out of a ducal coronet or, a demi-cockatrice azure, combed and wattled gules.

Edward Hutchensen of Wickham in com. Ebor. = Mary, daughter of Rich. Wood of Pickering in com. Eborum.

2. Charles Hutchenson, died without issue male.

1. Stephen Hutchenson of Wickham, Esqr, died in a° 1648. = Catherine, daughter of Sr Richard Musgrave of Norton juxta Rippon, in co. Ebor. Kn^t.

Edward Hutchenson of Wickham, Esqr, a Colonell of Horse in y^e Army of K. Charles y^e 1st, died in a° 1653. = Frances, daughter of Sr Richard Osbaldeston of the citty of Yorke, K^t.

Edward Hutchenson of Wickham, Esqr, æt. 21 an. 29 Aug. a° 1665. = Frances, daughter of Sr Philip Musgrave of Edenhall in com. Cumbr. K^t & Bar^t.

1. Catharine, wife of Thomas Coundon of Willerby in co. Ebor., afterwards of John Constable of Cathorpe in com. Ebor. Esqr.

2. Dorothy.

DICKERING WAPENTAKE. *Kilham*, 31 *Aug*. 1665.

OSBALDESTON OF HUNMANBY.

ARMS.—Quarterly of six:
1. Argent, a mascle sable between three pellets, a canton gules.
2. Azure, a cross moline square-pierced or.
3. Quarterly argent and sable, in each a leopard's face counterchanged.
4. Argent, two bars gules, on a canton of the second a rose of the first.
5. A lion rampant purpure.
6. As the first.

CREST.—A knight on horseback in complete armour brandishing a sword, on his shield the arms of Osbaldeston.

...... Osbaldeston, fourth son of ...... Osbaldeston of Osbaldeston in co. Lanc. Esqr. = ...

Edward Osbaldeston of Langscales in co. Lanc. died at Hunmanby in co. Ebor. circa annum 1639. = Margaret, daughter of ...... Molineux of Sefton in com. Lanc.

Sir Richard Osbaldeston of Hunmanby in co. Ebor. K^t, Attorney-generall to King Charles the first in y^e realme of Ireland, died at Dublyn in Ireland 11° Junij a° 1642. = Eleanor, daughter of William Westropp of Brunton in Pickering Lythe in com. Ebor.

William Osbaldeston of Hunmanby in com. Ebor. Esqr, æt. 34 ann. 31 Aug. a° 1665. = Anne, daughter and coheire of Sr George Wentworth, late of Wolley in com. Ebor. Kn^t.

Frances, wife of Edward Hutchenson of Wickham Abbey in com. Ebor. Esqr.

Richard, æt. 10 an. 31 Aug. 1665.

1. Anne.
2. Elizabeth.
3. Everald.
4. Eleanor.

BAYNTON BEACON. *Kilham*, 31 *Aug.* 1665.

MANBY OF MIDDLETON.

ARMS.—Argent, a lion rampant within an orle of escallops sable, a canton gules.
CREST.—A cubit arm in armour or, the gauntlet grasping a sword argent hilted of the first.

Willm. Mànby of Elsam, in com. Linc. = ...

2. Robert Manby of Farlington, in com. Ebor. = ...

1. Francis Manby of Elsham, son & heire. = ...

Richard Manby of Middleton in com. Ebor. died in aº 1658. = Elizabeth, daughter of George Barnes of .... in com. Wilts.

Willm. Manby of Cranswicke in co. Ebor. livinge aº 1612. =

Richard Manby of Middleton, æt. 38 ann. 31 Aug. aº 1665. = Frances, daughter of Francis Carlisle of Brandsburton in Holdernesse in com. Ebor.

1. Mary, wife of Stephen Hudson of Kellā in com. Eborū.
2. Eliz. wife of William Ringrose of South Dalton in com. Ebor.
3. Anne, wife of John Semar of Raisthorpe in co. Ebor.
4. Frances, wife of John Cotterell of Hugget in co. Ebor.
5. Hannah, wife of Francis Throckmorton of Burnbutts in co. Ebor.

Mary, æt. 9 ann. 31 Aug. 1665. Frances, æt. 6 an. 1665.

BAYNTON BEACON. *Kilham*, 31 *Aug.* 1665.

THROCKMORTON OF BURNEBUTTS.

ARMS.—Gules, on a chevron argent three bars-gemelles sable, a canton or.

Sr Richard Throckmorton of Higham Ferrers in com. Northampton, Knt. = ...

.... = John Throckmorton, a younger son = ...

Sr John Throckmorton, Kt, Governour of Flushing in ye time of Qu. Eliz., died in ye siege of Breda about the latter end of K. James his raigne. = Anne, daughter of John Sotherton, one of the Barons of the Excheqr.

Dr Raphaell Throckmorton, Arch-Deacon of Lincolne.

1. Sr Willm. Throckmorton, Kt, now Kt Marshall to K. Charles the 2d, aº 1665.

2. Francis Throckmorton of Burnebutts in com. Ebor. ætat. 47 ann. 31º Aug. aº 1665. = Hannah, daughter of Rich. Manby of Middleton in com. Ebor.

Philippa, wife of Sr Edmund Carey, Knt.

1. Mary, æt. 9 ann. 31 Aug. 1665. 2. Frances, æt. 3 an. 1665.

WHITBY STRAND. *Malton*, 28 *Aug.* 1665.

FARSIDE OF FILINGDALE.

ARMS.—Gules, a fess or between three bezants.

This coate is sayd to belong to the family of Farsides of Scotland, but no proofe made.

John Farside of Farside in the realme of Scotland came into England in the time of K. James, and was made Bowbearer in the Forest of Pickering in com. Ebor. = ...

William Farside, borne at Langdane bridge, wthin Whitby Strand, after resided at Ellis Close, wthin ye honour of Pickerg. = Mary, daughter of John Watson of Hakenes in Whitby Strand in com. Ebor.

3. James Farside of Fotheringhay in co. Northton.

2. Adam Farside of Scalby in Pickering Lythe.

1. John Farside of Huton Bushell in Pickering Lithe in com. Ebor. died in ao 1660. = Jane, eldest daughter of Marmaduke Wilson of Whitby in com. Ebor.

2. Thomas.

1. Willm. Farside of Filingdale in Whitby Strand, late Capt. Lieutenant to Sr Willm. Cholmeley for ye service of K. Charles ye 2d, æt. 44 an. 28o Aug. 1665. = Ursula, daughter of John Marshall of Filingdale in com. Ebor.

Mary, wife of Richard Etherington of Driffield in co. Ebor.

John Farside, ætatis 4 an. 28 Aug. 1665.

1. Jane.

2. Elizabeth.

3. Mary.

PICKERING LYTHE. *Malton*, 29° *Aug.* 1665.

STRANGWAYS OF SOUTH-HOUSE.

ARMS.—Quarterly of six:

1. Sable, two lions passant in pale paly of six argent and gules, a canton of the second.
2. Azure, three cinquefoils between nine cross-crosslets argent.
3. Azure, three bars-gemelles and a chief or.
4. Azure, a maunche or.
5. Or, five fusils in fess sable.
6. Argent, three chevronels braced in base sable, on a chief of the second as many mullets of the first.

Sr Richard Strangwayes of Ormesby and Sneton in com. Ebor. Kt. = Isabell, daughter of ...... Thwaytes of Lound in co. Ebor. 2 wife.

.... 2 wife. = 3. Edward Strangwayes of Middlesbrough in co. Ebor. 3d son. = Nelice, daughter of Wm Radcliffe of .... in com. Lanc. first wife.

4. Henry Strangways of South-House in Whitby Strand in co. Ebor. fourth son, died circa an. 1615. = ... daughter of ...... Millet of ...... in the Bishoprick of Durham.

James Strangwayes of Gisbrough in co. Eborum. =

Anne, wife of Will'm Chapman of Arsum in Cleveland.

James Strangways of South-House in com. Ebor. obijt circa ann. 1647. = Alice, daughter of ...... Key of ye Oldstede in com. Eborum.

1. Margery, ye wife of Richard Jones of Ampleforth in com. Ebor.
2. Thomasine, wife unto Robert Hudson of Whitby parish in co. Ebor.

2. Henry Strangways, of Sneton in com. Ebor. marr. Margt, daughter of Will'm Mitford of Kirby-Misterton in com. Eborum.
3. James.

1. Thomas Strangways of South-House, ætatis 45 ann. 29 Aug. a° 1665. = Jane, daughter of Luke Robynson of Thorneton-Risebrough by his 1st wife.

1. Dorothy, wife of John Moxon, a Merchant in Hull.
2. Isabella, first marr. to James Cosens of Whitby; 2dly, to Francis Knags of Whitby; thirdly, to Henry Lisle of Whitby.
3. Alice, wife of Will'm Smith of Swynton in com. Eborum.

Thomas, æt. 8 an. 29 Aug. 1665.

1. Jane, æt. 9 ann. 1665.

2. Elizabeth, æt. 3 ann. 1665.

PICKERING LYTHE. *Malton*, 29° *Aug.* 1665.

HUNTER OF THORNETON.

ARMS.—Or, a bugle-horn stringed and tasseled vert, between a mullet in chief and a crescent in base gules.

No proofe made of these armes.

Robert Hunter of Thorneton in com Ebor. died a° 1652 or thereabouts. = Ellen, daughter of William Spacye of Brackton.

- 2. Robert Hunter of Thorneton, married Anne, daughter unto Thomas Boys of Edston in co. Eborum.
- 1. Bethell Hunter of Thornton, died a° 1655, vel circa. = Magdalen, da. of Tho. Percehay of Ryton in co. Ebor. Esqr.
- 1. Christian, wife of Michaell Coppinson of Kingston super Hull.
- 2. Dorothy, wife of Christoph^r Hobman of Garton in com. Ebor.
- 3. Frances, wife of William Ives of Thornton in com. Ebor.
- 4. Mary, wife of Machabe Hollyes of Kingston super Hull.

Children of Bethell Hunter and Magdalen:

- Christopher Hunter of Thorneton, æt. 19 ann. 29° Aug. 1665.
- 1. Helen, wife of Samuell Robinson of Farnby in co. Ebor.
- 2. Mary, wife of John Hessell of Thornton in com. Ebor.
- 3. Frances.
- 4. Anne.

DICKERING WAPENTAKE. *Kilham*, 31 *Aug.* 1665.

STOUTVILLE OF HUMANBY.

ARMS.—Barry of twelve argent and gules, a lion rampant sable.

Charles Stouteville of Humanby in com. Ebor. died in a° 1622, or thereabouts. = Anne, daughter of Bryan Robinson of Boston in com. Linc.

- 2. Charles Stoutville of Humanby in co. Ebor. died in a° 1637. = Elizabeth, daugh. & coheire of Robert Knowseley of Burton Fleming in com. Ebor.
- 1. Henry Stouteville. (= ; issue)
- 1. Anna-Maria, wife of Thomas Acklam of Drinho in com. Ebor.
- 2. Elizabeth, wife of John Acklam.
- 3. Margaret, wife of ...... Shepheard.

Children of Charles Stoutville and Elizabeth:

- Mary, died unmarried.
- Robert Stouteville of Humanby in com. Ebor. æt. 31 ann. 31 Aug. a° 1665. = Jane, daughter of Humphrey Martin of Thorneton-le-Moore in com. Ebor.

Children of Robert Stouteville and Jane:

- Charles, æt. unius anni 31° Aug. a° 1665.
- 1. Elizabeth.
- 2. Jane.

HANG-EAST WAPENTAKE. *Richmund*, 19° *Aug.* 1665.

DODSWORTH OF THORNETON-WATLAS.

ARMS.—Argent, a bend engrailed sable between three annulets gules.

CREST.—A cubit arm in chain-mail or, the hand proper grasping a broken tilting spear of the first, the broken end imbrued proper.

John Dodsworth of Thornton Watlas in com. Ebor. = Anne, daugh. of Thomas Rokesby of Moreton in com. Ebor.

John Dodsworth of Thorneton-Watlas, Esqr, unto whom Richard St George, Esqr, Norroy King of Armes, granted this Crest to the Armes above exprest 2° Junij, 8° Jac. a° 1610, obijt a° 1644. = Winifride, da. and heire of John Warde of Barton in com. Ebor.

2. Robert, obijt sine prole.
3. Christopher Dodsworth, M^r of y^e Hospitall of Welle neere Snape in com. Ebor.
4. Francis, obijt sine prole.

1. John Dodsworth of Thorneton-Watlas in com. Ebor. Esqr, ætat 70 ann. 19 Aug. 1665. = Frances, daughter of Sr Timothy Hutton of Marske in com. Ebor. Kn^t.

1. Alice, wife of Mathew Smelt of Kirkby-Fletham in com. Ebor.
2. Winifred, wife unto George Clough of Sand-Hutton in co. Ebor.
3. Margaret, wife unto Thomas Atkinson of Yorke.

2. Timothy Dodsworth, married ..... daughter of .... Stringer of ...... in com. Staff.
3. Mathew.

1. John Dodsworth, died in his father's life-time. = Frances, youngest daughter to Sr John Lowther of Lowther in co. Westmerl. Kn^t.

1. Elizabeth, wife of Willm. Metcalfe, son and heire to Sr Francis Metcalfe of Louth-Parke in co. Linc. Kn^t.

2. Winifride y^e wife of Francis Purley of Farlesthorpe in co. Linc. Esqr.

John, æt. 16 an. 16 Aug. 1665.

Helen, died young.

GILLING EAST. *Richmund*, 19 *Aug.* 1665.

WYVILL OF CONSTABLE-BURTON.

ARMS.—Quarterly of six:
1. Gules, three cheTronels braced in base vair, a chief or.
2. Sable, three pickaxes argent, a crescent for difference.
3. Azure, a chief indented or.
4. Azure, a bend or, over all a label of three points argent.
5. Argent, on a pale sable a conger's head couped and erect or.
6. Or, on a fess between three crescents gules a lion passant of the field.

CREST.—A wyvern with the wings addorsed argent, breathing flames proper.

Christopher Wyvill, eldest son of Sr Marmaduke Wivill of Constable Burton in com. Ebor. Kt, died in his father's life time. = Jane, daughter of Sr Robert Stapleton, of Wighill in co. Ebor. Knt.

2. Edmund Wyvill, married .... daugh. of .... Lowther of .... neer Carlisle.
3. Will'm Wyvill, married ...... daugh. of Leonard Musgrave of Joneby in co. Westmerl. Esqr.
4. Henry, died unmarried.

1. Sr Marmaduke Wyvill of Constable Burton, Knt and Bart, died aº 1648. = Isabell, daughter and sole heire of Sr Will'm Gascoigne of Sedbury in co. Ebor. Kt.

1. Barbara, died an infant.
2. Elizabeth, ye wife of .... Bellingham of .... in com. Linc.
3. Olive, wife of Cuthbert Collingwood of Ellington in co. Northumb. Esqr.
4. Mary, wife of John Wilde of Hunton in com. Ebor. after marr. to Anth. Bulmer, 2d son to Sr Bertrã Bulmer, Knt.
5. Catherine, wife unto John Wharton of Kirkby-Theure in com. Westmerld, Esqr.
6. Philippa, wife of Richard Sale of Hopecare in com. Lanc. gent.

N

5. Robert Wyvill, marr. Mary, da. & heire of .... Parkinson of Slendingford in com. Ebor.
6. Henry Wyvill, Dr of Phisick.
7. Francis Wyvill of Rippon, marr. .... da. of .... widow of .... Percehay.

2. Will'm, died unmarried.
3. Marmaduke, a Merchant in the Isle of Scio, unmarried.
4. John.

1. Sr Christopher Wyvill of Constable Burton, Bart, æt. 50 an. 19º Aug. aº 1665. = Ursula, ye daughter of Conyers Ld Darcy & Conyers.

1. Mary, wife unto Arthur Beckwith of Aldbrough in co. Ebor.
2. Jane, wife of Robert Wilde of Hunton in com. Ebor.
3. Isabell, wife of James Darcy, 6th son of Conyers Ld Darcy and Conyers.
4. Grace, wife of George Wytham of Cliffe in co. Ebor. Esqr.
5. Olive, wife of George Meinill of Aldbrough in co. Ebor.
6. Eliz. wife of Sr Will. Dalton of Hawkswell in com. Ebor. Knt.
7. Anne, wife of Tho. Dalton, younger brother to Sr Will'm Dalton, Knt.
8. Dorothy.

5. Francis.
6. Robert, died young.
7. Christopher.

3. Darcy Wivill, died in his youth.
4. William Wyvill, æt. 20 an. 19º Aug. 1665.

1. Marmaduke, died in his father's life time unmarried.
2. Christopher, died young.

1. Dorothy, wife of Charles Tankard of Whixley, son and heire of Sr Richard Tankard of Whixley in co. Ebor. Kt.
2. Grace, died young.
3. Isabell, died young.
4. Barbara.
5. Ursula.

HANG-EAST WAPENTAKE. *Richmund*, 19º *Aug*. 1665.

LAWSON OF BROUGH.

ARMS.—Quarterly of six:
1. Argent, a chevron between three martlets sable. Lawson.
2. Barry of six argent and azure, in chief three annulets sable. Cramlington.
3. Argent, three boars passant sable. Swynnow.
4. Argent, on a saltire sable five swans of the field. Burgh.
5. Argent, a fess engrailed between six fleurs-de-lis sable. Richmund.
6. As the first.

CREST.—On a chapeau or, turned up ermine, a martlet sable.

Sr Raphe Lawson of Burgh in com. Richmund, Knt. = ...

Roger Lawson of Heton in co. Northumbr. Kt. died in the lifetime of his father. = Dorothy, daughter of Sr Henry Constable of Burton in com. Ebor. Kt.

Their children:

- 8. James Lawson. = ...
- 7. Edmund, of whom is noe issue remayning.
- 4. George, 5. John, 6. Thomas, died unmarried.
- 3. Roger, died unmarried.
- 2. Henry Lawson of Brough neere Cataract in com. Ebor. Esqr. obijt circa ann. 1636. = Anne, daughter of Robert Hodshon of Heburne in Episc. Dunelm.
- 1. Raphe, died unmarried.
- 1. Mary, a nunne at Gant in Flanders.
- 2. Catherine, died unmarried.
- 3. Elizabeth, wife of John Yorke of Gothwayt in co. Ebor. Esq.
- 4. Anne, wife of Henry Widdrington of Beautland in co. Northumb.

Children of James Lawson:

- 1. Raphe.
- 2. Henry.
- 1. Mary, wife of ...... Paston of .... in co. Norff.
- 2. Elizabeth.

Children of Henry Lawson and Anne:

- 2. Dorothy, wife of Will'm Blakeston of Sheildraw in com. Dunelm. Esqr.
- 1. Mary, a nunne at Gant in Flanders.
- 1. Roger, died unmarried.
- 2. Henry Lawson of Brough, Esqr. slayne in his Maties service in a fight at Melton Moubray in com. Leic. circa an. 1644. = Catherine, da. of Sr Will'm Fenwick of Meldon in com. Northumbr. Knt.
- 3. Sr John Lawson of Brough in co. Ebor. Bart. æt. 38 ann. 19 Aug. aº 1665. = Katharine, daughter to Sr Will'm Howard of Naworth Castle in com. Cumbr. Kt. sister to Charles Earle of Carlisle.
- 4. Francis.

Daughter of Henry Lawson and Catherine:

- Isabella, wife of Sr John Swynburne of Chap-Heyton in com. Northumbr. Bt.

Children of Sr John Lawson and Katharine:

- 1. Catherine.
- 2. Mary.
- 3. Elizabeth.
- 1. John, æt. 14 an. 19º Aug. 1665.
- 2. Henry.
- 3. Charles.
- 4. William.
- 5. Philip.

GILLING WEST WAPENTAKE. *Richmund*, 19 *Aug*. 1665.

ROBINSON OF KIRBY RAVENSWATH.

The entring of the armes is respited til proofe be made thereof.

Leonard Robinson of St. Ninians neere Richmund. = Anne, daughter of John Hilton of Hilton in com. Westmerland.

1. Jeromy, obijt sine prole.
2. Roger, obijt sine prole.
4. William Robinson of Ellerton in co. Ebor.
5. Christopher.

3. John Robinson of Aplegarth in in co. Ebor. died a° 1655. = Syth, da. of Leonard Smelt of Kirkby-Fletham in co. Ebor.

1. Jane, ye wife of Thomas Rud of Appleton in co. Ebor.
2. Margaret, wife of John Jaques of Kidston in com. Eborum.
3. Mary, ye wife of Gervase Lightfoot of Redmire in co. Ebor.
4. Elizabeth, wife unto James Collyns of Kirkby-Ravensweth in co. Ebor.

2. Thomas Robinson of Eseby in com. Eborum.
3. Mathew Robinson of Middleham in co. Ebor.

1. Leonard Robinson of Kirby-Ravenswath in com. Ebor. æt. 47 an. 19 Aug. 1665. = Lucie, daugh. of Percivall Philips of Wensley in com. Ebor.

1. Sythe, wife of Ninian Collins of Ravensweth in co. Ebor.
2. Elizabeth, ye wife of Mathew Berry of Downham-parke in com. Ebor.

Jerome, æt. 6 an. 19 Aug. 1665. | 1. Mary. | 2. Lucye. | 3. Sythe. | 4. Anne. | 5. Elizabeth.

HANG EAST WAPENTAKE. *Richmund*, 21 *Aug*. 1665.

CROFTS OF EAST-APPLETON.

He refers himselfe to the Visitation of Lancashire, in which there is nothing entred concerning any Croft.

Roger Crofts of East-Appleton in com. Ebor. Bowbearer in Wensdale to Qu. Eliz. descended from the family of Croft of Clawton in co. Lanc. = Anne, daughter and coheire of .... Mountfort of ...... in com. Ebor.

2. Edward Crofts of East-Appleton, Governour of Knaresborough Castle to K. Charles ye 1st, æt. 61 an. 21 Aug. 1665. = Anne, daughter of John Stanley of Dale-garth in com. Cumbr. Esqr.

1. Roger Crofts, æt. 65 an. 21 Aug. a° 1665.

1. Anne, wife of Walter Strickland of Nateby in com. Lanc.

2. Mary, wife of Richard Brathwayt of Burneside in com. Westmerl. Esqr.

1. Roger, æt. 22 an. 21 Aug. a° 1665. | 2. Richard. | 3. Raphe. | 4. Edward.

CLARO WAPENTAKE. *Richmund*, 21 *Aug.* 1665.

YORKE OF GOULTHWAYT.

ARMS.—Azure, a saltire argent.

Peter Yorke of Goulthwayt in com. Ebor. Esqr. = Elizabeth, daughter of Sr Will'm Ingleby of Ripley in com. Ebor. Knt.

4. Richard, died unmarried.

3. Will'm. = ...

2. Thomas Yorke, died in his elder brother's life time. = Frances, daugh. of .... Babthorpe of Babthorpe in com. Ebor. Esqr.

1. Sr John Yorke of Goulthwayt, Knt, died ao 1630, or thereabouts; died without issue. = Julian, daughter and coheire of Raphe Hansby of Beverley and Tickhill in co. Ebor. Esqr.

John Yorke. (son of Will'm.)

Florence, daughter of ...... Sharpe of .... in com. Westmerl. 1 wife. = John Yorke of Goulthwayt, Esqr, died in ao 1635, vel circa. = Catherine, daughter of Sr Ingleby Daniell of Besewicke in com. Ebor. Knt, 2 wife.

3. Jane, wife of David Lesley now Ld Newarke in Scotld.

2. Frances, wife of Tho. Barney of Dalebanke in co. Ebor.

1. Elizabeth, ye wife of Sr James Lesley Ld Londores in Scotland.

Sr John Yorke of Goulthwayt in com. Ebor. Kt, died in Apr. 1663. = Mary, daughter to Maulger Norton of St Nicholas neere Richmund in com. Ebor. Esqr.

Thomas Yorke, Esqr. æt. 6 ann. 19o Aug. ao 1665.

Mary, æt. 8 ann. ao 1665.

ALLERTONSHIRE. *Threske*, 23° *Aug.* 1665.

DANBY OF GREAT-LEAKE.

ARMS.—Quarterly of six:

1. Argent, three chevronels braced in base sable, on a chief of the second as many mullets of the first.
2. Gules, six billets ermine, three, two, and one.
3. Argent, a chevron between three crosses fleury sable.
4. Argent, five fusils in fess gules, in chief three bear's heads erased sable.
5. Argent, a fesse engrailed between three fleurs-de-lis in chief and one in base sable.
6. Per chevron-grady sable and argent, three stag's heads cabossed counterchanged.

CREST.—A crab-fish or.

Thomas Danby of Leake in co. Ebor. died in a° 1623, or thereabouts. = Anne, daughter and coheire to Ralphe Anger of ....

4. Will'm, died unmarried.
5. Francis.
6. Edmund Danby of Danby of Borroughby in com. Ebor. =

2. Miles Danby. =

3. John Danby of Borroughby in com. Ebor. =

1. Thomas Danby of Braworth, obijt patre vivente. = Eliz. daugh. of Christopher Carrus of Halghton in. com. Lanc. Esqr.

1. Eliz. wife of Michaell Metcalfe of Little Ottrington in com. Ebor.
2. Jane, wife of Thomas Middleton of Middleton in Cleveland.
3. Mary, wife of Thomas Appleby of great Smeaton in com. Ebor.

2. Thomas Danby, slayne at Navesby battell in the service of K. Charles the first.
3. Christopher Danby.

Mary, daughter of Will'm Swynbourne of Cap-Heaton in com. Ebor. 1 wife. = 1. John Danby of Great Leake in com. Ebor. Esqr. æt. 49 ann. 23° Aug. a° 1665. = Mary daughter of Anthony Meynill of Kilvington in co. Ebor. 2 wife.

Elizabeth, wife of James Shafto of Tanfeild-Leigh in y^e Bishoprick of Durham.

1. Anthony, æt. 12 an. 23° Aug. 1665.
2. Joseph, æt. 7 ann.
3. James, æt. 6 ann.
4. John, æt. 4 ann.

1. Eliz. æt. 10 an. a° 1665.
2. Agnes, æt. 3 ann.
3. Ursula, æt. 1 anni.

GILLING EAST WAPENTAKE. *Richmund,* 21° *Aug.* 1665.

PALLESER OF NEWBY.

ARMS.—Per pale sable and argent, three lions rampant counterchanged.
CREST.—Out of a ducal coronet gules a demi-eagle displayed or.
Respite given for proofe of these armes, but nothing done in it.

John Palleser of Newby super Wiske in com. Ebor. = Anne, daughter of Michaell Meeke of Maunby upon Swale in com. Eborum.

- 2. John Palleser of Kirby Wiske in co. Ebor.
- 1. Thomas Palleser of Newby, æt. 59 an. 21° Aug. 1665. = Joane, da. of Rich. Franklin of Blubber-houses in com. Ebor.
- 1. Mary, wife of Robert Wilson of Threske.
- 2. Anne, wife of Richard Metcalfe of North Aller-ton, afterwards of Mar-maduke Franke of Knighton in co. Ebor.
- 3. Jane, wife of Tho-mas Pybus of Fryer-garth in com. Ebor.
- 4. Elizabeth, y^e wife of George Llewelin of Danby upon Wiske.

Children of Thomas and Joane:

- John Palleser, æt. 26 ann. 21 Aug. 1665. = Ursula, daughter of Sr Hugh Bethell of Ellerton in com. Ebor. Kn^t.
- Willm.
- George.

Children of John and Ursula:

- 2. John, æt. 2 ann.
- 1. Thomas, æt. 3 an. 21 Aug. 1665.
- Frances.

ALLERTONSHIRE WAPENTAKE. *Threske,* 23 *Aug.* 1665.

SALTMERSH OF NORTH-KILVINGTON.

ARMS.—Argent, three cinquefoils between nine cross-crosslets gules.
CREST.—A rudder of a ship.

Thomas Saltmarsh de Saltmarsh in com. Ebor. ar'. died 5° Martij 20 Eliz. = ...

Robert Saltmarshe of Saltmarshe in com. Ebor. Esqr, died 19 March, 2 Jacobi Regis. = Cecilie, daughter of Thomas Grimston of Grimston-garth in Holdernesse in co. Ebor.

Philip Saltmarsh of Saltmarsh, Esqr, aged 18 yeares and five months at y^e death of his father, died in a° 1659. = Mary, y^e daughter of ...... Stanley of ......

- Mary, daughter of Sr Edw. Payler of Thoroldby, Bar^t, 1. wife; died w^th-out issue. = 2. Edward Saltmarsh of North Kilvington in com. Ebor. æt. 41 ann. 23° Aug. a° 1665. = Gerard, daughter of .... Ireland of Nostell in com. Ebor. Esqr. 2. wife.
- 1. Philip Saltmarsh of Saltmarsh, Esqr, æt. 46 ann. 23° Aug. a° 1665.

Children of Edward and Gerard:

- Elizabeth, æt. 8 an. 1665.
- 1. Philip, æt. 14 an. 23 Aug. 1665.
- 2. Gerard, æt. 12 ann.
- 3. Edward, ætat. 9 ann.
- 4. Peter, æt. 7 ann.

MEYNILL OF NORTH-KILVINGTON.

ARMS.—Quarterly:
1. Azure, three bars-gemelles and a chief or.
2. Argent, on a fess engrailed sable three quatrefoils or.
3. Checky argent and sable, a bordure of the first.
4. Argent, a bend between six martlets sable, a mullet for difference.

CREST.—A negro's head in profile couped at the shoulders sable, round the temples a wreath knotted behind argent and azure.

Thomas Meynill of North Kilvington in com. Ebor. Esqr, died in a° 1653, or thereabouts. = Winifride, daughter of Thomas Pudsey of Barforth in Richmondshire Esqr, first wife.

Children of Thomas and Winifride:
- 2. Richard Meynill of Broughton in com. Ebor. died in a° 1663 = Isabell, daughter of John Talbot of Thorneton in le Street in com. Ebor.
  - John Meynill, æt. 25 ann.
- 1. Anthony Meynill of North Kilvington, Esqr, ætatis 74 ann. 23° Aug. a° 1665. = Mary, daugh. of James Thwaytes of Marston in co. Ebor. Esqr.
  - 5. Anth. died unmarried.
  - 6. James, æt. 44 an. 23° Aug. a° 1665.
  - 2. John, died unmarried.
  - 3. Hugh, died unmarried.
  - 4. Will'm.
  - 1. Thomas Meynill. = Gerard, da. of Will. Ireland of Nostell in co. Ebor. Esqr.
    - 2. Will'm.
    - 1. Roger, æt. 25 an. 23 Aug. 1665. = Mary, daughter of Sr John Middleton of Thurntoft in co. Ebor. K^t.
    - Mary.
  - 1. Winifride, wife of Tho. Killingbeck of Allerton grange in com. Ebor.; afterward of Tho. Barlow of Barlow in co. Lanc. Esqr.
  - 2. Clare, wife of Sr Rich. Foster of Stokesley in co. Ebor. Bar^t.
  - 3. Collet, now unmarried.
  - 4. Mary, wife of John Danby of Leake in co. Ebor. Esqr.
  - 5. Julian.
  - 6. Cath.
  - 7. Frances.
- 1. Mary, wife of George Poole of Spinkhill in co. Derb.
- 2. Anne, wife of Tho. Grange of Harlsey in com. Ebor.

LANGBARGH WAPENTAKE. *Stokesley*, 25° *Aug*. 1665.

SALVEIN OF NEW-BIGGIN.

ARMS.—Quarterly:
1 and 4. Argent, on a chief sable two mullets or. Salveyn.
2 and 3. Or, a bend sable. Mawlee.

Dorothy, daughter of John Girlington of ......, first wife. = Will'm Salvein of New Biggin in com. Ebor. Esqr. = Anne, daughter of ...... Carnaby of .... in Northumbr.

William Salveyn of New Biggin ar'. æt. circa 40 ann. 25° Aug. a° 1665. = Anne, daughter of Marmaduke Cholmley of .... in com. Ebor. ar'.

4. Marmaduke. 5. John. 2. Thomas. 3. Will'm. 1. Francis, æt. 11 an. 25° Aug. 1665. 1. Mary. 2. Anne. 3. Ursula. 4. Dorothy.

LANGBARGH WAPENTAKE. *Stokesley*, 25° *Aug*. 1665.

LEE OF PINCHINGTHORPE.

Respite given for entring the armes and proofe of them; but nothing done.

Gervase Lee. = ... daughter of ...... Conyers.

Roger Lee of York, D^r^ in Phisick. = Muriell, daughter of ...... Gower of Stainsby in com. Eborum.

William Lee of Pinchingthorp in com. Ebor. died circa 1650. = Eleanor, daughter of Cutbert Morley of Normanby in co. Ebor.

Dorothy, first marr. to .... Young, and after to Sr Philip Hungate of Huddleston in com. Ebor. Kn^t^.

Roger Lee of Pinchingthorpe, æt. 33 ann. 25 Aug. 1665. = Mary, daughter unto John Turner of Welham in com. Ebor.

2. Robert. 1. George, æt. 6 an. 25 Aug. 1665. 1. Eleanor. 2. Dorothy. 3. Mary. 4. Elizabeth. 5. Isabell.

LANGBARGH WAPENTAKE. *Stokesley*, 25° *Aug.* 1665.

MALEVERER OF ARNCLIFFE.

ARMS.—Quarterly:
1 and 4. Sable, three greyhounds courant in pale argent.
2. Or, a fess gules, in chief three torteaux.
3. Azure, a maunche or.

CREST.—A maple-branch argent.

Will'm Maleverer of Wodersome in com. Ebor. Esqr. = Eleanor, daughter of Rich. Aldbrough of Aldbrough in co. Ebor. Esqr.

Their children:

4. Edmund Maleverer of Spalding in co. Linc.
3. Christopher Maleverer. = (issue)
2. Will'm, died unmarried.
1. James Maleverer of Arncliffe in com. Ebor. Esqr, died 24° Apr. 1664. = Beatrice, daugh. of Sr Timothy Hutton of Marske in com. Ebor. Kt.
Mary, wife of Henry Blakeston of Old Malton in co. Ebor.

Children of James and Beatrice:

2. James.
3. Edmund.
1. Timothy Maleverer of Arncliffe in com. Ebor. Esqr, æt. 37 ann. 25° Aug. 1665, now one of ye justices of this county. = Elizabeth, da. unto George Metcalfe of NorthAllerton in co. Ebor. Esqr.
1. Eliza, wife of Peter Blakeston of Ingleby under Arncliffe in com. Ebor.
2. Eleanor, wife of Anthony Nowers of Putney in com. Midd.
3. Beatrice, wife of George Wright of Bolton super Swale in co. Ebor.

Children of Timothy and Elizabeth:

Timothy, æt. 11 an. 25 Aug, 1665.
Beatrice, borne 6° Jan. 1651.

LANGBARGH WAPENTAKE. *Stokesley*, 25° *Aug.* 1665.

WRIGHT OF BOLTON UPON SWALE.

ARMS.—Quarterly:
1 and 4. Or, a fess componée argent and azure between three eagle's heads erased of the last, a canton gules.
2. Azure, three crescents or.
3. .... a lion rampant .... charged with an annulet.

CREST.—A unicorn passant regardant argent, armed or, unguled azure.

Will'm Wright of Plowland in co. Ebor. = ..., daughter of ...... Thorneton.

Robert Wright of Foston. = | Francis Wright of Sowerby in com. Ebor. = ...

Francis Wright of Bolton super Swale in co. Ebor. died in a° 1651, or thereabouts. = Grace, daughter of ...... Beckwith of Aldbrough in com. Ebor. | Christopher Wright of Sowerby in co. Ebor. =

Francis Wright of Bolton, died a° 1665. = Anne, daugh. of George Meryton, Deane of Yorke. | 1. Elizabeth, wife of Trinian alias Ninian Anderson of Gales in com. Ebor. | 2. Jane, wife of John Palleser of Kirby Wiske in com. Ebor. | 3. Grace, wife of Thomas Meryton of Castle Levinton in com. Eborum.

1. Francis Wright, obijt sine prole. | 2. George Wright of Bolton in co. Ebor. æt. 36 an. 25° Aug. a° 1665. = Beatrice, da. of James Maleverer of Arncliffe in co. Ebor. Esqr. | 3. Thomas. 4. Richard. 5. Christoph^r. 6. Will'm. | 1. Anne, wife of Thomas Hewardin of Maltby in co. Ebor. | 2. Grace, wife of John Blakeston of Old-Malton in co. Ebor.

3. Richard, æt. 1 ann. | 2. George, æt. 3 ann. | 1. Francis, æt. 7 ann. 25 Aug. 1665. | 1. Anne, æt. 9 ann. | 2. Beatrice, æt. 6 an. 1665.

LANGBARGH WAPENTAKE. *Stokesley*, 25° *Aug.* 1665.

TROTTER OF SKELTON CASTLE.

ARMS.—Argent, a chief ermine, over all a lion rampant azure.
CREST.—A lion's head erased argent, collared ermine.

Sr Henry Trotter of Skelton Castle in com. Ebor. Kt, obijt circa annu. 1625. = Catherine, da. of Anthony Wytham of Cliffe in com. Ebor.

...... daugh. of Sr Richard Cholmeley of Whitby in co. Ebor. Knt. 1 wife. = George Trotter of Skelton Castle, Esqr, died 5° Apr. 1647. = Mary, daughter of Sr Edw. Boyse of Fredvill in com. Cantij, Knt. 2 wife.

Robert, died young.

Dorothy, died unmarried.

Elizabeth, wife of George Nevill of.... in com. Hertf.

Henry, died unmarried.

Edward Trotter of Skelton Castle in com. Ebor. Esqr, æt. 27 ann. 25 Aug. a° 1665. = Mary, daugh. of Sr John Lowther of Lowther in com. Westmerl. Kt and Bart.

Hugh.

George.

Mary, wife of John Fullthorpe of Tunstall in com. Palat. Dunelm. arm.

John, æt. 5 an. 25° Aug. a° 1665.

1. Mary.

2. Catherine.

3. Elizabeth.

4. Margaret.

HALLIKELD WAPENTAKE. *Richmund*, 19° *Aug.* 1665.

WANDESFORD OF KIRKLINGTON.

ARMS.—Quarterly of six:
1. Or, a lion rampant double-queued azure.
2. Argent, a bend within a bordure engrailed gules.
3. Or, a fess gules, in chief three torteaux.
4. Azure, a maunche or.
5. Argent, a cross moline invertant sable.
6. Argent, on a bend sable three pheons or.

CREST.—A church proper, the spire azure.

Sr Christopher Wandesford of Kirklington in com. Ebor. Kt, living ao 1585. = Elizabeth, daughter to Sr George Bowes of Stretlam in com. Palat. Dunelm. Kt.

- 5. Francis, borne 31 Jan. 1581. = ⊥
- 3. Thomas, 4. John, ob. s. prole.
- 2. William Wandsford, married Margt, daughter of Robert Pamplyn, Citizen of London.
- Cath. da. & coh. of Raphe Hansby of Tickill and Beverley in co. Ebor. 1 wife. = 1. Sr George Wandesford of Kirklington, Kt, died circa ann. 1610. = Mary, da. of Robert Pamplin, an officer in ye great Wardrobe to Qu. Eliz. 2 wife.
- 1. Anna, died unmarried. 2. Ursula, wife of .... Savile. 3. Jane.
- 4. Anne, borne 4 July, 1583, wife of John Lancaster of Headlam in ye Bishoprick of Durham.

Children of Sr George and Cath. Hansby:

- Anne, wife of Mauger Norton of Cloberke in com. Ebor. Esqr.
- 3. MichaellWandesford, Deane of London-Derry in Ireland, died wthout issue.
- 2. John Wandsford, obijt sine prole.
- 1. Christopher Wandsford of Kirklington, Esqr. Master of ye Rolls in Ireland, Deputy of Ireland to Tho. Earle of Strafford, Ld Lieutenant of Ireld, died ao 1640. = Alice, da. of .... Osburne of Kiveton in co. Ebor.

Children of Sr George and Mary Pamplin:

- William Wandsford, married Rebecca, daughter of .... Reade.
- Margaret, wife unto James Blanchard.

Children of Christopher and Alice:

- 1. George Wandsford, died unmarried.
- Sr Christopher Wandesford of Kirklington in co. Ebor. Bart. æt. 39 ann. vel circa, 19 Aug. ao 1665. = Eleanor, daughter to Sr John Lowther of Lowther in co. Westmerland, Kt and Bart.
- 1. Catherine, ye wife of Sr Tho. Danby of Farneley in co. Ebor. Kt.
- 2. Alice, wife of WilliamThorneton of Newton in co. Ebor. Esqr.

Children of Sr Christopher and Eleanor:

- 2. George.
- 1. Christopher, æt. 9 ann. 19 Aug. 1665.
- 1. Marie.
- 2. Eleanor.
- 3. Anne.

HANG-EAST WAPENTAKE. *Richmund*, 19° *Aug.* 1665.

DAVILE OF KIRKBY-FLEETHAM.

ARMS.—Or, on a fess between four fleurs-de-lis gules two fleurs-de-lis of the field.
CREST.—A cubit arm erect, the hand holding a fleur-de-lis, all or.

- Richard Davile, borne at Cuckwould in com. Ebor., being a younger sonne of that family, became a Merchant in Newcastle upon Tine. = ... daughter of .... Horsley of .... in com. Northumbr.
  - Henry Davile of Kirby-Fletham in com. Ebor. died in a° 1646 vel circa. = Elizabeth, daughter of ...... Langley of Fletham in com. Ebor.
    - 2. Richard Davile of Fletham.
    - 1. Thomas Davile of Kirkby Fletham in co. Ebor. gen^t, died in a° 1648. = Elizabeth, daugh. of Thomas Perkinson of Burneston in co. Ebor.
      - Christopher Davile of Kirkby-Fletham, married Dorothy, da. of Henry Tenant of Scotton in co. Ebor.
      - Thomas Davile of Kirkby - Fletham, ætat. 40 an. 19° Aug. 1665. = Anne, daughter of Edward Caley of Brumpton in Pickering Lithe in co. Ebor.
        - 3. Henry.
        - 2. William.
        - 1. Thomas, æt. 17 an. 19 Aug. a° 1665.
        - 1. Elizabeth.
        - 2. Hesther.
    - Grace, wife of Sayth Agard of Stockton neere Yorke.

Richmund, 21 *Aug*. 1665.

NORTON OF ST. NICHOLAS JUXTA RICHMUND.

ARMS.—Quarterly of eight:

1. Azure, a maunche ermine, over all a bend or, a canton gules, a mullet argent for difference.
2. Argent, a chevron between three cushions sable.
3. Argent, a bend engrailed between six martlets sable.
4. .... two bars .... in chief three mullets ....
5. Gules, a chevron between three stag's heads cabossed or.
6. Argent, on a bend engrailed sable an escallop of the field.
7. Sable, a saltire argent.
8. Argent, a fess between three escallops sable.

CRESTS.—1. A stag's head cabossed .....
2. A moor's head couped at the shoulders proper, round the temples a laurel-wreath knotted behind vert, round the neck a torse argent and azure.

Richard Norton of Norton in com. Ebor. Esq[r], attainted in the time of Qu. Eliz. = Susan, daughter of Richard L[d] Latimer.

Edmund Norton of Clowbecke in com. Ebor died in a[o] 1610, vel circa. = Cecelie, daughter of Mathew Boynton of Barmston in Holdernes in com. Ebor. Esq[r], a Mayde of Honour to Qu. Eliz.

2. John, died without issue.

1. Francis Norton. = Albreda, sister of Thomas Wimbish of ...... in com. Lincoln.

4. Robert Norton of Swynton in com. Ebor. died circa annum 1629. = Catherine, daughter and heire of John Staveley of Swynton, Esq[r].

3. William Norton of Sawley, in com. Ebor. died a[o] 1644. = Margaret, sole daughter and heire of Will. Welburye of Newton in Cleveland.

1. Richard, 2. Francis, died unmarried.

Francis Norton, a naturall son. = Joane, daughter and heire of Thomas Exilby of Exilby in co. Ebor.

Elizabeth, wife of Richard Smurthwayt of Nutwith-Cote in com. Ebor.

1. Maulger Norton of St Nicholas juxta Richmund in com. Ebor. Esqr, æt. 72 ann. 19[o] Aug. 1665. = Anne, da. of Sr George Wandesford of Kirklington in com. Eborum, K[t].

2. Richard Norton. = Marg[t], da. and heire of Franc. Hall of Worsall in co. Ebor.

3. Will'm, died unmarried.

Peter Norton of Disford in com. Ebor. æt. 67 an. 19[o] Aug. 1665. = Mary, daughter and sole heire of .... Dickenson of Disford in co. Ebor.

2. William Norton, an Utter Barrister of Grayes Inne, æt. 38 an. 19 Aug. a[o] 1665.
3. Christopher, æt. 14 ann. a[o] 1665.

1. Edmund Norton, obijt sine prole. = Jane, daughter and sole heire of Toby Dudley of Chopwell in the Bishoprick of Durham.

Mary, wife of Sr John Yorke of Gothwayt in com. Ebor. Kn[t].

1. John Norton, æt. 35 ann. 19[o] Aug. 1665.
2. Michaell, citizen of Lond.

George Norton of Disford, now Captaine of Foote under Colonell Conyers Darcy, in the Trayned Bands of Yorkshire. = Margaret, daughter and heire of Anthony Pullen of Worton in co. Eborum.

MEYNILL OF WEST-DALTON AND ALDBROUGH.

ARMS.—Quarterly:
1. Azure, three bars-gemelles and a chief or, a canton gules.
2. Argent, on a fess engrailed sable three quatrefoils or.
3. Checky argent and sable, a bordure of the first
4. Argent, a bend between six martlets sable, a crescent for difference.

CREST.—A negro's head in profile couped at the shoulders proper, round the temples a wreath knotted behind argent and azure.

Roger Meynill of Kilvington, living a° 1585. = Margery, daughter and coheire of Anthony Caterick of Stanwick in com. Ebor.

2. George Meynill of Dalton-Royall alias West-Dalton in co. Ebor. = Elizabeth, daughter of Robert Trotter of Skelton Castle in co. Eborum.

1. Thomas Meynill of North Kilvington. = ...

Children of George Meynill and Elizabeth:

4. Anthony Meynill, capt of a troope of horse in the service of King Charles the First, slayne at Marston Moore a° 1644.

5. George Meynill of Aldbrough in com. Ebor. æt. 35 ann. 21 Aug. a° 1665. = Olivia, daugh. of Sr Marmaduke Wivill of Constable Burton in co. Ebor. Kt and Bt.

2. Roger Meynill of West-Dalton, æt. 60 ann. 21 Aug. a° 1665. = Mary, eldest daugh. of Sr Raphe Conyers of Layton in co. Palat. Dunelm. Kt.

1. John, 3. Thomas, died unmarried.

1. Elizabeth, wife unto Henry Messenger of Newsome in com. Eborum.
2. Dorothy, wife of Richard Harburn of Stillington in com. Dunelm.

3. Winifride, wife unto Christopher Tod of Stillington in co. Palat. Dunelm.
4. Margaret, wife unto John Mayre of Hardwick in com. Palat. Dunelm.
5. Agnes, died unmarried.

Children of George Meynill and Olivia:

George, æt. 6 an. 21 Aug. a° 1665. 1. Elizabeth. 2. Mary. 3. Olivia.

GILLING WEST WAPENTAKE. *Richmund*, 21 *Aug*. 1665.

LAYTON OF WHITEHOUSE.

ARMS.—Argent, a fess between six crosses botonnée fitchée sable.

William Layton of West-Layton in co. Ebor. Esqr, living a° 1585. = Elizabeth, daughter of Will'm Claxton of Winiard in co. Dunelm.

Thomas Layton of West-Layton, died a° 1624, vel circa. = Margaret, daughter of Richard Willands of Clints in com. Eborum.

3. Richard, died unmarried.

2. Robert Layton of West-Layton, died in Jan. 1655. = Jane, daughter of Robt Wyvill of High-Burton in com. Ebor.

1. Thomas, died unmarried.

Alice, wife of Will'm Tenant of Hubberam in co. Ebor.

......, wife of Robt Bowes of Appleton in co. Ebor.

Eliz. wife of Anth. Warde of Northcote in co. Ebor.

Dorothy, wife of Luke Wastell of Lasenby in com. Ebor.

1. Thomas Layton of White-house in com. Ebor. æt. 44 ann. 21 Aug. 1665.

2. Robert, æt. 40 ann.

3. Marmaduke.

HANGWEST WAPENTAKE. *Richmund*, 21 *Aug*. 1665.

SMELT OF KIRBY-FLEETHAM.

ARMS.—........ a chevron .... between three smelts naiant.

CREST.—A cormorant's head erased, per fess .... and ....

Richard Smelt of Fleetham in com. Ebor. = Anne, daughter of .... Conyers of Hutton Bonvile in com. Ebor.

Leonard Smelt, died circa ann. 1627. = Sythe, daughter of Edmund Allan of Gaterley in com. Ebor.

4. Thomas. = ⊥

3. Richard.

2. Leonard, died unmarried.

1. Mathew Smelt of Kirby Fleetham in com. Ebor. died a° 1652. = Alice, daughter of John Dodsworth of Thornton Watlas in com. Ebor.

1. Sythe, wife of John Robinson of Applegarth in com. Ebor.

2. Frances, wife of Tho. Robinson of Rokesby in co. Ebor.

7. Christopher Smelt of Brunton in com. Ebor. = .. ⊥

2. John.

3. Mathew, died unmarried.

4. Richard, died an infant.

5. Robert, died an infant.

6. Thomas. died an infant.

1. Leonard Smelt of Kirby Fleetham, æt. 40 ann. 21 Aug. a° 1665. = Anne, daughter of John Wastell of Scorton in com. Eborum.

2. John.

1. Leonard, æt. 7 ann. 21 Aug. a° 1665.

METCALFE OF NAPPA.

ARMS.—Quarterly of six:
1. Argent, three calves passant sable.
2. Argent, a lion rampant gules.
3. Sable, three pickaxes argent.
4. Argent, a chevron gules between three eagles displayed sable.
5. Argent, on a fess cottised gules three fleurs-de-lis of the field.
6. As the first.

James Metcalfe of Nappa in com. Ebor. Esq[r]. was a Cap[t] in the Battell of Agincourt, temp. H. 5. = ... daughter of .... Gibson of Ireby Hall.

3. Miles Metcalfe, Recorder of Yorke. 2. Brian Metcalfe of Beare Parke in co. Ebor. 1. Thomas Metcalfe, Chancellour of y[e] Dutchy of Lancaster, temp. R. 3. = Elizabeth, daughter and coheire of ...... Hartington.

2. Francis Metcalfe, marr. Joane, daugh. and coheire of Everard Seyton of Maidwell in co. North[ton]. 1. S[r] James Metcalfe of Nappa, K[nt]. = Margaret, daughter & coheire of Thomas Pigot of Clotherham in com. Ebor. 22 H. 7.

5. Robert. 4. Oswald. 3. Edmund. 2. Humphry. 1. S[r] Christopher Metcalfe of Nappa, K[nt]. = Elizabeth, daughter of Henry Earle of Cumberland.

2. John, 3. Ingram, 4. Charles, } died w[th]out issue. 1. James Metcalfe of Nappa, Esq[r]. died a° 22° Eliz. = Joane, daughter of John Savile of Stanley, in co. Ebor. Esq[r]. Margaret, wife of George Middleton of Leighton in com. Lanc. Esq[r].

S[r] Thomas Metcalfe, K[t], died in July, a° 1655. = Elizabeth, daughter of S[r] Henry Slingsby of Screvin in co. Ebor. K[t].

4. Henry. Frances, da. of Francis Burdet of Burthwayt in co. Ebor. 1st wife. = 3. Thomas Metcalfe. = Grace, da. of Robert Rokeley of Rokeley in co. Ebor. 2[d] wife. 2. Scroope Metcalfe, a Major in y[e] Army of King Charles y[e] 1st, died at Oxford, a° ...... of his wounds received at Henley upon Thames. 1. James Metcalfe of Nappa, Esq[r], now Recorder of y[e] Borough of Richmond, æt. 61 ann. 21 Aug. a° 1665. = Marg[t]. daugh. of William Hicks, Citizen of London. 1. Eliz. died young. 2. Mary, died unmarried. 3. Frances, y[e] wife of Sr Will. Robinson of Newby in com. Ebor. K[nt]. 4. Kath. died young. 5. Joane.

Elizabeth, sole daughter and heire apparent, æt. 18 ann. 21 Aug. a° 1665.

THE BURROUGH OF RICHMUND. *Richmund*, 21 *Aug*. 1665.

CRADOCK OF RICHMUND.

ARMS.—Argent, on a chevron azure three garbs or: an escutcheon of pretence, argent, a saltire sable between four swords erect azure, hilted and pomelled or.
CREST.—A bear's head couped sable, muzzled gules.

John Craddock of Newhouse in Baldersdale, in com. Ebor. of the family of the Cradocks in Staffordshire, died 40 Eliz. or thereabouts. = Anne, daughter of Anthony Latus of Becke in com. Cumbr.

Their children:

- 1. William Cradock of Newhouse. = ... daughter and sole heire of .... Dickenson of Salthouse in com. Cumbriæ, 1 wife.
  - Their children:
    - 1. John Cradock of Bishop Aukeland.
    - 2. William Cradock.
- 2. Anthony Cradock of Woodhouses in co. Palat. Dunelm. = Anne, daughter of ..... Williamson of St Ellen Aukland in com. Dunelm. 2 wife.
- 3. John Cradock, Dr in Divinity and Chancelor of Durham, died in a° 1627. = Margaret, daughter of William Bateman of .... in Wensdale in com. Ebor. widow of .... Robinson.
  - Their children:
    - 4. Tobye Cradock, an Utter Barrister of Grayes Inne. = ... daughter of ..... Bourne, citizen of London.
      - Their child: Richard.
    - 2. Francis, died unmarried.
    - 3. John Cradock, died without issue.
    - 1. Richard Cradock of Durham, Counceller at law. = Dorothy, eldest daughter to Thomas Heath of Kepier in co. Dunelm, Esqr.
      - Their children:
        - Anne, wife unto John Harrison of Scarborough.
        - 1. Elizabeth, wife of Raphe Hutton, of Mainsforth in com. Dunelm.
        - 2. Margaret, wife of Raphe Bowes of Bradley Hall in co. Dunelm.
        - 3. Anne.
    - 5. Sr Joseph Cradock Kt, Dr of Laws, and commissary of Richmund, æt. 60 an. 21° Aug. a° 1656.
      - First wife: Elizabeth, daughter of Robert Cruse, citizen of London, 1st wife.
        - Their children:
          - Joseph, died unmarried.
          - 1. Thomas Cradock, æt. 32 an. 21 Aug. 1665, now Attorney Generall to the Bpp of Durham. = Sibilla, daughter of Gabraell Clarke, Dr of Divinity and Archdeacon of Durham.
      - Second wife: Jane, daughter and heire of Anthony Maxton, Prebend. of Durham, 2d wife.
        - Their children:
          - 1. Jane.
          - 2. Peregrina.
          - 3. Maxton.

BIRDFORTH WAPENTAKE. *Threske*, 23° *Aug.* 1665.

LOCKWOOD OF SOWERBY.

ARMS.—........ a chevron .... between three cinquefoils ....
No proofe made of these armes.

Clare, daughter to Anthony Byerley of Pickhall in com. Ebor. first wife. = Richard Lockwood of Sowerby in com. Ebor. died a° 1645, or thereabouts. = Dorothy, daughter of Anthony Atkinson of Wensley in com. Ebor. second wife.

Issue by Clare:
2. Elizabeth, wife of Raphe Atkinson of Wensley in com. Ebor.
1. Clare, wife of .... Best of ...... in com. Ebor.

Issue by Dorothy:
2. John Lockwood.
1. Mathew Lockwood of Sowerby, æt. 35 ann. 23° Aug. a° 1665. = Barbara, daugh. and coheire of Thomas Beckwith of Aketon in com. Ebor. Esqr.
Dorothy, wife of John Hamerton of Purston in co. Ebor.

Issue of Mathew and Barbara:
2. Thomas, æt. 11 an. 1665.
1. Richard, æt. 12 an. 23° Aug. 1665.
Barbara, æt. 9 an. 1665.

LANGBARGH WAPENTAKE. *Stokesley*, 25° *Aug.* 1665.

MERYTON OF CASTLE LEVENTON.

ARMS.—Sable, on a chevron or three roses gules, a canton ermine.
No proofe made of these armes.

George Meryton, D[r] in Divinity, Chaplain to Qu. Anne (wife to K. James), Deane of Peterborough, and after of Yorke, died in a° 1624. = Mary, daughter of ...... Rande of ...... in com. Lincoln, son to ...... Rande, Bisshop of Lincolne.

Issue:
4. John Meryton of Moulton in com. Ebor. = (issue)
3. Robert, obijt sine prole.
2. Thomas Meryton of Castle Leventon in co. Ebor. died in a° 1652. = Grace, daugh. of Francis Wright of Bolton upon Swale in com. Ebor.
1. George Meryton, died without issue.
1. Mary, wife of Thomas Moyser of Nun-Appleton in com. Ebor.
2. Anne, wife unto Franc. Wright, son of Franc. Wright of Bolton upon Swale in co. Ebor.

Issue of Thomas and Grace:
4. Richard.
5. John.
2. Thomas.
3. Paul Meryton, marr. Meriam, daugh. of .... Lyster of .....
1. George Meryton of Castle Leventon, æt. 30 an. et 11 mensium 25 Aug. 1665. = Mary, daughter of John Palleser of Kirkby super Wiske in co. Ebor.
1. Grace, wife of Francis Palleser of Dublyn in Ireland.
2. Anne, wife of Thomas Palleser of the citty of Westminst[r], grocer.

Issue of George and Mary:
3. John.
2. George.
1. Thomas, æt. 8 annorum et 10 mens. 25 Aug. 1665.

THE BOROUGH OF RICHMUND. *Richmund*, 21 *Aug.* 1665.

DARCY OF RICHMUND.

ARMS.—Quarterly, a fleur-de-lis for difference:
1. Azure, three cinquefoils between nine cross-crosslets argent.
2. Azure, three bars-gemelles and a chief or.
3. Azure, a maunche or.
4. Sable, a saltire argent.

CREST.—On a chapeau gules, turned up ermine, a bull passant sable.

Conyers Ld Darcy and Conyers, died ao .... = Dorothy daughter of Sr Henry Bellasses of Newborough in com. Ebor. Bart.

6. James Darcy of Richmond in com. Ebor. Esqr, æt. 44 ann. 21 Aug. 1665. = Isabell, da. of Sr Marmaduke Wyvill of Constable Burton in com. Ebor. Kt and Bart.

5. Marmaduke Darcy, Gentleman Ussher to K. Charles the Second.

3. Henry Darcy of New Parke, neere Yorke.

4. Thomas Darcy of Winkeburne in com. Nott.

1. Conyers Ld Darcy and Conyers, now living, ao 1665. =

2. Sr Will'm Darcy, Kt. =

Children of James Darcy and Isabell:

1. Isabell.
2. Jane.
3. Elizabeth.

1. James, æt. 15 ann. 21 Aug. 1665.

2. Marmaduke, æt. 14 ann. ao 1665.

3. Christopher, æt. 12 ann. ao 1665.

GILLING WEST WAPENTAKE. *Richmund*, 21 *Aug.* 1665.

WYTHAM OF CLIFFE.

ARMS.—Quarterly :
1 and 4. Or, three eaglets sable, over all a bendlet gules.
2. Gules, a chief argent.
3. Argent, on a fess gules between three popinjays vert, as many escallops of the field.

CREST.—Out of a ducal coronet or, a demi-virgin with hair flowing proper, the dexter hand holding a gemmed ring of the first.

John Wytham of Cliffe in com. Ebor. Esqr, died ao 1656. = Dorothy, daughter and coheir of Will'm Wycliffe of Wicliffe, in com. Ebor. Esqr.

- 2. Anthony Wytham of Preston in co. Dunelm.
- 3. Roger Wytham, a Benedictine Monke at Doway.
- 1. William Wytham, son and heire, died in his father's lifetime. = Anne, daughter of George Collingwood of Eslington in co. Northumb. Esqr.
- 1. Margaret, wife of Cutbert Conyers, son and heire to Sr Raphe Conyers of Layton in Episc. Dunelm. Knt.
- 2. Catherine, died unmarried.

Children of William Wytham and Anne:

- 3. Will'm Wytham.
- 4. Thomas Wytham, marr. Cath. da. of Will'm Midleton of Stockheld in com. Ebor. Esqr.
- 5. Laurence, died unmarried.
- 2. George Wytham of Cliffe in com. Ebor. Esqr, æt. 36 an. 21 Aug. ao 1665. = Grace, da. of Sr Marmaduke Wyvill of Burton Constable in com. Ebor. Knt and Bart.
- 1. John Wytham, slayne at Preston fight in Lancashire ao 1648, being then Lieutenant Colonell to Colonell Raphe Pudsey, under the co'mand of Sr Marmaduke Langdale, for ye service of K. Charles the First.
- 1. Mary.
- 2. Dorothy, wife of Hillary Gray of Bitchburne in co. Northumbr. son of Edw. Gray, Esqr.
- 3. Jane.

Children of George Wytham and Grace:

- 1. John, æt. 13 ann. 21 Aug. 1665.
- 2. William, æt. 11 an.
- 3. George, æt. 10 ann.
- 4. Marmaduke, ætatis 8 ann.
- 5. Laurence, æt. 6 an.
- 6. Christopher, æt. 5 ann.
- Dorothy.

BIRDFORTH WAPENTAKE. *Threske*, 23 *Aug*. *a*° 1665.

THOMLINSON OF BYRDFORTH.

To expect a certificate from Sr Richard Maliverer Knt that this gent. is of his family.

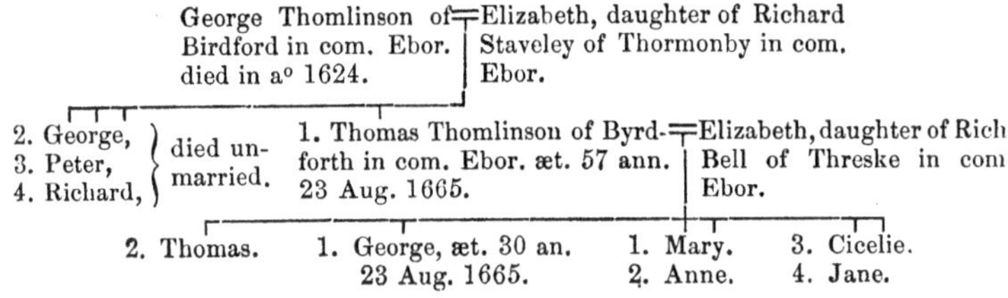

BAYNTON BEACON. *Kilham*, 31° *Aug*. 1665.

STAPLETON OF WARTRE.

ARMS.—Quarterly of nine:

1. Argent, a lion rampant sable, a crescent gules for difference.
2. Sable, fretty or.
3. Or, a saltire and a chief gules.
4. Checky or and azure within a bordure gules, a canton ermine.
5. Ermine, a crescent or.
6. Barry of eight, or and gules.
7. Bendy of six, argent and azure.
8. Argent, on a fess azure three fleurs-de-lis or.
9. Argent, a bend between six martlets gules.

CREST.—Out of a ducal coronet or, a Saracen's head affrontée, round the temples a wreath knotted behind, all proper.

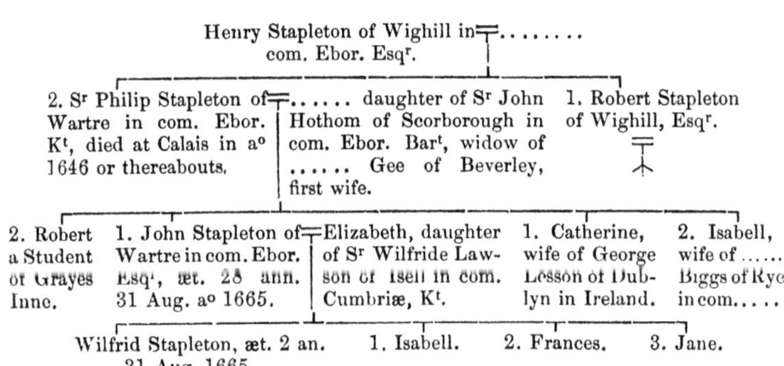

DICKERING WAPENTAKE. *Kilham*, 31° *Aug.* 1665.

LEGARD OF GANTON.

ARMS.—Quarterly of six:
1. Argent, on a bend between six mullets gules a cross pattée or.
2. Argent, on a bend gules three crescents of the field.
3. Gules, a bend or.
4. Argent, three water-bougets sable.
5. Argent, on a bend cottised sable three annulets of the field.
6. Or, a fess gules between three popinjays vert, collared of the second.

CREST.—A greyhound passant .... collared and ringed ....

John Legard of Ganton in com. Ebor. died in a° 1643. = Elizabeth, daughter of Sr William Mallory of Studley in com. Ebor., Kn^t.

2. Richard Legard, an Utter Barrister of y^e Middle Temple.
3. Will'm, obijt sine prole.
4. Christopher, died unmarried.
5. Henry, died unmarried.

1. John Legard of Ganton, died in his father's lifetime. = Mary, da. and sole heire of John Dawney of Potter Brunton in co. Ebor. Esqr.

1. Ursula, wife of Gregory Crake of Marton in com. Ebor.
2. Frances, wife of Sr John Hotham of Scorborough in co. Ebor. Bar^t.
3. Jane, died unmarried.

Grace, daughter to Conyers Ld Darcy and Conyers, of Hornby Castle, first wife. = Sr John Legard of Ganton, Bar^t, æt. 34 ann. 31 Aug. a° 1665. = Frances, daughter and co-heire of Sr Thomas Widdrington of Chisburne Grange in com. Northumbr. K^t, 2d wife.

1. Elizabeth.
2. Mary, wife of William Bernard of West-Heslarton in com. Ebor.

Issue by first wife:

1. Grace, æt. 8. ann. 31 Aug. 1665.
2. Dorothy, æt. 4 an. 1665.

Issue by second wife:

1. John, æt. 6 an. 31 Aug. 1665.
2. Thomas, æt. 5. an. 1665.
3. Will'm, æt. 1 anni et 6 mens.
4, Widdrington, æt. 3 mens. a° 1665, Aug. 31.

DICKERING WAPENTAKE. *Malton*, 29 *Aug.* 1665.

STRICKLAND OF BOYNTON.

ARMS.—Gules, a chevron between three crosses pattée or, on a canton ermine a buck's head erased sable.

CREST.—A Turkey-cock argent beaked sable crested gules.

Walter Strickland of Boynton in com. Ebor. Esqr. = Frances, daughter of Peter Wentworth of Lillingston in com. Oxon. Esqr.

Lady Frances Finche, eldest daughter to Thomas Earle of Winchelsey, of Eastwell in Kent, second wife. = Sr Will'm Strickland of Boynton in com. Ebor. K^t and Bar^t, æt. 69 an. 29° Aug. 1665. = Margaret, eldest daughter of Sr Rich. Cholmeley of Whitby in com. Ebor. Kn^t, first wife.

Thomas Strickland, ætatis 26 annorum 29 Aug. a° 1665. = Elizabeth, daughter and coheire of Sr Francis Pile of Compton Beauchamp in com. Berks, Bar^t.

1. Frances, wife of Barington Bourchier of Beningbrough in com. Ebor. Esqr.
2. Marg^t, wife of Sr John Cockeran of Ocletre in Scotl^d, 2^d son to Will'm Lord Cockeran of Passcle in Scotland.
3. Milcha, wife of Will'm Lawson, son & heire of Sr Wilfrid Lawson of Isell in co. Cumbr. Kn^t.
4. Eliz. wife of Will'm St Quintin Esqr, son & he. of Sr Henry St Quintin of Harpham in co. Ebor. Bar^t.

William, æt. 5 mens. 29° Aug. a° 1665. | 1. Frances, æt. 4 ann. 29° Aug. 1665. | 2. Jane, æt. 2. ann.

Malton, 29 *Aug. a*° 1665.

SKELTON OF MIDDLETON.

ARMS.—Azure, a fess between three fleurs-de-lis or, a canton argent.

Anthony Skelton, a younger son to Skelton of Armethwayt in Cumberland, setled at Sinington in com. Ebor. = ...

Children:

- 2. Anthony, died unmarried.
- 1. Thomas Skelton of Sinington in com. Ebor. died in May a° 1644. = Anne, daughter of ...... De-la-Poole of Pickering in co. Ebor.

Children of Thomas and Anne:

- 3. William Skelton of Sinington, married Marg[t], daugh. of Raphe Bromfield of Wilton in com. Ebor.
- 2. Thomas Skelton of Middleton in Pickering Lythe in com. Ebor. æt. 44 ann. 29 Aug. a° 1665. = Alice, da. of Will'm Newton of Chesterfield in com. Derbiæ.
  - 1. Anne.
  - 2. Alice.
  - 3. Mary.
  - Samuell, æt. 4 an. 29 Aug. 1665.
- 1. Robert Skelton of Sinington in com. Ebor. ætatis 59 annorum 29° Aug. 1665. = Anne, da. of Raphe Bromfeild of Wilton in co. Ebor.
  - Robert Skelton, æt. 27 ann. 29 Aug. a° 1665. = Mary, daughter of Will'm Smithson of Thornton in com. Ebor.
  - 2. Raphe.
  - 3. Thomas.
  - 4. George.
  - 5. Will'm.
  - 6. Samuell.
- 1. Mary, y[e] wife of Thomas Pearson of Hartoft in co. Ebor.
- 2. Christian, wife of George Hall of Sinington in com. Ebor. afterwards of James Grundon of Sinington afores[d].

PICKRINGE LYTHE WAPENTAKE. *Malton*, 29 *Aug.* *a*° 1665.

PERCEHAY OF RYTON.

ARMS.—Quarterly:
1. Argent, a cross fleury gules.
2. Azure, fretty argent.
3. Argent, a lion rampant azure, over all a bendlet or.
4. Argent, an inescutcheon sable within an orle of cinquefoils pierced gules.

CREST.—A bull's head couped azure, horns per fess or and azure.

Leonard Percehay of Ryton in Ryedale in co. Ebor. Esqr. = Prudence, daughter of Thomas Spenser of Old Malton in co. Ebor.

2. Robert, died w^th^-out issue.
3. Will'm.

4. Henry Percehay, citizen of London.
5. Leonard, of y^e^ guard to Henry the 4th, K. of France.

Anne, daughter of William Wivill of Osgodby in com. Ebor. first wife. = 1. Thomas Percehay of Ryton in com. Ebor. Esqr, died in a°. 1625. = Mary, daugh. of Sr Marmaduke Wyvell of Burton-Constable in co. Ebor. K^t^ and B^t^, 2d wife.

Anne, wife of Henry Johnson of Blackhurst in Sussex.

1. Anne, wife unto John Foyle of Tisburye in com. Wilts.
2. Elizabeth, wife unto Tho. Shirley, citizen of London.

William, eldest son, died in his father's lifetime unmarr.

1. Mary, wife of Christopher Philipson of Callgarth in com. Westmerl^d^, Esqr.
2. Magdalen, wife of Bethell Hunter of Thorneton in com. Ebor. Esqr.
3. Margerie, wife unto .... Edmonds of .... in Sussex.

Christopher Percehay of Ryton, Esqr, æt. 61 ann. 29 Aug. a° 1665. = Frances, daughter of Walter Strickland of Boynton in com. Ebor. Esqr.

2. Christopher Percehay, married Susan, daughter of Robert Gere of Barugh in com. Eborum.

1. Walter Percehay, died in his father's lifetime. = Barbara, daugh. of Basill Staveley of Rippon in com. Ebor. by Isabell his wife, da. and co-heire of .... Grant of Pickill in com. Ebor.

1. Frances, wife unto John Hames of Frome in com. Dorset.
2. Milcah, wife of Arthur Jegon, an Utter Barrister of Lincolnes Inne.

3. Ursula, wife of Will. Dove of Appleton in le Streete in com. Eborum.
4. Eliz. wife of Henry Simpson of Smeton in com. Ebor.

Christopher, æt. 11 ann. 29 Aug. a° 1665.

Frances.

CARLEIL OF SEWARBY.

ARMS.—........ on a chevron .... between three Cornish choughs .... as many mullets of six points ....

Qu.? the Colours and proofs of this Coate which he afferms to have beene allowed of in the E. Marshall's Court heretofore upon a sute heretofore commenced by one of this family.

John Carleil of Sewarby in com. Ebor.=......

Tristram Carleil of Sewarby.=Catherine, daughter of .... Rode of Rode in com. Cestr.

3. John, died unmarried.

2. Robert Carleil, a merchant in Hull, æt. 74 ann. 31 Aug. a° 1665.=Eliz. da. of Gilb[t] Crowther of Eland neer Halifax in co. Ebor.

1. Randle Carleil of Sewarby in co. Ebor. died in a° 1658 or thereabouts.=Elizabeth, da of Richard Knowseley of North-Burton in co. Ebor.

1. Anne, wife of .... Burges, a Merchant in Hull.
2. Catherine, wife unto Rich. Milner of Sutton in Holdernesse.

3. Jane, first marr. to ..... Grymston of Grimston-garth in com. Ebor.; after to Walter Hawkesworth of God-mundham in com. Ebor.

Robert, æt. 28 an. 31 Aug. a° 1665. (son of Robert Carleil of Hull)

2. John Carleil, marr. Jane, da. of ...... Hardy of Hilston in Holdernesse.
3. Thomas.

1. Robert Carleil of Sewarby, æt. 42 an. 31 Aug. 1665.=Anne, da. & coh. of Henry Vickerman of Fraystrope in com. Ebor.

1. Mary, wife of James Fisher of Sheffeild in com. Ebor.

2. Elizabeth, wife of Theodore Herring of Yorke; afterwards of Henry Beale of Knottingley in com. Ebor.

3. Hannah, wife of Timothy Preston of Bridlington in com. Ebor.

4. Dorothy, wife of Rob. Carleil of Hull.
5. Amie.
6. Susanna.

1. Elizabeth, æt. 7. an. 31 Aug. a° 1665. 2. Christian, æt. 3 ann. 1665. 3. Alathea, æt. unius anni.

PICKERING LITHE WAPENTAKE. *Malton*, 29° *Aug*. *a*° 1665.

SMITH OF SNEINTON.

ARMS.—Argent, on a bend azure between two unicorn's heads erased of the second maned or, three lozenges erminois, in chief a trefoil slipped gules.

......=......

1. Will'm Smith, Councellor at Law, resided in the Citty of Durham. =......

2. James Smith of Sneinton in Pickering Lythe in com. Ebor. died in a° 1643. = Helen, daughter of Francis Sare of Worsall in Cleveland.

2. James Smith of Cave in com. Ebor.
3. Raphe Smith of Cottingham in co. Ebor.
4. Francis Smith of Ruston in com. Ebor.

1. John Smith of Sneinton, ætatis 53 ann. 29° Aug. 1665. = Catherine, daugh. of Christophr Greene, citizen of London.

1. Anne.
2. Helen, wife of Will'm Hunter.
3. Susan, wife of John Sare of Rudby in co. Ebor.
4. Catherine, wife unto ....

Henry, æt. 11 an. 29 Aug. a° 1665.

1. Catherine, wife of Will. Fairfax of Furnivall's-Inne, in ye suburbs of London.

2. Helen.
3. Anne.

RYDALE WAPENTAKE. *Malton*, 30 *Aug*. 1665.

NARY OF MALTON.

ARMS.—Gules, on a fess argent three spear's heads of the field, in chief as many annulets or.

Enos Nary of Ardneverdneuagh in the province of Connaght and county of Roscomon in Ireland. = Margaret, daughter of Owen O'Ennis of Ballyburly, in the province of Leinster in Ireland.

Nicholas Nary of the Balleio of Will'm Roe in ye province of Leinster and county of Methe in Ireland. = Marion, daughter of .... Grant of ye Priory of Balliboggan in the county of Methe in Ireland.

Enos Nary of Armabreabagh in ye county of East Methe in Ireland, died in a° 1656 or thereabouts. = Dorothy, daughter and heire of Will. Vaughan of Ballecoune in ye King's County in Ireland.

2. Enos Nary of Ballennebrachy in the county of Methe in Ireland.

1. John Nary of Malton in co. Ebor. ætatis 47 ann. 30 Aug. a° 1665. = Anne, daughter of Thomas Hebletwayt of Norton juxta Malton in com. Ebor. Esqr.

DICKERING WAPENTAKE. *Kilham*, 1° *Sept.* 1665.

ROBINSON OF BUCKTON.

ARMS.—Vert, on a chevron between three bucks trippant or as many cinquefoils gules, a canton argent.

John Robinson, a Merchant in London, died a° ...., and lyeth interred in S[t] Helen's in Bishopsgate Streete. = ...

Henry Robynson, a Merch[t] in Lond. died in a° 1653. = Margaret, daughter of ...... Coulthurst, an alderman of the Citty of London, 1. wife.

John Robinson of Rither in com. Ebor. = ...

1. Henry Robinson, died without issue.

2. John Robinson of Buckton in co. Ebor. died in a° 1659 vel circa. = Margaret, daughter of John Woodhouse of Corneforth in y[e] Bishopprick of Durham.

2. Henry.
3. Humphry.
4. Arthur.

1. John Robinson of Buckton in com. Ebor. æt. 24 ann. 1 Sep. 1665. = Adeline, daughter of Richard Conyers of Filingdales in co. Ebor.

1. Margaret.
2. Dorothy.

WHITBY STRAND. *Kilham*, 1 *Sept.* 1665.

JACKSON OF WHITBY.

The entrance and proofe of the armes is respited.

Richard Jackson of Carhead in Whitby Strand in co. Ebor. died in a° 1648 or thereabouts. = ... daughter of Thomas Worfolke of Whitby Strand.

3. George Jackson of Pickering in co. Ebor.
. Richard Jackson of Maske in com. Ebor.
5. Peter Jackson of Whitby in com. Ebor.

2. William Jackson of Whitby, æt. 63 ann. 1 Sept. a° 1665. = Susanna, daugh. of Henry Russell of Whitby in com. Ebor.

1. John Jackson of Fosse in Whitby Strand.

1. Anne, wife of Nicholas Conyers of Pickering in com. Eborum.
2. Margaret, wife of .... Osburne of Whitby.

George Jackson of Whitby in com. Ebor. æt. 23 ann. 1° Sept. a° 1665. = Mercie, daughter of Thomas Broome of Howden in com. Ebor.

2. George. ætat. 5 mens.

1. William, æt. 2 an. et 10 mens. 1° Sept. a° 1665.

Mary, æt. 18 mens.

DICKERING WAPENTAKE. *Kilham*, 1° *Sept.* 1665.

HELLARD OF KILHAM.

ARMS.—Sable, a bend cottised between six fleurs-de-lis argent.

Thomas Hellard of Ruston parva in co. Ebor. = Elizabeth, daughter of Robert Bateson of Thorneholme in co. Ebor.

1. Elizabeth, wife of ...... Langton, a Merchant in Hull.
2. Frances, wife of Marmaduke Tenison of Long-Ruston in com. Ebor.

Thomas Hellard of Ruston parva, died a° 1665 vel circa. = Alice, daughter of John Cliffe of Burweston in com. Staff.

3. Dorothy, wife unto Henry Snell of Garton in com. Ebor.
4. Sarah, wife of John Ellerton of Boythorpe in com. Ebor.

1. Henry Hellard of Kilham in co. Ebor. æt. 63 ann. 1 Sept. a° 1665. = Mary, daughter of Thomas Wayte of Eland in com. Staff.

2. St Quintin Hellard of Ruston in co. Ebor. =

3. Thomas Hellard of Harpham in co. Ebor. =

4. Samuell Hellard of Langtoft in com. Ebor. =

5. John Hellard, died without issue.

NORTH BAYLIWICK OF HOLDERNESSE. *Hull*, 4° *Sept.* 1665.

FULTHORPE OF SIGLESTHORNE.

ARMS.—Argent, a cross moline sable, a crescent for difference.

CREST.—A horse passant argent, bridle azure, bit or.

Christopher Fullthorpe of Tunstall in com. Palat. Dunelm. Esqr. = Mary, daughter of Clement Colmer, Dr in Divinity.

Clement Fulthorpe of Tunstall in com. Palat. Dunelm. = Isabell, daughter of Sr John Calverley of Littleburne in com. Palat. Dunelm. Kt, 1 wife.

2. Christopher Fulthorp, Rector of Siglesthorne in Holdernesse, æt. 35 ann. 4 Sept. a° 1665.

1. John Fulthorpe of Tunstall in com. Palat. Dunelm. = ...

HOLME BEACON WAPENTAKE. *Pocklington*, 7 *Sept.* 1665.

CONSTABLE OF EVERINGHAM.

ARMS.—Quarterly of sixteen; on the fess point the badge of a baronet of England:

1. Quarterly gules and vair, a bend or. Constable.
2. Gules, a pale of lozenges or. Halton.
3. Or, a lion rampant purpure. Lacy.
4. Or, a chief azure. Lizures.
5. Checky, or and gules, on a chief argent a lion passant sable. Cumberworth.
6. Argent, two bars engrailed sable. Stanes.
7. Argent, a chevron between three martlets sable. Argum.
8. Gules, an eagle displayed argent. Suthill.
9. Gules, a cinquefoil argent. Poucher.
10. Argent, a bend sable. Paynell.
11. Or, on a mount a pear-tree vert. Pirton.
12. Or, on a cross sable five crescents argent. Ellis.
13. Gules, a lion rampant vair. Everingham.
14. Argent, a fess azure, in chief a label of five points gules. Birkin.
15. Sable, a chevron between three fleurs-de-lis argent. Cauz.
16. Argent, on a fess between two bars-gemelles gules three fleurs-de-lis or. Normanvill.

CREST.—A ship with three masts, sails furled, all or.

Marmaduke Constable of Everingham in com. Ebor. Esqr, died 3° Apr. a° D'ni 1632. = Frances, daughter of Thomas Metham of Metham in com. Ebor. Esqr.

1. Sir Philip Constable of Everingham, B^t, died 25° Febr. 1664. = Anne, onely daughter of Sr William Roper of Eltham in Kent, Kn^t.
2. Robert.
3. Michaell, 4. Marmaduke, 5. Thomas, } died unmarr.

2. Philip.
3. Thomas.
1. Sr Marmaduke Constable of Everingham, Bart. æt. 45 an. 7 Sept. a° 1665. = Anne, daughter of Richard Sherburne of Stanihurst in co. Lanc. Esqr.
1. Barbara.
2. Anne.
3. Catherine, wife of Edward Sheldon of Barton in com. Oxon.

Philip, æt. 14 an. 7 Sept. 1665. Anne. Elizabeth.

WILTON BEACON. *Pocklington*, 7° *Sept.* 1665.

WILBERFOSSE OF WILBERFOSSE.

ARMS.—Argent, an eagle displayed sable, beaked and membered gules.

Robert Wilberfosse of Wilberfosse in com. Ebor. died in a° 1640 vel circa. = Anne, daughter of Thomas Burland of Stockton in com. Ebor.

Marg^t^, daugh. of .... Eathrope of Kilpin in co. Ebor. ob. s. prole. 1st wife. = Roger Wilberfosse of Wilberfosse, died a° 1662. = Margaret, daughter of John Agard of Stockton in com. Eborum, 2 wife.

1. Dorothy, wife of ...... Cob of Full-Sutton in com. Ebor.
2. Elizabeth, wife of William Williamson of Newton in com. Ebor.
3. Anne, wife of Thomas Cooper of Barnby in com. Ebor.

2. Robert Wilberfosse, married Emmot, daugh. of Simon Newlove of Wetwang in com. Ebor.
3. William.
4. Thomas.

1. Roger Wilberfosse of Wilberfosse, æt. 31 ann. 7 Sept. 1665. = Anne, daughter of Will'm Plaxton of Pocklington in com. Ebor.

1. Anne, wife of Will'm Horseley of Beckhouse in Pickering Lythe.
2. Margaret.
3. Mary.

Roger, æt. 8 ann. 7 Sept. 1665. Anne.

RYDALE WAPENTAKE. *Malton*, 30° *Aug.* 1665.

PORTINGTON OF MALTON.

ARMS.—Gules, on a bend argent cotised or three martlets sable.

William Portington of Elloughton, a younger son to ...... Portington of Portington in com. Ebor. = ...

2. Francis Portington of Ellowton, æt. 62 ann. 30 Aug. a° 1665. = Ellen, daughter of Francis Scarfe of Ellowton in com. Ebor.

1. William Portington of Ellowton. =

Mary, daughter of Thomas Pye of Malton, first wife, ob. s. prole. = Timothy Portington of Malton in com. Ebor. æt. 35 ann. 30 Aug. a° 1665. = Mary, daughter of Robt Ruddock of Eglethorpe-grange in com. Ebor. 2^d^ wife. = Frances, daughter of Robert Thornton of Newton in com. Ebor. third wife.

Elizabeth, æt. 3 annor. et 10 mensium 30 Aug. 1665.

HOLME BEACON. *Pocklington, 7 Sept.* 1665.

GRYMSTON OF GRYMSTON-GARTH & GOODMADHAM.

ARMS.—Argent, on a fess sable three mullets of six points or, pierced gules.

CREST.—A stag's head with a ring round the neck argent.

Thomas Grimston of Grimston-garth in Holdernesse, Esqr. = Dorothy, daughter & sole heire of Marmaduke Thwayts of Smeton in com. Eborum.

- 3. Marmaduke Grimston of Grimston-garth, living in a^o 1612. = Anne, daughter of Sr William Dalton of Hawkeswell in co. Ebor. K^t.
- 2. Thomas, obijt sine prole.
- 1. Sir Marmaduke Grymston K^t, son and heire. = Frances, daughter of George Gill of .... in com. Hertf.
- 1. Dorothy.
- 2. Frances.

Children of Marmaduke Grimston and Anne Dalton:

- Theophan, wife of Leonard Beckwith of Handall Abby in Cleveland.
- Anne, daughter of Christopher Byerley of Midridge-grange in com. Palat. Dunelm, first wife. = Will'm Grymston of Grymston-garth & Goodmadham in com. Ebor. Esqr. died in Apr. a^o 1664. = Margaret, daughter of Sr Robert Strickland of Thorneton Brigge in com. Eborum, Kn^t, second wife.

Children of Sir Marmaduke Grymston and Frances Gill:

- Thomas Grimston, obijt sine prole.

Children of Will'm Grymston and Anne Byerley:

- 2. John.
- 3. Charles.
- 1. William Grymston of Grymston-garth and Goodmadham, Esqr, æt. 24 annor. 7 Sept. a^o 1665. = Dorothea, daugh. of Sr Thomas Norcliffe of Langton in co. Ebor. K^t.
- Dorothy, died a childe.

Children of Will'm Grymston and Margaret Strickland:

- Henry, Marmaduke, } died young.
- 1. Margaret.
- 2. Elizabeth.
- 3. Dorothy.

Children of William Grymston and Dorothea Norcliffe:

- 2. Thomas, ætatis 1 anni 7 Sept. 1665.
- 1. William, æt. 3 annorum et 11 mens. 7° Sept. 1665.
- Dorothea.

HOLDERNESSE MIDDLE BAYLIWICK. *Kingston super Hull*, 2° *Sept.* 1665.

THOMPSON OF HUMBLETON.

ARMS.—Per fess argent and sable, a fess counter-embattled between three falcons, all counterchanged, a crescent for difference.

William Thompson of Humbleton in Holdernesse, died a° 1630 or thereabouts. = ...

3. John, died unmarried. | 2. Richard Thompson of Kilham in com. Ebor. = | 1. Francis Thompson of Humbleton, died in a° 1657. = Elizabeth, da. of George Tocketts of Tocketts in com. Ebor. | 1. Mary, wife of Robert Jackson of Burlington in co. Ebor. | 2. Isabell, wife of Francis Beale of Scarborough in co. Ebor. | 3. Elizabeth, wife unto Richard Peacock of Scarborough. | 4. Eufemia, wife of Alexand^r^ Metcalfe of Leedes.

2. Christopher Thompson of Scarborough, married Sarah, daughter of James Boyse of Whitby in com. Ebor. = | 1. Stephen Thompson of Humbleton, Esqr, now one of his Maties Justices of the Peace in this county, æt. 63 ann. 2 Sept. 1665. = Mary, daughter of Henry Blakeston of Archdeacon-Newton in y^e^ Bishoprick of Durham. | 1. Isabell, wife unto Thomas Gent of Burbroke in co. Essex. | 2. Frances, wife unto Will'm Thorneton of Kingston super Hull in com. Ebor.

2. Stephen Thompson, Merchant of London. | 1. Will'm Thompson of Scarborough in com. Ebor. æt. 30 an. 2° Sept. 1665. = Frances, da. of Henry Bernard, an Alderman of Hull. | 1. Eliz. wife unto Charles Hotham, a younger son to Sr John Hotham of Scorborough in com. Ebor. B^t^. | 2. Juliana, wife unto Thomas Johnson, a merch^t^ in Hull. | 3. Frances, wife of Thomas Catterall of Crooke in com. Lanc. | 4. Isabell. | 5. Anne. | 6. Sarah. | 7. Margaret.

2. Henry, æt. 8 ann. | 1. Francis Thompson, æt. 10 ann. 2° Sept. a° 1665. | 1. Mary. | 2. Susanna. | 3. Arabella. | 4. Isabella. | 5. Anne.

DICKERING WAPENTAKE. *Kilham*, 31 *Aug*. 1665.

WHEATHE OF LANGTOFT.

Respite given for exhibiting the armes.

...... = Philip Wheathe of Hinderwell, in co. Ebor. = Ellen, daughter of ...... Walden of ...... in co. Derb.

Philip.

Joseph Weathe of Rullington in com. Ebor. died in a° 1641 vel circa. = Elizabeth, daughter of Dr Zachary Steward, a divine; of the Stewards of the Isle of Ely.

Elizabeth, daughter and soleheire of Thomas Hungate of Scampston in com. Ebor. 1st wife. = Philip Wheathe of Langtofte in com. Ebor. æt. 40 annorum 31 Aug. a° 1665. = Mary, daughter of Francis Topham of Upper-Bradley in Craven in com. Ebor. and widow of George Spenser of Langtoft, 2 wife.

4. Walter. 3. Philip. 2. Thomas. 1. John, æt. 20 an. 31 Aug. 1665. Anne.

BAYNTON BEACON WAPENTAKE. *Kilham*, 31° *Aug*. 1665.

REMINGTON OF LUND.

ARMS.—Barry of twelve argent and azure, over all a bend gules.

No proofe made of these armes.

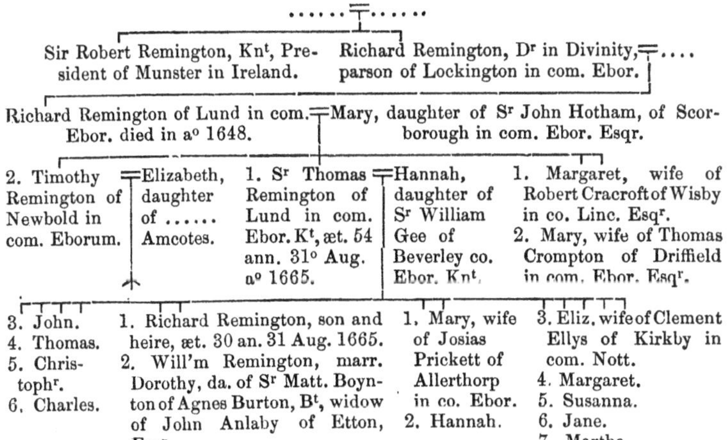

...... = ...

Sir Robert Remington, Knt, President of Munster in Ireland.

Richard Remington, Dr in Divinity, parson of Lockington in com. Ebor. = ...

Richard Remington of Lund in com. Ebor. died in a° 1648. = Mary, daughter of Sr John Hotham, of Scorborough in com. Ebor. Esqr.

2. Timothy Remington of Newbold in com. Eborum. = Elizabeth, daughter of ...... Amcotes.

1. Sr Thomas Remington of Lund in com. Ebor. Kt, æt. 54 ann. 31° Aug. a° 1665. = Hannah, daughter of Sr William Gee of Beverley co. Ebor. Knt.

1. Margaret, wife of Robert Cracroft of Wisby in co. Linc. Esqr.
2. Mary, wife of Thomas Crompton of Driffield in com. Ebor. Esqr.

3. John.
4. Thomas.
5. Christophr.
6. Charles.

1. Richard Remington, son and heire, æt. 30 an. 31 Aug. 1665.
2. Will'm Remington, marr. Dorothy, da. of Sr Matt. Boynton of Agnes Burton, Bt, widow of John Anlaby of Etton, Esqr.

1. Mary, wife of Josias Prickett of Allerthorp in co. Ebor.
2. Hannah.

3. Eliz. wife of Clement Ellys of Kirkby in com. Nott.
4. Margaret.
5. Susanna.
6. Jane.
7. Martha.

RYDALE WAPENTAKE. *Malton*, 29° *Aug*. 1665.

BARTON OF CAWTON.

ARMS.—Quarterly, a crescent for difference:
1 and 4. Ermine, on a fess gules three annulets argent.
2 and 3. Gules, three lions passant in bend argent cotised gobony of the second and azure.

CREST.—A wolf's head erased argent, a crescent gules for difference.

William Barton of Cauton in co. Ebor. descended by a younger son from ye Bartons of Whenby in com. Ebor. = Elizabeth, daughter of Will'm Botteresse of Ardenside in co. Ebor.

2. Robert Barton of Cawton, heire to his brother. = ... daughter of .... Brand of ....

1. Thomas Barton of Cauton, of whom there is no issue remayning.

2. John Barton of Cawton, died a° 1657 or thereabouts. = Ruth, daughter of George Watson of Old-Malton in co. Eborum.

1. William Barton of Cawton, obijt sine prole mascula. = Helen, daughter of Charles Tankard of Whixley in co. Ebor. Esqr.

Elizabeth, wife of Will'm Rosse of Cawton in com. Ebor.

2. Thomas.
3. William.

1. George Barton of Cawton in com. Ebor. æt. 26 ann. 29 Aug. 1665. = Mary, daughter of Francis Lascells of Ganthorpe in com. Ebor.

Barbara.

3. Lascells, æt. 12 septim.

2. George, æt. 2 an. et 9 mens.

1. Thomas, æt. 7 an. 29 Aug. 1665.

1. Elizabeth.
2. Mary.

PICKERING LITHE WAPENTAKE. *Malton*, 29 *Aug*. 1665.

SYMPSON OF RYTON.

ARMS.—Per bend nebulée or and sable, a lion rampant counterchanged.

CREST.—Out of a mural coronet argent a demi-lion rampant gardant per pale wavy or and sable, holding in the paws a sword erect hilted of the second.

He produced these armes depicted on a tablet. Qu. for better proofe?

Richard Simpson of Edgeston in co. Ebor. = Margaret, daughter of William Wytham of Britanby and Redeston in com. Ebor.

Will'm Simpson of Ryton in co. Ebor. = ... daughter of .... Atkinson, and widow of .... Mason of Welham in co. Ebor.

1. Roger Simpson, of whom there is noe issue male remayning.

3. Robert, died unmarried.

2. Henry Simpson of Smeaton in com. Ebor.

1. William Simpson of Ryton, died in a° 1638. = Ursula, daughter and heire of Tho. Silvestor of Great Driffeild in com. Ebor.

1. Ellen, first marr. to Will'm Hustler of Bridlington in co. Ebor., afterwards to Sr Edward Buckhock of ...... in Kent.
2. Mary, died unmarried.

Thomas Simpson of Ryton, æt. 34 ann. 29 Aug. a° 1665. = Mary, daughter of Sr Will'm Cayley of Brumpton in com. Ebor. Kt and Bart.

Ellen, died unmarried.

1. William, æt. 6 an. 29 Aug. 1665.
2. Thomas, æt. 4 an. 1665.

1. Dorothy, æt. 11 an. 1665.
2. Mary, died young.

3. Mary, æt. 1 anni.

PICKERING LYTHE WAPENTAKE. *Malton*, 29° *Aug*. 1665.

CALEY OF BRUMPTON.

ARMS.—Quarterly argent and sable, on a bend gules three mullets of the first.

CREST.—A demi-lion rampant or, charged with a bend gules, thereon three mullets argent, in the paws a battle-axe, head of the last, handle of the second, charged with a quatrefoil of the first.

¶ John Caley of Ouby in com. Norff.=....

John Cayley of Normanton=.... in com. Ebor.

Sr Will'm Cayley of Ouby in com. Norff. Kt, died without issue male.

¶ Edward Cayley of Brumpton in com. Ebor. died 6° Decemb. a° 1642.=Anne, daughter of William Walters of Cundall in com. Ebor.

2. Sr Arthur Cayley of Newland in co. civit. Coventr. Knt.

3. Thomas Cayley, died unmarried.

1. Sr Will'm Cayley of Brumpton in com. Ebor. Kt and Bart, æt. 56 ann. 29 Aug. a° 1665.=Dorothy, eldest daughter of Sr William St Quintin of Harpham in com. Ebor. Bart.

1. Elizabeth, wife of Robt Coulthurst of Up-Leatham in com. Ebor.

2. Catherine, wife of Arthur Ingram of Knottingley in co. Ebor. Esqr.

3. Anne, wife of Thomas Daivill of Kirkby Fletham in com. Ebor.

2. Arthur Cayley, married Eliz. daughter of Tho. Shipton, Alderman of London.

3. Cornelius.

1. William Cayley, son and heire, æt. 30 an. 29 Aug. 1665.=Mary, daugh. and heire of Barnabas Holbecke of Fillongley in com. Warr.

1. Mary, wife of Thomas Simpson of Ryton in com. Ebor.

2. Anne.

5. Thomas, æt. 6 ann.
6. Charles, æt. 5 ann.
7. Symon, æt. 4 ann.
8. Henry, æt. 2 ann.

Dorothy.

1. William, æt. 12 an. 30 Aug. 1665.
2. Arthur, æt. 10 ann.
3. Edward, æt. 9 an. 1665.
4. Barnabas, æt. 7 an. 1665.

DICKERING WAPENTAKE. *Kilham*, 31° *Aug.* 1665.

BOYNTON OF BARMSTON.

ARMS.—Quarterly :
1 and 4. Or, a fess between three crescents gules.
2. Gules, a cross moline or.
3. Azure, two bars wavy argent.

Sr Thomas Boynton of .... in co. Ebor. Knt. = Isabell, daughter of Sir Will'm Normanvill of Killingwick in co. Ebor. Kt. — a

1. Henry Boynton, Esqr. = Margaret, daughter and coheir to Sr Martin de la See of Barmeston, Knt. by Margt, coh. of Christopher Spenser.

Thomas Boynton of Barmston, Esqr. = Cecelye, daughter of Sr James Strangways of Smeton, Knt.

Mathew Boynton of Barmston in com. Ebor. Esqr. = Anne, daughter of Sr John Bulmer, Kt.

Sr Thomas Boynton of Barmston, Knt. = Frances, daughter of Francis Forbusher of Doncaster in com. Ebor. 1st wife.

Anne, wife of Francis Vaughan of Sutton super Darwent in co. Ebor.

Sr Francis Boynton of Barmston, Kt. = Dorothy, daughter and at length sole heire unto Sr Christopher Place of Hanaby in com. Ebor. Knt.

Dorothy, wife of Sr Henry Bellingham of Levens in com. Westmerl. Knt.

Sr Mathew Boynton of Barmston, Kt and Bart, died in ao 1646. = Frances, daughter to Sr Henry Griffith of Agnes Burton, Kt and Bart, and heire to Sr Henry Griffith, her brother.

3. Marmaduke.
4. Gustavus.

2. Mathew Boynton, slaine at Wigan in the advance of ye army of K. Ch. the second out of Scotland towards Worcester. = Isabell, da. of Robert Stapleton of Wighill in com. Ebor.

1. Sr Francis Boynton of Barmston, Bart, æt. 47 an. 31 Aug. ao 1665. = Constance, daugh. of William Viscount Say and Seale.

1. Mary.
2. Dorothy, wife of John Anlaby of Etton in co. Ebor. Esqr.
3. Elizabeth, wife unto John Herne, son of .... Herne of Bockenfield in co. ....
4. Margaret, wife unto John Robinson of Rither in co. Ebor.

Nathaniell, æt. 19 an. 1665.
Henry, æt. 17 ann.

Will'm Boynton, son and heire, æt. 22 an. 31 Aug. ao 1665. = Eliz. daughter & coheire of John Bernard, Alderman of Kingston sup' Hull.

Frances.

Griffith Boynton, æt. 1 anni 31 Aug. ao 1665.

Mary.

BOYNTON OF RAWCLIFFE.

a

2. Sr Christopher Boynton, Kn^{t}. = ... daughter to . . . . . . Conyers of Ormesby in com. Ebor.

Christopher Boynton of Sadborough in com. Eborum. = Elizabeth, daughter of Robert Strangways of Skelton in co. Ebor.

Sr Christopher Boynton of Sadborough, K^{t}. = Agnes, daughter of Henry Lord Scroope of Bolton.

1. Jane, wife of Sr William Nevill of Thorneton Briggs in com. Ebor. K^{t}.

2. Eliz. wife of Sr Gerard Widdrington, K^{t}.

1. Sr Henry Boynton, K^{t}. = Isabell, daughter & heire of Bertram Lumley.

2. John Boynton. = ... daughter of . . . . . . Leonard of . . . . in co. Ebor.

Isabell, daughter and sole heire, wife of Henry Gascoigne, 2^{d} son of Sr Wm Gascoigne of Gauthrope in com. Ebor. K^{t}.

Leonard Boynton of Willerby in co. Ebor. died a^{o} 29 Eliz. Reginæ. = Mary, daughter of Dr Stephen Tublay, Phisitian to King Henry the 8th.

Stephen Boynton of Rawcliffe in com. Ebor. died in a^{o} 1629. = Susan, daughter and coheir to John Harrison of Pollington in com. Ebor.

Thomas Boynton of Rawcliffe in com. Ebor. died a^{o} 1657. = Jane, daugh. of John Awnby of Sherwood in com. Ebor. gent.

1. Jane, wife of Will. Norman of Burton Salmon in com. Ebor.
2. Mary, wife of Francis Nuthall of Rawcliffe; after to Tho. Estoft of Estoft.
3. Lucie, wife of Robert Vicars of Scausby.

2. Stephen.
3. Francis.
4. Mathew.

1. John Boynton of Rawcliffe in com. Ebor. Esqr. æt. 44 ann. 31° Aug. a^{o} 1665. = Frances, daughter and coheire of John Bernard, Alderman of Kingston super Hull.

1. Anne, wife of William Ramsden, Alderman of Hull.
2. Susan, wife of . . . . . . Hodsall of London Merchant.
3. Mary, wife of Thomas Appleyard of Ulseby in co. Linc.

LISTER OF KINGSTON SUPER HULL.

ARMS.—Ermine, on a fess sable three mullets or, a fleur-de-lis for difference.

CREST.—Out of a ducal coronet or a stag's head couped ermine attired argent.

John Lyster of Kingston super Hull, living a° 1613.=Anne, daughter of Robt Geyton of Kingston super Hull.

Their children:

- Margaret, wife of Will'm Weddall of Erswick in com. Ebor. Esqr.
- Sr John Lyster of Kingston super Hull, Kt, died in Dec. 1640.=Elizabeth, daughter and sole heire unto Hugh Armyn of Kingston sup. Hull.

Children of Sr John Lyster and Elizabeth:

- 1. Elizabeth, wife unto Leonard Bernard, Alderman of Hull.
- 2. Anne, wife of Will'm Lutton of Knapton in com. Ebor.
- 3. Margaret wife unto John Hedlam of Kexby in com. Ebor.
- 4. Mary, wife of Toby Hodson of Bishop Burton in com. Ebor.
- 1. John Lyster of Lynton on the Woulds in co. Ebor. died in a° 1651 vel circa.=Jane, daughter of Christopher Constable of Hatfeild in co. Ebor.
- 2. Samuell Lyster of Estoft in co. Ebor. (married)
- 3. Will'm Lyster, an Utter Barister of the Inner Temple, and now Recorder of Kingston super Hull. (married)
- 4. Hugh Lyster of Kingston super Hull, æt. 46 ann. 4 Sept. a° 1665.=Jane, daughter and sole heire of Bernard Smith, an alderman of Kingston super Hull.
- 5. Thomas Lyster of Bawtre in com. Ebor. (married)
- 6. Walter Lyster, an alderman in Rippon in com. Ebor.
- 7. Benjamin Lyster, an Utter Barrister of ye Inner Temple Lond.

Children of John Lyster of Lynton and Jane:

- 1. Elizabeth, wife of Robert Southaby of Birdsall in co. Ebor. Esqr.
- 2. Frances.
- 3. Dorothye.
- John Lyster of Lynton, æt. 27 ann. 4 Sept. 1665.

Children of Hugh Lyster and Jane:

- 1. John, æt. 19 an. 4 Sept. 1665,
- 2. Bernard, æt. 18 an. 1665.
- 3. Hugh, æt. 9 ann.
- 1. Elizabeth, æt. 12 an. 1665.
- 2. Jane, æt. 5 ann.

HOLDERNESSE NORTH BAYLIWICK. *Pocklington*, 7 *Sept.* 1665.

GRYMSTON OF DRYNGE.

ARMS.—Argent, on a fess sable three mullets or pierced gules, a canton of the last.
CREST.—A stag's head with a ring round the neck argent.

Thomas Grymston of Grymston-garth in Holdernesse Esqr. = ...

3. John Grimston of Frastrope in co. Ebor. 3^d son. = Grace, daughter of Will'm Strickland of Boynton in com. Ebor. Esqr.

1. Thomas Grymston of Grymston, Esqr. = Dorothy, daughter of Sr Marmaduke Thwaytes of Syveton.

Children of John Grimston and Grace:

1. Marmaduke Grymston of Frastrope.
2. Francis Grymston of Frastrope.
3. Henry Grymston of Sherbourne in co. Ebor. died in a° 1645 vel circa. = Anne, daughter of William Strickland of Eston in com. Eborum.

Children of Henry Grymston and Anne:

John Grymston of Dringe in Holdernesse in com. Ebor. æt. 34 ann. 7 Sept. a° 1665.

Grace, wife of Marshall Ripley of Preston in Holdernesse.

HOLDERNESSE SOUTH BAYLIWICK. *Hull*, 2° *Sept.* 1665.

HOLME OF PALL-HOLME.

ARMS.—Quarterly:
1 and 4. Barry of six or and azure, on a canton argent a chaplet gules. Holme.
2. Sable, a lion rampant double-queued argent collared gules. Wastneys.
3. Argent, a fess sable between seven lozenges gules. Rockele.

Henry Holme of Pall-Holme in co. Ebor. Esqr, died in a° 1631 or thereabouts. = Dorothy, daughter of Thomas Grymston of Grymston-garth in com. Ebor.

2. Edward, died young.

1. Christopher Holme of Pall-Holme, Esqr, died a° 1657. = Marg^t, daugh. of Sr John Langton of Langton in com. Linc. K^t.

1. Frances, died unmarried.
2. Anne, died unmarried.
3. Dorothy, wife of John Catterall of Hollim in Holdernesse, and died without issue.
4. Eliz. wife of Thomas Hill of Tunstall in co. Ebor and died without issue.
5. Mary, wife of Richard Catherall of Hollim in Holdernesse.

Children of Christopher Holme and Margaret:

2. Christopher Holme of Skeffling in Holdernesse.

1. Henry Holme of Pall-Holme Esqr, ætatis 42 ann. 2° Sept. 1665. = Penelope, daughter of Sr Francis Rhodes of Barlbrough in co. Derb. K^t and Bar^t.

Catherine.

Children of Henry Holme and Penelope:

Henry, æt. 14 ann. 2° Sept. 1665.
1. Anne.
2. Margaret.
3. Lettice.

WILTON BEACON. *Pocklington*, 7 *Sept.* 1665.

PRICKET OF ALLERTHORPE.

ARMS.—Or, on a cross azure quarter-pierced of the field four mascles of the first.

Marmaduke Pricket, a younger son to ...... Pricket of Nateland in com. Westmerl[d]. = ...

Robert Pricket of Everingham in com. Ebor. died in Queene Eliz. time. = Margaret, daughter of Hugh Hindsley of Woodhouse in the parish of Sutton in com. Ebor.

Marmaduke Pricket of Allerthorpe in com. Ebor. died a° 1652. = Barbara, daughter of John Bew of the Citty of Yorke.

3. George Pricket.

2. Robert Pricket of Wressle in com. Eborum. = Mary, daughter of Marmaduke Lord Langdale.

1. Josias Pricket of Allerthorpe, ætatis 39 an. 7 Sept. 1665. = Mary, daughter of Sr Thomas Remington of Lund in com. Ebor. Kn[t].

Children of Robert Pricket: 1. Barbara, æt. 9 an. 7 Sept. a° 1665. 2. Lenox, a daughter, æt. 8 ann.

Children of Josias Pricket: Mary. Marmaduke, ætatis 3 ann. 7 Sept. a° 1665.

THE BOROUGH OF KINGSTON UPON HULL. *Hull*, 6° *Sept.* 1665.

RIPLEY OF KINGSTON SUPER HULL.

ARMS.—Per chevron or and azure, three lions rampant counterchanged.

Lionell Ripley of Rippon in com. Ebor. died in Hull tempore Eliz. Reginæ. = ...

Robert Ripley of Kingston upon Hull, died a° 1624, or thereabouts. = Emmot, daughter of John Boyse of Egton in com. Ebor.

2. Francis, 3. William, died young.

Mary, daughter of Francis Burrell of Kingston upon Hull, first wife. = Robert Ripley, Alderman of Kingston upon Hull, æt. 68 ann. 6 Sept. a° 1665. = Elizabeth, daughter of Edward Richardson, Alderman of Hull, 2[d] wife.

1. Elizabeth, wife unto George Carleil of Hull. 2. Margaret, wife unto John Scollet of Hull.

2. Lyonell Ripley. 3. Peregrine Ripley.

1. Marshall Ripley of Preston in Holdernesse, æt. 38 an. 6 Sept. 1665. = Grace, daughter of Henry Grymston of Sherburne in Holdernesse.

Elizabeth, wife of John Pearson of Kingston upon Hull.

RUDSTON OF HAYTON.

ARMS.—Quarterly of six:
1. Argent, three bull's heads erased sable, on a canton the badge of a Baronet of England. Rudston.
2. Argent, three bear's heads erased sable muzzled .... Barwick.
3. Per chevron sable and argent, in chief two etoiles of the second. Hayton.
4. Azure, a cross moline or. Molineux.
5. Gules, a chevron ermine between three bear's heads erased argent. Kighley.
6. Argent, a chevron between three lion's heads erased sable, a mullet or for difference. Gunhouse.

CREST.—A lion's gamb erased gules, holding a cross moline or.

Walter Rudston of Hayton in co. Ebor. Esq[r], died in a° 1640, or thereabouts. = Frances, daughter of S[r] Will'm Constable of Everingham in co. Ebor. K[t].

Children:

- 1. Barbara, wife of Samuell Saltonstall of Rogerthorpe in com. Ebor.
- 2. Mary, wife of John Rudston of Besonby in com. Ebor.
- 3. Catherine, wife unto Will'm Ley of Medley in co. Ebor.
- 1. S[r] Walter Rudston of Hayton, B[t], died a° 1651. = Mar[t], da. of S[r] Thomas Dawney of Cowick in co. Ebor. K[t].
- 2. Will'm Rudston, marr. Hesther, sister to S[r] George Savile of Rufford in co. Nott. Bar[t].
- 3. Charles, died unmarried.
- 4. Samuell Rudston. = Mary, daughter of Tho. Beckwith of Beverley in co. Ebor.
- 5. Mathew, died unmarried.
- 6. Marmaduke Rudston. = Bridget, daughter of .... Eyre of Rampton in com. Nott.
- 7. Philip, died unmarried.

Children of Sr Walter Rudston and Mar[t]:

- 2. Walter, æt. 21 an. 1565.
- 1. Sr Thomas Rudston of Hayton Bar[t], æt. 25 an. 7 Sept. a° 1665.
- 1. Fayth, wife of Cornelius Clarke of Cutthorpe in com. Derb.
- 2. Barbara.
- 3. Margaret.
- 4. Elizabeth.

HOLDERNESSE NORTH BAYLYWICK. *Hull, 2º Sep.* 1665.

BETHELL OF WRAYS.

ARMS—Argent, on a chevron between three boar's heads couped sable an etoile or.
CREST.—A griffin's head between two wings displayed azure, charged on the breast with an etoile or.

Thomas Bethell of Maunsell in com. Hereford. = ...

3. Roger Bethell of Wrays in Holdernesse in com. Ebor. died circa ann. 1625. = ...

2. Nicholas Bethell of Maidenhead in co. Heref. = ...

1. Sr Hugh Bethell of Ellerton in co. Ebor. Kt. = ...

2. Robert Bethell of Everthorpe in co. Ebor. = ...

1. Hugh Bethell of Wrays in com. Ebor. died aº 1657 vel circiter. = Helen, daughter of Thomas Johnston of Bisshop-Burton in com. Ebor.

Gresill, sole daughter and heir, wife to Sr John Wray of Glentworth in com. Linc. Kt.

2. Christophr, 4. Robert, died unmarr.

3. John Bethell of Skyrlow in co. Ebor. =

1. Sr Hugh Bethell of Wrays in com. Ebor. Knt, æt. 49 annorum 2 Sept. aº 1665. = Mary, daughter and coheire of Thomas Mitchelbourne of Carleton in com. Ebor.

Ellen, wife of Christopher Bacon of Ferriby in com. Ebor.

Hugh Bethell, æt. 13 annor. 2 Sept. 1665.

HOLDERNESS NORTH BAYLIWICK. *Hull, 4º Sept.* 1665.

HARRISON OF HORNESEY.

The proofe of the armes respited.

...... Harrison of Bigglesworth in com. Bedf. = ...

Thomas Harrison of Burwash in com. Sussex. = Susan, daughter of John Pollcil of Preston House in ye parish of Shoreham in Kent.

3. Robert Harrison of Icklesham in com. Sussex.

2. Thomas Harrison of Hornesey in Holdernesse, æt. 17 ann. 4 Sept. aº 1665.

1. John Harrison of Burwash in co. Sussex. = ...

RIPPON LIBERTYE. *Kilham*, 31 *Aug.* 1665.

CROSLAND OF NEWBY.

ARMS.—Quarterly argent and gules, a cross botonnée counterchanged, a crescent for difference; an escutcheon of pretence: Gules, a fret argent. Fleming of Rydale.

Roger de Crosland = Philippa, daughter of ...... Ufton.

Adam de Crosland, tempore Edw. I. = ...

Gilbert de Crosland = ...

Sr John de Crosland, K[t]. = ...

1. Sr Edward Crosland, K[t]. = ...
2. Thomas Crosland = ...

Grace, daughter and heire, wife of Sr Robert Beamont, Kn[t].

Richard Crosland = ...

Hugh Crosland = ...

John Crosland = ...

William Crosland = Agnes, daughter of ...... Clarke of Morton in com. Derbiæ.

Richard Crosland = Joane, daughter and heire of ...... Norman of .... in com. Nott.

2. Will'm. 3. Norman.
¶ 1. Thomas Crosland. = ... daugh. of ...... Hawksworth of Hawksworth.
Alice, wife unto Simon Sheild. Eliz. wife of Will'm Harbut. Margaret, wife unto John Broomby.

George.
John Crosland of Hemsley in com. Ebor. = Elizabeth, daughter of George Clapham of Beamsley in co. Ebor.
1. Anne. 2. Grace, wife of Leonard Calvert of Kipling in co. Ebor.

2. Peter.
1. John Crosland of Hemsley, died in Nov. 1636. = Jane, daughter of Henry Atkinson of Little Cattall in com. Ebor.
1. Elizabeth, wife of John Talbot of Thorneton in le street in com. Ebor. 2. Ellen, wife of Mich. Ernley of ......

2. Henry Crosland.
1. Sir Jordan Crosland of Newby in the Liberty of Rippon in co. Ebor. K[t], now Constable of Scarborough Castle in co. Ebor. æt. 45 an. 31 Aug. 1665. = Bridget, eldest da. to John Fleming of Rydale in co. Westmerl[d], Esq[r], and sister and coheir to Will'm her brother.
1. Eliz. wife of Charles Tankard of Arden. 2. Eleanor, wife of Colonell ...... Prideaux. 3. Jane.

3. George, æt. 5 mensium.
2. Charles, æt. 10 annor.
1. John, æt. 13 an. 31 Aug. 1665.
1. Dorothy. 2. Jane.

HOLDERNESSE MIDDLE BAYLIWICK. *Kingston super Hull*, 4 *Sept.* 1665.

THORPE OF DANTHORPE.

ARMS.—Quarterly of six :
1. Argent, a lion rampant gules between eight fleurs-de-lis azure.*
2. Argent, semée of fleurs-de-lis azure.
3 and 4. ....
5. Argent, a chevron between three mullets gules.
6. As the first.

¶ Robert Thorpe of Thorpe juxta Wellwyke in Holdernesse, temp. R. Joh'is.=Margery, daughter of John Holme of Pall-Holme in Holdernesse.

¶ Stephen Thorpe, tem. E. 1.=Maude.

¶ Stephen Thorpe, tempore Edw. 2.=Isolda.

Stephen Thorpe, died a° 17 E. 3.=......

Stephen Thorpe, died 10 Aug. a° 23 E. 3.=......

Sir Stephen Thorpe K[t]=Catherine. A° D'ni 1405.

Stephen Thorpe, a° 1405.=Joane, daughter of S[r] Robert Constable of Flamborough, K[t].

Stephen Thorpe, a° 1434, 12. H. 6.=Isabell.

Dionis, daughter of Will'm Eland of Hull.=Stephen Thorpe, died in a° 1502.=Isabell, sister of John Constable of Halsham in com. Ebor. Esq[r].

1. Dionis, wife of .... Musgrave.
2. Joane, wife of .... Handby.

John Thorpe of Thorpe, died a° 1533.=Ellen, da. & heire of Will. Wells of Anlaby in com. Kingston super Hull, married in a° 1503.

1. Lora.
2. Dorothy.
3. Elizabeth.
4. Margaret.
5. Alice.

1. Isabell.
2. Margaret.
3. Elizabeth.
4. Anne.

1. John,
2. Stephen, died without issue.

Margery, daughter of Christopher Hillyard, Esqr, first wife.=Will'm Thorpe of Thorpe, died 12 Martij a° 21 Eliz. Reginæ.=Elizabeth, sister of Thomas Estoft of Estoft in com. Linc. widow of Jasper Sheffeild of Croxby in com. Linc.

Christopher Thorpe, made his will in a° 1565.=Anne, daughter of Jasper Sheffeild of Croxby in com. Linc. married in a° 1543.

Stephen Thorpe of Thorpe, Esqr, made his will 1586.=Frances, daughter of Nicholas Rudston of Hayton in com. Ebor.

4. Thomas, obijt sine prole.

3. Will'm Thorpe of Danthorpe, Esqr, brother & heire, obijt circa 1620.=Eliz. daugh. of Peter Vavasour of Willytoft in com. Ebor.

2. John, obijt sine prole.

1. Robert Thorpe of Thorpe, Esqr, obijt sine prole.=Mary, daughter of .... Skerne of .... in co. Linc.

John Thorpe of Danthorpe, Esqre, æt. 51 ann. 4 Sept. 1665. He was Capt. of a Troope of Horse in the Regiment of Sr Walter Vavasour of Haslewood in com. Ebor. Bar[t], for the service of K. Charles y[e] 1st in the time of the late Rebellion.=Jane, daughter of Thomas Beckwith of Aketon in co. Ebor.

John Thorpe, son and heire, ætatis 27 annorum 4° Sept. a° 1665.=Elizabeth, daughter & coheire of George Daniell of Besewike in co. Ebor.

* Ex sigillo Stephani Thorp militis a° 6 H. 4.

Pocklington, 7° *Sept.* 1665.

ST. QUINTIN OF HARPHAM.

ARMS.—Quarterly:
1 and 4. Or, a chevron gules and a chief vair. St. Quintin.
2. ...... a lion rampant purpure within a bordure componée or and gules charged with seven bezants. Lacy of Foulkton.
3. Sable, a chevron between three buck's heads cabossed argent. Foulkton.

CREST.—Out of a ducal coronet gules, a pease-rise proper on the top of a fluted column between two horns or.

Sir Will'm St. Quintin of Harpham in com. Ebor. Bart. died a° 1648, or thereabouts. = Mary, daughter of Robert Lacy of Foulkton in com. Ebor. coheire to John her brother.

Their issue:

- 4. Thomas St Quintin of Flamborough in com. Ebor. æt. 45 an. 7 Sept. 1665. = Anne, daughter of Thomas Wood of Thorpe juxta Rudston in com. Ebor.
  - Anne.
  - William, æt. 8 an. 7 Sept. a° 1665.
- 3. John, died unmarried.
- 2. William St Quintin of Hayton in com. Ebor. æt. 56 ann. 7° Sept. a° 1665. = Margaret, daughter of Thomas Wood of Thorpe juxta Rudston in com. Ebor.
  - 1. Thomas, æt. 10 an. 7 Sept. a° 1665.
  - 2. George, æt. 5 ann.
  - 1. Margaret.
  - 2. Debora.
- 1. Sr Henry St Quintin of Harpham in com. Ebor. Bart. ætatis 59 annorū 7° Sept. 1665. = Mary, daughter of Henry Stapleton of Wighill in com. Ebor. Esqr.
  - 2. Henry.
  - 3. Philip.
  - 1. William St Quintin of Muston, son and heire, æt. 33 annorū 7° Sept. a° 1665. = Elizabeth, daughter of Sr William Strickland of Boynton in com. Ebor. Bart.
    - 3. Mary.
    - 4. Catherine.
    - 1. Frances.
    - 2. Margaret.
    - 1. Henry St Quintin, ætatis 11 annorum 7° Septembr. a° 1665.
    - 2. William, æt. 3 an. 1665.
  - 1. Mary.
  - 2. Debora.
- 1. Dorothy, wife of Sr William Caley of Brumpton in Pickering Lythe in co. Ebor. Bart.
- 2. Frances, wife of Francis Lascells of Stanke in com. Ebor.
- Everild, Elizabeth, } died young.
- 3. Catherine, first marr. to Mich. Wentworth, son of Sr George Wentworth of Wolley in co. Ebor. Kt; afterward to Sr John Kay of Woodsome in co. Ebor. Bt; lastly to ...... Sandes of ......

THE BOROUGH OF KINGSTON UPON HULL. *Hull, 4 Sept. a° 1665.*

DEWICK OF KINGSTON SUPER HULL.

No proofe made of the armes.

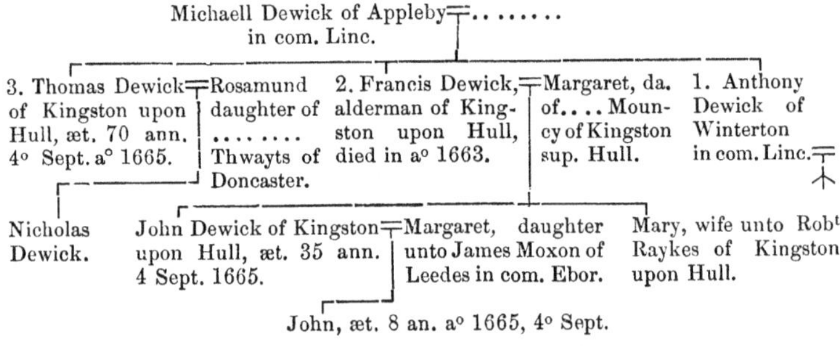

Michaell Dewick of Appleby = ... in com. Linc.

3. Thomas Dewick of Kingston upon Hull, æt. 70 ann. 4° Sept. a° 1665. = Rosamund daughter of .... Thwayts of Doncaster.

2. Francis Dewick, alderman of Kingston upon Hull, died in a° 1663. = Margaret, da. of.... Mouncy of Kingston sup. Hull.

1. Anthony Dewick of Winterton in com. Linc. =

Nicholas Dewick.

John Dewick of Kingston upon Hull, æt. 35 ann. 4 Sept. 1665. = Margaret, daughter unto James Moxon of Leedes in com. Ebor.

Mary, wife unto Robt Raykes of Kingston upon Hull.

John, æt. 8 an. a° 1665, 4° Sept.

HOLDERNESSE MIDDLE BAYLIWICK. *Burton Constable, 5° Sept.* 1665.

BRIGHAM OF BRIGHAM.

ARMS.—Quarterly:
1. Argent, a saltire engrailed vert. Brigham.
2. .... Garton of Garton in Holdernesse.
3. Gules, a fess ermine between three water-bougets argent. Rosse of Routhe in Holdernesse.
4. Argent, on a fess sable three mullets of six points or pierced gules, a crescent for difference. Grimston of Grimston.

CREST.—Out of a ducal coronet gules a double plume of ostrich feathers argent.

Francis Brigham of Brigham in com. Ebor. = Margaret, daughter of Gilbert Wartyr of Cranswick in com. Ebor.

Raphe Brigham of Brigham, died in a° 1656. = Mary, daughter of Raphe Creswell of Nonkelling in com. Ebor.

Alice, died unmarried.

3. Henry Brigham, æt. 43 an. 5° Sept. 1665

2. Will'm Brigham of Brigham, in co. Ebor. Esqr, æt. 53 ann. 5 Sept 1665. = Ursula, da. of Richard Langley of Millington in com. Ebor.

1. Henry, died young.

1. Mary, wife of Raphe Wilberfosse of Brigham in com. Ebor
2. Marg[t], died unmarried.
3. Frances, died unmarried.
4. Dorothy.

2. Richard.
3. Peter.

1. John Brigham, æt. 28 annorum 5 Sept. a° 1665.

1. Mary.

2. Dorothy.

HOLDERNESSE MIDDLE BAYLIWICK. *Burton Constable, 5 Sept.* 1665.

CONSTABLE OF BURTON-CONSTABLE, NOW VISCOUNT DUNBAR.

ARMS.—Quarterly of twelve:

1. Barry of six or and azure.
2. Argent, three chaplets gules.
3. Quarterly or and gules, on a bend sable three escallops argent, a crescent for difference.
4. Barry of six or and azure, on a canton gules a cross fleury argent.
5. Or, a cross sable.
6. Vert, three lions rampant argent, ducally crowned and maned or.
7. Gules, on a saltire argent a mullet pierced sable.
8. Or, fretty gules, on a canton sable a ship of the field.
9. Gules, a lion rampant erminois.
10. Or, a chief indented azure.
11. Azure, a cross fleury or.
12. Sable, a fess between three garbs argent.

CREST.—A dragon's head argent, charged with three bars gules, on each as many lozenges or.

Sr Henry Constable of Burton Constable of co. Ebor. Kt, living ao 1584. = Margaret, daughter of Sr Will'm Dormer of Ethrop in com. Buck. Kt.

Sr Henry Constable of Burton Constable, Kt, created Vicount Dunbar by King James, he died in ao 1645. = Mary, daugh. of Sr John Tufton of Hothfeild in Kent, Knt and Bart.

1. Catherine, wife of Sr Thomas Fairfax of Walton and Gilling in co. Ebor. Kt.
2. Dorothy, wife of Roger Lawson, son and heir to Sr Raphe Lawson of Burgh in co. Ebor. Knt.
3. Margt. wife of Sr Edward Stanhope of Edlington in com. Ebor, Kt of ye Bathe.
4. Mary, wife of Tho. Blakeston of Blakeston in ye Bishoprick of Durham, Kt and Bart.

2. Mathew.
. Henry.

1. John Viscount Dunbar, ætatis 50 ann. 5 Sept. 1665. = Mary, daugh. of Tho. Ld Brudenell of Staunton Wyvill in co Leic. created Earle of Cardigan by K. Charles the 2d.

1. Mary, wife of Robert Ld Brudenell & Earle of Cardigan.
2. Catherine, wife of Will'm Middleton of Stockheld in com. Ebor. Esqr.
3. Margaret.

3. Will'm, æt. 11 ann.

2. Robert, æt. 14 ann.

1. John Constablo, æt. 16 annor. 5 Sept. ao 1665.

1. Mary.

2. Cecelie, wife of Francis Tunstall of Hutton in com. Ebor. Esqr.

3. Catherine.

WILTON BEACON WAPENTAKE.

Pocklington, 7° *Sept.* 1665.

DOLMAN OF POCKLINGTON.

ARMS.—Azure, a fess dancettée or between eight garbs of the second banded gules.

CREST.—Two arms embowed, the dexter vested azure, the sinister or, the hands proper holding a garb of the second.

Another shield, quarterly of six:

1. Azure, a fess dancettée or between eight garbs of the second banded gules. Dolman.
2. Azure, two bars or, over all a lion rampant gules. Hawcliffe alias Hatcliffe.
3. Or, a fess dancettée sable, a crescent argent for difference. Vavasour of Spaldington.
4. Gules, three covered cups argent within a bordure engrailed or. Butler.
5. Argent, three escallops in bend gules cotised sable. De la Hay.
6. Quarterly azure and argent, in the first a fleur-de-lis or. Metham.

Sr Robert Dolman of Pocklington in com. Ebor, K^t, = Eleanor, daughter of Sr Will'm Mallory of Studley in com. Ebor. Kn^t.
died in a° 1626, vel circa.

Temperance, daughter of Sr Edward Watson of Rockingham-Castle, K^t, first wife. = 1. Thomas Dolman of Badsworth in com. Ebor. Esqr, died in a° 1639, or thereabouts. = Barbara, daugh. of Sr Thomas Metham of Metham in co. Ebor. Kn^t, second wife.

2. Robert, obijt sine prole.

3. Philip Dolman of Leade in com. Ebor. = ... daughter unto Walter Vavasour of Haslewood in com. Ebor. Esqr.

4. John Dolman, died without issue.

5. Peter Dolman.

1. Elizabeth, died unmarried.

2. Mary, wife of Robert Stapleton of Wressle in co. Ebor.

3. Ursula, wife unto John Ryder of Scarcrofte in co. Ebor.

4. Gresild, died unmarried.

Eleanor, wife of Raphe Evers of Washingbrough in co. Lincolniæ, Esqr.

Robert Dolman of Pocklington in com. Ebor. Esqr, ætatis 39 annorum 7° Sept. a° 1665. = Catherine, daughter of Edmund Thorold of Hough in com. Linc. Esqr.

1. Robert, æt. 28 annor. 7° Sept. a° 1665.

2. Thomas.

3. Philip.

1. Mary, died unmarried.

2. Helen.

1. Robert Dolman, æt. 6 annorū 7° Sept. a° 1665.

2. Thomas, ætatis 1 anni.

1. Catherine.

2. Barbara.

3. Frances.

METHAM OF METHAM.

ARMS.—Quarterly of nine:
1. Quarterly azure and argent, in the first a fleur-de-lis or.
2. Paly of six argent and gules, a bend paly of six counterchanged.
3. ...... an eagle displayed ...... over all a bend ......
4. Argent, on a bend sable three bezants.
5. Argent, a lion rampant sable.
6. ...... fretty ......
7. Argent, a lion rampant azure.
8. Argent, two bars gules, on a canton of the second a lion passant gardant or.
9. Gules, two bars-gemelles and a chief or.

CREST.—A bull's head barry of eight argent and azure.

Thomas Metham of Metham in com. Ebor. Esqr. = Catherine, daughter of Sr Will'm Bellassys of Newborough in co. Ebor. Kn^t^.

Issue:

- 3. Sr Jordan Metham, Kn^t^, died a° 1643. = Margaret, daughter of William Langdale of Lanthrope in Holdernesse in co. Ebor. Esqr.
- 2. John, died young.
- 1. Sr Thomas Metham, Kn^t^, slaine in the battail of Marston-Moore neer Yorke, being then Capt. of the Yorkeshire Gentry on the part of King Charles the First, against the rebells in June a° 1644. = Barbara, daughter unto Philip Constable of Everingham in com. Ebor. Esqr.
- Frances, wife of Marmaduke Constable of Everingham, Esqr.
- Bridget, first married to Tho. Hopton of ...... in co. Ebor.; after to Will. Langdale of Lanthrop in Holdernesse, Esqr.
- Dorothy, wife of Robert Thorneton of Newton in com. Ebor. Esqr.
- Eleanor, wife of Raphe Ellerker of Riseby in com. Ebor. Esqr.
- Cathering, wife of Geo. Creswell of Donington in Holdernesse.

Issue of Sr Thomas Metham and Barbara:

- 1. Jordan Metham, eldest son, slayne at Pomfret Castle, being in armes for K. Charles y^e^ First, at y^e^ raysing of the first seige there.
- 2. John Metham, died young.
- 3. George Metham of Metham, Esqr, æt. 47 ann. 7° Sept. a° 1665. = Catherine, da. of Tho. Visc. Fairfax of Emeley in Irel^d^.
- 4. Francis Metham.
- 5. Thomas, died unmarried.
- 6. Will'm Metham, married ...... daughter of .... and widow of Sr Tho. Tankard of Brampton in com. Ebor. K^t^.
- 7. Henry Metham.
- 8. John Metham.
- 1. Ursula, wife of Sr Tho. Brathwayt, K^t^, son and heire of Richard Brathwayt of Burneside in co. Westmerl. Esqr.
- 2. Jane, wife of Tho. Tempest, a younger son of S^r^ .... Tempest of Stanley in ye Bisshoprick of Durham.
- Thomas, died unmarried.
- 1. Cath. wife of Edward Smith of Ashe in co. Palat. Dunelm. Esqr.
- 2. Barbara, wife of Thomas Dolman of Badsworth in co. Ebor. Esqr.

Issue of George Metham and Catherine:

1. George Metham, ætatis 10 ann. 7° Sept. a° 1665. 2. Thomas. 3. Jordan. 4. Philip. 1. Catherine. 2. Anne. 3. Abigall.

BULMER WAPENTAKE. *Yorke*, 9° *Sept.* 1665.

BOURCHIER OF BENNINGBROUGH.

ARMS.—Quarterly :
1 and 4 Quarterly : 1. Argent, a cross engrailed gules between four water-bougets sable. Bourchier.
2. Gules, a fess argent between fourteen billets or. Lovaine.
3. Quarterly or and vert. Berners.
4. Argent, a chevron between three griffin's heads erased gules. Tilney.
2. Argent, a cross fleury sable, a crescent for difference. Banaster.
3. Argent, three bars sable, a bend ermine. Fyncham.

CREST.—An old man's head sidefaced proper, couped at the shoulders, habited vert, collared or, on his head a ducal coronet .. .. out of which a long cap hanging forward .... tasselled ....

Sr Raufe Bourchier of Beningborough in com. Ebor. Knt, living in a° 1584. = Elizabeth, daughter of Francis Hall of Grantham in com. Linc. Esqr, first wife.

2. Sr John Bourchier of Hanging Grimston in com. Ebor. Kt. = ...

1. Will'm Bourchier of Beningborough, Esqr, æt. 25 ann. a° 1584, died a° .... = Kathar. daughter of Sr Thomas Barrington of Hatfield-Broad-Oke in com. Essex.

Children of Sr John Bourchier:
1. Raphe Bourchier.
2. Richard, of whom there is issue remayng.
3. Will'm, a Divine.
4. Verney Bourchier.

Children of Will'm Bourchier:
3. Thomas Bourchier. = ...
2. Sir John Bourchier of Beningbrough, Kt, died a° 1659. = Anne, da. and sole heire of William Rolfe of Hadley in com. Suff.
1. Robert Bourchier, died unmarried.
1. Winifride, wife of .... Lyster, a Dr of Phisick in Yorke.
2. Eliz. wife of William Scudamore of Overton in co. Ebor. Esqr.
3. Anne, wife unto John Scudamore, brother to the aforesd William.

Children of Thomas Bourchier:
1. Elizabeth, wife of William Rokeby of Sandal in co. Ebor.
2. Abigall, wife of Andrew Taylor, a merchant in Yorke.

Children of Sir John Bourchier and Anne:
2. Will'm,
3. John, died unmarried.
Barrington Bourchier of Beningbrough, Esqr, ætatis 38 annorum 9° Sept. a° 1665. = Frances, eldest da. of Sr William Strickland of Boynton in com. Ebor. Kt and Bart.
1. Bridget, wife of Will'm Bethell of Swyneden in co. Ebor.
2. Dorothy, wife of Richard Beaumont, citizen of London.
3. Anne, wife unto Franc. Thompson, citizen of London.
4. Cath. wife unto John Eaton, citizen of London.
5. Eliz. wife of Gilbert Marshall of Sellaby in ye Bisshopprick of Durham.
6. Mary, wife of George Blakeston of Stapleton in co. Eborum.
7. Martha, wife unto John Blakeston of Newton in ye Bisshopprick of Durham.

Children of Barrington Bourchier and Frances:
Barrington Bourchier. eire, æt. 14 ann. 9° Sept. a° 1665.
Frances, died in her infancy.

Yorke, 9º *Sept.* 1665.

STAPYLTON OF MYTON.

ARMS.—Quarterly of eight:
1. Argent, a lion rampant sable.
2. Checky ...... and ......, a bordure ......, a canton ermine.
3. ...... fretty ....
4. Barry of six ...... and ......
5. Bendy of six ...... and ......
6. ...... on a fess ...... three fleurs-de-lis ......
7. Gules, between two flanches checky argent and azure, as many crosses pattée in pale of the second fimbriated or.
8. As the first.

...... daughter of Sr Marmaduke Constable of Everingham in com. Ebor, K^t^, first wife. = Sr Robert Stapylton of Wighill in co. Ebor. K^t^. = Oliva, daughter and coheir of Sr Henry Sherrington of Lacock in com. Wilts. K^t^, widow of John Talbot of Salwarp in com. Wigorn. Esqr, 2^d^ wife.

Children:

- Jane, wife of Christopher Wyvill, son of Sr Marmaduke Wyvill of Linton.
- Henry Stapleton of Wighill, Esqr. =
- 2. Robert.
- 3. William.
- 4. Edward.
- 1. Bryan Stapylton of Myton in com. Ebor. Esqr, died circa ann. 1658. = Frances, daughter of Sr Henry Slingesby of Scriven in com. Ebor. K^t^.
- 1. Oliva, wife of Sr Robert Dineley of ...... in com. Ebor. Kn^t^.
- 2. Ursula, wife of Sr Robert Baynard of Lackham in com. Wilts. Kn^t^.

Children of Bryan and Frances:

- 3. Miles Stapilton. = Elizabeth, daughter of ...... Hynde, citizen of London.
- 2. Robert Stapylton.
- 1. Sr Henry Stapylton of Myton, Bar^t^, æt. 48 an. 9 Sept. 1665. = Elizabeth, da. of Conyers Ld Darcy and Conyers of Hornby Castle in com. Eborum.
- 1. Oliva, wife of Sr Will. Vavasour of ......, K^t^ and Bar^t^, a younger son of Sr Thomas Vavasour, K^t^, Knight Marshall to King James.
- 2. Frances, wife of John Hutton, son and heire apparent of Mathew Hutton of Marske in co. Ebor. Esqr.
- 3. Ursula, wife of Thomas Pepys of Hatcham-Barnes in com. Surr. Esqr.

Children of Miles and Elizabeth:

1. Miles.
2. Brian.
3. Robert.

Children of Sr Henry and Elizabeth:

1. Henry Stapleton, æt. 9 ann. 9º Sept. aº 1665.
2. Brian.

1. Grace.
2. Ursula.
3. Margaret.
4. Elizabeth.
5. Frances.

OUSE AND DARWENT WAPENTAKE. *Yorke*, 9° *Sept.* 1665.

ROBYNSON OF THICKET.

ARMS.—Vert, on a chevron between three stags trippant or three cinquefoils gules, an annulet for difference.

CREST.—A stag trippant or, pellettée, attired of the first, gorged with a chaplet vert, on the breast an annulet azure.

John Robynson, Merchant of the Staple, and Alderm. of the Citty of London, died in February a° 1599. = Catherine, eldest daughter of Tho. Anderson, Citizen and Grocer of London.

Their children:

- 1. John Robinson of Ryther in com. Ebor. =
- 2. Henry.
- 3. Arthur.
- 4. Robert.
- 5. Humphry Robinson of ...... died in Sept. a° 1626. = Anne, daughter of Richard Pyot, Alderman of London.

Children of Humphry and Anne:

- 2. Humphry Robinson, died without issue.
- 1. Richard Robinson of Thicket in com. Ebor. Esqr, now one of his Maties Justices of the Peace in this county, æt. 52 an. 9 Sept. a° 1665. = Elizabeth, daughter unto John Bradley of Louthe in com. Lincoln, Esqr.
- 1. Elizabeth, first married to Will'm Breary, eldest son of William Breary, Alderman of Yorke; and after to Peter Bradley of Louthe in com. Linc.
- 2. Anne.

Children of Richard and Elizabeth:

- Jane, wife of Henry Edmunds of Worsbrough in co. Ebor. Esqr.
- Richard Robynson, son and heir, æt. 26 annorum 9 Sept. 1665. = Jane, daughter of John Aikeroyd of Folkerthorp in com. Ebor. Esqr.

Children of Richard and Jane:

- Elizabeth, æt. 2 an. et 6 mens.
- Humphrey, æt. 3 mensium 9° Sept. a° 1665.

HOLDERNESSE MIDDLE BAYLIWICK. *Hull*, 2° *Sept.* 1665.

DALTON OF SWYNE.

ARMS.—Azure, semée of cross-crosslets argent, a lion rampant gardant of the last.

CREST.—A dragon's head .... between two wings displayed ....

Robert Dalton of Myton, Sutton, South-Cotes, Stone-ferry and Dry-pole in Holdernesse, died in a°. 1626. = Elizabeth, eldest daughter and co-heire of Raphe Constable of North Park in Holdernesse.

5. Raphe, obijt sine prole.
6. James, a secular priest.
7. Ambrose, obijt sine prole.

2. Robert Dalton, a Carthusian Monke at Newport in Flanders.
3. Henry, obijt sine prole.
4. John Dalton of Barton sup. Humber in co. Linc.

1. Thomas Dalton of Myton, &c. died a° 1639. = Anne, daughter of John Ingleby, a younger son of S[r] Wm Ingleby of Ripley, K[t].

Anne, wife of Robert Bacon of Ferriby in com. Ebor.

3. Will'm, obijt sine prole.
4. Thomas.

1. John Dalton of Swine, Nuttles, Sutton, &c. Esqr, æt. 42 an. 2° Sept. 1665.
2. James Dalton, marr. Cath. daughter of James Clarke, Citizen and Chirurgeon of London.

1. Elizabeth, wife unto Samuell Snawsdell of ......
2. Catherine, wife of Robt Dickenson of Canwick juxta Lincolne, gen[t].

THE BOROUGH OF KINGSTON SUPER HULL. *Hull*, 4 *Sept.* 1665.

THOMPSON OF KINGSTON SUPER HULL.

ARMS.—Per fess argent and sable, a fess counter-embattled between three falcons, all counterchanged.

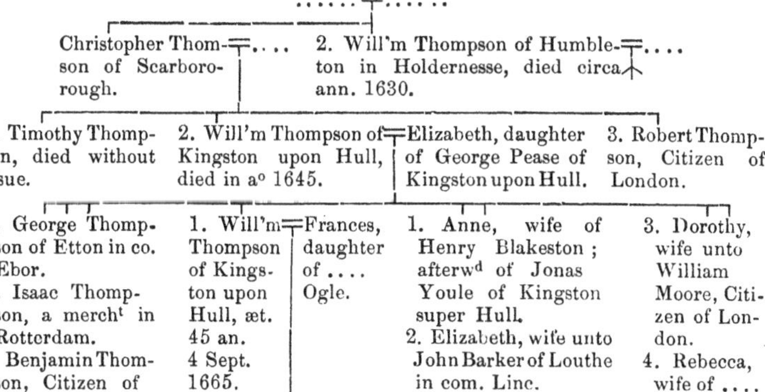

Elizabeth, æt. 16 ann. 4° Sept. a° 1664.

HUNSLOW BEACON WAPENTAKE. *Hull,* 2° *Sept.* 1665.

HILDYARD OF BEVERLEY.

ARMS.—Azure, three mullets or, on an inescutcheon the badge of a Baronet of England.

CREST.—A cock sable, crested wattled and membered gules.

Martin Hildyard of Wynestede in Holdernesse, Esqr. = Emme, daughter of Sr Robert Rudstone of London, Kn^t.

1. Sr Christopher Hildyard of Wynestede, K^t, living in a° 1584. = ...

2. Richard Hildyard of Routhe in Holdernesse. = Jane, daughter and heire of ...... Thweng of ......

Sr Christopher Hilyard, K^t, died circa ann. 1638. = Elizabeth, daughter and sole heire of Henry Welby of Gousell in com. Linc.

3. Christoph^r Hildyard, an Utter-Barrister of the Inner Temple.

Anne, daughter and coheir of Thomas Thackrey, Alderman of Hull, widow of Sr Edw. Mountfort of Bescote in com. Staff. Kn^t. = 2. Sr Robert Hildyard of Beverley, K^t & B^t, æt. 54 ann. 2 Sept. 1665. He was a Gentleman of y^e Privy-Chamber in Ordinary to K. Charles y^e 1st, as is also the like to K. Charles y^e 2^d. He was a Colonell of Foote in y^e Army of K. Charles y^e first, and commanded Sr Marmaduke Langdale's Brigade of Horse when he was Major-generall of all his late Majesties Horse in England and Wales. = Jane, da. of Christopher Constable of Hatfeild in com. Ebor. Esqr, widow of John Lyster, eldest son of Sr John Lyster, K^t.

1. Henry Hildyard of East Horsley in com. Surr. =

1. Elizabeth, died unmarried.
2 Anne, wife of Leonard Hildyard of Burstall in Holdernesse.
3. Susan, wife of Robert Moreton of Kingston upon Hull.
4. ....

2. Robert, æt. 23 ann.

1. Christopher, æt. 25 ann. 2° Sept. 1665.

Anne.

LANGBARGH WAPENTAKE. *Hull*, 5° *Sept*. 1665.

CRATHORNE OF CRATHORNE.

ARMS.—Quarterly:
1. Argent, on a saltire gules five crosses fleury or.
2. Sable, on a fess or between fourteen cross-crosslets argent three rooks of the field.
3. Argent, on a bend gules three escallops or.
4. Vert, a buck's head cabossed argent, between the attires a cross pattée of the last.

An escutcheon of pretence: Or, a fess counter-componée argent and azure between three eagle's heads erased of the last.

CREST.—On a mound vert a blackbird sable.

Thomas Crathorne of Crathorne in com. Ebor, Esqr, died a° 1637, or thereabouts. = Catherine, daughter & coheire of Edmond Richart of Swynington in com. Norff.

2. Edmund Crathorne of Hollins in Blakamore in com. Ebor., marr. .... daughtr of .... Cockerell. =

3. George, died unmarried.

Mary, sole daughter and heire of Robert Wright of Plowland in com. Eborum, first wife. = 1. Raphe Crathorne of Crathorne, Esqr, æt. 61 an. 5 Sept. 1665. = Margt, daughter of Robert Thorneton of Newton in com. Eborum, second wife.

1. Bridget, died unmarried.
2. Catherine.

Anne, wife of Gregory Grange of East Harlsey in com. Ebor.

1. Thomas Crathorne, son & heire, ætatis 42 ann. 5° Sept. a° 1665. = Frances, daughter of Charles Thimelby of Snidall in co. Ebor.

2. Raphe Crathorne, æt. 31 ann. 5 Sept. a° 1665.
3. Francis, æt. 26 ann. 1665.
4. John, æt. 23 ann. 1665.

Dorothy, wife unto Henry Swale, son & heire to Sr Solomon Swale of Swale Hall & South-Staineley in com. Ebor. Bart.

Thomas, æt. 8 an. 5 Sept. a°. 1665. 1. Mary. 2. Everild. 3. Catherine.

CLARO WAPENTAKE. *Yorke*, 12° *Sept.* 1665.

INGRAM OF CATTALL AND THORPE.

ARMS.—Ermine, on a fess gules three escallops or.
CREST.—On a perch ...... a parrot rising ......

Hugh Ingram, Mercht of London, died a° 1612. = Anne, daughter of ......

- Sr Arthur Ingram of Temple Newsom in com. Ebor. Knt.
- Sr William Ingram of the citty of Yorke, Kt, Dr of ye Civill Law, and of the King's Councell for the northern parts of this Realme, died a° 1623. = Catherine, daughter unto John Edmonds of Cambridge.
  - 3. Arthur Ingram of Kingston upon Hull in co. Ebor. ætatis 61 ann. 12 Sept. a° 1665. = Cath. daugh. of Edw. Caley of Brumpton in com. Ebor. Esqr.
    - Arthur Ingram of Thorpe on ye Hill in co. Ebor. æt. 28 ann. 12 Sept a° 1665. = Helen, daughter and heire of .... Gascoigne of Thorpe on ye Hill in co. Ebor. Esqr.
      - 2. Arthur.
      - 1. William, æt. 5 an. 12 Sept. 1665.
      - Essex, a daughter.
  - 2. Sr Will'm Ingram of Cattall parva in co. Ebor. Kt, æt. 65 an. 12 Sept. 1665. = Cath. daughter of Sr Edw. Grevill, late of Milcote in co. Warr. Knt.
  - 1. Hugh Ingram, citizen of London, now living, a° 1665. = ...
    - Will'm.
    - Mary, wife of ....
  - Anne, died unmarried.

YORKE CITTY. *Yorke*, 12° *Sept.* 1665.

AYSCOUGH OF YORKE.

ARMS.—Quarterly of ten:
1. Sable, a fess between three asses passant argent, a crescent for difference.
2. Argent, a saltire gules, on a chief of the second three cinquefoils or, a crescent for difference.
3. Vert, a cross counter-componée argent and gules.
4. Gules, two chevrons within a bordure or.
5. Sable, a chevron between three castles or, over all a label of three points argent.
6. Argent, three chevrons gules.
7. Ermine, two chevrons gules.
8. Gules, three mullets argent.
9. Argent, an inescutcheon within an orle of cinquefoils sable.
10. Vert, a saltire engrailed argent.

CREST.—An ass passant argent.

Sr Francis Ayscough of South-Kelsey in com. Linc. Knt. = ...

Sr Edward Ayscough of South-Kelsey in com. Linc. Knt. = ...

2. Francis Ayscough of Thorneton on the Moore in com. Linc. died circa ann. 1612. = Elizabeth, daughter of .... Hatcher of Carby in co. Linc. Dr of Phisick.

1. William Ayscough, eldest son, died in his father's lifetime.

John Ayscough, now residing in the Citty of Yorke, æt. 54 ann. 12 Sept. a° 1665. = Elizabeth, daughter of John Sherwood of Cambridge.

1. Francis, 2. John, died in their father's lifetime.

1. Elizabeth, 2. Catherine, 3. Jane, 4. Elizabeth, 5. Sarah, died young.

YORKE CITTY. *Yorke*, 12 *Sept.* 1665.

HERBERT OF YORKE.

ARMS.—Per pale azure and gules, three lions rampant argent within a bordure componée of the second and or, a canton of the last.

Richard Herbert came from Colebrooke in com. Monmouth, & resided in Yorkeshire. = Barbara, daughter of Christopher Pudsey of .... in Richmundshire.

2. Evan Herbert, buried in Christ's church in Yorke a° 1582. = ... daughter of ...... Aslaby.

1. Christopher Herbert, a Justice of Peace in y[e] Citty of Yorke, buried in Cruxchurche in Yorke a° 1589. = ...

Elizabeth, daughter and coheire of Thomas Thackray, a Merchant in Hull, 1 wife. = 2. Philip Herbert, Shireeve of Yorke a° 1633. = Ellen, daughter of Charles Tankard of Whixley, Esq[r], 2[d] wife.

1. John Herbert of the Citty of Yorke Merchant, buried in Christ's-church a° 1587. = Eufemia, daughter of George Wrightson of Alne in co. Ebor.

2. Thomas Herbert, borne a° 1629.

1. Philip Herbert, now Shireeve of the Citty of Yorke, æt. 39 an. 12 Sept. 1665. = Mary, daughter of Raphe Bell of Thruske in com. Ebor.

Thomas Herbert, Shireeve of the Citty of Yorke, a° 1634, ob. s. prole. = Sarah, daughter of William Breary, Alderman of Yorke.

1. Philip Herbert, ætatis 3 annorum 12 Sept. 1665.

2. Thomas, æt. 2 an. 1665.

HANGWEST WAPENTAKE. *Yorke*, 13° *Sept* 1665.

TOPHAN OF AGLETHORPE.

ARMS.—Argent, a chevron gules between three crane's heads erased sable.
CREST.—Two serpents proper entwined around a cross pattée fitchée or.

Edward Tophan of Aglethorpe in com. Ebor. Esqr, died about the yeare 1628. = Anne, daughter of John Scroope of Danby in co. Ebor.

2. Henry Tophan, Lieuten^{t} Colonell to Colonell Evers of a Regiment of Horse for the service of King Charles the first, & slayne at the battail of Marston Moore in co. Ebor. a° 1644, unmarried.

1. Francis Tophan of Aglethorpe, Esqr, died circa annū 1644. = Mary, daughter of Sr Edward Payler of Thoraby in co. Ebor. Bar^{t}.

1. Margery, the wife of Christopher Croft of Coverham in co. Ebor.
2. Eliz. wife to George Hemsworth of Roche in co. Ebor.

3. Anne,
4. Petronell, died unmarried.

2. Francis Tophan of Aglethorpe in com. Ebor. ætatis 34 ann. 13 Sept. a° 1665. = Clara, daughter of Lionell Robinson, a Barrister of the Middle Temple, London.

1. Edward Tophan, died in a° 1651, vel circa, sine prole. = Mary, daughter of Sr Peter Middleton of Stockheld in co. Ebor. Kn^{t}.

Anne, wife of Constable Bradshaw of Upsall in Cleveland.

1. Lyonell Tophan, ætatis 9 annorum 13 Sept. 1665.
2. Edward.
3. Francis.

BULMER WAPENTAKE. *Yorke*, 13 *Sept*. 1665.

HALL OF EAST LILLING.

ARMS.—Argent, a fess between two greyhounds courant sable.
CREST.—On a chapeau gules turned up ermine a greyhound sejant of the last.

Will'm Hall of Lenthrop in Swillington in com. Ebor. = Elizabeth, daughter and heire of Thomas Croswayte of Bawthorpe in com. Ebor.

5. Henry Hall, 5th son, Citizen and Alderman of Yorke. = ...

Henry Hall of East Lilling in com. Eboru. died a° 1622. = Mary, daughter of Will'm Towrye, of Kirby-Grindall in co. Ebor.

2. Francis Hall of Dunnington in com. Ebor.

1. Henry Hall of East Lilling in com. Ebor. æt. 45 an. 13 Sept. 1665. = Mary, daughter of William Hobson of Siston in com. Linc.

1. Alice, wife of John Ridgley of Brough in com. Linc.

2. Mary, wife of Dr Witty, D^{r} of Phisick, now residing in Yorke.

THE COUNTIE OF THE CITTY OF YORKE. *Yorke*, 13 *Sept.* 1665.

WICKHAM OF BOLTON-PERCY.

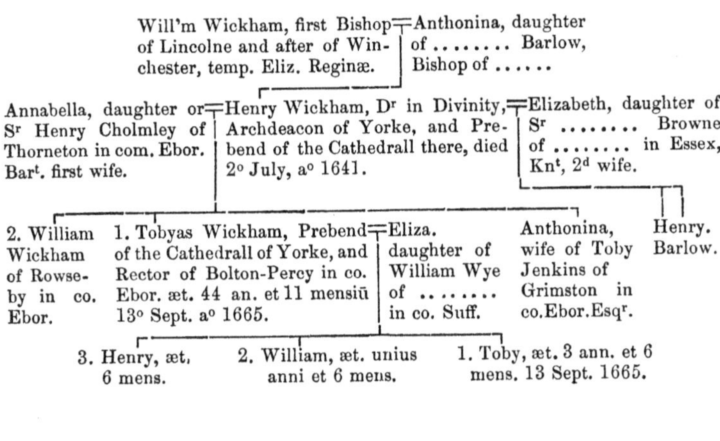

THE AINSTY OF YORKE. *Yorke*, 13 *Sept.* 1665.

SNAWSELL OF BILTON.

ARMS.—Quarterly:
1 and 4. Argent, on a chevron between three leopard's faces sable as many cross-crosslets fitchée of the field.
2. and 3. Argent, on a bend sable cotised gules three fleurs-de-lis of the field.

Hugh Snawsell of Bilton in co. Ebor. Esqr, died 29° Aug. a° 1661. = Isabell, daughter of Sr Thomas Beaumont of Stoughton in com. Leic. Kt.

3. John Snawsell, a Merchant of Turky.
4. Hugh died unmarried.

2. Thomas Snawsell of Bilton, Esqr, æt. 47 an. 13 Sept. 1665. = Anne, daugh. of Franc. Staresmore of Frowlsworth in com. Leic. Esqr.

1. Robert, died unmarried.

Elizabeth, wife of Sr John Anderson of Broughton in co. Linc. Bart.

YORKE CITTY. *Yorke*, 12 *Sept.* 1665.

BIGGE OF YORKE.

ARMS.—Ermine, on a fess engrailed between three martlets sable as many annulets or.

CREST.—On a wreath argent and sable a demi-eagle murally crowned ermine with wings displayed azure.

See the Visit. of Essex for proofe of these armes, there being none made.

Will'm Bigge of Shalford in com. Essex. = Anne, daughter of .... Jernegan.

Mathew Bigge, Vicar of St Martin's in Coney Street, in y[e] Citty of Yorke, æt. 55 ann. 12 Sept. 1665. = Frances, daughter unto John Shewood of Cambridge.

Will'm Bigge of Shalford in Essex. = ...

2. Roger.

Mathew Bigge, ætatis 30 ann. 12 Sept. 1665. = Mary, daughter of Will'm Blytheman of Newlathes in com. Ebor.

1. Sarah.
2. Elizabeth.
3. Dorcas.

YORKE CITTY. *Yorke*, 12 *Sept.* 1665.

OGLETHORPE OF OGLETHORPE.

ARMS.—Argent, a chevron between three boar's heads couped sable.

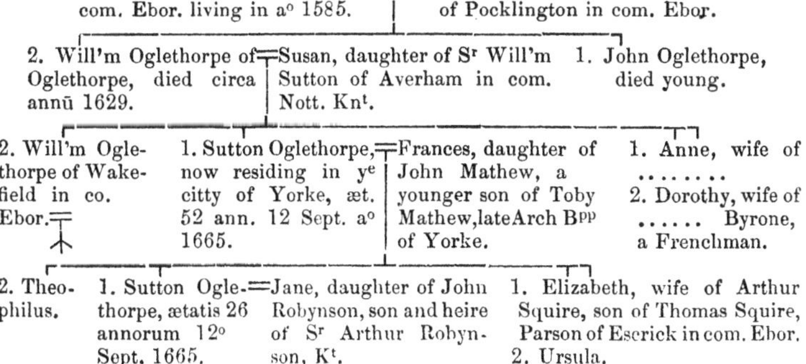

Will'm Oglethorpe of Oglethorpe in com. Ebor. living in a[o] 1585. = ... daughter of ...... Sotheby of Pocklington in com. Ebor.

2. Will'm Oglethorpe of Oglethorpe, died circa annū 1629. = Susan, daughter of Sr Will'm Sutton of Averham in com. Nott. Kn[t].

1. John Oglethorpe, died young.

2. Will'm Oglethorpe of Wakefield in co. Ebor. =

1. Sutton Oglethorpe, now residing in y[e] citty of Yorke, æt. 52 ann. 12 Sept. a[o] 1665. = Frances, daughter of John Mathew, a younger son of Toby Mathew, late Arch B[pp] of Yorke.

1. Anne, wife of ....
2. Dorothy, wife of ...... Byrone, a Frenchman.

2. Theophilus.

1. Sutton Oglethorpe, ætatis 26 annorum 12[o] Sept. 1665. = Jane, daughter of John Robynson, son and heire of Sr Arthur Robynson, K[t].

1. Elizabeth, wife of Arthur Squire, son of Thomas Squire, Parson of Escrick in com. Ebor.
2. Ursula.

STRAFFORD AND TICKHILL WAPENTAKE. *Rotherum*, 16 *Sept*. 1665.

HUNT OF STAINTON.

ARMS.—........ a bugle horn ...., on a chief .... three roses ....

Qu. the coloures in the Visit. of Lincolnsh. and Northton?

Nathaniell Hunt of Swaby in com. Lincoln. = Mary, daughter of Sr John Bolles of Louth in com. Linc. Knt.

all in Ireland or forrein countries: 2. Nathaniell, 3. Nicholas, 4. Zachary, 5. Edward, 6. Francis,

5. Abraham Hunt of Stainton in com. Ebor. æt. 24 an. 16 Sept. 1665. = Judith, daughter of .... Man of ye Isle of Man.

1. John Hunt of Skegmarsh in co. Linc. eldest son. = ...

Mary, wife of Roger Fretwell of Maltby in com. Ebor.

BULMER WAPENTAKE. *Yorke*, 13 *Sept*. 1665.

BELT OF OVERTON.

ARMS.—Gules, on a chevron argent between three bezants a cross pattée fitchée between two mullets pierced azure.

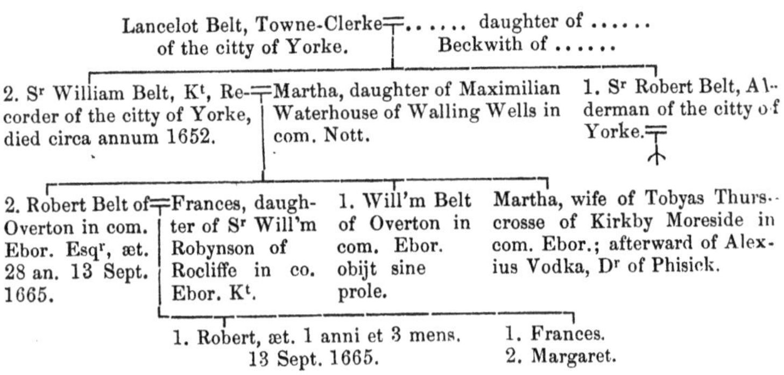

Lancelot Belt, Towne-Clerke of the citty of Yorke. = ... daughter of ...... Beckwith of ......

2. Sr William Belt, Kt, Recorder of the citty of Yorke, died circa annum 1652. = Martha, daughter of Maximilian Waterhouse of Walling Wells in com. Nott.

1. Sr Robert Belt, Alderman of the citty of Yorke. =

2. Robert Belt of Overton in com. Ebor. Esqr, æt. 28 an. 13 Sept. 1665. = Frances, daughter of Sr Will'm Robynson of Rocliffe in co. Ebor. Kt.

1. Will'm Belt of Overton in com. Ebor. obijt sine prole.

Martha, wife of Tobyas Thurscrosse of Kirkby Moreside in com. Ebor.; afterward of Alexius Vodka, Dr of Phisick.

1. Robert, æt. 1 anni et 3 mens. 13 Sept. 1665.

1. Frances.
2. Margaret.

YORKE CITTY. *Yorke, 13° Sept. 1665.*

AYSCOUGH OF YORKE.

ARMS.—Quarterly :
1 and 4. Sable, a fess or between three asses passant argent, a crescent for difference.
2 and 3. .... a fret ......, a crescent for difference.

CREST.—An ass's head argent, charged with a crescent gules.

Richard Ascough, buried at Bedall in com. Ebor. = ... daughter of Sr John Bassingburne.

Robert Ascough of Pot-grange in com. Ebor. = ...

John Ascough of Cowling in com. Ebor. Esqr, died 3 H. 6. = ...

Richard Ascough of Pot-grange. = Mary, daughter of Thomas Lascells of Brakenburgh, Esqr.

1. Robert Ascough. = Isabell, daughter of Tho. Strangwayes, Esqr. 2. Thomas. 3. John.

William Ascough of Pot-grange, Esqr. = ...

5. Thomas. 6. Miles. 7. Laurence.

2. Guy. 3. John. 4. Henry.

1. Raphe Ascough of Pot-grange Esqr. = ... daughter of .... Thackwreye of Sykesworth in com. Eborum.

1. Jane, wife of .... Steele. 2. Eliz. wife of .... Walker.

1. John Ascough of Pot-grange. = Alice, daughter of .... Cooper.

2. John. 3. Thomas.

3. Christopher Ayscough, Citizen of London. =

2. Thomas Ayscough, sometime Shireeve of Yorke. = Ursula, da. of Robt Sandwich of Yorke, 1 wife, ob. s. p.

1. Robert Ayscough, twice Ld Mayor of the Citty of Yorke. = Eliz. daugh. & sole heire of Tho. Cartmele of Yorke.

Margaret, wife of .... Barton of Yorke. Maudlin, wife of John Ascough of Kilburne ; afterwards of Tho. Browne.

Thomas. Christopher. Alice.

1. Eliz. wife of Richard Hodgson of Cherry Burton in York co. Ebor. 2. Catherine, wife of Robert Meares of Yorke.

1. Sr Robert Ayscough, Kt, twice Ld Mayor of Yorke, ob. s. prole. 2. Thomas, obijt sine prole. 4. Philip Ayscough of Yorke.

3. George Ascough of Yorke, died ao 1626. = Sarah, daughter of Leonard Belt of the Citty of Yorke.

William Ayscough, died unmarried.

1. Robert Ayscough of the City of Yorke, æt. 59 an. 13 Sept. ao 1665. = Elizabeth, da. & heire of Thomas Peake of Toynton in co. Linc.

1. Mary, wife of Josias Bellwood Clerke. = ; son: Roger.

2. Elizabeth, wife of Christopher Geldart, a Merchant in Yorke ; after of Abraham Bynns, Merchant in Yorke. 3. Frances, wife of John Morret, Citizen of London. 4. Anne, wife of Anth. Plaice of Yorke.

Robert Ayscough.

1. Will'm Ayscough, Dr of Phisick, æt. 29 an. 13 Sept. ao 1665.

1. Elizabeth. 2. Martha, died young. 3. Mary.

BULMER WAPENTAKE. *Yorke*, 9° *Sept*. 1665.

SCUDAMORE OF OVERTON.

ARMS.—Gules, three stirrups leathered and buckled or, in chief a cinquefoil argent,

Thomas Scudamore of Overton in com. Ebor. died in Aprill a° 1621. = Mary, daughter to John Jenkins of the City of Yorke Esqr.

- 7. Richard.
- 3. Francis, 5. Thomas, 6. Edward, obierunt sine prole.
- 4. Hugh Scudamore, Rector of Holtby in com. Ebor. =
- 2. John Scudamore of Burstallgarth in com. Ebor. =
- 1. Will'm Scudamore of Overton, died 4 Apr. a° 1661. = Eliz. 2^d daugh. of Will. Bourchier of Beningbrough-grange in co. Ebor. Esqr.
- 1. Jane, wife of Charles Menill of Hornby in co. Ebor. Esqr. 2. Eliz. wife of William Manby of Hutton Cranswike in co. Ebor.

Children of Will'm and Eliz.:

- 2. William Scudamore. 3. Henry Scudamore.
- 1. Thomas Scudamore of Overton, æt. 49 ann. 9° Sept. a° 1665.
- Mary.

HUNSLOW BEACON WAPENTAKE. *Yorke*, 9° *Sept*. 1665.

ORME OF SOUTH-NEWBOLD.

ARMS.—.......... six escallops .... three, two, and one.

No proofe made of the armes.

Robert Orme of Elston in com. Nott. = Jane, sister of Sr John Meares of the manour in Kirton, in Holland in com. Linc.

Robert Orme of Elston in com. Nott. = Barbara, sister to Sr Will'm Sutton of Averham in com. Nott. K^t.

- Robert Orme of South-Newbold on the Woulds in co. Ebor. æt. 63 an. 9° Sept. a° 1665. = Frances, daughter of Sr John Vavasour of Spaldington in com. Ebor. K^t.
- Barbara, wife of Will'm Leat[illegible] of Newarke upon Trent; afterwards of Henry Drewell of Headley in com. Ebor.

Children of Robert and Frances:

- 2. Thomas Orme of Copenthorp in co. Ebor. = Frances, daughter of Thomas Bankes of Bilbrough in com. Ebor.
  - John, æt. 3 annorū 9 Sept. 1665.
  - Barbara, ætatis 2 annorum.
- 1. Robert Orme, son and heire, æt. 28 annor. 9° Sept. 1665. = Frances, daughter of Sr Ferdinando Lee o[f] Middleton in com. Ebor. Kn^t.
  - John, æt. unius anni 9° Sept. a° 1665.

BETHELL OF ELLERTON AND FALTHROP.

ARMS.—Argent, on a chevron between three boar's heads couped sable an etoile of the field.

CREST.—A demi-eagle with wings displayed azure, on the breast an etoile or.

Nicholas Bethell of Maydenhead in com. Heref. = ...

3. Sr Walter Bethell of Alne in com. Ebor. K^t, died in January a° 1623. = Mary, daughter of Sr Henry Slingsby of Scriven in com. Ebor. K^t.

1. Will'm, 2. John, } died without issue.

Children of Sir Walter and Mary:

1. Elizabeth, died unmarried.
2. Frances, wife of Sr George Marwood of Busby in Cleveland, Bar^t.
3. Mary, wife of Thomas Hesket of Heslington in com. Ebor. Esqr.
4. Matilda, wife of Robert Goodwyn, a Divine in Norf.

1. Sr Hugh Bethell of Ellerton in com. Ebor. K^t, died in January a° 1662. = Frances, daughter of William Franklyn of Thirkelby in com. Ebor. Esqr.

2. Henry Bethell of Falthrop in com. Ebor. Esqr, now one of his Maties Justices of Peace in this county, æt. 59 ann. 9° Sept. a° 1665.

3. Slingesby Bethell, a Merchant. = Mary, daughter of ..... Burrell of ..... in co. Hunt.

4. Walter Bethell. = Mary, daughter of Sr John Poynes of Acton in co. Glouc. Kn^t.

5. Will'm Bethell, Rector of Kirkby-Overblows in com. Ebor. = Bridget, da. of Sr John Bourchier of Beningbrough-grange in co. Ebor. K^t.

6. Nicholas, died without issue. = Frances, daughter of Sr Anthony Dering of Pluckley in Kent.

Children of Sir Hugh and Frances:

2. Henry Bethell.
3. Hugh Bethell.
4. William Bethell.

Anne, daughter of Sr George Palmes of Naburne in co. Ebor. K^t, first wife. = 1. Walter Bethell of Ellerton, Esqr, æt. 37 an. 9 Sept. a° 1665. = Mary, daughter of Peter Vavasour of Spaldington in com. Ebor.

1. Mary.
2. Lucie, wife of John Mattrum of Bisshops-Dike in co. Ebor.
3. Ursula, wife of John Palleser of Newby super Wiske in co. Ebor.
4. Frances.
5. Elizabeth.

Child of Walter and Anne: Mary.

Child of Walter and Mary: Hugh, æt. 7 annor. 9 Sept. a° 1665.

Children of Will'm and Bridget:

1. William, ætatis 14 annorum 9 Sept. a° 1665.
2. Bourchier.
3. Walter.
4. Slingesby.
5. Nicholas.
6. Hugh.

1. Anna.
2. Frances.

THE ANSTY. *Yorke, 9° Sept.* 1665.

LACOCK OF COPPENTHORPE.

ARMS.—Argent, a chevron between three cocks gules.

No proofe made of the armes.

Richard Laycock of Leedes in co. Ebor. = ... daughter of Sr Richard Brooke of Norton in com. Cestr. K^t.

Martin Laycock of Leedes in co. Ebor. = Frances, daughter of Rich. Walker of Leedes.

2. Martin Laycock of Leedes. = Eliz. daughter of . . . . Clapham of Beamsley in com. Ebor.

Mary, da. of . . . . . . Pollard of . . . . . . in com. Ebor. first wife. = Walter Laycock of Leedes, cheif Aulnager to y^e Northern Counties of England, died 18 Oct. a° 1634. = Eliz. daughter of John Wood of Wetherby in co. Ebor. gen^t, second wife.

1. Dorothy, wife of Edw. Fairfax, broth^r to Tho. 1st Visc. Fairfax of Cameron.
2. Mary, wife unto William Pannet, a Merchant in Yorke.

1. Frances, wife unto Francis Shan of Medley in com. Ebor.
2. Mary, wife of Edward Burbeck of Orton in co. Westmerl.
3. Eliz. wife of Robert Sykes of Loftus in com. Ebor.

1. Richard,
2. William,
3. Martin,
died unmarried.

Walter Laycock of Coppenthorpe in com. Ebor., one of the Captaines of his Maties Trayned Bands for y^e county of Yorke, ætatis 36 ann. 9 Sept. 1665. = Thomasine, daughter unto William Bilbye of Micklethwayt grange in com. Ebor. Esqr.

6. Peter.
7. Will'm.
8. Thomas.

3. Francis.
4. Richard.
5. Martin.

1. Walter, æt. 15 ann. 9 Sept. a° 1665.
2. John.

1. Susan.
2. Thomasine.

BULMER WAPENTAKE. *Yorke*, 12° *Sept.* 1665.

LOVELL OF SKELTON.

ARMS.—Argent, a chevron sable between three wolf's heads erased gules.
CREST.—A talbot courant argent.

Thomas Lovell of Skelton in com. Ebor. Esqr. died in the 20th yeare of Qu. Eliz. vel circa. = Jane, daughter of William Hungate Esqr.

Thomas Lovell of Skelton Esqr. died a° 1603. = Mary, daughter of Christopher Herbert of Yorke.

1. Isabell, wife of .... Blundell, citizen of Lond.
2. Eliz. wife of Robert Jackson of ...... in y^e Bpprick of Durham.
3. Mary, wife of Seth Lasenby of Earswick in co. Ebor.

1. Thomas Lovell of Skelton Esqr, died in a° 1655. = Mary, daughter of John Boothe of Burnham in com. Linc.

2. John Lovell, citizen of Yorke.
3. Marmaduke Lovell of Leedes in com. Ebor. died without issue.
4. Philip Lovell, a Merchant in the Barbados.

2. Will'm Lovell, marr. Anne, daughter of Roger Cockhill of Brigg in com. Linc.
3. John Lovell, of Tadcaster in co Ebor. marr. Mary, daughter of Francis Cundell citizen of Yorke.

1. Thomas Lovell of Skelton Esqr, æt. 45 ann. 12. Sept. a° 1665. = Philadelpha, daughter of Thomas Atkinson citizen of Yorke.

1. Frances, wife of Thomas Cockhill, of Brigg in com. Linc.
2. Beatrice, wife of Arthur Atkinson of Skelton in co. Ebor.
3. Susanna, wife of Will'm Belt of Overton in com. Ebor. Esqr.; 2dly of Edward Stanhope of Grimston in com. Ebor. Esqr.; lastly of Sr Henry Thompson of the citty of Yorke Kn^t.
4. Hesther, wife of Benjamin Masterman citizen of Yorke.

John, æt. 6 ann. 12 Sept. 1665.

Philadelphia, ætatis 3 ann. a° 1665.

BIRDFORTH WAPENTAKE. *Yorke*, 13 *Sept.* 1665.

MORE OF ANGRAM GRANGE.

ARMS.—Argent, a chevron sable between three heath-cocks of the second crested and wattled gules.

CREST.—A Moor's head in profile sable, the temples bound with a wreath knotted behind gules and argent.

James More of Angram grange in com. Ebor. a Justice of the Peace in the borough of Rippon, ætatis 67 annorum, 13 Sept. 1665. = Anne, daughter and coheire of Mich. Ascough of Angram in com. Ebor.

2. Will'm More of How in com. Ebor. now Clerke of ye Peace for ye North-Riding of Yorkshire. = Eleanor, daughter and sole heire of John Raper of of How.

1. Thomas More, an Utter Barrister of the Inner Temple London, ætatis 36 an. 13 Sept. a° 1665. = Margt, daughter of Sr Raphe Blakeston of Gibside in the Bisshoprick of Durham, Bt.

1. Anne, wife unto John Ernley of Cockwould, in co. Ebor. gent.
2. Dorothy, wife of Alan Chambers of Oulston in com. Ebor. gent.
3. Mary.

2. James, æt. 6 ann.
1. Thomas, æt. 7 an. 13 Sept. a° 1665.
1. Bridget, ætatis 4 ann.
2. Mary, æt. unius anni et dim.

YORKE CITTY. *Yorke*, 12 *Sept.* 1665.

NESBIT OF YORKE.

ARMS.—Argent, three boar's heads couped azure langued gules, a crescent for difference.

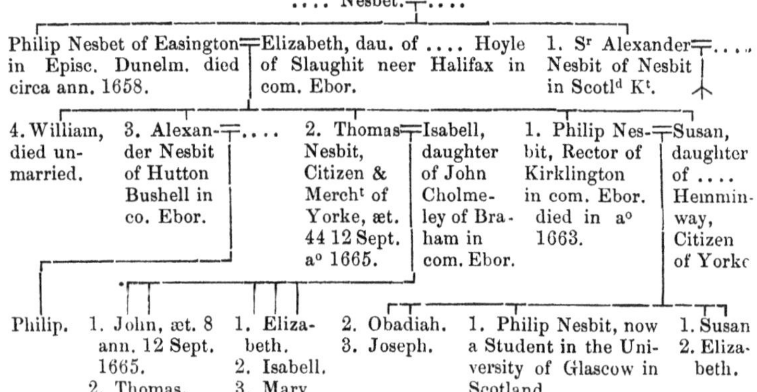

CLARO WAPENTAKE. *Yorke*, 13 *Sep*. 1665.

GOODRICK OF RIBSTAN.

ARMS.—Argent, on a fess gules between two lions passant gardant sable a fleur-de-lis of the field between as many crescents or.

CREST.—A demi-lion rampant regardant erminois, holding in his paws a battle-axe or.

S[r] Henry Goodrick of Ribston in com. Ebor. Kn[t], died in Julij a° D'ni 1641. = Jane, daughter of Sr John Savile of Medley in co. Ebor. K[t], one of y[e] Barons of y[e] Exchequer.

9. Sr Francis Goodrick of Manby in co. Linc. K[t], now living a° 1665.	Elizabeth, daugh. and coheir of Stephen Norcliffe of ...... in com. Ebor. Esq[r], 1st wife. =	8. S[r] John Goodrick of Ribston, K[t] and B[t], æt. 48 ann. 13 Sept. a° 1665. =	Eliz. Vicountesse Emley in y[e] Realme of Ireland, da. of Alex. Smith of Stulton in com. Suff. Esq[r], relict of Will. Ld Fairfax Visc. Emlay in Ireland (of Gilling Castle in co. Ebor.)	3. Toby, 4. Edward, 5. Thomas, 6. Rouland, died young.	1. Richard, 2. Henry, 7. Savile, died unmarried.	1. Mary, wife of S[r] Richard Hawkesworth of Hawkesworth in co. Ebor. Kn[t].	2. Jane, died young. 3. Elizabeth, died unmarried.

Henry Goodrick, æt. 22 an. 13 Sept. 1665. (son of Sr John and Elizabeth)

John Goodrick, æt. 10 an. 13 Sept. 1665. (son of Sr John and Eliz.)

LANGBARGH WAPENTAKE. *Yorke*, 13° *Sept.* 1665.

MARWOOD OF LITTLE BUSKEBY.

ARMS.—Gules, a chevron ermine between three goat's heads erased argent.
CREST.—On a mound vert a ram couchant argent attired or.

James Marwood of Nunthorpe in com. Eborum. = ... daughter of James Cleasby of Cleasby in co. Ebor.

2. Henry Marwood of Little Buskeby, heire to his brother, died about the yeare 1639. = Anne, daughter of John Constable of Dromonby in com. Ebor. Esqr.

1. William Marwood of Little Buskeby, died without issue.

1. Margerie, wife of .... Warde of Nunthorpe.
2. Dorothy, wife of .... Winterton of .... in com. Warr.

1. Anne, wife of Gyles Wetherell of Stockton in com. palat. Dunelm.
2. Barbara, wife of Josias Mathews, grandson to Toby Mathews, Archbysshop of Yorke.

1. Sr George Marwood of Little Buskeby in com. Ebor. Bar^t^, æt. 64 an. 13 Sept. 1665. = Frances, daugh. of Sr Walter Bethell of Alne in com. Ebor. K^t^.

2. William Marwood of Stubby in co. Linc.
3. Francis Marwood, Citizen of London.

2. George Marwood, a Hamborough Merchant.
3. Walter.

Margaret, daugh. of Conyers Ld Darcy and Conyers, 1. wife. = 1. Henry Marwood Esqr. ætatis 30 annor. 13° Sept. a° 1665. = Dorothy, daughter of Alan Bellingham of Levens in com. Westmerland Esqr. 2. wife.

1. Barbara, wife of Sr Thomas Heblethwayt of Norton in co. Ebor. Kn^t^.
2. Frances, wife of Richard Weston, an Utter Barrister of Grayes Inne.
3. Anna, wife of Will. Metcalfe of Allerton in co. Ebor. Esqr.

Margaret, æt. 4 an. 13 Sept. a° 1665.

George, æt. 5 mens. 13 Sept. 1665.

BAYNTON-BEACON WAPENTAKE. *Yorke*, 12 *Sept.* 1665.

CROMPTON OF SUNDERLANDWYKE.

ARMS.—...... a fess wavy ...... between three lions rampant ......, a mullet for difference.
No proofe made of these armes.

Thomas Crompton of Houndslow in co. Middlesex. = ... daughter of ...... Hudson.

...... daughter of ...... Culverwell of Cherriburton in com. Ebor. 1st wife. = ... daughter of .... Holdenby, 2d wife. = Robert Crompton, a Clerke in the Alienation Office in London, afterwards resided at Great Driffeild in com. Ebor. and died there Sept. 1646. = Ceziah, daughter of Walter Strickland of Boynton in co. Ebor. Esqr, 3d wife.

1. Mary, wife of George Fairweather of Cottingham in co. Ebor.	2. Frances, wife of .... Williamson of Cottingham in co. Ebor.	1. Thomas Crompton of Great Driffeild in com. Ebor. 2. John.	4. Walter Crompton of Sunderlandwyke in com. Eborum, æt. 32 ann. 12° Sept. 1665.	= Anne, da. of John Pearson of Settrington in com. Ebor.	3. Robt Crompton, married Anne, daughter of .... Wheale of Hingerwell in co. Ebor.	3. Anne, wife of Arthur Jegon of .... in co. Ebor. 4. Ceziah, wife of Inglebert Leedes of North-Milford in co. Ebor.

YORKE CITTY. *Yorke*, 13 *Sept.* 1665.

HULEY OF YORKE.

ARMS.—Argent, three piles sable, one issuing from the chief and two from the base, a crescent for difference.
No proofe made.

John Hule of ...... in Cheshire, came first into Yorkeshire with Edwyne Sands, Arch-Bpp of Yorke. = ...

Ellen, daughter of ...... Warde of .... 1st wife. = Thomas Hule of Wistow in com. Ebor. died circa annum 1615. = Anne, daughter of ...... of .... in .... 2d wife.

John Hewley of Wistow, died circa annū 1630. = Dorothy, daughter of John Wood of Copmanthorpe in com. Civit. Ebor. | Anne, wife of William Smith of Cawood in com. Ebor.

Sr John Hewley of the Citty of Yorke, Kt, æt. 46 an. 13° Sept. 1665. = Sarah, sole daughter and heire of Robert Wolriche of Grayes Inne Esqr. | Margaret, wife of John Baynes of Wistow in com. Eborum.

1. Wolriche,
2. John, } died young.

OUSE AND DARWENT WAPENTAKE. *Yorke*, 12 *Sept.* 1665.

JAQUES OF ELVINGTON.

ARMS.—Sable, on a fess engrailed argent between three escallops or a lion passant of the field.

CREST.—A lion's head erased gules langued azure, pierced through the neck with a sword argent hilted and pomelled or.

Sr Roger Jaques, Kt, Ld Mayor of ye Citty of Yorke ao 1639, died circa an. 1654. = Mary, daughter to Sr Marmaduke Rawdon of Hodsden in com. Midd. Knt.

- 4. Will'm Jaques, a Merchant of London.
- 5. Robert.
- 3. John Jaques, died unmarried.
- Anne, da. of Sr William Allason of the Citty of Yorke, Kt, 1 wife. = 2. Henry Jaques. = ... da. of ..... Dawson of Heworth in com. Ebor. 2 wife.
- 1. Roger Jaques of Elvington in com. Ebor. Esqr, æt. 35 ann. 12 Sept. ao 1665. = Frances, da. of John Lockton of Swinsted in co. Linc.
    - Mary.
    - Roger Jaques, æt. 14 ann. 12 Sept. 1665.
- 1. Eliz. wife of John Robynson of Rither in com. Ebor. Esqr.
- 2. Mary, wife of ..... Taylor, a Divine.
- 3. ..... wife of Charles Allason, eldest son of Sr William Allason, Kt.

STRAFFORD AND TICKHILL WAPENTAKE. *Rotheram*, 16 *Sept*. 1665.

JESSOP OF BROMEHALL.

ARMS.—Quarterly:
1 and 4. Barry of six argent and azure, on each piece of the first three mullets gules. Jessop.
2 and 3. ...... a chevron vair between three stags trippant ...... Swift.

CREST.—A turtle-dove argent, neck and wings azure, standing upon an olive-branch vert.

Richard Jessop of Bromehall in com. Ebor. a° 1575. = Anne, daughter and coheire of Robert Swift Esqr, and of Helen his wife, daughter and heire of Nicholas Wickersley.

William Jessop of Bromehall, ætatis 13 ann. a° 1575. = ...

Wortley Jessop of Bromehall, drowned at sea. = ... daughter of .... D'Oyle.

George Jessop of Brantcliffe in com. Ebor. =

Anne, wife of ...... Wade of ......

William Jessop of Bromehall, died in a° 1641. = Jane, daughter of Sr Francis South of Kelsterne in co. Linc. Kn[t].

2. Will'm, died unmarried.

1. Francis Jessop of Bromehall in co. Ebor. ætatis 27 ann. 16 Sept. 1665. = Barbara, daughter of Robert Eyre of Highlow in com. Derb. Esqr.

Anne.

William, æt. 6 mensium 16 Sept. 1665.

STAINECROSSE WAPENTAKE. *Barnesley*, 15 *Sept*. 1665.

MONKETON OF HODROYD.

ARMS.—Sable, on a chevron or between three martlets ...... as many mullets of the field, a canton argent.

Marmaduke Monketon of Cavell in com. Ebor. = Elizabeth, daughter of Matt. Wentworth of Breton Hall in co. Ebor. Esqr.

2. John Monketon of Garton & of Burland in com. Ebor. died in a° 1625. = Susanna, daughter of William Berrye of Walesby in com. Linc.

1. Philip Monketon, son and heire. =

4. Marmaduke Monketon of Hodroyde in com. Ebor. a Capt of Foote in the Army of the late King Charles y[e] first, æt. 42 ann. 15 Sept. a° 1665, who hath now assumed y[e] Sirname of Berry by a speciall Covenant made in marriage wth Mary his wife, and by y[e] last will and Testament of Richard Berry her father. = Mary, sole da. of Rich. Berry of Hodroyd in co. Ebor. & heire.

3. Edmond, of whom there is now no issue remayning.

2. John Monkton of Melton super montem in co. Ebor. a Major of Foot in the Army of K. Charles the 1st, died circa ann. 1653. = Mary, daughter of Samuell Oldfeild of Oldfeild in co.....

1. William Monkton, died unmarried.

Elizabeth, æt. 13 an. et 10 mens. 15 Sept. 1665.

BULMER WAPENTAKE. *Yorke*, 13 *Sept*. 1665.

WEDDELL OF EARSWICK.

ARMS.—Gules, on a chevron counter-embattled or, between three martlets argent, an eagle displayed between two escallops sable.

The proofe of these armes respited.

Leonard Weddall of Clifton in com. Ebor.=. . . . .

1\. . . . . wife of Robert Shaw of Ipswich in Suffolke.
2\. Margaret, wife of William Stot, Alderman of Yorke.
3\. . . . wife of John Richardson of Wharram Percy in co. Ebor.
4\. Mary, wife of John Lasenby of Huntington in co. Eborum.
5\. Jane, wife of John Mason a Merchant of Yorke.

1\. Robert Weddall, obijt sine prole.

2\. Will'm Weddall of Earswick in co. Ebor. died in July a° 1665.=Marg[t]. daughter of John Lyster of Kingston super Hull.

3\. Leonard Weddall, obijt sine prole.

2\. Leonard.

1\. William Weddall of Earswick, Esqr, æt. 31 an. 13 Sept. a° 1665, now one of his Maties Justice of the Peace for this county.=Margaret, the daughter of Sr Will'm Robynson of Rocliffe in com. Ebor. Kn[t].

Margaret, wife of John Agar of Huntington in co. Ebor.

Metcalfe Weddell, son and heire, æt. 5 an. et 6 mens. 13 Sept. a° 1665.

1\. Margaret, ætatis 6 annorum 1665.

2\. Frances, æt. 4. ann.

3\. Elizabeth, æt. 3 an. 1665.

4\. Dorothy, æt. 6 mens.

STRAFFORD & TICKHILL WAPENTAKE. *Doncaster*, 14 *Sept*. 1665.

RAWSON OF PICKBURNE.

ARMS.—Argent, a castle azure between three raven's heads erased sable.
CREST.—A raven sable rising from a castle or.

Per me W. Dugdale Norroy concessa.

John Rawson of Pickburne in co. Ebor. died in a° 1622 vel circa.=Alice, daughter of Barnaby Vickars of Scawsby in com. Ebor.

John Rawson of Pickburne, died in a° 1628 or thereabout.=Ursula, daughter and sole heir of John Rawson of Carcroft in com. Ebor.

John Rawson of Pickburne, æt. 40 annor. 14 Sept. 1665.=Mary, daughter of Darcy Washington of Adwick in com. Ebor.

2\. Darcy, æt. 4 ann.
3\. Thomas, ætatis 2 annor.

1\. Richard, æt. 12 an. 14 Sept. a°. 1665.

1\. Anne.

2\. Sarah.

3\. Ursula.

YORKE CITTY. *Yorke*, 12° *Sept.* 1665.

HERBERT OF MIDDLETON-WHERNHO.

ARMS.—Per pale azure and gules, three lions rampant argent within a bordure componée of the second and or.

MOTTO.—Pawb-ŷn ŷ Arver.

Gwillim ap Iankin, 50 E. 3.=..........

Thomas ap Gwillim, 22 R. 2=.........

William ap Thomas, 9 H. 5.=Gladis de Gam.

*Sr Richard Herbert, 2d son 6 E. 4.=..........

Richard Herbert of Tynterne in com. Monmouth, descended from * Sr Richard Herbert of Colbroke in co. Monmouth, Knt, came first into Yorkeshire upon the account of the Lady Mawde Herbert Countesse of Northumberland, which Countesse lyes buried at Beverley in com. Ebor.=....

Christopher Herbert=Elizabeth, daughter of Tho. Hemsworth.

Alfonsus Fowles of Westminster, Esqr.=Eleanor da. of Edward Medley, Esqr.

Thomas Herbert, Lord Mayor of Yorke, borne a° 1554, and died in a° 1614.=Mary, dau. of Tho. Harrison of Acaster in com. Eborum.

Sr Walter Alexander, Kt, Gentleman Usher Daylie wayter to King Charles ye first.=Anne.

Christopher Herbert, borne in a° 1583, of Ottrington in com. Ebor. died in 1624.=Jane, daughter of John Akeroyd of Folkerthorpe in com. Ebor.

1. Charles, died unmarried.

2. Henry Alexander, Cupbearer to K. Charles ye 2d.=Margery, daughter of John Noble of Midhurst in Sussex.

2. Anne, the wife of James Davenport, Esqr.

1. Lucie.=Sr Thomas Herbert of Tinterne in com. Monmouth, Bart, ætatis 58 annorum 12 Sept. 1655.

1. Barbara, wife of Thomas Bulmer, gent.
2. Lucy, wife of Edward Harrington, son of Sr Sapcote Harrington, Knt.

1. Terresia, wife of Alex. Bratield of Hanslap in com. Bucks, ob. s. prole.
2. Eliz. wife of Robert Phaire of Rostillon in co. Cork in Ireland.
3. Lucie, wife of John Frost of Clapham in com. Surrey.
4. Anne.

1. Henry Herbert of Middleton Whernho in com. Ebor. Esqr. son and heire, ætatis 25 an. 12 Sept. 1665.=Anne, da. of Sr Tho. Harrison of Allerthorpe in com. Ebor. Kt, by Dame Margaret his wife, daughter to Conyers Lord Darcy and Conyers.

2. Alexander, ætatis 23 an. 1665.

3. Philip, 4. Montgomery, 5. Will'm-ap-Thomas, 6. Thomas, died young.

1. Terresia, died in August, a° 1665.

2. Margaret, æt. 2 ann. 1665.

1. Lucie, æt. 3 ann. 12 Sept. 1665.

Thomas, died young, at the age of 10 months.

CLARO WAPENTAKE. *Yorke*, 13 *Sept.* 1665.

SYKES OF SPOFORTH.

See the Visit. of Cumberland for the armes.

Richard Sykes of Sykes-dike neer Carleill ═ .... in Cumberland.

William Sykes, a younger son, came into Yorkeshire and setled at Leedes ═ ....

.... Sykes of Leedes ═ ....

Richard Sykes, an Alderman of Leedes ═ Elizabeth, daughter of .... Mawson.

3. Richard Sykes, Rector of Kirk-Heaton in com. Ebor. died in a° 1653. ═ Grace, daughter of AlexanderStock, Rector of Kirk-Heaton in com. Ebor.

2. Henry Sykes of Hunslet Hall in com. Ebor. ═

1. John Sykes of Leedes, died circa annum 1622. ═ ...

1. Rebecca, wife of John Kershaw, Rector of Ripley in com. Ebor.
2. Eliz.

1. Richard Sykes, Rector of the Church of Spoforth and Prebend of ye Cathedrall of St Peter in Yorke, æt. 36 an. 13 Sept. 1665. ═ Anna, daughter of Marke Mickle-thwayt, Rector of LongMarston in co. Ebor.

2. John Sykes, a Merchant in Dort.
3. Samuell Sykes, a Merch[t] in Leedes.
4. Bernard Sykes, a Merch[t] in Lond.
5. Charles, died young.

1. Sarah, wife of William Horne of Leedes.
2. Elizabeth, wife of William Lodge of Leedes, afterward of Will'm Aldborough of Aldborough in com. Ebor. Esqr.

3. Micklethwayt Sykes, ætatis 3 annorum.

2. Marke, died young.

1. Richard, æt. 12 an. 13 Sept. a° 1665.

1. Anna, æt. 9 ann.

2. Sarah, 3. Rebecca, died young.

STRAFFORD AND TICKHILL WAPENTAKE. *Doncaster*, 14 *Sept.* 1665.

BATTIE OF WADWORTH.

ARMS.—Sable, a chevron argent between three goats passant of the second attired or, each charged with two pallets gules, on a chief of the third a demi-savage holding in his right hand a club, between two cinquefoils, all of the fourth.

James Battie of ...... in com. Eborum.=......

John Battie of Alverthorpe in com. Ebor. died in a° 1628 vel circa.=Elizabeth, daughter of Christopher Stanley of Wakefield in com. Ebor.

John Batty of Alverthorpe, died a° 1632.=Dorothy, daughter of Thomas Marshall of Moore-Allerton in com. Ebor.

Mary, daughter and heire of John Pierpont of Wadworth in com. Eborū, 1st wife.=John Batty of Wadworth in com. Ebor. æt. 49 an. et 11 mens. 14 Sept. 1665.=Anne, daughter of Stephen Kelham of Rotherham in com. Eborū, second wife.

1. Margaret. 2. Elizabeth. | 1. Francis, æt. 20 ann. 14 Sept. a° 1665. | 2. John, æt. 2 ann. | 3. Henry, æt. 6 ann. 14 Sept. 1665. | 3. Dorothy. 4. Anne.

STRAFFORD & TICKHILL WAPENTAKE. *Doncaster*, 14 *Sept.* 1665.

ROKEBY OF WARMESWORTH.

ARMS.—Argent, a chevron between three rooks sable, a canton gules.

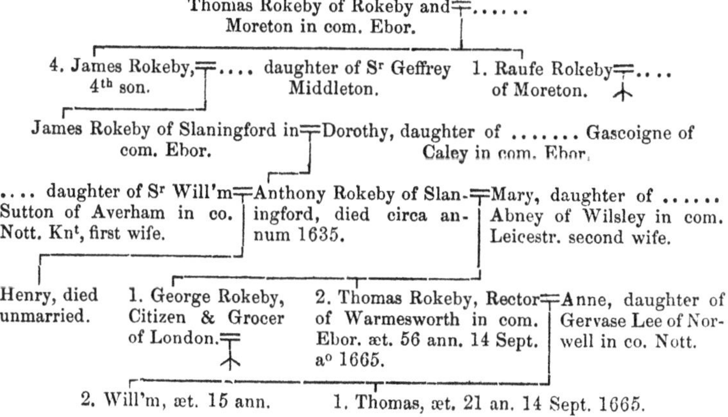

Thomas Rokeby of Rokeby and Moreton in com. Ebor.=......

4. James Rokeby, 4th son.=.... daughter of Sr Geffrey Middleton. | 1. Raufe Rokeby of Moreton.=....

James Rokeby of Slaningford in com. Ebor.=Dorothy, daughter of .... Gascoigne of Caley in com. Ebor.

.... daughter of Sr Will'm Sutton of Averham in co. Nott. Knt, first wife.=Anthony Rokeby of Slaningford, died circa annum 1635.=Mary, daughter of ...... Abney of Wilsley in com. Leicestr. second wife.

Henry, died unmarried. | 1. George Rokeby, Citizen & Grocer of London.= | 2. Thomas Rokeby, Rector of Warmesworth in com. Ebor. æt. 56 ann. 14 Sept. a° 1665.=Anne, daughter of Gervase Lee of Norwell in co. Nott.

2. Will'm, æt. 15 ann. | 1. Thomas, æt. 21 an. 14 Sept. 1665.

DONCASTER BOROUGH. *Doncaster*, 14 *Sept.* 1665.

SCORAH OF DONCASTER.

ARMS.—Vair, a bend engrailed ....

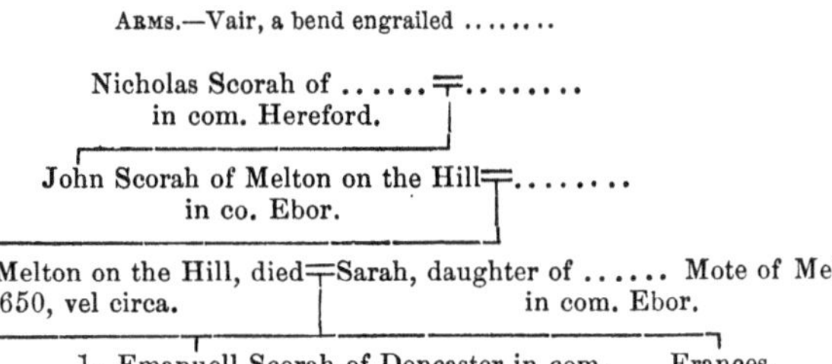

STRAFFORD AND TICKHILL WAPENTAKE. *Doncaster*, 14 *Sept.* aº 1665.

PORTINGTON OF BARNBY SUPER DUN.

ARMS.—Quarterly:
1. Gules, on a bend argent three martlets sable. Portington.
2. Argent, a chevron between three mullets pierced sable. Passelow.
3. Argent, a lion rampant sable charged on the shoulder with an escallop of the field. Barnby.
4. Sable, a saltire raguly argent. Keddall.

Robert Portington of Barnby=Isabell, daughter of Sr Richard Darley in com. Ebor. Esqr. of Buttercrambe in co. Ebor. Knt.

2. Robert Portington.=Grace, daugh. of Gilbert Gregory of Barnby super Dun in com. Ebor.

Joane, da. of Raphe Hopton of Armeley Hall in com. Ebor. 1. wife=Roger Portington of Barnby super Dun in com. Ebor. Esqr, æt. 55 ann. 14 Sept. 1665.=Jane, daugh. of .... Ramsden of Lascells-Hall neer Wakefield in co. Ebor. widd. of Leonard Wray of Cusworth in co. Ebor. 2. wife.

1. Mary, wife unto Joseph Holden, Citizen and Haberdasher of London.
2. Eliz. wife of Thomas Taylor of Thurne in com. Ebor.

1. Roger. 2. Robert. 3. Gilbert. 4. Francis. 1. Grace. 2. Elizabeth. 3. Anne.

1. Roger Portington, son and heire, æt. 27 an. 14 Sept. aº 1665.

2. Raphe Portington.

THE COUNTIE OF Y^e CITTY OF YORKE. *Yorke*, 13° *Sept.* 1665.

YARBOROUGH OF APPLETON.

ARMS.—Per pale argent and azure, a chevron between three chaplets all counterchanged, a canton gules.

Charles Yarborough of Yarborough in com. Linc. = ...

Will'm Yarborough of Yarborough in com. Linc. = Helen, daughter of . . . . . . Clifford of Brakenborough in com. Linc.

Will'm Yarborough of Appleton in y^e County of y^e Cittie of Yorke, æt. 65 ann. 13 Sept. 1665. = Margaret, daughter of Robert Jephason of Kellingley in co. Ebor. gent.

Nicholas Yarborough, æt. 3 an. 13 Sept. 1665. | 1. Elizabeth. | 2. Mary.

WILTON BEACON. *Yorke*, 13° *Sept.* 1665.

HORSLEY OF FULL-SUTTON.

ARMS.—Gules, three horse's heads erased argent bridled sable.

Will'm Horsley of Skirpenbeck in com. Eborum. = ...

Francis Horsley of Full-Sutton in com. Ebor. died in a° 1630, or thereabouts. = Gartrude, daughter of . . . . Wytham of Wytham in com. Ebor.

3. Edward Horsley of Stamford Briggs in com. Ebor. = | 2. Richard Horsley, died unmarried. | 1. Francis Horsley of Skirpenbeck in com. Ebor. died in his father's lifetime. = Isabell, daughter of James Fryar of . . . . | Gartrude, wife of Caleb Procter of . . . . in com. Eborum.

2. George. | 1. Francis Horsley of Full-Sutton, æt. 35 annor. 13 Sept. 1665. = Mary, daughter of John Spoforth of Howsham in com. Ebor. widow of Francis Dawtre of Full-Sutton.

Francis, æt. 10 an. 13 Sept. 1665. | 1. Triphena. | 2. Mary.

STAINECROSSE WAPENTAKE. *Barnesley*, 15 *Sept*. 1665.

NEVILL OF CHEVET.

ARMS.—Argent, a saltire gules.
CREST.—A bull's head erased sable.

Sr John Nevill of Leversege in com. Ebor. Knt. = Maude, daughter of Sr Raphe Rither of Rither in com. Eborum.

2. Robert Nevill. = ... 1. Thomas Nevill, son and heire. = ...

Sr John Nevill, Kt. = Elizabeth, daughter and coheir of William Bosvile of Chevet, in com. Ebor. Esqr.

Henry Nevill of Chevet, Esqr. = Dorothy, daughter of Sr John Dawney of Seazy in co. Ebor. Knt.

Gervase Nevill of Chevet, Esqr, = Anne, daughter and coheire of ...... Greenehalgh of Tevershall in com. Nott.

Henry Nevill of Chevet in com. Ebor. Esqr, died ...... = Eleanor, daughter and coheire of Henry Samford of Thorpe Salvein in com. Ebor.

2. Gervase Nevill of Beeston in co. Ebor. juxta Leedes. = Barbara, da. to John Bullock of Derley in co. Derb. Esqr.

Rosamund, daughter of Cyrill Arthington of Arthington in com. Ebor. Esqr, 1 wife. = 1. Francis Nevill of Chevet, Esqr, æt. 73 ann. 15 Sept. 1665. = Anne, daugh. of Tho. Tankerd of Brampton in com. Ebor. Esqr, widow of .... Arthington of Arthington, 2 wife. = Anne, daughter and coheire of Charles Markham of Ollerton in co. Nott. Esqr, 3 wife.

3. Roger Nevill, dyed unmarried.

Children of Gervase Nevill of Beeston:

Francis.
Gervase Nevill of Beeston, marr. to .... da and coheire to .... Cavendish.

Children of Francis Nevill of Chevet:

Dorothy, da. to Humphry Shalcrosse, citizen of London, 1st wife. = Sandford Nevill of Chevet and Kildwick in co. Ebor. = Anne, da. to Sr John Wolstenholme, Kt, one of the Farmers of the King's Customes, 2d wife.

1. Mary, wife of Sr Richard Tankard of Whixley in com. Ebor. Kt.
2. Rosamund, first marr. to Sr Tho. Bland of Kippax-park in co. Ebor. Bart; 2dly, to Walter Welsh of Houghton, Esqr.

Eleanor.

Gervase Nevill of Milnthorpe juxta Wakefield. = Eliz. da. to Sr Tho. Beaumont of Whitley in co. Ebor. Knt.

Children of Sandford Nevill:

Dorothy, wife to Algernon Cicill, 2d son to Will'm E. of Salesbury.

1. Francis, æt. 17 ann. 15 Sept. 1665.
2. Sandford Nevill.

1, Anne.
2. Rosamund, wife to John Estoft of Estoft in co. Ebor. Esqr.

3. Catharine.
4. Dorothy.

AGBRIGG AND MORLEY WAPENTAKE. *Barnesley*, 15 *Sept.* 1665.

KAY OF WOODSOME.

ARMS.—Quarterly of six:

1. Argent, two bendlets sable.
2. Argent, on a chevron gules three goldfinches or.
3. Sable, a fess or between three trefoils slipped erminois.
4. Argent, a chevron between three cross-crosslets fitchée sable.
5. Argent, a chevron between three cross-crosslets fitchée gules.
6. Argent, three boar's heads erect and erased sable, a crescent gules for difference.

CREST.—A goldfinch proper.

John Kay of Woodsome in com. Ebor. Esqr, died in a° 1641. Justice of peace dum vixit. = Anne, daughter of Sr John Ferne, K^t, one of the Councell of Yorke for the Northern parts of this realme.

Margaret, daughter and coheire of John Moseley of Northcroft, by Elizabeth, daughter and coheire of Tho. Triget of South Kirkby in com. Ebor. Esqr, 1st wife. = Sr John Kay of Woodsome, B^t, created by K. Charles y^e first 4° Febr. 17° of his reigne, died 25 Julij, a° 1662. = Eliz. daughter of Sr Ferdinando Leigh of Middleton juxta Leedes in com. Ebor. K^t, widow of Francis Burdet of Burthwayt in com. Ebor. Esqr, 2 wife. = Cath. daughter of Sr Will. St Quintin of Harpham in co. Ebor. Bar^t, widow of Michaell Wentworth, son and heire of Sr George Wentworth late of Wolley in com. Ebor. K^t, by whom there is noe issue. 3 wife.

Elizabeth, wife unto Raphe Asshton of Middleton in co. Lanc. Esqr.

Children of the first wife:

2. Robert, æt. 22 ann.

1. Sr John Kay of Woodsome, Bar^t, æt. 24 an. 15 Sept. 1665. = Anne, daughter of Will. Lyster of Thorneton in com. Ebor. Esqr.

- Anne, æt. unius anni et 9 mens. 15 Sept. a° 1665.

1. Margaret.

Children of the second wife:

2. Grace.
3. Anne.

3. George, ætatis 18 ann.

4. Mathew, æt. 15 an.

THE COUNTY OF THE CITTY OF YORKE. *Yorke*, 13 *Sept.* 1665.

HARRISON OF ACASTER.

ARMS.—Azure, three demi-lions rampant erased or, a canton argent.
CREST.—A demi-lion rampant or, holding in his paws a laurel-wreath vert.

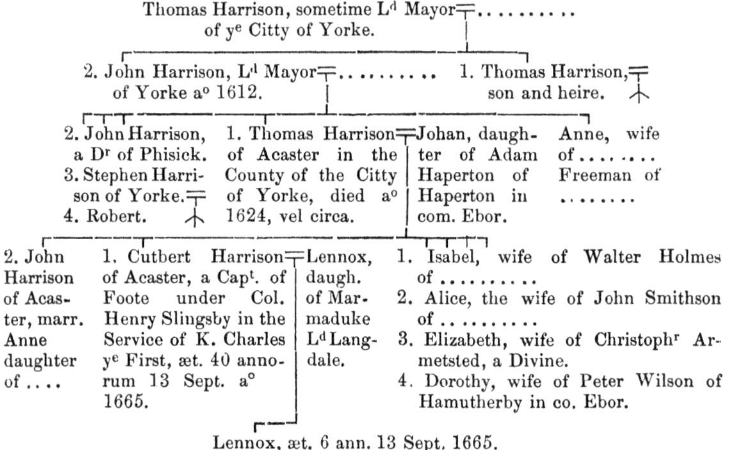

THE COUNTIE OF THE CITTY OF YORKE. *Yorke*, 13 *Sept.* 1665.

HUTTON OF POPPLETON.

ARMS.—Gules, on a fess argent between three cushions of the second tasselled or as many fleurs-de-lis of the field, a crescent for difference.

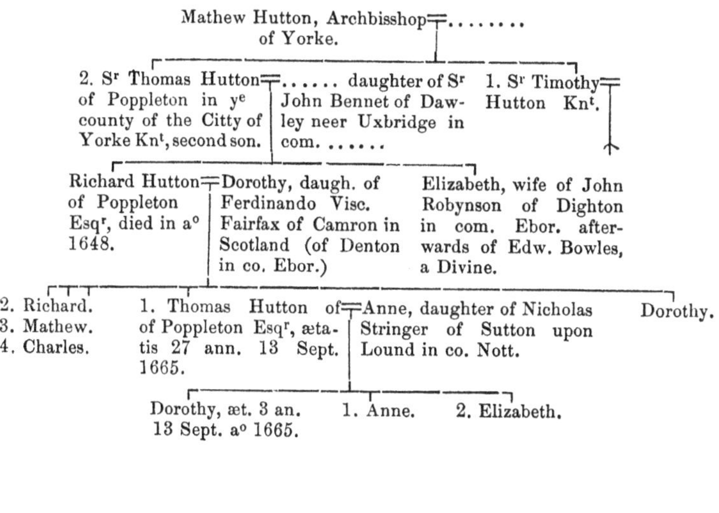

Mathew Hutton, Archbisshop of Yorke.=........

2. S[r] Thomas Hutton of Poppleton in y[e] county of the Citty of Yorke Kn[t], second son.=...... daughter of S[r] John Bennet of Dawley neer Uxbridge in com. ......

1. S[r] Timothy Hutton Kn[t].=

Richard Hutton of Poppleton Esqr, died in a[o] 1648.=Dorothy, daugh. of Ferdinando Visc. Fairfax of Camron in Scotland (of Denton in co. Ebor.)

Elizabeth, wife of John Robynson of Dighton in com. Ebor. afterwards of Edw. Bowles, a Divine.

2. Richard.
3. Mathew.
4. Charles.

1. Thomas Hutton of of Poppleton Esqr, ætatis 27 ann. 13 Sept. 1665.=Anne, daughter of Nicholas Stringer of Sutton upon Lound in co. Nott.

Dorothy.

Dorothy, æt. 3 an. 13 Sept. a[o] 1665. 1. Anne. 2. Elizabeth.

[S]TRAFFORD & TICKHILL WAPENTAKE. *Rotheram*, 16 *Sept.* 1665.

SYMPSON OF SHEFFEILD.

ARMS.—Per bend sinister or and sable, a lion rampant counterchanged.

Lancelot Sympson of .... neer Maidstone in Kent.=....

2. Samuell Sympson of Blithe in com. Nott. died in a[o] 1635, vel circa.=Fayth, daughter of Alexander Nevile of Wyston in com. Nott.

1. John Sympson of Mount-bures in Essex clerke, died unmarried.

. Will'm Sympson of [S]heffeild in com. Ebor. [æ]t. 31 annor. 16 Sept. [a]o 1665.=Elizabeth, daughter of Will'm Linley of Kingston super Hull in com. Eborum.

1. Lancelot Simpson of Stoke-Neyland in co. Suff.

Elizabeth.

Eleanor, æt. 3 mens. 16 Sept. a[o] 1665.

STRAFFORD AND TICKHILL WAPENTAKE. *Rotheram*, 16 *Sept*. 1665.

WESTBY OF RAVENFIELD.

ARMS.—Argent, on a chevron azure three cinquefoils pierced of the field.
CREST.—A martlet sable, in his beak a stalk of wheat, leaves vert, ears or.

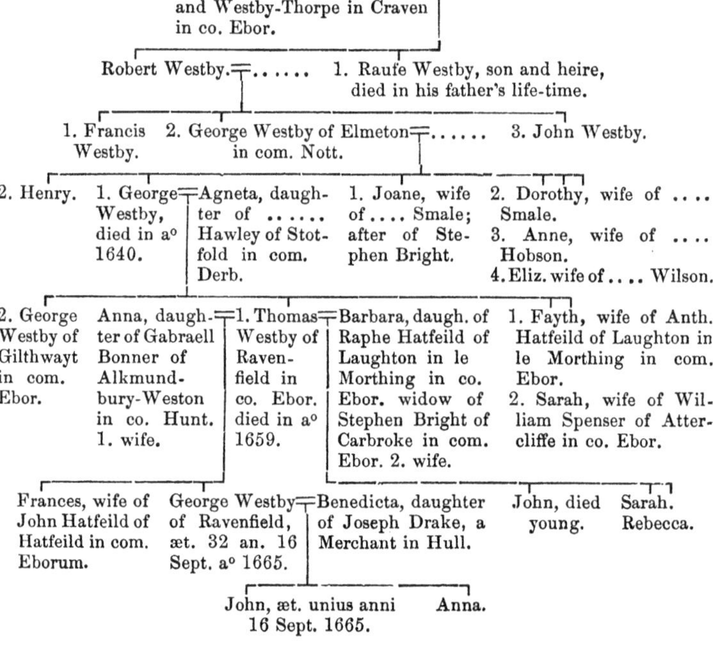
Raufe Westby of Leyton-Hall and Westby-Thorpe in Craven in co. Ebor. = ...

Robert Westby. = ...
1. Raufe Westby, son and heire, died in his father's life-time.

1. Francis Westby.
2. George Westby of Elmeton in com. Nott. = ...
3. John Westby.

2. Henry.
1. George Westby, died in a° 1640. = Agneta, daughter of ...... Hawley of Stotfold in com. Derb.
1. Joane, wife of .... Smale; after of Stephen Bright.
2. Dorothy, wife of .... Smale.
3. Anne, wife of .... Hobson.
4. Eliz. wife of .... Wilson.

2. George Westby of Gilthwayt in com. Ebor.
Anna, daughter of Gabraell Bonner of Alkmundbury-Weston in co. Hunt. 1. wife. = 1. Thomas Westby of Ravenfield in co. Ebor. died in a° 1659. = Barbara, daugh. of Raphe Hatfeild of Laughton in le Morthing in co. Ebor. widow of Stephen Bright of Carbroke in com. Ebor. 2. wife.
1. Fayth, wife of Anth. Hatfeild of Laughton in le Morthing in com. Ebor.
2. Sarah, wife of William Spenser of Attercliffe in co. Ebor.

Frances, wife of John Hatfeild of Hatfeild in com. Eborum.
George Westby of Ravenfield, æt. 32 an. 16 Sept. a° 1665. = Benedicta, daughter of Joseph Drake, a Merchant in Hull.
John, died young.
Sarah.
Rebecca.

John, æt. unius anni 16 Sept. 1665.
Anna.

STRAFFORD AND TICKHILL WAPENTAKE. *Rotheram*, 16 *Sept.* 1665.

MORETON OF SPOUTHOUSE.

(See Moreton of Wrathhouse for the upper part of this descent.)

ARMS.—Or, three ravens sable within a bordure azure.

Richard Moreton of Spouthouse in the parish of Bradfeild in com. Eborum. = ...

Nicholas Moreton of Spouthouse, died circa ann. 1630. = Gertrude, daughter of Raufe Ward of Morehall in com. Ebor.

2. Thomas Moreton of Thorne House in com. Ebor. =

1. Francis Moreton of Spouthouse, died in a° 1654. = Anne, daughter of John Slater of Hunshelfe in com. Ebor.

1. Anne, wife of John Scott of Thurston in co. Ebor.
2. Dinas, wife of Raufe Lee of Greenaforth in com. Ebor.

Francis Moreton of Spouthouse, æt. 50 ann. 16 Sept. 1665. = Mary, daughter of Will. Revell of Dungworth in com. Ebor.

1. Gartrude, now wife of Edward Ratcliffe of Thriber in com. Ebor. and widow of Thomas Sotterthwayt of Grasebrooke in com. Ebor.
2. Anne, wife of William West of Round-green in com. Ebor.
3. Mary, wife of John Drew of Rotheram in com. Ebor.

1. Anne.
2. Mary.

3. Elizabeth.
4. Sarah.
5. Martha.

1. Thomas Moreton, Mr of Arts, ætatis 26 ann. 16 Sept. 1665.

2. Nicolas, ætatis 12 ann.
3. Francis, æt. 10 ann.
4. Joseph, æt. 8 ann.

DONCASTER BOROUGH. *Doncaster*, 14 *Sept.* 1665.

MARSHALL OF DONCASTER.

ARMS.—........ three bars ...., a canton ermine.

Miles Marshall of Marston in com. Linc. = Anne, daughter of Robert Spendola of Dene in com. Northton.

1. Winifride, wife of Thomas Allen of Colby in com. Linc.
2. Isabell, wife of Edward Downer of Great-Ponton in com. Linc.
3. Mary, wife of Thomas Goodburne of Marston in co. Linc.

Thomas Marshall of Marston in com. Linc. died 22° Jan. a° 1653. = Mary, daughter of Thomas Barnes of the Citty of Lincolne.

Thomas [M]arshall, [ci]tizen of [Lo]ndon.

2. Benjamin Marshall of Doncaster in co. Ebor. æt. 41 ann. 14 Sept. a° 1665. = Elizabeth, daugh. of John Farnley of Thornhill in com. Ebor. widow of Will. Madocks of Doncaster.

1. Gervase Marshall of Whatton in the Vale in co. Nott. =

1. Alice, wife of Obadiah Martin of Doncaster.
2. Eliz. wife of Robt Walcot of Scredinton in com. Linc.
3. Mary.

BULMER WAPENTAKE. *Yorke*, 13 *Sept.* 1665.

MORLEY OF NEWTON UPON OUSE.

ARMS.—Quarterly:

1. Sable, a leopard's face jessant-de-lis argent.
2. Gules, a fess between three Katherine-wheels argent.
3. Argent, on a bend gules three garbs or.
4. Gules, two wings conjoined and inverted or, in chief a fleur-de-lis argent.

CREST.—On a chapeau gules turned up ermine a leopard's face argent jessant-de-lis or.

Anne, daughter of Christopher Thornaby of Thornaby, first wife. = Cuthbert Morley of Normanby in co. Ebor. = Isabell, daughter of ...... Wilson of ...... in Northumberland, second wife.

1. James Morley of Normanby in Cleveland. = (issue by first wife)

2. Robert Morley of y^e Citty of Yorke, an Utter Barrister of the Inner Temple, died in a° 1651. = Elizabeth, daughter of Sr John Scorey of ...... in com. Hereford, Kn^t.

Eleanor, wife of ...... of .... in com. ......

2. James Morley of Newton upon Ouse in com. Ebor. æt. 38 an. 14 Sept. a° 1665. = Cordelia, daughter of Thomas Dodsworth of ...... in co. Ebor. widow of ...... Higginbotham.

1. Cuthbert Morley.

1. Isabell.
2. Anne.

STRAFFORD AND TICKHILL WAPENTAKE. *Doncaster*, 14 *Sept.* 1665.

ADAMS OF SCAUSBY.

ARMS.—Gules, a lion rampant between three escallops or, on a chief argent as many pallets engrailed sable.

CREST.—A demi-griffin segreant ermine, beaked and winged azure, holding an escallop or.

Philip Adams of Ouston in com. Ebor. died circa annum 1622. = Gertrude, daughter of Thomas Boswell of Warmesworth in com. Ebor.

Will'm Adams of Owston, died in a° 1637 vel circa. = Margaret, daughter of Sr Thomas Ellys of Grantham in com. Linc. Kn^t.

1. Jane, wife of Thomas Young, son and heire of Sr George Young, K^t, son to ...... Young, Arch B^pp of Yorke.

2. Mary, wife of Christopher Wormley of Rickall in com. Ebor.

1. Sr William Adams of Scausby in com. Ebor. K^t, æt. 38 an. 14 Sept. 1665. = Mary, daughter of John Dawney, Esqr, son and heire apparent of Sr Tho. Dawney of Cowick in com. Ebor. Kn^t.

2. Thomas, 3. Philip, 4. Benjamin, } died unmarried.

3. Thomas, ætatis 10 ann.
4. Philip, æt. 3 ann.

1. William, died in his childhood.
2. John Adams, now son and heire, ætat. 12 annor. 14 Sept. 1665.

1. Elizabeth, ætatis 14 annorum.
2. Margaret, ætatis 7 annorum.

3. Mary, æt. 5 ann.
4. Jane, æt. 1 anni.

OSGODCROSSE WAPENTAKE. *Yorke*, 13° *Sept.* 1665.

HUMFREY OF ASKERNE.

ARMS.—Gules, a cross botonnée ermine.
CREST.—An otter passant argent, vulned in the breast gules.
No proofe made of these armes.

Nicholas Humfrey of ..... in com. Dorset, resided afterwards in y^e Citty of Worcester. = ...

Will'm Humfrey, D^r in Divinity & Chaplain to King James, resided at Averham in com. Nott. a Justice of Peace and Quorum, died a° 1626, or thereabouts. = Anne, daughter and heire of Charles Hall, a younger son of .... Hall of Gretford in com. Linc.

2. Francis Humphrey, a Merchant in Yorke, died without issue male.
3. Mathew, died without issue male.

1. Toby Humfrey of Askerne in co. Ebor. now one of the Masters of y^e Chancery Extraordinary, æt. 45 an. 13 Sept. 1665. = Anne, daugh. unto Francis Bayne of Netherdale in com. Ebor. gent.

1. Anne, wife of James Sturton of great Ayton in Cleveland gent.
2. Mary, wife of Edmund Woodroofe, Citizen of London.

Toby, æt. 17 an. 13 Sept. 1665.

ALLERTONSHIRE WAPENTAKE. *Yorke*, 13 *Sept.* 1665.

METCALFE OF NORTH-ALLERTON.

ARMS.—Argent, three calves passant sable, a canton gules.

George Metcalfe, second son to James Metcalfe. = ...

Richard Metcalfe of North-Allerton in co. Ebor. = Anne, daughter of Roger Wilson of Danby-Wiske in com. Ebor. gent.

[Ri]chard Metcalfe of North-[A]llerton. = [issue]

1. George Metcalfe of Allerton, one of the Justices of Peace in the North Riding of Yorkesh. died a° 1642. = Elizabeth, daughter of William Talbot of Knaton in com. Ebor. gent.

Cecelie, wife of Marmaduke Bell of Elmer in com. Ebor. gent.

Richard.

1. Will'm Metcalfe of North-Allerton, æt. 30 an. 13 Sept. 1665. = Anna, daugh. of Sr George Marwood of little Buskby in co. Ebor. Bart.

1. Eliz. wife of Timothy Maleverer of Arncliffe in co. Ebor. Esqr.
2. Cath. wife of Henry Crosland of Hemsley in com. Ebor. gent.
3. Mary, wife of Lancelot Pinkney of Silton in co. Ebor. gent.

Thomas, æt. 4 an. 13° Sept. 1665. 1. Elizabeth. 2. Margaret.

2 A

STAINECLIFFE WAPENTAKE. *Barnesley*, 15 *Sept.* 1665.

LYSTER OF THORNETON AND MIDHOPE.

ARMS.—Quarterly:
1. Ermine, on a fess sable three mullets or.
2. Gules, a chevron between three mullets argent, in the dexter and sinister chief two bird-bolts in pale or.
3. Argent, a water-bouget between four fleurs-de-lis sable.
4. Argent, on a bend sable three roses or.

CREST.—A stag's head proper erased or attired sable.

Sr Will'm Lyster of Thorneton in co. Eborū K^t, died a^o 1650. = Mary, daughter of Sr Henry Bellasses of Newborough in co. Ebor. K^t and Bar^t.

Their issue:

- 8. Edmund.
- 2. Laurence, 4. Henry, 7. Michaell, died unmarried.
- 5. Martin, married Cath. da. of Sr Will. Fairfax of Steeton in co. Ebor. K^t.
- 6. Mathew Lyster, now Consull at Ciprus.
- 3. Christopher Lyster, marr. Winifride, da. of ...... Fletcher & widow of Sr Richard Dacres K^t. Their daughter:
  - Anne.
- 1. Will'm Lyster of Thorneton & Midhope in co. Ebor. Esqr, died in his father's lifetime. = Cath. da. of Sr Rich. Hawkesworth of Hawkesworth in com. Ebor. K^t. Their issue:
  - 1. Will'm Lyster, son and heire, æt. 28 annor. 15 Sept. 1665. = Martha, daughter of Stephen Bright of Carbrooke in com. Ebor.
  - 2. Christopher.
  - Anne, wife of Sr John Kay of Woodsome in co. Ebor. Bar^t.
- 1. Ursula, wife of Sampson Staveley of Ripponparke in co. Ebor.
- 2. Frances, wife of John Lambert of Calton in com. Ebor. Esqr.

Rotheram, 16 *Sept*. 1665.

BLYTHMAN OF NEWLATHES.

ARMS.—Vert, on a fess or between three bears rampant argent as many fleurs-de-lis gules.
No proofe made of these armes.

Thomas Blythman of Newlathes in com. Eborum. = Ursula, daughter and heire of John Normanvell of Oldham, widow of Raphe Rearesby of Ashwood in co. Derb. Esqr.

Thomas Blytheman of Newlathes. = ... daughter of Percivall Whitley.

3. Henry. 2. Michaell. 1. Thomas Blythman. = Jane, daughter of Owen Hopton of Armeley in com. Ebor. Margaret. Catherine. Helen.

Thomas, a merchant in Newcastle sup. Tine. William Blytheman. = Elizabeth, daughter and heire of ...... Bardon of ......

William Blythman. = ... daughter and heire of John Burton of ...... Elizabeth, wife unto James Crosby.

2. Will'm Blytheman, marr. .... daughter of .... Tankerd of Burrough-brigg in co. Ebor. ...... da. of Hugh Lacy of Burlay, 1 wife. = 1. Jasper Blytheman. = ... 2^{d} wife. 1. Dorothy, wife of ...... Dennam of West-Retford in com Nott. 2. Winifrid, wife of Bryan Lascells of Gateford in com. Eborum.

3. William Blythman, died in a^{o} 1659. = Elizabeth, daughter of Sr John Stanhope of Mellwood Parke in com. Linc. Kn^{t}. 2. John Blythman, marr. ...... daugh. of ...... Burdet of Denby in co. Ebor. obijt sine prole. 1. Jasper Blythman, marr. ...... daughter of Tho. Wentworth of Woodhouse in co. Ebor. Esqr, obijt sine prole. 1. Mary, wife of Stephen Skypwith of .... in Hartfordsh. 2. Elizabeth.

1. Fulljambe Blythman, marr. Mary, da. and heire of Tho. Boswell of Warmesworth in com. Ebor. Esqr, and died without issue in a^{o} 1658.
2. Will'm Blythman, marr. Jane, daughter of Tho. Butler, Citizen of London.

3. Jasper Blythman of Newlathes in co. York, æt. 23 ann. 16 Sept. 1665. = Catherine, daugh. of Richard Mountney of Rotheram in co. Ebor. Esqr.

4. Michaell. 1. Mary, wife of Mathew Biggs of Yorke. 2. Hesther, 3. Eliz. } died unmarried. 5. Elizabeth, wife unto Philip Lutton of Yedingham in co. Ebor. 4. Rachell. 6. Rachell. 7. Everilda.

Elizabeth, æt. 1 anni 16 Sept. 1665.

STRAFFORD & TICKHILL WAPENTAKE. *Rotheram*, 16 *Sept.* 1665.

WOMBWELL OF WOMBWELL.

ARMS.—Gules, a bend between six unicorn's heads couped argent.

Will'm Wombwell of Blacker in co. Ebor. son and heire of Tho. Wombwell of Wombwell in com. Ebor. Esqr. = Oliva, daughter of William Burnell of Wynkeburne in com. Ebor. 3^d^ wife.

Children:

- 6. Fulljambe Wombwell. = — issue: John.
- 5. Roger Wombwell. = — issue: George.
- 3. John, 4. Francis, died without issue.
- 2. Thomas Wombwell, Fellow of St John's Colledge in Cambridge, died unmarried.
- 1. William Wombwell Esqr, died in Febr. a^o^ 1662. = Margaret, da. of Michaell Wentworth of Wolley in com. Ebor. Esqr.
- 1. Eliz. wife to John Blythe of Finchamsted in com. Berks.
- 2. Oliva, wife of Stephen Taylor, D^r^ of Phisick in Yorke.
- 3. Dorothy, wife of Thomas Brooke, Citizen of Lond.
- 4. Mary, wife of Francis South of Bradfeild parish in com. Ebor.

Thomas Wombwell of Wombwell Esqr, died in Aug. a^o^ 1663. = Martha, eldest daughter of Sr Thomas Wentworth of Empsall in comitatu Eborum K^t^.

William, æt. 7 an. 16 Sept. a^o^ 1665.

STRAFFORD AND TICKHILL WAPENTAKE. *Rotheram*, 16 *Sept.* 1665.

SAVILE OF MEXBROUGH.

ARMS.—Argent, on a bend sable three owls of the field, in chief a trefoil slipped gules.
CREST.—An owl argent, charged on the breast with a trefoil as in the arms.

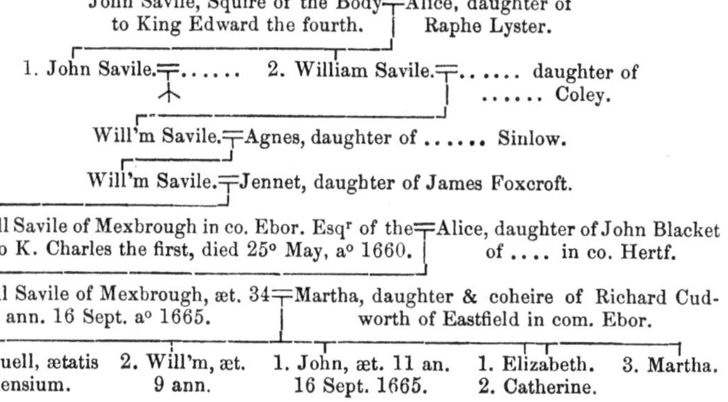

STRAFFORD AND TICKHILL WAPENTAKE. *Rotheram*, 16 *Sept.* 1665.

RERESBY OF THRIBERGH.

ARMS.—Quarterly of nineteen:

1. Gules, on a bend argent three cross-crosslets fleury sable.
2. Azure, billetté or, a fess dancetté of the last.
3. Argent, on a fess double-cotised gules three fleurs-de-lis of the field.
4. Gules, on a chevron between three trefoils slipped argent as many pellets.
5. Argent, three bars-gemelles gules, on a canton of the second as many fusils in fess of the field.
6. Gules, three goats passant argent.
7. Argent, three bendlets gules.
8. Argent, a fess dancetté between three cock's heads erased sable wattled gules.
9. Argent, a chief gules, over all a bend engrailed azure.
10. Gules, three garbs argent within a bordure sable bezantée.
11. Sable, a chevron between three church-bells argent.
12. Azure, semée of fleurs-de-lis argent, a lion rampant gardant of the last.
13. Gules, three mullets of six points or, a quarter ermine.
14. Argent, three pairs of pincers sable.
15. Ermine, a talbot passant gules.
16. Azure, a fleur-de-lis argent, a crescent for difference.
17. Azure, a fess between three escallops or.
18. Azure, a chevron engrailed between three eagles displayed or.
19. Argent, on a chevron sable between three pellets as many mullets pierced or, on a chief of the second three cinquefoils of the third.

CREST.—On a chapeau gules turned up ermine a goat passant argent.

Thomas Reresby of Thribergh in com. Ebor. Esqr, living a^{o} 1585. = Mary, daughter of Thomas Babington of Dethick in com. Derb. Esqr.

7. Gervase Reresby of Wood-Lathes in co. Ebor. = ...
(a)

6. Michaell, died unmarried.

5. Godfrey Reresby. = ..., daughter of . . . . Swift of Rotheram.
(b)

2. Francis Reresby, died young.
3. William, died unmarried.
4. Raphe Reresby, of whom there is noe issue remayn^{g}.

1. Sr Thomas Reresby of Thriberg K^{t}, died in May a^{o} 1619. = Margery, daughter of Sr John Mounson of South-Carleton in com. Linc. Kn^{t}.
(c)

1. Anne, wife of Tho. Trygot, son and heire of Bartholomew Trigot of South Kirkby.
2. Edith, wife of Thomas Coxson of Crockhill in co. Ebor. Esqr.
3. Mary, wife of Sr Richard Harpur of Littleover in co. Derb. Kn^{t}.
4. Margaret, wife of . . . . Eland of . . . .

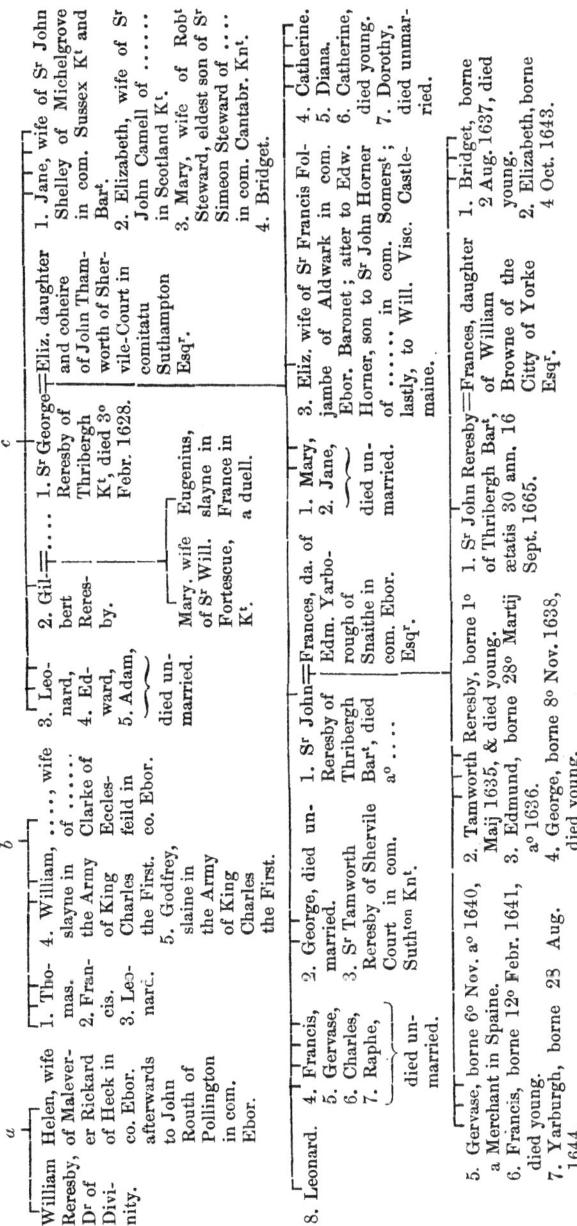
a
William Reresby, Dr of Divinity.
Helen, wife of Malever-er Rickard of Heck in co. Ebor. afterwards to John Routh of Pollington in com. Ebor.
1. Thomas.
2. Francis.
3. Leonard.
b
4. William, slayne in the Army of King Charles the First.
5. Godfrey, slaine in the Army of King Charles the First.
. . . ., wife of . . . . . . Clarke of Ecclesfeild in co. Ebor.
3. Leonard,
4. Edward,
5. Adam,
died unmarried.
2. Gilbert Reresby.
. . . .
c
1. Sr George Reresby of Thribergh Kt, died 3o Febr. 1628.
Eliz. daughter and coheire of John Thamworth of Shervile-Court in comitatu Suthampton Esqr.
1. Jane, wife of Sr John Shelley of Michelgrove in com. Sussex Kt and Bart.
2. Elizabeth, wife of Sr John Camell of . . . . . . in Scotland Kt.
3. Mary, wife of Robt Steward, eldest son of Sr Simeon Steward of . . . . in com. Cantabr. Knt.
4. Bridget.
Mary. wife of Sr Will. Fortescue, Kt.
Eugenius, slayne in France in a duell.
8. Leonard.
4. Francis,
5. Gervase,
6. Charles,
7. Raphe,
died unmarried.
2. George, died unmarried.
3. Sr Tamworth Reresby of Shervile Court in com. Suthton Knt.
1. Sr John Reresby of Thribergh Bart, died ao . . . .
Frances, da. of Edm. Yarborough of Snaithe in com. Ebor. Esqr.
1. Mary,
2. Jane,
died unmarried.
3. Eliz. wife of Sr Francis Foljambe of Aldwark in com. Ebor. Baronet; after to Edw. Horner, son to Sr John Horner of . . . . . . in com. Somersst; lastly, to Will. Visc. Castlemaine.
4. Catherine.
5. Diana.
6. Catherine, died young.
7. Dorothy, died unmarried.
5. Gervase, borne 6o Nov. ao 1640, a Merchant in Spaine.
6. Francis, borne 12o Febr. 1641, died young.
7. Yarburgh, borne 23 Aug. 1644.
2. Tamworth Reresby, borne 1o Maij 1635, & died young.
3. Edmund, borne 28o Martij ao 1636.
4. George, borne 8o Nov. 1638, died young.
1. Sr John Reresby of Thribergh Bart, ætatis 30 ann. 16 Sept. 1665.
Frances, daughter of William Browne of the Citty of Yorke Esqr.
1. Bridget, borne 2 Aug. 1637, died young.
2. Elizabeth, borne 4 Oct. 1643.

STRAFFORD AND TICKHILL WAPENTAKE. *Rotheram*, 16 *Sept.* 1665.

ROKEBY OF HOTHAM AND SKIRES.

ARMS.—Quarterly:
1 and 4. Argent, a chevron sable between three rooks of the second legged azure, a crescent for difference.
2 and 3. Argent, three chevronels braced in base sable, on a chief of the second as many mullets of the first.

Thomas Rokeby of Hotham in com. Ebor. Esqr. = Catherine, daughter of Laurence Legh, Serjeant at Armes.

2. Raphe, died unmarried.

1. William Rokeby of Hotham. = Dorothy, daughter of William Rokeby of Skyres in com. Ebor. Esqr.

1. Eliz. wife of Rich. Vincent of Firsby in com. Ebor.
2. Susan, wife of Will'm Cartwright of Normanby in com. Linc.

2. Alexander Rokeby of Sandall in co. Ebor. marr. Susan, da. of Gervase Boswell of Warmesworth in com. Ebor.
3. Thomas Rokeby, marr. Eliz. daugh. of .... Bury of Grantham in com. Linc.
4. Philip Rokeby, married Jane, daughter of ...... Godfrey of Thunnock in com. Linc.

Sir William Rokeby of Hotham and Skyres in co. Ebor. Bar^t. æt. 64 ann. 16 Sept. a^o 1665. = Frances, daughter of Sr Will'm Hickman of Gaynesborough in com. Linc. Kn^t.

Mary, wife of Christopher Legard of Anlaby in com. Kingston sup. Hull.

3. Willoughby Rokeby, æt. 33 ann. 16 Sept. 1665.
4. Francis, died unmarried.

2. Alexander Rokeby, æt. 36 ann. 16 Sept. 1665. = Margaret, da. of John Cooke of Holkam in com. Norff. Esqr.

1. William Rokeby, died unmarried.

1. Mary, died unmarried.
2. Elizabeth.
3. Mildred.
4. Bridget.

William, æt. 9 ann. 16 Sept. a^o 1665.

STRAFFORD AND TICKHILL WAPENTAKE. *Rotheram*, 16 *Sept*. 1665.

HATFEILD OF LAUGHTON IN LE MORTHING.

ARMS.—Ermine, on a chevron engrailed sable three cinquefoils or.

CREST.—A cubit-arm vested sable cuffed argent holding in the hand proper a cinquefoil slipped or

Stephen Hatfeild of Hatfeild in Holdernesse in com. Ebor. to whom Will. Flower, Norroy, granted the Armes here depicted (as it is affirmed) a° 1563, in his Visitation of Yorkeshire. = ...

...... Hatfeild of Ecclesfield in com. Ebor. and there resided at Shire-greene alias Hatfeild house. = ...

Alexander Hatfeild of Shire greene. = ...

Raphe Hatfeild of Shire-greene, afterward of Laughton in the Morning, died circa an. 1635. = Margaret, daughter of Robert Merfield of Thurcroft in com. Ebor.

Children:

4. Barbara, wife of Stephen Bright of Carborough in co. Ebor.; after of Tho. Westby of Ravenfield in co. Ebor.
5. Elizabeth, wife of James Fisher of Sheffeild in co. Ebor.

1. Margaret, wife of Thomas Lord of Brampton in com. Ebor.
2. Anne, wife of James Trubshaw of Bawtre in co. Ebor.
3. Isabell, wife of Will'm Stanniforth of Rotheram in co. Ebor.

1. Anthony Hatfeild of Laughton in the Morthing in com. Ebor. æt. 67 ann. 16 Sept. 1665. = Fayth, daughter of Thomas Westby of Gilthwayt in com. Ebor.

2. Alexander Hatfeild of Ranfield in co. Ebor. Clerke.
3. John Hatfeild.

Children of Anthony and Fayth:

John Hatfeild, ætatis 30 an. 16 Sept. 1665.

1. Rosamund, wife of Charles Laughton of Howorth in com. Eborum.
2. Martha.
3. Fayth.
4. Prudence.

DONCASTER BOROUGH. *Doncaster*, 14 *Sept*. 1665.

YARBURGH OF DONCASTER.

ARMS.—Quarterly of eight:
1. Per pale argent and azure, a chevron between three chaplets all counterchanged.
2. Argent, semée of cross-crosslets fitchée ...., a rose gules.
3. Sable, a chevron between six cross-crosslets in chief and four in base argent.
4. Argent, a chevron engrailed .... between three birds azure legged gules.
5. Sable, two lion's gambs in saltire erased argent.
6. Gules, a fess humetté argent, in chief three griffin's heads erased or.
7. Gules, on a chief indented argent three lions rampant azure.
8. Argent, a bend engrailed sable cotised gules.

CREST.—A falcon close or trussing a duck proper.

Eustacius de Yarburgh.=........

Robert de Yarburgh.=...... daughter of Sr Lambert Munby.

Lambert de Yarburgh.=...... daughter of Arthur Ormesby.

Sr John de Yarburgh K^t, 9 E. 2.=Ursula, daughter to Sr Raphe Humberston K^t.

Raphe de Yarborough.=Anne, daughter of Sr William Staine Kn^t.

Robert de Yarborough.=...... daughter of Sr John Bussam Kn^t.

William Yarburgh.=Beatrix, daughter of Sr Geffrey Auke Kn^t.

Richard Yardburgh.=Cassandra, daughter of Sr Robert Maplethorpe.

Robert Yarburgh.=Isabell, daughter of Sr John Ewrby Kn^t.

William Yarburgh.=...... daughter of Thomas Anguine.

Richard Yarburgh.=Joane, daughter and heire of John Atwell.

a

a

William Yarburgh. = Isabell, daughter and heire of Sr John Billing Knt.

Richard Yarburgh of Yarburgh Esqr. = Elizabeth, daughter of Thomas Moyne.

Agnes, daughter of Sr John Skipwith Kt, first wife. = Charles Yarburgh of Yarburgh Esqr. = Elizabeth, daughter of Martin Newcomyn, second wife.

1. Richard Yarburgh. = Margaret, daughter of Thomas Portington.

2. Edmund Yarburgh of Lincolne Esqr. = Margaret, daughter of Sr Vincent Grantham Knt.

3. Christopher Yarburgh. = ... daughter and heire of John Michell alias Copeland.

4. Bryan Yarburgh.

1. Ursula, wife unto Thomas Wall.
2. Margaret, wife unto John Dyan.
3. Bridget, wife of ...... Radley.
4. Barbara, wife of William Darby.
5. Jane, wife of Nicholas Thornecock.

Charles Yarburgh of Kelstern and Yarburgh. = Elizabeth, daughter of Humphrey Littlebury of Hagworth Ingham.

Charles Yarburgh of Willoughby in com. Nott. = Barbara, daughter of Will'm Whalley.

Elizabeth, daughter of Robert Farmour, first wife. = Francis Yarburgh of Northampton, Serjeant at Law, died aº 37 Eliz. Reginæ. = Frances, daughter of Leonard Wray of ..... in com. Ebor. 2 wife.

William Yarburgh. = Eleanor, daughter of Thomas Clifford.

Robert Yarburgh Esqr. = Mary, daughter of Sr Gervaise Elwish.

Edmund Yarburgh of Balne Hall in co. Ebor. died 6º Maij, aº 1631. = Sarah, daughter and coheire of Thomas Wormeley.

Henry Yarburgh.

3. Edmund Yarburgh of Doneaster, Dr of Phisick, æt. 40 annorum 14 Sept. 1665. = Anne, daughter of Thomas Stanhope of Stotfold in com. Ebor. 3d son of Sr John Stanhope of Melwood in com. Linc.

2. Thomas Yarburgh of Campsall in com. Ebor. now one of the Justices of Peace in this county. = Anne, daughter of Thomas Ellys of Notthill in co. Bedf. Esqr.

1. Sr Nicholas Yarburgh of Snaith-Hall in com. Ebor. Knt. = Fayth, daughter of John Dawney of Cowick Knt.

Frances, wife of Sr John Reresby of Thribergh in co. Ebor. Bart.

Thomas, æt. 4 mensium 14 Sept. 1665.

Sr Thomas Yarburgh of Snaith in co. Ebor. Kt.

AGBRIGG AND MORLEY WAPENTAKE. *Yorke*, 13 *Sept.* 1665.

CROSLAND OF CROSLAND HILL.

ARMS.—Quarterly argent and gules, a cross botonnée counterchanged.

Thomas Crosland of Crosland Hill in the parish of Almondbury in com. Ebor. died in a° 1587. = ...

Thomas Crosland of Crosland Hill. = Dorothy, daughter and coheire of ...... Key of Thorpe in co. Ebor.

5. Nathaniell Crosland of Crosland Hill, died circa ann. 1644, being a Capt of Horse in the Army of K. Charles the first. = Jane, daughter of Gawyn Hymers of Shields in the Bisshopprick of Durhā.

1. Thomas,
2. Gyles,
3. Mathias,
4. William,
ob. s. prole.

1. Judith, wife of ... Booth, D^r of Phisick.
2. Lucie, wife of .... Hurst of Grenehead in co. Ebor.
3. ...... wife of .... Lancashire of Manchester.

Thomas Crosland of Crosland Hill, æt. 28 an. 13 Sept. 1665. = Elizabeth, daughter of Christoph^r Breary, Alderm. of Yorke.

1. Thomasin, wife of George Good of Kingston upon Thames in com. Surrey.
2. Lucie, wife of Thomas Hill of Fulham in co. Midd.
3. Mary.
4. Jane, wife of Thomas Sympson of Braferton in co. Ebor.
5. Esther.
6. Susan.

2. Christopher, æt. 3 ann.

1. Thomas Crosland, ætatis 4 annor. 13 Sept. a° 1665.

1. Elizabeth.
2. Jane.

BEALE OF WOODHOUSE.

ARMS.—Quarterly of six:
1. Sable, on a chevron between three griffin's heads erased or as many mullets of the field, a crescent for difference.
2. Argent, on a mound vert a bull passant gules horns or.
3. Gules, a chevron argent between three falcons of the second beaked or.
4. Sable, a bend between six crosses pattée-fusilly fitchée argent.
5. Quarterly argent and sable, on a bend gules three mullets of the first, a martlet for difference.
6. As the first.

CREST.—A unicorn's head erased or, crined sable.

Oliver Beale of Woodhouse in the parish of Drax in com. Ebor. living in a° 1612. = Anne, daughter and sole heire of Tho. Lake of Barley in co. Ebor.

Their issue:

- 3. John, died without issue.
- 4. Amiell Beale, of ......
- 5. Thomas, died without issue.
- 6. Joseph.
- 7. Edward.
- ...... 1 wife. = 2. Paul Beale, an Alderman of Yorke. = ... 2 wife.
- Ellen, da. of Marmaduke Constable, son of .... Constable of ye house of Everinghã, 1 wife. = 1. George Beale of Woodhouse, died a° 1643 vel circa. = Alice, daugh. of .... Haslewood of Maydwell in co. Northton, widow of Christophr Twysleton of Barley in co. Ebor., 2 wife.
- 1. Anne, wife of ...... Squire, Clerke.
- 2. Mary, the wife of George Hewley, Citizen of Yorke.

Issue of George Beale and Ellen:

- 2. John Beale of Monke Fryston in com. Ebor. = Frances, da. of .... Ickringall, widd. of Will. Louther of Monkefryston.
- 1. Henry Beale of Woodhouses, died 15° Febr. a° 1664. = Eliz. 4th daugh. of Randolfe Carleile of Sowerby in co. Ebor. Esqr. widd. of Samuell Heron, Clerke.
- Everild, died unmarried.

Issue of Henry Beale and Eliz.:

- 2. Henry, æt. unius anni.
- 1. George, æt. 3 ann. 15 Sept. 1665.
- 1. Elizabeth.
- 2. Helen.

PLUMPTON OF PLUMPTON.

ARMS.—Quarterly :
1. Azure, five fusils in fess or, each charged with an escallop gules.
2. and 3. Sable, a bend between six escallops or.
4. Argent, six lions rampant azure, three, two, and one.

Eldredus, tenuit terras in Plumpton de Gulielmo de Percy = ... ut patet per librum vocatam Domesday.

Petrus de Plumpton, miles a° 6 R. 1. = Helena.

Maria consanguinea Joh'is Alb. . . . . de Eboraco, uxor 1ª. = Nigellus de Plumpton, defunctus a° 15 Joh'is. = Julian de Warwick, uxor 2ª, vidua 15 Joh'is.

Robertus de Plumpton, vixit a° 10 H. 3. | Petrus de Plumpton, filius et hæres, in Bello contra Regem Joh'em, 16 Joh'is. = ...

Johannes Plumpton. | Nigellus de Plumpton, fil. et hæres, obijt a° 55 H. 3. = Avicia de Clare.

Gulielmus de Plumpton. = ... | Robertus de Plumpton, miles 16 E. 1, defunctus a° 26 E. 1. = Isabella, filia Serlonis de Westwick. | Alicia de Plumpton. | Avicia, uxor Jordani de Nesfield.

Henricus de Beaufits, D'n's de parva Ribstane a° 28 E. 1. = Cecyllia, filia et hæres Will'mi de Plumpton. | Rob'tus de Plumpton, miles 2. E. 2, defunctus a° 19 E. 2. = Lucia, filia D'ni Will'mi de Rosse, vidua 5 E. 3. | Willielmus de Plumpton, 9 E. 2. | Nigellus, a° 9 E. 2. | Rogerus, a° 9 E. 2. | Olivia, soror Rob'ti, 9 E. 2.

Alicia, filia et hæres, uxor 1, a° 2 E. 2. = Will'mus de Plumpton, petit Parliamentũ pro jure suo in Forrestâ de Knaresborough 5 E. 3, miles 13 E. 3, fundavit Cantariam apud Rippon 19 E. 3, Vicecom. Ebor. 23 E. 3, defunctus a° 43 E. 3. = Christiana Moubray, relicta Ric'i Ellenden, uxor secunda 12 E. 3, obijt 38 E. 3. | Marmaduke, a° 15 E. 2. | Isabella, uxor Ingrami Knowts, militis, 5 et 14 E. 2.

a

a

Johannes Gisburne, Major Civitatis Ebor. 45 Edw. 3. ═ Ellena, 9. H. 4.

Isabella, filia Henrici D'ni Scroope, soror Ric'i Archi-Ep'i Ebor. obijt 11 Edw. 3, uxor 1ª. ═ Rob'tus Plumpton, mil. 47 E. 3, obijt 8 H. 4, in servitio maritimo 46 E. 3. ═ Isabella, vocata de Kirkswold, 23 R. 2, uxor 2ª, postea nupta Nicholao de Midleton militi, 1 H. 5.

Alicia de Plumpton, 25 E. 3, primo nupta Richardo filio et hæredi Johannis Sherburne de Stonihurst, postea Roberto Butler de Warington militi, aº 47 E. 3.

Alicia, filia et hæres, ob. 2 H. 6. ═ Willielmus de Plumpton miles, Regi Ricardo secundo fidus et ideo decollatus, patre vivente.

Isabella, uxor Steph. Thorpe, aº 3 H. 6.

Kath. ux. Will'i la Zouch, militis.

Alison, soror Thomæ Remston, mil. uxor 1. ═ Robertus de Plumpton, miles, in exercitu Ducis Bedford. 3 H. 5. ═ Alicia, filia et hæres Galfridi Foljambe per quam habuit diversas terr. nupta 16 R. 2.

Ricardus Plumpton, condidit testam. 22 H. 6.
Georgius Plumpton, Clericus, condidit testam. 29 H. 6.
Thomas Plumpton, 4 H. 5.
Bryan Plumpton, aº 4 H. 5.

Jennet, uxor Will'mi Slingsby, arm'i 7 H. 5.

Eliz. filia Briani Stapleton, mil. uxor. 1ª, nupta 3 H. 5. ═ Will's de Plumpton miles, obijt 20 E. 4. ═ Joanna de Wintringham, uxor 2ª.

Galfridus de Plumpton. ═ Alicia, filia Thomæ Wintringham.

Jana, uxor Thomæ filio et hæredi Willielmi Middleton de Stockheld, 8 E. 4.
Agnes, uxor Ric'i Aldbrough militis, aº 3 E. 4.
Eliz. uxor Will'mi filij et hæredis Tho. Beckith, arm'i 34 H. 6.
Jana, uxor Thomæ filio Roberti Rosse armigeri.

Rob'tus de Plumpton, natus 1430, ob. 1450, sine prole.

Will's de Plumpton, natus 1435, ob. 1 E. 4, duxit Eliz. fil. Tho. D'ni Clifford. ═ . .

Isabella, filia .... 20 H. 8. ═ Robertus de Plumpton, miles, aº 22 E. 4, condidit testam' 15 H. 8. ═ Agnes, soror Will'mi Gascoigne de Gawthrop, in co. Ebor.

Ricardus Plumpton, Clericus, aº 15 H. 8.
Georgius Plumpton.
Johannes Plumpton.

Alicia.

Margareta, filia et cohæres ux. Joh'is, fil. et hær. Briani Rawcliffe, nupta 3 E. 4.

Eliz. altera fil. et cohæres ux. Joh'is, fil. et hær. Henrici Suthill ar. nupta 3 E. 4.

Robertus Plumpton, aº 2 E. 6.
Marmaduke Plompton.
Neale Plumpton, aº 2 E. 6.

Will'ms de Plumpton, arm. obijt apud Waterton 2 E. 6. ═ Isabella, filia Rob'ti Babthorpe, hæres Will'mi Babthorpe, et consanguineus et hæres Isabellæ nuper uxor Joh'is Hastings mil. nupta 11 H. 7.

a

Elizabetha.
Dorothea.
Clare.
Magdalena.

Anna, uxor Germani Poole de Redburne in co. Derb. ═ . . . . .

b

a *b*

Dionisius Plumpton de Rufforlington, filius 2dus. = Ursula, filia ...... Audbrough de Audbrough.

Robertus Plumpton, filius et hæres, obijt patre vivente. = Anna, filia Joh'is Norton de Norton Tower mil. relicta 2 E. 6, postea nupta Rob. Morton de Bawtre.

Germanus = Dorothea, filia Poole. .... Cockain.

Isabella Plumpton, infra æt. 2 E. 6.

Maria Plumpton, infra æt. 2 E. 6.

Anna Plumpton, 2 E. 6.

Anna, filia Edwardi Griffin de Dingley in com. Northampton, = Willielmus Plumpton, consanguineus et hæres Willielmi. = Maria, filia Willielmi Vavasour de Haslewood in com. Ebor. ob. s. prole.

Willielmus Plumpton, a° 1663. = Maria Lovick, obijt a° 1661.

Richardus Plumpton, obijt sine prole.

Johannes Plumpton.

Thomas Plumpton, obijt a°. 1663. = Maria, filia .... Buskeld.

Petrus Plumpton, obijt in insula de Axholme, a° 1661, sine prole.

Francesca, filia Will. Arthington de Arthington in co. Lanc. ar. nupta 41 Eliz. = Edwardus Plumpton, miles factus per R. Jac. obijt a° 1658, æt. suæ 77. = Francesca, filia Ric'i Chamney ar. ux. 2a, nupta 16.., obijt 1663.

Francesca.

Maria, uxor Francisci Scroope, postea Johannis Cottam.

.... uxor Henrici Scroope de Danbi, armigeri.

Katherina.

8. Edwardus Plumpton, a° 1665. = Anna, filia Anthonij Morgan.

7. Anthonius, ob. sine prole. a°. 1659.

5. Will'ms, 5. Rob'tus, obiere infantes.

9. Will'ms, 10. Carolus, 11. Francis, obiere infantes.

4. Johannes Plumpton, arm. lethaliter vulneratus in prœlio de Marston Moore, adversus rebelles fortissime dimicans, obijt a° 1644. = Anna, filia unica Ric'i Towneley de Towneley in com. Lanc. arm. nupta 3 Car. 1. ob. a° 1643.

1. Will'mus, 2. Franciscus, 3. Henricus, obiere infantes.

6. Dorothea, uxor Clementis Paston de Barningham in co. Norff. arm. nupta 1654, ob. a°. 1662.

3. Maria, 4. Clara, 5. Anna, in pueritiâ obiêre.

2. Francesca, uxor Thomæ Gage de Bentley, armigeri, ob. a° 1664.

1. Jana, nata a° 1630, ux. Thomæ filij et hær. Will. Worthington de Blainsco in co. Lanc. arm.

1. Edwardus, 2. Johannes, in cunis obiere.

Robertus Plumpton, filius et hæres, natus 13° Martij 1643, æt. 21 annor. 13 Sept. a° 1665.

LANGBARGH WAPENTAKE. *Yorke*, 13 *Sept.* 1665.

FOULIS OF INGLEBY-MANOUR.

ARMS.—Argent, three laurel-leaves proper, on an inescutcheon the badge of a baronet of England.
CRESTS.—1. A demi-unicorn winged ....
2. Out of a crescent .... a cross pattée fitchée ....

William Foulis, Keeper of the Privy Seale to James ye 1st, K. of Scotland, a° 1430. = ...

William Foulis. = Elizabeth, daughter of Sr Walter Ogleby Knt.

2. James Foulis. = Margaret, daughter to Sr Tho. Henderson Knt. | 1. Will'm, died wthout issue.

James Fowlis, heire to Will'm his uncle, purchased the lands of Collington from Will. Master of Glencarne, a° 1519. He was Keeper of the Register to James the 5th, King of Scotland, a° D'ni 1530. = Barbara, daughter of ...... Browne of the House of Fordee in Fife.

...... = ... daughter of the Earle of Marr, and her mother of the Earle of Monteith, and hers of Argyle.

Henry Foulis. = Mary Hadden, daughter of ...... Glennageis.

4. Thomas. | 2. David Foulis, came into England with James the sixth King of Scotland and first of England, and was made Knt and after Bart by him. He was agent from K. James to Qu. Eliz. and cofferer to Prince Henry and K. Charles the first, died in a° 1642. = Cordelia, daugh. of William Fleetwood of Great Missenden in com. Buck. Esqr, Serjeant at Law and Recorder of London in Qu. Eliz. time. | 1. James.

4. Edward, died unmarried. 5. Will'm Foulis. | 2. Robert, died unmarried. 3. John Foulis. | 1. Sr Henry Foulis of Ingleby Manour in Cleveland Bt. = Mary, eldest daughter of Sr Thomas Layton of Sexho in com. Ebor. Kt. | Anne, wife of George Purves, Dr of Phisick. Eliz.

2. Henry. 3. Edw. died unmarried. 4. Thomas. | 1. Sr David Foulis of Ingleby Manour Bart, æt. 32 ann. 13 Sept. 1665. = Cath. eldest da. of Sr David Watkins of ye county of Midd. Kt. | 1. Cordelia, died unmarried. 2. Mary, wife of Rob. Shafto of Benwell in com. Northumb. | 3. Cath. wife of Raphe Cole, son & heire of Sr Nich. Cole of Keeper in ye Bisshopprick of Durham Bart. 4. Eliz.

1. Honora, æt. unius an. et 9 mensiū. 2. Mary, æt. 6 mens. | 1. David, æt. 9 ann. 13 Sept. 1665. 2. Henry, died young. | 3. Will'm, æt. 6 ann. 4. Thomas, æt. 5 ann. | 5. Charles, died young. 6. John, æt. 3 ann.

YORKE, THE ANSTY. *Yorke*, 13 *Sept*. 1665.

NEWARKE OF ACHAM.

ARMS.—Sable, three saltires engrailed argent.
No proofe made.

Thomas Newarke of Acham in the county of the citty of Yorke. = Alice, daughter of ...... Redmers of ......

1. Peter Newarke of Ascham, Esqr of the Body to Qu. Mary, living in a° 1584. = Joane, daughter of Thomas Vavasour of Coppenthorpe in co. Ebor.

2. Robert Newark of Acham. = ... daughter of ...... Cawood, widow of ...... Casbut.

Issue of Peter:
1. Thomas, died unmarried.
2. Henry, died unmarried.

Issue of Robert:
Henry Newarke of Askham Bryan in the county of the citty of Yorke, died a° 1635, or thereabouts. = ... daughter of ...... Vavasour.

Issue of Henry:
2. Robert Newark. =
3. Will'm Newark of Askham Bryan in com. civitatis Ebor. =
4. Henry Newark of Askham Bryan.

1. Thomas Newark of Acham, died in a° 1657, or thereabouts. = Susan, daugh. of John Robynson of Ryther in com. Ebor.

1. Anne, wife of Will'm Hunter of Copmanthorp in co. civit. Ebor,
2. Cath. wife of .... Ferby of Askham Bryan.
3. Mary, wife of John Fox of Askham Richard.

Issue of Thomas and Susan:
2. John Newarke of Richmund in com. Ebor.
3. Arthur, died unmarried.
4. Henry.
5. Edward.

1. Thomas Newarke of Acham, æt. 31 annor. 13 Sept. 1665. = Winifride, daughter of Francis Childers of Carhouse in the parish of Doncaster in co. Ebor.

Susan.

Issue of Thomas and Winifride:
3. Henry, æt. 9 mens.
2. Francis, æt. 2 ann. 13 Sept. 1665.
1. Thomas, died young.
Elizabeth, died young.

Yorke, 13 *Sept*. 1665.

WYCLIFFE OF THORPE.

ARMS.—Quarterly:
1 and 4. Argent, a chevron between three cross-crosslets sable.
2 and 3. Argent, on a chevron sable three stag's heads cabossed of the field.

CREST.—A stag's head cabossed ...., between the attires a cross-crosslet ....

John Wicliffe of Thorpe in com. Ebor. died circa annum 1638.=......

Children:

- 3. Anne, wife of Anthony Wharton of Eppleby in com. Ebor.
- 2. Beale, wife of Henry Girlington of Girlington in com. Ebor.
- 1. Mary, wife of Martin Dethick of Gretham in the Bisshoprick of Durham.
- John Wycliffe of Thorpe in com. Ebor. died in his father's lifetime.=Margaret, daughter of Henry Dethick of Gretham in the Bisshoprick of Durham.

Children of John Wycliffe and Margaret:

- 4. Henry Wycliffe of Melmorby in com. Ebor. died circa ann. 1655.=......
  - John ......
- 3. Francis Wycliffe of ......=Jane, da. of Dr Mathew Levet, Rector of Fingell in co. Ebor.
- 2. George, died unmarried.
- 1. John Wycliffe of Thorpe in co. Ebor. æt. 50 an. 13 Sept. aº 1665; now Gentleman of the Horse to George Duke of Buckingham.=Mary, daughter of Robert Talbot of Worvill in com. Salop.
- 1. Mary, wife of Emanuell Trotter of ...... in com. Ebor.
- 2. Beale, wife of Tho. Trotter of the Ashes in the Bisshoprick of Durham.

Children of John Wycliffe and Mary:

- 3. Susan.
- 2. Margaret, wife of Thomas Rokesby of Mortham in com. Ebor. Esqr.
- 1. Mary, wife of ...... Lascelles of ...... in com. Ebor.
- 1. John Wycliffe, æt. 22 ann. 13 Sept. 1665.
- 2. Robert, æt. 20 ann.

CAYLEY OF BRUMPTON.

Hugh de Cayley of Owby in com. Norff. died a° 14° Edw. I. A° Domini 1286 = Agnes, daughter and heire of Hamo de Hamsted.

Sr William Cayley of Owby Kn^t. = ...

John Cayley of Owby Esqr. = ...

1. Sr William Cayley of Owby Kn^t, eldest son. = Alice, daughter of Sr John Bruse Knight.

2. John Caley of Normanton in com. Ebor. = ...

Children of Sr William Cayley and Alice:

1. Agnes, eldest da. and coheire, wife of John Harsicke of . . . . . . in com. Norff.

2. Eva, second daughter and coheire, wife of Edmund Clipsby of Clipsby in com. Norff.

Children of John Caley of Normanton:

1. Hugh Caley, eldest son, ob. sine prole.

2. William Cayley of Normanton in com. Ebor. = ...

3. John Cayley. = ...

John Lake of Normanton [in right of his wife Jennet], which continewed with the name for 6 generations, till the raigne of Qu. Eliz. when Anne, daughter and heire of John Lake, the last of that name, married to Oliver Beale of Woodhouse in the parish of Drax in com. Ebor. in whose right a parte of Normanton passed to that family. = Jennet, daughter and sole heire of William Caley of Normanton.

William Cayley. = ...

1. John Caley, eldest son, ob. s. prole.

2. Edward Caley of the citty of Yorke, 2^d son. = ...

1. William Caley, eldest son. = ...

2. John Caley, Parson of Thormondby in com. Ebor.

John Cayley of Malton, in com. Ebor. = ...

1. Edward Caley of Malton. = ...

2. William Cayley, Parson of Thormonby in com. Ebor.

3. Lawrence Cayley, third son.

1. William Cayley of Thormonby, eldest son, died at Thormonby a° 1586. = Joane, daughter of Richard Gouldthorpe, Alderman and Mayor of the citty of Yorke a° 1588. She died at Brompton in Pickering-Lithe in com. Ebor. [one other of whose daughters was marr. to Hugh Ingram, citizen of London, father of Sr Arthur and Sr Will'm Ingram K^ts, from whom all the family of the Ingrams in com. Ebor. are descended.]

a

2. Richard Cayley, second sonne.

a

1. Edward Caley of Brompton in Pickering Lyth, eldest son, died about the yeare 1633. = Anne, daughter of William Watters of Cundall in co. Ebor. Esqr, married in a° 1604.

2. James Cayley of Thormonby in com. Ebor. = Mary, daughter of Ralphe Bell of Sommerby in com. Eborum.

1. Sr William Cayley of Brompton Kn^t, eldest son, knighted by King Charles y^e 1st at Theobalds 2 March 1641, created Bar^t 20 April 1661, æt. 56 an. 29 Aug. 1665. = Dorothy, eldest daughter of Sr William St Quintin of Harpham in the county of Yorke Bar^t, married a° 1633.

2. Sr Arthur Cayley of Newland in com. Warr. Kn^t, knighted at London 13° Junij 1660, marr. Mary, daughter of ...... Oldfeild of Spalding in com. Linc. relict of Barnabas Holbech, of Birchley-Hall in y^e parish of Fillongley in com. Warr. first wife, died without issue. = Hesther, daughter of .... Simonds of London, relict of Charles Hayles of Newland in com. Warr. 2^d wife.

Thomas Cayley.

Mary, died unmarried.
Elizabeth, wife of Robert Colthurst of Upleatham in Cleveland gent.
Catherine, wife of Arthur Ingram of Knottingley Esqr.
Anne, wife of Tho. Davile of Kirby Fleetham neer Richmond in com. Ebor. Esqr.

Edward.
Richard.
Peter.
Mathew.

Anne.
Mary.

1. Edward Caley, eldest son, died without issue.

2. William Cayley of Brompton Esqr, second son, æt. 30 an. 29 Aug. 1665. = Mary, onely daughter and sole heire of Barnabas Holbech of Birchley Hall in co. Warr. by Mary, daughter of ...... Oldfeild of Spalding in the county of Linc., after married to Arthur Caley, now Sr Arthur Caley of Newland, ut supra.

3. Arthur Caley, third son. = Eliz. daughter of Thomas Shipton of Lyth.

4. Cornelius Cayley.
5. Hugh Cayley.

Mary.

Dorothy.

1. William Caley, eldest son, æt. 12 an. 29 Aug. 1665.
2. Arthur Cayley, æt. 10 ann.
3. Edward, ætatis 9 ann.
4. Barnabas, æt. 7 an.
5. Thomas, æt. 6 an.
6. Charles, æt. 5 ann.
7. Symon, æt. 4. an.
8. Henry, æt. 2 an.

LANGBARG WAPENTAKE. *Yorke*, 21 *Mart.* 1665.

PENNYMAN OF ORMESBY.

ARMS.—Gules, a chevron ermine between three half spears with broken staves or headed argent, on an inescutcheon the badge of a baronet of England.

CREST.—Out of a mural coronet gules a lion's head erased or, pierced through the neck with a broken spear as in the arms.

Robert Pennyman Esqr.=......

Will'm Pennyman of Ormesby in com. Ebor. Esqr.=......

....=James Pennyman of Ormesby in com. Ebor. Esqr, unto whom Will'm Segar Esqr, Norroy King of Armes, by his Instrument under the seale of his office, bearing date 1 May a^o^ 1599, granted the Crest here depicted to his coate of armes.=Anne, daughter of ..... Burnet of ..... in Cleveland in com. Ebor.

Children of James Pennyman by his first wife:

- Will. Pennyman Esqr, one of y^e^ six Clerks in Chancery.=Anne, da. of Robert Aske of Aughton in com. Ebor. Esqr.
  - Sr William Pennyman B^t^, Governour of Oxford a^o^ 1645, died without issue.=Anne, da. and sole heire of Will'm Atterton, by .... his wife, da. & coheir of Christopher Ld Conyers of Hornby Castle in com. Ebor.
- Reginald, Thomas, Robert, John, ob. s. prole.

Children of James Pennyman and Anne Burnet:

- 2. Will'm Pennyman.
- Cath. da. of Will'm Kingsley of Canterbury, 1 wife.=1. James Pennyman of Ormesby Esqr, died on St Luke's day a^o^ 1655.=Joane, da. of ...... Smith, Citizen of London.
- Ellen, wife of Alan Certain of Red Carr in co. Ebor.
- Mary, wife of Thomas Pilley of Skeldersheugh in co. Ebor.
- Anne, wife of Henry Yoward of Westerdale in co. Ebor.
- Eliz. wife of Strangwayes Bradshaw of Upsall in co. Ebor.

Children of James Pennyman by Cath. Kingsley:

- 2. Thomas Pennyman, D^r^ in Divinity, now Rector of the Parish Church of Stokesley in com. Eborum.
- 1. Sr James Pennyman of Ormesby Kn^t^ & Bar^t^, made Kn^t^ by K. Charles y^e^ 1st, and Bar^t^ by K. Charles the 2^d^, æt. 58 ann. 21 Martij 1665.=Eliz. da. & coheir of Stephen Norcliffe of Yorke.

Children of James Pennyman by Joane Smith:

- Will'm Pennyman of Ormesby, marr. Joane, daughter of ..... Tocketts of ..... in Kent.
- John Pennyman.
- Joane, wife unto John Gybson of Welburne in co. Ebor.

Son of Sr James Pennyman and Eliz. Norcliffe:

Thomas Pennyman, son and heire, æt. 24 annorum, 21° Martij a^o^ D. 1665.=Frances, daughter of Sr John Lowther of Lowther in co. Westmerland Bar^t^.

- 2. John, æt. 2 ann. 1665.
- 1. James, æt. 4 ann. 21 Mart. 1665.

STAINECROSSE WAPENTAKE. *Barnesley*, 15 *Sept.* 1665.

ELMEHIRST OF HOUNDHILL.

ARMS.—Barry-wavy of six argent and sable, a canton of the second.

The proofe of these armes respited. Nothing done.

Robert de Elmehirst, temp. Edw. 1 et Edw. 2.=........

1. John de Elmehirst, 15 E. 3, of Worsbrough.=......
2. Richard de Elmehirst, 41 Edw. 3.=......
3. Will'm de Elmehirst.

Maud, daughter and heire, wife of Roger Genne of Ouzlethwayt, ob. s. prole.
John Elmehirst, Lord of Elmehirst a° 1409.=......

2. Will'm Elmehirst, brother and heire.=Alice.
1. John Elmehirst, died w[th]out issue.=Margaret, afterwards marr. to George Tingle.

Robert Elmehirst.=Margaret.

3. Will'm Elmehirst.=Agnes, daughter of ...... Hall of Smethley.
2. James Elmehirst, Priest, Crosse Bearer to Card. Wolsey, and Parson of S[t] Swythens in Lond.
1. Robert, died w[th]out issue.
1. Agnes, y[e] wife of .... Benson.
2. Margaret, wife of Robert Genne of Ouzletwayt.

Roger Elmehirst, a° 17 Eliz. Reginæ.=Eliz. daughter of .... Marshe of Deyhouse in the parish of Darton.
1. Agnes, first married to John Forster; and after to Thomas Addye of Ederthorpe.
2. Jennet, wife unto John Cawood of Worsbrough.

3. Will'm.
4. Roger, Custom[r] of Lymrick in Ireland, ob. sine prole.
2. John.=
1. Rob[t] Elmehirst.=Eliz. da. of Will. Thorneton of Tiresall, widd. of Marke Foxcroft.
1. Eliz. first marr. to Rob[t] Castleforth of Darley cliffe; after to John Booth, L[d] of the Manour of Worsbrough.
2. Joane, wife of Nicholas Stamforth of Tunslaw.
3. Margaret, wife to Roger Genne of Ouzletwayt.
4. Agnes, wife of .... Needome of Rotheram.
5. Mary, wife unto John Allot of Doncaster.

Margaret, daughter and coheire of Richard Micklethwayt of Swayth-Hall, first wife.=1. Richard Elmehirst, died in a° 1653, or thereabouts.=Eliz. daughter of Tho. Wayte of Haxby, 2. wife.
2. William Elmehirst of Wadham Colledge in Oxford.

Eliz. died unmarried.
2. Will'm.
3. Tho.
1. Richard Elmehirst of Houndhill in co. Ebor. æt. 25 annor. 15 Sept. a° 1665.=Alice, da. of Gervase Dixon of Upper-Woodhall in co. Ebor.
1. Eleanor, wife of Hastings Rasby of Smeton in co. Ebor.
2. Rebecca, died unmarried.
3. Elizabeth, wife of Edward Canby of Thurne in com. Ebo.
4. Anne.
5. Mary.

Elizabeth, æt. 4 ann. 14° Sept. a° 1665.
Eleanor, died young.

STRAFFORD & TICKHILL WAPENTAKE. *Rotheram*, 16 *Sept.* 1665.

MOUNTNEY OF ROTHERAM.

ARMS.—Gules, a bend between six martlets or.

Sir John Mountney Knight, a° 22 H. 6. = ...

2. Thomas Mountney. = ...

1. Robert Mountney Esqr. 20 E. 4. = ...

Thomas Mountney. = ...

Barbara, daughter and heire. = Robert Thwayts of Marston in co. Ebor. ar.

Nicholas Mountney Esqr. = ...

Anne, wife of Will'm Ingleby, who had by her Sherclyffe Hall and other lands, and died w^th^out issue.

...... a son, who died in his childhood.

John Mountney = Maud, daughter of George Wastneys of Headon in co. Nott.

1. Thomas Mountney of Wheatley in com. Ebor. = Mary, da. of John Draycote of Paynesley in co. Staff. Esqr.

2. Arnold Mountney, died without issue.

3. Nicholas Mountney of Rotheram in com. Ebor. died a° 1616, or thereabouts. = Ellen, daughter of Richard Burrows of Rotheram.

Thomas Mountney Esqr. died in a° 1635, or thereabouts. = Eliz. daughter of Sr William Cave of Walterstoke in com. Oxon.

2. John, died unmarried.

1. Richard Mountney of Rotheram, æt. 67 annorum 16 Sept. a° 1665. = Katherine, eldest daughter of Sr George Fitz-Geffrey Kn^t.

Anne, wife of Anthony Wright of Maltby in com. Ebor.

Arnold Mountney of .... in com. Northumberland.

1. Elizabeth, wife of .... Brawne.
2. Jane, wife of ..... Brawne of ......

Francis, æt. 32 an. 16 Sept. a° 1665.

1. Anne, wife of Charles Tucker of .... in com. Wilts, now residing in Rotheram.
2. Catherine, wife of Jasper Blythman of Newlathes in com. Ebor. Esqr.

Sciant præsentes et futuri, quod ego Johanna Mountney, filia et hæres Thomæ Mounteney, quondam uxor Thomæ Furnivall ch'r, dedi, concessi, &c. Johanni Mountney filio meo manerium meũ de Bulcotes, cum omnibus pertinentijs in Comitatu Nottyngham ; Dedi etiam prædicto Johanni omnia terras et tenementa, prata, &c. in Rissheton juxta Rothewell in com. Northampt. &c. ac in Swynton et Scoles in com. Ebor. Habendũ, &c. prædictis Johanni hæredibus et Assignatis suis, &c. Data apud Shircliffe in com. Ebor. in festo Sancti Martini Episcopi in Hyeme, 15° Ric. 2.

Circular seal appended: device, two shields suspended from a tree, each bearing a bend between six martlets: inscription "+ SIGILLUM JOHANNE DE FURNIVALL."

Stokesley, 8° *Sept*. 1666.

CHALONER OF GISBROUGH.

ARMS.—Quarterly of nine:
1. Sable, a chevron between three cherub's heads or.
2. Gules, a chevron argent between three buck's heads cabossed of the second attired or.
3. Or, a lion rampant azure.
4. Per pale gules and or, a Roman P in pale argent between two lions counter-rampant counterchanged.
5. Argent, a cross engrailed fleury between four Cornish choughs sable.
6. Vert, a chevron between three wolf's heads erased argent.
7. Sable, a chevron between three fleurs-de-lis argent.
8. Sable, a chevron between three goat's heads erased or.
9. Azure, a lion passant gardant argent.

CREST.—A demi sea-wolf rampant ....

Elizabeth, daughter of S[r] Willm. Fleetwood Serjeant at Law and Recorder of the Citty of London, first wife. = S[r] Thomas Chaloner of Steeple Claydon in com. Buck. and Gisbrough in com. Ebor. Kn[t]. = Judith, daughter of Sr William Blount of the Citty of London, second wife.

Children:

4. James Chaloner, died circa an. 1659. = Ursula, daugh. of .... Fairfax, and sister to S[r] Wm Fairfax of Steeton in com. Ebor. K[t].
   - Edmund, æt. 25 ann. 8 Sept. 1666.
   - 1. Mariana, wife of Richard Brathwayt of Warcop in com. Westmerland.
   - 2. Jemieta.
   - 3. Veriana.

3. Thomas, obijt sine prole.

2. Edward Chaloner, dyed in a° 1625, æt. 35 ann. = Eliz. da. of Dr Ovenden, a Prebend of Canterbury.
   - 3. Edward Chaloner of Gisbrough Esqr, æt. 41 annor. 8 Sept. 1666. = Anne, daughter of Sr Richard Ingoldsby of Lenborow in com. Buckingh. Kn[t].
     - 3. Edward, æt. 6 an. 1666.
     - 2. Thomas, æt. 10 an. 1666.
     - 1. William Chaloner, son and heir, æt. 11 ann. 8° Sept. a° 1666.
     - 1. Elizabeth, æt. 14 an. 1666.
     - 2. Anne, æt. 12. ann.
     - 3. Mary, æt. 9 ann.
     - 4. Dorothy, æt. 8 ann.

1. Sr Will'm. Chaloner, Bart., obijt sine prole.

1. Mary.
2. Elizabeth.
3. Dorothy.

STRAFFORD AND TICKHILL WAPENTAKE. *Rotheram*, 16 *Sept*. 1665.

VINCENT OF BARONBROUGH.

ARMS.—Quarterly:
1 and 4. Argent, two bars gules, on a canton of the second a trefoil stalked and slipped or.
2 and 3. Gules, on a chief indented argent three lions rampant azure.

CREST.—A trefoil stalked and slipped ....

John Vincent of Braywell in com. Ebor. slayne in the battail of Wakefield 39 H. 6, being then Reciever of Rich. Duke of Yorke. = Agnes, daughter of ...... Barlow of Barlow in com. Derb.

Bryan Vincent, temp. Edw. quarti. = Beatrix, daugh. of Sr Tho. Cockaine of Ashburne in co. Derb. Kt. 1. Allison. 2. Isabell.

John Vincent of Braywell, ao 1 Henr. 7. = Anne, daughter ...... Rowlesley of Rowlesley in com. Derb.

Christophr, died unmarried. Agnes, daugh. of ....., Lacy of Beverley in co. Ebor. 24 H. 7. = John Vincent of Braywell. = Margery, daughter of ...... Page of Bunney in com. Nott.

1. Thomas Vincent of Braywell, 7o Edw. 6. = Dionisia, da. of Rich. Pewtinger of Carleton in Lindrick in com. Eborum.

2. John Vincent of Braywell, 16 Qu. Eliz. = Margt, daugh. of .... Hudson of Brocher neere Bradfeild in com. Eborum.

3. Richard Vincent of Firsby neere Braywell in com. Eborum. = Alice, daughter of Thomas Allen of Rowley neer Wetherby in com. Ebor. widow of Robert Lepton of Firsby.

Dorothy, sole dau. and heire, wife of Thomas Waterhouse of Hallifax in co. Ebor. died in ao 1627.

Francis Vincent, Standerd Bearer to Sr John Norreys, Generall of ye English Forces in the Netherlands, aged 62 years ao 1630. = Susan, daughter of John Gifford of Laughton in le Morthing in com. Ebor.
a

Richard Vincent of Firsby in com. Ebor., died ao 1617. = Elizabeth, daughter of Thomas Rokeby of Hotham in com. Ebor.
b

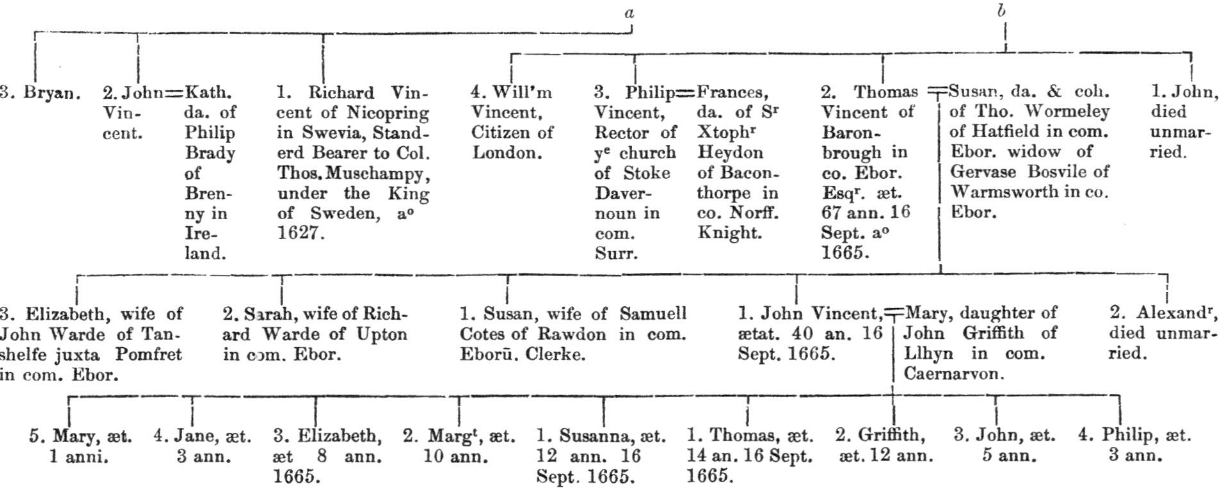
a
b
3. Bryan.
2. John Vincent. = Kath. da. of Philip Brady of Brenny in Ireland.
1. Richard Vincent of Nicopring in Swevia, Standerd Bearer to Col. Thos. Muschampy, under the King of Sweden, a° 1627.
4. Will'm Vincent, Citizen of London.
3. Philip Vincent, Rector of y[e] church of Stoke Davernoun in com. Surr. = Frances, da. of Sr Xtoph[r] Heydon of Baconthorpe in co. Norff. Knight.
2. Thomas Vincent of Baronbrough in co. Ebor. Esqr. æt. 67 ann. 16 Sept. a° 1665. = Susan, da. & coh. of Tho. Wormeley of Hatfield in com. Ebor. widow of Gervase Bosvile of Warmsworth in co. Ebor.
1. John, died unmarried.
3. Elizabeth, wife of John Warde of Tanshelfe juxta Pomfret in com. Ebor.
2. Sarah, wife of Richard Warde of Upton in com. Ebor.
1. Susan, wife of Samuell Cotes of Rawdon in com. Eborū. Clerke.
1. John Vincent, ætat. 40 an. 16 Sept. 1665. = Mary, daughter of John Griffith of Llhyn in com. Caernarvon.
2. Alexand[r], died unmarried.
5. Mary, æt. 1 anni.
4. Jane, æt. 3 ann.
3. Elizabeth, æt 8 ann. 1665.
2. Marg[t], æt. 10 ann.
1. Susanna, æt. 12 ann. 16 Sept. 1665.
1. Thomas, æt. 14 an. 16 Sept. 1665.
2. Griffith, æt. 12 ann.
3. John, æt. 5 ann.
4. Philip, æt. 3 ann.

AGBRIGG & MORLEY WAPENTAKE. *Yorke*, 11° *Aug*. 1666.

FORSTER OF ROTHWELL.

ARMS.—Argent, a chevron engrailed vert between three bugle-horns sable stringed of the second.

No proofe made of these armes.

Ralph Forster of .... in co. Northumbr. dyed in a° .... ætatis 50 ann. = ... daughter & heire of ......

- 1. Richard Forster, died young.
- 2. James Forster of .... in co. Northumbr. died in a° .... æt. circa 76 an. = Joane, daughter of Robert Roode of .... in co. Ebor.
  - Frances, dyed young.
  - 1. Christopher, dyed young.
  - 2. Ralph Forster of Rothwell in co. Ebor. æt. circa 40 an. 11° Aug. a° 1666. = ... daughter of Philip Nisbet of Essington in com. Ebor.
  - 3. John Forster æt. circa 36 an. 11 Aug. 1666. = Elizabeth, daughter and coheir of Henry Hoyle of ..... neer Halifax in com. Ebor.
    - 1. James, dyed young.
    - 2. John Forster, æt. 3 annor. 11° Aug. 1666.
    - 3. Raphe, æt. unius anni 11 Aug. a° 1666.
    - 1. Mary, dyed young.
    - 2. Hannah, æt. 9 ann.
    - 3. Ruth, æt. 7. ann.
    - 4. Elizabeth, æt. 5 ann.

OUSE AND DARWENT WAPENTAKE. *Yorke*, 13° *Aug*. 1666.

HEADLAM OF KEXBY.

ARMS.—Gules, a chevron or between three lamb's heads erased argent.

CREST.—A demi-griffin segreant holding a spear, all argent.

Raphe Headlam, Citizen of Yorke. = ...

- 2. John.
- 3. Robert Headlam, Citizen of London.
- 1. Leonard Headlam, Towne-Clerke of Yorke, died in a° 1641. = Jane, daughter and heir of John Knaggs of Kendall neer Otley in com. Ebor.
  - 1. John Headlam of Kexby in com. Ebor. died in a° 1664. = Margaret, 2d daughter of Sr John Lyster of Kingston super Hull in co. Ebor. Knt.
    - 1. William Headlam of Kexby, æt. 18 annor. 13 Aug. 1666.
    - 2. John.
    - 3. Walter.
    - 4. Charles.
    - 5. Richard.
    - 1. Eliz.
    - 2. Susan, } dyed young.
    - 3. Frances.
  - 2. William Headlam, died unmarried.
- 1. Mary, died unmarried.
- 2. Elizabeth, died unmarried.

BUCKROSE WAPENTAKE. *Malton*, 12° *Sept.* 1666.

HEBLETHWAYTE OF NORTON.

ARMS.—Argent, two pales azure, on a canton or a mullet pierced sable.
CREST.—Out of a ducal coronet or a demi-wolf rampant ermines.

Anne, daughter of Rich. Hillyard & sister to Sr Christoph^r Hillyard of Wynestead in Holdernesse, 1 wife. = Thomas Heblethwayt, a Barrister of the Middle Temple, London (on whom James Heblethwayt of Norton setled all his lands), died at Hull a° D. 1647. = Mary, daughter of Tho. Sutheby of Birdsall in com. Ebor. relict of Thomas Hungate of North-Dalton in co. Ebor. 2 wife.

Anne, wife of Raphe Yoward of Westerdale in com. Ebor.

1. James Heblethwayt of Norton in com. Ebor. died in anno. 1653. = Anne, youngest daughter of Tho. Hungate of North-Dalton in co. Ebor.

2. Thomas Heblethwayt, slayne at Manchester in the service of King Charles the first a° 1641 sine prole. = Isabell, daughter of Isaac Mountaine of Wistow in com. Ebor.

Sr Thomas Heblethwayte of Norton in com. Ebor. Kn^t. æt. 37 annorū 12° Septembr. a° 1666. = Barbara, daughter of Sr George Marwood of Little Buskby in com. Ebor. Bar^t.

3. Charles, æt. 7 ann.
4. Mountagne, æt. 3 ann. et amplius.
5. George æt. 2 mens.

1. James Heblethwayt, son & heire, æt. 14 ann. 12° Sept. 1666.
2. Thomas, æt. 10 ann.

1. Frances.
2. Barbara.
4. Theodosia.
6. Margaret.

3. Anne,
5. Eliz.
dyed young.

YORKE CITTY. *Yorke*, 19 *Martij*, 1665.

LANGLEY OF YORKE.

ARMS.—Argent, a cockatrice with the tail nowed sable crested and membered gules, a canton of the last.
He refers himselfe to the Visitation of Berk. for proofe of y^e armes.

Henry Langley of Hill-End in com. Berks. = ...

Thomas Langley of Clifton in com. Oxon. = ...

William Langley of Akington in com. Berks. died in a° .... = ... daughter of John Carryer of ...... in com. ......

Anne, daughter of Henry Langley of Hill-End in com. Berks. 1. wife, obijt sine prole. = William Langley, M^r of Arts, sometime of Pembroke-Colledge in Oxford, now residing in y^e Citty of Yorke, ætatis 57 ann. 19° Martij, a° Domini 1665. = Priscilla, daughter of Henry Ayscough of the Citty of Yorke, 2^d wife.

BULMER WAPENTAKE. *Yorke*, 19° *Martij*, 1665.

FRANKLAND OF ALDWARKE.

ARMS.—Azure, a dolphin naiant embowed argent, on a chief or three saltires gules.
CREST.—A demi-dolphin argent.

Hugh Franklin, alias Frankland, of Nelsing in com. Ebor. 8° Eliz. = ...

Richard Frankland. = ... daughter of . . . . . . Young, Arch-Bishop of Yorke.

Jane, daughter of Sr Charles Wren of Binchester in the Bishoprick of Durham, 1 wife. = Sr Henry Frankland of Aldwarke in com. Ebor. K^t^, died in a° 1624, vel circa. = Frances, daughter of Sr Henry Windham of . . . . in com. Norff. Kn^t^, 2 wife.

Anthony Frankland of Ellerton in com. Ebor.

1. Thomas Frankland, Lieutenant Colonell to Sr Wm Pennyman K^t^, in the service of y^e^ late King Charles, died unmarried.

2. Henry Frankland of Aldwarke in co. Ebor. æt. 47 ann. 19° Mart. 1665. = Dorothy, daughter of Thomas Holcroft of . . . . . . in com. Wilts.

Frances, wife of William Browne.

2. Henry, æt. 14 ann.
3. Will'm, æt. 13 ann.
4. Francis, æt. 11 ann.

1. Anthony Frankland, ætatis 18 ann. 19 Martij, 1665.

1. Dorothy, wife of Sr Gervase Cutler of Stainbrough in com. Ebor. Kn^t^.
2. Rebecca.

YORKE CITTY. *Yorke*, 20 *Mart.* 1665.

WATKINSON OF YORKE.

ARMS.—Quarterly argent and azure, on a bend gules three roses of the first.
CREST.—An eagle's head erased azure, in the beak a rose-branch slipped, leaves vert, flower argent.

Henry Watkinson of Leedes in com. Ebor. died a° 1638, or thereabouts. = Bridget, daughter of Robert Lodge of Leedes.

Henry Watkinson, D^r^ of Law, now residing in Yorke, æt. 38 an. 20 Martij, 1665. = Elizabeth, daughter of Jonathan Jennings of Rippon in com. Ebor. widow of Christopher Hodgson of Newhall in com. Ebor.

Henry, ætatis 8 mensium 20 Martij, a° 1665.

Mary.

Yorke, 19° *Martij*, 1665.

ROBINSON OF NEWBY.

Arms.—Vert, a chevron between three stags standing at gaze or.

Crest.—In a coronet composed of fleurs-de-lis or on a mound vert a stag as in the arms.

...... daughter of John Redman of Fullforth in the county of Yorke, first wife. = William Robinson, Mercht of Yorke, and twice Ld Mayor of yt citty, died about the yeare 1610, being aged 82 yeares. = ... daughter of Tho. Harrison, Mercht of Yorke.

William Robinson, Citizen and Mercht of Yorke, and once Ld Mayor of yt citty, dyed circa annū 1618. = ... da. of Sr Henry Jenkins of Grymston in co. Ebor. Kt.

Thomas, died unmarried.

Mary, daughter and coheire of Sr William Brambrough of Ouseham in com. Ebor. Kt, 1 wife. = Sr William Robinson of Newby in com. Eborū, knighted at the Coronation of K. Charles ye First in Scotland, died 1 Sept. 1658, æt. 78 ann. = Frances, daughter of Sr Thomas Metcalfe of Nappa in co. Ebor. Kt, 2d wife.

Will'm, died unmarried.

3. John, dyed young.

2. Thomas Robinson, a Turkey Merchant, now residing in Yorke. = Eliz. daugh. of Charles Tankard of Arden in co. Ebor. Esqr.

1. Sr Metcalfe Robinson of Newby in com. Ebor. Bart, æt. 36 an. 19 Martij, 1665, now residing at Rocliffe in Bulmer Wapentake. = Margt, da. of Sr Will'm Darcy of Witton in com. Palat. Dunelm. Knt.

1. Eliz. wife of Philip Rycot, an East India Merchant.
2. Margt, wife of Will. Weddell of Erswike in co. Ebor. Esqr.
3. Frances, wife of Rob. Belt of Overton in co. Ebor. Esqr.

Mary and 3 more, dyed young.

1. William Robinson.
2. Tankard Robinson.

1. Elizabeth.
2. Margt.

William, died in his infancy.

THE AYNSTYE. *Yorke*, 19° *Mart*. 1665.

ROUNDELL OF MARSTON.

Respite given for exhibiting ye armes.

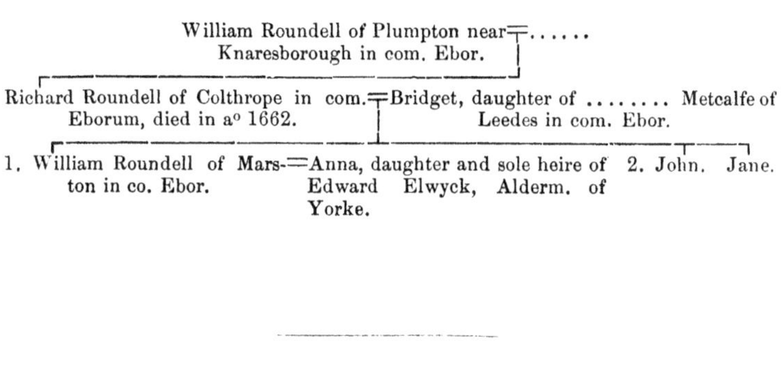

OUSE & DARWENT WAPENTAKE. *Yorke*, 20 *Martij*, 1665.

ROBINSON OF DIGHTON.

ARMS.—Vert, on a chevron between three bucks trippant or as many cinquefoils gules, a mullet for difference.

CREST.—A stag trippant or, pellettée, attired of the first, gorged with a chaplet vert, a mullet for difference.

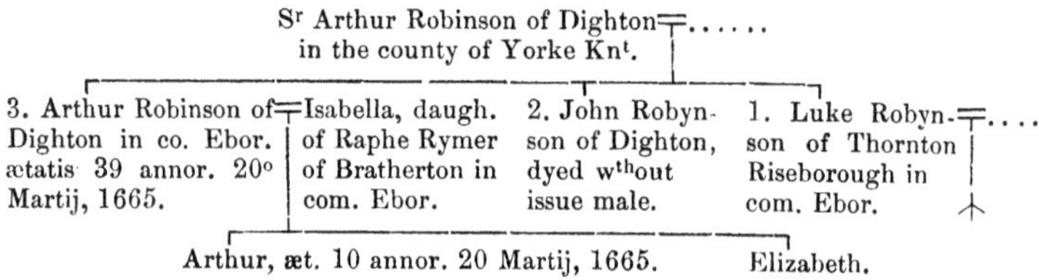

BULMER WAPENTAKE. *Yorke*, 20 *Martij*, 1665.

DARCY OF COLBURNE.

ARMS.—Quarterly, a mullet gules for difference :
1. Azure, three cinquefoils between nine cross-crosslets argent.
2. Azure, three bars gemelles and a chief or.
3. Azure, a maunche or.
4. Sable, a saltire argent.

CREST.—On a chapeau gules turned up ermine a bull passant sable, a mullet for difference.

Coniers Lord Darcy and Conyers. = Dorothy, daughter of S[r] Henry Bellasses Kn[t].

3. Henry Darcy of Colborne in com. Ebor. 3[d] son, æt. 55 annorum 20 Martij, a° D. 1665. = Mary, daughter unto William Scrope of Highley in com. Palat. Dunelm. Esq[r].

1. Coniers Lord Darcy & Conyers. = ...

2. Henry.
3. Thomas.

1. Philip, æt. 34 annor. 20 Martij, 1665.

1. Frances, wife of Robert Colingwood of Durhã in Epãtu.

2. Mary.
3. Dorothy.

BULMER WAPENTAKE. *Yorke*, 20 *Mart.* 1665.

APPLEBY OF LINTON.

ARMS.—Azure, six martlets or, three, two, and one.

Ambrose Appleby of Lynton upon Ouse in co. Ebor. died in a° 1649, or thereabouts. = Mary, daughter of Thomas Crompe of Bradforton in com. Wigorn.

2. Francis Appleby of Lortington in the county of Yorke, died in a° 1663. = ... daughter of Gerard Salvein of Croxdell in y[e] B[p]prick of Durhã Esq[r].

Ellen, daughter of S[r] Thomas Gascoigne of Barnbow in co. Ebor. Bar[t], 1 wife. = 1. Thomas Appleby of Lynton, ætat. 47 annor. 20 Martij, a° 1665. = Elizabeth, daughter unto John Johnson of Osmotherley in com. Ebor. 2[d] wife.

1. Ambrose, dyed in his father's life time, then aged 12 years.
2. Francis, æt. 7 an. 1665.
3. Gerard, æt. 5 ann.

1. Mary.
2. Marg[t], dyed young.

1. Mary, æt. 14 annor. 20 Martij, 1665.
2. Ellen, æt. 11 ann.

Thomas, æt. 9 mensiũ 20 Martij, 1665.

3. Elizabeth, æt. 5 an. 1665.
4. Julian, æt. 3 ann.

THE AYNSTIE.

Yorke, 20 *Mart.* 1665.

BREAREY OF YORKE.

ARMS.—Argent, a cross potent gules between four torteaux, a canton azure.

Walter Breary of Leedes in com. Ebor. gent.=...... daughter of Robert Brooke.

Children:

- William Brearey, twice Ld Mayor of the Citty of Yorke, died in a^o 1637.=Elizabeth, daughter of Thomas Casson of Leedes.
- 1. Mary.
- 2. Sibill.

Children of William and Elizabeth:

- 3. Samuell, married Ellen y^e daught^r of Aldermā Topham (L^t Co^ll in y^e Army of K. Ch. y^e 1st).
- 4. James, marr. Helen, da. of Henry Acroyd of Fogerthorp.
- 5. Henry, marr. Mary, da. of Marke Micklethwayt of Marston, Clerke.
- 2. Christopher Breary, now Alderm. of the Citty of Yorke, æt. 64 an. 20 Mart. 1665.=Elizabeth, daughter unto Thomas Key, a Merchant in Yorke (and sole heire).
- 1. Will'm Breary, obijt sine prole.=Eliz. da. of Humphry Robinson of Thicket in com. Eborū.
- 1. Sarah, wife of Thomas Herbert, a Merchant in Yorke.
- 2. Eliz. y^e wife of Edmund Bracken, a Merchant in Yorke.
- 3. Susan, wife of Robert Hemsworth, Ld Mayor of Yorke.
- 4. Franc. wife of Leonard Thompson, twice Ld Mayor of the Citty of Yorke.
- 5. Mary, wife of Crescy Burnet, Alderm. of the Citty of Yorke.

Children of Christopher and Elizabeth:

- 3. Walter.
- 2. Christopher Breary, æt. 32 annor. 20 Martij, 1665.=Elizabeth, daughter of Francis Spachhurst of the Middle Temple, London (and sole heire), Lieu^t Co^ll in y^e Army of K. Ch. y^e First.
  - Elizabeth, æt. 5 mensium 20 Martij, a^o 1665.
- 1. William, died without issue.
- 1. Elizabeth, wife of Thomas Crosland of Crosland-Hill in co. Ebor.
- 2. Mary.

Yorke, 20 *Martij*, 1665.

WORMELEY OF RIKHALL.

ARMS.—Gules, on a chief indented argent three lions rampant azure.

John Wormeley of Hatfeild in com. Ebor. = Margaret, daughter of ...... Hutchins.

Their children:

- 3. Thomas Wormeley. = Thomasin, daughter of Nicholas Waller of Sikehouse in co. Ebor.
  - 2. Sarah, wife of Edmund Yarbrough of Snayth in co. Ebor.
  - 1. Susan, wife of Gervase Bosvile of Warmsworth in co. Ebor.; after to .... Vincent of Warmsworth.
- 2. Christopher Wormeley of Kingston super Hull. = Elizabeth, daughter of Richard Hogge of Marflete near Hull in Holdernesse.
  - Jane.
  - 1. Edward Wormley of Hatfeild, dyed without issue.
  - 2. Henry Wormeley of Rikhall in co. Ebor. dyed in a° 1657. = Margaret, y[e] daughter of Christopher Conset, twice L[d] Mayor of Yorke.
    - 3. John Wormley. = Jane, daughter of Christoph[r] Wormley of Adwick in co. Ebor.
      - 1. Mary.
      - 2. Jane.
      - 1. Edward, æt. 18 ann. 20 Mart. 1665.
      - 2. Henry.
    - 2. Christopher Wormeley. = Marg[t], daughter to Rich[d] Newsome of Fishlake in com. Ebor.
    - 1. Edward Wormeley of Rikhall in com. Ebor. Esq[r], æt. 53 annorum 20 Martij, a° 1665. = Anne, daughter of Christopher Wormley of Adwick in com. Ebor.
      - Edward, æt. 23 ann. 20 Martij, 1665.
      - 1. Elizabeth.
      - 2. Mary.
  - 3. Christopher Wormeley of Adwick in com. Eborum. = Mary, daughter of William Adams of Austin in com. Ebor.
- 1. Symon Wormeley of Hatfeild in com. Ebor. obijt sine prole.
- Jane, wife of Thomas Moseley, a Merch[t] in Yorke.

STRAFFORD AND TICKHILL WAPENTAKE. *Yorke*, 20 *Martij*, 1665.

CRASHAW OF BENTLEY.

The armes referred to the Bookes of Lancash.

Richard Crashaw of Crashaw in com. Lanc. = ...

4. Thomas, 5. Edward, dyed without issue.

3. Richard Crashaw of Dodworth in co. Ebor.

2. Robt Crashaw of Bentley in co. Ebor. died circa an. 1642. = Joane, da. and coheire of Williã Rymer of Bentley in co. Ebor.

1. Richard Crashaw of Crashaw in com. Lanc.

1. Dinas, wife of Francis Stafford of Dodworth in co. Ebor. 2. Helen.

Will'm Crashaw of Bentley in com. Ebor. æt. 65 annor. 20 Martij, aº 1665. = Audrey, daughter and coheire of William Turner of Doncaster in com. Ebor.

1. Joane, wife of Robt Pettie of Sutton upon Lound in com. Nott.
2. Anne, wife of John Jaques of Epworth in co. Linc.

BAYNTON-BEACON WAPENTAKE. *Yorke*, 20 *Martij*, 1665.

MOYSER OF BEVERLEY.

ARMS.—Azure, on a chevron argent, between three falcons of the second beaked or, as many lion's heads erased sable collared of the third.

CREST.—A demi-horse rampant sable gutté d'or, bit and reins of the last.

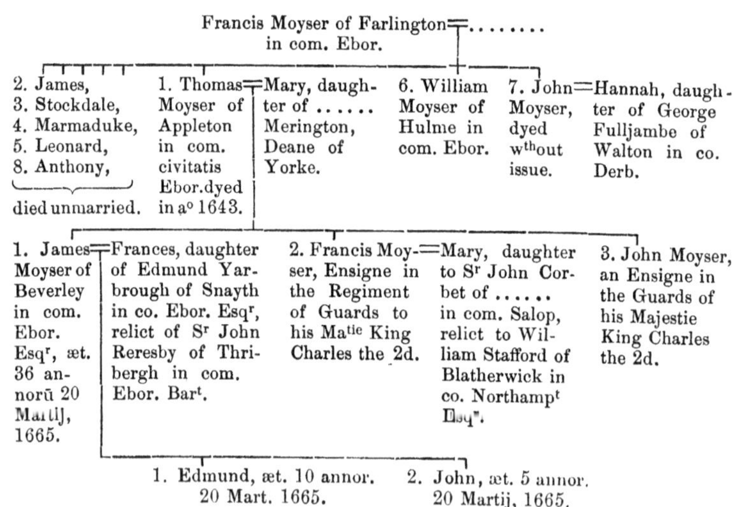

Francis Moyser of Farlington in com. Ebor. = ...

2. James, 3. Stockdale, 4. Marmaduke, 5. Leonard, 8. Anthony, died unmarried.

1. Thomas Moyser of Appleton in com. civitatis Ebor. dyed in aº 1643. = Mary, daughter of ...... Merington, Deane of Yorke.

6. William Moyser of Hulme in com. Ebor.

7. John Moyser, dyed wthout issue. = Hannah, daughter of George Fulljambe of Walton in co. Derb.

1. James Moyser of Beverley in com. Ebor. Esqr, æt. 36 annorũ 20 Martij, 1665. = Frances, daughter of Edmund Yarbrough of Snayth in co. Ebor. Esqr, relict of Sr John Reresby of Thribergh in com. Ebor. Bart.

2. Francis Moyser, Ensigne in the Regiment of Guards to his Matie King Charles the 2d. = Mary, daughter to Sr John Corbet of ...... in com. Salop, relict to William Stafford of Blatherwick in co. Northampt Esqr.

3. John Moyser, an Ensigne in the Guards of his Majestie King Charles the 2d.

1. Edmund, æt. 10 annor. 20 Mart. 1665.

2. John, æt. 5 annor. 20 Martij, 1665.

BULMER WAPENTAKE.

Yorke, 21 *Mart.* 1665.

GELDART OF WIGGINTHORPE.

ARMS.—Vert, a lion rampant regardant between three arrows in pale or.
No proofe made of these armes.

John Geldart of Wigginthorpe in com. Eborũ, æt. 34 annorum 21 Martij, 1665. = Sarah, daughter of Dr Robert Hitch, Deane of Yorke.

John Geldart, æt. unius anni 21 Mart. 1665.

YORKE CITTY.

Yorke, 21o *Martij*, 1665.

BELLWOOD OF LEATHLEY.

ARMS.—Gules, three caltraps argent.

Roger Bellwood, a Mr of Arts, lived in the citty of Yorke, dyed in ao 1646, or thereabouts. = Catherine, daughter of . . . . . . Jackson.

Josias Bellwood of Leathley in com. Eborum, died in ao 1652. = Mary, daughter of George Aiscough of Yorke.

Anne, died unmarried.

Roger Belwood, now a Student of ye Middle-Temple, London, æt. 25 an. 21 Mart. 1665.

1. Anne, died unmarried.
2. Elizabeth.

YORKE CITTY. *Yorke*, 22 *Mart.* 1665.

TAYLOR OF YORKE.

ARMS.—Argent, on a pale sable three lions passant of the field.
CREST.—An ounce passant proper resting the dexter paw on a shield of the arms.

John Taylor of Bickerton in co. Civit. Ebor. = ...

2. John Taylor of Bickerton in com. Civit. Ebor.

1. Stephen Taylor of Bickerton. = Dulcibell, daughter of William Grimston of Newport in the Isle of Wight.

1. Dulcibell, wife of John Eckton of Appleby in co. Westmerl^{d}.
2. Elizabeth, wife of Robert Traps of Nid in com. Ebor.

1. John Taylor, Envoy for his Matie King Charles the first to the Emperour Ferdinando at Vienna.

2. Stephen Taylor, D^{r} in Phisick and now resident in y^{e} Citty of Yorke, æt. 58 an. 22 Martij, a^{o} 1665. = Olive, daughter of William Wombwell of Wombwell in com. Ebor. Esqr.

3. Francis Taylor, Almoner to the Empero^{r} at Vienna, died in Sept. 1665.

Stephen, æt. 19 ann. 22 Martij, 1665. 1. Mary. 2. Olive. 3. Elizabeth.

SKYRACKE WAPENTAKE. *Yorke*, 23° *Martij*, 1665.

HALL OF LENTHORPE.

ARMS.—Argent, a fess between two greyhounds courant sable.
CREST.—On a chapeau gules turned up argent a greyhound sejant ermine.
No proofe made of these armes.

William Hall of Lenthrop in Swillington in co. Ebor. = Elizabeth, daughter of Thomas Croswayt of Bawthorp in co. Ebor.

Mathew Hall of Lenthorpe, living a^{o} 1585. = Alice, daughter of ...... Bates of Clarehall in com. Ebor.

Charles Hall of Lenthorpe, æt. 72 an. (vel circa) 23 Martij, 1665. = Priscilla, daughter of Francis Bunney of Newland in com. Eborū.

.... wife unto George Bracebridge.

2. Charles Hall.

Mathew Hall, æt. 38 an. 23 Martij, 1665. = Mary, daughter of Raphe and sister and coheire to William Metcalfe, an Alderman of Yorke.

1. Priscilla, wife of Thomas Bywater of Newsham in co. Ebor.
2. Margerye, wife of Rich. Daniell of Biggin-Greene in com. Ebor.

1. Frances.
2. Mary.

1. Philip, æt. 12 ann. 23° Mart. 1665.

2. Mathew.
3. Peter.

STILLINGTON OF KELFIELD.

ARMS.—Quarterly:
1 and 4. Gules, a fess between three leopard's faces argent.
2. Or, on a cross gules five escallops argent.
3. Argent, a cross engrailed sable.

John Stillington of Acaster in com. Eborum. = Elizabeth, daughter and coheire of John Fitz-Henry of Kelfield in com. Eborum.

Thomas Stillington of Kelfield in com. Eborum. = ... daughter of ...... Hungate of Saxton in com. Eborum.

Isabell, wife of ...... Hungate of Saxton in co. Ebor.

3. Thomas Stillington, Divinity Professor at Lovaine.

2. Robert Stillington of Kelfeild in com. Ebor. = Olive, daughter to S[r] William Sutton of Averham in com. Nott. Kn[t].

1. William Stillington, died unmarried.

1. ...... wife of ...... Wetherhead.

2. ...... wife of ...... Oglethorpe.

3. .... wife of .... Vavasour of Willowtoft.

4. .... wife of .... Hodgson of Allerton-grange.

1. John Stillington of Kelfeild in com. Ebor. died in a° 1658. = Ursula, 2[d] daughter of Conyers L[d] Darcy and Conyers.

2. William Stillington. = ...

3. Thomas Stillington. = ...

1. Olive, died unmarried.

2. Margaret, wife of Legard of Beverley in com. Ebor. Clerke.

5. John Stillington.

4. Thomas Stillington of Kelfield, Esq[r], æt. 36 annorum 22 Martij, a° 1665. = Dorothy, da. of Joseph Micklethwayt late of Yorke D[r] of Phisicke.

1. John, 2. Robert, 3. William, died unmarried.

1. Marg[t], wife of John Shaw of Rotheram in co. Ebor. Clerke.
2. Mary, wife of Will'm Drake of Barnoldswicke-Cotes in com. Ebor. Esqr.
3. Olive.

4. Ursula, wife of George Tolson of Stakes in com. Ebor.
5. Elizabeth, died unmarried.

(Children of William:) William, died unmarried. Elizabeth, wife of Rich. Hooke, D[r] in Divinity and Vicar of Halifax in co. Ebor.

(Children of Thomas:) Elizabeth. Thomas, dyed young.

2. Thomas, æt. 6 mens. 22 Mart. 1665. 1. John, dyed an infant. 1. Anne, dyed young. 2. Ursula.

HANG-EAST WAPENTAKE. *Yorke*, 23° *Martij*, 1665.

HARRISON OF ALLERTHORP.

ARMS.—Azure, three demi-lions rampant erased or, a crescent for difference : an escutcheon of pretence, Azure, a maunche or.

CREST.—A demi-lion rampant or holding a wreath vert.

Thomas Harrison, sometime Ld Mayor of the Citty of Yorke. = ...

3. Robert Harrison, Alderm. of ye Citty of Yorke aº 1612. = Frances, daughter of Will. Robinson, Alderman of Yorke.

2. John Harrison, Ld Mayor of Yorke aº 1612.

1. Thomas Harrison, son and heire. = ...

1. Sr Thomas Harrison, late of Copgrave in co. Ebor. Knt, died aº 1664. = Margaret, daughter unto Conyers Ld Darcy and Conyers.

2. Robert Harrison of Wyke in co. Ebor.

Thomas Harrison of Caton, living aº 1612. = ...

2. Henry Harrison of Holtby in com. Ebor. æt. 31 an. 23º Mart. 1665. = Eliz. da. & sole heire to Darcy Conyers of Holtby in co. Ebor.

1. Thomas Harrison of Allerthorpe in Richmundshire in co. Ebor. Esqr, æt. 38 annor. 23º Martij, aº 1665. = Mary, daughter of Sr William Roberts of Wilsden in the county of Middlesex.

1. Margaret, wife of Rich. Musgrave Esqr, son & heire to Sr Philip Musgrave of Hartley-Castle in com. Westmerland Bart.

2. Anne, wife of Henry Herbert Esqr, son and heire to Sr Tho. Herbert of Tinterne in com. Monmouth Bart.

3. Dorothy, died unmarried.

4. Mary.

1. Conyers Harrison, son and heire, æt. 2 an. 23 Martij, 1665.
2. Thomas.

1. Margt.
2. Eliz.

1. Eleanor.
2. Margaret.
3. Sarah.
4. Frances.

1. Thomas, æt. 15 ann. 23 Mart. 1665.
2. William, æt. 13 annor.

3. Robert, æt. 12 annor.
4. Edward, æt. unius anni.

CLARO WAPENTAKE. *Yorke*, 23 *Martij*, 1665.

HARRISON OF CATON.

ARMS.—Azure, three demi-lions rampant erased or.
CREST.—A demi-lion rampant or, holding a wreath vert.

Thomas Harrison, sometime Ld Mayor of ye City of Yorke. = ...

1. Thomas Harrison, son and heire. = ...
2. John Harrison. =
3. Robert Harrison. =

Thomas Harrison of Caton in com. Ebor. died in a° 1642. = Elizabeth, daughter of Henry Atkinson of Little Cattall in com. Eborum.

3. Robert Harrison of Caton, æt. 36 annor. 23 Mart. 1665.
1. Thomas, died unmarried.
2. Will'm, died unmarried.
1. Beatrice,
2. Joane, died unmarried.
3. Mary, wife of Edward Wise of Burton Leonard in com. Ebor.
4. Alice, wife unto John Warenner of Knaresborough in com. Ebor.

BULMER WAPENTAKE. *Yorke*, 19° *Martij*, 1665.

AGARD OF HUNTINGTON.

Respite given for showing the Armes.

John Agard of Stockton in co. Ebor. died a° 1636, or thereabouts. = Ellen, daughter of . . . . . . Lasenby.

Elizabeth, daughter of Thomas Wayte of Haxby in com. Ebor. 1 wife. = John Agard of Stockton, dyed in a° 1662. = Isabell, daughter of Edw. Gibson of Bugthorpe in comitatu Eborum, 2 wife. = Alice, daughter of George Porter of Warthell in com. Ebor. 3 wife.

Issue by 1st wife:
- Margaret, wife of Hamond Dawtrey of Catton in com. Ebor.

Issue by 2nd wife:
- Margaret, daughter of Will'm Weddell of Erswike in com. Eborū. 1 wife. = John Agard of Huntington in com. Ebor. æt. 38 annor. 19 Martij, 1665. = Anne, daugh. of Thomas Lasenby of Huntington in com. Eborū, 2 wife.
- Jane, wife of Richard Mason of Yorke.

Issue by 3rd wife:
1. Thomas.
2. Laurence.
3. William.

Issue of John Agard of Huntington:
1. William, æt. 10 annorū 19 Martij, 1665. (by 1st wife)
2. John, æt. 6 annor. 19 Martij, 1665.
3. Thomas.
4. Lawrence.

ALLERTONSHIRE WAPENTAKE.

Yorke, 23 *Mart.* 1665.

WAKEFIELD OF SEASSEY.

ARMS.—Argent, three bars sable, on a chief of the second as many owls of the first.

Edward Wakefield of Kingston upon Hull, living a° 1584. = Joane, daughter of Ninyon Bee of ...... in com. Northumbriæ.

Joshua Wakefield of Pomfret in co. Ebor. dyed in a° 1650, or thereabouts. = Jane, daughter of Robert Legerd of Hull, a younger brother to ...... Legard of Anlaby in com. Eborũ.

4. Edward Wakefield of Grasfield in co. Linc. =

3. Richard Wakefield of Kildale in Cleveland. =

2. Thomas, died unmarried.

1. Will'm Wakefield of Seassey in com. Ebor. dyed in June, a° 1665. = Anne, daughter to John Franke of Pomfret in com. Ebor.

1. Anne, wife of Rowland Simson of Cambridge.

2. Mary, wife of William Cropley of Cambridge.

3. Jane, y^e wife of ...... Spenlove of Norw^ch.

4. Eliz.
5. Fayth, died young.

Thomas Wakefield of Seassy in com. Ebor. æt. 25 an. 23° Martij, 1665.

1. Fayth, wife of John Hitchin of Carleton juxta Pomfret in com. Ebor.

2. Anne.

Yorke, 19° *Martij*, 1665.

THOMPSON OF KILHAM.

ARMS.—Per fess argent and sable, a fess counter-embattled between three falcons all counterchanged, a canton gules.

William Thompson of Humbleton in com. Eborū. = ...

1. Francis Thompson of Humbleton. =

2. Richard Thompson of Kilham in co. Ebor. dyed circa ann. 1653, aged 70 yeares. = Anne, daughter of Edward Nelthorpe of . . . . in com. Ebor.

5. Edward Thompson, æt. 26 ann. 1665.

4. Richard Thompson, marr. Jane, da. and heire of . . . . Dun of . . . . in Holdernesse, æt. 28 an. =
- 1. Henry.
- 2. Richard.

3, Stephen Thompson, marr. Mary, daughtr of Leonard Thompson, Alderman of Yorke, æt. 30 ann. 1665.

Mary, da. of John Thompson, Merchant of Yorke, died without issue, 1 wife. = 2. Sr Henry Thompson of Kilham in com. Ebor. Kt, æt. 39 ann. 19 Martij, a° 1665. = Jane, daughter and coheire of Richard Newton of the Citty of Yorke, 2 wife. = Susanna, daugh. of Thomas Lovell of Skelton in com. Ebor. Esqr, 3 wife.
- Issue by Jane:
  - 1. Henry Thompson, son and heire, ætatis 8 ann. 19° Martij, 1665.
  - 2. Richard Thompson.
  - 1. Mary.
  - 2. Anne.
- Issue by Susanna:
  - 3. Allathea.
  - 4. Susanna.

1. Jonas Thompson. = Frances daughter unto William Beilby of . . . . . . in co. Ebor. Esqr.
- Richard.

BULMER WAPENTAKE. *Yorke*, 19 *Martij*, 1665.

CHOLMELEY OF BRANDESBY.

ARMS.—Quarterly:
1. and 4. Gules, in chief a crescent ermine between two helmets argent, in base a garb or.
2. and 3. Barry-nebuly of four argent and gules, a bordure azure bezanté.

CREST.—On a royal helmet argent a garb or.

Margaret, daughter of Will'm Lord Conyers, 1 wife. = Sr Richard Cholmeley of Roxby in the county of Yorke Knt. = Catherine, daughter to Henry Earle of Cumberl. 2d wife.

1. Francis Cholmeley of Roxby Esqr, dyed leaving no issue.

2. Roger Cholmeley of Brandesby Esqr, com. Ebor. = Jane, daughter and coh. of Thomas De-la-Rivere of Brandesby in co. Ebor. Esqr.

Henry Cholmeley of Roxby, married Margt, da. of Sr Will. Babthorpe Knt.

4. William Cholmley, slaine in ye warrs in Ireland, unmarr.

3. Tho. Cholmeley of Brandesby in co. Ebor. dyed circa 1630. = Anne, da. of John Pullen of Scotton in com. Ebor. Esqr.

2. Richard Cholmley, married Mary daughter of Will. Saxton of Saxton in co. Ebor. obijt sine prole.

1. Marmaduke Cholmeley, married Ursula, daughter and sole heire of Raphe Aslaby of South Dalton in co. Ebor. obijt s. prole.

1. Catherine, wife of Leonard Chamberlain of Bugthorpe in co. Ebor.
2. Alice, wife of John Wright of Blansby-Parke in com. Ebor.
3. Eliz. wife of Robert Harrison of Rockley in com. Linc.

Marmaduke Cholmeley of Brandesby in com. Ebor. Esqr, ætat. 62 ann. 19 Martij, 1665. = Ursula, daughter of William Thorneton of Newton in com. Ebor.

2. Francis.

1. Thomas Cholmeley, son and heire, æt. 37 annorū 19 Martij, 1665. = Catherine, daughter of Marmaduke Tunstall of Wycliffe in com. Eborum.

1. Mary, wife of Will'm Fairfax, a younger son to Thomas Viscount Fairfax of Emeley in Ireland.

2. Anne, wife of Will. Salvein of New Biggin in co. Ebor. Esqr.

3. Dorothy.
4. Alathea.

Thomas, æt. 3. annorum, 19 Martij, ao 1665.

Catherine.

YORKE CITTY. *Yorke*, 19 *Mart.* 1665.

WITTIE OF YORKE.

ARMS.—Gules, a chevron between three serpents erect nowed or.
CREST.—Two serpents in pale embowed and interlaced.........

John Wittie of Beverley in co. Ebor. = ... dyed in a° 1645, or thereabouts.

2. Richard Wittie of Beverley in com. Eborum.

1. George Wittie of Beverley in com. Ebor. died in a° 1650. = Anne, daughter of Will'm Roward of Therne in co. Eborum.

Elizabeth, wife of Richard Cooke of Winterton in com. Linc.

Robert Wittie, Dr in Phisick, now residing in the Citty of Yorke, ætatis 51 annorum 19 Martij, a° 1665. = Mary, daughter of Henry Hall of Lilling in com. Ebor.

OSGODCROSSE WAPENTAKE. *Yorke*, 20° *Mart.* 1665.

STEPHENSON OF SWYNFLETE.

ARMS.—Gules, on a bend argent three leopard's faces vert.

John Stephenson of Swynflete in com. Ebor. = ... daughter of ...... Sympson of Swynflete in com. Ebor.

John Stephenson of Swynflete, dyed in a° 1632, or thereabouts. = Mary daughter of Stephen Skelton of Usflete in com. Ebor.

3. Nicholas, died unmarried.

2. Thomas Stephenson of Swynflete, æt. 54 annorū 20° Martij, 1665. = Dorothy, daughter of Gerard Drury of Adlingflete in com. Eborum.

1. John Stephenson of Swynflete, dyed in anno 1652, or thereabouts. = ..

Children of Thomas Stephenson and Dorothy Drury:

2. Nicholas.

1. John Stephenson, æt. 21 ann. 20 Mart. 1665.

1. Dorothy, wife of Joseph Howorth of Rawcliffe in com. Ebor.

2. Mary.
3. Elizabeth.
4. Sarah.

Daughter of John Stephenson (d. 1652):

Dorothy, sole daughter and heire, wife of Leonard Stables, an Alderman in Pontefract in com. Ebor.

OUSE AND DARWENT WAPENTAKE. *Yorke*, 21 *Mart*. 1665.

PALMES OF NABURNE.

ARMS.—Gules, three fleurs-de-lis argent, a chief vair.

CREST.—A cubit-arm vested azure cuffed ermine, the hand holding a palm-branch all proper.

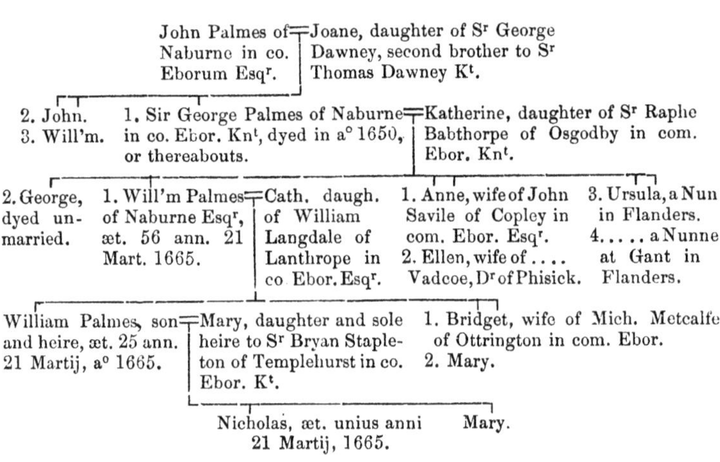

BARKESTON-ASHE WAPENTAKE. *Yorke*, 21 *Martij*, 1665.

MOTTRAM OF BISHOPDIKE-HALL.

ARMS.—Sable, on a chevron argent between three cross-crosslets or as many cinquefoils gules.

No proofe made of these armes.

Thomas Mottram, son of ...... Mottram of ...... in Maxfeild Hundred in com. Cestriæ, resided at Eckering in com. Nott. = ... daughter of ...... Bristow of ...... in com. Hertf.

Samuell Mottram of Wistowe in co. Ebor. died aº 1646, or thereabouts. = Elizabeth, daughter of .... Forde of ...... in com. Staff.

John Mottram of Bishop-Dike-Hall in the parish of Kirk-Fenton in com. Ebor. æt. 36 an. 21 Martij, 1665. = Lucie, daughter of Sr Hugh Bethell of Ellerton in ye county of Yorke Knt.

Frances, wife of John Hanses, a German.

Bethell Mottram, son and heire, æt. 6 annorum 21 Martij, aº 1665.

YORKE CITTY. *Yorke*, 21 *Mart.* 1665.

MOULD OF YORKE.

ARMS.—Sable, two bars wavy argent, in chief a lion passant gardant of the second.
CREST.—A demi-lion rampant gardant or.
No proofe made of these armes.

John Mould of Kydbie in com. Linc. = Joane, daughter of ...... Margrave of Croule in com. Linc.

3. Richard.
4. Thomas.

2. Edmund Mould of Kidbie in co. Linc. died in a° 1658, vel circa. = Elizabeth, daughter of Thomas Fydling of Luddington in com. Linc.

1. John Mould of Kydbie in com. Linc. =

Eliz. wife of Henry Fydling of Luddington in com. Linc.

John Mould, now a Cittizen of Yorke, æt. 30 annorum 31 Martij, 1665. = Elizabeth, daughter of William Stockham of Retford in com. Nott. Esqr.

William, died an infant.

1. Margaret, æt. 3 ann. 21 Martij, 1665.

2. Elizabeth.

YORKE CITTY. *Yorke*, 23 *Mart.* 1665.

MASCALL OF YORKE.

ARMS.—Sable, six fleurs-de-lis or, three, two, and one, within a bordure engrailed argent.

Richard Mascall of Rikhall in com. Eborum. = Helen, daughter of ...... Clarkson of North Duffeild in com. Eborũ.

1. Will'm, died without issue.

2. Thomas Mascall, Citizen of Yorke, died in a° 1662. = Mary, daughter of Rogor Spocie of Thorpe-Under-Wood in com. Eborum.

Jonas Mascall of the Citty of Yorke, æt. 41 an. 23 Martij, 1665. = Jane, daughter of Bartholomew Philips of Leconfield in com. Eborum.

Thomas, æt. 17 annor. 23 Martij, 1665.

Mary.

Yorke, 21 *Martij*, 1665.

STAPLETON OF WIGHILL.

ARMS.—Quarterly of six:
1. Argent, a lion rampant sable.
2. Checky or and azure within a bordure gules, a canton ermine.
3. Sable, fretty or.
4. Barry of six or and gules.
5. Bendy of six argent and azure.
6. Argent, on a fess azure three fleurs-de-lis or.

Sr Miles Stapilton of Wighill in co. Ebor. Kt. = ...

1. Gilbert, dyed without issue. | 2. Sr Nicholas Stapilton Kt. = Sibill, daughter and heir of Sr John de Bellâ-aquâ. | 3. Gilbert.

Sr Miles Stapilton Knt, one of the founders of the Noble Order of the Garter, tempore E. 3. = ... to John Duke of Britannie and Richmund. | Gilbert, a Priest.

2. Sr Gilbert Stapilton Knt. = Anne, daughter and coheire to Sr Bryan Fitz-Alan of Bedall in com. Ebor. Knt. | 1. Sr Nicholas Stapilton Kt. = ...

* Sr Bryan Stapilton Kt of the Garter. = ..., daughter and heire to Sr John St Philibert. — *a* | Sr Miles Stapilton of .... in com. Norff. = ... — *b* | Thomas, died without issue. | Elizabeth, sister and heire, wife of Sr Thomas Metham of Metham in com. Ebor. Knt.

* This Sr Bryan slew a Sarazin in open battaile, in ye presence of three Kings, vizt. England, France, and Scotland.

a — b

Sr Bryan Stapilton. = ... daughter and heire of Sr Will. Alcbrough Kt. — Sr Miles Stapilton of Wighill. = ... daughter and coheir of Sr Gerard Usflete Knt. — John, dyed without issue. — Sr Miles Stapleton of ...... in com. Norff. Knt. = ...

Sr Bryan Stapleton Knt. = ... daughter and heir of Sr John Goodard. — Sr John Stapilton of Wighill Kt. = Margaret, daughter of ...... Norton. — Sr Bryan Stapilton Knt. = ...

Sr Brian Stapilton Knt. = Isabell, daughter and heire of Sr Thomas Remston Kt. — Sr William Stapilton of Wighill Knt. = Margt, daughter of Sr James Pickering Knt. — Sr Miles Stapilton Knt. = ...

Sr Bryan Stapilton Knt. = Jane, daughter of John Vicount Lovell, sister and coheir to her brother. — Sr Bryan Stapilton of Wighill Knt. = Jane, daughter of Sr Lancelot Thirkeld Knt. — Elizabeth, daughter and coheir, wife of Richard Harecourt. — Joane, daughter and coheire, wife of Sr Philip Calthorp Knt.

Sr Bryan Stapilton Kt. = Elizabeth, daughter to the Lord Scroope of Bolton. — 3. Eleanor, wife of Thomas Lord Wharton. 4. Margt, wife of John Copley Esqr. — 1. Elizabeth, wife of Edward Saltmarshe Esqr. 2. Jane, wife of Robt Conyers of Kelton Esqr. — Alice, daughter of William Aske of Aske, 1 wife. = Christopher Stapilton of Wighill Esqr. = Elizabeth, daughter to Sir John Nevill, 2d wife,

Richard Stapilton Esqr. = Thomasine, daughter of Robert Amades. — 2. Sr Robert Stapilton Knt. = Elizabeth, daughter to Sr William Mallory of Studley in com. Ebor. Kt. — 1. Bryan Stapilton. = Margaret, daughter of Sr John Constable of Holdernesse Kt. — 1. ...... wife of John Lampton Esqr. 2. ...... wife of John Urton Esqr. 3. ...... wife of Henry Eser.

Catherine, daughter of Sr Marmaduke Constable Kt, 1 wife = Sr Robert Stapilton of Wighill Knt. = Olive, daughter of Sr Henry Sherington Kt, 2 wife. — 1. Elizabeth, wife of Bryan Hamond. 2. Bridget, wife of John Norton Esqr.

c — b

a — *b*

2. Philip.

1. Henry Stapilton of Wighill Esqr. = Mary, daughter of Sr John Forster of Alnwicke Kn^t.

1. Jane, wife of Christopher Wyvill Esqr.
2. Dorothy.

3. Bryan Stapilton of Myton Esqr. = Frances, daughter of Sr Henry Slingsby of Scriven in com. Ebor. Kn^t.

4. Robert.
5. Edward.
6. Will'm.

...... da. of Sr John Hothom of Scarborough in co. Ebor. Kn^t, 1 wife. = 2. Sr Philip Stapleton of Wartre in com. Ebor. K^t, died at Calais circa ann. 1647. = Barbara, daughter of Leonard Lord Dacres of Hurst Monceaux, 2^d wife.

1. Robert Stapilton of Wighill Esqr, died 12 Martij, a^o 1634. = Catherine, daughter of Sr Thomas Fairfax of Walton in co. Ebor. K^t, afterwards made Visc^t Fairfax of Emelye in Ireland.

1. Sr Henry Stapleton of Myton K^t and Bar^t. = ... daughter of Conyers Ld Darcy and Conyers.

2. Robert.
3. Miles.

---

2. Robt.

1. John Stapilton of Wartre Esqr. = Mary, daughter of Sr Wilfrid Lawson of ...... in com. Cumbr.

1. Isabell.
2. Catherine.
3. Mary.

1. Sr Miles Stapilton of Wighill K^t, ætatis .... annorū 22 Martij, a^o D'ni 1665. = ... daughter and sole heire of Sr Ingram Hopton Kn^t.

2. Henry Stapilton. = ... daughter of Sr Arthur Ingram K^t.

Catherine, wife of William Fairfax of Steeton Esq.
Mary, wife of Walter Moyle of ...... in com. Midd.
Elizabeth, wife of Mathew Boynton.

Robert, dyed young.

Catherine.

Ellen, Mary, } dyed young.

Yorke, 23 *Martij*, 1665.

WASTELL OF SCORTON.

ARMS.—......, on a bend between two martlets ...... three garbs bendways ......, on a chief quarterly ...... and ermine a unicorn courant ......
No proofe made of these armes.

Christopher Wastell of Scorton in Richmundshire in com. Eborum. = ... daughter of ...... Smelt of Anderby in com. Ebor.

Leonard Wastell of Scorton in co. Ebor. died circa annum 1629. = Anne, daughter of Edmund Danby of Kirkby-Knole in com. Ebor.

3. Luke, marr. .... da. of ...... Layton of West-Layton; afterwards Eliz. da. of ...... Patison of ...... relict of Christoph^r^ Allison.
4. Marke Wastell, died unmarried.

2. Mathew Wastell of Ellerton in com. Eborū, died in a° 1664. = Ellen, da. of Christopher Smithson of Moulton in com. Eborū.

1. John Wastell of Scorton in com. Eborum, died in a° 1659, æt. 66 ann. = Anne, daughter unto John Robinson of Hackforth in comitatu Eborum.

1. Isabell, wife of Raphe Swalldale of Caterig in com. Eborū.
2. Sith, wife of William Robinson of Ellerton super Swale in com. Eborum.
3. Mary, wife of Richard Curle of Scorton in com. Eborū.
4. Elizabeth, wife of Marmad. Danby of Askew in com. Ebor.
5. Margaret, wife of Cuthbert Wetenhale of South-Coton in co. Ebor.

2. John, died unmarried.

1. Leonard Wastell of Scorton in com. Ebor. dyed in Sept. 1664. = Eliz. daugh. of John Savile of Methley in com. Ebor. Esqr.

1. Dorothy, wife of Will. James of Washington in Episcopatu Dunelm. arm.
2. Anne, wife of Leonard Smelt of Kirkby-Fleetham in com. Ebor. Esqr.
3. Susanna, wife of Tho. Pepper of Temple-Coton in com. Ebor.

John Wastell, æt. 5 annorum 23 Martij, a° 1665.

Elizabeth, æt. 3 annor. et amplius, 1665.

THE AYNSTIE OF YORKE. *Yorke*, 23 *Martij*, 1665.

SLINGSBY OF SCRYVEN.

ARMS.—Quarterly:
1 and 4. Gules, a chevron between two leopard's faces in chief and a bugle-horn in base argent.
2 and 3. Argent, a griffin segreant sable debruised with a fess gules.

CREST.—A lion passant vert.

Francis Slingsby of Scryven in co. Ebor. Esqr, living a^o D. 1586. = Mary, daughter of Sr Thomas Percy, second brother to Henry Earle of Northumbr'.

- 2. Francis, 3. Henry, dyed young.
- 4. Henry Slyngsby of Scryven Esqr, died in Decemb^r 1634. = Frances, daughter of Wm Vavasour of Weston in co. Ebor. Esqr.
- 1. Thomas Slingsby, died in France unmarried.

Children of Henry and Frances:

- 3. Thomas.
- 2. Sr Henry Slingsby Bar^t, beheaded upon Tower Hill 8 Junij, 1658, in the time of Oliver Cromwell's Usurpation, for his signall loyaltie to our present Soveraign King Charles y^e second. = Barbara, daughter unto Thomas Viscount Fauconbridge.
- 1. Will'm Slingsby, died unmarried.
- 1. Elizabeth, wife of Sr Tho. Metcalfe of Nappa in co. Ebor. Kn^t.
- 2. Mary, wife of Sr Walt^r Bethell in com. Ebor. K^t.
- 3. Alice, wife of Tho. Waterton of Walton Hall in com. Ebor. Esqr.
- 4. Cath. wife of Sr John Fenwick of Wallington in com. Northūbr' K^t.
- 5. Frances, wife of Bryan Stapleton of Myton in com. Ebor. Esqr.
- 6. Eleanor, y^e wife of Sr Arthur Ingram of Temple-Newsome in co. Ebor. Kn^t.

Children of Sr Henry and Barbara:

- 2. Henry.
- 1. Sr Thomas Slyngsby of Scryven Baronet, ætatis 30 annorum 23 Martij, a^o 1665. = Dorothy, daughter and coheire of .... Cradock of Caverswall-Castle in com. Staff. Esqr.
- Barbara, wife of Sr John Talbot of Lacock in co. Wilts. K^t.

Child of Sr Thomas and Dorothy:

- Henry, æt. 4 ann. et 6 mens. 23 Mart. 1665.

STRAFFORD AND TICKHILL WAPENTAKE. *Yorke*, 16 *Martij*, 1665.

BRADFORD OF ARKSEY.

ARMS.—Quarterly:
1 and 4. Argent, a wolf's head erased between three bugle-horns sable.
2 and 3. Argent, on a bend cotised sable three roses of the field.

CREST.—A peacock's head proper, in the beak and entwined round the neck a serpent argent.

Robert Bradford of Stainley Esqr, living in a[o] 1585. = Elizabeth, daughter of Anthony Thorney of .... in co. Nott.

Robert Bradford, son and heire, æt. 22 annor. a[o] 1585. = ... daughter of ...... Fletcher.

2. Thomas Bradford of Doncaster in com. Eborum.

1. William Bradford of Arksey, æt. 58 annorum a[o] 1658, being the yeare of his death. = Elizabeth, daughter of Hector Cooper of Walkington in Holdernesse.

2. Robert Bradford.

1. John Bradford of Arksey near Doncaster in com. Ebor. æt. 30 annor. 22 Martij, a[o] 1665. = Isabell, eldest daughter of Lancelot Roper, Alderman of Kingston upon Hull in com. Eborum.

1. Jane.
2. Dorothy, wife of Thomas Burdon of Burdon in com. Palat. Dunelm.
3. Elizabeth.

YORKE CITTY. THE AYNSTIE. *Yorke*, 22 *Mart.* 1665.

FAIRFAX OF SLEDMER.

ARMS.—Argent, three bars-gemelles gules, over all a lion rampant sable, a canton azure.

Gabraell Fairfax of Steeton in co. Ebor. = Elizabeth, daughter of Robert Aske of Aughton in co. Ebor. Esqr.

1. Sr William Fairfax of Steeton, K[t]. =

2. Thomas Fairfax of Sledmer, died a[o] 1641, or thereabouts. = Dorothy, daughter of ...... of ...... in com.

Anne, daughter of ..... Johnston of Long Preston in Holdernesse, 1 wife. = Charles Fairfax of Sledmer, now residing at Whitby in com. Ebor. æt. 54 an. 22 Martij, 1665. = Mary, daughter of William Rousby of Crome in the County of Yorke, 2 wife.

Mabell, wife of Dr Johnson of Langtoft in com. Ebor.

2. Will'm Fairfax, marr. Cath. daugh. of John Smith of Snaynton in com. Ebor.

1. Thomas Fairfax, æt. 32 ann. 22 Martij, 1665, marr. Anne, da. of Cuthbert Conyers of Layton in co. Palat. Dunelm. Esqr, 1 wife. = Mary, daughter & coheire to Henry Anderson of Long-Couton in com. Ebor. Esqr, 2 wife.

1. Dorothy, wife of Wm Faucet of Sunderland in co. Palat. Dunelm.
2. Elizabeth.

Charles.

Mary.
Jane.

1. John, æt. 11 an. 22 Mart. 1665. 2. Conyers, ætatis 5 annor.

Per uxorem primã.

WHITBY STRANDE WAPENTAKE. *Yorke*, 22 *Martij*, 1665.

FAIRFAX OF DUNSLEY.

ARMS.—Argent, three bars-gemelles gules, over all a lion rampant sable, a canton of the last.

Sr Nicholas Fairfax of Walton and Gilling in co. Ebor. Kt. = Jane, daughter of Guy Palmes, Sergeant at Law.

1. Will'm Fairfax of Gilling Kt. =

2. Henry.

3. Cuthbert Fairfax of Acaster in com. Ebor. = ... daughter of ...... Whitmore of ...... in com. Ebor.

2. Thomas, 3. Francis, } died unmarr.

1. Nicholas Fairfax of Sand-Hutton-grange in com. Eborum. = Jane, daughter and coheire to Raphe Hungate of Sand-Hutton-grange in com. Ebor.

3. Nicholas, died unmarried.

2. Thomas Fairfax of Dunsley in com. Ebor. æt. 60 annor. 22 Mart. 1665. = Eliz. daugh. of Isaac Mountaigne of Westow in com. Eborum.

1. Hungate Fairfax, marr. .... daughter of .... Thwenge of Heworth in co. Ebor. ob. s. prole.

1. Elizabeth, wife of .... Forster of Moreton in com. Palat. Dunelm. 2. ...... wife of John Clement of Newton-Morrell in Richmundshire in co. Ebor.

2. Thomas. 3. Nicholas. 4. George.

1. Isaac Fairfax, æt. 32 annor. 22 Mart. 1665. = Catherine, daughter of James Herbert, a Merchant in London.

Elizabeth. Melior.

Lucretia. Anne.

1. Frances, æt. 8 ann. 22 Mart. 1665. 2. Catherine. 3. Mary.

YORKE CITTY. *Yorke*, 23 *Mart.* 1665.

ALLENSON OF YORKE.

ARMS.—Paly-wavy of six or and azure, on a chief gules a lion passant gardant of the first.

CREST.—On a mount vert a demi-lion rampant gardant or, holding a cross gules.

Sr William Allenson Knt, twice Lord Mayor of the Citty of Yorke, dyed 6 Dec. aº D. 1656. Knighted by K. Charles ye first in his progresse into Scotland to his Royall Coronation. = Anne, daughter of Charles Tankard of Whixley in com. Eborū Esqr.

2. Will'm, died unmarried. 3. Joseph, died unmarried.

Frances, daughter of Sr Thomas Whorwood of Sturton Castle in com. Staff. Bart. ob. s. prole. 1. wife. = 1. Charles Allenson of the Citty of Yorke Esqr, ætatis 32 annorum 23 Martij, 1665. = Grace, daughter of Sr Roger Jaques Kt, late Ld Mayor of the Citty of Yorke, 2. wife.

1. Barbara, 2. Mary, died unmarried.

3. Anne, wife of Henry Jaques, 2d son to Sr Roger Jaques Kt, late Ld Mayor of the Citty of Yorke, ob. s. p.

1. Charles, æt. 3 ann. 23 Mart. 1665. 2. Marmaduke. 1. Anne. 2. Mary. 3. Barbara. 4. Grace.

STAINECLIFFE AND EWECROSSE WAPENTAKE. *Skypton*, 30 *Martij*, 1666.

CURRER OF SKIPTON.

ARMS.—Ermine, three bars sable each charged with a closet argent, on a chief azure a lion passant of the third, a canton or.

CREST.—A lion's head erased argent, gorged with a collar sable charged with three roundlets.

Henry Currer of Hollinghall in com. Ebor. = Dorothy, daughter of William Mawde.

2. Walter Currer, obijt sine prole.

1. William Currer of Skipton in Craven in co. Ebor. son and heire, dyed in anno 1644. = Ellen, daughter of Bryan Parker of Brousholme in com. Lanc.

Elizabeth, wife of Nicholas Walker of Gorthrop-Hall in com. Eborum.

2. William Currer of Wighill in co. Ebor.

1. Henry Currer of Skipton in co. Ebor. dyed circa an. 1658. = Cath. daugh. of Ambrose Loraine of Tinmouth in com. Northumbr.

Mary, wife of Henry Goodgeon of Skipton in com. Eborum.

William Currer, ætatis 19 an. 30 Martij, 1666.

Grace.

AGBRIGG AND MORLEY WAPENTAKE. *Hallifax*, 2° *Apr.* a° 1666.

HORSFALL OF STORTHESHALL.

Respite given for proving and exhibiting ye armes.

Richard Horsfall of Stortheshall in com. Ebor. = ... daughter of Peter Scarborough of Glusburne in the parish of Kildwick in in com. Eborū.

ichard Horsfall of ortheshall in co. bor. dyed a° 1644. = Mary, daughter of Thomas Lewes of Marr in co. Ebor. Esqr.

1. ...... wife of John Couper of Denehouse in Coley in com. Ebor.
2. .... wife of Ambrose Grenewood.

. John, .George, died unmarried.

1. Richard Horsfall of Stortheshall in com. Ebor. æt. 53 annor. 2 Apr. 1666, a Capt of Foot in Sr George Savile's Regimt. = Anne, da. of Gervase Ricard of Hock in the parish of Snayth in com. Ebor. Esqr.

1. Mary, wife of Thomas Fenney of Fenney in com. Ebor.
2. Jane, wife of John Ricard of Heck Esqr.
3. Anne, died unmarried.
4. Susan, wife unto John Linley of Snayth, Clerke.
5. Cath. wife of Charles Nettleton of Honley in co. Ebor.

Thomas, æt. 26 annor.

1. William Horsfall, ætatis 28 ann. 2° Apr. 1666. = Dorothy, daughter of John Ellerker of the Citty of Yorke.

1. Anne. 2. Susan.

2. William. 1. John, æt. 4 ann. 2. Apr. 1666. 1. Elizabeth. 2. Dorothy. 3. Anne.

SKYRACKE WAPENTAKE. *Leedes*, 4 *Apr.* 1666.

FAIRFAX OF MENSINGTON.

ARMS.—Quarterly of eight:—

1. Or, three bars gemelles gules, over all a lion rampant sable.
2. Argent, a bend sable, a chief indented gules.
3. Checky or and azure, on a canton sable an etoile argent.
4. Argent, a chevron between three hind's heads erased gules.
5. Barry of eight argent and gules, on a canton sable a cross fleury or.
6. Or, a bend sable.
7. Or, a bend azure.
8. Argent, on a fess sable between three fleurs-de-lis gules as many bezants.

An escutcheon of pretence: Argent, a cross potent gules between four torteaux.

CREST.—On a wreath or and sable a lion passant gardant of the last.

Sr Thomas Fairfax of Denton in com. Ebor. Knt. created Baron Fairfax of Cameron in Scotland 3 Caroli primi. = Helen, daughter of Robert Aske of Aughton in com. Ebor. Esqr.

Their children:

- 3. Charles Fairfax of Mensington in co. Ebor. Esqr. æt. 70 annorum 4o Apr. ao D. 1666. = Mary, daugh. of John Brerehay of Mensington alias Menston aforesaid gent. sister and sole heire to Thomas her brother, died 18 Oct. ao 1657.
- 2. Henry Fairfax of Oglethorpe. = ⊥
- 1. Ferdinando Ld Fairfax. = ⊥

Children of Charles and Mary:

- 2. Mary.
- 3. Dorothy.
- 4. Elizabeth.
- 1. Eleanor, wife unto George Smithson of Moulton in co. Ebor. Esqr.
- 1. Thomas Fairfax, son and heire, æt. 38 ann. 4 Apr. 1666. = Eleanor, daugh. of James Hinchcliffe of Kirkstall-Abby in co. Ebor. gent.
  - Eleanor, ætatis 7 mens. 4 Apr. 1666.
- 2. Charles, died a child.
- 3. Will'm, an East India mercht, dyed at Saratt, unmarr.
- 4. Bryan, died in his infancy.
- 5. John, a twyn with Henry, æt. 31 ann.
- 6. Henry, a twyn with John, now Batchelour of Divinity, æt. 31 an. 4 Apr. 1666.
- 7. Ferdinando, Citizen and Grocer of London, died unmarried.
- 8. Peregrine, ætatis 22 annor. 4 Apr. 1666.
- 9. Charles, æt. 21 an. in his Maties Navy wth Sr John Lawson in the great fight with the Dutch 3 June, 1665, Sr John Lawson receiving his death's wound, and now in ye Mediterranean Sea with Sr Jeremy Smith, 4o Apr. 1666.

AGBRIGG AND MORLEY WAPENTAKE. *Halifax*, 2 *Apr.* 1666.

BATTE OF OKEWELL.

ARMS.—Argent, a fess sable between three bats proper.
CREST.—A bat proper.

Henry Batte, purchased Okewell in com. Ebor. from Thomas Hussey, Esqr. 7o Eliz. Reginæ. = ...

2. Robert Batte, brothr and heire of John, died circa an. 1617. = Eliz. daughter of . . . . Parrey of. . in com. Heref.

1. John Batte of Okewell, dyed without issue male. = ... daughter of. . Thurgarland of Ley-ley in com. Ebor.

2. Henry, setled in Virginia.
3. William, setled in Virginia.
4. Robert Batte of Middleham in co. Ebor.

1. John Batte of Okewell in co. Ebor. died in ao 1652. = Martha, dau. of Tho. Mallory, Dr in Divinity and Deane of Chestr.

1. Eliza. wife of Rich. Marshe, Dr in Divinity and Deane of Yorke.
2. Mary, wife of Reresby Eyre of Darton in com. Ebor.; afterwards to Henry Hurst, Clerke.
3. Cath. wife of Philip Mallory, a younger son to Dr Mallory, Deane of Chester.
4. Rebecca, died unmarried.

2. Thomas,
3. Henry,
now in Virginia.

1. William Batte of Okewell in com. Ebor. Esqr, now one of his Majesties justices of ye Peace in the West-Riding, ætatis 33 annor. 2o Apr. 1666. = Elizabeth, daughter unto William Horton of Barkislond in com. Eborum.

Martha.

3. John. 2. Gleddill. 1. William, æt. 7 annorum 2 Apr. ao D. 1666. 1. Elizabeth. 2. Martha.

AGGBRIGG AND MORLEY WAPENTAKE. *Hallifax*, 2o *Apr.* 1666.

HORTON OF BARKISLAND.

Respite given for exhibiting the Armes of Horton.

William Horton of Barkisland in com. Eborum. = Elizabeth, daughter of Thomas Hanson of Toothill in com. Eborum.

William Horton of Barkisland in com. Eborū, died in ao1655. or thereabouts. = Eliz. daughter of Thomas Gledhill of Barkesland in com. Ebor. and now cosyn and next heire of Thomas Gledhill, grandchild to the said Thomas late deceased.

1. Thomas Horton, ætatis 15 annorum 2 Apr. ao 1666.
2. William Horton.
1. Elizabeth, wife of Will'm Batte of Okewell in co. Ebor. Esqr.
2. Sarah, wife of Alexandr Butterworth of Belfield in com. Lanc. Esqr.
3. Judith.

AGBRIGG AND MORLEY WAPENTAKE. *Hallifax*, 2° *Apr*. 1666.

LANGLEY OF RATHORP-HALL.

ARMS.—Argent, a cockatrice with wings addorsed and tail nowed sable, crested gules.

Arthur Langley of Rathorpe-Hall in com. Ebor. = ...

Richard Langley of Rathorp-Hall = ...

Arthur Langley of Rathorp-Hall, æt. , dyed in ye month of June, a° D'ni 1659. = Dorothy, daughter of William Cartwright, Clerke of the Assize in com. Eborum.

1. Richard Langley of Rathorp-Hall, æt. 61 an. 2 Apr. 1666. = Mary, daughter of William Bentley of Heptonstall in com. Ebor.

2. William Langley.

1. Mary, wife of John Fox of . . . . near Scarborough in com. Ebor.
2. Sarah.
3. Eliz. wife of John Browne of Leedes.
4. Winifride, wife unto Will. Swale of Kippus in co. Ebor.
5. Cath. wife of John Dixson of Lepton in com. Ebor.
6. Grace.

1. Arthur, æt. 32 an. 2 Apr. a° 1666. = Sarah, daughter of William Garlicke of Dinting in com. Derb.

2. John.

1. Susannah, wife of Philip Rippon of Darlington in co. Dunelm.
2. Barbara, wife of William Brooke of Heckmonwyke in com. Ebor.
3. Mary, wife of . . . . . . Wilson of Thornehill in com Ebor. Clerke.
4. Catherine.
5. Sarah.

THE BOROUGH OF LEEDES. *Leedes*, 3° *Apr*. 1666.

NEALE OF LEEDES.

ARMS.—Or, two lions counter-rampant azure supporting a sinister hand couped at the wrist gules.

Henry O'Neale of . . . . . . in the Province of Ulster in Ireland temp. Eliz. Reg. = ... daughter of . . . . Caruddor of . . . . . . in Scotland.

John Neale of Bolton in Craven in co. Ebor. died in a° . . . . = ...

2. Henry Neale of Otley, now living, scilt 3° Apr. a° 1666.

1. William Neale of Otley in com. Eborum, died in November, anno Domini 1665. = Isabell, daughter of Christopher Pickard of Cotehouse neare Otley in com. Ebor.

2. George Neale, Dr of Phisick, now residing in Leedes, æt. 41 ann. 3 Apr. 1666. = Elizabeth, daughter of Francis Jackson an Alderman of Leedes in com. Ebor.

John, æt. 10 an. 3 Apr. 1666.
1. Elizabeth.
2. Mary.
3. Isabella.

1. John Neale of Otley in com. Ebor. æt. 45 annorum 3° Apr. a° 1666. = Anne, daughter of Thomas Barker of Otley.

2. John.
1. William, æt. 13 annor. 3 Apr. a° 1666.
1. Anne.
2. Mary.

Mary, wife of Thomas Mason of Leedes.

RYTHER OF SCARCROFT.

ARMS.—Azure, three crescents or.

CREST.—A leg in armour couped at the thigh ....

Sr Will'm Rither of Ryther in co. Ebor. Kn^t^ 1443. = Eleanor, daughter of Sir Will'm Fitz-Williams of Malberthorpe in com. Linc. Kn^t^.

Children:

- 1. Sr Robt Rither K^t^, Shireeve of Yorkeshire a° 2 H. 7, obiijt sine prole. = Cath. da. of Sr Robt Constable of Flamborough, 1 wife.
  - Eleanor, wife of John Aske of Aughton in co. Ebor. Esqr.
  - 1. Robert, 2. Thomas, ob. s. prole.
- 2. Sr Raphe Ryther of Ryther K^t^. = Maude, da. of Henry Percy E. of Northumberland, 2^d^ wife.
  - Henry Ryther, of whom noe issue is remayning.
  - Elizabeth, wife of William Aclom.
- 3. Thomas.
- 4. Nicholas Ryther. = ...
  - John Ryther, Cofferer to King Edward the Sixt. = Anne, daughter of ...... Hussey.

John Ryther of Ryther. = Frances, daughter of Sr Will'm Vavasour Kn^t^.

Henry Ryther of Scarcroft in com. Ebor. died in a° 1615 vel circa. = Anne, daughter of Edmund Clough of Thorpe-Hall in com. Ebor.

Children:

- 4. Richard Ryther. = ... daughter of ...... Blakestone of Monk-Fryston in co. Ebor.
  - Mary.
  - Elizabeth.
- 2. Robert, 3. Thomas, ob. s. prole.
- 1. John Ryther of Scarcroft Esqr. æt. 74 ann. 4 Apr. 1666. = Ursula, daughter of Sr Robt Dolman of Gunby in co. Ebor. K^t^.
- 1. Ellen, died unmarried.
- 2. Frances, wife of Henry Rawlins, Merch^t^ Taylor of London.
- 3. Eliz. wife of Robt Barston of Thorner in co. Ebor.
- 4. Mary, died unmarried.
- 5. Anne, wife of ...... East, citizen of London; afterwards of Christoph^r^ Favell, a younger son to ...... Favell of Altofts in com. Ebor.

Children of John Ryther and Ursula:

- 1. John Ryther, ætatis 35 an. 4 Apr. a° D. 1666. = Mary, daughter of Philip Langdale of Lanthrop in com. Ebor.
  - 4. Henry, æt. 3 mens.
  - 3. Thomas, æt. 2 ann.
  - 2. Robert, dyed young.
  - 1. John, æt. 6 annor. 4 Apr. a° 1666.
  - Mary, æt. 7 ann.
- 2. Robert.

TALBOT OF THORNETON.

ARMS.—Quarterly, a crescent for difference:

1. Argent, three lions rampant purpure.
2. Per pale gules and sable, a lion rampant ducally crowned argent.
3. .... a lion rampant ....
4. Gules, three cross-crosslets fitchée and a chief or.

Ex Order. Vitali, fol. 844.

Hugo Talebot, nepos Hugonis de Gornaico, et cognatus Rogeri D'ni de Molbray, fuit Capitaneus municipij de Plessey in Essex 18 H. 1. = Beatrix, soror Galfridi Comitis Essexiæ, amita et tandem hæres Willi. de Mandeville comitis Essexiæ, avia Rob'ti Talbot, fuit dotata in terris de Berkamstede, obijt a° 4 R. Joh'is. *(a)* = Willielmus de Say, maritus 2dus.

Willielmus Talbot, filius Hugonis, Capitaneus Castri Herefordensis ex parte Matildæ Imperatricis; tenuit 2 feoda militum in Geinsberge, de Rogero de Molbray (14 H. 2, Certificationes de feodis Militum in com. Linc.) Solvit finem Regi, pro venando in R. Forresta de Knaresbrough. (Nova Placita et Conventiones, 22 Henr. 2.) *(b)* = ...

Ricardus Talbot, habet terras in Appletrewick in Craven in com. Ebor. de feodo Bertrami de Bulmer. *(c)* = ... filia Stephani Bulmer.

Rogerus Talebot de Gainsberge, dedit Eccl'iam de Gainsberge cum duabus bovatis terræ & 3 toftis ib'm Miliciæ Templi. (Inq° capta de Terrarum donatoribus Hospitali Sci Johīs Jer'lem anno 1185, ut patet in lib. Monasticon.) *(d)*

Silvester Talbot, tenuit terras in Thorpe in com. Ebor. fuit Balistarius Abbatis de Selby, et avunculus Johannis Talbot, cui dedit terras suas. (Ex libro Coucher de Selby.)

Robertus Talebott de Geinberge, hæres fr'is Rogeri, cui Hugo de Lacy dedit terras in Brakenberge in Craven, (Pat. 18 R. Joh. m. 5.) cui Rex dedit terras in Arnethorpe et Scaleberge in Craven ibidem. (Claus. 17 Joh. m. 12.) Cui etiam dedit terras Rob'ti de Ropesley, rebell. in Wulrickby in co. Linc. (Claus. 17 Joh. m. 12.) Dedit terras in Yarum in Cleaveland Monach. de Gisburgh. (Nova Oblata p' co. Essex et Hartf. 12 Jo. Rob. Talbot dat 1 marcam.) *(e)* *(f)* = Ermintruda, fil. et una cohæred. Roberti filij Walkelini de Ferrarijs, quæ attulit viro maner. de Heginton in com. Derb. (Plīta in Thesaur. Receptæ Scaccarij 13 H. 3, Rot. 13.) Altera cohæres Margeria erat.

a

a

Willielmus Talbot de Geinberge, filius et hæres, dedit terras in Sledmer in com. Ebor. Monachis de Beverlaco; fuit Senesch. Ric'i R. Alemaniæ. Ipse cum Galfrido de Neville fuit Custos Galliarum, et Regis Navium apud Scardeburgh, Pat. 1 H. 3. Idem missus ad provisionem faciend. pro Regis transfretatione in Vasconiã, Pat. 1 E. 3, m. 3. Idem missus ad provisionem faciend. pro Regis transfretatione ex Britannia in Angliã, Pat. 14 H. 3. m. 1. Idem habet custodiam Castri Gloverniæ, et Alianoræ Regis Consanguiniæ, quam sanam et incolumem reddidit Regi apud Wodestock, Pat. 22 H. 3, m. 11ª. (g) (h) = Alicia, supervixit virum, dotata in Sledmere.

Johēs Talbot de Thorpe, ex dono avunculi Silvestris, Dominus de Geinberge, cui R. dedit liberam warennam et 1am feriam in Geinsberge. Cartæ et Pat. 27, 28, H. 3. Habuit terras in Sneyth et Cowyck de feodo Edmundi de Lascy Constabularij Cestr. Esc. 35 H. 3. Nº 19. (i)

Gerardus Talbot D'n's de Geinberge post obitum fratris Johannis.

In Regis Servicio in Wallia cum fratre Johanne. Claus. 28 H. 3. mª 6ª. Obijt aº 42 H. 3. = Eufemia fuit dotata in Geinberge. Com'unia de Termº Mich. aº 42 H. 3. rot. 5º.

Robertus Talbott, fil. Rob'ti, tenuit duas partes unius feodi militis in Wulrickby in comitatu Lincolniæ, de feodo Lascy, ex dono patris sui 20 H. 3. tenuit duo feoda et dimidium de eisdem feodis, quæ assignantur in dotem M. Comitissæ Lincolniæ, tempore H. 3. (Ex Rotulo in Turre London.) (j) = Matildis. (k) = Robertus de Berevile, maritus secundus.

Robertus, filius Willielmi de Stuteville. Rot. Claus. 45 H. 3, mª. 16ª. (l) = Johanna, sola filia et hæres, quæ attulit viro manerium de Hegginton in com. Derbiæ, et manerium de Aldham sive Dedham in Essex.

Escaetria 10 Edw. 1.

a

Ricardus Talebott, filius Girardi, Dominus de Geinberge, concessit manerium de Geinberge, D'no Regi, dandum Willielmo de Valencia fratri Regis, si obiret sine exitu.

Cartæ, aº 43 H. 3, pars 1ª, mª 5ª.

Robertus filius Rob'ti Talbot tenet terras in Wulrickby, et terras in Hudresfield in com. Ebor. de Constabularia Cestriæ. (m)

Nova oblata pro com. Ebor. 25 H. 3, Rob. Talbot, terras in Hudresfield, &c.

Escaetria in co. Derb. post mortem Edmundi fratris Regis 25 E. 1, Nº 15.

Rob'tus de Tolebutt tenet terras in co. Derb. in servicio, pro dimid. feodi militis.

Thomas Talbot, filius Rob'ti tenuit terras in co. Linc. Rot. Pipe 46 H. 3.

Cui Edmund' Lascy Constabularius Cestriæ dedit maneria de Bashall et Mitton in com. Ebor. inter 35 et 42 H. 3.

Fuit Seneschallus de Clyderhou. = ...

b

Robertus filius Roberti de Berevile ob. (Esc. pro com. Linc. et Ebor. 2 E. 1.)

a

Willielmus de Stuteville, filius et hæres matris, et de jure ejus D'n's manerij de Hegginton, &c. aº 10 E. 1. =....

Edmundus Talbott of Bashall, fil. et hær. Receptor pecuniar. Henr. Comitis Lincolniæ, 21 E. 1, postea fuit Seneschallus Dominij de Blackburnshire in com. Lanc. 31 E. 1. ivit in Scotiā cum E. 1. ubi idem R. per Cartā dedit ei liberā warennā pro M. de Bashall in co. Ebor. et Hapton in co. Lanc. (Cartæ 32 E. 1. n. 31.) Factus miles 34 E. 1. Inter Escaetria de aº 23 E. 1. pro com. Ebor. fit mentio quod M. de Thorpe recuperatur versus Ed. Talbot. *(n)* = Johana, filia Rob. Holland de Holland, fuit dotata in Hapton. Assiza capta apud Cliderow coram Joh. de Hopton, &c. 2 E. 3. = Hugo Dutton de Dutton, maritus secundus. = Johannes Radcliffe de Ordsall, maritus tertius.

b

Robertus Talebot, frater Edmundi, habet annualem redditum de terris in Huddresfield.

Egidius Talbott de Bashall, temp. Edw. 1.

Rob. D'n's Stuteville filius et hæres, obijt seisitus de manerio de Heginton et Manerio de Dedham in Essex, et Kirby in com. Nott. Escaetr. 34 E. 1.)

Thomas Talbot de Bashall infra ætatem, et in custodia Edw. 2, ut apparet in Inq. post mortē Tho. de Altaripa, 19 E. 2. Placita de Banco termº Hillarij 6 E. 3, inter Gilbertū de Ruisshton et Joh. de Radcliffe et Johanam uxorē ejus pro M. de Ruishton. Thomas Talbot vocatus ad warantizand. inter bundellas Indenturarum de Guerra, de eis qui Regem secuti sunt in Francia 20 E. 3. Tho. Talbot miles, &c. idem (ex viginti hominibus ad arma in le Westriding Ebor.) eligitur iturus cum equis et armis ad partes Scotiæ pro defensione regni. (Rot. Scotiæ 12 Edw. 3. m. 19.) =....

Ricūs Talbott Justiciarius Villæ Berwici, et omnium aliarum Regis terrarum in Scocia. (Rot. Scociæ 14 E. 3. Nº 24.) Idem testis in Causa Armorum inter Scroope et Grosvenour ex parte Grosvenour.

Johannes Talbot filius Edmundi Dominus Manerij de Hapton in com. Lanc. ex dono patris, exutus de Constabularia Castri Lincolniæ ab. E. 2. (Veteres Escaetr. pro com. Linc. 19 E. 2.) Cui idem Rex dedit manerium de Segebrooke in com. Linc. (Cartæ 15 E. 2. membra 1ª.) *(o)*

Edmundus Talebot de Bashall, filius et hæres, miles, obijt aº 46 E. 3. Ex Registro Johannis Ducis Lancastriæ, apud Graye's Inne. =........

a

Johannes Talbot, filius Thomæ, habet custodiam Castri de Athlone in Hiberniâ ex dono Regis, 3 pars Pat. 31 E. 3.

Margeria, uxor Thomæ De la Legh de Middleton in com. Ebor. 34 E. 3.

a

Thomas Talbot de Bashall, filius et hæres, infra ætatem ad mortem patris, et in custodia Thomæ Banester militis, 46 E. 3. (Ex Registro Johannis Ducis Lancastriæ apud Greye's Inne.) Fuit miles et Capitaneus Villæ Berwici contra Scotos, 2ª pars Pat. 10 R. 2. mª 25ª. Capitaneus Castri de Guisnes in Picardia, 1ª pars Pat. 12 R. 2. m. 26; quem idem Rex penes se moraturum cepit, et cui dedit 40 marcas annuas, pro vitâ, vel quousq. pro statu suo aliter ordinaret, 2 Pars Patentium 16 R. 2. m. 26; indicatus de supersedendo Johannem Ducem Lancastriæ in Parliamento tento apud Westmonasterium 17 R. 2. (Ex Rotulo Parliamenti 17 R. 2. m. 4.) Committitur Prisonæ Turris London, Dorso Clausarum 17° R. 2. m. 2.*(p)* ═ Elizabetha, filia et una cohæredum Jacobi filij Rogeri Bellars et Leticiæ (filiæ et hæredis Walteri Prest de Melton-Mowbray in comitatu Leicestriæ) uxoris ejus. Fines de anno 51 Edw. 3.

Thomas Talbot de Bashall miles, filius et hæres, cui Rex dedit 40 marcas pro vitâ (8 pars Pat. 1 H. 4. m. 3.) Capitaneus Castri de Montgomery (Pat. 8 H. 4. m. 22.) ivit in Hiberniâ (in Comitivâ Thomæ de Lancastriâ filij Regis, et Locumtenentis R. pro salvâ custodiâ ejusdem terræ (Rot. Pat. 9 H. 4. m. 20); factus Capitaneus Castri de Guisnes in Picardiâ pro tribus annis; cujus pro salvâ custodiâ habet 40 Homines ad Arma, 40 Archeatores equis insidentes, et 500 pedites, per Indenturas datas 10 H. 6. inter Regem et ipsum.*(q)* ═ Agnes, filia et hæres Alani Catterall de Wiglesworth in Craven ex Isabella uxore, filiâ et hærede Nigelli Halton de Halton in Craven, quæ attulit marito manerium de Halton, Pathorne, Swinden (pertinentia ad matrem), et terras in Wiglesworth et Horton (pertinentia ad patrem), &c. ibidem. Post obitum viri, contulit se in domo Religiosorum infra Civitatem Ebor. 9 H. 4, ut apparet in libro pergameneo remanent. inter Recorda in Owsebrigg, Ebor.

Henricus Talebot, frater Thomæ, habet 20 marcas pro vitâ ex concessione Regis (8 pars Pat. 1 H. 4. m. 3), fuit Capitaneus Castri de Montgomery post Thomam Talbot militem.

Ricardus Talebot, frater Thomæ, de Esington in Bolland, obijt ante 3 H. 4. ═ Avelina.

Edmundus Talebot miles, filius et hæres; Vic. Ebor. 22 H. 6. In pugna apud Wakefield ex parte Ricī Ducis Ebor. (Rot. Pat. 36 H. 6. de pardon.) Cui et Agneti uxori Archiepiscopus Ebor. indulsit habere Oratoriū in omnibus Oratorijs et locis congruis in terra Diocesios Ebor. (Ex Registro Archiepī Kempe.) Eandem indulgentiam concessit eisdem in manerio de Holt in co. Lanc. Epūs Coventrensis. (Ex Registro ipsius Episcopi.)*(r)* ═ Agnes, filia tertia et una cohæredum Johannis Arderne, quæ attulit viro suo Manerium de Nether-Derwind in com. Lanc. Supervixit virum.

a

Johannes Talebot de Holt, frater Edmundi.

Elizabetha, obijt 9 H. 6. uxor Joh'is Stanhope de Rampton in com. Nott. antecessoris Comitis Cestrefeldiæ.

Petrus Talbot, filius Ricī, ex parte Ricī Ducis Ebor. contra H. 6. Rot. Pardon. 15 H. 6. m. 6. Petrus Talbot de Newland in com. Ebor. gen. alias dictus Petrus Talbot, nuper de Bashall in com. Ebor. alias dictus Petrus Talbot de Arnthorpe in com. Lanc. generosus, alias dictus Petrus Talbot de Scaleberge in Bolland in co. Ebor. gen. alias dictus Petrus Talbot nuper unus Collectorum in le Westriding Ebor. vel quocunq. alio nomine censeatur habet pardon.

a

Thomas Talbot, filius et hæres, habet visum franciplegij, bona estreata et waveata, et bona felonum et fugitivorum infra Dominium de Bashall (Cartæ de anno 5 E. 4.) habet licentiam includendi unum clausum vocat. Bashall Parke, Cartâ suâ de Bolland non obstante: proviso quod non sit Saltus (Cartæ de a° 5 E. 4.) Fuit ex parte E. 4. contra H. 6. et ipsum cepit ut apparet per cartā de anno 2, 3, Ric. 3. per quam dedit huic Thomæ Talbot militi et servienti suo et hæredibus masculis 40li per annum, de exitibus Comitatus Palatini Lanc. pro capturâ magni adversarij nostri Henrici nuper de facto (sed non de jure) R. Angliæ; Dedit Monachis de Whalley in com. Lanc. (ubi sepultus erat) annualem redditum exeuntem de omnibus terris 13s 4d per Cartam datam a° 13 H. 7..... obijt Inquisitio 15 H. 7.(*s*) = Alicia, filia Johannis Tempest de Bracewell militis, ex Aliciâ uxore, (filiâ Richardi Sherbourne de Stannyhurst,) vivens a° 13 H. 7. cui frater ejus Johannes Tempest miles, legavit per Testamentum suum totum apparatum Capellæ suæ de Bracewell.

Ex Registro Testament. Ebor. temp. Archiepisc. Savage 21 H. 7.

Johannes Talbot, frater Thomæ, de Burnsall in Craven, condidit Testamentū 20 Jan. 15 E. 4. (sepultus in Ecclīâ ibidem) fecit fratrem hæredem; obijt sine prole. = Johana, filia Johīs Rythre, obijt ante virum.

Elizabetha, 21 H. 6. uxor Johannis Boteler de Roucliffe in comitatu Lancastriæ armigeri.

Agnes, uxor Johīs Crosby militis, qui condidit Testament. 11 E. 4. Per quod dedit omnes terras filiæ suæ Johannæ Talbot, et 200 marcas cum ad ætatem pervenerit. (Ex Reg'ro Wattys.) = ...

Johanna, filia Johannis et Agnetis, fecit se vocari Talebot, infra ætatem 11 H. 4.

Thomas Talbot, filius et hæres, cui Rex Ric. 3, dedit 20li per annum pro vitâ (3 pars. Pat 2. R. 3. (Obijt ante patrem sine prole.(*t*) = Florentia Pudsey de Bolton in Craven, postea nupta Henrico D'no Clifford.

Edmundus Talbot de Bashall, fil. et hæres cui Rex Ric. tertius dedit 20li p' vitâ (1 pars Pat. 2 R. 3.), condidit Testam' apd London per qd dedit Joh. Talbot f'ri annualē redditum 6l 13s 4d pro vitâ 21 H. 8. Jacet sepultus in Abbīa Westm..... obijt Inq° 21 H. 8. = Jana, filia unica Roberti Harrington (ex uxore filia et una cohæredum Ricī Baldreston de Baldreston, et soror et hæres Jacobi Harrington Decani Ebor. 13 H. 7.)

Johannes Talbot, D'n's Manerij de Hymsworth jure uxoris, perquisivit manerium de Thornton de Henr. Everingham de Birkin, et Henrico Everingham de Stainbergh filio ejus, obijt ante 31 H. 8. = Isabella, sola filia et hæres Thomæ Wortley militis quæ attulit viro manerium de Hymsworth et alias terras.

Anna, uxor. Hugonis Sherburne de Sherburne ar. 7 H. 7.

Eliz. uxor. Gilberti Scaresbreke de Scaresbreke arm. 3 H. 7.

Nich. Talbot de Hymsworth, filius et hæres Johīs et Isabellæ 33 H. 8. = ...

Johēs Talbot filius secundus, habuit maner. de Thornton et terras in Otterington, cum advocatione Ecclīæ ejusdem, ex dono patris 31 H. 8, obijt 4° Mariæ R. sepultus in Ecclīa de Thornton. = Eliz. filia Will. Lambert de Oulton in Episc. Dunelm. ex Elizabethâ sorore Tho. Tempest de Epātu Dunelm. militis, vidua ...... Wethereld de Thorpefield.

Anthonius Talbot.

Rogerus Talbot.

a | b

Antonius Talbot, filius et hæres, vendidit Hymsworth Tho. Gargrave militi 19 Eliz. Reginæ.

Antonius Talbot, filius et hæres, obijt apud interius Templum innuptus.

Rogerus Talbot, frater et hæres, D'n's de Thornton, obijt 31 Eliz. sepultus in Ecclesia de Thornton. = Cath. filia Willī Bate de Dighton, ex Eliz. filiâ Leonardi Warcop de Tanfeild, obijt a° 1620, sepulta in Ecclesia de Thornton.

Thomas Talbot, frater Rogeri, habet terras in Otterington ex dono patris.

Ricūs Talbot de Woodend, obijt a° 1634, sepultus in Eccl'ia de Thornton.

1. Johēs Talbot, filius et hæres, D'n's de Thornton, obijt a° 1638, sepultus in Eccl'iâ de Thornton. = Jana, filia Johīs Crosland de Harum, ex Janâ filiâ .... Clapham de Beaumesley.

2. Will'mus Talbot de Knaton, filius secundus, obijt anno Domini 1635. = Alicia, supervixit virum.

3. Michaell Talbot de Danby super Wiske, filius 3. = ...

4. Thomas Talbot, filius 4tus, habet terras in Appleton, obijt apud Ebor. et ibidem sepultus 1657. = Anna, filia Jacobi Ward de Rokewith, ex Annâ filiâ Joh. Smith, filij junioris Georgij Smith de Esh in Epātu Dunelm. et soror et una cohæred. Johīs Ward, obijt a° 1635, sepulta in Ecclīa de Thornton.

Johēs Talbot, filius et hær. Colonellus ex parte R. ob. 1659, sepultus in Eccl. de Thornton. = Jana, filia Rogeri Sothaby, Ar. ex Eliz. filiâ Rob'ti Hungate de Saxton in com. Ebor.

Carolus, obijt innuptus.

Maria, uxor Christopheri Fauconberge de Otterington. Jana, obijt cœlebs.

Rogerus Talbot, filius et hæres, obijt a° D'n'i 1664. = ...

Eliz. uxor Georgij Metcalfe de Allerton, jurisperiti. Caterina, uxor Willī Pinkney de Silton.

Willielmus Rogerus.

Franciscus Talbot, occisus in bello a° Domini 1643.

Thomas Talbot, jam vivens a° D'ni 1666. = Anna, soror Joh'is Rushworth.

Anna, uxor Will. Kennet de Hunwick in Epātu Dunelm. Armī. Eliz. ux. Tob. Wright de Winaldston in Episc. Dunelm. postea Willī Blackett de Wodecross.

Rogerus Talbot, filius et hæres, jam D'n's de Thornton, a° Domini 1666. = Elizabetha, filia Ambrosij Pudsey de Bolton Armigeri.

Johannes Talbot, Capitaneus ex parte Regis (in nuperrima Rebellione) jam vivens et innuptus a° D'ni 1666.

Isabella, uxor Richardi Meynille, filij secundi Thomæ Meynille de Kilvington Armigeri, obijt ille a° 1663.

Maria, uxor Timothei Cleburne de Cleburne (filij et hæredis Edwardi Cleburne).

Rogerus, filius et hæres a° D'ni 1666.

Johannes Talbot, obijt in pueritiâ.

Rogerus Talbot, ætatis 7 annor. 1666.

Ambrosius Talbot, ætatis 3 annor.

Benedicta.

Jana.

Elizabetha.

Notes to Pedigree of Talbot of Thorneton.

(a) Vide liber 1. Monasticon, fol. 450, for proofe of her marriage with Hugh Talbot, and with William de Say.

Placita de Banco termino Michælis, temp. Regis Johīs, Rotulo 5. ind.

(b) Rotulo Pipæ, temp. R. Steph. Ada de Tisum reddidit compotum de 32[li] 2[s] et 15 m'cis ne plītetur de terra sua, donec filius Nigelli de Albanie (id est Molbray), sit miles. This was in regard he had intruded into Geinberge.

Math. Paris, fol. 76.

Nova Placita et novæ Conventiones pro com. Ebor. Ex Rot. Pipæ, 22 H. 2.

Will's Talbot reddit compotum de 2 m'cis pro transgressione in venando in R. Foresta de Knaresbrough.

Idem, testis cartæ fundationis Hosp[lis] fundat. per Petrum filium Serlonis de Arthington in com. Ebor. Vide Monasticon Anglicanum.

(c) Notum sit omnibus &c. quod ego Ricūs Talebott, dedi Hospitali beati Petri Ebor. 1 toftum, cum 2 acris et dimid. terræ in Cunegston, et communam pasturæ ejusdem villæ ad 100 oves et agnos, ad 20 animalia et 2 equos, pro aīa mea et aīa Stephī Bulemer, ut sumus participes orationum et eleīar. quæ in illa Sta Domo, tam in vita quam in morte. Test. Gaufrido de Percy, Petro de Marton, Willō Talebott, Willielmo Granordei, Alano de Cunegeston. Ex lib. 2. b'ti Petri et Leonardi Hospitalis Ebor. The witnesses all Craven men, where the land did lye.

(d) Scutagium ad redemptionem R. Ricī (Essex. et Hertf.) de Rogero Talebot pro 2 feodis Militū et dim. 50[s].

Idem Scutagiū p. co. Linc. de Rogero Talbot pro 1. feodo in Geinberge.

Inquisitio de Capitalibus honoribus per totam Angliam, et de Servicijs Militum tentis de eisdem Honoribus temp. Regis Johīs (Ex libro rubro Scaccarij), Rogerus Talbot tenet 1 feodum militis in Geinberge, tent' de Honore de Bullingbrooke. Insula de Axholme in com. Linc.

(e) Omnibus, &c. Robertus de Tolebutt salutē, &c. me dedisse Canonicis de Gisburne pro salute aīæ D'ni Petri de Bruce et aīæ meæ, unam carucatam terræ in villa de Jarum de Dominico meo, cum dimid. prati mei. Habend. in p'petuā Eleīam. Testibus, Alano de Wilton, Willō de Tameton, Ph[o] de Colville, Henrico filio Conani, Rob. Engeram, Willō de Thwenge, Ewdone Hamett.

(f) Robertus de Tolebut petit versus Gaufridum filium Petri, et Alivam uxorem ejus, quam idem Gaufr. vocat ad warrant', terras in Berchamstede cum pertinentijs sicut jus suum, unde avia sua fuit sesita ut de feodo et jure. (Nova Oblata p. com. Linc. 8 R. Joh.) Ada Tyson debet 13 m'cas de misericordia sua pro dissesina quam fecit Roberto de Talebut de terra sua in Geinberge.

(g) Willielmus Talbot confirmat D'no Willō Præposito Beverlaci totam terram in Sledmer, &c. reddendo inde per annum tota vita sua, 5 m'cas; et post decessum, reddendo Aliciæ uxori ejus prædictū reddit. nōie dotis; et post ejus decessū reddendo hæredi ipsius Willī, &c. Test. D'nis Willielmo de Lund, Willō de Aumbly, Galfrido Baddel, Gerardo Salveyne, Tho. de Heslarton.

Willielmus de Montecanisio confirmat D'no Willielmo Præposito Beverlaci servicium Rogeri Bigot in Heyke, &c. Test. Rogero de Thurkelby, Gilberto de Preston,

Willō Aumbly, Willō Britone, Petro filio Tany, Willō Talebot Senesch° Ricī R. Alemaniæ, et Ducis Cornubiæ.

Pat. 9 H. 3. m. 4. Will's Talebot profecturus cum Ricō fratre Regis et Willielmo Comite Sarum in Vasconiam.

(h) This Elianor was daughter of Geoffry Plantaginet Earle of Britayne, sister and heire of Arthur, right heir to the Crowne.

(i) Ex Coucher de Selby.

Johannes Talbot de Thorpe relaxat totū clamiū et jus in ōib'z illis terris quæ fuerunt avunculi sui Silvestris, quondam venatoris Domus de Selby. Testibus Roberto de Lascy et Johanne Birne, &c.

(j) In rotulis diversar. inquisitionū in Scaccario, 20 H. 3. Ex parte Fanshawe. Robertus Talebot tenet 2 partes 1 feodi militis in Wulrickby de Constabularia Cestriæ.

(k) Communia de Termino Michaelis, 21 H. 3. rot. 11°. m. 1°. Linc. Matildis de Berevile non est distringenda pro una marca, quæ exigitur per summonitionē Scaccarij, de Roberto Talebutt, quondam viro suo.

(l) Robertus de Stutville, et Johanna uxor, petentes pro manerio de Gainsberge.

(m) Memorand. Hudresfield went away with a daughter and heire to Beaumont of Whitley in Yorkeshire, and still is in that family; also in the windowes of the Church of Hudresfield are yet seen painted the Armes of Beaumont and Talbot quarterly. Vide Fines de annis 28, 29 E. 3. inter Will'm de Merfield et Agnet' uxorē Quer. et Joh'em de Bellomont Chr Def. de 12 bovatis terræ in Hudresfield esse jus ipsius Willī et Agnetis pro vita ipsius (sororis Jo. de Bellomonte).

(n) In dorso Brevis R. Vic. Ebor. direct. 14 E. 1. ad sectam Rob. de Clyderhow versus Edm. Talbot, de placito debiti, ita habetur: Plura bona ipsius Edmundi super terram suam in Cunegeston et Scaleberge nuper distringi et sesinare feci in manu mea, quæ adhuc restant invendita pro defectu emptorū.

Ex libro Coucher de Whalley: Anno 1306 Edw. Princeps Walliæ filius R. factus fuit miles a patre suo apud Westm. et plus quam 300 milites ab eodem Rege et filio suo facti fuere die Pentecostes, qui fuit annus ætatis dicti Principis 23. inter quos fuere Edm. Talebot et Henr. le Scroope.

(o) The manour of Sedgbrooke went with a daughter and heire of this family to the Markhams, in whose tenure it still remayns.

(p) Fines de anno 49 Edw. 3. inter Thomam de Talbot Quærentem, et Johannem filium Ivonis et Sibillam uxorem Deforcient. de terris in Scaleberge, &c. esse jus Thomæ, &c.

(q) Fines de 11 H. 4. inter Alanum Caterall et Thomam Talbot militem, pro terris, &c. quiet. de hæredibus Isabellæ uxoris ipsius Alani.

(r) Pat. 12 H. 6. pars 2a m. 26. Edmundus Talebot miles prestitit juramentum servare articulum in Parliamento.

(s) Thomas Talbot miles dedit per Cartam Johanni filio suo annualē reditū decem marcarum, exeuntem de villâ de Pathorne. Test. Tho. Tempest, Nicō Tempest, et Johē Talebot de Salebury Arm°, Johē Talbot frē Tho. Talbot militis, et Ricō filio Egidij Talbot. Datum apud Bashall, 11 E. 4.

Thomas Talbott miles dedit per Cartam Tho. Tempest militi et alijs feoffatoribus Maneria de Bashall, Mitton et Halton in com. Ebor. de Ruyshton et Derwind in com. Lanc. et de Banke in com. Cestriæ, cum terris in Swynden, Paythorne, Scales, Thornbarre, Austwick, Lounsdale, Arncliffe, Wykesworth, Mitton, Pathnall, Horton, et Clederow, in usū ipsius Tho. Talbot pro vitâ, remanere Edmundo Talbot filio et hæredi, et hæredibȝ masculis, remanere Joh. Talbot fratri dicti Edm. et hæredibus masculis, remanere Antonio Talbot et hær. masculis, rem. Willō Talbot et hær. rem. Gilberto Talbot et hær. masculis. Datum apud Bashall, 24 Apr. 13 H. 7. Testibus Ricō Sherburne, Johē Townley, Stephano Hamerton, militibus, Ricō Banester arm. Joh. Livesay gen.

(t) Ex Reg'ro Archiepī Ebor. Thomas Talbot et Florentia Pudsey de Bolton habent licentiam maritandi 7 Jan. 1449, 9 H. 7.

SKYRACK WAPENTAKE. *Leedes,* 4 *Apr.* 1666.

HAWKESWORTH OF HAWKESWORTH.

ARMS.—Quarterly :
1 and 4. Sable, three falcons argent.
2 and 3. Argent, three chevronels braced in base sable, on a chief of the second as many mullets of the first.

Will'm Haukesworth of Hawkesworth in com. Ebor. Esqr, living in ao 1585. = Rosamund, daughter of Thomas Lyster of Westby in com. Ebor. Esqr.

Walter Haukesworth Esqr. = Isabell, daughter and coheir of Thomas Colthurst of Edisforth in com. Ebor.

2. Walter Hawkesworth.

Anne, daughter of Thomas Wentworth of Emsall in co. Ebor. Esqr, 1 wife. = 1. Sr Richard Haukesworth of Haukesworth Knt, died 11 Febr. ao 1657. = Mary, daughter of Sr Henry Goodrick of Ribstan in com. Ebor. Knt, 2 wife.

Isabell.

Katherine, first married to Will'm Lyster of Thornton in com. Ebor, Esqr, afterwards to Sr John Bright of Badsworth in com. Ebor. Bart.

Jane, wife of Francis Baylden of Baylden in com. Ebor. Esqr.

Walter Hawkesworth of Hawkesworth Esqr, æt. 40 ann. 4 Apr. 1666, now one of the Justices of the Peace for this county. = Alice, daughter of Sr Will'm Brownlowe of Humby in com. Linc. Bart.

Walter Hawkesworth, æt. 5 annorum 4o Apr. ao D'ni 1666.

WADE OF KINGCROSSE.

ARMS.—.......... on a bend .... two gillyflowers proper, a bordure engrailed ....

CREST.—A griffin's head erased ...., in his beak a gillyflower proper.

No proofe made of these armes.

Henry Wade of Kingcrosse neer Hallifax in com. Ebor. = Elizabeth, daughter of ...... Ramsden of ......

- 2. Mary, wife of .... Longbotham of Longbotham in co. Ebor.
- 1. Judith, wife of Robert Dene of Exley in com. Ebor.
- 1. Anthony Wade of Kingcrosse, died in aº 1620, or thereabouts. = Judith, daughter of Tho. Foxcrofte of Newgrange in com. Ebor.
- 2. Will'm Wade of Ballgreene neer Hallifax.

Children of Anthony Wade and Judith:

1. Eliz. wife of Cotton Horne of Wakefield.
2. Sarah, wife of John Hargreves of Leedes.
3. Judith, wife of Henry Power, Clerke, afterwards of Joseph Stocke.
4. Priscilla, wife of Will. Favour, Citizen of London.
5. Susan, wife of Dr Jennison of Newcastle upon Tine.

- 1. Benjamin Wade of Newgrange, æt. 74 ann. 4 Apr. 1666. = Edith, daugh. of John Shan of Leedes.
- 2. John Wade of Kingcrosse, died in aº 1645, vel circa. = Mary, daughter of Anthony Waterhouse of Woodhouse in co. Ebor.

Children of John Wade and Mary:

- 3. John,
- 2. Anthony Wade, ætatis 30 ann. 4 Apr. aº D. 1666. = Mary, daughter of John Moore f Greenhead in com. Lanc.
  - Benjamin, æt. 6. mens. 4 Ap. 1666.
- 1. Benjamin Wade, died unmarried.
- Judith.

AGBRIGG AND MORLEY WAPENTAKE. *Halifax*, 3° *Apr.* 1666.

LISTER OF SHIPDEN-HALL.

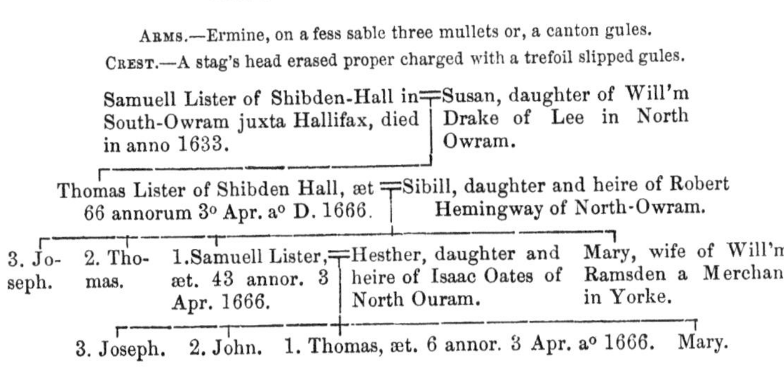

ARMS.—Ermine, on a fess sable three mullets or, a canton gules.

CREST.—A stag's head erased proper charged with a trefoil slipped gules.

Samuell Lister of Shibden-Hall in South-Owram juxta Hallifax, died in anno 1633. = Susan, daughter of Will'm Drake of Lee in North Owram.

Thomas Lister of Shibden Hall, æt 66 annorum 3° Apr. a° D. 1666. = Sibill, daughter and heire of Robert Hemingway of North-Owram.

3. Joseph. | 2. Thomas. | 1. Samuell Lister, æt. 43 annor. 3 Apr. 1666. = Hesther, daughter and heire of Isaac Oates of North Ouram. | Mary, wife of Will'm Ramsden a Merchant in Yorke.

3. Joseph. | 2. John. | 1. Thomas, æt. 6 annor. 3 Apr. a° 1666. | Mary.

AGBRIGG AND MORLEY WAPENTAKE. *Wakefield*, 5 *Apr.* 1666.

GREENWOOD OF WEST-ARDESLEY.

ARMS.—Sable, a chevron ermine between thr[e]e saltires argent.

CREST.—A leopard sejant ....

The proofe of these Armes respited.

Robert Greenewood, a younger son to .... Greenewood of Greenewood Lee in com. Eborum. = Alice, daughter of ...... Shaw of Hanging-royd in the parish of Heptonstall in com. Ebor.

James Greenewood, died in his father's lifetime. = Mercia, daughter of ...... Broome of Broome Hall in com. Ebor.

Robert Greenewood of West-Ardesley in co. Ebor. died in a° 1638, or thereabouts. = Jane, daughter of John Halliwell of Pykehouse in co. Lanc.

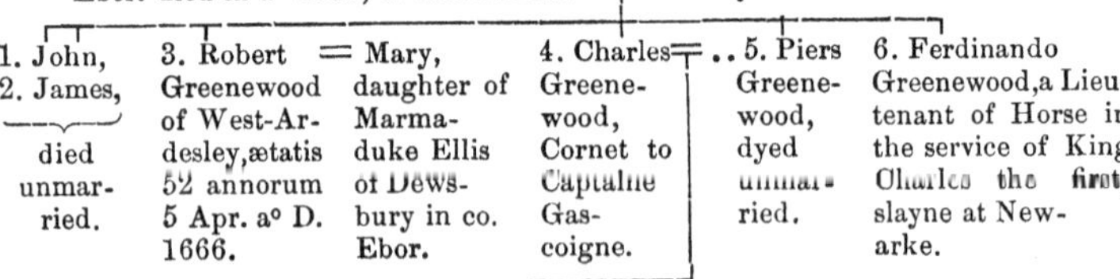

1. John, 2. James, died unmarried. | 3. Robert Greenewood of West-Ardesley, ætatis 52 annorum 5 Apr. a° D. 1666. = Mary, daughter of Marmaduke Ellis of Dewsbury in co. Ebor. | 4. Charles Greenewood, Cornet to Captaine Gascoigne. = .. | 5. Piers Greenewood, dyed unmarried. | 6. Ferdinando Greenewood, a Lieutenant of Horse in the service of King Charles the first, slayne at Newarke.

Jane.

Pomfret, 7° *Apr*. 1666.

BULKLEY OF SOUTH EMSALL.

John de Bulkley, Lord of the mannour of Bulkley in com. Lanc.=......

Adam de Bulkley.=....

Geffrey de Bulkley, slaine in the Battail of Evesholme,=...... a° 49 E. 3, and buryed in the Abby there.

John de Bulkley.=......

Adam de Bulkley,=Alice, daughter of Thomas son of a° 44 E. 3. | William de Legh, 44 Edw. 3.

John de Bulkley, a° 19 Edw. 3.=......

Robert de Bulkley, 16 Ric. 2.=......

John de Bulkley, a° 2 H. 4.=Alice, daughter and heire of Roger de Wolstuden.

Raph de Bulkley.=Catherine, 7 H. 5.

James de Bulkeley, a° 38 H. 6.=Margaret.

Robert de Bulkley,=Margaret, 10 Edw. 4. | 10 Edw. 4.

Isabell, wife of Gilbert, son of Lambert de Legh, 13° E. 4.

1. Thomas de Bulkley=...... 21 Henr. 7.

2. John Bulkley, Clerke, Vicar of Wasperton in co. Warr. 11° H. 7.

James Bulkley.=Alice, daughter of .... Howorth.

3. Arthur Bulkley, married Jane, da. of Henry Hamond.

2. Hugh.

1. Thomas=Margaret, dau. Bulkley, 14 H. 8. | of Ranulph Howorth, 14 H. 8.

1. Catherine.

2. Eliz. wife of Tho. Chadwick of Heigh in co. Lanc.

Robert Bulkley, baptized=Grace, daughter and heire of John Holt 6 July, a° D'ni 1578. | of Ashworth in com. Lanc.

Thomas Bulkley.=Grace, daughter of Arthur Asshton of Clegg in com. Lanc.

3. Thomas Bulkley, Chaplaine to Will. Cecill Earle of Salisbury and Rector of Damoram in Wiltsh. died in a° 1627, and was buried in St John's colledge in Cambridge, whereof he was Fellow.

2. Abell=Anne, daughter and sole Bulkley. | heire of Robert Norfolke of Barnesley in com. Ebor.

1. Robert Bulkley, died at Cambridgo, unmarried.

Priscilla, wife of John Hopwood of Spotland in com. Lanc.

1. Robert, 2. Samuell. died young.

3. Joshua=Cath. da. of Bulkley of .... in com. Lanc. | John Smith of Rachdale in com. Lanc. relict of Joseph Rither of Smedley.

4. Thomas Bulkley, married Eliz. eldest daughter and coheir of Michaell Butterworth of Little Howorth in co. Lanc.

5. Jonas=Margery, daughter of Bulkley of South-Emsall, in co. Ebor. æt. .. annor. 7 Apr. a° D. 1666. | Robert Lord Bishop of Clonfert and Kilmachough in Ireland, and relict of Collonell John Morris, Governour of Pomfret Castle for K. Charles the first.

2. Elizabeth. 1. Margery. 2. Morris. 1. Thomas, æt. .... an. 7 Apr. 1666.

THE BOROUGH OF LEEDES. *Leedes*, 4° *Apr.* 1666.

THORESBY OF SYKEHOUSE AND LEEDES.

ARMS.—Argent, a chevron between three lions rampant sable.
Qu. for proofe of these Armes?

Robert Thoresby of Thoresby, Dent, and Sedburgh in co. Ebor. = ...

George Thoresby of Thoresby, Barden, Dent, and Sedburgh, in com. Ebor. = Agnes, daughter to Mathew Ellerton and Katherine his wife, one of the daughters and coheirs to John Barden.

* Christopher Thoresby of Thoresby, &c. = Elizabeth.

George Thoresby of Thoresby, &c. 7 H. 7. = Agnes, daughter to Humphry Sedgwick. Elizabeth.

† William Thoresby of Thoresby, obijt 11 July, 20 H. 8. = Marg[t], daughter and coheire to Richard Errington of Cokell in com. Northumbr.

a

* Obijt 20 Nov. 7 H. 7.

† Esc. 20 H. 8, Will'mus Thoresby tenet manerium de Thoresby in com. Ebor. de D'no Scroop de Bolton, et Will'mus est filius et hæres.

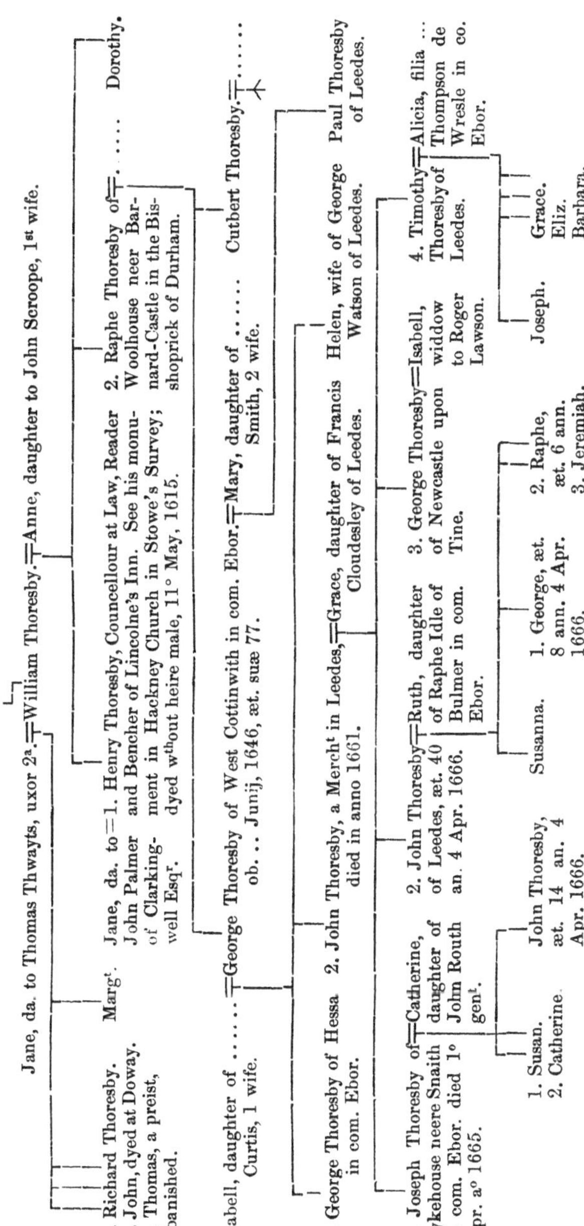
a
Jane, da. to Thomas Thwayts, uxor 2a.=William Thoresby.=Anne, daughter to John Scroope, 1st wife.
1. Richard Thoresby.
2. John, dyed at Doway.
3. Thomas, a preist, banished.
Margt.
Jane, da. to John Palmer of Clarking-well Esqr.=1. Henry Thoresby, Councellour at Law, Reader and Bencher of Lincolne's Inn. See his monument in Hackney Church in Stowe's Survey; dyed wthout heire male, 11° May, 1615.
2. Raphe Thoresby of Woolhouse neer Barnard-Castle in the Bishoprick of Durham.=.....
Dorothy.
Isabell, daughter of ...... Curtis, 1 wife.=George Thoresby of West Cottinwith in com. Ebor. ob. .. Junij, 1646, æt. suæ 77.=Mary, daughter of ...... Smith, 2 wife.
Cutbert Thoresby.=.....
1. George Thoresby of Hessa in com. Ebor.
2. John Thoresby, a Merch't in Leedes, died in anno 1661.=Grace, daughter of Francis Cloudesley of Leedes.
Helen, wife of George Watson of Leedes.
Paul Thoresby of Leedes.
1. Joseph Thoresby of Sykehouse neere Snaith in com. Ebor. died 1° Apr. a° 1665.=Catherine, daughter of John Routh gent.
2. John Thoresby of Leedes, æt. 40 an. 4 Apr. 1666.=Ruth, daughter of Raphe Idle of Bulmer in com. Ebor.
3. George Thoresby of Newcastle upon Tine.=Isabell, widdow to Roger Lawson.
4. Timothy Thoresby of Leedes.=Alicia, filia ... Thompson de Wresle in co. Ebor.
1. Susan.
2. Catherine.
John Thoresby, æt. 14 an. 4 Apr. 1666.
Susanna.
1. George, æt. 8 ann. 4 Apr. 1666.
2. Raphe, æt. 6 ann.
3. Jeremiah.
Joseph.
Grace.
Eliz.
Barbara.

THE BOROUGH OF LEEDES. *Wakefeild*, 5° *Apr.* 1666.

ROSSE OF CHAPELL-ALLERTON.

ARMS.—Azure, three water-bougets or.

William Rosse, who held certain lands in Igmanthorpe in com. Ebor. for terme of life, of Robt Rosse of Igmanthorpe, as appeareth by the last Will and Testament of the said Robert, bearing date 22 H. 8. ═ ....

William Rosse of Bramley in com. Eborum. ═ ....

Robert Rosse of Bramley in com. Ebor. ═ .... daughter of .... Beaumont of Honley in com. Ebor.

1. Robert Rosse of Bramley, died in a° 1625, or thereabouts. ═ Agnes, daughter of John Wood of Bramley in com. Ebor.

2. William Rosse, an Atturney of Furnivall's Inne, died in anno 1648.

2. John Rosse, a Merchant in Leedes.

3. William Rosse, died unmarried.

1. Robert Rosse of Chapell Allerton in the parish of Leedes in co. Ebor. æt. 48 annor. 5° Apr. a° D'ni 1666. ═ Anne, daughter of Raphe Yoward of Westerdale in Blackamore in com. Ebor, gent.

Hannah, wife of William Waugh of Leedes.

1. Robert, æt. 16 annor. 5° Apr. a° 1666. | 2. Raphe. | 3. Richard. | 4. William. | Susan.

AGBRIGG AND MORLEY WAPENTAKE. *Wakefield*, 5 *Apr.* 1666.

THORNTON OF TIERSALL.

ARMS.—Argent, on a chevron sable between three hawthorn bushes vert a trefoil slipped or.

Richard Thornton of Tiersall in com. Ebor. descended from Thornton of Thornton in Bradford-dale in com. Ebor. ═ Eliz. daughter of John Hobson.

2. Will'm,
3. Richard,
4. John,
} of whom noe issue is remayning.

1. Tempest Thornton of Tiersale, died in a°. 1630, vel circa. ═ Margaret, daughter of John Lockwood of Linthwayt in com. Ebor.

1. Richard Thornton, dyed in a°. 1617, or thereabouts. ═ Rose, daughter of ...... Arthington of Arthington in com. Ebor.

2. John Thornton of Tiersall, æt. 35 annorum 5 Apr. a°. 1666. ═ Judith, daugh. of Richard Richardson of Bierley in com. Ebor.

1. Anne, wife of Ro^t Walmisley of Coldcotes in com. Lanc.
2. Elizabeth, wife of Joshua Witton, clerke.

Children of Richard and Rose: 1. Anne, æt. 19 annor. 5° Apr. a° 1666. | 2. Margaret, ætatis 18 annor.

Children of John and Judith: Richard, æt. 6 an. 5 Apr. a° 1666. | 1. Margaret. 2. Elizabeth. | 3. Jane, non baptizata 5° Apr. 1666.

ARMITAGE OF KIRKLEES.

ARMS.—Gules, a lion's head erased between three cross-crosslets argent.

CREST.—A dexter arm embowed, couped at the shoulder, vested or, cuffed argent, the hand proper holding a pilgrim's staff gules, handle or.

John Armitage of Kirklees in com. Ebor. Esqr, some time High Shireeve of Yorkeshire. = Winifride, daughter and heire of Henry Knight of Knight-Hill and Brockholes in the parish of Lambeth.

Their issue:

- 2. John Armitage. = Dorothy, daughter of Sirell Ardington of Ardington in com. Ebor. Esqr.
- 1. Sr Francis Armitage of Kirklees Bar^{t}, died in a° 1646, or thereabouts. = Katherine, daughter of Christopher Danby of Farnley in com. Ebor. Esqr.
- Elizabeth, wife of Sr John Savile of Lupset in com. Ebor. Kn^{t}.

Issue of Sr Francis and Katherine:

- 4. Will'm Armitage of Killinghall in com. Ebor. = Eliz. da. of Robt Trapps of Nidd in com. Ebor. Esqr.
- 3. Thomas died unmarried.
- 2. Francis Armitage of Kirby in the West-Riding in co. Ebor. = Mary, da. of Robt Trapps of Nidd in com. Ebor. Esqr.
- 1. Sr John Armitage of Kirklees Bar^{t}, ætatis 38 annor. 6° Apr. a° 1666. = Marg^{t}, da. of Tho. Thornhill of Fixby in com. Ebor. Esqr.
- 1. Cath. 2. Eliz. 4. Prudence, 5. Anne, died unmarr.
- 3. Mary, wife of ......
- 6. Winifride.

Issue of Will'm and Eliz.:

- Catherine.

Issue of Francis and Mary:

- Francis, æt. 18 mens. 6 Apr. a° 1666.

Issue of Sr John and Marg^{t}:

- 1. Thomas Armitage, son and heire, æt. 13 annor. 6 Apr. a° 1666.
- 2. John. 3. Michaell. 4. Will'm. 5. Francis. 6. Christopher. 7. George.
- 1. Margaret. 2. Catherine. 3. Allathea. 4. Anne. 5. Beatrix.

STAINECLIFFE & EWECROSSE WAPENTAKE.

Skipton, 30 *Martij*, 1666.

CURRER OF KILDWICK.

ARMS.—Ermine, three bars gules each charged with a closet argent, on a chief azure a lion passant of the third.

CREST.—A lion's head erased argent, collared sable.

Henry Currer of Hamelthorpe in co. Ebor. = ...

Hugh Currer of Kildwick in com. Ebor. died circa annum 1623. = Eleanor, daughter of John Halsted of Rewley in com. Lanc. gent.

4. Christophr, died unmarried.

3. William Currer of Kildwick grange in co. Ebor.

2. Hugh Currer of Steeton in co. Ebor.

1. Henry Currer of Kildwick, dyed in aº 1653, or thereabouts. = Anne, daughter and sole heire to John Harrison of Flasby in com. Eborum.

2. Henry Currer, Citizen of London.

3. John Currer, Citizẽ of London.

Blanch, daughter of Tho. Farrand of Carleton in com. Eborum gent. 1 wife. = 1. Hugh Currer of Kildwick, æt. 56 ann. 30 Martij, aº 1666. = Anne, da. of Peter Howorth of Tharcroft in co. Lanc. widd. of Roger Winkley of Winkley in co. Lanc. gent, 2 wife.

1. Ellen, wife of Roger Whalley of Winterburne in co. Ebor.

2. Mary, wife of Thomas Hamond of Threshfield in co. Ebor. gent.

3. Anne, wife of William Watson of Silsden-Moore in com. Ebor.

4. Martha, wife of Edmund Bawdwyn of Stonegap in co. Ebor.

(Issue of 1st wife) Henry, died in his infancy.

(Issue of 2nd wife) Henry, æt. 13 annor. 30 Martij, 1665.

1. Anne.

2. Eleanor.

3. Grace.

4. Mary.

5. Elizabeth.

AGBRIGG & MORLEY WAPENTAKE. *Hallifax*, 2 *Apr. a*° 1666.

BEAUMONT OF WHITLEY.

ARMS.—Azure, a lion rampant within an orle of nine crescents or.

CREST.—A bull's head erased, quarterly argent and gules, the horns per fess, the dexter or and the second, the sinister or and the first.*

¶ Willielmus de Bellomonte, temp. H. 3.=........

- Will'mus de Bellomonte miles, temp. Edw. 1.
- D'n's Ricardus de Bellomonte.

¶ Robertus Beaumont miles, 10 Edw. 2.=Gracia, sola filia et hæres Edwardi Crosland de Crosland militis, 10 E. 2.

- 3. Johannes Beaumont miles, D'n's de Whitley, 21 Edw. 3.=......
- 1. Adam, 2. Thomas, obiere sine prole.

Johannes Beaumont, filius et hæres, 21 E. 3.=Alicia, filia Adæ de Hopton, 21 E. 3.

¶ Ric'us Beaumont ar. a° 35 H. 6, 1 E. 4.=Elizabetha, filia Roberti Nevile de Leversege arm. a° 35 H. 6.

¶ Thomas Beaumont de Whitley, arm. 18 E. 4.=........

Robertus Beaumont, fil. et hæres, a° 18 Edw. 4.=Isabella, filia Ricĩ Woodrove armĩ.

¶ Thomas Beaumont.=Elizabeth, 10 H. 7.

Joanna, fil. Joh'is Sandford, de .... in co. .... ar. ux. 1.=Ricũs Beaumont ar. 4 H. 7, 19 H. 7, 22 H. 7.=Elizabetha, filia Jacobi Harrington, 22 H. 7 (ux. 2[a]).

¶¶ Henricus Beaumont de Lascell-Hall.=........

Johannes Beaumont.=........

Thomas Beaumont de Lascell-Hall, 1 et 2 Ph. et M.=........

- Thomas Beaumont de Lascell-Hall, 14 H. 8, et 1 et 2 Ph. et Ma.=.... (a)
- * Ricardus Beaumont, a° 14° Henr. 8.=Margareta, fil. Roberti Wyvell de Burton Parva in com. Ebor. arm. 14 H. 8. (b)

* The Crest was granted to Richard Beaumont of Whitley in com. Ebor. Gentilman, 10 Maij, 1503, by Thomas Wryothesley, Garter K. of Armes, & John Younge, Norroy K. of Armes.

a *b*

Henricus, 1 et 2 Ph. et Ma. | 1. Willielmus Beaumont de Lascell-Hall in com. Ebor. 9 Eliz. Reg. ═ Rosamund. | Edwardus Beaumont de Whitley in com. Ebor. arm. ═ Elizabeth, filia Joh'is Ramsden de Longley in com. Ebor.

2. Thomas Beaumont de Heaton in com. Ebor. | 1. Ricardus Beaumont, obijt circa ann. 1656. ═ Anna, filia Roberti Kay de Wakefield in com. Ebor. | Ricardus Beaumont miles et Baronettus, obijt sine prole. | 1. Gracia, uxor Thomæ Pilkington armigeri. 2. Margeria, uxor Christopheri Wray de Cursworth in com. Ebor. arm.

Elizabetha, filia Gregorij Armitage de Netherton in com. Ebor. (uxor 1a). ═ Thomas Beaumont de Whitley miles, æt. 60 an. 2 Apr. 1666. ═ Maria, filia Ricī Burdet de Denby in com. Ebor. arm. (uxor 2a).

2. Ricardus. 3. Willielmus. | Adam Beaumont, obijt vitâ patris. ═ Elizabetha, filia Radulphi Asshton de Middleton in com. Lanc. arm. | 1. Elizabetha, uxor Gervasij, filij junioris Francisci Nevill de Chevet in com. Ebor. arm. 2. Sarah.

Ricardus, æt. 10 annorum 2o Apr. 1666.

Sciant presentes et futuri, quod ego* Johannes de Lacy Comes Lincoln. et Constabularius Cestriæ, dedi, &c. Johanni Muncebot et hæredibus suis, vel uno assignato, scil. Willielmo de Bellomonte, si ipsum assignare voluerit, pro homagio et servicio suo, totam terram quam habui de Thomâ de Dranefeld in villâ de Wittiley, cum capitali messuagio, et omnibus libertatibus et aisiamentis, &c. Tenendum, &c. sibi et hæredibus suis, vel assignato suo, scil: prædicto Willielmo de Bellomonte, de me et hæredibus meis imperpetuum. Reddo inde annuatim mihi et hæredibus meis, unas [duas] cirotecas albas ad Pascha, &c. Hijs testibus, D'no Ada de Nairford, Roberto de Stapeltona, D'no Ricō Grammatico, D'no Willo de Swinlington, D'no Ada Prestona, D'no I. de Wridlesford, et alijs.

Sciant presentes et futuri, quòd nos Isabella de Bellomonte D'na de Vescy, dedimus, &c. Willo Hastyngs valetto nostro, et hæredibus et assignatis suis, totum messuagium nostrum, cum ædificijs, &c. in Hoveden; vizt illud messuagium quod quondam fuit Magistri Johannis de Snaynton, Tenendum, &c. præfato Willielmo, hæredibus et assignatis suis, &c. imperpetuum. Data apud Sandhall die Jovis proximâ ante Festum S. Jacobi Apostoli, ao Gratiæ MCCCXXXIIo et Regni Regis Edwardi tertij a Conquestu sexto.

A circular seal is appended to the second charter, the inscription + S'ISABELLE : DE : BEAVMONT : DNE : DE : VESCY. surrounding a shield bearing a cross dimidiated impaling a lion rampant between six fleurs-de-lis.

* Erectus in Comitem Lincolniæ, 17o H. 3.

AGBRIGG AND MORLEY WAPENTAKE. *Halifax*, 2° *Apr.* 1666.

HOLDSWORTH OF ASTLEY.

ARMS.—Argent, the stem of a tree in bend couped and eradicated proper.

John Holdsworth of Astley in com. Ebor. died circ. 1620. =Elizabeth, daughter of Henry Savile of Bradley in com. (father to Sr John Savile Knt, one of the Barons of the Exchequer.)

1. John Holdsworth, dyed without issue.
2. Robert Holdsworth, Parson of Modbury in com. Devon.
3. Henry, obijt sine prole.
4. Thomas Holdsworth of Astley, died in a° 1650, or thereabouts. =Mary, daughter unto Daniell Northend of Crumbwell bottome in co. Ebor.

Thomas Holdsworth, son and heire, ætat. 16 annor. 2 Apr. 1666.

AGRRIGG AND MORTEY WAPENTAKE. *Hallifax*, 2a *Apr.* a° 1666.

WILKINSON OF MANNINGHAM.

ARMS.—Gules, a fess vair, in chief a unicorn passant between two mullets or, all within a bordure engrailed of the last and pellettée, a canton azure.

CREST.—A fox's head erased, per pale wavy vert and or, charged with a trefoil slipped gules, in the mouth a wing argent.

Richard Wilkinson of Manningham in com. Ebor. a branch of the family of the Wilkinsons of Bolton upon Dearne in com. Ebor. died in anno 1648, or thereabouts. =Anne, daughter of John Mortimer of Clayton in com. Ebor.

3. Nicholas Wilkinson.= (issue)
2. William Wilkinson.= (issue)
1. Thomas Wilkinson of Manningham, æt. 66 annorum 6 Apr. 1666. =Martha, daughter of Thomas Mallison of Bradford in com. Ebor.
1. Anne, wife of Thomas Ellinson of Shipley in com. Ebor.
2. Mary, wife unto Thomas Killingbeck of Ollerton-Gledho in com. Ebor.

Thomas Wilkinson of Manningham, ætatis 35 annor. 2° Apr. a° D. 1666. =Anne, daughter of Ellis Nutter of the Forest of Pendle in com. Lanc.

3. John. 2. Ellis. 1. Thomas, æt. 8 annor. 2° Apr. a° 1666. Martha.

AGBRIGG AND MORLEY WAPENTAKE. *Hallifax*, 2 *Apr*. 1666.

SAVILE OF BOWLINGS.

ARMS.—Argent, on a bend sable three owls of the field, a mullet for difference.

Mary, daughter of George Earle of Shrewsbury, 1 wife. = Sr George Savile of Baroughby in co. Linc. made Bart by King James. = Elizabeth, daughter of Sr Edw. Ayscough of Kelsey in com. Linc. Knt, 2 wife.

Children of the first wife:

- Sr George Savile of Thornhill in co. Ebor. Bart. = Anne, eldest da. of Sr Will. Wentworth of Wentworth Woodhouse in co. Ebor. Bart.
  - 1. George, died unmarried.
  - 2. Sr William Savile of Thornhill in co. Ebor. Bart. died in ao. 1644 vel circa. = ⅄

Children of the second wife:

- 2. Sr John Savile of Lupsete in com. Ebor. Kt. = ⅄
- 3. Henry Savile of Bowlings in co. Ebor. æt. 67 an. 2 Apr. 1666. = Anne, da. of Robert Cruse of London Merchant.
  - 1. Elizabeth.
  - 2. Anne.
  - 3. Mary.
  - 1. George Savile, son and heire, æt. 22 ann. 2 Apr. 666.
  - 2. John.
  - 3. Henry.
  - 4. Robert, dyed young.
  - 5. Edward.
- 4. Richard, died unmarried.
- 1. Eliz.
- 2. Mary.
- 3. Hesther.
- 4. Margaret, wife of John Archer, an Utter Barrister of Grayes Inne.

AGBRIGG AND MORLEY WAPENTAKE. *Halifax*, 4 *Apr.* 1666.

HANSON OF WOODHOUSE.

ARMS.—Quarterly:

1. Or, a chevron counter-componé argent and azure between three martlets sable. Hanson.
2. Argent, a chevron between three roses gules. Rastrick.
3. .... a chevron between three mullets pierced .... a crescent for difference. Woodhouse.
4. Or, on a chevron sable three crescents argent, a crescent for difference. Toothill.

CREST.—On a chapeau azure turned up argent a martlet with wings addorsed sable.

¶ Rogerus de Rastrick vixit temp. R. Henr. tertij (scil[t] a° 1251) et tenuit terras in Rastrick, Clayton, Bradforddale, prædium quoq. in Rastrick vocatum Linland, et habuit servicium diversorum nativorum in eadem villa.

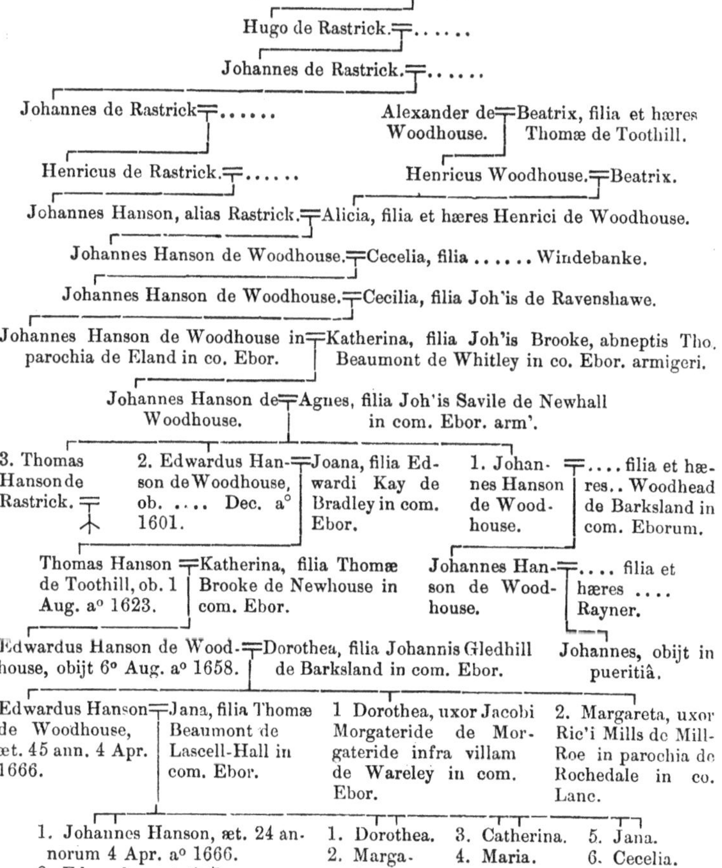

AGBRIGG & MORLEY WAPENTAKE. *Hallifax*, 2° *Apr.* 1666.

RAWSON OF SHIPLEY.

ARMS.—Per fess wavy sable and azure, a castle with four towers in perspective argent.

CREST.—An eagle's head erased sable guttée d'or, in the beak an annulet gules.

William Rawson of Shipley in com. Ebor. = ...

Laurence Rawson of Shipley in com. Eborum. = ... daughter of ..... Hawkesworth of Hawkesworth in com. Ebor.

Laurence. John. Thomas.

1. William Rawson of Shipley in com. Eborum, dyed in December a° 1662. = Martha, daughter of ...... Pollard of Tonge in com. Eborum.

Rose, wife of Richard Pollard of Tonge in com. Eborum.

2. John.

1. Will'm Rawson, æt. 25 annor. 2 Apr. 1666.

1. Mary, wife of Richard Riblesden of Wike in co. Ebor.

2. Martha. 3. Sarah. 4. Hellen.

AGBRIGG AND MORLEY WAPENTAKE. *Wakefield*, 6° *Apr.* 1666.

LEEKE OF HORBURY.

ARMS.—Argent, on a saltire engrailed sable five annulets or, in chief a trefoil slipped gules.

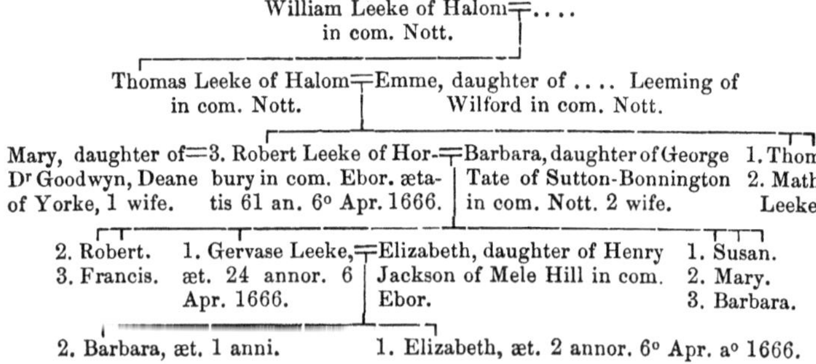

William Leeke of Halom in com. Nott. = ...

Thomas Leeke of Halom in com. Nott. = Emme, daughter of .... Leeming of Wilford in com. Nott.

Mary, daughter of Dr Goodwyn, Deane of Yorke, 1 wife. = 3. Robert Leeke of Horbury in com. Ebor. ætatis 61 an. 6° Apr. 1666. = Barbara, daughter of George Tate of Sutton-Bonnington in com. Nott. 2 wife.

1. Thomas. 2. Mathew Leeke.

2. Robert. 3. Francis.

1. Gervase Leeke, æt. 24 annor. 6 Apr. 1666. = Elizabeth, daughter of Henry Jackson of Mele Hill in com. Ebor.

1. Susan. 2. Mary. 3. Barbara.

2. Barbara, æt. 1 anni.

1. Elizabeth, æt. 2 annor. 6° Apr. a° 1666.

COPLEY OF BATLEY.

ARMS.—Argent, a cross moline lozenge pierced sable.

John Copley of Batley in com. Ebor. = Agnes, daughter of Geffrey Pigot.

1. John Copley of Batley in com. Ebor. = Margt, da. of Sr Bryan Stapleton of Wighill in co. Ebor. Knt.

2. Sr Will'm Copley Knt, from whom the Copleys of Sprotborough are descended. = ...

Jane, daughter of Richard Beaumont of Whitley in co. Ebor. Esqr, first wife. = Alvery Copley of Batley in com. Ebor. = Grace, daughter of Bryan Bradforth of Stanley in co. Eborum, second wife.

2. Alvery Copley, died unmarried.

1. Edward Copley of Batley Esqr, died ao 1605, or thereabouts. = Dorothy, da. of Sr Wm Mallory of Hutton Parke & Studley in com. Ebor. Kt.

Catherine, wife of Edward Savile of Stanley in com. Ebor.

Robert Copley, died unmarried.

1. Dorothy, wife of Francis Boswell of Gunthwayt in com. Ebor.

2. Isabell, wife of Sr Robt Savile of Howley in com. Ebor. Knt.

2. William, 3. John, dyed unmarryed.

1. Alvery Copley of Batley, died circa annū 1623. = Elizabeth, 2d daughter of John Ld Savile of Howley.

1. Grace, 2. Jane, died unmarried.

3. Elizabeth, wife of Robert Howorth, son and heire of Edmund Howorth of Howorth in com. Lanc. Esqr.

4. Troth, wife of Thomas North of ...... in com. Ebor.

5. Ursula, dyed unmarried.

1. John Copley, marr. Sarah, 2d daughter of Bryan Cooke of Doncaster in com. Ebor. obijt sine prole.

2. Richard Copley, died unmarried.

Susan, daughter of Will'm Butterworth of Belfield in com. Lanc. first wife. = 3. Edward Copley of Batley in com. Ebor. Esqr, æt. 43 annor. 6 Apr. 1666. = Beatrix, daughter of Adam Hulton of Hulton Parke in com. Lanc. Esqr, second wife.

4. Savile Copley, slayne at Tredagh in Ireland, in ye service of K. Charles ye 1st.

5. Godfrey Copley, now residing in Ireland, marr. ...... daughter of ...... Nugent.

Frances, æt. 12 an. 6o Apr. ao 1666.

Edward, æt. 2 mensiū 6o Apr. ao 1666. 1. Elizabeth. 2. Catherine. 3. Jane.

AGBRIGG AND MORLEY WAPENTAKE. *Wakefield*, 6 *Apr.* 1666.

CLAYTON OF OKENSHAW.

ARMS.—Argent, a cross engrailed sable between four torteaux.
No proofe made of these Armes.

Thomas Clayton, descended from the Claytons of Clayton Hall in com. Ebor. = ...

William Clayton of Okenshaw in com. Ebor. died a° 1627, or thereabouts. = ... daughter of ...... Cholmeley of ...... in the East Riding of Yorksh.

...... Clayton, from whom Thomas Clayton, now of Clayton Hall in com. Eborum, is descended. =

John Clayton of Okenshaw, æt. 74 ann. 6 Apr. 1666. = Elizabeth, daughter of ...... Citterne of ...... in Kent.

2. James Clayton, æt. 42 annor. 6 Apr. 1666.

1. John Clayton, æt. 46 annor. 6 Apr. 1666.

1. Margaret, wife of John Spenser of Cannon Hall in com. Ebor.

2. Elizabeth, wife of ...... Hoskins, Citizen of London.

OSGODCROSSE WAPENTAKE. *Pomfret*, 7° *Apr.* 1666.

YARBROUGH OF SNAYTH.

ARMS.—Per pale argent and azure, a chevron between three chaplets, all counterchanged.

Edmund Yarbrough of Yarbrough in co. Linc. Esqr. = Sarah, daughter of .... Wormeley of Hatfeild in com. Ebor.

Sr Nicholas Yarbrough of Snayth in com. Ebor. Kn^{t}, died in a° 1655, or thereabouts. = Fayth, daughter of John Dawney, son and heire to Sr Thomas Dawney of Seazy in com. Ebor. Kn^{t}.

4. John.
5. Edmund.
6. Christopher.

2. Nicholas, died unmarried.
3. Richard Yarbrough, a Merch^{t} in London.

1. Sr Thomas Yarbrough of Snayth Kn^{t}, æt. 27 ann. 7° Apr. a° 1666. = Henrietta Maria, daughter of Thomas Blague of Hollinger in com. Suff. Esqr, a Colonell in the army of K. Charles y^{e} 1st, and Governour of Wallingford Castle.

1. Eliz.
2. Fayth.

2. Thomas, æt. 3 mens.

1. James, æt. 18 mens. 7 Apr. 1666.

Agbrigg and Morley Wapentake. *Wakefield*, 6 *Apr*. 1666.

THURGARLAND OF LYLEY.

Arms.—Argent, a cross moline in saltire between four mullets sable.
No proofe made of these Armes.

George Thurgarland of Lyley in com. Ebor. = Anne, daughter of Henry Mitton of Colne in co. Lanc.

Children:

- 5. John, obijt sine prole.
- 1. Edward, 2. Richard, 3. Averye, ob. s. prole.
- Marg^t, da. of Tho. Nettleton of Thornhill-Lees in com. Ebor. gent. first wife, ob. s. prole. = 4. George Thurgarland of Lyley, ætatis 60 annor. 6 Apr. 1666. = Mary, daugh. of Jonas Binns of Horbury in co. Ebor. gent. second wife.
    - Anne.
    - 1. Richard Thurgarland, ætatis 19 annorum 6° Apr. a° D'ni 1666.
    - 2. George.
- 1. Mary, wife of ...... Blakburne of ...... juxta Leedes in co. Ebor.
- 2. Catherine, wife of ...... Crosley of ...... in com. Linc.
- 3. Dorothy.
- 4. Eliz. wife of John Hill, Citizen of London.
- 5. Jane, wife of Henry Gillot of Woodsome Lees in com. Ebor.; afterwards of Richard Hare of Woodsome Lees.
- 6. Anne, first married to Thomas Doget of St Edmundsbury in Suffolke; after to Miles Towe, Citizen of London.

OSGODCROSSE WAPENTAKE. *Pomfret,* 7° *Apr.* 1666.

OGLETHORPE OF BRANDESBY.

ARMS.—Argent, a chevron engrailed between three boar's heads couped sable

John Oglethorpe of Oglethorpe in com. Ebor. = ...

1. Richard Oglethorpe of Oglethorpe. = (no issue)

2. Thomas Oglethorpe of Beall. = ... daughter of ...... Vavasour of Haselwood in com. Ebor.

2. William Oglethorpe, Rector of Kellingtō in co. Ebor. = ...

1. Henry Oglethorpe of Beall. = ...

3. John Oglethorpe, a Fellow of Trinity Colledge in Cambridge, died unmarried.

2. Stephen Oglethorpe of Kellington in co. Ebor. = Eliz. daughter of ...... Dewhurst of Wadworth in com. Ebor.

1. Gervase Oglethorpe, of Kellington in co. Ebor. = Margaret, daughter of ...... Sainter of West Haddlesey in com. Ebor.

1. Richard Oglethorpe.

2. Thomas Oglethorpe.

1. William Oglethorpe, ætatis 47 annor. 7° Apr. a° 1666. = Joane, daughter of John Walton of Kellington in com. Ebor.

2. John Oglethorpe. = ...

1. ...... wife of ...... Wickham of Kellington in com. Ebor.

Katherine, wife of Will'm Bywater of Water-Fryston in com. Ebor.

2. Marg[t], wife of Henry Verdon of Beale.

Alice, sole daughter and heire, wife of Thomas Style of Sutton neer Ouston in com. Ebor. = ...

John Oglethorpe, Rector of Bransby in com. Ebor. æt. 28 an. 7 Ap. 1666. = Elizabeth, daughter of William Lete of Newarke super Trent in com. Nott. Esqr.

1. Jane, wife of William Thorpe of Beall in com. Ebor.

2. Anne, wife of Tho. Dickon of Water-Fryston in com. Ebor.

1. Gervase.
2. Stephen.
3. Will'm.

Thomas Stile of Kellington in co. Ebor. = Susan, da. of ...... Welburn of Kingston upon Hull.

 Pomfret, 7° *Apr.* 1666.

BRIGHT OF BADSWORTH.

Arms.—Per pale azure and gules, a bend or between a mullet in chief argent, and another in base of the third, on an inescutcheon the badge of a baronet of England.

Crest.—A sun in splendour or, issuing from a cloud argent.

Thomas Bright of ...... = ...

2. James.
3. John.

Joane, daughter of George Westby of Elmley in com. Derb. 1. wife. = 1. Stephen Bright of Carbroke in com. Ebor. unto whom Sr John Borough Garter (considering him to be a man of 1000li a yeare estate, and of credit and respect in the affections of the gentrye, and extraordinary merits), did grant these armes, 2° Dec. 17 Caroli primi. = Barbara, daughter of Ralph Hatfeild of Laughton in le Morthing, 2d wife.

.... wife of .... Parker of .... in com. Derb.

Children of Stephen and Joane:

1. Thomas,
2. Stephen,

died unmarried.

Catherine, only daughter of Sr Richard Hawksworth of Hawksworth in com. Ebor. Knt, relict of Will'm Lyster of Thornton in Craven in co. Ebor. Esqr, first wife. = 3. Sr John Bright of Badsworth in com. Ebor. Bart, created 16° Julij a° 1660, æt. 46 ann. 7° Apr. a° D. 1666. = Elizabeth, daughter of Sr Thomas Norcliffe of Langton in co. Ebor. Knt, second wife.

Children of Stephen and Barbara:

1. Mary.
2. Sarah.
3. Ruthe.

Martha, wife of Will'm Lyster of Thornton in Craven in co. Ebor. Esqr.

Child of Sr John and Catherine: John, æt. 8 annor. 7° Apr. a° 1666.

Children of Sr John and Elizabeth:

1. Catherine.
2. Dorothea.

OSGODCROSSE WAPENTAKE. *Pomfret*, 7° *Apr*. 1666.

DAWNEY OF COWICK.

ARMS.—Quarterly of six:

1. Argent, on a bend cotised sable three annulets of the field.
2. Gules, a man's head in profile couped at the neck argent, the temples encircled with a wreath knotted behind of the last and sable, issuing from the dexter and sinister chief and the middle base points three lion's gambs or each pointing to the centre.
3. Azure, a lion rampant or, ducally crowned argent.
4. Azure, five fusils in fess or within a bordure argent semée of torteaux.
5. Or, on a chief indented azure two mullets of the field.
6. Barry of eight argent and gules, on a canton sable a cross fleury or, a crescent for difference.

CREST.—A demi-man in armour, wreathed about the temples, holding in his dexter hand a gemmed ring, and in his sinister a lion's gamb erased.

Sr John Dawney of Seazay in com. Ebor. Knt. = Elizabeth, daughter of Sr Marmaduke Tunstall of Thurland-Castle in com. Lanc. Knt.

1. Sr Thomas Dawney of Seasay in co. Ebor. Knt, died in a° 1641. = Fayth, daughter of Richard Legard of Rysomegarth in Holdernes.

2. Marmaduke Dawney of Sutton-Colfeild in com. Warr. = ... daughter of ...... Gardner.

2. Thomas, 3. George, 4. Richard, died unmarried.

1. John Dawney, son and heir, died in the life-time of his father, a° 1628. = Elizabeth, eldest daughter of Sr Richard Hutton of Gouldesborough Kt, late one of the Justices of the Court of Common Pleas.

1. Elizabeth, wife of Sr Will'm Acclome of Moreby Hall in com. Ebor. Knt.
2. Frances, wife of Sr Henry Vaughan of Sutton upon Darwent in co. Ebor. Knt.
3. Margaret, wife of Sr Walter Rudstone of Hayton in co. Ebor. Bart.

1. Thomas Dawney, Citizen of London. = Catherine la Gouse, a Dutchwoman.

2. John, died without issue.

Thomas. John.

1. Fayth, wife of Sr Nicholas Yarborough of Snaith in co. Eborum Knt.
2. Mary, wife of Sr Will'm Adams of Scawseby in com. Ebor. Knt.

1. Thomas, died unmarried.

2. Sr Christopher Dawney of Cowick in co. Ebor. created Baronet by K. Charles the first a° 1641, died in a° 1644. = Jane, daughter and coheire of John Moseley of Uskelfe in com. Ebor. Esqr.

Elizabeth, daughter of Sr John Melton Knt, Secretary to the Councell of Yorke for the Northern parts of this Realme, 1 wife. = 3. Sr John Dawney of Cowick in co. Ebor. Knt, ætatis 41 ann. 7 Apr. 1666. = Dorothy, daughter of Will'm Johnson of Wickham in co. Linc. Esqr.

2. Sr Thomas Dawney Bart, died in his childhood.

1. John, died in his infancy.

1. George Dawney, son and heir, ætat. 13 ann. 7° Apr. 1666.

1. Anne.
2. Margaret.

3. Catherine.

2. Henry, æt. 2 annor.
3. Will'm, æt. 2 mens.

STAPLETON OF CARLETON.

ARMS.—Argent, a lion rampant sable.
CREST.—A talbot passant ....

The Lady Eleanor, daughtr to the Earle of Westmerld, 1st wife. = Brian Stapleton of Carleton in com. Ebor. Esqr. = Elizabeth, daughter of George Ld Darcy, 2d wife.

Issue:

- 1. John Stapilton, died young.
- 2. Miles, dyed young.
- 3. Richard Stapilton of Carleton Esqr, died circa an. 1614. = Eliz. daughter of Sr Henry Pierpont of Holme-Pierpont in com. Nott. Knt.
- 4. George Stapilton of Linton in co. Ebor. = ... — Issue: Elizabeth.
- 5. Robert Stapilton of Temple-hurst in com. Eborū. = ... daughter of Sr Robt Dolman of Gunby in co. Eborum Knt.
- 6. Bryan.
- 1. Thomasine, wife of Robert Gale of Acombe-grange in co. Ebor.
- 2. Dorothie.

Issue of Richard and Eliz.:

- 2. Epiphanius, died unmarried.
- 3. Sr Robt Stapilton Kt, one of ye Gentlemen Huishers of the Privy Chamber to K. Charles the second, married ...... daughtr of ...... Manwaring of ...... widow of ...... Hamond.
- 1. Gilbert Stapilton of Carleton Esqr, died 17 Apr. 1636. = Eleanor, da. of Sr John Gascoigne of Barnbow in com. Ebor. Kt and Bt.
- 1. Jane, 2. Elizabeth, 3. Grace, died unmarried.

Issue of Robert and .... Dolman:

- 2. Robt, 3. Henry, died unmarried.
- 1. Sr Bryan Stapleton of Temple-hurst, slayne in the service of King Charles the first in the fight neer Chester ao 1644. = Margt, daughter of ...... Langley of Millington in com. Ebor.
- 1. Mary, wife of Charles Bacon of Ferriby in com. Ebor.
- 2. Eliz. died unmarried.
- 3. Eleanor, wife of Michaell Anne of Frickley in com. Ebor. Esqr.
- 4. Ursula, wife of Will'm Langdale of Langthorpe in com. Ebor. (afterwards knighted.)

Issue of Gilbert and Eleanor:

- 4. John, died unmarried.
- 3. Sr Miles Stapleton of Carleton Bart, æt. 38 annorum 7° Apr. ao D. 1666. = Elizabeth, daughter to Robert late Earle of Lindsey, Ld Great Chamberlain of England.
- 1. Richard.
- 2. Gregory, a Monke at Doway.
- 1. Mary, a Nunn at Cambray.
- 2. Anne, wife of Marke Errington of Pont-Eland in com. Northumbr. Esqr.

Issue of Sr Bryan and Margt: Mary, wife of Will'm Palmes, son & heir of Will'm Palmes of Naborne in co. Ebor. Esqr.

Issue of Sr Miles and Elizabeth:

- Bryan, died in his infancy.
- Elizabeth, dyed an infant.

STRAFFORD AND TICKHILL WAPENTAKE.

Pomfret, 7° *Apr.* 1666.

RHODES OF GREAT-HOUGHTON.

ARMS.—Argent, on a bend cotised .... a lion passant between two acorns ...., in chief a trefoil slipped .....

...... daughter of ...... Samford, 1 wife. = Francis Rhodes Esqr, one of the Justices of the Court of Common Pleas temp. Eliz. Reg. = Mary, daughter of ...... Charleton of ...... in com. Salop, 2^d^ wife.

Children of the first wife:

- ...... wife of ...... Basset.
- 2. Peter Rhodes of Hickleton in com. Ebor.
- 3. Francis.
- 1. Sr John Rhodes of Barlbrough in co. Derb. K^t^. = ...

Children of the second wife:

- 2. Robert, 3. Francis, died unmarried.
- 1. Sr Godfrey Rhodes of Great Houghton in com. Ebor. K^t^, died in anno 1634, or thereabouts. = Anne, daughter of Sr Edward Leuknor of Denham Hall in Sussex.
- 1. Mary, wife of Sr John Thorney of .... in com. Linc.
- 2. Ruth, wife of Sr Richard Tempest of Bracewell in com. Ebor.
- 3. ...... wife of .... Pilkinton of Stanley neer Wakefeild in com. Ebor.
- 4. Cecelie, 5. Atheline, died unmarried.
- 6. Judith, wife of .... Waterhouse of ....
- 7. Bridget, wife of ...... Bruer.
- 8. ....

Children of Sr Godfrey Rhodes and Anne:

- 2. Godfrey Rhodes, D^r^ in Divinity and Deane of London Derry in Ireland.
- 1. Sr Edward Rhodes of Great Houghton Kn^t^, ætatis 65 an. 7° Apr. 1666. = Mary, daughter of Sr Hamon Whitchcote of Harpswell in com. Linc. Kn^t^.
- 1. Anne, wife of John Nevill of Mattersey in com. Nott. Esqr.
- 2. Elizabeth, wife of Thomas Earle of Strafford.

Children of Sr Edward Rhodes and Mary:

- 3. Will'm. 4. Hamon.
- 2. Edward Rhodes, an Utter Barrister of Grayes Inne, died unmarried.
- 1. Godfrey Rhodes, son and heire, ætat. 34 ann. 7 Apr. a° D. 1666.
- 1. Mary. 2. Anne.
- 3. Elizabeth. 4. Milicent.

OSGODCROSSE WAPENTAKE. *Pomfret*, 7° *Apr.* 1666.

MORRIS OF NORTH EMSALL.

ARMS.—Azure, three eagles displayed or, on a canton argent a castle gules.

Edward Morris of Emsall in co. Ebor.=......

Robert Morris of Emsall=......

Nicholas Morris of North-Emsall.=Lucie, sole daughter and heire of John Lathum of Carleton Hall neer Pomfret.

1. Thomas Morris of Emsall.=Barbara, daughter of John Wentworth of Emsall Esq[r].
2. Edward.
3. Richard.
4. John.

...... daughter of .... of Newarke in com. Nott. 1 wife.=Mathias Morris of Emsall, dyed ....=Jane, daughter of George Holgate of Grimsthorpe in com. Ebor. 2 wife.

Children of the first wife: Elizabeth. 2. Nicholas. 3. Edward. *1. John Morris, Governour of Pomfret Castle for King Charles y[e] first, put to death at Yorke .... Aug. 1649.=Margery, eldest daughter of D[r] Robert Dawson, late L[d] B[pp] of Clonfert and Kilmackdough in Ireland, died 28 Oct. 1665, æt. suæ 38.

Children of the second wife: 4. Mathias. 5. Wentworth. 6. Richard. Sarah.

Children of John Morris and Margery:
1. Robert Morris of North Emsall, æt. 21 annorū 7° Apr. a° 1666.
2. Castilian Morris, borne in the time of the Seige of Pomfret Castle.
Mary.

* This John Morris being bred up under the right Ho[ble] Thomas late Earle of Strafford was first an Ensigne to his guards after the said Earle became Lord Lieutenant of Irel[d], and when the Rebellion brake forth in that Kingdome was made Serjeant Major to S[r] Francis Willoughby Kn[t], Major Generall of his late Ma[ties] Army there: Where amongst many other his valiant exploits, this one is not a little remarkable, viz. that after he had recieved some dangerous wounds in the Storming of Rosse Castle, whence he was brought of in a Litter, the English Forces in another encounter against Generall Preston being routed and flying by him, when by perswasions he could not prevaile with them to stand, he got upon his led horse (though with much difficulty) and by his couragious example rallyed the disordered troops, and, charging the enemy in the very head of them, obtained an absolute and honourable victory.

After that he surprized the strong Castle of Pontfract, for King Charles the first, with the helpe of eight men besides himselfe, upon the 3[d] of June, a° 1648, and valiantly defending it, during a long siege, untill after the murther of that King; and then being excluded the benefit of the articles, upon delivery thereof to those inhumane Regicides, it being the last in England that had held out against their usurped power, himselfe with two more excepted persons (whereof Michaell Blackburne his Cornet was one) and two servants, with great courage and resolution, made their way through two workes, guarded by about five hundred foot and horse, and got clere from them into Lancashire; having had a promise from Generall Lambert (who besieged him)

BARKESTON ASHE WAPENTAKE. *Pomfret*, 7° *Apr.* 1666.

ADAMS OF CAMBLESFORTH.

ARMS.—Gules, a lion rampant between three escallops or, on a chief argent as many pallets engrailed azure.

CREST.—A demi-griffin segreant ermine, winged and armed azure, holding an escallop gules.

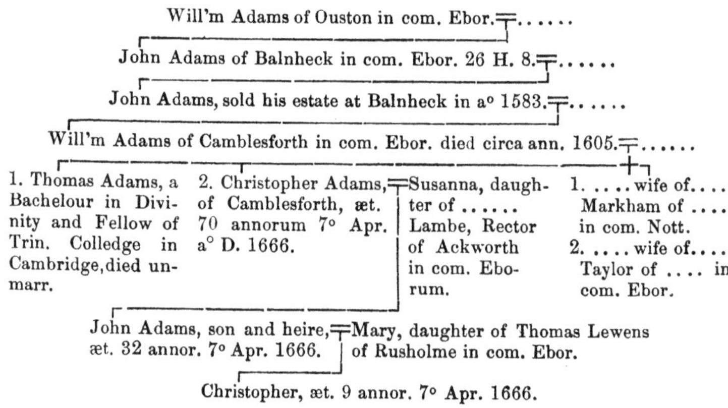

---

that if he could escape but 5 miles from that Castle, he should not be lyable to any farther question: notwithstanding which assurance, they most perfidiously tooke him at Oreton in Furnesse Fells, one Bell a presbiterean minister and Wrench a Parliament Captaine first discovering him, and Sawrey a Justice of Peace, with Fell a Colonell, committing him to the castle of Lancaster; whence he was conveyed to Yorke, where being brought before Thorpe and Pulisdon, two of their then bloudy judges, and indicted upon the Statute of 25 E. 3, for levying war against the King, though he produced his late Maties Commissions for all his most valiant and loyall actings for him, the Jury being then packt finding him guilty they condemned him to death, which with much Christian magnanimity he accordingly suffred upon the .... day of August a° 1649, his body being afterwards buried according to his desire at Wentworth in this county of Yorke, neer unto the grave of his worthy Ld and Master the late famous Earle of Strafford.

Margery, wife of the aforesaid John Morris, was afterwards married to Jonas Bulkley, 4th son of Abell Bulkley of Bulkley in com. Lanc. Esqr. by whom she had issue 4 children, vizt. Thomas, Morris, Margery, Elizabeth.

See ye Descent of Bulkley, p. 247.

CRESSY OF BIRKIN.

ARMS.—Quarterly:

1 and 4. Argent, a lion rampant double-queued sable.
2. Gules, a lion rampant vair.
3. Or, a fess azure, in chief a label of three points gules.

An escutcheon of pretence: ...... three calves passant in pale, a mullet for difference.– Metcalfe.

CREST.—A stag's head erased......

Everingham Cressy of Birkin in com. Ebor. Esqr. died in a° 1644, or thereabouts. = Mary, daughter to Sr Will'm Fairfax of Steeton in com. Ebor. K^t^.

- 2. Everingham Cressy of Birkin Esqr, æt. 54 annorum 9 Apr. a° D. 1666. = Sarah, daughter and sole heire of Marke Metcalfe of the Citty of Yorke Esqr.
  - 1. Sarah.
  - 2. Mary.
  - 3. Alice.
  - 4. Anne.
  - 5. Elizabeth.
  - 1. Everingham Cressy, son and heire, æt. 25 annorum 9° Apr. a° D. 1666.
  - 2. Gervase Cressy.
  - 3. Nathaniell.
  - 4. Joseph.
- 1. Gervase Cressy, died in his father's lifetime. = Elizabeth, daughter to Sr Anthony Chester of ...... in the county of Lincolne Kn^t^.
  - Everingham Cressy, died unmarried.
- 1. Mabell, wife of Marmaduke Constable of of Kexby in co. Ebor. Esqr.
- 2. Mary, 3. Anne, } died unmarried.
- 4. Eliz. wife of Edw. Wingate of ...... in com. Ebor.

STRAFFORD AND TICKHILL WAPENTAKE. *Doncaster*, 9 *Apr*. 1666.

HATFEILD OF HAITFEILD.

ARMS.—Ermine, on a chevron engrailed .... three cinquefoils ...., a canton gules.

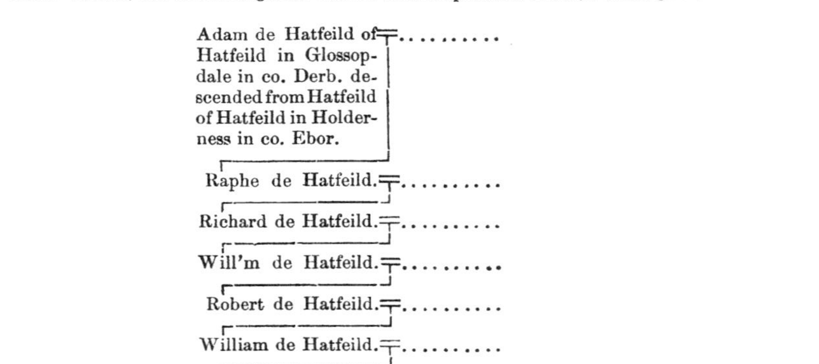

Adam de Hatfeild of Hatfeild in Glossopdale in co. Derb. descended from Hatfeild of Hatfeild in Holderness in co. Ebor. = ...

Raphe de Hatfeild. = ...

Richard de Hatfeild. = ...

Will'm de Hatfeild. = ...

Robert de Hatfeild. = ...

William de Hatfeild. = ...

Robert de Hatfeild. = ...

2. Nicholas Hatfeild of Hatfeild house in y[e] parish of Ecclesfield in com. Ebor. 2 E. 6. = Anne, daughter of ...... Sanderson of ....

a

1. John de Hatfeild.

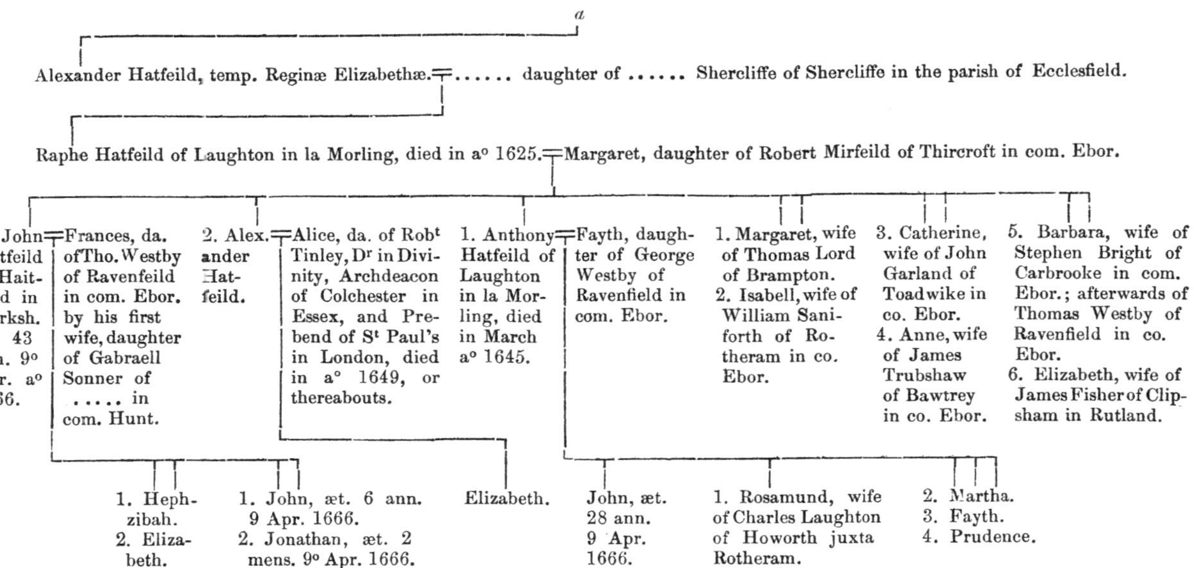
a
Alexander Hatfeild, temp. Reginæ Elizabethæ.=...... daughter of ...... Shercliffe of Shercliffe in the parish of Ecclesfield.
Raphe Hatfeild of Laughton in la Morling, died in aº 1625.=Margaret, daughter of Robert Mirfeild of Thircroft in com. Ebor.
3. John Hatfeild of Haitfeild in Yorksh. æt. 43 ann. 9º Apr. aº 1666.
=Frances, da. of Tho. Westby of Ravenfeild in com. Ebor. by his first wife, daughter of Gabraell Sonner of ..... in com. Hunt.
2. Alexander Hatfeild.
=Alice, da. of Robt Tinley, Dr in Divinity, Archdeacon of Colchester in Essex, and Prebend of St Paul's in London, died in aº 1649, or thereabouts.
1. Anthony Hatfeild of Laughton in la Morling, died in March aº 1645.
=Fayth, daughter of George Westby of Ravenfield in com. Ebor.
1. Margaret, wife of Thomas Lord of Brampton.
2. Isabell, wife of William Saniforth of Rotheram in co. Ebor.
3. Catherine, wife of John Garland of Toadwike in co. Ebor.
4. Anne, wife of James Trubshaw of Bawtrey in co. Ebor.
5. Barbara, wife of Stephen Bright of Carbrooke in com. Ebor.; afterwards of Thomas Westby of Ravenfield in co. Ebor.
6. Elizabeth, wife of James Fisher of Clipsham in Rutland.
1. Hephzibah.
2. Elizabeth.
1. John, æt. 6 ann. 9 Apr. 1666.
2. Jonathan, æt. 2 mens. 9º Apr. 1666.
Elizabeth.
John, æt. 28 ann. 9 Apr. 1666.
1. Rosamund, wife of Charles Laughton of Howorth juxta Rotheram.
2. Martha.
3. Fayth.
4. Prudence.

STRAFFORD & TICKHILL WAPENTAKE. *Doncaster*, 9 *Apr.* 1666.

COPLEY OF DONCASTER.

ARMS.—Argent, a cross moline sable, a canton gules.

Francis Copley of Doncaster, died in anno 1610, or thereabouts. = Dorothy, daughter of Hugh Wyrrall of Leversall in com. Ebor.

3. Robert, 4. Richard, 5. Thomas, died without issue.

2. Will'm Copley of Doncaster, died in his father's life-time. = Sarah, daughter of Christoph[r] Copley of Wadworth in com. Ebor.

1. Francis, died unmarried.

1. Anne, died unmarried.
2. Margaret, wife of .... Wentworth, a younger son of the House of Wentworth Woodhouse.

2. William, dyed young.

1. John Copley of Doncaster, now living, aº sc. 1666, ætatis 63 ann. 9 Apr. = Elizabeth, daughter of Nicholas Stringer of Sutton upon Lound in com. Nott.

2. Thomas Copley, Citizen of London.

1. Robert Copley, an Utter Barrister of Gray's Inne, ætatis 32 annor. 9º Apr. 1666. = Elizabeth, daughter of George Sitwell of Renishaw in com. Derb.

1. Mary.
2. Anne, wife of Samuell Jackson of Leedes in com. Ebor.
3. Sarah, wife of John Lambe of Hardwick juxta Pontefract in com. Ebor.

1. John Copley, æt. 6 ann. 9 Apr. 1666. 2. George. Elizabeth.

STRAFFORD & TICKHILL WAPENTAKE. *Sheffeild*, 10 *Apr.* 1666.

KNIGHT OF LANGOLD.

ARMS.—Or, on a chief sable three griffins segreant of the field.
CREST.—An eagle displayed or.
Qu. for proofe of these Armes ?

Will'm Knight of .... neer Newbury in com. Southampt. descended from the family of the Knights of St Dens neer Suthampt. = Alice, daughter of ...... Worthington of ......

Sr Raphe Knight of Langold in co. Ebor. K[t], ætatis 47 ann. 10 Apr. aº D. 1666. = Fayth, daughter of William Dickenson of Rotheram in com. Ebor. Clerke.

Dina, wife of Joseph Payne of Letwell in com. Ebor.

2. Isaac.
3. Raphe.

1. John, ætatis 17 annorũ 10 Apr. aº 1666.

1. Hesther.
2. Christian.

3. Bridget.
4. Fayth.

STRAFFORD AND TICKHILL WAPENTAKE. *Doncaster*, 9 *Apr*. 1666.

WASHINGTON OF ADWICKE.

ARMS.—Argent, two bars and in chief three mullets gules, a crescent for difference.

Richard Washington of Adwicke in com. Ebor. Esqr.=.....

- 4. Will'm Washington, resided in Ireland.=
- 2. Philip, 3. Godfrey, 5. Richard, died without issue.
- 1. Darcie Washington of Adwicke in co. Ebor. Esqr, died in a^o^ 1657.=Anne, daughter of Mathew Wentworth of Bretton in com. Ebor. Esqr.
- 1. Frances, wife of .... Kilvert, a Merchant in London.
- 2. Elizabeth, 3. Mary, died unmarried.

Children of Darcie Washington and Anne:

- 3. Darcy Washington, died in the Garrison of Newarke, being a Captaine there for the King, unmarr.
- 2. Robert Washington, a Merchant in Holland.=.....
- 1. James Washington, son and heire, died in the last siege of Pomfret Castle, being there in armes for the King, obijt patre vivente.=Eliz. da. of William Copley of Sprotborough in com. Ebor. Esqr.
- 1. Anne, wife of George Gill of Lightwood in co. Derb.
- 2. Grace, wife of Thomas Stanhope of Mellwood in co. Linc. Esqr.
- 3. Mary, wife of John Rawson of Pickburne in com. Ebor.
- 4. Sarah, wife of Godfrey Copley of Skelbrough in com. Ebor.

Children of Robert Washington: Hannah. 1. James. 2. Joseph.

Children of James Washington and Eliz.:

- 2. Fuljambe. 3. Godfrey. 4. Francis.
- 1. Richard Washington of Adwicke in com. Ebor. Esqr, æt. 28 annorū 9 Apr. a^o^ 1666.=Elizabeth ap Rees, daughter of ...... ap Rees of Washingley in com. Hunt.
- 1. Dorothy, wife of Henry Dove of Folkeworth in com. Hunt.
- 2. Mary.

BECKWITH OF ACTON.

ARMS.—Argent, a chevron between three hind's heads erased gules.

Marmaduke Beckwith of Acton in com. Ebor. sold his Lands in Clynt in com. Ebor. = Anne, daughter of ...... Dynely of Bramup in com. Ebor.

Their children:

- ...... daughter of ...... Currer of ...... = 2. Roger Beckwith of Aldbrough in com. Ebor. died in anno 1634. = Susanna, daughter of ...... Brakenbury of Sellaby in the Bishopprick of Durham.
- 1. Thomas Beckwith of Acton, living in anno 1612. = Frances, daughter and heire of Will. Frost of Acton in com. Ebor.

Children of Roger and his first wife:

- 1. ...... wife of ...... Norton.
- 2. ...... wife of ...... Robinson of Bolton super Swale in com. Ebor.
- Thomas Beckwith of Beverley in co. Ebor. = ...

Children of Roger and Susanna:

- 1. Arthur Beckwith of Aldbrough in com. Ebor. Esqr, died in a° 1642. = Mary, da. of Sr Marmaduke Wyvill of Constable Burton in com. Ebor. K^t and Bar^t.
- 2. Mathew Beckwith of Tanfeild in co. Ebor. now living. scil^t 9 Apr. 1666. = Elizabeth, da. of Sr John Buck of Filey in com. Ebor. K^t.
- 3. Will'm Beckwith of Thurcroft in Laughton in co. Ebor. æt. 42 an. 9° Apr. a° 1666. = Marg^t, da. of Bernard Ellis, Recorder of Yorke.
- 1. Susan, wife of John Anlaby of Anlaby in co. Ebor.
- 2. Judith, wife of William Parker, D^r of Phisick of .... in Kent.
- 3. Hesther, wife unto John Odingsells of Eperston in co. Nott.

Son of Thomas and Frances:

- Thomas Beckwith of Acton, ætat. 43 annorū 1612. = Barbara, daugh. of John Milborne of Hinderskelfe in co. Ebor.

Children of Arthur and Mary:

- 1. Marmaduke, died unmarried.
- 2. Roger Beckwith of Aldbrough Esqr, now living, a° 1666.
- 1. Mary.
- 2. Isabell.
- 3. Susan.

Children of Mathew and Elizabeth:

- 1. John Beckwith, ætat. 14 annor. 1666.
- 2. Will'm.
- 1. Susan.
- 2. ....

Son of Thomas and Barbara:

- Thomas Beckwith of Acton, æt. 14 annor. a° 1612. = ... daughter of .... Wandesford of Pickhill in co. Ebor.

Their children:

- 2. Barbara, wife of John Lockwood of Soureby in co. Ebor.
- 1. Isabell, wife of Nicholas Fairfax, second brother to Thomas late Viscount Fairfax of Emelyn in Ireland.

Doncaster, 9° *Apr.* 1666.

COPLEY OF SPRODBOROUGH.

ARMS.—Quarterly : on an inescutcheon the badge of a baronet of England.

1. Argent, a cross moline sable, a crescent for difference.
2. Lozengy, argent and gules.
3. Or, a maunche gules.
4. Argent, five fusils in fess gules, in chief three bear's heads erased sable.

CREST.—Out of a ducal coronet or a plume of five ostrich feathers argent.

John Copley of Batley in co. Ebor. Esqr. = ...

Will'm Fitz-Williams of Sprodborough in com. Ebor. Esqr. = Eliz. da. of Sr John Conyers Knt.

1. .... Copley of Batley Esqr. = ... (issue)

2. Sr Will'm Copley of Sprodborough in com. Ebor. Knt. = Dorothy, daughter of Will'm Fitz-Williams of Sprodborough, sister and coheir to John her brother.

Margery, wife of Thomas Sutill of Sutill Hall in com. Ebor. =

1. John, 2. Will'm, } died without issue.

Mary, daughter of Sr Bryan Hastings Knt, 1 wife. = Philip Copley of Sprotborough in com. Ebor. Esqr. = ... 2 wife.

Elizabeth, daughter and heire, wife of Sr Henry Savile of Thornhill in com. Eborum Knt.

Margaret, wife of Henry Sandford.

1. Will'm Copley of Sprotborough in com. Ebor. Esqr. = Eliz. da. & coheire of Godfrey Boswell of Gomelthwayt, sister & heire to Francis Boswell of Gomelthwayt in co. Ebor. Esqr.

2. Avery Copley of Warren Hall in co. Ebor. died circa an. 1605. = Joane, daughter of Simon Gonby of ..... in com. Ebor.

3. John Copley, from whom the Copleys of Skelbrough are descended. = Jane, daughter and coheir of Raphe Anger.

Elizabeth, wife of Henry Sacheverell of Ratcliffe upon Sore in com. Nott.

1. Godfrey Copley of Sprodborough Esqr, died unmarried.
2. Raphe Copley, dyed without issue.

1. Mary, wife of Edmd Hastings of Braunston in com. Leic.
2. Anne, wife of Emanuell Moote of Melton in com. Ebor.
3. Isabell, wife of James Pinkney of Newton in com. Ebor.

Will'm Copley of Sprodborough Esqr, heir unto Raphe his Uncle's son, died 1644. = Dorothy, da. of Will. Rooth of Romley in co. Derb.

Thomas. Godfrey. Mary. Elizabeth.

Eleanor, daughter of Sr Thomas Walmisley of Dunkinhalgh in co. Lanc. Knt, 1 wife. = Sr Godfrey Copley of Sprodborough, created Baronet by K. Charles ye 2d 17 Junij, 17 of his Reigne, æt. 40 annor. 9 Apr. aº 1666. = Eliz. daughter of Will'm Stanhope of Linby in com. Nott. Esqr, 2 wife.

Eliz. wife of James Washington of Adwick upon Street in com. Ebor. Esqr.

Godfrey Copley, son and heire, ætat. 13 ann. 9º Apr. 1666.

1. Dorothy. 2. Elizabeth. 3. Catherine.

STRAFFORD AND TICKHILL WAPENTAKE. *Doncaster*, 9° *Apr*.1666.

BOSVILE OF WARMSWORTH.

ARMS.—Argent, five fusils in fess gules, in chief three mullets sable, a crescent for difference.

Gervase Boseville of Warmsworth in com. Ebor. died a° 1621. = Susan, daughter and coheir of Tho. Wormeley of Hatfeild in com. Ebor.

Their issue:

- Mary, daughter of Francis Stringer of Whiston in co. Ebor. 1 wife. = 4. Gervase Bosvile of Warmsworth in com. Ebor. æt. 47 ann. 9 Apr. a° D'ni 1666. = Jane, daughter of Marmaduke Wilson of Kirk-Dighton in co. Eborum Esqr, second wife.
- 2. Edward, 3. Godfrey, died unmarried.
- Barbara, da. & coh. of Sr Franc. Babington of Rampton in com. Nott. Kn^t^, first wife. = 1. Thomas Bosvile of Warmsworth in co. Ebor. died in a° 1659. = Isabell, daughter of John Bullock of Norton in co. Derb. Esqr, second wife.
- 1. Jane, wife of Thomas Atkinson of Barton upon Humber in com. Linc.
- 2. Gartrude, dyed young.
- 3. Susan, wife of Alexander Rokeby of Skyres in comitatu Eborum.
- 4. Elizabeth, y^e^ wife of Christoph^r^ Copley of Wadworth in comitatu Eborum.
- 5. Mary, wife of Robert Sanderson of Blythe in comitatu Nott.
- 6. Margaret, died unmarried.

Issue of Gervase and Mary (1st wife):

- 1. Thomas, ætatis 15 annor. 9 Apr. 1666.
- 1. Susan, 2. Sarah, 3. Mary, died young.

Issue of Gervase and Jane (2nd wife):

- 2. Gervase, ætatis 10 annor. 9° Apr.1666.
- 3. Marmaduke.
- 4. Godfrey.
- 1. Jane.
- 2. Elizabeth, dyed young.
- 3. Anne.

Issue of Thomas:

- 1. Susan, wife of Thomas Ashhurst of Ashhurst in com. Lanc. Esqr.
- 2, Mary, wife of Fuljambe Blytheman of Newlathes in com. Ebor. afterwards of George Nevill of Thorney in com. Nott. Esqr.
- 3. Elizabeth, wife of Sr Edward Stanley of Bickerstaff in com. Lanc. Esqr.

STRAFFORD AND TICKHILL WAPENTAKE. *Sheffeild*, 10 *Apr.* 1666.

GILL OF CARR-HOUSE.

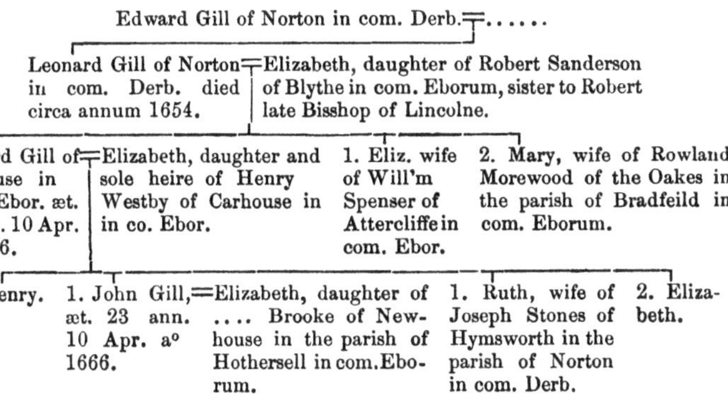

STRAFFORD AND TICKHILL WAPENTAKE. *Sheffeild*, 10 *Apr.* 1666.

RATCLIFFE OF SHEFFEILD.

Respite given for exhibiting ye Armes.

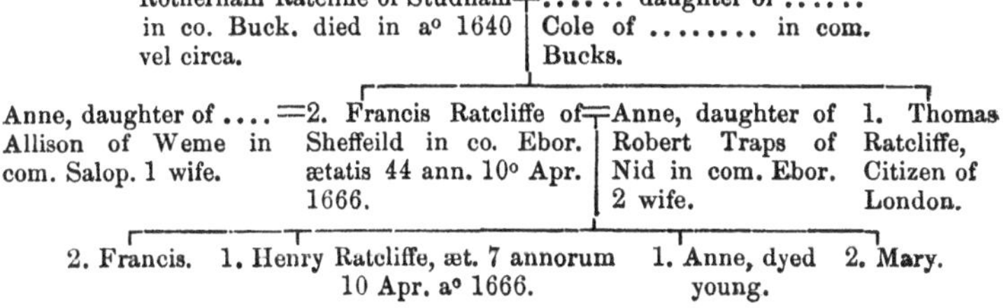

STRAFFORD & TICKHILL WAPENTAKE. *Sheffeild*, 10 *Apr*. 1666.

WESTBY OF GILTHWAYT.

ARMS.—Argent, on a chevron azure three cinquefoils of the field, a crescent for difference.
CREST.—A martlet sable, holding in the beak three ears of wheat or, stalk and leaves vert.

George Westby of Ravenfield in co. Ebor. died in a° 1640. = Frances, daughter of Richard Boroughs of Gilthwayt in com. Ebor.

2. George Westby of Gilthwayt in co. Ebor. ætatis 50 annor. 10 Apr. 1666. = Alice, daughter of Francis Stringer of Whiston in co. Ebor. Esqr.

1. Thomas Westby of Ravenfield in com. Ebor. = ...

1. Samuell, ætatis 17 annorum 10 Apr. a° 1666.
2. George.
3. Thomas.
4. John.
1. Sarah.
2. Mary.
3. Dorcas.
4. Frances.
5. Elizabeth.

STRAFFORD & TICKHILL WAPENTAKE. *Sheffeild*, 10 *Apr*. 1666.

GOODWIN OF RAWMARSH.

ARMS.—Argent, on a bend raguly gules a lion passant of the field.
No proofe made of these Armes.

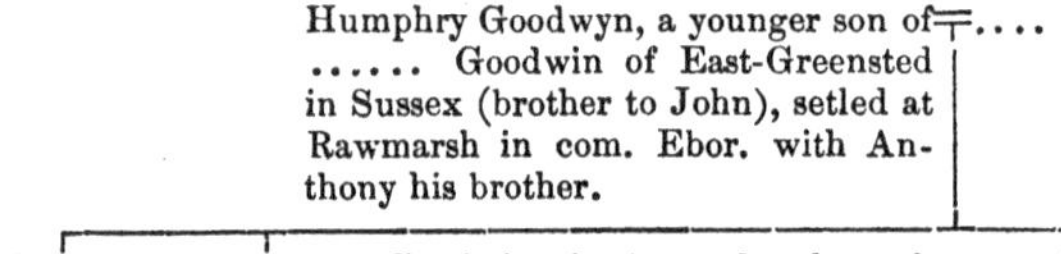

Humphry Goodwyn, a younger son of ...... Goodwin of East-Greensted in Sussex (brother to John), setled at Rawmarsh in com. Ebor. with Anthony his brother. = ...

2. Edward Goodwin of Yorke.

1. Anthony Goodwin of Rawmarsh in com. Ebor. died in anno 1664. = Anne, daughter of .... Slack of Emley in com. Ebor. 1 wife.

Anne, wife of Charles Laughton of Howorth in com. Ebor.

Edward Goodwin of Rawmarsh, æt. 34 ann. 10 Apr. 1666.

Margaret, wife of Richard Townend of Hoyland in com. Ebor.

THE CITTY OF YORKE. *Yorke*, 19 *Mart.* 1665.

LINDLEY OF YORKE.

ARMS.—Argent, on a chief sable three griffin's heads erased of the field, in the fess point a trefoil slipped gules.

.... 1 wife. = Nicholas Lindley, Merchant and Alderman of Kingston upon Hull, descended by a younger son from the antient family of Linley of Linley in com. Ebor. = ... 2 wife.

3. Thomas Linley of Beverley in com. Ebor.
4. Nicholas, died unmarried.

2. Will'm Lindley, a Mercht in Kingston upon Hull, died in a° 1635, vel circa. = Dorothy, daughter and coheire of Bryan Bateson of the Citty of Yorke.

1. John, died unmarried.

Lancelot, died unmarried.

Francis Lindley of the City of Yorke Esqr, an Utter Barrister of Gray's Inne, and Vice-Chamberlain of Chester, æt. 32 ann. 19 Mart. 1665. = Elizabeth, sole daughter of John Lightbound of Manchester in com. Lanc.

1. Fayth.
2. Elizabeth, wife of Will'm Simpson of Sheffeild in com. Ebor.

Elizabeth, æt. 9 mens. 19° Apr. a° 1665.

AGBRIGG AND MORLEY WAPENTAKE. *Pomfret*, 7° *Apr.* 1666.

BUNNY OF NEWLAND.

ARMS.—Quarterly of nine:

1. Argent, a chevron between three goat's heads erased sable.
2. Gules, a cross fleurée or, on a chief azure three round buckles of the second.
3. Per saltire gules and ermine.
4. Argent, three bendlets sable.
5. Gules, three lions rampant argent ducally crowned or.
6. Sable, three lions rampant argent.
7. Gules, a fess or between three saltires argent.
8. Argent, three bendlets gules.
9. Argent, in bend three boar's heads couped sable cottised potent counterpotent of the last.

Francis Bunny of Newland in com. Ebor. æt. 83 ann. 7 Apr. a° 1666. = Mary, daughter of Will'm Cartwright of Newland in com. Ebor.

Theodosia, daughter of Sr Francis Molineux of Teversall in com. Nott. Bart, 1. wife. = 4. Edmund Bunny, son and heire, æt. 47 ann. 7 Apr. 1666. = Elizabeth, daughter of Will'm Palmer of Southwell in com. Nott. Esqr, 2. wife, died leaving noe issue. = Mary, daughter of Will'm Bosseville of Gunthwayt in com. Ebor. Esqr, 3d wife.

1. Richard,
2. Henry,
3. William,
dyed young.

Theodosia, dyed young. Richard, dyed young.

GILLING EAST WAPENTAKE. *Darneton*, 6 *Sept.* 1666.

GYLL OF BARTON.

ARMS.—Sable, a pale between four fleurs-de-lis or, a canton argent.

CREST.—A moor's head in profile couped at the shoulders sable, charged on the cheek with a crescent argent, ducally crowned and collared or, a chain of the last passing from the rim of the crown behind to the back of the collar.

Thomas Gyll of Barton in com. Ebor. = Anne, daughter of Peter Ward of Barton in com. Ebor.

2. Christopher Gyll of Barton in co. Ebor., died circa an. 1646. = Margaret, daughter of Christopher Langley of Langton super Swale in com. Ebor.

1. John Gyll of the Citty of Durham. =

2. John, died unmarried.

1. Thomas Gyll of Barton, died in his father's lifetime. = Elizabeth, daugh. of Richard Wandsford of Pickhall in com. Ebor. Esqr.

1. Agnes, died unmarried.
2. Elizabeth, wife of George Middleton of South Sheilds in co. p. Dunelm. gent.
3. Mary, wife of William Glover of Barton in com. Ebor.

1. Christopher, dyed unmarried.

2. Thomas Gyll of Barton, an Attorney at Law, æt. 34 an. 6 Sept. 1666. = Elizabeth, daughter of Thomas Smithson of Barton in com. Ebor.

2. Thomas, æt. 2 ann. 6 Sept. 1666.

1. Christopher, died in his infancy.

1. Elizabeth, dyed young.

2. Margaret, dyed young.

HOLDERNESSE MIDDLE BAYLIWICK. *Yorke*, 11 *Aug.* 1666.

MICKLETHWAYT OF SWYNE.

ARMS.—Checky argent and gules, on a chief indented azure a crescent or.

Universis et singulis Christi fidelibus, ad quos præsentes Literæ pervenerint, Johannes Borough Miles, Norroy Rex Armorum partium Borealium Angliæ ultra Trentam, salutem in Domino sempiternam. Cum præclarissimus vir D'ns Leonardus Besson Major Civitatis Eborac.: ad instantiam egregij viri Eliæ Micklethwayt, per literas suas propriâ manu consignatas, et Sigillo Officij sui munitas, mihi fidem fecerit quod Scutum Armorum uti hic in margine depictum existit in vetusto quodam Codice penes Edwardum Binckes, rerum antiquarū in eadem Civitate studiosum remanente ad antiquam Micklethwaytorum familiam pertinere reperitur, et inter nonnulla ali virorum illustrium partium illarum borealium Insignia eidem familiæ adscribi conspicitur; Ego indubitato hoc testimonio ductus, idem Scutum, sicut in margine depingitur, et hic inferius Anglicè recensetur, vizt Checquy Argent and Gules, on a Che indented Azure a Cressant Or, esse ejusdem Micklethwaytorum Familiæ Insign gentililia credo ac censeo, et quantum in me est eidem Familiæ per præsentes ratific et confirmo. In cujus rei testimonium, ego præfatus Johannes Borough præsentib hijs literis, nomen meum propriâ manu subscripsi et Sigillum Officij mei apposui. Datum sexto die Novembris, anno regni Serenissimi Principis D'ni nostri Caroli Angliæ, Scotiæ, Franciæ, et Hiberniæ Regis secundo 1626.

JOHANNES BOROUGH Miles, Norroy Rex
Armorum Partium Borealiū ultra Trentā.

Adam de Micklethwayt,=...... temp. H. 3.

Henricus de Mickelthwayt.

Will's filius Will'i de Michelthwayt concessit terras in Kerreby et Michelthwayt per Cartam sine datâ. (temp. H. 3.)

Robertus de Micklethwait, 31 E. 1.

Joh'es de Mictylthwayt, a° 1409.

John Micklethwayt.=......

John Micklethwayt of Ingbirch-worth in com. Ebor.=......

Dorothy, da. of ...... Jaques, 1 wife.=3. Elias Micklethwayt, a Merch^t in Yorke, twice Ld Mayor of that Citty, & a Burgesse in Parliam^t in K. James his time, died circa 1630.=...... widow of ...... Arding-ton, 2 wife.

1. John Micklethwayt, of Ingbirch-worth in the parish of Penyston & West-Riding of Yorksh.=

2. Francis Micklethwayt, a Merch^t in Yorke, dyed without issue.

3. Elyas Mickle-thwayt of the Inner Temple, London, of whom no issue remains.

2. Marke Mickle-thwayt, Rec-tor of Mar-ston in y^e Aynstie of Yorke.=

1. Joseph Mickle-thwayt of Swine in Holderness, one of y^e Justices of Peace in this county, died in Sept. 1658, and buried in the Min-ster at Yorke.=Anne, daugh. of Percevall Levett, Citizen of Yorke.

1. Mary, wife of Samuell Pawson, a Merch^t in Yorke.
2. Susan, wife of Chris-topher Topham, Mer-chant in Yorke.
3. Tabitha, wife of John Geldart, Alderman of the Citty of Yorke.

1. Mary.
2. Han-nah.

Elias.

2. Joseph Mickle-thwayt, æt. 26 ann. 11 Aug. 1666.

1. John Mickle-thwayt of Swine, an Utter Barrister of the Inner Temple London, and a Jus-tice of Peace in the East Riding of Yorkshire, died in Apr. a° 1660.=Barbara, daugh. of Timothy Middleton of Stansted Mount-Fitchet in com. Essex Esqr.

1. Anne, wife of Thomas Dicken-son of Kirby-Hall in the West-Riding of York-shire.
2. Dorothy, wife of Thomas Stil-lington of Kelfeild in com. Ebor.

Joseph, æt. 10 ann. 11 Aug. 1666.

Anne.

AGBRIGG AND MORLEY WAPENTAKE. *Pomfret*, 7 *Apr*. 1666.

STRINGER OF SHARLETON.

ARMS.—Sable, three eagles displayed erminois.

CREST.—An eagle's head erased erminois.

This Crest was assigned to Francis Stringer of Sharleton in co. Ebor. Gent. with a confirmation of the Coat by Richard St. George Esqr. Norroy K. of Armes, 2o Aug. ao 1612. (10 Jac. R.)

Thomas Stringer of Whiston in com. Ebor. as appeareth by an Inquisition taken at Barnesley 10o Apr. ao 30 Eliz. R. dyed 15 Febr. 30 Eliz. R. = ... daughter of ...... Fenton of ......

2. George Stringer of Whiston in com. Ebor. died in ao 1637, or thereabouts. = Frances, daughter of .... Routhe of Roundley in com. Derb. Esqr, first wife.

Isabell, daughter and coheire of Thomas Wombwell of Greisbrooke and Thurnercliffe-grange in com. Ebor. first wife. = 1. Francis Stringer of Sharleton, ætatis 23 annorum 10 Apr. 30 Eliz. Reginæ, died 14 Julij 13o Car. 1. = Dorothy, daughter of John Thorney of Fenton in com. Ebor. second wife.

2. Francis Stringer of Whiston, died in anno 1658. = Mary, daughter of Christopher Michell of Morden in com. Ebor.

1. George Stringer, a Mercht in London.

1. Frances, wife of William Worseley of Usflete in Marshland in com. Ebor.

2. Eliz. wife of Richard Franklin of Roche Abbey in com. Ebor.

Thomas Stringer of Sharleton, æt. 50 annor. 6. Mart. 13 Car. 1, died in ao 1649, or thereabouts. = Barbara, daughter and coheir of Cutbert Fleming of Sharleton.

2. George.

1. Thomas Stringer of Sharleton in com. Ebor. Esqr, by conveyance from the last Thomas Stringer of Sharleton. Now one of his Maties Justices of Peace in the West-Riding of this County of Yorke, ætat. 41 annorum 7 Apr. anno D'ni 1666. = Anne, d. of Sr John Melton, Knt, Sec. to the Councell at York.

1. Frances, w. of George Taylor of Chesterfield in co. Derb.

2. Mary, w. of Gervase Boswell of Warmsworth co. Yk.

3. Alice, wife of George Westby of Gilthwayt in com. Ebor.

4. Anne, w. of Robert Armitage of Netherton in co. Ebor.

5. Constance.

6. Elizabeth.

7. Sarah.

John, dyed in his childhood.

1. Thomas Stringer, son and heir, æt. 8 annor. 7 Apr. 1666.

2. William, æt. 2 annorū 1666.

Catherine.

Pomfret, 7 *Apr*. 1666.

WATSON OF EASTHAGE.

ARMS.—Argent, on a chevron azure between three martlets gules as many crescents or.
CREST.—A griffin's head erased sable, holding in his beak or a rose-branch slipped vert.
For proofe hereof there is an old glasse window in an house at Loftus which was antiently belonging to this Family, as Mr John Hopkinson affirmes.

Richard de Bolton.=......

Joh'es, filius Ricardi, a° 1307.=......

Walterus, filius Joh'is, a° 1321.=Cecilia, a° 1321.

Will's, filius Walteri, a° 1316.=......

Will'm Watson, a° D'ni 1391.=Margaret, daughter of Robert Tup.

Christopher Watson, 14 Edw. 4.=......

Will'm Watson, 7 H. 7.=......

Richard Watson, 2 H. 8.=Elen ......

Thomas Watson, borne 12 Nov. a° 1524.=Elizabeth .....

2. Rowland Watson of Silsden More in com. Ebor.=Agnes, daughter of .... Currer of Kildwick in com. Ebor.

1. William Watson of Bolton upon Dearne in com. Ebor.=....

Alice, wife of Thomas Wentworth of Thurnscough grange in com. Ebor.

1. Will'm Watson of Silsden-More.=..

2. Hugh, dyed without issue.

3. Edmund Watson of Crosse-yate in the parish of Bingley in com. Ebor. died in Nov. a° D'ni 1660.=Mary, daughter of .... Shakelton of ...... in com. Ebor.

Jane, daughter of .... Elliot of Billingley in com. Ebor. 1 wife.=Rowland Watson of Bolton, 15 Jac.=.... daughter of.... Scofeild of Ankeridge juxta Doncaster in com. Ebor. 2 wife.

Alice, daughter and coheir of Nathaniell Birkhead of Eastage in com. Ebor. Esqr, widow of Edmund Rogers of Barnsley in com. Ebor. 1 wife.=Edmund Watson of Easthage in co. Ebor. æt. 39 an. 7 Apr. 1666.=Jane, daughter of Robert Wood of Burton in com. Eborum, 2 wife.

Mary, wife of Edward Bouling of Shelley in com. Ebor.

1. Mary, æt. 12 ann. 7 Apr. 1666.

2. Jane.

1. Edmund, æt. 3 ann. 7 Apr. a° 1666.

2. Robert.

OSGODCROSSE WAPENTAKE. *Pomfret*, 7° *Apr*. 1666.

WENTWORTH OF SOUTH EMSALL.

ARMS.—Sable, on a chevron between three leopard's faces or as many mullets gules.

Thomas Wentworth of Emsall in com. Ebor. Esqr. = Jane, daughter and coheire of Oliver Merfeild of Howley in com. Ebor.

2. Roger Wentworth of South Kirkby in com. Ebor. = Elizabeth, daughter and heir of John Went of Pomfret in com. Ebor. | 1. John Wentworth, from whom the Wentworths of Emsall are descended. = ...

Thomas Wentworth of South-Kirkby. = Eliz. daughter and heire of Edward Flintell of Kirby. | 1. Isabell, wife to Lyonell Portington of Barnby super Dun in co. Ebor. | 2. Elizabeth, wife of Nicholas Fitz-Williams of Bentley in com. Ebor.

4. Christopher. | 3 Hugh Wentworth of Thurnscough grange in co. Ebor. = Beatrice, sister of Sr Tho. Waterton of Walton in com. Ebor. K^t, widd. of Raph Barnby of Barnby Hall in co. Ebor. 1 wife. | 2. Roger Wentworth of Stubs-Walden in com. Eborum. = | 1. Thomas Wentworth of South-Kirkby. = Ursula, daughter ... Swinho.

Thomas Wentworth of Thrunscough-Grange, died in anno 1624. = Alice, daughter of Will'm Watson of Bolton upon Dearne in com. Ebor. | William Wentworth of South Kirkby. = ...

2. Christopher, died unmarried. | 1. Hugh Wentworth of South Emsall in com. Ebor. æt. 58 annor. 7 Apr. 1666. = Elizabeth, daughter of John Brown of Manston in the parish of Whitchurch in com. Ebor. | Mary, wife of Thomas Day of South-Emsall in com. Ebor.

1. Thomas, æt. 30 ann. 7 Apr. 1666. | 2. John. | 3. Darcy. | 4. Hugh.

ANNE OF FRICKLEY.

Arms.—Argent, on a bend sable three martlets of the field.

Crest.—A woman's head couped at the breast ...., hair dishevelled ....

George Anne of Frickley in com. Ebor. Esqr. living in anno 1585. = Margaret, daughter and sole heire of Richard Fenton of .... in co. Derb.

Their children:

- 4. Thomas Anne of Sutton in com. Wilts. = (had issue)
- 5. John Anne of Rippon in com. Ebor.
- 1. John, died in his childhood.
- 3. George, died unmarried.
- 2. Philip Anne of Frickley in com. Ebor. Esq[r], died in a° 1647. = Ellen, da. and coheir of Hugh Shirbourn of Eshold in com. Ebor. Esq[r].
- 1. Mary, wife of ...... Conyers of ....
- 2. Bridget, 3. Frances, Nunns in Flanders.
- 4. Catherine, wife of D[r]. Bright of Beverley, D[r] of Phisick.
- 5. Martha, wife of Charles Forster, son and heir to S[r] Richard Forster of Stokesley in co. Ebor. B[t].
- 6. Elizabeth, wife of Thomas Lepton of Kebeck in com. Ebor.
- 7. Jane.

Children of Philip Anne and Ellen:

- 5. Philip, died w[th]out issue.
- 4. Michaell Anne of Frickley, Esq[r], æt. 40 annor. 7 Apr. a° 1666. = Eleanor, daughter of Robert Stapleton of Templehurst in com. Ebor. Esq[r].
- 1. John, 2. Richard, 3. George, died unmarried.
- 1. Jane, 2. Elizabeth, 3. Helen, 4. Margaret, died unmarried.

Children of Michaell Anne and Eleanor:

- 2. George, æt. 10 an. 1666.
- 1. Michaell, æt. 12 ann. 7 Apr. a° 1666.
- 1. Ursula, 2. Ellen, died unmarried.
- 3. Elizabeth.

BARKESTON ASHE WAPENTAKE. *Pomfret*, 7 *Apr.* 1666.

LEEDES OF HOPENTHORNE.

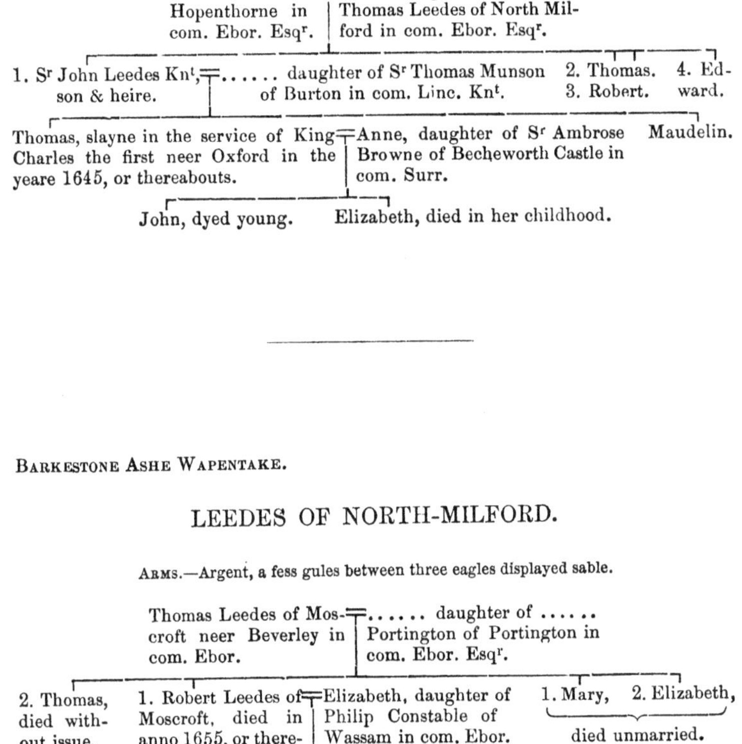

BARKESTONE ASHE WAPENTAKE.

LEEDES OF NORTH-MILFORD.

ARMS.—Argent, a fess gules between three eagles displayed sable.

Thomas Leedes of Moscroft neer Beverley in com. Ebor. = ... daughter of ...... Portington of Portington in com. Ebor. Esqr.

- 2. Thomas, died without issue.
- 1. Robert Leedes of Moscroft, died in anno 1655, or thereabouts. = Elizabeth, daughter of Philip Constable of Wassam in com. Ebor. Esqr.
- 1. Mary, 2. Elizabeth, died unmarried.

Children of Robert:

- 2. Edward.
- 3. John.
- 4. Robert.
- 1. Englebert Leedes of North-Milford in com. Ebor. Esqr, æt. 28 annor. 7 Apr. 1666. = Seceziah, daughter of Robert Crompton of Great Driffeild in com. Ebor.
- 1. Lenox.
- 2. Everill.

Children of Englebert:

- John Leedes, son and heir, ætatis 10 annorum 7 Apr. ao D. 1666.
- 1. Frances.
- 2. Elizabeth.

STRAFFORD & TICKHILL WAPENTAKE. *Pomfret*, 7° *Apr.* 1666.

DODSWORTH OF BADSWORTH.

ARMS.—Argent, a chevron between three bugle-horns sable.

Simon Dodsworth of Settrington in com. Ebor. = ...

Mathew Dodsworth, Chancelour to Toby Mathews, Arch Bpp of Yorke, died in a° 1628, or thereabouts. = Helen, daughter of .... Sandwith of Hutton-grange in com. Ebor.

1. Roger Dodsworth, eldest son, died in anno 1654, or thereabouts. = ... daughter of .... Hesketh of Rufford in com. Lanc. widdow of .... Rosthorne.

2. Edward Dodsworth, Rector of Badsworth in com. Ebor. æt. 70 ann. 7 Apr. 1666. = Isabell, daughter of Tho. Wood, Clerke, Rector of Badsworth in com. Eborum.

.... daughter of .... Wilkinson of .... = Robert Dodsworth, Clerke. = Alice, daughter of Thomas Stirrup of the Citty of Lincolne, widow of Robt Stamford of High-Ashe in com. Lanc.

Mathew, æt. 12 an. 7° Apr. a° 1666.

1. Elizabeth.
2. Isabell.
3. Eleanor.
4. Margaret.

Roger, died in his youth, unmarried.

Robert, æt. 8 ann. 7 Apr. 1666.

STRAFFORD AND TICKHILL WAPENTAKE. *Doncaster*, 9 *Apr.* 1666.

EATON OF DARFIELD.

ARMS.—Quarterly argent and sable, a cross fleurée counterchanged.

Robert Eaton of Barrow Lane in the Lordship of Whitley in com. Cestr. = Anne, daughter of Will'm Port of Ilam in co. Staff. brother to Sr John Port Kt, sometime one of the Justices of the K. Bench.

Robert Eaton, Rector of the Churches of Mobberley and Grapenhall in com. Cestr. died in anno 1619, or thereabouts, æt. 70 ann. = Ellen, sole daughter and heire of Robert Hatton of Weverham in co. Cestr.

3. Richard Eaton, Vicar of Aldlim in co. Cestriæ.

...... 1 wife. = 2. Thomas Eaton of Grapenhall in com. Cestr., died 4° Sept. a° 1657, ætatis 70 ann. = Hellen, daughter of Richard Harper of Mooro in com. Cestr., second wife.

1. Samuell Eaton, Rector of Grapenhall, died in anno 1634, or thereabouts. = Anne, daughter of ...... Byrom of Byrom in com. Lanc.

1. Eleanor, wife of John Hulton of Berterton in com. Cestr.
2. Christian, wife of Edw. Taylor of Ashton under Lime in com. Cestriæ.

1. William, slaine at the siege of Busse in the Netherlands.

2. Raphe Eaton, Rector of Darfield in com. Ebor. æt. 32 ann. 9 Apr. 1666.

Byrom Eaton, Dr of Divinity, Principall of Gloucester Hall in the University of Oxford a° D. 1666. = Frances, daughter of John Vernon, Rector of Hanbury on the Hill in com. Wigorn. 1 wife.

OSGODCROSSE WAPENTAKE. *Pomfret*, 7° *Apr.* 1666.

WENTWORTH OF EMSALL.

ARMS.—Quarterly of six:
1. Sable, a chevron between three leopard's faces or.
2. Paly of four argent and sable, on a bend gules three mullets ....
3. Gules, three fleurs-de-lis argent.
4. Vert, two lions passant gardant in pale argent.
5. Gules, on a bend argent three escallops azure.
6. Azure, a chevron between three birds argent.

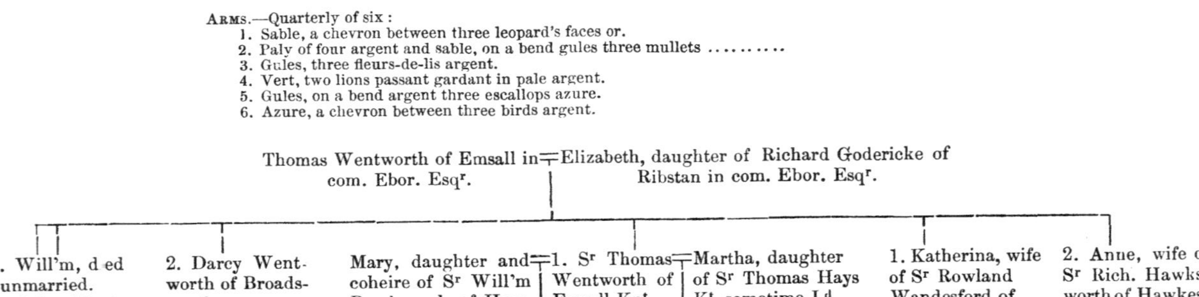

Thomas Wentworth of Emsall in com. Ebor. Esqr. = Elizabeth, daughter of Richard Godericke of Ribstan in com. Ebor. Esqr.

3. Will'm, died unmarried.
4. John Wentworth.

2. Darcy Wentworth of Broadsworth.

Mary, daughter and coheire of Sr Will'm Bambrough of Howson in co. Ebor. Knt, first wife. = 1. Sr Thomas Wentworth of Emsall Knt, died a° 1650, or thereabouts. = Martha, daughter of Sr Thomas Hays Kt, sometime Ld Mayor of London, second wife.

1. Katherina, wife of Sr Rowland Wandesford of Kirtlington in com. Ebor. Knt.

2. Anne, wife of Sr Rich. Hawksworth of Hawkesworth in com. Ebor. Knt.

Thomas Wentworth of Emsall Esqr, died in May, anno D. 1653. = Agnes, daughter of Sr Henry Bellingham of Levens in com. Westmerland Bart.

1. Martha, wife of Thomas Wombwell of Wombwell in com. Ebor. Esqr.

2. Mary, wife of Will'm Middleton of Belsey in com. Northumb. Esqr.

2. Henry, æt. 19 ann.

1. John Wentworth of Emsall Esqr, æt. 21 ann. 7 Apr. 1666.

Dorothy, wife of Edward Gower, son and heire of Sr Thomas Gower of Stitnam in com. Ebor. Bart.

Leedes, 4 *Apr*. 1666.

GASCOIGNE OF BARNBOW.

ARMS.—Quarterly of six:

1. Or, on a pale sable a conger's head couped and erect of the field. Gascoigne.
2. Argent, on a bend gules three leopard's faces of the field. Bolton.
3. Vert, a saltire engrailed or. Franke.
4. Gules, a saltire engrailed or, a mullet for difference. Clitherow of Salisbury.
5. Gules, a lion rampant or, maned argent. Grace.
6. Vert, a lion rampant within a bordure engrailed argent. Heyton.

John Gascoigne of Lasingcroft in co. Ebor. = Anne, daughter of John Vavasour, 3d son to Sr Henry Vavasour of Haselwood in co. Ebor. Knt.

3. John Gascoigne of Parlington, living in anno 1584. = Mawde, daughter of .... Ardington of Adwyke in the Street in com. Ebor.

2. Richard Gascoigne of Lasingcroft, died wthout issue.

1. Thomas Gascoigne of Lasingcroft, died without issue.

Mary, wife of .... Crofte of ......

1. Sr John Gascoigne of Lasingcroft and Barnbow in com. Ebor. made Bart by King Charles the first of Nova Scotia, dyed circa annum 1638. = Anne, daughter of .... Ingleby of Laukland in com. Ebor. a younger son of Ingleby of Ripley.

2. Thomas Gascoigne, of whom there is now noe issue remayning.

3. Avery, 4. Leonard, } of whom noe issue remayneth.

2. John Gascoigne, Abbot of Lamspring in Lower Saxony, now living ao 1666.
3. Michaell, dyed unmarried.
4. Francis Gascoigne.

1. Sr Thomas Gascoigne of Barnbow Bart, æt. 70 annorum, 4 Apr. 1666. = Anne, daughter of ...... Simonds of Brightwell in com. Oxon. sister to Sr George Simonds of Watlington Parke in com. Oxon.

1. Helen, wife of Gilbert Stapleton of Carleton in com. Ebor. Esqr.
2. Mary, wife of Will'm Houghton of Parkehall in com. Lanc.

3. Catherine, now Abbesse at Cambray ao 1666.
4. Anne, wife unto George Thwenge of Kilton Castle in Cleveland in com. Ebor

5. Margaret, 6. Christian, } died unmarried.

5. John Gascoigne.

4. George Gascoigne. = ... daughter and coheir of Ellis Woodroofe of Hope in com. Derb. widd. of ...... White-hall.

3. Thomas Gascoigne, son and heir, æt. 43 ann. 4 Apr. 1666. = Eliz. daughter of Will'm Sheldon of Beoley in com. Wigorn. Esqr.

1. John Gascoigne, died unmarried.
2. Francis Gascoigne, died unmarried.

1. Anne, wife of Sr Stephen Tempest of Broughton in Craven in com. Ebor. Knt.
2. Catherine, Prioresse of the English Nunnery in Paris, of the Benedictine Order, now living ao 1666.

3. Helen, wife of Tho. Appleby of Linton upon Ouse in co. Ebor. Esqr.
4. Mary, died unmarried.
5. Frances, now a Nunne at Cambray.

1. Thomas, æt. 7 annor. 4 Apr. ao 1666.

2. John, æt. 4 ann. et amplius.

BARKESTON ASHE WAPENTAKE. *Yorke*, 13 *Sept.* 1665.

LEWIS OF LEDSTON.

ARMS.—Sable, a chevron between three trefoils slipped or, on an inescutcheon the badge of a Baronet of England.

CREST.—Out of a ducal coronet or a plume of five ostrich feathers, three or and two sable, charged with a chevron of the first.

Morgan.═╤ . . . .

Jorder.═╤Philippa.

Philip.═╤ . . . . daughter to Guillam Says ap Madock ap Howell.

David.═╤ . . . . daughter of Will'm Robnet.

Thomas.═╤Anne, daughter of John Evans of Northop in Flyntshire. Lewis.═╤ . . . . . daughter of Will'm Robnet.

John Lewis.═╤Mary, daughter of Will'm Morgan of Gulgreve. William Lewis.═╤Anne, daughter of Sr John Welch, Ld of Lanwer.

Hope Lewis.═╤Margaret, daughter of Morgan Kevillin ap Guilliam. George Lewis Esqr.═╤Catherine, daughter of John Hearle.

Roger Lewis. . . . . . . Lewis of Waverclow in Northwales.═╤ . . . . . George Lewis. Henry Lewis.═╤Bridget, daughter of Thomas Kemis.

. . . . Lewis of Doncaster in com. Ebor.═╤ . . . . daughter of . . . .═ . . . . Ellis, 2d husband. George Lewis. William Lewis.═╤Margaret, daughter unto Robert Gamage. Richard Lewis. John Lewis.

Robert Lewis of Marr in co. Ebor. 4 E. 6—36 Eliz. R.═╤Elizabeth, daughter and heire of John Hanley of High Melton in co. Ebor. Peter. Edward. Hugh. Thomas.

a

a

* 1. John Lewis of Marr Esqr, died 31 Eliz. R. = Mary, daughter of Lyonell Reresby of Thrybergh in com. Ebor. Esqr.

2. Richard Lewis. 3. Thomas Lewis. 4. Robert Lewis.

1. Thomas Lewis of Marr, died in anno 1663. = Jane, daughter of Edward Munday of Marketon in com. Derb. Esqr.

2. Richard Lewis, died in anno 1661. = Jane, eldest daughter and coheir of Gervase Brinsley of Brinsley in com. Nott.

1. Margaret, wife of John Maleverer of Letwell in com. Ebor. Esqr.
2. Ellen, wife unto John Ramsden of Lascells Hall.
3. Edith, wife of Timothy Bright, a Counceller at Law.
4. Mary, wife of Richard Horsfeild of Startheshall in com. Ebor.

Mary, wife of Tho. son of Sr William Cheytor of Crofte, of whom there is noe issue remayning.

Theobald Burgh Viscᵗ Mayo in Ireld, 1627. = Eliz. da. & coh. of Tho. Talbot of Bashall in co. Ebor. = 1. Thomas Lewis, son and heir, obijt sine prole.

2. Francis, died unmarried.

¶1. Brinsley Lewis, slain in the late warrs on the King's part, unmarried.

2. Sr John Lewis of Ledston in co. Ebor. Bt, æt. 50 an. 13 Sept. 1665. = Sarah, 2d da. and coh. of Sr Thomas Foote, Citizen of London, Kt & Bart.

3. Edward Lewis of Marr in co. Ebor. marr. . . . . da. and heire of Ellis Woodrove of Hope.
4. Richard, dyed young.
5. Philip, died unmarried, slain in the late warrs on the King's part.

1. Mary, wife of George Wortley, Citizen of London.
2. Anne, wife of Edward Rumball, Citizen of London.
3. Isabell, wife of Nathaniell Newdigate, Citizen of London.
4. Jane, first marr. to Valentine Crome, a Mercht in London; after to Sr Freschevill Hollies Knt.
5. Eliz. wife of Henry Harnes, Citizen of London.
6. Margaret, died unmarried.

1. Thomas, dyed young.
2. John, dyed young.

1. Elizabeth, æt. 11 an. 1665.

2. Mary, ætatis 7 ann. 1665.

3. Sarah, died in her infancy.

* Upon a Tombstone in the Church of Marr in Yorkeshire:—

Here lyeth John Lewis, late of Marr Esqr, deceased, sonne and heire of Robert Lewis of the same, gent. Lawyer, and one of the Justices of our Lady the Queene of Peace and Quorum within the West Riding of the County of Yorke and Recorder of the Towne of Doncaster, who died 17 day of October, in the 31 yeare of the Raigne of Qu. Elizabeth, and in the xlvjth yeare of his age, who married Mary Reresby, daughter of Lyonell Reresby of Thribergh Esqr deceased, by whom he had issue six Children, vizt two sons and foure daughters.

STRAFFORD & TICKHILL WAPENTAKE. *Doncaster*, 9° *Apr.* 1666.

*WEST OF ASTON.

ARMS.—Argent, a fess dancettée between three leopard's faces sable.

CRESTS.—1. Out of a mural coronet .... a griffin's head argent charged with a fess dancettée sable.

2. A demi-dragon vert, holding in the dexter claw a sword erect argent hilted or.

John West of Aghton in co. Ebor. = Anne, daughter of Raufe Ayre of Offerton in the Peake in co. Derb.

3. Thomas West of Beiston in com. Nott. = Anne, daughter Will. Bradbury of Ollerset in the Peake in co. Derb.

2. George West of Aughton. = Jane, daughter of Thomas Trygot of Kirkby in co...

1. John, obijt sine prole.

Will'm West† of Rotherham, living in a° 1585. = Winifride, daughter of Adam Eyre of Offerton in com. Derb.

John West of Aughton. = Anne, daughter of John Moore of Chelsey in com. Midd.

5. Gilbert West of Beiston in com. Nott. = ; 6. Robert West of .... in co. Nott.

3. Thurstan West of ....

4. George West of Masborough neer Rotherham in co. Ebor. of whom there is noe issue remayning.

Susan, daughter of ...... Baxter of Tickhill Castle in com. Ebor. 1 wife, of whom there is noe issue remayn^g. = 2. Thomas West of Doncaster in co. Ebor. died in anno 1647. = Susan, daughter of Richard Baker of Much-Munden in com. Hertf. (a)

1. Marg^r, wife of Peter Frechwell of .... in com. Derb.

2. Edith, wife of Godfrey Columbell of Darley in com. Derb.

3. Mary, wife of Edmund Bradbury of Ollerset in co. Derb.

1. William West of Firbeck in com. Ebor. died in anno 1649, or thereabouts. = Catherine, eldest daughter of Sr Edward Darcy of Dertford in Kent. (b)

Godfrey West of Aughton, living in anno 1585, of whom there is now noe issue remayning. = ... daughter of Thomas Revell.

† He wrote the booke called *West's Presidents*.

¶ FANE OF ASTON.

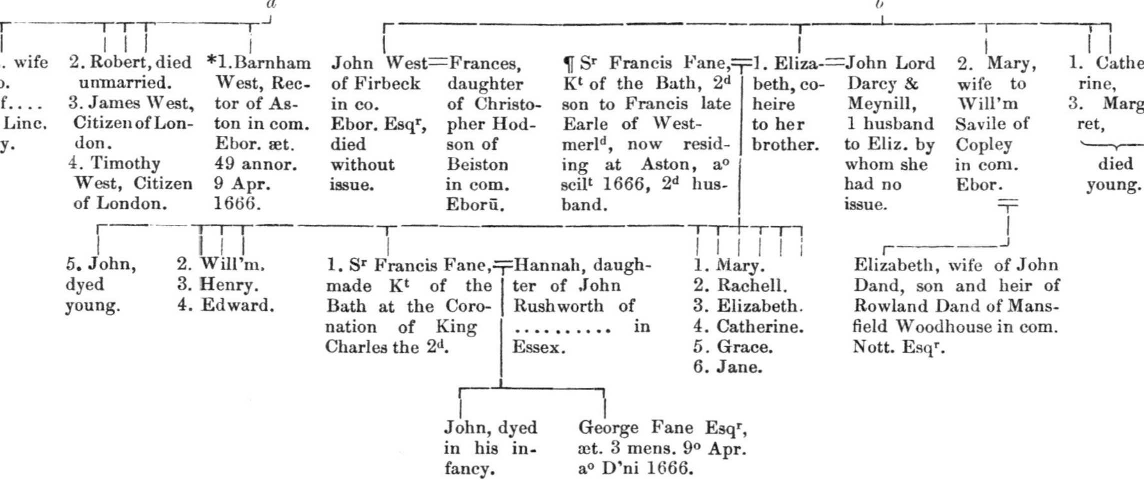

STRAFFORD AND TICKHILL WAPENTAKE. *Doncaster*, 9 *Apr*. 1666.

STANHOPE OF HAMPULL.

ARMS.—Quarterly ermine and gules, in the fess point a cinquefoil or.

CREST.—A tower .... charged with a cinquefoil ...., issuing from the battlements a demi-lion rampant azure.

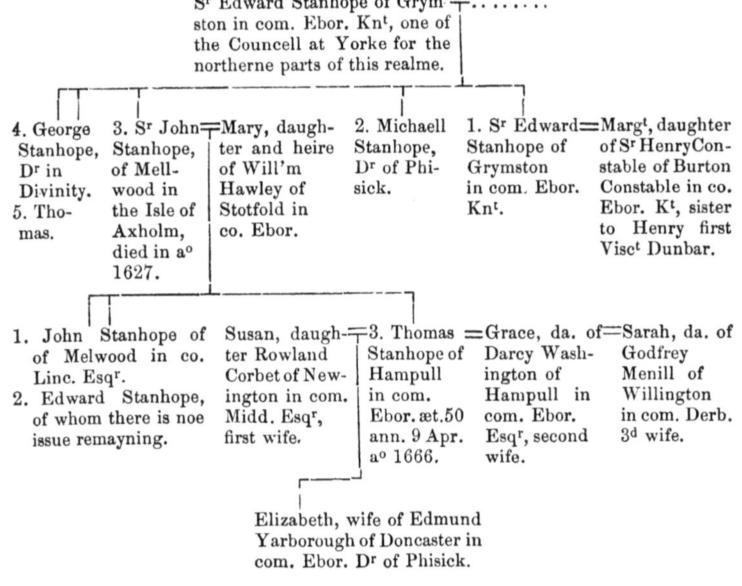

ELLERKER OF YOLTON.

ARMS.—Gules, a fess or between three water-bougets argent.

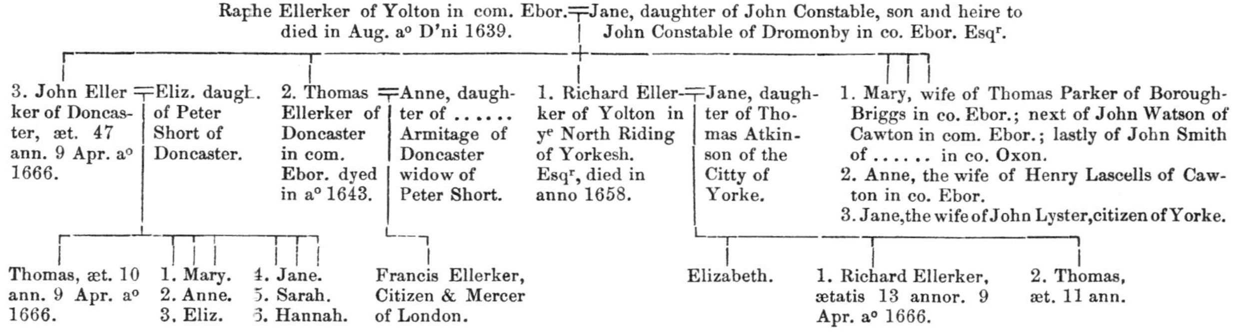

Raphe Ellerker of Yolton in com. Ebor. died in Aug. a° D'ni 1639. = Jane, daughter of John Constable, son and heire to John Constable of Dromonby in co. Ebor. Esqr.

3. John Ellerker of Doncaster, æt. 47 ann. 9 Apr. a° 1666. = Eliz. daught. of Peter Short of Doncaster.

2. Thomas Ellerker of Doncaster in com. Ebor. dyed in a° 1643. = Anne, daughter of ...... Armitage of Doncaster widow of Peter Short.

1. Richard Ellerker of Yolton in y^e North Riding of Yorkesh. Esqr, died in anno 1658. = Jane, daughter of Thomas Atkinson of the Citty of Yorke.

1. Mary, wife of Thomas Parker of Borough-Briggs in co. Ebor.; next of John Watson of Cawton in com. Ebor.; lastly of John Smith of ...... in co. Oxon.
2. Anne, the wife of Henry Lascells of Cawton in co. Ebor.
3. Jane, the wife of John Lyster, citizen of Yorke.

Thomas, æt. 10 ann. 9 Apr. a° 1666.

1. Mary.
2. Anne.
3. Eliz.
4. Jane.
5. Sarah.
6. Hannah.

Francis Ellerker, Citizen & Mercer of London.

Elizabeth.

1. Richard Ellerker, ætatis 13 annor. 9 Apr. a° 1666.

2. Thomas, æt. 11 ann.

BARKESTON ASHE WAPENTAKE.

Pomfret, 7° *Apr.* 1666.

HUNGATE OF SAXTON.

ARMS.—Gules, a chevron engrailed between three hounds sejant argent.

CREST.—A hound as in the arms.

Will'm Hungate of Saxton in com. Eborum. = ...

1. William Hungate of Saxton in com. Ebor. Esqr. = ... daughter and heire of .... Sotheby of ......

2. Robert Hungate, marr. ...... daughter of ...... Thimelby of Irnham in com. Linc.

3. Raphe Hungate of Sand-Hutton in co. Ebor. living in a° 1584. = ...

Children of William Hungate:

3. Roger, 4. Robert, died unmarried.

1. Sr Will'm Hungate of Sotheby Kn^t, dyed without out issue. = ... daughter of .... Middleton of ...... in com. Lanc.

2. Sr Philip Hungate of Saxton Kn^t, died in a° 1655, or thereabouts. = Dorothy, da. of .... Lee of Hatfeild in co. Ebor. widow of Andrew Younge of Bourne in com. Ebor.

1. Eliz. wife of Gilbert Stapleton of Carleton in com. Ebor. Esqr.

2. Mary, wife of Sr Henry Browne of Kiddington in co. Oxon. Bart.

3. Catherine, wife of ...... Cholmeley of Bransby in co. Ebor.; afterward of Sr Will'm Howard, younger son to the Ld William Howard of Naworth Castle in com. Cumbr.

Children of Raphe Hungate:

1. Jane. 2. Frances.

Francis Hungate of Saxton in com. Ebor. Esqr, slayne in the service of K. Charles the first in the late warrs. = Joane, daughter of Robert Middleton of Leighton in com. Lanc.; afterwards married to Will'm Hamond of Scarthingwell Esqr.

1. Sr Francis Hungate of Saxton in com. Ebor. Bar^t, æt. 23 annor. 7° Apr. a° D'ni 1666. = Margaret, daughter to Charles Lord Carrington of Wotton in com. Warr.

2. Will'm.

Mary, wife of John Fairfax, a younger brother to Charles Visc^t Fairfax of Emeley in Ireland.

1. Philip Hungate, son & heire, æt. 5 an. 7 Apr. 1666.

2. Francis.

1. Marg^t.

2. Elizabeth.

STRAFFORD AND TICKHILL WAPENTAKE. *Doncaster*, 9° *Apr*. 1666.

MELLISH OF DONCASTER.

ARMS.—Azure, between two flaunches ermine as many swans in pale proper, a mullet for difference.

Edward Mellish, Citizen and Mercht of London. = Alice, sister and heire of William Reason of Askham in co. Nott.

Their children:

3. William Mellish of Doncaster in com. Ebor. æt. 60 annor. 9° Apr. a° 1666. = Martha, daughter of Samuell Goldsmith, Merchant of London.
2. Robt Mellish of Ragnall in com. Nott. = (with issue)
1. John Mellish, Merchant of London. = (with issue)

Children of William and Martha:

- Anne, wife of ...... Calcot, Citizen of London.
- 1. Samuell Mellish, an Utter Barrister of the Inner Temple, æt. 31 ann. 9 Apr. a° D. 1666. = Joane, daughter of ...... Sprouse of ...... in co. Devon, widdow of John Harvey, Citizen of Lond.
  - Their son: William, æt. 1 anni 9 Apr. 1666.
- 2. Robert, a Turkey Merchant.
- 3. William, a Turky Mercht.

STRAFFORD AND TICKHILL WAPENTAKE. *Doncaster*, 9° *Apr*. 1666.

BOSSEVILE OF BRAYWELL.

ARMS.—Quarterly of six:

1. Argent, five fusils in fess gules, in chief three mullets sable, a mullet for difference. Bosvile.
2. Or, a saltire vair. Darfeild.
3. Argent, a lion rampant azure debruised with a bendlet gules. Vescye.
4. Argent, a lion rampant gules, ducally crowned or, charged on the breast with a mullet azure. St. Paull.
5. Argent, a saltire between four butterflies volant sable. Travers.
6. ...... a chevron between three round buckles ...... Barber.

Thomas Bossevile of Braywell in co. Ebor. = Alice, daughter of Raphe Fretwell of Hellaby in co. Ebor.

Their children:

- 2. Nicholas Bossevile of Doncaster in co. Ebor.
- 3. Jasper.
- 4. John.
- 1. Thomas Bossevile, Mr of Arts & Vicar of Braywell in com. Ebor. æt. 50 annor. 9 Apr. a° D. 1666. = Mary, daughter of John Richardson of Blackwell in com. Derb.
- Dorothy, wife of John Blithe of Norton in com. Derb.

Children of Thomas and Mary:

- Thomas, æt. 22 annorū 9 Apr. 1666.
- 1. Alice.
- 2. Mary.

Osgodcrosse Wapentake. *Doncaster*, 9° *Apr.* 1666.

WINNE OF NOSTELL ABBEY.

Arms.—Ermine, on a fess vert three eagles displayed or.

Edmund Wynn of Thorlton Curtis in co. Linc. died circa ann. 1645. = Mary, daughter of Rowland Berkley of the citty of Worcester, sister to Sr Robert Berkley Knt, one of the Justices of the Kings Bench.

Children:

- 3. Marke Winne of Little Warley in com. Essex. = Constance, daughter of . . .
- 2. Rowland Winne, Merchant and Alderman of London, now living, scilt a° D. 1666.
- Rachel, dau. of John Turner of Hame in co. Surr. 1st wife, died without issue. = 1. Sr George Winne of Nostell Abby in com. Ebor. Bart, æt. 59 an. 9° Apr. a° 1666. = Eliz. da. of Robt Jeffreys, Alderm. of the citty of London, 2 wife. = Anne, da. of Sr Will'm Pelham of Brocklesby in co. Linc. Knt, 3 wife.
- 1. Margaret, wife unto Roger Fletcher, Citizen and Draper of London.
- 2. Mary, wife of Thomas Glover, Citizen and Ironmonger of London.
- 3. Joyce, wife unto John Ramsden, a Mercht in Kingston super Hull, in com. Ebor.
- 4. Anne, the wife of John Aynsworth, Mercht in London.

Children of Sr George Winne and Eliz. Jefferys:

- 1. Edmund Winne, son and heire, æt. 22 annorum 9° Apr. a° 1666.
- 2. George, æt. 21 ann.
- 3. Robert, æt. 20 ann.
- 4. Marke, æt. 17 ann.
- 5. Rowland, ætatis 14 ann.

STRAFFORD AND TICKHILL WAPENTAKE. *Doncaster*, 9 *Apr.* 1666.

COOKE OF WHEATLEY.

ARMS.—Or, a chevron gules between two lions passant gardant sable.

CREST.—Out of a mural coronet argent a demi-lion rampant gardant sable ducally gorged or.

Bryan Cooke of Sandall juxta Doncaster in co. Ebor. = ...

Bryan Cooke of Doncaster in com. Ebor. gent. dyed 26° Dec. a° 1653. = Sarah, daughter and sole heire of Henry Ryley of Doncaster in com. Ebor.

3. Henry Cooke of Carlingho neer Batley in com. Ebor. a Student of the Inner Temple, æt. 32 an. 9 Apr. 1666. = Diana, daughter of Anthony Butler of Cotes in com. Linc. Esqr.

1. Bryan Cooke, an Utter Barrister of y^e^ Inner Temple, died unmarried in Jan. a° 1660.

2. Sr George Cooke of Wheatley juxta Doncaster in co. Ebor. Bart. æt. 36 annorum 9 Apr. 1666.

2. Sarah, wife of John Copley of Batley in com. Ebor. Esqr; secondly married to George Nevill of Thorney in com. Nott. Esqr; thirdly to Christopher Ayscough, a younger son to Sr Edward Ayscough of Kelsey in com. Linc. K^t^.

1. Susan, wife of Charles Butler of Cotes in com. Linc. Esqr.

3. Margaret, wife unto Acton Burnell of Winkburne in co. Nott. Esqr.

1. George Cooke, æt. 3 annorum et 10 mens. 9 Apr. 1666.

2. Henry, æt. 1 anni.

AGBRIGG AND MORLEY WAPENTAKE. *Pomfret*, 7° *Apr.* 1666.

LACY OF THORNHILL.

ARMS.—Argent, a lion rampant purpure within a bordure gobonée or and gules charged with eight bezants.

Thomas Lacy of Folton in Dickering in com. Ebor. = ... daughter of S^r^ ...... Gower of Stitnam in co. Ebor.

2. Lancelot Lacy of Sherburne in Dickering in com. Ebor. = ... daughter of ...... Moreton.

1. Robert Lacy of Folton in Dickering in co. Ebor. = Elizabeth, daughter of ...... Leighton of Sproston.

Thomas Lacy of Beverley. = Anne, daughter of William Whitehouse of Barnby super Man in com. Nott.

2. William Lacy. = Elizabeth, daughter of ...... Newby.

1. Thomas Lacy of Beverley, living a° 1612. = Elizabeth, daughter of Richard Franceys of Beckingham in co. Nott.

Thomas, died unmarried.

William Lacy, D^r^ in Divinity, Rector of Thornhill, æt. 56 ann. 7 Apr. 1666. = Anne, daughter of William Sherman of Newarke neer Leycester gent.

William, died an infant.

BULMER WAPENTAKE. *Yorke*, 19° *Mart.* 1665.

LANGLEY OF SHERIFF-HUTTON PARKE.

ARMS.—Quarterly, on an inescutcheon the badge of a Baronet of England :
1 and 4. Paly of six argent and vert.
2 and 3. Argent, a cockatrice with wings addorsed sable, beaked and membered gules.

CREST.—Out of a ducal coronet or a plume of five ostrich feathers three argent and two vert.

William Langley of Langley 2 H. 6.=Alice.

Thomas Langley of Langley.=......

Henry Langley of Dalton in y[e] West Riding of Yorkeshire.=...... daugh. of...... Kay of Woodsome in com. Ebor.

Thomas Langley, L[d] Chancellour of England, Bisshop of Durham, and Cardinall a° 1417.

1. Thomas Langley of Rathorp Hall in Dalton in com. Ebor.=Marg[t], daughter of ...... Wombwell of Wombwell.

2. Robert Langley of Langley, 2 son.=......

Richard Langley of Rathorp-Hall.=Jane, daughter of ...... Beaumont of Mirfeild.

George Langley of Langley, son and heire.=......

Richard Langley of Owthorpe in co. Ebor.=Agnes, da. of Richard Hansby of Malton.

Thomas Langley of Melton.=Agnes, da. of Will'm Tates.

2. Will'm Langley, 2 sonne.=...

1. Robert Langley of Langley, son and heire.=...

George Langley of Stainton in com. Ebor.=Jane, daughter of John Hall of Sherbourne in co. Ebor.

Katherine, daughter and heire, wife of Thomas Leigh of Boothes.

Sr William Langley of Higham-Gobion in com. Bedford Bar[t], died in Holborne and buried at St Andrewes Church a° 1651.=Elizabeth, daughter of Roger Lumley and sister of Richard Viscount Lumley of Waterford in Ireland.

2. Sr Roger Langley of Sheriff-Hutton Parke in co. Ebor. Bar[t], æt. 38 an. 19 Mart. 1665.=Mary, daughter of Tho. Keightley of Hartingfordbury in com. Hertf.

1. William Langley, 1 son, died unmarried a° D. 1634.

Dorothy, wife of Will. Bristow of .... in com. Somerset.

2. Richard, æt. 16 ann.
3. Roger, æt. 14 an.
4. Thomas, æt. 4 ann.

1. William Langley, eldest son, æt. 18 an. 19 Mart. 1665.

1. Mary, æt. 11 ann.
2. Rose.

3. Elizabeth.
4. Frances.

Malton, 10° *Sept.* 1666.

LANGLEY OF NORTH-GRIMSTON.

ARMS.—Paly of six argent and vert, a canton gules.

Christopher Langley of ..... neer Durham in the County Palatine of Durham. = ...

Francis Langley of great Langton upon Swale in com. Ebor. died circa an. 1636, and was there buried. = ... daughter of ..... Robinson of ..... in com. Ebor.

3. Francis Langley of Little Danby in com. Ebor.
4. John Langley of Langton in com. Ebor.

2. George Langley of great-Langton, æt. 72 ann. 10 Sept. 1666. = Anne, daughter of Christopher Danby of Langton aforesaid.

1. Christopher Langley of South-Cowton in com. Ebor.

1. Anne, wife of .... Conyers of Rawker in y[e] parish of Danby super Wiske in co. Ebor.; afterward of John Fall.

2. Jane, wife of .... Richardson of Kirkby super Wiske in com. Ebor.; afterwards of Richard Mason of Kirkby super Wiske.

3. Francis Langley, Citizen of London.
4. George Langley of North-Allerton in co. Ebor.

2. Charles Langley, a Captain in Portugall, marr. Mary, daugh. of .....

1. Thomas Langley of North-Grimston in co. Ebor. æt. 41 ann. 10 Sept. a° 1666. = Elizabeth, daughter of Henry Metcalfe, a Merchant in Kingston upon Hull.

1. Mary.
2. Anne.
3. Muriell, wife unto Richard Robinson of Cundall in com. Ebor.

1. Henry, ætatis 10 ann. et 4 mens. 10 Sept. 1666.
2. Thomas, æt. unius anni.

1. Anne.
2. Frances.
3. Elizabeth.

GILLING EAST WAPENTAKE. *Stokesley*, 8° *Sept.* 1666.

CHAYTOR OF CROFTE.

ARMS.—Quarterly:
1 and 4. Per bend indented azure and argent, three cinquefoils two in chief and one in base counterchanged, a crescent for difference.
2 and 3. Sable, a saltire or, a crescent for difference.

CRESTS.—1. A stag's head lozengy argent and azure, the dexter attire of the first, the sinister of the second, a crescent for difference.
2. A heron argent.

Christopher Chaytor of Butterby in com. palat. Dunelm. = ...

1. Anthony Chaytor, son and heire. = Margery, daughter of William Thorneton of Newton in co. Ebor. Esqr.

2. Thomas Chaytor of Butterby in com. palat. Dunelm., dyed circa annum 1618. = Jane, daughter of Sr Nicholas Tempest of Stella in com. pal. Dunelm. Kn^t.

Children of Anthony and Margery:

2. Richard, 3. Thomas, dyed without issue.

1 Sr Will'm Chaytor of Crofte in co. Ebor. Kn^t. = Frances, daughter of Sr James Bellingham of Levens in com. Westmerland Kn^t. (a)

1. ...... wife of ...... Hutton of Mainsforth in com. palat. Dunelm.
2. ...... wife of ...... Hutton, brother to ...... Hutton of Mainsforth.

Children of Thomas and Jane:

3. Thomas, 5. Robert, died unmarried.

4. George.

2. Nicholas Chaytor of Butterby, dyed 10 Febr. 1665. = Anne, da. & coh. of Will. Lambton of Haughtonfield in co. p. Dunelm. Esqr. (b)

1. Henry Chator of Butterby, died in a° 1630, vel circa, unmarried.

1. Jeronima, wife of Tho. Swinburne of Barmton in com. palat. Dunelm. Esqr.
2. Isabell, wife unto James Bellasses of Aughton in com. Palat. Dunelm.
3. Marg^t, wife of Raphe Bates of Halliwell in co. Northumbr. Esqr.

4. Troth, 5. Mary, died unmarried.

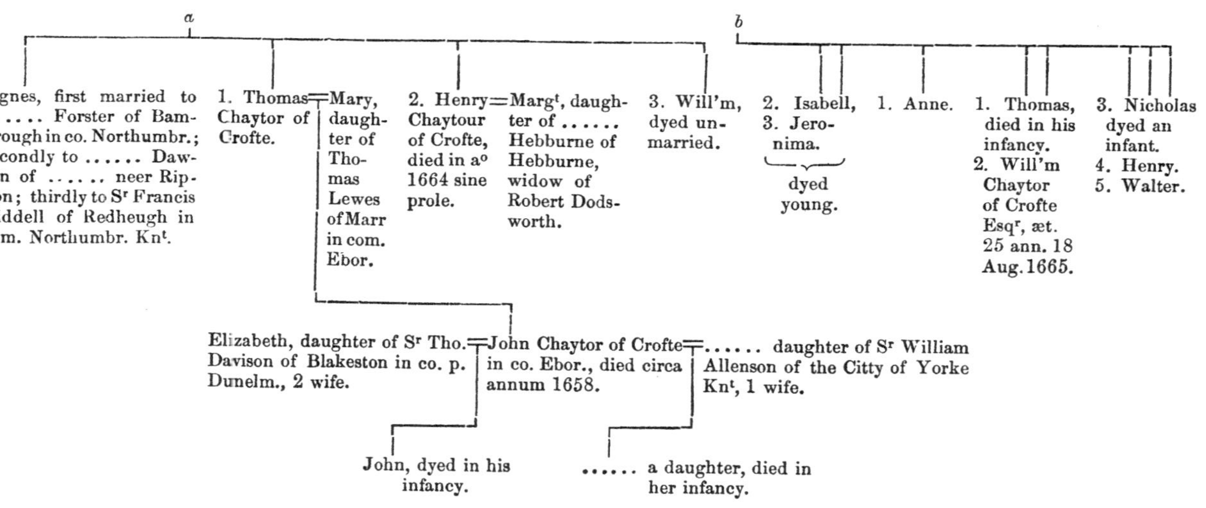
a
b
Agnes, first married to ...... Forster of Bambrough in co. Northumbr.; secondly to ...... Dawson of ...... neer Rippon; thirdly to Sr Francis Liddell of Redheugh in com. Northumbr. Knt.
1. Thomas Chaytor of Crofte.
Mary, daughter of Thomas Lewes of Marr in com. Ebor.
2. Henry Chaytour of Crofte, died in aº 1664 sine prole.
Margt, daughter of ...... Hebburne of Hebburne, widow of Robert Dodsworth.
3. Will'm, dyed unmarried.
2. Isabell, 3. Jeronima. dyed young.
1. Anne.
1. Thomas, died in his infancy.
2. Will'm Chaytor of Crofte Esqr, æt. 25 ann. 18 Aug. 1665.
3. Nicholas dyed an infant.
4. Henry.
5. Walter.
Elizabeth, daughter of Sr Tho. Davison of Blakeston in co. p. Dunelm., 2 wife.
John Chaytor of Crofte in co. Ebor., died circa annum 1658.
...... daughter of Sr William Allenson of the Citty of Yorke Knt, 1 wife.
John, dyed in his infancy.
...... a daughter, died in her infancy.

STAINECROSSE WAPENTAKE. *Pontefract*, 7 *Apr*. 1666.

SOTWELL OF CATLINGHILL.

ARMS.—Gules, a chevron between two mullets in chief and a lion rampant in base or.

Another shield.—Quarterly of fifteen [the tinctures are omitted]:

1. A chevron between two mullets in chief and a lion rampant in base.
2. A fess dancettée between three pheons.
3. A rook within a bordure engrailed.
4. Two bars each charged with as many cross-crosslets.
5. Six escallops, three, two, and one.
6. Two wings conjoined and inverted, a crescent for difference.
7. Vairée.
8. On a chief a label of three points.
9. Three escallops.
10. Three demi-lions rampant couped.
11. Ermine, three bars.
12. Per bend, three roses in bend counterchanged,
13. A chevron between three bird's heads erased.
14. ....
15. Three falcons.

CREST.—Out of a mural coronet a lion's head pierced through the neck with an arrow.

Francis Sotwell of Chute in co. Wilts Esq[r]. = ...

John Sotwell of Andover in com. Suthampt. and Catling-hill in Hoyland Swaynes in the parish of Silkston in com. Ebor. = ...

1. John Sotwell of Chute, D[r] of the Civill Lawe, dyed unmarried.

Richard Sotwell.

* Will'm Sotwell of Greenham in com. Wilts. Esq[r]. By Indenture 29 Mart. 11 Car. 1, conveys to Eliz. his daugh. & heire, y[e] Manour of Tudworth in com. Wilts. & lands in Lurcashall, &c. 1 Nov. 16 Car. 1, upon y[e] same daugh. & sole heire, lands in Andover in co. Suthampt. and in Apples.... and on her heires; and the remainder to y[e] right heires of the said William William Sotwell Esq[r]. = ... sister unto Roger Knight of Greenham in co. Wilts. Esq[r].

a

2. Richard Sotwell of Catling-hill in Hoyland Swaine, died circa annū 1622. = Alice, daughter of Roger Micklethwayte of Ingbirchworth in com. Ebor.

b

Edward, John, died unmarried.

1. Frances, wife of Rob[t] Hepworth of Cumberworth in com. Ebor.
2. Ellen, wife of John Deane of Sandleford in com. Berks.
3. Jane, wife of George Burdet of Carrhead in the parish of Silkston in com. Ebor.; afterward of William Field of Thurnsco in com. Eborum.
4. Elizabeth, wife of John Micklethwayt of Ingbirchworth in com. Eborum.

Francis Trenchard of Normanton in com. Wilts. Esqr. ═ Elizabeth, daughter & co-heire. ═ John Bulkley of Fordingbridge in co. Suthampt. Esqr.

a — Constance, da. & co-heire, wife of Thomas Fauconer of King's-Clere in co. Suth^ton Esqr; had issue 2 children, who dyed in their infancy.

b — 1. Francis Sotwell, died unmarried. 3. Richard Sotwell, died an infant.

2. John Sotwell of Catlinghill in com. Ebor. and Andover in co. Suthampt. gent. æt. 52 annor. 7 Apr. a° 1666. ═ Dinah, daughter of Thomas Hanson of Nether Eastfield in the parish of Silkston in com. Eborum.

1. Jane, wife of De-la-River Burdet of Danby.
2. Ellen, wife of Will. Milner of Bentley neer Doncaster.
3. Margaret, 1st married to Will. Hewet of Rawroyde neer Cawthorn; 2dly of Will. Greathead.

Elizabeth, died under age. (child of Francis Trenchard and Elizabeth)

.... a son, dyed an infant. (child of Elizabeth and John Bulkley)

Children of John Sotwell and Dinah:

2. Ellen. 3. Mary.

1. Elizabeth, wife of John Kay of Milshaw in the parish of Burton.

William, Richard, died unmarried.

John Sotwell, son and heire, æt. 24 annor. 7 Apr. 1666. ═ Elizabeth, daughter of Richard Streete of Langsett in the parish of Penyston.

Mary, æt. 1 anni et 3 mensiū. (child of John Sotwell and Elizabeth)

Upon a Monument in the Church of Thatcham in co. Berks.
are these Armes & this Epitaph:—

1. Sotwell.
2. Standen.
3. Fort.
4. Elburie.
5. Deane.
6. Estcott.
7. Seymour.
8. Beauchamp.
9. Belfeild.
10. Mallet.
11. Esturmy.
12. Hussey.
13. Mackwilliams.
14. Bray.
15. Falconer.

Here lyeth buried the Body of * William Sotwell Esqr, Councelour
at Law, sometimes Justice of Peace in this County, &
heire and eldest of the antient Family of the Sotwells
of Chute in ye County of Wilts: Who departed this life
at his house in Greeneham wth in this parish (where
he had lived a most religious & vertuous life by
the space of 35 yeares) the 18 day of June, 1639, in the 68
yeare of his age. He left behind him one only childe
named Elizabeth, being his sole heire, and widdow of
Francis Trenchard Esqr.

STAINECROSSE WAPENTAKE. *Pomfret*, 7° *Apr*. 1666.

GREENE OF BANCKE.

ARMS.—Azure, three demi-lions rampant erased erminois.

CREST.—Out of a mural coronet gules a demi-lion rampant erminois.

Raphe Green of Micklethwayt in the parish of Cawthorn in com. Ebor. 36 H. 8. = ...

Children:

- Richard.
- Will'm Greene of Micklethwayt in com. Ebor. = 1. . . . . . daughter of . . . . Swift of Nabbs, 1 wife. = 2. Mary, daughter of George Cressy of Elmhirst, in the parish of Cawthorn in com. Ebor. . . . wife. = 3. Jennet, daughter of Thomas Beaumont of Flockton in co. Ebor.
- Jane, wife of Richard Slack of Woodhouse.

Children of Will'm Greene by . . . . . . daughter of . . . . Swift:

- Robert, William, died unmarried.

Children of Will'm Greene by Mary Cressy:

- John Greene of Elmhirst in the parish of Calthorn in co. Ebor. = ...
- Richard Greene of Micklethwayt vulgò Bancke, in ye parish of Calthorne in co. Ebor. died in anno . . . . = Gertrude, daughter of Godfrey Ellison of Cotes in parish of Silkston in com. Ebor.
- Mary, wife of Thomas Barnby of Barnby Esq.

Child of Will'm Greene by Jennet Beaumont:

- Will'm, died at the Innes of Court.

Children of Richard Greene and Gertrude Ellison:

- Robert, dyed an infant.
- Will'm Greene of Micklethwayt vulgò Bancke, in the parish of Calthorne in co. Eborum, æt. 33 annor. 7° Apr. 1666. = Mary, daughter of Michaell Portington of Portington in co. Ebor. Esqr.
- Mary.
- Anne.

Children of Will'm Greene and Mary Portington:

- William Greene, son and heire, ætatis 9 annor. 7° Apr. a° 1666.
- Richard.
- Grace.

Pomfret, 7 *Apr*. 1666.

WENTWORTH OF WEST-BRETTON.

ARMS.—Quarterly:
1 and 4. Quarterly, a crescent for difference: 1 and 4. Sable, a chevron between three leopard's faces or within a bordure argent.
2 and 3. Gules, on a bend argent three escallops azure.
2 and 3. Paly of six argent and sable, on a bend gules three mullets or.
An escutcheon of pretence: Argent, on a bend cotised sable three eagles displayed of the field.

Mathew Wentworth of West-bretton in com. Ebor. Esq[r]. = Dorothy, daughter and coheir of Richard Charlesworth of Tottys in y[e] parish of Birton in com. Ebor.

Their children:

- Anne, wife of Darcy Washington of Adwick in com. Ebor. Esq[r].
- 1. George Wentworth of West-brettor in com. Ebor. Esq[r]. = Mary, daughter of .... Ashburnham, and sister of S[r] John Ashburnham of Ashburnham in Sussex Kn[t].
- 2. Mathew Wentworth, obijt sine prole, married Dorothy, daughter of ..... Whitacres.
- 3. Robert.
- 4. Henry Wentworth, Citizen of London. = Dorothy, daughter of Will'm Towerson of Portsmouth gent.

Children of George Wentworth and Mary:

- 1. William Wentworth of West-bretton Esqr. died 22 Oct. 1642, sine prole. = Hesther, daughter and co-heire of Richard Arthington of Castley in com. Ebor.
- 2. Sr Thomas Wentworth of West-bretton K[t] & Bart. æt. 56 an. 7 Apr. 1666, a Colonell of foote and Lieutenant Colonell of Horse in the service of K. Charles the 1st, & now Deputy Lieutenant & Captain of Horse in the Trayned bands for the West Riding of Yorkshire. = Grace, daughter and sole heire of Francis Popeley of More-house in co. Ebor. gent.
- 3. Matthew Wentworth of Bretton in co. Ebor. gent. = Judith, daughter of Thomas Rhodes of Flockton.
- 4. John Wentworth of Towthornfield in com. Derb. = Susan, daughter of Thomas Eyre of Towthornfield in com. Derb.
- 1. Dorothy, wife of Michaell Portington of Portington Esqr.
- 2. Mary, died unmarried.
- 3. Anne, wife of Richard Allot of Bilhā Grange in co. Ebor.
- 4. Grace.

Children of Henry Wentworth and Dorothy:

- 1. William.
- 2. Henry.
- 3. Matthew.

Children of John Wentworth and Susan:

- Thomas, ætatis circa 19 ann. 7 Apr. a° 1666.
- Mary.

Pontefract, 7° Apr. 1666.

THORNHILL OF FIXBY.

ARMS.—Quarterly of eight:
1. Gules, two bars-gemelles and a chief argent. Thornhill.
2. Or, on a chevron sable three crescents argent. Totehill.
3. Azure, a saltire between four cross-crosslets or. Ficksby.
4. Gules, a horse's head couped argent, a mullet for difference. Marsh.
5. Argent, a chevron between three cross-crosslets fitchée sable. Trigot.
6. Argent, a chevron between three cross-crosslets fitchée gules. Byrton.
7. Argent, three boar's heads erect and erased sable, a crescent for difference. Booth.
8. As the first.

An escutcheon of pretence:
Quarterly: 1. .... a chevron between three leopard's faces .... within a bordure .... Wentworth of Wolley.
2. Azure, on a bend or three torteaux. Whitley.
3. Argent, three pallets wavy sable. Downes of Herefordshire.
4. As the first.

Ascelphus de Thornhill.=......

Johannes Thornhill.=...... 2. Jordanus Thornhill. 3. Thomas Thornhill.

Johannes Thornhill.=......

Richard Thornhill of Thornhill, died in a° 1287.

Johannes Thornhill.=......

Sr Bryan Thornhill Kn^t.=......

Sr John Thornhill Kn^t.=......

Sr Bryan Thornhill Kn^t.=......

Sr Bryan Thornhill Kn^t.=......

Sr Bryan Thornhill of Thornhill=...... Kn^t, a° 23 E. 3.

a

Willielmus Fekisby.=......

Roger. Thomas Fekisby al's Fixby.=......

Thomas Tothill, a° 20 E. 2.=Modesta, daughter and coheire. Beatrix, daughter and coheire.

b

a · *b*

Sr Simon Thornhill of = ... Thornhill, eldest son. | Thomas Thornhill, 8 E. 3, = Margaret, daughter of ...... Lascy. Thomas Thornhill, second sonne. | William Tothill of = Sibilla, vidua 14 E. 3. William Tothill of Fixby, Esc. 13 E. 3. | ...... other sons and daughters.

Elizabeth, daughter and heire, wife of Sr Henry Savile of Thornhill Knt. | Richard Thornhill of = Margaret, daughter and coheire to her brother. Richard Thornhill of Fixby, ao 8 E. 3. | Thomas Tothill, ob. s. prole. | Roger Tothill, obijt sine prole.

William Thornhill of Fixby Esqr, 5. H. 5. = Joane, daughter of ...... Hopton of Swillington.

Bryan Thornhill Esqr, 22 H. 6. = ... daughter of ...... Acton, Alderman of Yorke.

William Thornhill of Fixby Esqr. = Elizabeth, daughter of Robert Mirfeild of Mirfeild Esqr.

John Thornhill of Fixby, 6 H. 8. = Jennet, daughter of John Savile of Newhall in co. Ebor.

John Thornhill of Fixby Esqr, 6 H. 8. = Elizabeth, daughter of Thomas Grice of Wakefeild.

John Thornhill of Fixby Esqr. = Jennet, daughter and heire of Edmund Marsh of the Knowles in the parish of Eland in com. Ebor.

Richard, dyed an infant. | Thomas Thornhill of Fixby Esqr, living ao 1612, a Justice of Peace and Quorum, obijt circa an. 1663. = Anne, daughter and coheire of Thomas Trigot of South-Kirkby in co. Ebor. Esqr. | 1. John Thornhill of Fixby Esqr., a Justice of Peace & Quorum, obijt sine prole. | Jane, wife of William Rookes of Rodes Hall.

Dorothy, daughter and sole heire of George Columbell of Darley in com. Derb. gent. 1 wife. = John Thornhill of Fixby Esqr, now one of his Maties Justices of Peace and Quorum in the West Riding of Yorkshire, as also a Major of Foot in the Regiment of Sr George Savile Bart, æt. 50 annorū 7 Apr. ao D. 1666. = Everilde, daughter and coheire of Sr George Wentworth of Wolley in com. Ebor. Knt, 2 wife. | Thomas, Bryan, ob. s. prole. | William, Thomas, Francis, ob. s. prole. | Anne, Mary, Frances, Rebecca, died unmarried. | Elizabeth, wife of Langdale Sunderland of Aygbton in com. Ebor. Esqr. | Margaret, wife of Sr John Armitage of Kirklees in com. Ebor. Bart.

Anne, dyed an infant. | John, dyed an infant. | 1. George, æt. 10 an. et 11 mens. 7 Apr. 1666. 2. Thomas, æt. 7 an. 1666. | 1. Everild, borne 3 Sept. ao 1651, on which day was the Battail of Worcester. | Elizabeth, dyed an infant. Frances.

AGBRIGG AND MORLEY WAPENTAKE. *Pomfret*, 7° *Apr*. 1666.

SAVILE OF COPLEY.

ARMS.—Quarterly:
1 and 4. Argent, on a bend sable three owls of the field, a crescent for difference. Savile.
2. Argent, a cross moline sable. Copley.
3. Azure, three cinquefoils between nine cross-crosslets argent. Darcy.

Robt Savile of Copley in com. Ebor. Esqr. = Jane, daughter of Roger Ellis of Kiddall.

Their children:
- William Savile of Copley in co. Ebor. Esqr. = Isabell, daughter of John Lacy of Breareley.
- Mary, wife of John Bentley of Shipden.
- Bridget, wife of Robert Cawden of Sowerby.

Children of William and Isabell:
- 1. Henry Savile of Copley Esqr, æt. 7 ann. a° 1585. = Anne, daughter of Michaell Darcy, son and heire of John Lord Darcy of Aston, and sister and heire to John Lord Darcy.
- 2. John Savile, second son. = ... daughter of ...... Lawe.

Children of Henry and Anne:
- 6. Darcy, 7. Anthony, 8. Henry, obiere sine prole.
- 5. William Savile of Copley in co. Ebor. = Rosamund, the daughter of John Franch of Pontefract.
- 4. John Savile of Copley in com. Ebor. Esqr, dyed about the yeare 1644. = Anne, daughter of Sr George Palmes of Naburne in com. Ebor. K^t^; afterwards married to Walter Bethell Esqr, son and heir to Sr Hugh Bethell of Ellerton in com. Ebor. Knight.
- 2. Henry, 3. Michaell, dyed without issue.
- 1. Thomas Savile of Copley in co. Ebor. Esqr. = Frances, daughter of ...... Dawson of Azerley Esqr.
- Margaret, wife unto Rowland Dand of Mansfield Woodhouse in com. Nott. Esqr.
- Jane.
- Anne, wife of Thomas Squire of Thornhill in com. Ebor. gent.
- Elizabeth, wife unto George Pulleyn, D^r^ of Phisick.

Child of John Savile and ...... Lawe:
- Robert Savile. = ... (issue).

Child of William and Rosamund:
- William Savile. = ... daughter of Arthur Ingram of Knottingley in com. Ebor. Esqr.

Child of John and Anne:
- Sr John Savile of Copley in com. Ebor. Bart. æt. 26 ann. 7 Apr. 1666. = Mary, daughter of Clement Paston of Berningham in com. Norff. Esqr.

Children of Thomas and Frances:
- William Savile died without issue.
- Mary, died without issue.

Child of Sr John and Mary:
- Mary-Elizabeth Savile, æt. 3 ann. 7 Apr. a° 1666.

GREENWOOD OF STAPLETON.

ARMS.—Sable, a chevron ermine between three saltires or, a mullet for difference.
An escutcheon of pretence ......, on a chevron ...... between three church bells ...... as many eagles displayed ......

CREST.—A demi-lion rampant sable holding a saltire argent.

James Greenwood, a younger brother to the Greenwoods of Greenwood Lee in com. Ebor. = Elizabeth, daughter of ...... Chapellholme of ......

Robert Greenwood. = Anne, daughter of ...... Warriner of Wakefield in com. Eborū.

Anne, daughter of ...... Marsh of Thornill in co. Ebor. 1 wife. = John Greenwood of Wrenthorp juxta Wakefield in com. Ebor. a French merchant. = Ellen, daughter of ...... Cutts of ...... in Essex, 2d wife.

Isabell, wife of Richard Lyster of New-Lathes in co. Eborū.

Margaret, wife of Richard Ibbotson of Leedes in com. Ebor.

Elizabeth, wife of William Ingleton of Rotheram in co. Ebor.

Anne, wife of Richard Waterhouse of Wakefield in com. Ebor.

¶ Francis Belhouse of Newsome juxta Swillington in com. Ebor. = Bartholina, daughter of ...... Wilkinson of Towthorp.

Anne, wife of Christopher Naylor of Wakefield in com. Ebor. a Barrister at Law.

Sarah, daughter of Samuell Burdet of Moregrange in com. Ebor. 1 wife. = James Greenwood, æt. 9 ann. 1612. Served in the Low Countries under Coll. Edw. Harwood. He is now of Stapleton near Darington in com. Ebor. = 3. Mary, daughter of Francis Bellhouse of Newsome in com. Ebor. sister & coheir to Francis her brother, 2 wife.

1. Eliz. eldest daughter and coheire, wife of George Tofthouse of Osmondthorpe juxta Leedes in co. Ebor.
2. Ellen, 2d daughter and coheir, wife of Robert Milner of Cowton neer Temple Newsome, co. Ebor.
4. Jane, 4th daughter and coheire, wife of .... Thompson of Killingbeck neare Leedes in co. Ebor.
5. Katherine, 5th daughter and coheire, wife of John Nunns of Houghton juxta Pontefract in com. Ebor.
6. Margery, 6th da. & coheire, wife unto Richard Wilkes of Newsome in com. Eborum.

1. William Belhouse, died unmarried.
2. Francis Bellhouse, married Jane, daughter of .... et obijt sine prole.

Isabell.

1. Samuell Greenwood, æt. 30 an. 7° Apr. a° 1666. = Anne, daughter of ......

2. James Greenwood, ætatis 22 annor. 7° Apr. 1666.

3. Francis. 4. Henry. 5. John. 6. Charles. 7. William.

OSGODCROSSE WAPENTAKE. *Yorke*, 13° *Aug*. 1666.

BIRKBECK OF SHEFFEILD AND CASTLEFORD.

ARMS.—Quarterly:
1 and 4. Argent, a fess between two lion's heads erased in chief and a boar's head erased in base gules. Birkbeck.
2 and 3. Argent, two bendlets sable, in the dexter chief a mullet gules. Kay.

An escutcheon of pretence: Quarterly, 1 and 4. Argent, a saltire vert, a crescent for difference. 2 and 3 ....

This Escocheon of Pretence is here inserted as belonging to Peter Birkbeck of Castleford.

Thomas Birkkeck of Orton in com. Westmerl. of the Family of Morton-Tinmouth in com. Palat. Dunelm. = ... daughter of .... Wharton.

Richard Nelson of Altofts. = Alice, daughter of ...... Beckwith of Aghton in com. Ebor.

2. Robert Birkbeck.

Anne, daughter and sole heire of William Kay of Woodsome, a 3d son of the family of Kay of that place, 1 wife. = 1. Edward Birkbeck of Orton, Batchelour of Divinity, Domestick Chaplain to John Ld Darcy, Fellow of Trinity Colledg in Cambridg, & Rector of Staveley in com. Derb. = Barbara, daughter of .... Kay, 2 wife.

Thomas Nelson of Altofts in com. Ebor. = Grace, daughter of Christopher Saxton of Dunningley in co. Ebor. Surveyor and compiler of the Mapps of England, and heir to her brothers, they dying without issue.

Anne, wife of Cotton Faram of Doncaster in co. Ebor. afterwards of Will'm Waleby of Nottingham.

1. Thomas Birkbeck of Sheffeild in com. Ebor. ætatis 55 ann. 13 Aug. 1666. = Sarah, ye daughter of James Creswick of Sheffeild.

2. Edward Birkbeck, died without issue.

3. Peter Birkbeck, Rector of Castleford in co. Ebor. æt. 51 ann. 13 Aug. a° 1666. = Mary, sole daughter and heire.

Samuell, æt. 16 ann. 13 Aug. 1666.

Sarah.

4. Edward.

1. Thomas, 2. Peter, 5. John, died in their infancies.

3. Thomas, æt. 18 an. 13 Aug. a° 1666.

Barbara, died young.

Mary, wife of Wm Smithson of Methley.

Jane, Eliz. Sarah, died infants.

OSGODCROSSE WAPENTAKE. *Yorke*, 13° *Aug.* 1666.

AWNBY OF SHERWOOD HALL.

ARMS.—Argent, on a pale sable three demi-lions rampant couped of the field.
CREST.—On a mount vert a beagle couchant or collared and chained azure.

Anne, daughter of Charles Gerard of Heck Esqr, 1 wife. = John Awnby of Sherwood Hall in co. Ebor. died circa ann. 1647. = Marg^t^, daughter of Roger Lepton Esqr, widow of Sr George Ellis Kn^t^, and of Edm^d^ Clough Esqr, 2 wife.

2. John Awnby.

1. George Awnby of Sherwood-Hall, died 21 Maij a° 1666. = Frances, eldest daughter of Richard Bowes of Bapthorp in com. .... Esqr.

1. Jane, wife of Thomas Boynton of Rawcliffe in com. Ebor.
2. Elizabeth, wife of George Empson of Gowle in com. Ebor.
3. Alice, wife of Thomas Wood of Thorpe Awdlin in co. Ebor.

2. William, died unmarried.
3. John, died an infant.

Jane, daugh. of Francis Bunney of New-land Esqr, 1 wife. = 1. John Awnby of Sherwood-Hall, ætatis 38 ann. 13° Aug. a° 1666. = Mary, daugh. & coheir of Robert Nettleston of Thornhill-Lees, 2 wife.

1. Mary, wife of .. de Witt, Major to Prince Rupert.
2. Anne, wife of Francis Nuttall of Rawcliff.
3. Mary, wife of Savile Jackson of Carleton.

George, died in his infancy. — Francis, ætatis 9 annor. 13° Aug. a° 1666. — Jane, died an infant.

GILLING-EAST WAPENTAKE. *Stokesley*, 8° *Sept.* 1666.

DODSWORTH OF BARTON.

ARMS.—Argent, on a chevron between three bugle-horns sable as many bezants.

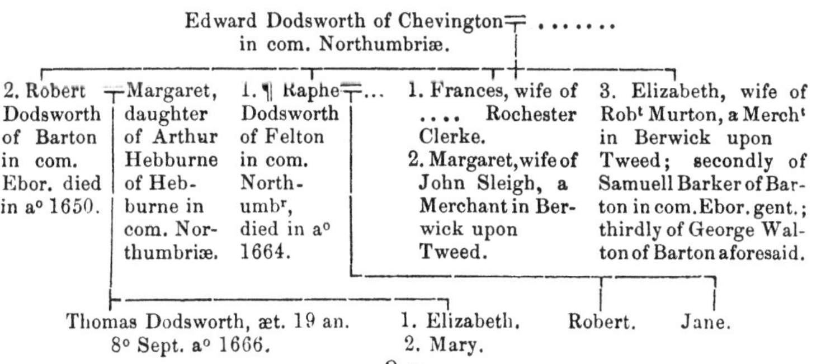
Edward Dodsworth of Chevington in com. Northumbriæ. = ...

2. Robert Dodsworth of Barton in com. Ebor. died in a° 1650. = Margaret, daughter of Arthur Hebburne of Hebburne in com. Northumbriæ.

1. ¶ Raphe Dodsworth of Felton in com. Northumb^r^, died in a° 1664. = ...

1. Frances, wife of .... Rochester Clerke.
2. Margaret, wife of John Sleigh, a Merchant in Berwick upon Tweed.

3. Elizabeth, wife of Robt Murton, a Merch^t^ in Berwick upon Tweed; secondly of Samuell Barker of Barton in com. Ebor. gent.; thirdly of George Walton of Barton aforesaid.

Thomas Dodsworth, æt. 19 an. 8° Sept. a° 1666. — 1. Elizabeth. 2. Mary.

Robert. — Jane.

BARKESTON ASHE WAPENTAKE. *Yorke*, 13° *Aug*. 1666.

TAYLER OF COATES.

ARMS.—Argent, on a pale sable three lions passant of the field, a canton gules.

CREST.—A leopard passant proper, charged on the shoulder with a trefoil slipped gules, the dexter paw resting on a shield argent bearing a pale sable.

Hugh Tayler of Hemingbrough in in co. Ebor. a branch of ye Taylors of Bickerton in com. ...... = ...

Hugh Taylor of Coates neer Carleton in co. Ebor. died circa ann. 1640. = Elizabeth, daughter of Rowland Revill of Rotheram in com. Ebor.

Elizabeth, wife of Robt Walker of Brayton neer Selby in com. Eborum.

Hugh Taylor of Coats in co. Ebor. æt. 38 ann. 13 Aug. a° 1666. = Elizabeth, daughter of George Lodge of Barlby in co. Ebor.

1. Elizabeth, 1st marr. to Marmaduke Dolman of Pocklington; 2dly to Will'm Beverley of Wistow; & 3dly to Tho. Horsman.

2. Jane, wife of Thomas Ricard of Cowick.

3. Mary, wife of Gervase Ashley of Eston on ye Woulds in com. Ebor.

4. Anne, wife of Amwell Beale of Barlow in com. Ebor.

5. Cath. wife of Edw. Kirlton of Woodhall neer Hembrough in co. Ebor.

6. Isabell, wife of John Bacon of Welton in com. Ebor.

7. Dorothy, died unmarried.

1. Hugh Taylor, æt. 14 annor. 1666. 2. John. 1. Jane. 2. Elizabeth.

THE CITTY OF YORKE. *Yorke*, 11° *Aug*. 1666.

CHADDERTON OF YORKE.

Edmond Chadderton descended from the house of Chadderton of Nutthurst in com. Lanc. = ...

2. Edward Chadderton, died circa ann. 1634. = Muriell, eldest daughter of Sr Francis Baildon of Baildon in co. Ebor. Knt.

1. William Chadderton. = ... daughter of .... Columbell.

Francis Chadderton of the Citty of Yorke, son and heir, æt. 43 ann. 11° Aug. a° 1666. = Jane, daughter of Christopher Parker of the Citty of Yorke.

Roger, obijt sine prole. Edward, obijt sine prole.

1. Katherine, died young. 2. Frances, æt. 11 ann. 11° Aug. a° 1666.

CLARO WAPENTAKE. *Yorke*, 11° *Aug*. 1666.

CHOLMELEY OF BRAHAM.

ARMS.—Quarterly :

1 and 4. Gules, in chief a fleur-de-lis ...... issuing from a crescent ermine between two helmets argent, in base a garb or.
2 and 3. Barry nebuly of four argent and gules, a bordure azure bezantée.

CREST.—On a royal helmet argent a garb or charged with a cinquefoil gules.

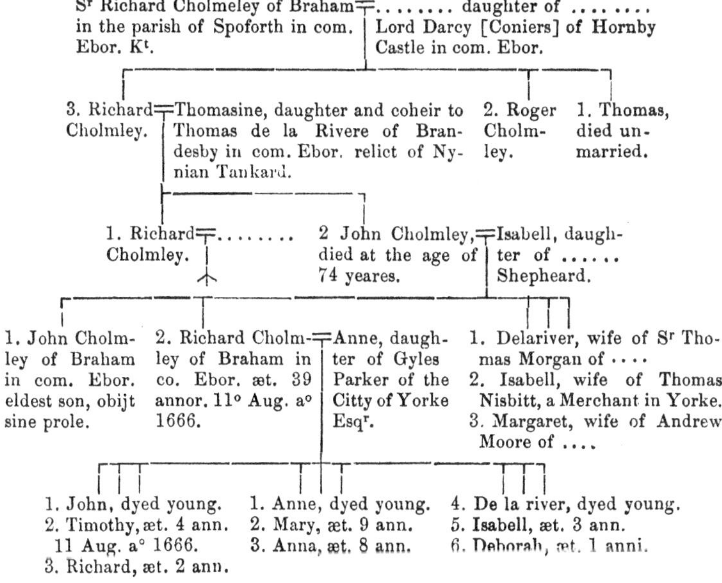

BUCKROSE WAPENTAKE. *Yorke*, 11° *Aug.* 1666.

LISTER OF LINTON.

ARMS.—Ermine, on a fess sable three mullets or, in chief a fleur-de-lis gules.
CREST.—Out of a ducal coronet or a stag's head erminois attired argent.

Sr John Lyster of Kingston upon Hull Kt, dyed 23 Dec. 1640. = Elizabeth, daughter and coheir of Hugh Armin Esqr.

1. John Lyster of Linton, Esqr. died 30 Martij, 1651. = Jane, daughter and sole heire of Christopher Constable of Great-Hatfeild in Holdernesse.
2. Samuell. 3. William. 4. Hugh.
5. Thomas. 6. Walter. 7. Robert.
8. Benjamin.

John Lyster Esqr. son and heire, æt. 28 annor. 11° Aug. 1666.
I. Elizabeth, wife of Robert Sothaby of ... in co. Ebor. Esqr.
2. Frances, wife of Constable Bradshaw of Upsall in Cleaveland in com. Ebor.
3. Dorothy.

PICKERING LITHE. *Malton*, 11° *Sept.* 1666.

MARSHALL OF AISLABY-GRANGE.

ARMS.—Quarterly : a crescent for difference:

1. Barry of six argent and sable, a canton ermine.
2. Or, a saltire engrailed gules, a chief per fess indented of the first and second.
3. Gules, a lion rampant argent within an orle of bezants.
4. Ermine, a chief per pale indented gules and or.

CREST.—A man in complete armour proper, holding in his dexter hand a baton or, a crescent for difference.

Roger Marshall of Aislaby-grange in Pickering Lithe in com. Ebor. = ... daughter of Thomas Curtes of Clee.

Thomas Marshall of Aislaby-grange, dyed circa annum 1621. = Susannah, daughter of .... Brooke, Alderman of Yorke.
1. Mary. 2. Margaret.

1. Henry Marshall, died without issue.
2. Samuell Marshall of Aislaby-grange, in co. Ebor. æt. 48 annor. 11 Sept. 1666. = Annie, daughter of ...... Page of Finchley in com. Midd.
1. Jane, wife of Hugh Ingram, son and heire to Sr William Ingram of Yorke Knt.
2. Mary, wife of Robert Horner, Alderman of Yorke.

2. Arthur, æt. 10 ann.
1. Samuell Marshall, æt. 15 annorum, 11° Septembr. 1666.
1. Susanna.
2. Annie.

Buckrose Wapentake. *Malton*, 11° *Sept.* 1666.

PAYLER OF THOROBY.

Arms.—Gules, three lions passant gardant in pale argent, over all a bend or charged with as many mullets of six points sable.

No proofe made of these Armes.

Sr Edward Payler of ...... in com. Ebor. Bart, died circa an. 1642. = Anne, daughter of William Watkinson of ......

Watkinson Payler Esqr, died in his father's lifetime. = ... 3d daugh. of ...... Ld Visc. Fairfax of Emeley in Ireland, of Gilling in com. Ebor.

1. Mary, wife of Francis Tophan of Aglethorpe in co. Ebor.
2. Frances, dyed young.

Sr Watkinson Payler of Thoroby in co. Ebor. Bart, æt. .. ann. 11 Sept. 1666. = Alathea, daughter of Sr Thomas Norcliff of Langton in co. Ebor.

1. Mary, wife of Thomas Ingram Esqr, eldest son of Sr Arthur Ingram of Temple-Newsam in com. Ebor. Knt.
2. Anne, died unmarried.

Thomas Payler, dyed young.

Dorothy Payler, æt. 1 anni 1666.

Citty of Yorke. *Yorke*, 11° *Aug.* 1666.

SOWRAY OF YORKE.

Arms.—Argent, a bend gules between six lions rampant sable, a canton or.

James Sowray, came first from Furnace-fells in Lancashire, and setled at Stathes in com. Ebor.; he died about the yeare 1626. = ...

2. James Sowray, now living, æt. 78 an. vel circa 11 Aug. a° 1666. = Cicily, daughter of ...... Adamson of ......

1. Richard Sowray. = ...

John Sowray, marr. Isabell, daughter of ...... Whitlamb.

Richard Sowray of the Citty of Yorke, ætat. 40 an. 11 Aug. 1666. = Mercia, daughter of John Morton of the Citty of Yorke.

Edward Sowray. = ...

Richard Sowray, son and heire, æt. 2 annorū 11° Aug. 1666.

1. Mary, ætatis 5 ann. 1666.
2. Sarah, æt. 4 ann.
3. Rachell, æt. 2 mens.

...... a daughter.

BUCKROSE WAPENTAKE. *Malton*, 11° *Sept.* 1666.

SOWTHEBY OF BIRDSALL.

ARMS.—Argent, on a fess vert between three cross-crosslets sable as many talbots passant of the field.
CREST.—A demi-talbot rampant proper, ears argent.

Robert Sowtheby of Birdsall in co. Ebor. Esqr, dyed 16 Nov. a° 1626. = Cath. daughter of Will'm Payler of Yorke Esqr.

1. Robert Sowtheby of Birdsall Esqr, died 24 Dec. a° 1636. = Jane, daughter of ...... Moseley, Alderm. of Yorke.
2. Thomas Sowtheby.
3. Will'm.
4. John.
5. Henry.

1. Thomas, dyed without issue.
2. Robert Sowtheby of Birdsall Esqr, æt. 36 ann. 11 Sept. 1666. = Elizabeth, eldest daughter of John Lyster of Lynton in co. Ebor. Esqr.
1. Jane, wife of Henry Tophan of ......
2. Isabell, wife of John Place.

1. Thomas Sowtheby, son heir, æt. 10 an. 11° Sept. 1666.
2. Robert, æt. 8 ann.
1. Jane, æt. 14 ann.
2. Elizabeth, æt. 12 ann.
3. Fidelia, dyed young.
4. Frances, æt. 6 ann.

CITTY OF YORKE. *Yorke*, 11° *Aug.* 1666.

WITTON OF YORKE.

ARMS.—Sable, a water-bouget argent, in chief three bezants.
CREST.—An owl argent, ducally gorged or.
No proofe made of these Armes.

Oliver Witton of Skipton in Craven in com. Ebor. died in a° 1502, temp. H. 7. = Elizabeth, daughter and heire of John Illingworth of Illingworth.

Elizabeth, daughter of John Whitlay of Whitlay in Craven in com. Ebor., 1 wife. = Oliver Witton of Skipton in Craven. = Susan, daughter of John Dickson of Bentley-Royd in Craven, second wife.

Edward Witton.
Joshua Witton of Skipton in Craven in com. Ebor., dyed circa annū 1615. = Sibell, daughter of Gilbert Drake of Hallifax in com. Ebor.

Joshua Witton of the Citty of Yorke, æt. 51 ann. 11° Aug. 1666. = Elizabeth, daughter of Tempest Thorneton of Tiersall in com. Ebor. Esqr.

Richard, æt. 16 an. 11° Aug. 1666.
1. Elizabeth, æt. 12 ann.
2. Margaret, æt. 10 ann.

Malton, 12° *Sept.* 1666.

TEMPEST OF TONGE.

ARMS.—Quarterly of eight:
1. Argent, a bend between six martlets sable, a crescent for difference.
2. .... a bend ermine.
3. Ermine, five fusils in fess ....
4. ...., an inescutcheon within an orle of martlets ....
5. ...., a fox's head erased between three bugle-horns ....
6. ...., a bend cotised between six martlets ....
7. ...., two lions passant in pale ....
8. ...., on a bend .... three owls ....

CREST.—A griffin's head erased ...., a crescent for difference.

Richard Tempest of Tonge in com. Ebor. Esqr, living a° 1612. = Alice, daughter of Will'm Maleverer of Arncliffe in com. Ebor. Esqr.

Their children:

- 3. Henry Tempest. = ...
- 2. Christopher Tempest of Tonge in com. Ebor. = ...
- 1. John Tempest of Tonge Esqr, dyed circa an. 1622. = Catherine, daughter of Robert Duckenfield of Duckenfeild in co. Cestr. Esqr.
- 1. Eleanor.
- 2. Elizabeth.
- 3. Beatrix.

Children of John Tempest and Catherine:

- John, died unmarried.
- Henry Tempest of Tonge Esqr, dyed in anno 1657. = Mary, daughter of Nicholas Bushell of Bagdell in co. Ebor.

Children of Henry Tempest and Mary:

- 4. Richard, æt. 19 ann.
- 5. Nicholas, æt. 17 ann.
- 6. Percy, æt. 13 ann.
- 3. Sr John Tempest of Tonge in com. Ebor. Bar^t, æt. 21 an. 12° Sept. 1666. = Henrietta, daughter of Sr Henry Cholmeley of Newton-grange in com. Ebor. Kn^t.
  - Henry, æt. 3 septiman. 12 Sept. 1666.
- 1. Henry, 2. Richard, dyed young.
- 1. Catherine, 2. Dorothy, dyed young.
- 3. Mary, wife of Will. Rogers of Woodhouse neer Malton in co. Ebor.
- 4. Eleanor, died unmarried.
- 5. Anabella.

LANGBERGH WAPENTAKE. *Stokesley*, 8° *Sept.* 1666.

TOCKETTS OF TOCKETTS.

ARMS.—Quarterly:
1 and 4. Argent, a lion rampant azure debruised with a bendlet gules.
2. Argent, a chevron between three hind's heads erased gules.
3. Sable, a chevron between three chaplets argent.

George Tocketts of Tockets, died circa ann. 1626, æt. 70. = Elizabeth, daughter of ...... Hutton of Hunwyke in com. Palat. Dunelm.

- 4. Robert, died without issue.
- 3. Will'm Tocketts of Tocketts Esqr, died circa ann. 1665, æt. 68. = Mary, da. of Joseph Constable of New-Building in com. Ebor.
- 2. James, died unmarried.
- 1. Roger Tocketts of Tocketts Esqr, died circa ann. 1650 sine prole. = Jane, daughter of ...... Cooke of Newcastle super Tine.
- Elizabeth, wife of Francis Thompson of Scarborough in com. Ebor.

Children of Will'm Tocketts and Mary:

- 4. George, obijt sine prole.
- 5. Joseph Tocketts, marr. Cath. daughter of .... Eddon.
- 2. Thomas, died in his infancy.
- 3. James, died unmarried.
- 1. Roger Tocketts of Tocketts Esqr, ætatis 46 an. 8 Sept. 1666. = Cornelia, daughter of Marcus Van Valkinburgh of Valkinburgh in Holland.
- 1. Elizabeth, wife of Robert Ward of Darneton in co. Palat. Dunelm.
- 2. Cath. wife of John Kirton of ...... in Holdernesse.
- 3. Bridget, wife of Musgrave Ridley of Fetherston-halgh in co. Pal. Dunelm.

Children of Roger Tocketts and Cornelia:

- Roger, dyed young.
- George Tocketts, son and heire, æt. 9 ann. 8 Sept. a° D. 1666.
- 1. Marg^t^, dyed young.
- 2. Catherine, æt. 3 an. 1666.
- 3. Cornelia, dyed young.
- 4. Elizabeth, dyed young.
- 5. Cornelia, died in her infancy.

Beverley, 15 *Sept.* 1666.

GEE OF BISHOP-BURTON.

ARMS.—Gules, a sword in bend argent, hilt gripe and pomel or.

Thomasine, daughter of Mathew Hutton, Archbisshop of Yorke, 1 wife. = Sr William Gee of Bishop Burton in co. Ebor. Kt, Secretary to his Maties Councell at Yorke for the Northern parts of this Realme, died in ao 1611. = Mary, daughter of Thomas Crompton of Hounsley in Surr. one of the Auditors to Qu. Eliz. for her Revenue, 2 wife.

Jane, wife of Roger Gregory of ...... in com. Lanc.

3. Thomas Gee of Killinggreaves in com. Ebor. = ...

2. William Gee of Bentley in co. Ebor. = ...

1. John Gee of Bishop-Burton Esqr, died in ao 1626. = Frances, daugh. of Sr John Hothom of Scorborough in co. Ebor. Kt & Bart.

Elizabeth, died unmd.

Hannah, wife of Sr Thomas Remington of Lund in com. Ebor. Knt.

Rachell, daughter of Sr Thomas Parker of Willington in com. Sussex Kt, first wife. = William Gee of Bishop-Burton Esqr, ætatis 41 annor. 15 Sept. 1666. = Mary, daughter of Richard Spenser of Orpington in com. Cantij Esqr, brother to the Lord Spenser of Wormleigton, second wife.

William Gee, ætatis 18 an. 15 Sept. 1666. = Elizabeth, daughter of Sr John Hothom of Scorborough in co. Ebor. Bart.

1. Richard Gee, æt. 9 ann. et 10 mens. 15 Sept. 1666.

2. Robert, æt. 6 ann.

Mary, dyed young.

BAYNTON-BEACON WAPENTAKE.

Beverley, 15 *Sept.* 1666.

CROMPTON OF GREAT DRIFFEILD.

ARMS.—Gules, a fess wavy between three lions rampant or, a crescent for difference.

CREST.—A talbot sejant or.

Thomas Crompton of Hounsley in com. Sussex Esqr, Auditor to Queene Elizabeth for her Revenue. = Mary, daughter of Henry Hudson of .... in com. Surr. Esqr.

Ceziah, daughter of Walter Strickland of Boynton in com. Ebor. Esqr, 3^d wife. = 3. Robert Crompton of Great Driffeild in com. Ebor. dyed in a^o 1646. = Anne, daugh. of Francis Haldenby of Haldenby in com. Ebor. second wife. = Jane, da. of .... Culverwell of Cherry-Burton in com. Ebor. Clerke, 1 wife.

2. Sr John Crompton of Skerne in com. Ebor. Knt. = ... daughter of Sr Henry Crofts of ..... in com. Suff. K^t.

1. Sr Thomas Crompton K^t, slaine at Abbeville in France by a Robber. = ... daughter of Sr Henry Carey K^t.

1. Mary, wife of Sr Will'm Gee of Bpp-Burton in com. Ebor. Kn^t.

2. Frances, wife of Sr Robert Fen K^t, Clerke Comptroller of his Maties Houshold.

4. Cesaia, wife of Englebert Leedes of North-Milford in com. Ebor.

3. Anne, wife of Will. Metcalfe, an Alderm. of Yorke; afterwards of Arthur Jegon of Wansworth in com. Ebor.

3. Walter.

4. Robert.

1. Thomas Crompton of Great-Driffeild Esqr, æt. 47 annor. 15 Sept. 1666. = Mary, daughter of Rich. Remington of Lund in co. Ebor. Esqr.

2. John. = ...

2. Frances.

1. Mary, wife of .... Fairweather of Cottingham in com. Ebor.

Sr Robert Crompton of Skerne in com. Ebor. Kn^t. = Cath. da. of .... Holland, sister of Sr John Holland of .... in co. Norff. Kn^t.

Cath. wife of Sr Tho. Littleton of Frankley in com. Wigorn. B^t, sole daughter & heire.

Thomas, æt. 24 ann. 15° Sept. a^o 1666.

Anne.

HOLDERNESSE, THE NORTH BAYLIWICK. *Beverley*, 15 *Sept.* 1666.

CONSTABLE OF CATFOSSE.

ARMS.—Quarterly:
1 and 4. Sable, a cinquefoil pierced within an orle of cross-crosslets or.
2 and 3. Argent, two bars each of five lozenges sable.

Christopher Constable of Catfosse, Freshmarshe, and Hampton in com. Ebor. Esqr. = Averill, daughter of George Fowberye of Newbold in com. Ebor. Esqr.

Children:

- John Constable of Catfosse in com. Ebor. Esqr, died in a° 1659. = Mary, daughter of Raphe Moore of Bewick in co. Ebor., widow of Philip Constable of Wassand in com. Ebor. Esqr.
- 1. Frances, wife of John Beverley of Ganstede in com. Ebor.
- 2. Ellyn, wife to Richard Hillyard of Ottringham in com. Ebor.; afterwards of Sr Francis Cobb of Beverley in co. Ebor. K^t^.
- 3. Cath. wife of ...... Langdale of Eberstone in com. Ebor.

Children of John and Mary:

- 3. Christoph^r^, 4. Raphe, died unmarried.
- 1. John Constable of Catfosse Esqr, æt. 45 annor. 15 Sept. 1666.
- 2. Robert, a Merch^t^ in Portugall.
- 1. Jane, wife of Christopher Smith of Awdby in co. Linc.
- 2. Frances.
- 3. Mary, wife of John Moore of Bewick in com. Eborũ.
- 4. Lenox.
- 5. Bridget.

LANGBERGH WAPENTAKE. *Stokesley*, 8° *Sept.* 1666.

COULSON OF AYTON.

ARMS.—Argent, two dolphins haurient respecting each other sable, collared and chained together by their necks, the chain pendent between them, of the last.

Christopher Coulson of South-Mimmes in com. Midd., died in anno 1641. = Susan, daughter and coheire of Richard Mahew of South-Mimms in com. Middlesex.

Children:

- 2. William Coulson of Greenwich in Kent. = (issue)
- 1. John Coulson of Ayton in co. Ebor., æt. 60 annorũ 8 Sept. a° 1666. = Elizabeth, daughter of Richard Hovell of Hillington in com. Norff. Esqr.
- Dorcas.

Children of John and Elizabeth:

- 2. John, æt. 21 ann.
- 3. William, æt 12 ann.
- 4. Edward, æt. 10 ann.
- 1. Christopher Coulson, son and heir, now a Barrister of the Middle Temple, London, æt. 25 ann. 8 Sept. 1666. = Elizabeth, daughter of John Man, Alderman of the Citty of Norwich.
- 1. Frances.
- 2. Susan.
- 3. Elizabeth.
- 4. Anne.

LANGBARGH WAPENTAKE. *Yorke*, 13° *Aug.* 1666.

TURNER OF KIRK-LEATHAM.

ARMS.—Sable, on a cross argent five mill-rinds of the field.

CREST.—A lion passant gardant or, the dexter paw resting upon a mill-rind sable.

John Turner of .... in com. Hereford, afterwards setled at Kirk Leatham in com. Ebor. died in anno 1644. = Elizabeth, daughter of Robert Colthurst of Up-Leatham in com. Ebor.

7. Richard Turner of Tunstall in com. Ebor. = Elizabeth, daughter of William Wiggener of Whitby in com. Ebor.

4. Henry Turner, died unmarried.
5. George, dyed unmarried.
6. Thomas, dyed unmarried.

2. Robt Turner, died unmarried.
3. Sr Will'm Turner Knt, Alderman of the Citty of London.

1. John Turner of Kirk-Leatham in com. Ebor. Esqr. a Bencher of the Middle Temple, London, one of his Maties Justices of the Peace and Quorum in the county of Yorke, and Recorder of the Citty of Yorke, æt. 53 ann. 13° Aug. aº 1666. = Jane, daughter of John Pepys of Creake in co. Norff. aunt and coheire to Anne Pepys, daughter and soleheire to Edward Pepys of Bromesthorpe in co. Norff.

1. Elizabeth, died unmarried.
2. Elizabeth, wife of Nicholas Johnston, Citizen of London.
3. Dorothy, died unmarried.
4. Mary, died unmarried.
5. Alice, first married to Richard Seton of Skinningrave in com. Ebor.; afterwards to Bryan Laton, a younger brother to Robert Layton of Sexho in com. Ebor. Esqr.
6. Sarah, wife unto Thomas Pennyman, Dr in Divinity.

Children of Richard and Elizabeth:

1. William, æt. 18 annor. 13° Aug. aº 1666.
2. John.
3. Richard.
4. Thomas.
5. Timothy.
6. Charles.
7. Robert.
8. James.

1. Sarah.
2. Elizabeth, dyed young.
3. Mary.

Children of John and Jane:

1. John, dyed in his infancy.
2. John, died also in his infancy.
3. Charles Turner, æt. 14 annor. 13° Aug. aº 1666.
4. William.

1. Anne, died in her infancy.
2. Theophila.
3. Elizabeth.

ALLERTONSHIRE WAPENTAKE. *Stokesley*, 8° *Sept. a°* 1666.

PEIRSE OF LASENBY.

ARMS.—Gules, a ducal coronet between three cross-crosslets fitchée or.
CREST.—On a cross-crosslet fitchée or a mural coronet gules.

Peter Peirse of Bedall in com. Ebor.=........

Thomas Peirse.=........

Marmaduke Peirse.=........

Henry Peirse.=........

Richard Peirse, Gentleman Sewer in Ordinary to King Charles the first, died unmarr.

John Pierse of East-Greenwich in Kent, Gentleman Sewer in ordinary to K. Charles ye 1st.=........ daughter of ....

2. Richard Peirse of Lasenby in com. Ebor. æt. 26 ann. 8 Sept. a° 1666.=Mary, daughter of Mathew Hutton of Maske in com. Ebor.

1. John Peirse, dyed unmarried.

1. .... 2. .... 3. .... 4. .... daughters.

1. John Peirse, son and heir, æt. 4 annor. 8 Sept. 1666.

2. Henry, æt. 2 ann. 1666.

ALLERTONSHIRE WAPENTAKE. *Stokesley*, 8° *Sept.* 1666.

METCALFE OF THORNBOROUGH.

ARMS.—Argent, three calves passant sable, a canton azure.

George Metcalfe, 2d son to James Metcalfe, which James was grandson to Thomas Metcalfe, Chancelour of the Dutchy of Lancaster.=......

4. Anthony Metcalfe.= ⅄

3. Richard Metcalfe of North-Allerton, died in a° 1616, or thereabouts.=Margaret, daughter of Roger Wilson of Danby-Wiske in co. Ebor.

2. John Metcalfe.

1. Gilbert Metcalfe.= ⅄

1. George Metcalfe of North-Allerton in com. Ebor.= ⅄

2. Richard Metcalfe of North-Allerton in com. Ebor. died in a° 1640. (vel circa.)=Anne, daughter of John Palleser of Newby-Wiske in com. Ebor.

2. Richard Metcalfe, a Merch^t^ in Yorke.
3. Gilbert Metcalfe, a Merchant in London.
4. Peter Metcalfe, a Merchant in the City of Yorke.

1. George Metcalfe of Thornborough neer Romonby in com. Ebor. æt. 42 ann. 8° Sept. a° D. 1666.=Anne, daughter and sole heire of Henry Danby of Romonby in co. Ebor.

Margt, wife of John Pecket, a Merchant in Yorke.

3. Gilbert, æt. 10 ann.

1. Richard, æt. 15 ann. 8 Sept. 1666.

1. Anne, wife of Michaell Pemberton of Aislaby Hall in com. Pal. Dunelm. Esqr.

2. Mary.
3. Margaret.
4. Catherine.

LANGBARGH WAPENTAKE. *Stokesley*, 8° *Sept.* 1666.

STEWARD OF LOFTHOUSE.

Respite given for inserting the Armes, refers to the Visit. of Cambridgshire.

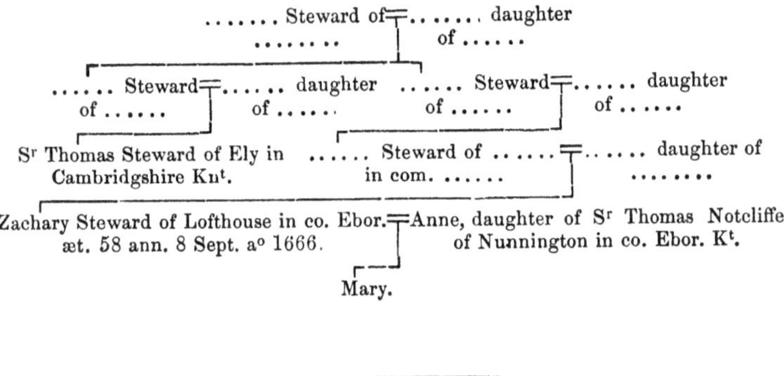

BIRDFORTH WAPENTAKE. *Stokesley*, 8° *Sept.* 1666.

PINKNEY OF SILTON-PAYNELL.

ARMS.—Argent, five fusils in pale within a bordure engrailed sable.

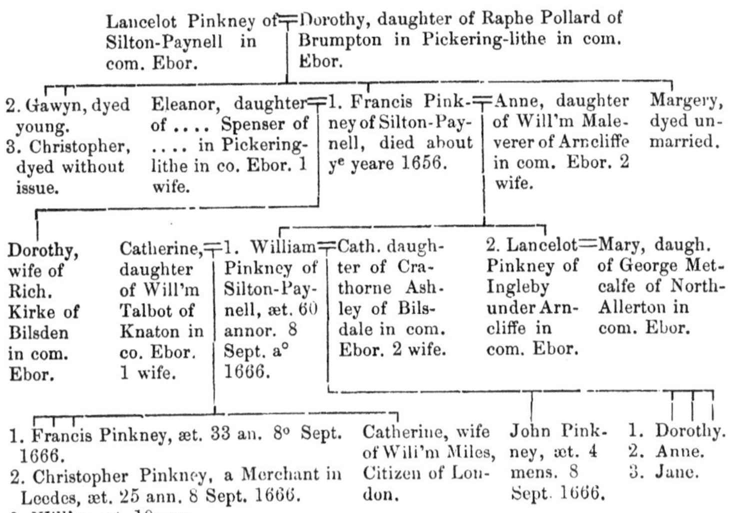

LANGBARGH WAPENTAKE. *Stokesley*, 8° *Sept.* 1666.

YOWARD OF WESTERDALE.

Robert Yoward of Stokesley in com. Ebor. = Muriell, daughter of Henry Warcopp of Grenow.

4. Charles.
3. John Yoward, Dr of Phisick. =
2. William.
1. Henry Yoward of Westerdale in co. Ebor., dyed circa ann. 1626. = Anne, daugh. of James Pennyman of Ormesby in co. Ebor. Esqr.
1. Muriell, wife of ...... Gower of Stanesby in com. Ebor.
2. Anne, wife of Samuell Bras of Hilton in com. Ebor.
3. Mary, wife of ...... Wandsford.

3. Robert Yoward.
4. Henry, obijt sine prole.
2. Raphe Yoward of Westerdale in co. Ebor., died circa annum 1640. = Susan, daughter of ...... Willis of ...... in com. ......
1. William Yoward, died unmarried.
Jane, wife of Robert Stope of Tunstall in com. Eborum.

2. Henry, dyed young.
1. Richard Yoward of Westerdale, died 5° Oct. a° 1664. = Frances, daughter of Josias Mathews of Kirby-under-hill in Cleveland in com. Ebor.
Anne, wife of Robert Ros of Leedes in com. Ebor.

2. Matthew, æt. 13 ann.
3. Richard, æt. 8 ann.
4. Charles, æt. 6 ann.
1. Raphe Yoward. æt. 17 annorū 8 Sept. a° 1666.
1. Anne.
2. Barbara.
3. Susanna.
4. Frances.
5. Eleanor.
6. Jane.
7. Catherine.

DICKERING WAPENTAKE. *Beverley*, 15° *Sept.* 1666.

CREYKE OF MARTON.

ARMS.—Quarterly:
1 and 4. Per fess argent and sable, a pale and three "creyks alias crowes" counter-changed. Creyke.
2. .... Eglinton.
3. Paly of six or and gules, on a chief argent three lozenges of the second. Arden.

CREST.—On a garb .... a "creyk alias crowe" with wings elevated sable.

Catherine, daughter of Thomas Crathorne of Crathorne in co. Ebor. 1 wife. = Raphe Creyke of Marton in com. Ebor. Esqr. = Anne, daughter of George Pate of Flamborough in com. Ebor. 2 wife.

4. Gregory Creyke of Marton in co. Ebor. æt. 71 an. 15° Sept. a° 1666. = Ursula, daughter of John Legard of Ganton in co. Ebor. Esqr.

2. William, 3. Alexander, died unmarried.

1. Robert Creyke of Cottingham in com. Ebor. =

Jane, died unmarried.

Marg^t, wife of Francis Wright of Plowland in com. Ebor. Esqr; afterwards to Hugh Cholmeley, son and heir to Sr Henry Cholmeley of West-Newton in com. Ebor. Kn^t.

1. Raphe Creyke, æt. 40 annor. 15° Sept. 1666.
2. Gregory, æt. 34 ann.
3. Christopher, æt. 28 ann.
4. Henry, æt. 26 ann.
5. Richard, æt. 25 ann.
6. George, æt. 24 ann.

Beverley, 15° *Sept*. 1666.

WYVELL OF OSGODBY.

ARMS.—Gules, three chevronels braced in base vair, on a chief or a trefoil slipped azure.

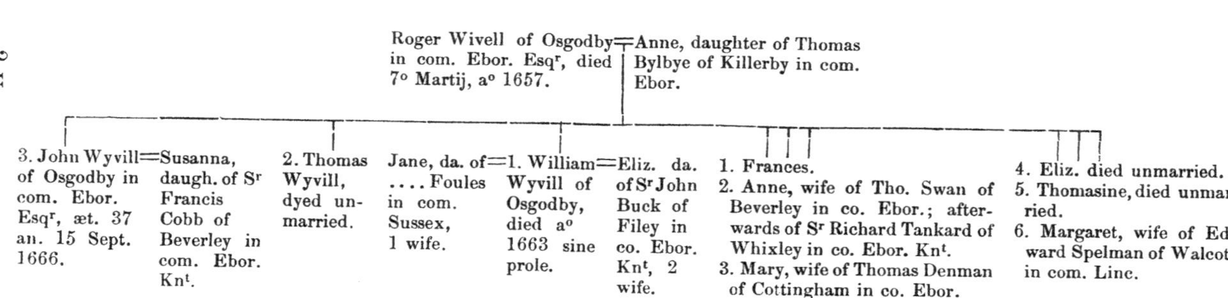

Roger Wivell of Osgodby in com. Ebor. Esqr, died 7° Martij, a^o 1657. = Anne, daughter of Thomas Bylbye of Killerby in com. Ebor.

3. John Wyvill of Osgodby in com. Ebor. Esqr, æt. 37 an. 15 Sept. 1666. = Susanna, daugh. of Sr Francis Cobb of Beverley in com. Ebor. Kn^t.

2. Thomas Wyvill, dyed unmarried.

Jane, da. of .... Foules in com. Sussex, 1 wife. = 1. William Wyvill of Osgodby, died a^o 1663 sine prole. = Eliz. da. of Sr John Buck of Filey in co. Ebor. Kn^t, 2 wife.

1. Frances.
2. Anne, wife of Tho. Swan of Beverley in co. Ebor.; afterwards of Sr Richard Tankard of Whixley in co. Ebor. Kn^t.
3. Mary, wife of Thomas Denman of Cottingham in co. Ebor.

4. Eliz. died unmarried.
5. Thomasine, died unmarried.
6. Margaret, wife of Edward Spelman of Walcote in com. Linc.

HOLDERNESSE. *Beverley*, 15 *Sept.* 1666.

LEVYNS OF ESKE.

ARMS.—Argent, on a bend sable three escallops of the field.

No proofe made of these Armes.

...... Levyns of ...... in com. Westmerl[d].=......

James Levyns.=.... daughter of .... Bacchus of Milton in co. Somerset.

Thomas Levyns of Bedminster in com. Somerset.=Jane, daughter to .... Kemise of Bedminster in com. Somerset.

James Levyns of Swynflete in com. Ebor.=Ellen, daughter of ...... Lee of Maxfield in the edge of Wales.

Anne, daughter of Vincent Beverley of Selby in co. Ebor. 1 wife.=Thomas Levyns of Rusholme in com. Ebor. died circa an. 1626.=Anne, daughter of Henry Browne of Selby in com. Ebor. 2 wife.

1. Alice, wife of Robert Anby of Selby in com. Ebor.

2. Anne, wife of Roger Marshall of Selby in com. Ebor.

2. Lucyan Levyns of Rusholme in com. Ebor.

1. Lewys Levyns of Eske in Holdernesse in com. Ebor. æt. 50 ann. 15 Sept. 1666.=Eleanor, daugh. and heire of Will'm Wytham of Ledston in com. Ebor.

1. Marg[t], wife of Elias Micklethwayt of Marston in co. Ebor.
2. Mary, wife of John Adams of Rawcliffe in co. Ebor.
3. Sarah, wife of Alexander Stocke, Rector of ...... in com. Ebor.

1. William, æt. 20 ann. 15 Sept. 1666.
2. Thomas, æt. 18 ann.
3. Lewis, æt. 15 ann.
4. Wytham, æt. 13 ann.
5. Lucyan, æt. 11 ann.
6. Charles, æt. 6 ann.

WARTON OF BEVERLEY.

ARMS.—Quarterly:

1 and 4. Or, on a chevron azure a martlet between two pheons of the field. Warton.
2 and 3. .... Maltby.

CREST.—On the stump of a tree couped and sprouting a squirrel sejant, all proper, holding in his paws a nut or.

Sr Michaell Warton of Beverley Parke in com. Ebor. Knt, dyed 12° Oct. a° D. 1655. = Elizabeth, 3d daughter and coheire of Raphe Hansby of Beverley.

Michaell Warton of Beverley Esqr, died in his father's lifetime, being slayn by a canon bullet at Scarborough Castle in the time of the late warrs, it being then a garrison for the King. = Catherine, daughter and coheire of Christopher Maltby of Maltby in com. Ebor.

Their children:

- 1. Michaell Warton of Beverley Esqr, æt. 42 annorū 15 Sept. a° 1666. = Susan, daugh. of John Ld Pawlet of Hinton St George in co. Somerset.
- 2. Raphe Warton, æt. 38 ann. 15 Sept. a° 1666.
- 1. Everill, dyed without issue.
- 2. Cath. wife of Eldred Curwen, brother to Sr Patricius Curwen of Workinton in com. Cumbr. Knt.
- 3. Eliz. wife of Salveyn Carleil of Brandsburton in com. Ebor.
- 4. Jane, wife of Francis Trapps of Midd. in com. Ebor.
- 5. Mary, wife of Symon Scrope of Danby super Yore in co. Ebor.

Children of Michaell Warton and Susan:

- 1. Michaell, æt. 17 annor. 15 Sept. 1666.
- 2. Raphe, æt. 10 ann.
- 3. Charles, æt. 8 an. 1666.
- 1. Elizabeth.
- 2. Susan.
- 3. Mary.

HOLDERNESSE BAYLIWICK. *Beverley*, 15° *Sept.* 1666.

COBB OF OTTRINGHAM.

ARMS.—Quarterly:

1. Per chevron gules and sable, in chief two shovellers respecting each other argent, in base a fish naiant or, a crescent for difference.
2. Sable, three ewers with covers argent.
3. Argent, a chevron gules between three martlets sable.
4. Argent, three bars gules, an inescutcheon ermine.

CREST.—A shoveller's head erased proper, holding in the beak gules a fish or.

.... Cobb of Sandringham in com. Norff. from whom William Cobb, now of Sandringham in com. Norff. Esqr, as the chief Male Branch is also lineally descended. = ...

.... Cobb of Sandringham in com. Norff. = ... daughter of .... Walpole of .... in co. Norff.

...... Cobb of Snettesham in co. Norff. = ... daughter and heire of ..... Martin of ..... in Kent.

Francis Cobb of Burnham in com. Norff. = ... daughter and coheire of ...... Fiske of Wells in co. Norff.

2. Will'm Cob, died without issue.

1. Sr Francis Cobb of Burnham in Norfolke K^t, and afterwards of Ottringham in Holdernesse in com. Ebor. first Esquier of the Body to K. James and K. Charles, afterwards Knighted by King Charles the first, died in a° 1648. = Mary, youngest daughter of Will'm Daniell of Beswyke in co. Ebor. Esqr.

1. Margaret, wife of .... Percy of .. .. in co. Norff.
2. Fayth, wife of Nicholas Browne of Walsingham in co. Norff.
3. .... wife of .... Newark of Burnham in co. Norff.
4. .... wife of Will'm Davye of Little-Gayton in com. Norff.

2. William, dyed young.

1. Sr Francis Cobb of Ottringham in co. Ebor. Kn^t, æt. 60 ann. 15 Sept. 1666. = Ellen, daughter of Cristopher Constable of Catfosse in com. Ebor. Esqr.

1. Jane, wife of Robert Haldenby of Haldenby in Marshland in co. Ebor. Esqr.
2. Mary, wife of Christopher Hillyard of Ottringham in Holdernesse, Esqr.

2. Francis, died unmarried.

1. Sr William Cobb Kn^t, son and heire, æt. 37 annorũ 15° Sept. a° 1666. = Winifride, daughter of John Cooke of Holkam in com. Norff. Esqr.

1. Mary, died unmarried.
2. Susan, wife of John Wyvill of Osgodby in com. Ebor. Esqr.

Bridget, æt. 11 ann. 15° Sept. 1666.

Francis, died in his childhood.

Beverley, 14 *Sept.* 1666.

GREY OF BEVERLEY.

ARMS.—Barry of six argent and azure, as many fleurs-de-lis or, three, two, and one.

CREST.—On a chapeau gules turned up ermine a wyvern with wings addorsed or, charged on the breast with a trefoil slipped of the first.

Edward Grey of Beverley in co. Ebor., came out of Northumberland, being a branch of the House of Chillingham. = ...

Edward Grey of Beverley, dyed circa ann. 1636. = Elizabeth, daughter of William Thompson of Humbleton in Holdernesse in com. Ebor.

3. Edward Grey of Beverley, æt. 66 ann. 14 Sept. 1666. = Marg[t], daugh. of ...... Skelton of ...... in co. Ebor.

2. Will'm Grey, Rector of the parish Church of Rosse in Holdernesse, died in Scarborough Castle in y[e] service of K. Ch. y[e] first.

1. Robert Grey of Beverley. = ...

1. Anne, wife of Will'm Forde of Scarborough in com. Ebor.

2. Mary, wife of Christopher Headlam of Scarborough.

Edward Grey of Beverley, æt. 35 an. 14 Sept. 1666. = Elizabeth, daughter of John Wardall of Hull-banke in co. Ebor.

Timothy Grey of Beverley, now living a[o] 1666.

Edward, ætatis unius anni et 8 mens. 14 Sept. 1666.

1. Anne.

2. Elizabeth.

3. Margaret.

HUNSLOW BEACON. *Beverley*, 15° *Sept.* 1666.

ANLABY OF ETTON.

ARMS.—Argent, a chevron between three chess-rooks sable.

Thomas Anlaby of Etton in com. Ebor. Esqr, dyed in a° 1641. = Ursula, daughter of William Palmer of Yorke, 1 wife. = Sarah, daughter of Gervase Crescy of Berking in com. Ebor. second wife.

Children of Thomas Anlaby and Ursula:

- Anne, wife of ...... Waters of Yorke.

Children of Thomas Anlaby and Sarah:

- Susan, daughter of Roger Beckwith of Aldbrough in com. Ebor. Esqr, 1st wife. = 2. John Anlaby of Etton, Esqr, dyed 10° Dec. a° 1661. = Dorothy, daughter of Sr Matthew Boynton of Barmston in com. Ebor. K^t and Bar^t. 2^d wife.
- 1. Edward, dyed young.
- 1. Sarah, 5th wife of Sr John Hothom of Scorborough in co. Ebor. K^t and Bar^t.
- 2. Eliz., wife of Henry Barnardeston of ...... in com. Leic.
- 3. Susanna, wife of Charles Bowes of Babthorpe in co. Ebor.

Children of John Anlaby and Susan:

- Susan.
- Thomas Anlaby of Etton, Esqr, æt. 28 annor. 15° Sept. a° 1666. = Susan, daughter of Dr Will'm Parker of Margets in the Isle of Thanet in Kent, D^r of Phisick.
  - Susan, æt. 2 annor. et 6 mens. 15 Sept. 1666.

Children of John Anlaby and Dorothy:

- Matthew Anlaby.
- Elutherea.

Beverley, 15° *Sept*. 1666.

CONSTABLE OF WASSAND.

ARMS.—Quarterly:

1 and 4. Quarterly gules and vair, over all a bend or charged with an annulet of the first.
2 and 3. ......, a fess dancettée paly of four gules and sable between three mullets pierced ....

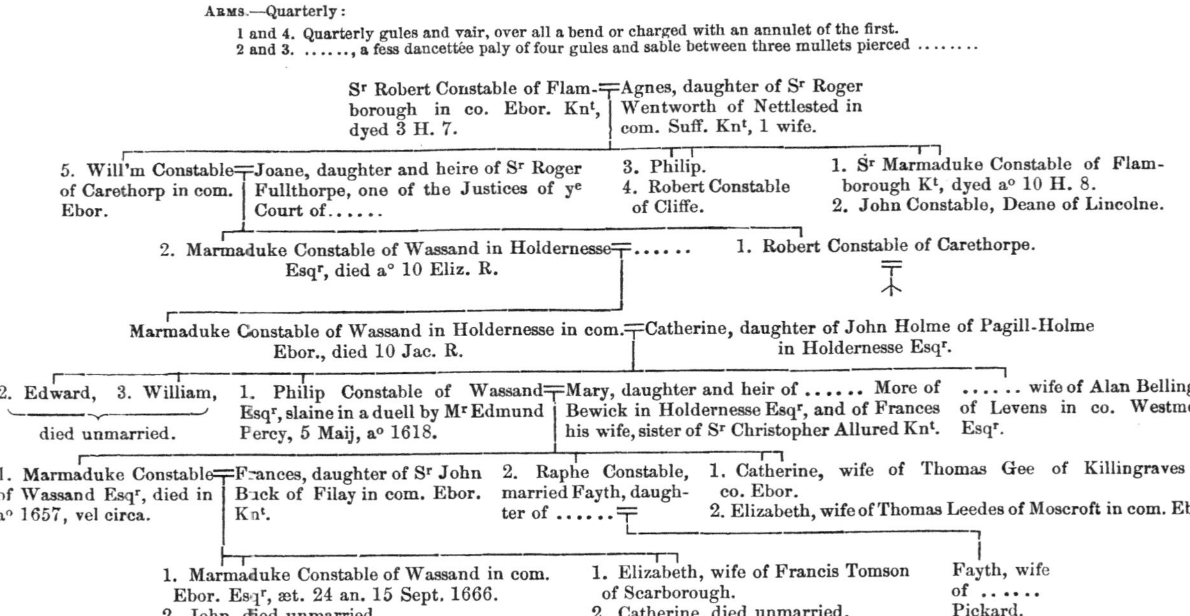

Sr Robert Constable of Flamborough in co. Ebor. Knt, dyed 3 H. 7. = Agnes, daughter of Sr Roger Wentworth of Nettlested in com. Suff. Knt, 1 wife.

5. Will'm Constable of Carethorp in com. Ebor. = Joane, daughter and heire of Sr Roger Fullthorpe, one of the Justices of ye Court of......

3. Philip.
4. Robert Constable of Cliffe.

1. Sr Marmaduke Constable of Flamborough Kt, dyed a° 10 H. 8.
2. John Constable, Deane of Lincolne.

2. Marmaduke Constable of Wassand in Holdernesse Esqr, died a° 10 Eliz. R. = ...

1. Robert Constable of Carethorpe.

Marmaduke Constable of Wassand in Holdernesse in com. Ebor., died 10 Jac. R. = Catherine, daughter of John Holme of Pagill-Holme in Holdernesse Esqr.

2. Edward, 3. William, died unmarried.

1. Philip Constable of Wassand Esqr, slaine in a duell by Mr Edmund Percy, 5 Maij, a° 1618. = Mary, daughter and heir of ...... More of Bewick in Holdernesse Esqr, and of Frances his wife, sister of Sr Christopher Allured Knt.

...... wife of Alan Bellinghā of Levens in co. Westmerld Esqr.

1. Marmaduke Constable of Wassand Esqr, died in a° 1657, vel circa. = Frances, daughter of Sr John Buck of Filay in com. Ebor. Knt.

2. Raphe Constable, married Fayth, daughter of ...... =

1. Catherine, wife of Thomas Gee of Killingraves in co. Ebor.
2. Elizabeth, wife of Thomas Leedes of Moscroft in com. Ebor.

1. Marmaduke Constable of Wassand in com. Ebor. Esqr, æt. 24 an. 15 Sept. 1666.
2. John, died unmarried.

1. Elizabeth, wife of Francis Tomson of Scarborough.
2. Catherine, died unmarried.

Fayth, wife of ...... Pickard.

Baynton Beacon Wap.

Beverley, 15° *Sept.* 1666.

HOTHAM OF SCORBOROUGH.

Arms.—Quarterly of eight; on an inescutcheon the badge of a Baronet of England:

1. Barry of ten argent and azure, on a canton or a Cornish chough sable legged gules.
2. Or, on a bend sable three mullets pierced argent.
3. Argent, on a bend between six mullets gules a cross pattée or.
4. Argent, on a bend gules three crescents or.
5. Argent, in fess between two bars gules three torteaux, a chief indented of the second.
6. Argent, a pale of lozenges sable.
7. Gules, a bend or.
8. Argent, three water-bougets sable.

Crest.—A demi-seaman issuing out of water proper, holding in the dexter hand a sword wavy .... and in the sinister a shield of the arms of Hotham.'

John Hotham of Scorborough in com. Ebor. Esqr. died circa an. 1605. = Jane, daughter of Richard Lydiard of Rysome in Holdernesse in com. Ebor. 3 wife.

Children:

- Sarah, daughter of Thomas Anlaby of Etton in co. Ebor. Esqr, 5th wife. = Katherine, daughter of Sr Will. Bambrough of Ousan in com. Ebor. Kn^t. 4 wife = Frances, daughter of John Legard of Ganton in co. Ebor. Esqr. 3 wife. = Anne, daughter of Raphe Rookesby, Secretary to y^e Councell of Yorke for the Northern parts of this realme, 2 wife. = Sr John Hotham of Scorborough K^t and Bar^t, created by K. James, a° 19 Regni sui, dyed 2° Jan. 1644. = Katherine, daughter of Sr John Rhodes of Barlbrough in com. Derb. Kn^t, 1 wife.
  - (by Katherine Bambrough) Francis, died unmarried. Jane, died young. — *a*
  - (by Frances Legard) 1. Eliz. 2. Frances, 3. ...... 4. ...... } died young.
  - *b*
  - *c*
- 1. Mary, wife of Richard Remington of Lund in in com. Ebor. Esqr.
- 2. Elizabeth, 3. Fayth, } died unmarried.

a | b | c

1. Sarah. 2. Cath. wife of Sr Will'm Cholmley of Whitby n com. Ebor. Bart.

3. Dorothy, 4. Alathea, died young.

5. Durand Hotham of Lockinton in co. Ebor. æt. 47 an. 15 Sept. 1666. = Frances, da. of Rich. Remington of Lund in com. Ebor. Esqr.

3. Charles. Hotham, Clerke, married Eliz. da. of Stephen Tompson of Humbleton in co. Ebor. Esqr.
4. Will'm.

Frances, eldest daughter of Sr John Wray of Glentworth in com. Linc. Kt and Bart, 1 wife. = 1. John Hotham Esqr, dyed 1o Jan. a° 1644. = Margt, daughter of Thomas Visct Emeley, 2 wife. = Isabell, daughter of SrHenry Anderson of Long-Cowton in com. Ebor. Knt. 3 wife.

Henry, dyed young.

2. Richard. =

1. Margt, died an infant.

2. Frances, first marr. to John Gee of Beverley in com. Ebor. after to Sr Philip Stapleton of Wartre in co. Ebor. Kt.

---

5. Durand, 6. Thomas, 7. William, dyed young.

3. Walleran, æt. 17 ann. 4. Edmund, dyed young.

1. Durand Hotham, dyed young. 2. Jeffrey Hotham, æt. 19 annor. 15 Sept. 1666.

3. Elizabeth. 4. Anne, dyed young.

1. Frances, 2. Alathea, dyed young.

Sr John Hotham of Scorborough, Bart, æt. 31 ann. 15 Sept. a° 1666. = Elizabeth, only daughter of Sapcote Ld Beaumont, Vicount Beaumont of Swords in Ireland.

1. Grisild, wife of Peter le Gay a Mercht in London, afterwards of . . Hay, Alderm. of London.

2. Frances, wife of John Daniell, 3d son of Sr Ingleby Daniell of Beswick in co. Ebor. Knt.

---

1. John Hotham, son and heire, æt. 10 an. 15 Sept. 1665.

2. Robert, æt. 3 ann.

1. Elizabeth, wife of William Gee, son and heir of Will'm Gee of Bishop-Burton and Beverley in com. Ebor. Esqr.

2. Bridget.

MORTON OF WRATH-HOUSE.

ARMS.—Argent, three ravens sable within a bordure azure, in chief a trefoil slipped ......

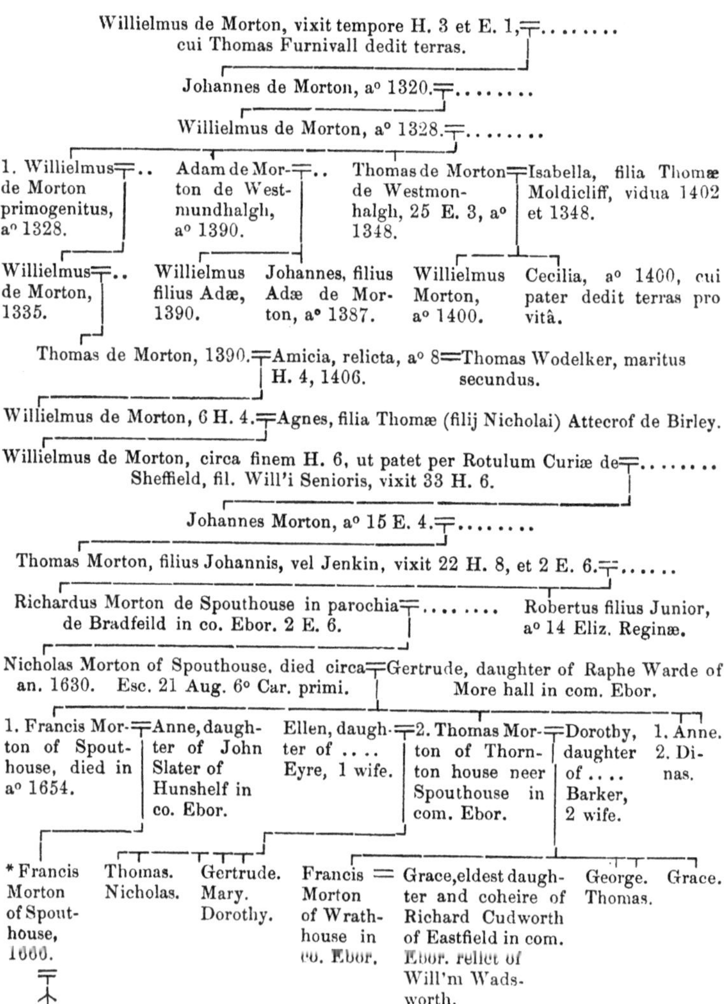

* Vide Morton of Spouthouse, p. 175.

HUNSLEY BEACON WAPENTAKE. *Beverley*, 15° *Sept.* 1666.

CONSTABLE OF CLIFFE.

ARMS.—Quarterly:

1. Quarterly gules and vair, over all a bend or, a crescent for difference.
2. ....
3. ...., billetté .... a lion rampant .....
4. Vairé sable and or.

Sr Robert Constable, 2d son of ...... Constable of Flamborough in com. Ebor. Serjeant at Law. = Beatrix, daughter and heire of ...... Hatcliffe of ...... in com. ...... Relict to ...... Lord Graystock.

Marmaduke Constable of Cliffe in com. Ebor. Esqr. = ... daughter of Sr James Metcalfe of Napper in com. Ebor. Knt.

James Constable of Cliffe Esqr. = ... daughter to Sr Geffrey Middleton of Middleton in com. ...... Knt.

James Constable of Cliffe in com. Ebor. Esqr. = ...

2. Robert, died unmarried.

1. Marmaduke Constable of Cliffe in com. Ebor. Esqr. = Frances, daughter and coheir of Sr Raphe Bulmer of Bulmer in com. Ebor. Kt.

2. Robert Constable, dyed without issue.

1. James Constable of Cliffe in com. Ebor. Esqr. = Margery, daughter of John Hedworth of Chester in ye streete in com. Palat. Dunelm.

2. Robert, died unmarried.

1. Marmaduke Constable of Cliffe, Esqr, æt. 20 annor. a° 1612. = Anne, daughter of Edward Barker of Dore in com. Derb.

1. Eliz, wife of Robert Bethell of Althorpe in com. Ebor.
2. Mary, wife of .... Sergeant.
3. Susan, wife of .... Richardson.

2. James, died unmarried.

1. Robert Constable of Cliffe, Esqr, died circa annum 1631. = Frances, daugh. and coheir of Thomas Oldfeild of Oldfeild in com. Ebor.

1. Anne, wife of .... Arksey of Beverley; afterwards to ...... Bamford; Lastly of .... Tucker, Citizen of London.

2. Frances, wife of William Legard of Beverley.
3. Alice, wife John Constable of the Citty of Yorke.

Robert Constable of Cliffe in com. Ebor. Esqr, æt. 28 annor. 15 Sept a° 1666. = Elizabeth, daughter of John Milward of Snitterton in co. Derb. Esqr.

Frances, wife of John Eyre, son and heire to Rowland Eyre of Bradway in com. Derb.

John, æt. 6 ann. 15 Sept. 1666.

Frances.

LANGBARGH WAPENTAKE. *Stokesley*, 8° *Sept*. 1666.

CONYERS OF BOWLBY.

ARMS.—Azure, a maunche or, over all a bend gobony gules and ermine.

CREST.—A bull's head erased or, horned and maned sable, pierced through the neck with an arrow of the last feathered and barbed argent, vulned gules.

Leonard Conyers of Whitby in com. Ebor. = ...

1. Nicholas Conyers of Bowlby in com. Ebor. Esqr. died in a° 1636, vel circa. = Catherine, daughter of Robert Trotter of Skelton-Castle in com. Ebor. Esqr.

2. George Conyers of Filingdale in co. Ebor.
3. Robert Conyers of Gisbrough in com. Ebor. dyed without issue.
4. James Conyers, dyed young.
5. Francis Conyers, died unmarried.
6. Raphe Conyers, died unmarried.

1. Margaret, wife of Robert Lakin of Yedingham in com. Ebor.
2. Mary, wife of William Conyers of Scarborough in com. Ebor.

1. Robert Conyers of Bowlby Esqr, died in a° 1640 or thereabouts. = Anne, daughter of Sr Raphe Conyers of Layton in the County Palatine of Durham.

2. Nicholas Conyers of Cleasby in co. Ebor. = Grace, daughter of . . . . . . Smithson of Moulton in com. Ebor.

3. Henry,
4. Anthony, } died unmarried.

5. Leonard Conyers, a Capt. of Foote in the Army of K. Charles ye 1st, wounded at Newarke by a canon bullet whereof he dyed.
6. Edmund Conyers, slaine at Scarborough Castle, in the service of King Charles the first.

Nicholas. (son of Nicholas Conyers of Cleasby and Grace)

2. Raphe, died in his childhood.
3. Thomas, died unmarried.

Margt, daughter of Nicholas Frevile of Hardwick in com. palat. Dunelm. Esqr, 3 wife. = 1. Nicholas Conyers of Bowlby Esqr, æt. 37 annor. 8 Sept. a° 1666. = Jane, daughter of Sr Will'm Lambton of Lambton in co. Palat. Dunelm. Kt, 2 wife. = Elizabeth, daugh. of Marmaduke Norcliffe of Nunnington in com. Ebor. ob. s. prole, 1 wife.

1. Catherine, died unmarried.
2. Mary.
3. Anne, wife of Will'm Hodshon of Mannour-house in co. Palat. Dunelm.
4. Margaret, wife of Roger Reade of . . . . in co. Northumbriæ.

Issue of Nicholas and Margt (3 wife): Mary.

Issue of Nicholas and Jane (2 wife):
Catherine.
1. Nicholas, æt. 11 annor. 8° Sept. a° 1666.
2. William, æt. 9 an. 1666.
3. Robert, æt. 7 ann.
4. Raphe, æt. 5 ann.

NORCLIFF OF LANGTON.

ARMS.—Azure, five mascles in cross or, a chief ermine.

CREST.—A greyhound sejant or, collared and ringed azure, the dexter paw resting upon a mascle argent.

This Coat and Crest granted to ...... Norcliffe of Great-Somersall in com. Ebor. by .... 11° Julij, a° 4° Jac. R.

Stephen Norcliffe.=......

Thomas Norcliffe of Great Somersall in com. Ebor. a° 1612. = Eliz. daugh. of Robt Ealand of Carlinghow in com. Ebor.

1. Francis Norcliff, æt. 36 ann. a° 1612, died without issue.

2. Sr Thomas Norcliff of Nunnington in com. Ebor. Kn^{t}. = Cath. daugh. and coh. of Sr Will'm Bamburgh of Howson in com. Ebor. Bart.

3. Stephen Norcliff. = ... daugh. of .... Udal, married to her 2^{d} husband Richard Scot of Barnshall in com. Ebor.

4. Marmaduke Norcliff of Oswaldchurche. = Mary, daughter and heire of Will'm Dolman.

Children of Sr Thomas Norcliff:

2. Benjamin Norcliffe, a Barrister at Law.
3. Will'm Norcliffe, married Mary, da. of Will'm Armitage of Doncaster, a Barrister at Law, & coheir to her brother W^{m}.
4. John Norcliff.

1. Sr Thomas Norcliff of Langton in com. Ebor. Kn^{t}, æt. an. 13 Aug. 1666. = Dorothy, daugh. of Sr Tho. Fairfax of Gilling in com. Ebor. B^{t}, & Viscount Emely in Ireland.

1. Anne, wife of Zachary Steward of Lofthouse in com. Ebor.
2. Eliz. 1st marr. to .... Pulleyn, afterwards to .... Stockdale.
3. Mary, wife of John Scriven.
4. Martha.
5. Cath.

Children of Stephen Norcliff:

1. Elizabeth, daughter and coheir, wife of Sr James Pennyman, of Maske in com. Ebor. Kn^{t} & Bar^{t}.
2. Cath. daughter and coheire, wife of Sr John Goderick of Ribstan in com. Ebor. Kn^{t} & Bar^{t}.

Children of Marmaduke Norcliff:

Thomas Norcliff. = ... daugh. & coheire of ...... Anderson.

Marmaduke.

Elizabeth, wife of Nicholas Conyers of Bolby in com. Ebor, Esqr.
Anne, wife of ...... Wood,

Children of Sr Thomas Norcliff of Langton:

Thomas Norcliff Esqr, æt. 24 annor. 13 Aug. 1666.

1. Alathea, wife of Sr Watkinson Payler of Thoroby in co. Ebor. Bar^{t}.

2. Dorothy, wife of Will'm Grimston of Goodmadham in com. Ebor. Esqr.

3. Elizabeth, wife of Sr John Bright of Badsworth in com. Ebor. Bar^{t}.

4. Cath. wife of Christopher Lister of Thornton in com. Ebor. Esqr.
5. Anthonia.
6. Frances.

BULMER WAPENTAKE. *Yorke*, 11° *Aug*. 1666.

AYSCOUGH OF SKEWSBY.

ARMS.—Quarterly, a crescent for difference:
1 and 4. Sable, a fess between three asses passant argent.
2. Azure, a bend or.
3. Argent, a cross moline sable.

CREST.—An ass's head erased argent.

John Ayscough of Cowling in the parish of Bedall cum Ayscough in com. Ebor. 9 R. 2, died 8 Jan. 1425, 3° H. 6. = ... daughter of Sr John Arncliffe Knt.

Sr Will'm Ayscough Knt, one of the Justices of the Court of Common Pleas. = Elizabeth, daughter and one of the coheires of John Calthrop Esqr.

2. William Ayscough of Cowling in com. Ebor. Esqr, died circa 35 H. 8 a° D. 1544. = ... one of ye daugh. and coheires of a younger son of Fulthrope of Fulthrope in Episc. Dunelm. & Hipswell in co. Ebor.

1. John Ayscough, from whom Sr Edward Ayscough of South-Kelsey in com. Linc. Knt is descended. = Margaret, daughter and heir of John Talboise of ...... in com. Linc. Esqr.

George Ayscough of Cowling in com. Ebor., died circa ann. 1556, 3° Mar. R. = Alice, sister to Sr Christopher Wray of Glentworthe in co. Linc., Cheife Justice of ye King's Bench temp. Eliz. R.

a

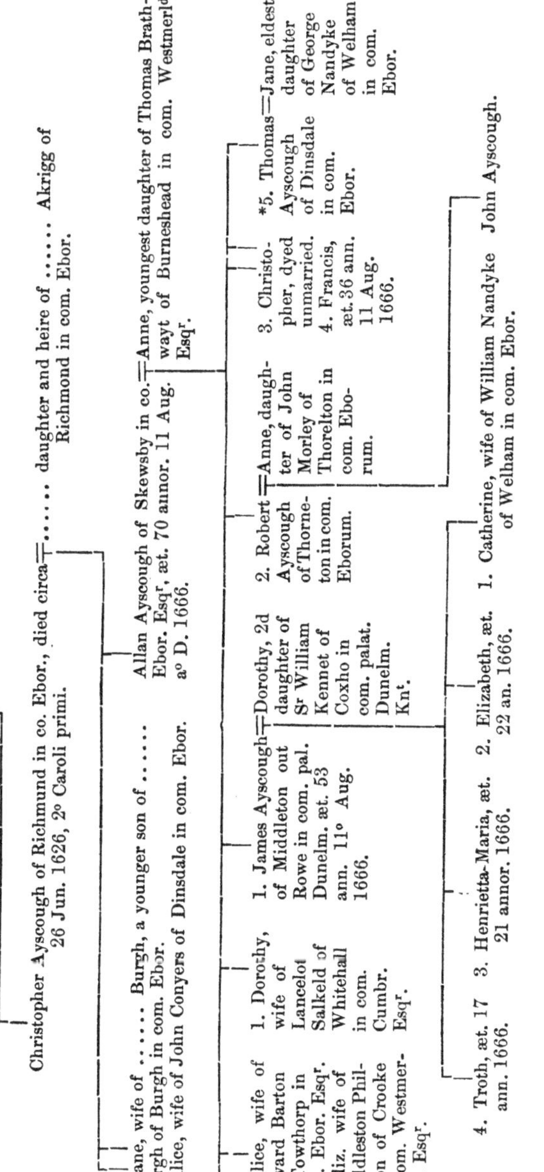

* Upon this marriage the lands in Dinsdale were setled by Indenture bearing date 10 Apr. aº 1656, and 20 Nov. 1660, 12 Car. 2.

In the Church of Bedall in com. Ebor.

Here lyeth the body of S[r] William Ayscough who dyed in the yeare of our Lord MCCCCLVI. in the xxxiiij yeare of the reigne of King Henry the vj[th].

By indenture dated the 5th of March, 1658, betwene Francis Topham Esq[r], Francis Wycliffe and John Tonge in Episc. Dunelm. gent. on the one part, Allan, James and Francis Ayscough on the other part, the mannours of Skewsby and Middleton on Rowe, six Oxganges of Land in Newby in the possession of Christopher Marshall and other Tenants in Cleveland in com. Ebor.: By which Indenture amongst other things, part of the Lands are limitted to Allan and Anne his wife for their lives, & part to James & Dorothy his wife for their lives, with provision for the daughters of James, as by Decree in Chancery dated 30 July, 16 Car. 2. and also entayled upon the first and tenth issue male of the severall and respective bodyes of James, Francis and Thomas Ayscough, succesively one after another ; And for default of such issue to the right heires of James, with severall other limitations in the said endenture expressed, by Sale of severall lands in the County of Durham, the west part of Sowerby Parke in the parish of Threske and ...., six Oxganges of Land in Newby in com. Ebor. for the payment of the Debts of James, and provision for Robert, John, Christopher, and Allan Ayscough his sons, and the abovesaid daughters of James; upon which said Manours and Lands there was severall Fines and Comon Recoveries levyed and suffered by Allan and Anne his wife, James and Dorothy his wife, Robert and John Ascough his eldest son, to dock all former Settlements, in consideration of which, Allan, James, Francis and Thomas Ayscough releaseth to John Ayscough and the heires males of his body, all their right and title in any the Lands in Thorneton, Stainton, and Worsell in com. Ebor., with a considerable sume of money paid by them to Robert and his sons John and Christopher for all their right and title in any the mann[rs] or Lands in Skewsby, Middleton on Rowe, Sowerby Parke, and Newby, by mediation of Serjeant Archer, now one of y[e] Justices of the Court of Common Pleas, & Joseph Ayliffe Esqr, 21 Jan. 1658 [10 July, 13° Car. 2.] 27 Julij, 1661. 26 Apr. 1662.

VAVASOUR OF HASELWOOD.

ARMS.—Or, a fess dancettée sable, in a canton the badge of a Baronet of England.

CREST—Out of a ducal coronet .... a goat's head ....

...... = ...

Walter Vavasour of Haslewood in com. Ebor. Esqr. = Anne, daughter of Sr Thomas Manners K^{t}, son of Thomas Earle of Rutland.

Frances, wife of Francis Hercy of Scotton Esqr.

Children of Walter Vavasour and Anne:

- 1. Sr Thomas Vavasour of Haslewood Bar^{t}, died ...... = Ursula, daughter of Walter Giffard of Chillington in co. Staff. Esqr.
- 2. Henry Vavasour, a Secular Preist.
- 3. John Vavasour, a Lay Brother in y^{e} Jesuits' Colledge.
- 4. Francis Vavasour, a Franciscan Frier at Doway.
- 5. George, died unmarried.
- 1. Jana, wife of Raphe Hansby of Tickhill in co. Ebor. Esqr.
- 2. Theodosia, 3. Bridget, 4. Anne, died unmarried.
- 5. Mary, a Nunne at Bruxells.
- 6. Frances, wife of James Lawson of Neesam.
- 7. Marg^{t}, a Nunne at Cambray.
- 8. Catherine, a Nunne at Cambray.

Children of Sr Thomas Vavasour and Ursula:

- 1. Sr Walter Vavasour of Haselwood Bar^{t}, Colonell of a Regiment of Horse under the right hob^{le} Will'm Marquesse of Newcastle for the service of K. Charles the first in the times of the late Rebellion, æt. 53 ann. 13 Aug. 1666. = Ursula, daughter of Thomas Visc^{t} Fauconbridge.
- 2. Will'm Vavasour, a Major in that Regim^{t} of Horse under his brother.
- 3. Thomas Vavasour, slayne in y^{e} Bataile of Marston Moore neer Yorke, fighting on the behalfe of K. Ch. the first, a^{o} 1644.
- 4. John Vavasour.
- 5. Peter Vavasour, a Doctor of Phisick. = Elizabeth, daughter of Philip Langdale of Lanthorp in com. Ebor. Esqr.
- 1. Anne.
- 2. Frances, wife of Alphonso Thweng of Kilton Castle in com. Ebor. Esqr.

Children of Sr Walter Vavasour and Ursula:

- 1. Thomas, died in his infancy.
- 2. Walter, æt. 22 ann. 13 Aug. 1666.
- 3. Henry, died in his infancy.
- 4. John, æt. 13 ann. 13 Aug. 1666.
- Ursula, died in her infancy.

Children of Peter Vavasour and Elizabeth:

- 1. Walter.
- 2. ......

AGBRIGG AND MORLEY WAPENTAKE.

Yorke, 13 *Aug*. 1666.

SAVILE OF METHLEY-HALL.

ARMS.—Quarterly of eight:

1. Argent, on a fess sable three owls of the field.
2. Sable, a cross pattée or.
3. Argent, a bend sable between an eagle displayed of the last in chief and a cross fleurée vert in base.
4. Gules, two bars between nine martlets, three, three, and three, argent.
5. Sable, an inescutcheon within an orle of martlets argent.
6. Argent, on a bend gules three escallops or.
7. Gules, two bars-gemelles argent.
8. Argent, a cross moline sable.

Henry Savile, second son of John Savile of Newhall in com. Ebor. = Elizabeth, daughter of Robert Ramsden.

2. S[r] Henry Savile K[t], Provost of Eaton-Colledge juxta Windsor in co. Berks.	= Marg[t], daughter of George Dacres of Chesham in co. Hunt. Esq[r]. (c)	Jane, daughter of Richard Garth of Morden in com. Surr. Esq[r], 1 wife.	= 1. S[r] John Savile Kn[t], one of y[e] Barons of y[e] Exchequer in y[e] time of Qu. Eliz. & K. James. (b)	= Eliz. da. of Thomas Wentworth of Emsall in co. Ebor. Esq[r], 2 wife. (c)	3. Thomas Savile, dyed Proctor of the University of Cambridge a[o] 1592.	1. Jennet, wife of William Wilkinson. 2. Margery, wife of John Clayton of Clay in com. Ebor. 3. Mary, wife of Marmaduke Peirson of ...... in Richmundshire.	4. Elizabeth, wife of John Holdesworth of Astley. 5. Dorothy, wife of Richard Sproxton, Steward of the Starr Chamber.

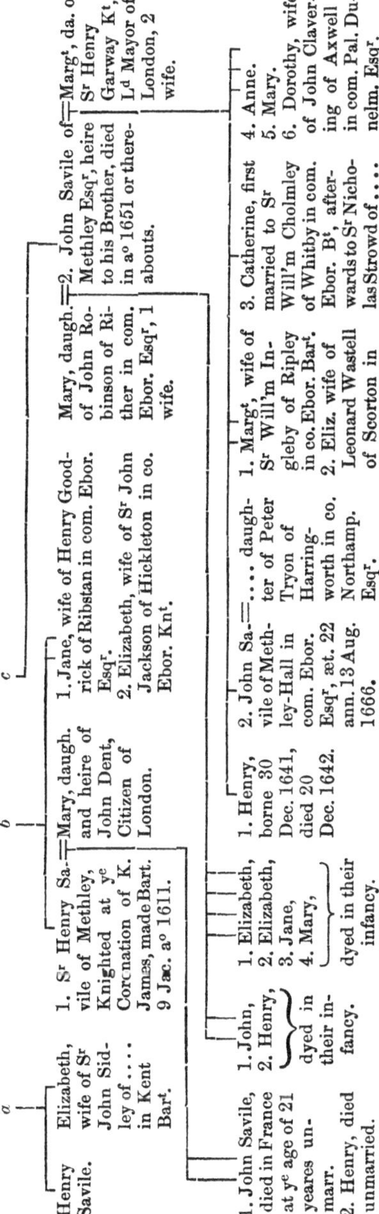
a
b
c
Henry Savile.
Elizabeth, wife of Sr John Sidley of .... in Kent Bart.
1. Sr Henry Savile of Methley, Knighted at ye Coronation of K. James, made Bart. 9 Jac. ao 1611.
Mary, daugh. and heire of John Dent, Citizen of London.
1. Jane, wife of Henry Goodrick of Ribstan in com. Ebor. Esqr.
2. Elizabeth, wife of Sr John Jackson of Hickleton in co. Ebor. Knt.
Mary, daugh. of John Robinson of Rither in com. Ebor. Esqr, 1 wife.
2. John Savile of Methley Esqr, heire to his Brother, died in ao 1651 or thereabouts.
Margt, da. of Sr Henry Garway Kt, Ld Mayor of London, 2 wife.
1. John Savile, died in France at ye age of 21 yeares unmarr.
2. Henry, died unmarried.
1. John,
2. Henry,
dyed in their infancy.
1. Elizabeth,
2. Elizabeth,
3. Jane,
4. Mary,
dyed in their infancy.
1. Henry, borne 30 Dec. 1641, died 20 Dec. 1642.
2. John Savile of Methley-Hall in com. Ebor. Esqr, æt. 22 ann. 13 Aug. 1666.
.... daughter of Peter Tryon of Harringworth in co. Northamp. Esqr.
1. Margt, wife of Sr Will'm Ingleby of Ripley in co. Ebor. Bart.
2. Eliz. wife of Leonard Wastell of Scorton in com. Ebor. Esqr.
3. Catherine, first married to Sr Will'm Cholmley of Whitby in com. Ebor. Bt, afterwards to Sr Nicholas Strowd of .... in Kent, Bart.
4. Anne.
5. Mary.
6. Dorothy, wife of John Claverting of Axwell in com. Pal. Dunelm. Esqr.

CLARO WAPENTAKE. *Yorke*, 13 *Aug*. 1666.

FAVELL OF KEIRBY.

ARMS.—Sable, a chevron between three escallops argent.

Christopher Favell of Burnsey neer Skipton in co. Ebor. = Elizabeth, daughter of ......, widow of Will'm Shute of Shutenooke in the Forrest of Knaresburgh.

James Fauvell of Keireby in the parish of Kirkby Overblows in com. Ebor. died in a° 1653, or thereabouts. = Isabell, daughter of ...... Warde of Monmoth neer Burrougbrigg in com. Ebor.

3. John Favell.

2. Christopher Favell. = Anne, daughter of Robert Rither of Seacroft in com. Ebor.

1. Henry Favell of Kireby, Steward to Algernon Earle of Northumberl^d & Secretary to Oliver Ld Grandison, died circa ann. 1656. = Dorothy, da. of Christopher Wright of Maltby, Sollicitor to George Earle of Cumberl^d.

1. Barbara, wife of .... Brearcliffe of Righton in co. Ebor.

2. Mary, wife of .... Dusheld of Grantley neer Rippon.

3. Marg^t, wife of .... Speare, Harbinger to y^e Prince of Leigne.

Henry Favell, an Atturney at Law. = Katherine, daughter & sole heire of ...... Stocks of Doncaster, widd. of Richard Layton of Barrowby Grange in co. Ebor.

Christopher Favell of Keirby, æt. 25° an. 13 Aug. 1666. = Johanna, da. of John Jaques of ...... in co. Linc. widd. of Thomas Levet of Normanton in com. Ebor.

1. Cecelie, wife of George Gamble of Lofthouse in co. Ebor.

2. Marg^t, wife of Will'm Bennison of Foxholes in co. Ebor.

3. Dorothy.

4. Mary, wife of Tho. Hardisty of Hampsthwayt in com. Ebor.

Margareta de Lund concessit Abbatiæ de Selby redditum xi[d] e terris Alani Fauvell. S. date. Ex Chartulario de Selby.

Edwardus de Fauvell tenet in Thoralby, de Rege in Capite, ut de Honore de Skipton, unum Capitale Messuagium et tres Carucatas, de quibus una carucata et dim. est in Thoralby et Stretton et una carucata et dim. in Broughton. Ex Inquis. Joh. de Kirkeby.

Adam de Fauvell tenet dim. feodum in Stretton. In Lib. feod. mil. 7 Edw. 2. tentorum de Roberto de Clifford.

Robertus de Eston, frater Thomæ, ut filius Johannis, dedit Monachis de Bolton duas carucatas terræ in Hulton, &c. Testibus D'no Joh'e Vavasour, d'no Roberto Plompton, Edwardo Fauvell, Eliâ de Kighley, &c. Ex Chartulario nup. Edwardi Plumpton militis.

Richardus Fauvell tenet septem carucatas in Steton. Robertus Fauvell tenet tres carucatas in Fearnhill in Conyngley. Esc. 12. E. 2. n° 41. post mortem Margaretæ de Nevill.

D. Henricus de Kighley tenet 1. carucat. in Skipton, et Constantinus Fauvell tenet dim. car. In Rentali incerti temporis.

In Stainford sunt quatuor carucatæ, quarum Abbas de Selby tenet 1. carucatam et sex bovatas de hæred. D. Percy, et ille de Rege, Constantinus Fauvell et Alicia uxor ejus tenent decem bovatas de W° Maleverer, et tres de Radulfo de Normanvill, et Radulfus de hærede de Percy. Inquis. Joh's de Kirkby.

In Broughton Constantinus Fauvell tenet 1. carucatam. Et infra, Constantinus Fauvell 1. bovatam, et Ric. de Fauvell thorp quinq. bovatas. Inq. Joh'is de Kirkby. In Stretton Ric. Fauvell tenet dimid. carucatam; Adam Fauvell tres bovatas; Everardus Fauvell sex bovatas. Ibid.

Juratores dicunt, quod Everardus Fauvell tenuit die quo obijt de Honore de Skipton 1. messuagium et tres carucatas in dominico et servicio ; de quibus una carucata in Thoralby et Stretton, et 1. carucata in Broghton, et 1. carucata in Stretton in servicio ; et Thomas est filius et heres æt. 40 annor. Esc. 1. E. 2. n° 28.

SKYRACK WAPENTAKE. *Yorke*, 13º *Aug*. 1666.

BLAND OF KIPPAX-PARKE.

ARMS.—Quarterly of ten:

1. Argent, on a bend sable three pheons of the field.
2. Sable, six escallops or, three, two, and one.
3. Azure, a cross fleurée or.
4. Barry of ten azure and argent, on a canton or a martlet sable.
5. Argent, on a fess azure three fleurs-de-lis or.
6. Barry of six ermine and gules, three crescents sable.
7. Gules, a lion rampant argent.
8. Sable, a chevron between three leopard's faces argent.
9. Sable, three pheons argent, a chief of the second.
10. Argent, a chevron gules between three boar's heads couped sable tusked or.

CRESTS.—Out of a ducal coronet or a lion's head tenné.

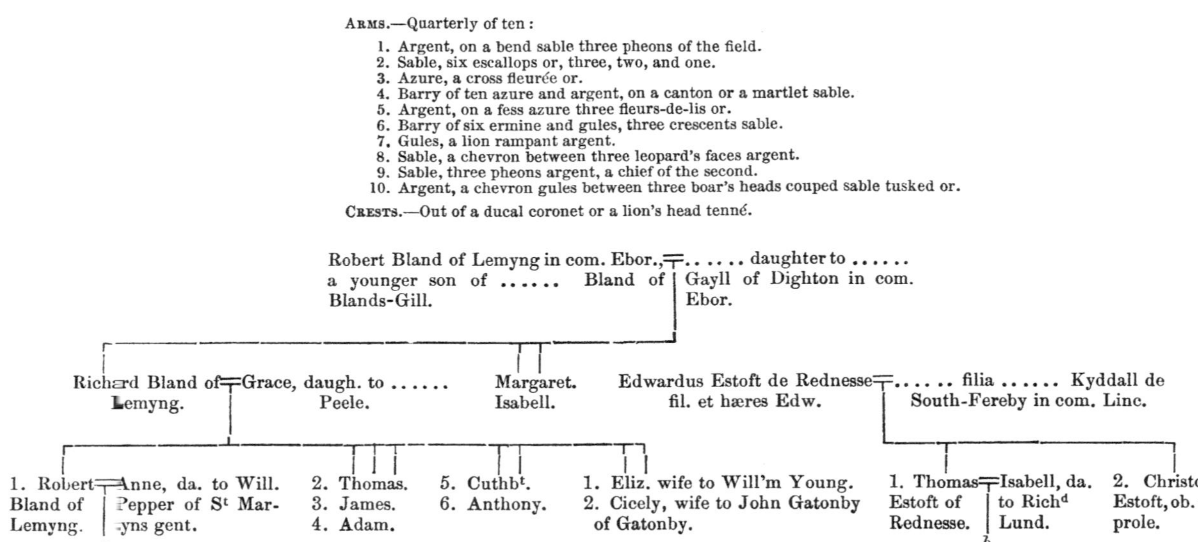

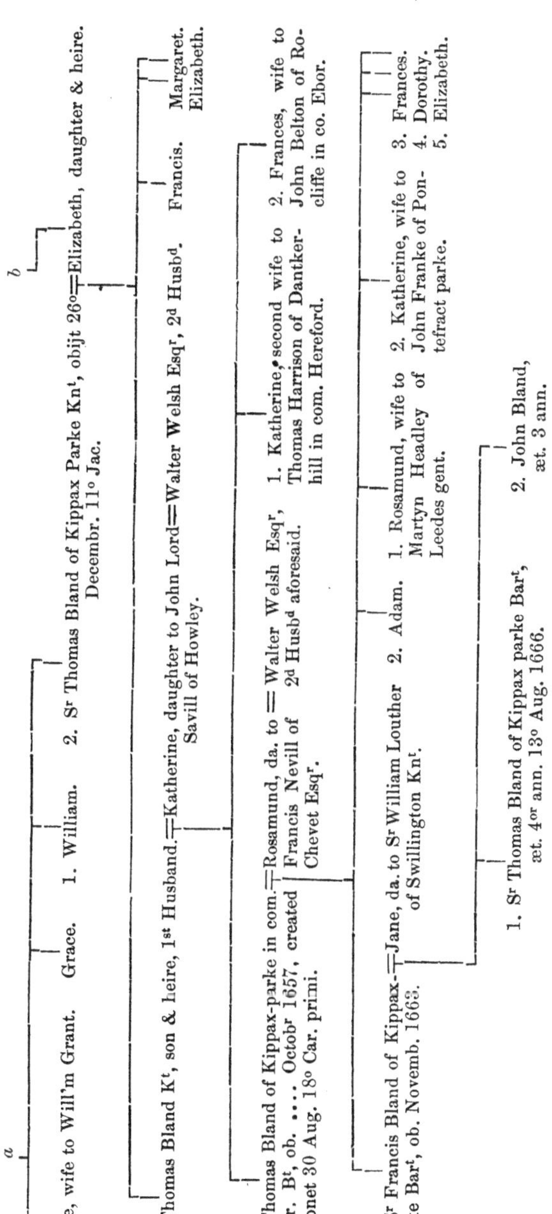

a
b
Jane, wife to Will'm Grant.
Grace.
1. William.
2. Sr Thomas Bland of Kippax Parke Knt, obijt 26o Decembr. 11o Jac.
Elizabeth, daughter & heire.
Sr Thomas Bland Kt, son & heire, 1st Husband.
Katherine, daughter to John Lord Savill of Howley.
Walter Welsh Esqr, 2d Husbd.
Francis.
Margaret.
Elizabeth.
Sr Thomas Bland of Kippax-parke in com. Ebor. Bt, ob. .... Octobr 1657, created Baronet 30 Aug. 18o Car. primi.
Rosamund, da. to Francis Nevill of Chevet Esqr.
Walter Welsh Esqr, 2d Husbd aforesaid.
1. Katherine, second wife to Thomas Harrison of Dantker-hill in com. Hereford.
2. Frances, wife to John Belton of Ro-cliffe in co. Ebor.
1. Sr Francis Bland of Kippax-parke Bart, ob. Novemb. 1663.
Jane, da. to Sr William Louther of Swillington Knt.
2. Adam.
1. Rosamund, wife to Martyn Headley of Leedes gent.
2. Katherine, wife to John Franke of Pon-tefract parke.
3. Frances.
4. Dorothy.
5. Elizabeth.
1. Sr Thomas Bland of Kippax parke Bart, æt. 4or ann. 13o Aug. 1666.
2. John Bland, æt. 3 ann.

BARKESTON-ASH WAP. *Yorke*, 13° *Aug.* 1666.

TINDALL OF BROTHERTON.

ARMS.—Quarterly:
1. Argent, a fess dancettée gules, in chief three crescents of the second.
2. Or, a lion rampant gules.
3. Gules, six escallops argent, three, two, and one.
3. .... three fleurs-de-lis ....

CREST.—Out of a ducal coronet or a plume of five ostrich feathers ermine banded of the last.

John Tindall of Brotherton in co. Ebor. Esqr. = Dorothy, daughter of Martin Anne of Frickley in co. Ebor.

Their issue:
- 1. Francis Tindall of Brotherton Esqr, dyed in a° 1637 or thereabouts. = Edith, daughter and sole heire to Leonard Reresby of Barnburgh, third son to Lionell Reresby of Thribergh in com. Ebor. Esqr.
- 2. Will'm Tindall.
- 3. Barthelmew Tindall, married Mary, da. of ...... Farmer of Hamilton, ob. s. prole.

Issue of Francis and Edith:
- 1. Henry Tindall, obijt patre vivo. = Lucie, da. of Sr John Jackson of Edderthorpe in com. Ebor. K^t, one his Maties Councell at Yorke for y^e Northern Parts of this Realme.
- 2. Leonard Tindall, Lieuten^t Coll. under Sr John Ramsden Kn^t in the service of K. Charles 1st.
- 3. George.
- 4. Francis Tindall, marr. .... da. & coh. of .... Palmer of .... in co. Linc.
- 5. John, died unmarr.
- 1. Anne, wife of Edward Lowdon of Wrenthorpe in co. Ebor.
- 2. Eliz. wife of John Cartwright of Wheatley Woods in co. Ebor.
- 3. Cath. wife of John Lincoln.
- 4. Mary.
- 5. Ellen.

Issue of Henry and Lucie:
- Bradwardine Tindall of Brotherton Esqr, æt. 27 annor. 13 Aug. 1666. = Mary, daughter and sole heire of Francis Bayldon of Bayldon in co. Ebor. Esqr.
- Will'm Tindall, Citizen of London.
- Lucie, wife of Sr Will'm Jobson of Cudworth, Bar^t of Nova Scotia. =
- Fienes Tindall (a daughter) died unmarr.

Issue of Lucie and Sr Will'm Jobson:
- Thomas, dyed in his infancy.
- 1. Elizabeth.
- 2. Lucie.

Yorke, 13° *Aug.* 1666.

HORNE OF MEXBURGH.

ARMS.—Or, a fess between two chevrons gules, each chevron between three bugle-horns sable stringed azure.

Cotton Horne of Hemsworth, Bayliff to S[r] Cotton Gargreave of Nostall in co. Ebor. = ...

Cotton Horne of Hemsworth in com. Ebor. = Jane, daughter to ...... Burton of Kinsley-parke in com. Eborū.

- 4. Francis Horn of Almondsbury in co. Ebor. = Mary, daugh. to Robert Pickles.
- 3. Richard, dyed unmarried.
- 2. Will. Horn of Havercroft in com. Ebor. = Ellen, daugh. to Will. Wood of Warldsend in y[e] parish of Ecclesfield in co. Ebor.
  - William.
- 1. Cotton Horn, Steward of the Honour of Pontefract. = Eliz. da. to Anth. Wade of Kingcrosse neer Hallifax in co. Ebor.
  - .... 2[d] wife. = 1. Will'm Horn of Mexburgh, æt. 50 an. 13° Aug. 1666. = Sarah, daugh. to John Sykes of Leedes, 1st wife.
    - 2. William
    - 3. Alexander.
    - 4. Benjamin.
    - 1. Judith, wife to Nicholas Maskall of Yorke.
    - 2. Elizabeth.
    - 3. Sarah.
    - 1. Thomas Horn, æt. 24 an. 1666. = Mary, daughter to .... Eyre of Stroxton in co. Linc.
      - Anne.
  - 2. John Horn of Wakefield in co. Ebor. = Elizabeth, daughter to .... Parker of Ottley in co. Ebor.
    - William.
    - 1. Agnes.
    - 2. Judith.
    - 3. Elizabeth.
  - Judith.
  - Mary, wife to Lucian Lewins of Rusholme in co. Ebor.
- 1. Anne, wife to Frances Heaton of Morehouse in co. Ebor.
- 2. Elizabeth, wife to Samuell Norfolke of South-Hindley in com. Ebor.

OSGODCROSSE WAPENTAKE. *Yorke*, 13° *Aug*. 1666.

HAMERTON OF PRESTON-JACKLYN.

ARMS.—Argent, on a chevron between three hammers sable a trefoil slipped or.

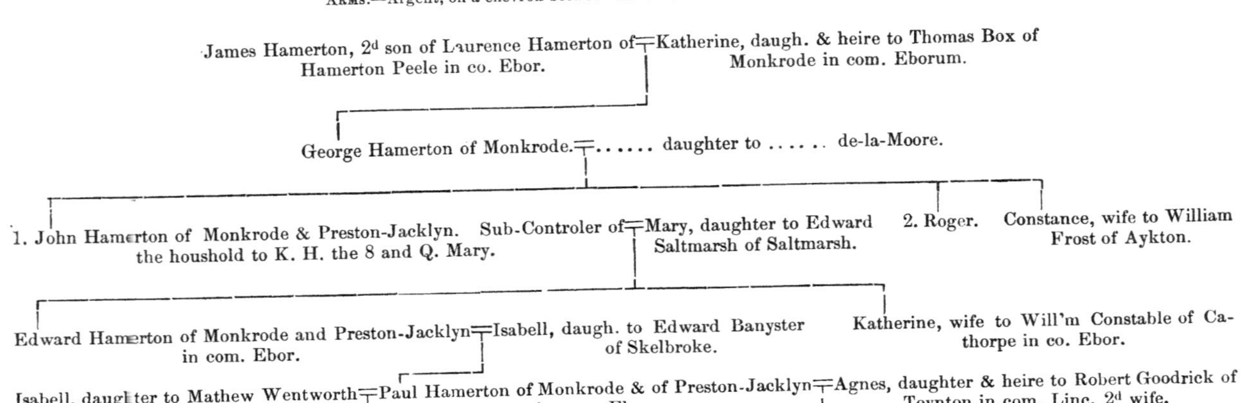

James Hamerton, 2d son of Laurence Hamerton of Hamerton Peele in co. Ebor. ═ Katherine, daugh. & heire to Thomas Box of Monkrode in com. Eborum.

George Hamerton of Monkrode. ═ ...... daughter to ...... de-la-Moore.

1. John Hamerton of Monkrode & Preston-Jacklyn. Sub-Controler of the houshold to K. H. the 8 and Q. Mary. ═ Mary, daughter to Edward Saltmarsh of Saltmarsh.

2. Roger.

Constance, wife to William Frost of Aykton.

Edward Hamerton of Monkrode and Preston-Jacklyn in com. Ebor. ═ Isabell, daugh. to Edward Banyster of Skelbroke.

Katherine, wife to Will'm Constable of Cathorpe in co. Ebor.

Isabell, daughter to Mathew Wentworth of Bretton Esq[r], 1st wife. ═ Paul Hamerton of Monkrode & of Preston-Jacklyn in com. Ebor. ═ Agnes, daughter & heire to Robert Goodrick of Toynton in com. Linc. 2[d] wife.

a *b*

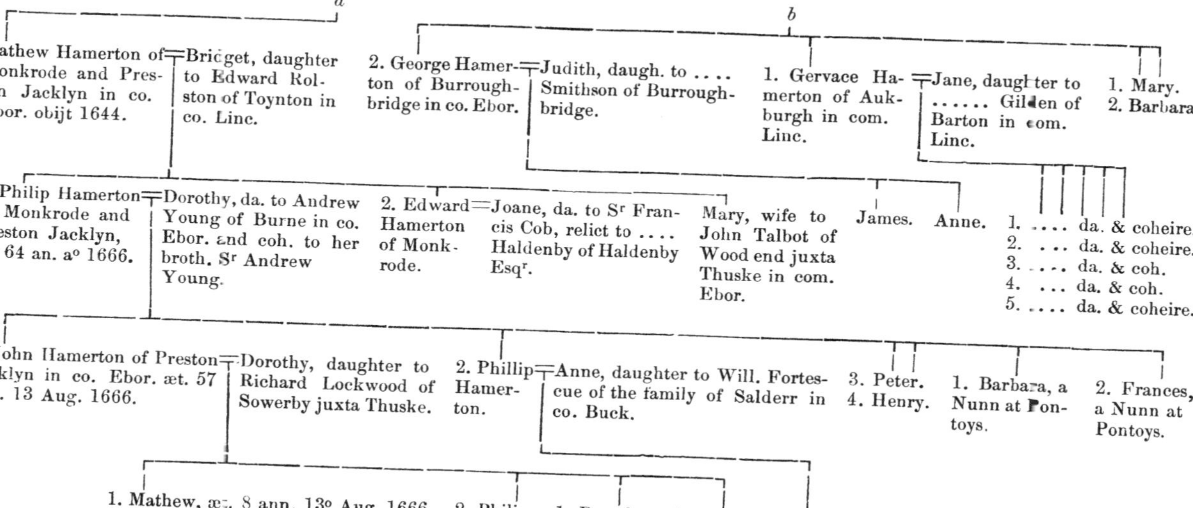
a
b
Mathew Hamerton of Monkrode and Preston Jacklyn in co. Ebor. obijt 1644.
Bricget, daughter to Edward Rolston of Toynton in co. Linc.
2. George Hamerton of Burroughbridge in co. Ebor.
Judith, daugh. to .... Smithson of Burroughbridge.
1. Gervace Hamerton of Aukburgh in com. Linc.
Jane, daughter to ...... Gilden of Barton in com. Linc.
1. Mary.
2. Barbara.
1. Philip Hamerton of Monkrode and Preston Jacklyn, æt. 64 an. aº 1666.
Dorothy, da. to Andrew Young of Burne in co. Ebor. and coh. to her broth. Sr Andrew Young.
2. Edward Hamerton of Monkrode.
Joane, da. to Sr Francis Cob, relict to .... Haldenby of Haldenby Esqr.
Mary, wife to John Talbot of Wood end juxta Thuske in com. Ebor.
James.
Anne.
1. .... da. & coheire.
2. ... da. & coheire.
3. .... da. & coh.
4. ... da. & coh.
5. .... da. & coheire.
1. John Hamerton of Preston Jacklyn in co. Ebor. æt. 57 ann. 13 Aug. 1666.
Dorothy, daughter to Richard Lockwood of Sowerby juxta Thuske.
2. Phillip Hamerton.
Anne, daughter to Will. Fortescue of the family of Salderr in co. Buck.
3. Peter.
4. Henry.
1. Barbara, a Nunn at Pontoys.
2. Frances, a Nunn at Pontoys.
1. Mathew, æt. 8 ann. 13º Aug. 1666.
2. Philip.
1. Dorothy.
2. Frances.
Phillip, æt. unius anni 1666.

OSGODCROSSE WAPENTAKE.

Yorke, 13° *Aug.* 1666.

KELLAM OF PONTEFRACT.

ARMS.—Gules, a bicorporate lion gardant, sejant counter-sejant coward, or, ducally crowned azure, within a bordure argent.
D. 4. fol. 8 a. in Off. Armor.

[A]

¶ ...... Kellom vel Kyllom de Hickleton. ╤ Agnes, filia et cohæres, habuit Hickleton.

1. Thomas Kyllom sold Hickleton. ╤ ....

2. Andreas Kyllom de Cudworth in com. Ebor. 30 H. 8.

Francis Killom, 4 and 5 P. and M. ╤ ....

Francis Killam of Hickleton, ob. circa an. 1610. ╤ Elizabeth, daughter to Thomas Normanvill of Billingley in com. Ebor. gent.

1. John Killam of London, publique Notary, died unmarried.

2. Bartholomew Killam of London, dyed unmarried.

3. Stephen Kellam of of Rother- in co. Ebor. ╤ ...... daughter to Gervace Westall of Grelbrooke in com. Ebor. — a

4. William Kellam, Alderman of Pontefract, ætat. 76 an. 15 Aug. a° 1666. ╤ Anne, daughter to Stephen Cooper, Alderman of Pontefract. — b

Dorothy, wife to George Berry, Citizen of London.

ARMS.—Argent, a lion rampant sable ducally gorged and crowned or.

¶ Roger de Preston, d'n's de Hickleton et Preston super montem in co. Ebor. sans date. ╤ ......

Adā Preston, 6 Edw. 1. ╤ ......

Adā de Preston, 11° E. 2. = Idonea, soror et hæres Henrici de Potterton, d'ni de Rouhall in com. Eborum.

Roger, frater Adæ. ╤ Agnes.

1. Willielmus, filius Rogeri de Preston, 33 E. 3, 8 R. 2. ╤ Agnes.

2. Alexander, 20 R. 2.

3. Adā, 33 E. 3.

Rogerus de Preston, 10 H. 4. ╤ ......

Thomas de Preston, 6 E. 4. ╤ Agnes.

Agnes, filia et cohæres, habuit Hickleton.
[A]

Katherina, filia & cohæres, habuit Preston & Rouhall. = Joh'es Anne de Frickley arm.

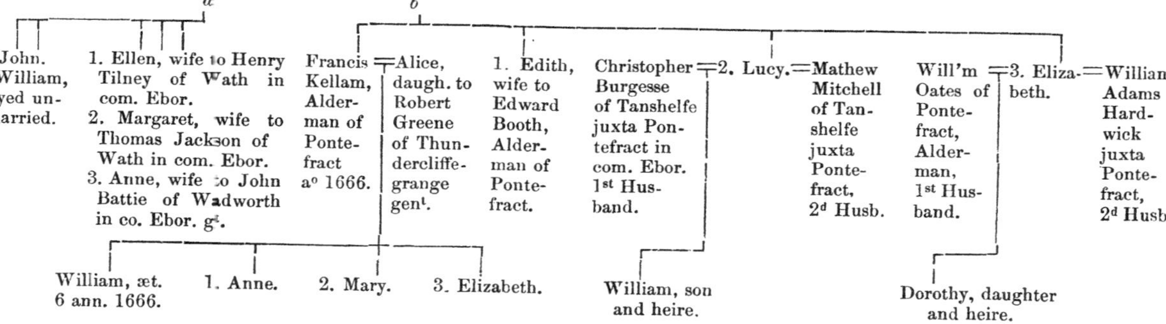

a

1. John.
2. William, dyed unmarried.

1. Ellen, wife to Henry Tilney of Wath in com. Ebor.
2. Margaret, wife to Thomas Jackson of Wath in com. Ebor.
3. Anne, wife to John Battie of Wadworth in co. Ebor. g[t].

b

Francis Kellam, Alderman of Pontefract a° 1666. = Alice, daugh. to Robert Greene of Thundercliffe-grange gen[t].

William, æt. 6 ann. 1666.
1. Anne.
2. Mary.
3. Elizabeth.

1. Edith, wife to Edward Booth, Alderman of Pontefract.

Christopher Burgesse of Tanshelfe juxta Pontefract in com. Ebor. 1st Husband. = 2. Lucy. = Mathew Mitchell of Tanshelfe juxta Pontefract, 2[d] Husb.

William, son and heire.

Will'm Oates of Pontefract, Alderman, 1st Husband. = 3. Elizabeth. = William Adams of Hardwick juxta Pontefract, 2[d] Husb[d].

Dorothy, daughter and heire.

Yorke, 13° *Aug.* 1666.

BOOTH OF PONTEFRACT.

ARMS.—Argent, three boar's heads erect and erased within a border engrailed sable.

CREST.—A lion passant ducally gorged ....

¶ Robert Booth of Glossop in com. Derbiæ. = Jane, daughter to .... Bramhall.

- 1. John Booth of Glossop in co. Derb. ob. a° 1636. = Dorothy, daugh. to Allan Austwick of Pontefract.
- 2. Nicholas Booth of Pontefract. = Jane, daughter of John Tatham of Pontefract.
  - 1. Gervace, an Ensign bearer under the Lord Vere in the Netherlands.
  - 2. John Booth, Leivet[nt] of Horse under the Duke of Ormond in Ireland, a serv[t] to D[r] Usher, Arch B[pp] of Armagh. = Jane, da. to .... Walker of Wakefield.
    - Robert Booth.
  - 3. William Booth, Keeper of Pontefract-parke 13 Aug. 1666. = Ellen, daughter of Robert Wildman.
    - Ellen, dyed unmarr.
  - 4. George, dyed in Pontefract Castle during the seige their.
  - 5. Thomas Booth of Pomfret. = Mary, daughter to John Turner of Pontefract.
  - 6. Edward Booth, Alder. of Pomfret, a° 1666. = Edith, da. to. Will'm Kellam, Alder. of Pomfret.
    - William Booth.
    - 1. Sarah.
    - 2. Elizabeth.
    - 3. Jane.
  - 7. Robert Booth of Seazey. = Katherine da. to Will. Nelson of Thorpfield neer Thuske in co. Ebor.
    - 1. Emanuell.
    - 2. Robert.
    - 3. Will'm.
    - 4. Timothy.
    - 5. Joseph.
    - 6. John.
    - Elizabeth.
    - Mary, wife to Samuell Halleley of Turnbridg in co. Ebor.
  - 1. Anne, wife to John Wagstaff of Glossop.
  - 2. Elizabeth, wife to Richard More of Carleton.
  - 3. Marg[t]. wife to William Collet of Fetherston.
  - 4. Mary, wife to Edward Methley.
  - 5. Jane, wife to George Crosland.
- 3. George Booth of Glossop. = ...
  - Thomas Booth of Glossop.

 Hull, 18 *Sept.* 1666.

CORBET OF KINGSTON UPON HULL.

ARMS.—Or, a raven sable.
Respite for proofe of the descent from Corbet of Shropshire.

Thomas Corbet of Agnes Burton in com. Ebor., came out of Staffordshire. = ...

- 1. William Corbet of Bridlington in com. Ebor. obijt aº 1638. = Alice, daughter to Thomas Rode of Rode in co. Cestr. Esqr.
  - 2. Thomas Corbet of Bridlington. = Anne, daughter to Thomas Ricaby of Bridlington Key in com. Ebor.
    - 1. Henry Corbet of Kingston upon Hull, Dr of Phisick, æt. 41 ann. 1666. = Euphemia, daugh. & heire to Peter Paulin of Rudston in co. Ebor.
      - 1. Thomas Corbet, ætatis 13 a. 18º Sept. 1666.
      - 2. William, æt. 7º annor. 1666.
      - 3. Henry, æt. 2 annor. 1666.
      - 1. Anne. 2. Mary. 3. Elizabeth.
- 2. Francis Corbet, Rector of Pottrington in Holdernesse in com. Ebor. = Anne, daughter to .... Lamplough of Leverston in co. Ebor.
  - 1. Elizabeth. 2. Alice. 3. Faith. 4. Francis.
  - William Corbet, æt. 16 ann. 1666.
  - 1. Elizabeth. 2. Anne. 3. Naoma. 4. Fayth.
- 3. Henry Corbet of Agnes Burton in com. Ebor. = Mary, da. of ...... Penyfather of Burton in com. Staff.
  - Thomas Corbet, ætatis 26 an. 1666.

TEMPEST OF BROUGHTON.

ARMS.—Quarterly:

1 and 4. Argent, a bend between six martlets sable, an annulet for difference.
2. Argent, a fess between six martlets sable.
3. Argent bordured with demi-fleurs-de-lis azure, a lion rampant gules.

CREST.—A griffin's head erased, per pale wavy argent and sable, beaked gules, an annulet for difference.

Anne, daughter to Edmund Eltofts of Farnhull in com. Ebor. Esqr. = Sr Stephen Tempest of ..... in co. Ebor. Kn^t. = Katherine, daughter to Henry Lawson of Neesham in Epātu Dunel. Esqr.

Children of Sir Stephen and Anne:

- 1. Anne, wife to Henry Yonge of Hebden in com. Ebor. gent.
- 2. Frances, wife to Simon Blackey of Blackey in co. Lanc. gent.
- 3. Isabell, wife to Francis Malham of Elslake in co. Ebor.
- 4. Jane, died unmarr.
- ...... / ...... dyed young.

Children of Sir Stephen and Katherine:

- 1. Roger, dyed young.
- 2. Stephen Tempest of .... = (1) Susan, da. & coh. to Will. Ogletharp of Roundey grange in co. Ebor. Esqr, 1st wife. (a) = (2) Frances, da. to .... Gargrave of Nostell in com. Ebor, ob. s. prole, second wife.
- 3. Thomas, dyed unmarried.
- 4. Richard Tempest. = Elizabeth, daugh. to Nicholas Grymshaw of Clayton de-la-Mares in com. Lanc. Esqr. (b)
- 5. George Tempest of ...... = Frances, wid. to Will'm Baildon of Baildon in com. Ebor. Esqr.
- 6. Robt Tempest of ...., Capt. of a Foot Company in the service of K. Ch. the first, & slayn in his wares. = Thomasine, wid. to Nicholas Michell.
- 7. James, 8. Henry, dyed young.
- 9. John Tempest, Major of a Regim^t of Horse in the service of K. Charles the first, slayne at the taking of Tredagh in Irel^d.

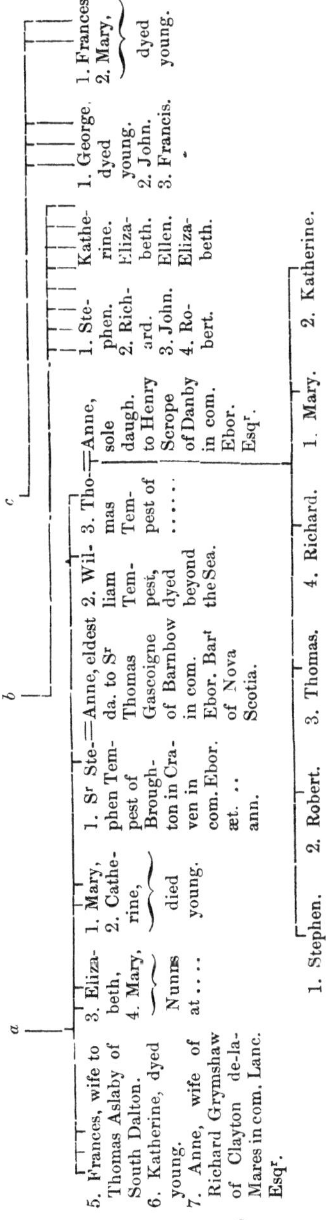
a
b
c
5. Frances, wife to Thomas Aslaby of South Dalton.
6. Katherine, dyed young.
7. Anne, wife of Richard Grymshaw of Clayton de-la-Mares in com. Lanc. Esqr.
3. Eliza-beth,
4. Mary,
Nunns at . . . .
1. Mary,
2. Cathe-rine,
died young.
1. Sr Ste-phen Tem-pest of Brough-ton in Cra-ven in com. Ebor. æt. . . ann.
Anne, eldest da. to Sr Thomas Gascoigne of Barnbow in com. Ebor. Bart of Nova Scotia.
2. Wil-liam Tem-pest, dyed beyond the Sea.
3. Tho-mas Tem-pest of . . . . . .
Anne, sole daugh. to Henry Scrope of Danby in com. Ebor. Esqr.
1. Ste-phen.
2. Rich-ard.
3. John.
4. Ro-bert.
Kathe-rine.
Eliza-beth.
Ellen.
Eliza-beth.
1. George, dyed young.
2. John.
3. Francis.
1. Frances,
2. Mary,
dyed young.
1. Stephen.
2. Robert.
3. Thomas.
4. Richard.
1. Mary.
2. Katherine.

PICKERING LITH WAPENTAKE. *Malton*, 29° *Sept.* 1666.

HORSLEY OF BECKHOUSE.

ARMS.—Gules, three horse's heads couped argent, bridled sable.

William Horsley.=....

2. Thomas.
3. Jeremiah.

1. Robert Horsley of Beckhouse in com. Ebor.=Elizabeth, daughter to .... Gidney of Ancaster in com. Lincolniæ.

William Horsley of Beckhouse in com. Ebor. obijt a° 1637.=Elizabeth, daughter to Richard Waynd of Foutroyst in com. Ebor.

Elizabeth, daughter and sole heire to John Agard of Stockton in co. Ebor. second wife.=William Horsley of Beckhouse in co. Ebor. æt. 28 ann. 1666.=Anne, eldest daugh. to Roger Wilberfosse of Wilberfosse in co. Ebor. 1st wife.

2. Mary, dyed young. 1. Anne. William Horsley, ætatis unius anni. Elizabeth, dyed young.

BUCKROSE WAPENTAKE. *Yorke*, 13° *Aug.* 1666.

MOUNTAIGNE OF WESTOW.

ARMS.—Barry-lozengy or and azure, on a chief gules three cross-crosslets of the first.
CREST.—A crane's head issuing out of rays, all or.

Thomas Mountaigne of Westow in co. Ebor.=.... daughter to .... Hungate of Saxton in co. Ebor.

1. George Mountaigne, Arch-Bisshop of Yorke.

2. Isaak Mountaigne of Westow in co. Ebor. obijt a° 1648.=Elizabeth, daughter to Thomas Bell of Rochester in Kent.

1. George Mountaigne of Westow in com. Ebor. Esqr, æt. 46 annor. a° 1666.=Mary, 4th daughter to Sr Thomas Gore of Stitnam in co. Ebor. Kt & Bt.

2. James Mountaigne.=Mary, daughter to William Wiggoner of Whitby Merchant.

3. Richard Mountaigne.

1. Elizabeth, æt. 17° ann. 1666. 2. Catherine, ætatis 14° an. 1666.

OUSE & DARWENT WAPENTAKE. *Yorke*, 13° *Aug.* 1666.

JENKYN OF GRIMSTON.

ARMS.—Or, a lion rampant regardant sable.
CREST.—On a mural coronet sable a lion passant regardant or.

John Jenkyn of the Citty of Yorke Esqr. = Margaret, daugh. to ...... Carance, an Ittallian.

Sr Henry Jenkyn of Busby in co. Ebor. K^{t}, living 1612. = Dorothy, daughter & heire to Will'm Tanckard of .... Esqr.

1. Mary, wife to Thomas Scudamore Esqr, Receiver generall of Yorke.
2. Margaret, wife to William Robinson, Alderman of Yorke.

1. Will'm Jenkyn, dyed wthout issue.

2. Toby Jenkyn of Grimston in co. Ebor. Esqr, ætat. 52 ann. 1666. = Anthonyna, da. to Henry Wickham, D^{r} in Divinity, & one of the Prebend^{s} of St Peters Cathedr.

3. Henry a Sergeant Major in the Army of K. Charles y^{e} 1st, died wthout issue.

1. Anne.
2. Dorothy.
3. Grace.

1. Henry Jenkyn, dyed in Spane a° 1665.
2. William Jenkyn, æt. 16 an. 1666.
3. Toby, æt. 6 ann. 1666.

1. Anthonyna.
2. Elizabeth, dyed young
3. Dorothy.

BUCKROSE WAPENTAKE. *Malton*, 29 *Sept.* 1666.

CARTER OF SETTRINGTON.

ARMS.—Quarterly :
1 and 4. Azure, a talbot passant between three round buckles or.
2 and 3. Argent, four lions passant in bend double-cotised sable.

CREST.—A lion's head erased or, frettée sable.
No proofe made of this Crest.

John Carter of Lisle neer Luton in co. Bedf. = Prudence, daughter & coheire to Sr Philip Hawtre of Luton Kn^{t}.

Abraham Carter of Lisle aforesaid, dyed in a° 1612. = Elizabeth, daugh. to ...... Carlton of ......

John Carter of Settrington in com. Ebor. D^{r} in Divinity, ætat. 59 an. 1666. = Frances, eldest daughter to Will'm Fuller, Deane of Durhã.

1. Charles, ætatis 16° ann. 29° Sept. 1666.
2. John, æt. 9° ann. 1666.
3. William, æt. unius anni a° 1666.

1. Elizabeth.
2. Katherine.
3. Prudence.
4. Frances.

BULMER WAPENTAKE. *Yorke*, 13° *Aug.* 1666.

ATKINSON OF SKELTON.

ARMS.—Ermine, on a fess .... three pheons ....

No proofe made of these Armes.

Richard Atkinson of Thrintoft in com. Ebor. obijt circa annum 1600. = Margaret, daughter to ...... Lumley.

- 1. Simon.
- 2. Thomas Atkynson of Yorke, obijt ætat. suæ 63 a° 1656. = (1) Elizabeth, daugh. to Rowland Ward of the Citty of Yorke, gent. 1st wife. = (2) Margaret, daughter to John Dodsworth of Watlas, in com. Ebor. second wife.
  - (by 1st wife):
    - 1. Arthur Atkinson of Skelton in co. Ebor. æt. 45 an. a° 1666. = Beatrix, da. to Tho. Lovell of Skelton in co. Ebor. Esqr.
      - Margaret, Rebecha, dyed young.
      - Margaret. Susanna. Jane. Mary. Elizabeth.
      - Thomas Atkinson, æt. 15 an. 1666.
      - Arthur, dyed young.
    - 2. Phenyas Atkinson of Belthrop in co. Ebor. = Frances, da. to Will. Harper of B^pp Wilton in co. Ebor. Esqr.
    - 3. William Atkinson, Citizen & Grocer of Londō. = Barbara, da. to ... Hobson of Kirk-Merrington in Epātu. Dunelm.
    - 1. Philadelphia, mar. to Tho. Lovell, eldest son to Thomas Lovell of Skelton Esqr.
    - 2. Jane, mar. to Richard Ellerker of Youlton in co. Ebor. Esqr.
  - (by 2nd wife):
    - 1 Marg^t, wife to John Lambert of Strensall in com. Ebor. gent.
    - 2. Winifred.
    - 3. Mary.
- 3. George.

Yorke, 13° *Aug.* 1666.

SHAW OF SHEPPARD-CASTLE.

ARMS.—Vert, a chevron between three covered cups or.
Qu. for proofe of these Armes.

John Shaw of Hall-Broom in com. Ebor. = Elizabeth ....

1. William Shaw, dyed young.

2. John Shaw of Hall-Broom in com. Ebor. = Emot, daughter to Nicholas Stead of Onsacre.

Dorothy, daughter to George Heathcoat of Calthorp Hall in co. Derb. first wife. = John Shaw of Sheppard-Castle in com Ebor. æt. 57 ann. 1666. = ... daughter to ...... Stillington of Kelfield in co. Ebor. Esqr. 2^d^ wife.

Children by the first wife:

1. Emot, mar. to Francis Blunt of Kingston upon Hull.
2. Dorothy, mar. to Jonathan Staynforth of Rotheram in co. Ebor.
3. Rebeca, mar. to Richard Sheldon of Monyash in com. Derbiæ.
4. Rachell, mar. to Francis Burdet of Wolley in com. Ebor.
5. Hesther, mar. to Humphry Marler of Manchester in co. Lanc.
6. Ruth, mar. to George Dale of Monyashall in com. Derb.

Children by the second wife:

John Shaw æt. 3 ann. 1666.

7. Marg^t^, æt. 5 an. 1666.

Yorke, 13° *Aug.* 1666.

LLOYD OF HARDWICK.

ARMS.—Per fess argent and gules, a lion rampant counterchanged, a canton azure.

David Lloyd of Towyn in com. ...... = ... daughter to Mathew Price of Trenewith Esqr, sister to Sr John.

Thomas Lloyd of Kilnach in com. Cardigan, æt. 70 an. 1666. = Mary, daughter to David Lloyd of Kryngbryn in co. Cardigan Esqr.

Richard Lloyd of Hardwick mannour in com. Ebor. æt. 44 ann. 1666. = Mary, daughter to Aaron Belt of .... neer Hallifax in com. Ebor.

1. Richard, ætat. 11 ann. 1666.
2. Samuell, æt. 5 ann. a° 1666.
1. Mary, æt. 16 ann. 1666.
2. Anne, æt. 15 ann. 1666.
3. Margaret, ætatis 13 ann. 1666.

BIRDFIRTH WAPENTAKE. *Yorke*, 13° *Aug*. 1666.

CHAMBER OF OULSTON.

ARMS.—Or, a cross ermines between four birds azure, on a chief of the last a serpent coroné devouring a woman or between two roses gules.

No proofe made of these Armes.

Robert Chamber of the Haws in com. Westmerl. vixit 19° H. 8. = Jane, daughter and coheire to Thomas Washington of Hallid Hall in co. Westmerl[d].

Walter Chamber of the Hawes in co. Westmerl. = Anne, da. to ...... Travers of Nateby in com. Lanc. Esq[r].

2. Anne, wife to Christopher Bainbrigg of ...... in com. Westmerl.

1. Mary, wife to ...... Ripley, Alderman of Rippon in co. Ebor.

Allan Chamber of the Hawes in co. Westmerl., ob. ætatis suæ 50 a° 1613. = Anne, daughter to John Carlton of Beeforth in com. Eborum gent.

6. James, 7. Allan, dyed young.

3. John, 4. Thomas, 5 Christoph[r], dyed young.

2. Robert.

1. Walter Chamber of the Hawes in com. Westmerl., ob. æt. suæ 68 a° 1666. = Elizabeth, da. to Will. Prickett of Natland in co. Westmerl.

1. Anne, wife to Allen Pricket of Natland in co. Westmerl.

2. Marg[t], wife to Jeffrey Braythwayt of Beamond-Hall in com. Lanc.

3. Helen, wife to Thomas Smith of Kendall in com. Westmerl.

3. Elizabeth. 4. Margaret.

1. Anne. 2. Dorothy.

1. Allan Chamber of Oulston in com. Ebor., æt. 50 ann. 1666. = Dorothy, daughter to James Moore of Angram in com Ebor. gent.

2. Robert. 3. Edward.

4. William, dyed young.

4. Allan.

3 Robert, dyed young.

2. James, æt. 5 ann. 1666.

1. Thomas Chamber, ætatis 6 ann. 13° Aug. 1666.

HARTHILL WAPENTAKE. *Kingston upon Hull*, 18 *Sept.* 1666.

LAMBERT OF KINGSTON UPON HULL.

ARMS.—Gules, on a chevron between three lambs passant argent a trefoil slipped ...., a chief checky or and azure.

William Lambert, who came out of Craven in co. Ebor. = ...

Anthony Lambert of Holme in Spaldingmore. = ...

Robert Lambert of Kingston sup. Hull, æt. 60 ann. 1666. = ...

1. Robert Lambert, ætatis 38 ann. 1666.

2. Anthony Lambert of Kingston upon Hull in co. Ebor. = Anne, daughter to George Saltmarsh of Kingston upon Hull.

1. Anthony Lambert, æt. 9 an. 1666. 2. George, æt. 5 an. 1666. 3. Henry, æt. unius anni. Anne. Dorothy.

AGBRIGG AND MORLEY WAP. *Hallifax*, 2° *Apr.* 1666.

PEEBLES OF DEWSBURY.

ARMS.—Argent, on a chevron engrailed sable between three parrots vert a fleur-de-lis .... An escutcheon of pretence: Vert, a saltire engrailed or.

John Peebles, Dr in Divinity, and Bpp of .... in Scotland, obijt circa ann. 1604. = Jane, daughter to Will'm Middleton of ...... in Scotland.

Andrew Peebles, Dr in Divinity and Chaplaine to K. James wth whom he came first into England a° 1603, dyed in a° 1632. = Anne, daughter of William Ramsey of Drackton in Scotland Esqr.

1. John Peebles, Batchelour in Divinity and Rector of Would-Newton in com. Ebor. æt. 70 ann. 2° Apr. 1666. = Sarah, daughter of William Booth of .... in co. Cestr. gent.

2. Andrew Peebles of Would-Newton in co. Ebor. marr. Beatrice daughter to ...... Conyers of .... in com. Ebor.

John Peebles of Dewsbury in com. Ebor. Esqr, one of the gentlemen of the privy Chamber in ordinary to his Matie K. Charles the 2d, æt. 35 ann. 2° Apr. 1666. = Elizabeth, daughter and sole heire to Robert Franke of Alwoodley in com. Ebor.

John Peebles, æt. 1 anni & dim. 2° Apr. 1666. 1. Elizabeth. 2. Jane, died young. 3. Anne. 4. Mary.

RYDALL WAPENTAKE.

Yorke, 13 *Aug.* 1666.

RAYNES OF APLETON IN THE STREETE.

ARMS.—Azure, a chevron engrailed between three crane's heads erased argent, each holding in the beak an oak-branch, leaves vert, acorns or.

No proofe made of these Armes.

James Raynes of Apleton in the Streete in com. Ebor. = Margaret, daughter to . . . . . Atkinson of Thusk in co. Ebor.

Their children:

- 4. Ursula, wife to Ambrose Clarke of Ryton; afterwards to James Deane of Thorne in co. Ebor.
- 3. Elizabeth, wife to James Storr of Hutton-Bushell in com. Ebor.
- 2. Seazy, wife to John Story of Apleton in the Street in co. Ebor. Clarke.
- 1. Frances, wife to Thomas Tratle of Apleton in yͤ Street in co. Ebor.
- 1. James Raynes of Apleton in the Street in com. Ebor. obijt 1642. = Sarah, 3d daughter to Richard Letby of Skirterbeck in com. Ebor.
- 2. William Raynes of Apleton in yͤ Street in co. Ebor. = Elizabeth, daughter to Thomas Cooper.
- 3. Peter Raynes of Apleton in the Street in com. Ebor. = Anne, daughter to Robert Tratle of Apleton in the Street in co. Ebor.

Children of James Raynes and Sarah:

- James, Thomas, dyed young.
- 3. Thomas Raynes of the Citty of Yorke, Attorney of the Court of Common Pleas of Westminst., æt. 25 ann. 1666. = Mary, daughter of Nich. Conyers of Boleby in co. Ebor. Esqr.
  - 1. Alice.
  - 2. Sarah.
- 2. William Raynes of the Citty of London, æt. 28° ann. 1666. = Alice, daugh. to . . . . Ipswich.
  - James.
- 1. John Raynes of Apleton in the Street, a Capt. of Foot in yͤ King's service, æt. 35 ann. 1666. = Dorothy, daughter to . . . . . . Layths of Dalehead in co. Cumbriæ.
  - Sarah, æt. 2 annor.
  - James, newly borne.
- Sarah, obijt ætatis suæ 20.
- Mary, dyed young.

Yorke, 13° *Aug*. 1666.

WALLER OF SYKEHOUSE.

ARMS.—Argent, a bend engrailed cotised sable.

Thomas Waller, Mayor of Beverley a° 1605.=....

Children of Thomas Waller:
- Nicholas Waller of Sykehouse, Mayor of Beverley a° 1624.=Elizabeth, daughter to Will'm Parkinson, twice Mayor of Beverley.
- Jane, wife to .... Haughton of Sykehouse in co. Ebor.
- Mary, dyed young.

Children of Nicholas Waller and Elizabeth:
- 1. Nicholas Waller, died at Cambridge & buried in Allhallows Church there.
- Olive, da. of Thomas Beckw^th of Beverley Esqr.=2. Edward Waller of Sykehouse in co. Ebor.=Eliz. da. of Gilbert Gregory of Barnby-Dun in co. Ebor.
- 3. Thomas Waller of Bentley in co. Ebor. Cornet to Sr Franc. Cob K^t under Pr. Rupert & now Capt. of Foot in y^e Regim^t of Sr John Hotham Bar^t.=Hannah, da. & coheire to Gervase Hamerton of Aukeburgh in com. Linc.
- 4. John Waller, marr. Dorcas, da. of Christopher Ridley of Beverley.=
- 5. Nicholas Waller of Sykehouse.=Eliz. da. & co-heire to Luke Colson of Doncaster.
- 1. Eliz. wife to .... Beckwith of Burnby.
- 2. Anne, wife to George Blakiston of Sandall.

Children of Edward Waller and Olive: Edward, ob. s. prole. 1. Eliz. 2. Jane. 3. Fayth.

Children of Edward Waller and Eliz. Gregory: Nicholas. Edward. Gregory. Elizabeth. Grace. Mary. Frances. Anne.

Children of Thomas Waller and Hannah: 1. Thomas, æt. 12° an. 1667. 2. Edmund. Elizabeth, Frances, dyed young. Theodosia. Elizabeth. Hannah. Jane.

Children of John Waller: Nicholas. Christoph^r. John.

Children of Nicholas Waller and Eliz. Colson: Elizabeth. Thomas. Nicholas. Edward. Luke. Anne. Mary.

LANGBARGH WAPENTAKE. *Stokesley*, 8° *Sept*. 1666.

COLTHURST OF UP-LEATHAM.

To see the bookes of Lancashire for proofe of the Armes; noting of it there.

Henry Coulthurst of Up-Leatham in co. Ebor., a branch of ye family of Colthurst of ...... in com. Lanc. = Elizabeth, daughter of ...... Rudd of ......

Children:

- 1. George Colthurst, obijt sine prole.
- 2. Robert Colthurst of Up-Leatham in com. Ebor. = Dorothy, daughter to William Craw of Up-Leatham in co. Ebor.

Children of Robert and Dorothy:

- 3. William Colthurst. = ...
  - Divers daughters.
- 2. George Colthurst. = ...
  - Robert Colthurst.
- 1. Robert Colthurst of Up-Leatham, æt. 68 an. et amplius 8° Sept. 1666. = Elizabeth, da. to Edw. Caley of Brumpton in co. Ebor. Esqr.
  - 1. Robert.
  - 2. Edmund.
  - 1. Anne, wife to Robt Cooke of Up-Leatham in co. Ebor.
  - 2. Dorothy, wife to George Smalwood of Up-Leatham.
  - 3. Elizabeth, wife to Henry Rousby of Crome in co. Ebor.
- 1. Elizabeth, wife to John Turner of Kirk-Leatham in co. Ebor. gent.
- 2. Anne, wife to Richard Wynne of Gisbrough in co. Ebor.
- 3. Dorothy, wife of George Powell of Stokesley in co. Ebor.

Stokesley, 8° *Sept.* 1666.

SMALWOOD OF UP-LEATHAM.

Refers to the Visit. of Staff. for proofe of his Armes. There is nothing there of it.

Alan Smalwood of Egton in com. Ebor. a younger branch of the Smalwoods of ...... in com. Stafford, obijt 3° Decembr. 1614. = ...

Children:

- 5. George Smalwood of Yorke.
- 4. James Smalwood, Clerke.
- 3. Raphe Smalwood. = ...
  - John Smalwood.
- Alice, daugh. to Robt Watson of Rosedale in co. Ebor. 2d wife. = 2. Thomas Smalwood of Egton. = Jane, da. of Will'm Garnet of the Hee in com. Westmerld, 1st wife.
  - By Alice (2d wife):
    - 3. Thomas Smalwood of Norton in co. Palat. Dunelm. æt. 36 ann. 8° Sept. 1666.
    - 2. George Smalwood of Up-Leatham in com. Ebor. æt. 39 ann. 8° Sept. 1666. = Dorothy, da. of Robert Coulthurst of Up-Leatham in co. Ebor.
      - Dorothy, æt. 8° annor. a° 1666.
  - By Jane (1st wife):
    - 1. Alan Smalwood, Rector of Greistocke in com. Cumbr. & Dr in Divinity, æt. 58 ann. 1666.
    - 1. Mary, wife to Richd Pursglove of Glasedale.
    - 2. Jane, wife to John Twisley of Danby.
    - 3. Eliz. wife to Samuell Dickenson of Scarborough.
- 1. Richard, obijt sine prole.

OSGODCROSSE WAPENTAKE. *Pontefract*, 16° *Martij*, 1665.

ROKEBY OF ACKWORTH-PARKE.

ARMS.—Quarterly :
1 and 4. Argent, a chevron sable between three rooks of the second legged azure, a crescent for difference.
2 and 3. Argent, three chevrons braced in base sable, on a chief of the second three mullets of the first.

Thomas Rokeby of Hotham in com. Ebor. Esqr. = Catherine, daughter to Lawrence Leigh, Serjeant at Armes.

- 2. Raphe, died unmarried.
- 1. William Rokeby of Hotham. = Dorothy, daughter to Will'm Rokeby of Skyres in co. Ebor.
- 1. Elizabeth, wife to Richard Vincent of Firsby in co. Ebor.
- 2. Susan, wife to William Cartwright of Normanby in co. Linc.

Issue of William Rokeby and Dorothy:

- Mary, wife to Christopher Legard of Anlaby in co. Kingston super Hull.
- 4. Philip Rokeby, mar. Jane, da. to. ...... Godfrey of Thunnock in in com. Linc. = (issue)
- 3. Thomas Rokeby. = Elizabeth, da. to Robert Bury of Granthā in com. Linc.
- 2. Alexander Rokeby of Sandall in co. Ebor. marr. Susan da. to Gervase Boswell of Warmesworth in co. Ebor. of whom there is no issue remaining.
- 1. Sir Will. Rokeby of Hotham and Skyres Bar^t, æt. 64 ann. 16° Sept.1665. = Frances, da. of Sr Will. Hickman of of Gaynesbrough in co. Linc. K^t.

Issue of Thomas Rokeby and Elizabeth:

- 4. Susanna.
- 3 Emme, wife to Leonard Weddall of Erswick in co. Ebor.
- 2. Anne, wife to Raphe Waterhouse of Burnby in co. Ebor.
- 1. Mary, wife to Francis Hall of Dunnington in co. Ebor.
- 1. Will'm Rokeby of Ackworth parke in co. Ebor. æt. 35 an. 16° Martij a° 1665. = Emme, da. to Sr Will. Bury of Linwood in co. Linc. Kn^t.
- 2. Thomas Rokeby, an Utter Barrister of Gray's Inne. = Ursula, da. to James Danby of New-building juxta Threske in co. Ebor.
- 3. John.
- 4, Joseph.
- 5. Benjamin.

Issue of Will'm Rokeby and Emme:

- 1. William, æt. 9° ann. 16 Mart. 1665.
- 2. George.
- 3. Alexander.
- 1. Emme.
- 2. Elizabeth.

SKYRACK WAPENTAKE. *Yorke*, 13° *Sept.* 1665.

ELLIS OF KIDDALL.

ARMS.—Or, on a cross sable five crescents argent.
CREST.—A woman naked proper, her hair dishevelled or.

John Ellis of Kiddall Esqr, a° 1612. = Mary, daughter of Martin Anne of Frickley in co. Ebor.

Issue:

- 8. Thomas. 9. Gervase. 10. Samuell.
- 5. Robert. 6. Richard. 7. Francis.
- 2. Nicholas. 3. Martin. 4. Henry.
- 1. John Ellis, Esqr. slain at his house called Rowell by the Parlmt soldiers, a° .... = Elizabeth, da. of .. Plompton of Plompton, Esqr.
- 1. Anne.
- 2. Frances, wife of Tho. Burley of Egglesfeild.
- 3. Mercy. 4. Mary.

Issue of John Ellis and Elizabeth:

- 3. Charles, slayn in the service of King Charles the first.
- 2. Henry, slayn in the service of King Charles the first.
- 1. William Ellis of Kiddall in co. Ebor. Esqr. Captain under the Ld Inchequin in Ireland, in the service of K. Ch. ye first, and slayn there a° 1647. = Mary, da. of John Austin, Alderman of London; afterwards married to Tho. Culpeper of Penton in co. Hants.
- Mary, wife of Sr Anthony Chester Bart.

Issue of William Ellis and Mary:

- 2. Henry.
- 1. Will'm Ellis of Kiddall Esqr, æt. 22° an. 13° Sept. 1665. = Mary, daughter of Sr Will'm Lowther of Swillington in com. Ebor. Knt.
- Fridiswide, wife of Will'm Culpeper, Citizen of London.

SKYRACK WAPENTAKE. *Yorke*, 13° *Sept.* 1665.

WYTHAM OF GARFORTH.

ARMS.—Quarterly: a crescent for difference:

1 and 4. Or, three ravens sable, over all a bendlet gules.
2. Gules, a chief argent.
3, Argent, on a fess gules between three popinjays vert collared and membered of the second, as many escallops of the field.

CREST.—Out of a ducal coronet or a demi-woman proper, hair dishevelled of the first, holding in her dexter hand a gemmed ring of the last.

.... first wife. = Mathew Wytham of Brettonby in co. Ebor. = ... second wife.

3. Cuthbert Wytham, Rector of the Church of Garforth in co. Ebor. Batchelour of Law, Chaplain to ye Lady Margaret Lennox, condidit testamentum 10 Aug. 1581. = Dorothy, da. to ...... Walker.

2. Thomas, ob. sine prole.

1. Henry Wytham, who purchased Ledston in co. Ebor. marr. Margaret da. of Tho. Middleton of Stockeld in in co. Ebor. Esqr. =

Catherine, widow of Will'm Walker of Balnhall in co. Ebor. 2d wife. = Cuthbert Wytham of Garforth. = Anne, da. of Tho. Hemsworth of Great-Preston neer Swillington in co. Ebor. first wife. (a)

Elizabeth.

Jennet.

John Flower of Louth in com. Linc. = Jennet, dau. to ...... Hall.

John Flower of Methley in in co. Ebor. a° 1612. = Jane, da. of John Nelson of Methley.

John Flower of Methley. = Jane, daughter of Richard Shann of Woodroofe in Methley co. Ebor. (b)

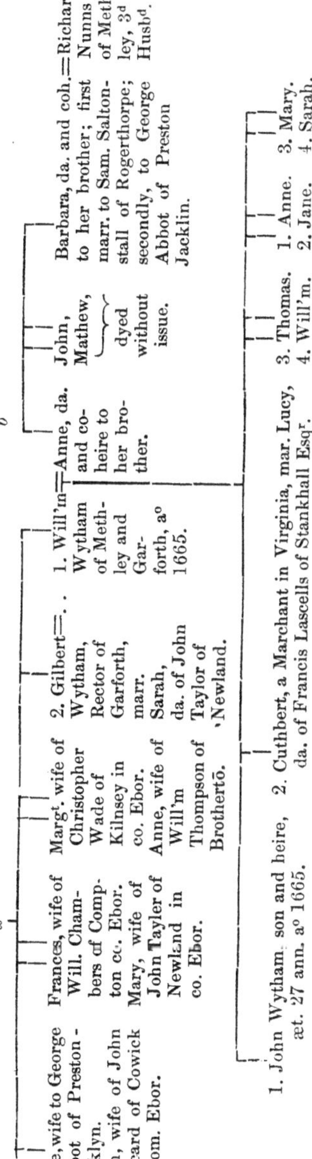
a
b
Joane, wife to George Abbot of Preston-Jacklyn.
Sarah, wife of John Riccard of Cowick in com. Ebor.
Frances, wife of Will. Chambers of Compton co. Ebor.
Mary, wife of John Tayler of Newland in co. Ebor.
Margt. wife of Christopher Wade of Kilnsey in co. Ebor.
Anne, wife of Will'm Thompson of Brothertō.
2. Gilbert Wytham, Rector of Garforth, marr. Sarah, da. of John Taylor of Newland.
1. Will'm Wytham of Methley and Garforth, aº 1665.
Anne, da. and coheire to her brother.
John, Mathew, dyed without issue.
Barbara, da. and coh. to her brother; first marr. to Sam. Saltonstall of Rogerthorpe; secondly, to George Abbot of Preston Jacklin.
Richard Nunns of Methley, 3d Husbd.
1. John Wytham, son and heire, æt. 27 ann. aº 1665.
2. Cuthbert, a Marchant in Virginia, mar. Lucy, da. of Francis Lascells of Stankhall Esqr.
3. Thomas.
4. Will'm.
1. Anne.
2. Jane.
3. Mary.
4. Sarah.

Yorke, 13° *Sept.* 1665.

THOMLINSON OF THORGAMBY.

ARMS.—Per pale vert and argent, three greyhounds in pale courant counterchanged, on a chief or a garb of the first surmounted of a sword gules in saltire.

It behoveth Captain Thomlinson, being a branch of the Family of Thomlinson of Byrdforth, to procure a Certificate from Sr Richard Maleverer, that they are descended from his Family, as they pretend (and as Mr. Thomlinson of Byrdforth did undertake to prove); wch done, he may then beare these Armes of Maleverer thus counterchang'd, whereunto he pretends, wth this Cheife to distinguish himselfe from Thomlinson of Byrdforth.

Anthony Thomlinson of Burne in co. Ebor. descended from Thomlinson of Byrdforth in com. Ebor. ═ ....

Will'm Thomlinson of Burne in co. Ebor. died in a° 1652. ═ Jennet, da. of Tho. Monet of Hadlesey in com. Ebor.

John Thomlinson. ═ Anne, da. to .... Baxter of Cliff in co. Ebor.

Andrew Thomlinson of .... in com. Ebor. ═ Jennet, da. of ...... Howle.

.... wife to .... Sympson of Goldale in com. Ebor.

Anne, wife to Edward Wood of Hathelsay in com. Ebor.

Margaret.

Bridget, da. and heire, wife of Will'm Langthorn of Drewton in com. Ebor.

1. John Thomlinson of Thorgamby in co. Ebor. Capt of Horse under the Ld Mansfeild (son and heire to the Marquess of Newcastle) in the service of K. Charles the first, æt. 42 an. a° 1665. ═ Marg^t^, da. of Rich. Herbert of Skipwith in com. Ebor.

2. Peter Thomlinson of Burne in co. Ebor. ═ Elizabeth, da. of Calisthenes Brooke of Gateford in co. Ebor.

3. Will'm Thomlinson of Aldwaldley in co. Ebor. ═ Jane, da. of Henry Metcalfe of Holbeck in co. Ebor.

1. Kath. wife of Tho. Dalby of Barleby in co. Ebor.
2. Anne, wife of Will'm Stables of Allerton juxta Wate in com. Ebor.
3. Jane, wife of Rich. Linley of Houghton neer Pontefract.

Children of John: 1. Richard, æt. 3 ann. 1665. John. Joseph, Benjamin, } twins. Mary. Margaret. Elizabeth.

Children of Peter: John. 1. Hannah. 2. Rebecca.

Skyrack Wapentake. *Yorke*, 13° *Aug.* 1666.

LAYTON OF BARROUGHBY.

Arms.—Argent, a fess between three cross-crosslets botonnée fitchée sable.

...... = ...

George Layton of Barroughby in com. Ebor. = ... da. to ...... Reynolds. — Lancelot Layton.

Susan, da. of Abraham Key of Almondbury, first wife. = 1. Gabraell Layton of Barroughby, ob. circa annum 1640. = Mary, da. of Francis Arthington of Castley, 2d wife. — 2. John Layton of Berwick in Elmet in com. Ebor. = Rosamund, da. of John Taylor of Morwick. — 3. George Layton. — 4. Bryan Laytō. = Susan, da. of Capt. Kighley. — 5. Cuthbt Layton, under Shireeve to Sr Richard Gargrave, died unmarried. — Anne, wife of Will. Morell of Shireburne.

Anne, wife of Thomas Langdale of Ebberton Esqr. (child of Gabraell and Susan) — Gabrael Laytō of Barroughby, æt. 55 ann. a° 1666. (child of Gabraell and Mary) = Mary, da. of Marke Brereclose. — 1. George. 2. Francis. 3. Richard. 1. Eliz. 2. Susan. (children of John and Rosamund) — Cuthbert. 1. Alice. 2. Mary. (children of Bryan and Susan)

1. Rich. Layton, died wthout issue a° 1662. = Cath. da. & heire of John Stock of Doncaster. = Henry Favell, second husband. — 2. Stephen Layton, æt. 14 an. a° 1666. — Philip Jackson of great-Askham, first husband. = Rosamund. = Rich. Wright Vicar of Whitkirke, 2d husbd.

BARKESTON-ASHE WAPENTAKE. *Yorke*, 13 *Sept.* 1665.

HAMOND OF SCARTHINGWELL.

ARMS.—Quarterly:
1 and 4. Argent, a chevron engrailed between three mullets pierced sable.
2. Gules, two lions passant gardant in pale argent.
3. .... a hawk's lure argent stringed or braced gules.

CREST.—A lion's gamb gules between two bat's wings erect proper, the paw holding an almond slip fructed vert, blossoms of the first.

Anthony Hamond of Scarthingwell in ye parish of Saxton in co. Ebor. ob. 11 Aug. anno 1554. = ... cousen and heire of Alex. Leedes, Ld of the Mannour of Scarthingwell.

Will. Hamond of Scarthingwell, a Justice of Peace in K. Edward ye 6ths time, vixit 18 Eliz. = Frances, da. of Sr Thomas Metham Knt, 35 H. 8 (12 Sept).

Eliz. da. of Sr Robert Stapleton of Wighill Knt, 1 wife. = 1. Bryan Hamond of Scarthingwell Esqr, ob. 11 Apr. ao 1601. = Sarah, da. of Gervase Cressy, Esqr, 2d wife.

2. Richard Hamond 13 Eliz.

3. Will'm Hamond, cheif Collector of ye Subsidie for Barkeston-Ashe Wapentake.

4. Christopher Hamond of Arras.

5. Thomas.

6. Robert Hamond of Freston.

Anne, da. of Ralph Salveyne of New-Biggin Esqr, 1st wife. = 1. Gervase Hamond Esqr, ob. 4 Oct. 21 Car. 1. = Elizabeth, daughter of Bartholomew Fletcher Esqr, widdow of ...... Wilson of Monk-Friston, and of Mathey Keys of Beghall.

2. Will'm, 45 Eliz.

3. Edward, 45 Eliz.

1. Will'm Hamond of Scarthingwell Esqr, now one of ye Justices of the Peace in ye West-Riding of Yorkshire, 13 Sept. 1665. = Frances [Joane ?], da. of Robert Middleton Esqr, and widdow of Francis Hungate Esqr.

2. Bryan, 3. Gervase, died unmarried.

Mary, died unmarried.

Gervase Hamond, ætat. 15 ann. 13 Sept. 1665.

GREENE OF LEVERSEDGE.

John Green of Osset, a branch of y[e] family of Horsforth in com. Eborum. = ...

John Greene of Leversedge in com. Eborum. = Anne, da. of .... Drake of Clifton in co. Eborum.

- 1. Will'm Greene of Leversedge in co. Eborum. = Anne, da. of Edw. Rayner of Clack-Heaton in co. Ebor.
- 2. John Greene of Leversedge. = Winifride, da. of Michaell Drake of Blacob in Leversedge.
- 3. James Greene of Leversedge. = Mary, da. of .... Crawthorn of Howley.
- 4. Richard Greene of Ridings in Gomersall in co. Ebor. = Alice, da. of Rich. Armitage of Gomersall.
  - 1. Richard, ob. s. p'le. 2. Will'm. 3. John.
- 5. Thomas Greene of Leversedge. = Grace, da. of Tho. Shepley of Morfeild.
  - 1. Will'm. 2. Thomas. 3. Joshua.
- 6. Michaell Greene of Leversedge. = Elizabeth, daughter of Thomas Wheatly of White-crosse.
  - ...... Greene of Wortley.

Children of Will'm Greene and Anne Rayner:

- 1. John Greene, L[d] of y[e] Moiety of y[e] Mannour of Leversedge, Lieutenant to Capt. Batt in y[e] Regim[t] of Foot of George Visc[t] Halifax, æt. 48 an. 1666. = Mary da. of John Farrer of Ewgod in com. Ebor.
  - 1. John Greene, æt. 25 ann. 1666. = Mary, daughter of John Crookes of Monke-Bretton.
    - William.
  - 2. William.
- 2. Will'm Greene of Leversedge. = Mary, da. of .... Sugdē.
  - 1. Will'm. 2. John. 3. Richard.
  - 1. Mary, wife of John Rayner of Leversedge.
  - 2. Anne, wife of Richard Leversedge of Gomersall.
- 3. Rich. Greene of Leversedge, marr. Mary, da. of Will'm Bankes of Morley.
- 4. Edw. Greene of Leversedge, marr. Eliz. da. of Edw. Crosland of Newall-Grange.
- 1. Barbara, wife of Edward Robinson of Leversedge.
- 2. Susan, wife of John Crowder of Morley.

Child of John Greene and Winifride Drake:

- John Green of Leversedge, marr. Eliz. da. & heire of Tho. Lee of Batley in co. Ebor. = ⅄
- 1. Dorothy, wife of Abraham Beaumont of Almonbury in co. Ebor.
- 2. ..... wife of Henry Wordsworth of Ovenden.

Children of James Greene and Mary Crawthorn:

- 1. Joshua Greene, mar. Alice, da. of John Hargrave of Wiskit hill in y[e] parish of Tonge in co. Ebor.
- 2. John Greene, mar. Alice, da. of .... Stables of Tong in co. Ebor.

AGBRIGG AND MORLEY WAP. *Yorke*, 13° *Sept.* 1665.

SUNDERLAND OF AYKTON.

ARMS.—Per pale argent and azure, three lions passant in pale counterchanged.

CREST.—A goat's head erased azure, attired or.

Respite given for proofe of these Armes.

Abraham Sunderland of High Sunderland neer Hallifax in com. Ebor. Esqr. = Judith, da. of Thomas Oldfeild.

Mary, da. of Robt Moore of Midgley, first wife. = Richard Sunderland of Sunderland Esqr. = Anne, da. of John Rushworth of Ridlesden, 2^d^ wife.

1. Abraham Sunderland. = Susan, da. of Raphe Waterhouse of Burstall.

2. Richard Sunderland of Copley Esqr, heire to his brother. = Mary, da. of Sr Rich. Saltonstall Kn^t^, Ld Mayor of London.

...... a son, died young.

3. Sam. Sunderland of Harden in co. Ebor., æt. 67 an. 11 Aug. 1605.

2. Robt Sunderland, a Turkey Marchant, died in a° 1613, and lyeth buried in y^e^ Church of Hallifax, wth Armes on his Gravestone.

1. Abrahã Sunderland of Sunderland & Coley Esqr, died in Pontefract Castle 25 March 1644, during y^e^ Seige there, it being then kept for K. Charles y^e^ first. = Eliz. da. of Peter Langdale of Beverley Esqr. (father to Marmaduke Ld Langdale).

4. Richard Sunderland, Clerke.

5. Peter Sunderland of Faireweither Greene neer Bradford in co. Ebor. = Mary, da. of Rich. Buck of ...... neer Bradford in co. Ebor.

1. Susan, wife of William Beilby of Micklethwayt Grange Esqr.
2. Mary, wife of Edward Parker of Browholm Esqr.
3. Judith, died unmarried (she was a twinne wth Peter.)

Langdale Sunderland of Aykton in co. Ebor. Esqr, Capt. of a Troop of horse under y^e^ command of Marmaduke late Lord Langdale, in y^e^ service of K. Ch. y^e^ 1st, æt. 44 ann. a° 1665. = Eliz. da. of Thomas Thornhill of Fixby in com. Ebor. Esqr.

1. Abraham Sunderland, æt. 15 ann. 13 Sept. 1665.

2. Bryan Sunderland, æt. 12 an. 1665.

GILLING-WEST WAPENTAKE. *Yorke*, 13° *Aug.* 1666.

WILKINSON OF KIRKBRIGG.

ARMS.—Azure, a fess erminois between three unicorns passant argent, a canton or.

CREST.—Out of a mural coronet gules, a demi-unicorn rampant erminois, erased of the first.

1615, Sept. 18. These Arms and Crest were granted to Laurence Wilkinson of Ferry-hill in co. Durham by Richd St George, Norroy.

Christopher Wilkinson of Barton in co. Ebor. descended from the family of Wilkinson of Harpley and Ferrey in the B'pprick of Durham, died circa ann. 1632. = Helen, daughter of ...... Bucke of Sedberge in com. Palat. Durham Esqr.

1. John Wilkinson of Barton, died circa ann. 1640. = Margery, daughter of Francis Foster of Darnton in com. Pal. Dunelm.

2. Thomas Wilkinson of Kirkbrigg in the parish of St John's neere Gilling, died in a° 1664. = Elizabeth, daughter of Thomas Clement of Newton neere Barton aforesaid.

Margery, died unmarried.

Francis Wilkinson, of Monkend in the parish of Croft in co. Ebor.

3. Jane, wife of Thomas Jones, an Utter-Barister of Lincoln's-Inne.

1. Elizabeth, wife of John Weddal of Widdington neere Yorke.

2. Mary.

4. John Wilkinson, an Utter-Barister of Gray's-Inne, and one of the six Clerkes in Chancery.

5. Francis Wilkinson of the Inner Temple, London.

2. Mathew Wilkinson of Greenhead in the parish of Huddersfeild in com. Ebor.

3. Christopher Wilkinson of Lincolns-Inne.

1. James Wilkinson of Kirkbrigg, borne a° 1625. = Mary, daughter of John Garth of Headlam in co. Palat. Dunelm.

2. James.

3. Christopher.

1. Thomas, ætatis 7 ann. 13 Aug. a° 1666.

Elizabeth.

AGBRIGGE AND MORLEY WAPENTAKE. *Halifax*, 2° *Apr.* 1666.

CALVERLEY OF CALVERLEY.

ARMS.—Sable, an inescutcheon within an orle of six owls argent.
CREST.—Out of a ducal coronet or a calf's head couped and erect sable.

¶ See the Visitation of Yorksh. by W. Flower, Norroy, a° 1563 et 1564.

Elizabeth, daughter of Richard Sneyd of Bradwell in co. Staff. Esqr, 2^d wife. = Sr Will'm Calverley K^t, Shireeve of Yorkesh. 3° Edw. 6. = Elizabeth, daughter of Sr Will. Middleton of Stockeld in co. Ebor. K^t, 1 wife.

1. Beatrix, wife of Robert Hyde of Norbury in com. Cestr. Esqr. — 2. Jane. — 3. Elizabeth. — Walter Calverley of Calverley Esqr. = Anne, daughter of Sr Christopher Danby of Farnley K^t.

1. Will'm Calverley Esqr, Lord of the Mannours of Calverley, Pudsey, and Burley in Wharfedale, in com. Ebor. = Katherine, daughter of John Thorneholme of Hasthrope Esqr. — 2. Christopher. — 3. Edward.

1. Walter Calverley of Calverley Esqr, died at Yorke a° 1605 (3 Jac. R.) = Philippa, daughter of Sr George Brooke K^t, Ld Cobham; afterwards married to Sr Thomas Burton of Stokerston in com. Leic. K^t and Bar^t. — 2. Will'm. — 3. John. — 4. Thomas. — 5. Shefeild. — 6. Raphe.

Joyce, daughter of Sr Walter Pye K^t, Attorney of the Courte of Wards and Liveries, 2^d wife. = Henry Calverley of Calverley Esqr, died 1 Jan. 1661. = ... daughter to John Moore of Grantham in com. Linc. Esqr, died w^th^out issue. — Will'm, Walter, died young.

1. Walter Calverley, an Utter Barister of Grays Inne and one of his Maties Justices of Peace for the West Riding of Yorkeshire, ætatis ... ann. a° 1666. = Frances, daughter and heire to Hen. Thomson of Esholt in com. Ebor. Esqr. — 2. John.

1. Anne. — 2. Bridget.

LANGBARGH WAPENTAKE. *Yorke*, 13° *Aug*. 1666.

BECKWITH OF HANDALE-ABBEY.

ARMS.—Argent, a chevron gules frettée sable between three hind's heads erased of the second, on a chief of the last a saltire engrailed between two roses in fess and as many demi-fleurs-de-lis joined to the dexter and sinister sides all or.

CREST.—A stag's head erased, quarterly per fess indented or and azure, the dexter attire of the second the sinister of the first.

Roger Beckwith of Handale-Abby in com. Ebor. Esqr. = ... daughter of Peter Newark of Aickham in co. Ebor. Esqr.

- 1. Mary.
- 2. Anne.
- 2. Philip.
- 1. Newark Beckwith of Handale-Abby Esqr, died in a° 1656, ætatis 66 ann. = Mary, daughter of ...... Fisk of Laxfeild in co. Suff.
  - 2. Elizabeth, wife of Robert Lassels of Ariholme in com. Ebor. Esq[r].
  - 1. Mary.
  - Theophania, daughter of ...... Grimeston of Grimeston-garth in Holdernes, 1 wife. = Leonard Beckwith of Handale-Abby Esq[r], æt. 47 ann. a° 1666. = Anne, daughter of George Thweng of Heworth in co. Ebor. Esq[r], 2[d] wife.
    - Issue by the first wife:
      - 1. Anne.
      - 2. Mary, wife of Philip Garnet of Dalesmill in co. Ebor.
      - 5. Marmaduke, æt. 9 ann. 1666.
      - 4. Leonard, æt. 14 1666.
      - 3. Newark, æt. 16 1666.
      - 2. Will'm, died young.
      - 1. Roger Beckwith, son and heir, æt. 18 ann. 1666.
    - Issue by the second wife:
      - Albert Beckwith, ætatis unius anni 1666.
      - Helen, ætatis 3 ann. 1666.

BULMER WAPENTAKE. *Yorke*, 13° *Aug*. 1666.

DRIFFEILD OF EASINGWOLD.

ARMS.—Ermine, on a bend sable three boar's heads erased argent.

Thomas Driffeild of Easingwould in com. Ebor. = Margaret, daughter of ..... Cundall, Merchant of London.

3. Cundall, died w^th^out issue.
2. Thomas, died w^th^out issue.
Mary, daughter of .... Thornton of ...... in com. Ebor. 1 wife. = 1. Will'm Driffeld of Easingwould. = Ursula, daughter of Bryan Rosse of Herst-thwayt in com. Ebor. 2d wife.

3. Christopher Driffeild of Rippon, Barister at Law. = Bridget, daughter of Lewes West of ...... in com. Cumbr.
2. Mathias Driffeild of Easingwould. = Ursula, daughter of Will'm Dowman of Duncoates in co. Ebor.
1. Francis Driffeild of Easingwould Esqr, now one of his Maties Justices of Peace in com. Ebor. æt. 45, 1666. = Frances, daughter and coheir of Nicholas Towers, a Merchant in Yorke.
4. Stephen Driffeild.
1. Margaret, wife of Timothy Wright, a Merchant in London.
2. Ursula.
3. Hester.

2. Margaret. 1. Mary. Towers Driffeild, ætatis 10 annor. 1666.

WEST-RIDING. *Yorke*, 13° *Aug.* 1666.

OTWAY OF INGMER-HALL.

ARMS.—Argent, a chevron sable, over all a pile azure counterchanged.

CREST.—Out of a ducal coronet or two wings displayed sable.

For proofe of these armes he voucheth his father's seale, who died at the age of 88 yeares.

Thomas Otway of Middleton in com. Westmerl.=........

Thomas Otway of Middleton=........

George Otway, Clerke. | Roger Otway of Middleton in com. Westmerl. died 10 Febr. a° 1648, then aged 88 yeares.=Anne, daughter of John Mayer of Sedbergh, in com. Ebor. | Edward Otway of Bocking in co. Hartf. Clerke.

Mary, daughter of Robert Riggs of Fareham in co. Suth^t^, 1 wife.=John Otway, a Bencher of Gray's-Inne, Vice-Chancelour of the County Palatine of Lancaster, and the King's Attorney Gen^ll^ there; now also of Ingmer Hall in the parish of Sedbergh in com. Ebor. ætatis 47 ann. a° 1666.=Elizabeth, only daughter of John Brathwayt of Ambleside in co. Westmerl. 2^d^ wife. | Abigal, wife of Daniel Redman of Balylinch in com. Kilkenny in Ireland. | George Otway, died unmarried.

1. John, ætatis 16 ann. 1666. | 2. Charles. | 1. Anne. 2. Mary. | 3. Elizabeth. | 4. Margaret. | 5. Katherine.

Yorke, 13° *Augusti*, 1666.

SHILLETO OF YORKE.

ARMS.—Or, a chevron engrailed between ten cross-crosslets sable.

CREST.—A greyhound's head per fess or and sable charged with a cross-crosslet counterchanged.

These armes were granted to Francis Shilleto of Houghton in com. Ebor. 24° Jan. 1602, by Will'm Dethick, Garter, and now in the custody of Edward Shelleto of the Citty of Yorke.

Francis Shilleto of Houghton in co. Ebor. a° 1602.=........

Will'm Shilleto of Pontfract in com. Ebor.=Elizabeth, daughter of ...... Stonehouse of.... in Cleveland.

1. Will'm Shilleto, died w^th^out issue. | Judith, daughter of Robert Deane of the Grange-house called Bale-Stubing in com. Ebor. 2^d^ wife.=2. Edward Shellito of the Citty of Yorke, ætatis 44 ann. 1664.=Bridget, daughter of Edward Robinson of Perith in com. Cumbr. 1 wife. | 1. Anne, wife John Berry of Monke-Fryston in co. Ebor. | 2. Elizabeth, wife of John Marrow of Doncaster.

Edward, ætatis 14 ann. 1666.

OSGODCROSSE WAPENTAKE. *Yorke*, 13° *Aug.* 1666.

DAVYE OF FOCKERBY.

ARMS.—Paly of six argent and gules, a chief ermine.

John Davye of Shelly in com. Suff. gent. = Jane.

David Davy of Shelly in co. Suff. = Mary, daughter of Thomas Ellis.

Robert Davy, Citizen of Yorke. = Anne, daughter of Martin Laurence, Citizen of Yorke.

Will'm Davye of Fockerby in com. Ebor. ætatis 35 ann. a° 1666. = Mary, daughter of Samuel Lister of Kingston upon Hull.

- Will'm Davye (borne since, vz^t in a° 1667).
- 1. Anne, ætatis 3 ann. a° 1666.
- 2. Mary, ætatis 2 ann. a° 1666.
- 3. Barbara (borne since, sc^t in a° 1670).

INDEX.

WESTMINSTER:
PRINTED BY J. B. NICHOLS AND SONS.
1860.

THE SURTEES SOCIETY.

REPORT FOR THE YEAR MDCCCLIX.

(Read at the General Meeting on the 24th of June.)

THE Surtees Society has now been in existence for a quarter of a century. During this long period it has not been idle. Thirty-five volumes, all illustrating the manners or the religion of the North of England, bear witness to its industry, and the increasing demand for these volumes is a sufficient test of their usefulness and popularity. There are at the present time very few public libraries in England of any importance that do not possess a set of the publications of the Surtees Society.

When the Society commenced its labours in 1834 it had a roll of one hundred and nine members, very many of whom were personal friends of the great historian of the Palatinate of Durham. Of these gentlemen nearly eighty are now no more. And as they are being gradually removed from us the Surtees Society must rely for its support not on those feelings of regard and attachment towards him in whose honour it was founded which called it, many years ago, into being, but on the excellence of its publications. This is now the true basis of its strength and the earnest of its future prosperity. The names of more than two hundred gentlemen are now enrolled upon the list of members, a number which tempts the Council to think that the Society has not laboured altogether in vain.

The Council most sincerely congratulate the members upon the present state of the finances of the Society. After several years of difficulty and almost of embarrassment a considerable and most satisfactory balance has been secured. For this the Council feel that they are greatly indebted to the painstaking and disinterested efforts of the late treasurer. It is impossible to estimate too highly the valuable services that Mr. Henderson has rendered to the Surtees Society. It was with great regret that the Council were obliged to accept his resignation, but it is most gratifying to them to find that in their present treasurer they have an officer who will vie with Mr. Henderson in his efforts to advance the best interests of the Society.

A suggestion has been made, and a most important one it is, that the Surtees Society should undertake the compilation of a Glossary of Old North Country Words and Phrases. Such a work, although necessarily laborious, would be most useful and acceptable. Were it merely explanatory of the curious words and terms that occur in the volumes which the Society has already issued the value of the work, especially to the members of the Surtees Society, would be very great. Such an undertaking would, perhaps, be more efficiently carried out by a combination of editors than by one; although, for the sake of arrangement and unity of plan, it might be necessary that some one person should superintend the whole. Several distinguished philologists have expressed a wish that the work should be undertaken and have promised their assistance. The Council hope, before long, to be able to carry this suggestion into effect.

THE SURTEES SOCIETY,

ESTABLISHED IN THE YEAR 1834,

In honour of the late Robert Surtees, of Mainsforth, Esquire, the Author of the History of the County Palatine of Durham, and in accordance with his pursuits and plans; having for its object the publication of inedited Manuscripts, illustrative of the intellectual, the moral, the religious, and the social condition of those parts of England and Scotland, included on the East between the Humber and the Frith of Forth, and on the West between the Mersey and the Clyde, a region which constituted the ancient Kingdom of Northumberland.

NEW RULES AGREED UPON IN 1849.

The Report of the Committee appointed at a General Meeting, held on the 7th February last, to revise the Rules of the Society, was taken into consideration, and the following Rules were adopted for the future government of the Society:—

I. The Society shall consist of an unlimited number of members.

II. There shall be a Patron of the Society, and the Right Reverend Edward Maltby, D.D., F.R.S., Lord Bishop of Durham, shall be the first Patron.

III. The Warden of the University of Durham for the time being shall be the President of the Society.

IV. There shall be twenty-four Vice-Presidents, of whom four shall be such of the Professors, Tutors, or Fellows of the University of Durham as shall be members of the Society. There shall also be a Secretary and two Treasurers.

V. The Patron, the President, the Vice-Presidents, the Secretary, and the Treasurers, shall form the Council, any five of whom, including the Secretary and a Treasurer, shall be a quorum competent to transact the business of the Society.

VI. The twenty-four Vice-Presidents, the Secretary, and the Treasurers, shall be elected at a general meeting, to continue in office for three years, and be capable of re-election.

VII. Any vacancies in the offices of Secretary or Treasurers shall be provisionally filled up by the Council, subject to the approbation of the next general meeting.

VIII. Three meetings of the Council shall be held in every year, one in each academical term of the University of Durham, at such place, and on such a day, as shall be fixed upon by the President, to be communicated by the Secretary to the members of the Council.

IX. The meeting in the Easter Term of each year shall be the anniversary, to which all the members of the Society shall be convened by the Secretary.

X. The President shall have the power of convening extraordinary meetings of the Council.

XI. Members may be elected by ballot at any one of the terminal meetings, upon being proposed in writing by three existing members. One black ball in ten shall exclude.

XII. Each member shall pay in advance to the Treasurer the annual sum of one guinea. If any member's subscription shall be in arrear for two years, and he shall neglect to pay his subscription after having been reminded by the Treasurer, he shall be regarded as having ceased to be a member of the Society.

XIII. The money raised by the Society shall be expended in publishing such compositions, in their original language, or in a translated form, as come within the scope of this Society, without limitation of time with reference to the period of their respective authors. All editorial and other expenses to be defrayed by the Society.

XIV. One volume, at least, in a closely printed octavo form, shall be supplied to each member of the Society every year, free of expense.

XV. If the funds of the Society in any year will permit, the Council shall be at liberty to print and furnish to the members, free of expense, any other volume or volumes of the same character, in the same or a different form.

XVI. The number of copies of each publication, and the selection of a printer and publisher, shall be left to the Council, who shall also fix the price at which the copies not furnished to members shall be sold to the public.

XVII. The armorial bearings of Mr. Surtees and some other characteristic decoration connecting the Society with his name, together with the armorial bearings of the University of Durham, shall be used in each publication.

XVIII. A list of the officers and members, together with an account of the receipts and expenses of the Society, shall be made up every year to the time of the annual meeting, and shall be submitted to the Society to be printed and published with the next succeeding volume.

XIX. No alteration shall be made in these rules except at an annual meeting. Notice of any such alteration shall be given, at least, as early as the terminal meeting of the Council immediately preceding, to be communicated to each member of the Society.

PUBLICATIONS OF THE SURTEES SOCIETY,

With their respective Sale Prices.

N.B. Of several of these volumes, especially of 2, 4, *and* 24, *the number of copies on hand is very small.*

---

1. REGINALDI Monachi Dunelmensis Libellus de Admirandis BEATI CUTHBERTI Virtutibus. 15s.
2. WILLS and INVENTORIES, illustrative of the History, Manners, Language, Statistics, &c., of the Northern Counties of England, from the Eleventh Century downwards. [Chiefly from the Registry at Durham.] 15s.
3. The TOWNELEY MYSTERIES; or, MIRACLE-PLAYS. 15s.
4. TESTAMENTA EBORACENSIA; Wills illustrative of the History, Manners, Language, Statistics, &c., of the Province of York, from 1300 downwards. Vol. I. 15s.
5. SANCTUARIUM DUNELMENSE et SANCTUARIUM BEVERLACENSE; or, Registers of the Sanctuaries of Durham and Beverley. 15s.
6. The Charters of Endowment, Inventories and Account Rolls of the PRIORY of FINCHALE, in the County of Durham. 15s.
7. CALALOGI Veteres Librorum ECCLESIÆ CATHEDRALIS DUNELM. Catalogues of the Library of Durham Cathedral at various periods, from the Conquest to the Dissolution, including Catalogues of the Library of the Abbey of Hulne, and of the MSS. preserved in the Library of Bishop Cosin at Durham. 10s.
8. MISCELLANEA BIOGRAPHICA. Lives of Oswin, King of Northumberland; Two Lives of Cuthbert, Bishop of Lindisfarne, and a Life of Eata, Bishop of Hexham. 10s.
9. Historiæ Dunelmensis Scriptores Tres. GAUFRIDUS de COLDINGHAM, ROBERTUS de GRAYSTANES, et WILLIELMUS de CHAMBRE, with the omissions and mistakes in Wharton's Edition supplied and corrected, and an Appendix of 665 original Documents, in illustration of the Text. 15s.

10. RITUALE ECCLESIÆ DUNELMENSIS; a Latin Ritual of the Ninth Century, with an interlinear Northumbro-Saxon Translation. 15s.
11. JORDAN FANTOSME'S ANGLO-NORMAN CHRONICLE of the War between the English and the Scots in 1173 and 1174, with a Translation, Notes, &c., by Francisque Michel, F.S.A. 15s.
12. Correspondence, Inventories, Account Rolls, and Law Proceedings of the PRIORY of COLDINGHAM. 15s.
13. LIBER VITÆ ECCLESIÆ DUNELMENSIS; NECNON OBITUARIA DUO EJUSDEM ECCLESIÆ. 10s.
14. The Correspondence of ROBERT BOWES, of Aske, Esq., Ambassador of Queen Elizabeth to the Court of Scotland. 15s.
15. A Description or Briefe Declaration of all the ANCIENT MONUMENTS, RITES and CUSTOMS belonging to, or being within, the MONASTICAL CHURCH of DURHAM, before the Suppression. Written in 1593. 10s.
16. ANGLO-SAXON and EARLY ENGLISH PSALTER, now first published from MSS. in the British Museum. Vol. I. 15s.
17. The Correspondence of Dr. MATTHEW HUTTON, Archbishop of York. With a Selection from the Letters of Sir Timothy Hutton, Knt., his Son, and Matthew Hutton, Esq., his Grandson. 15s.
18. The DURHAM HOUSEHOLD BOOK; or the Accounts of the Bursar of the Monastery of DURHAM from 1530 to 1534. 15s.
19. ANGLO-SAXON and EARLY ENGLISH PSALTER. Vol. II. 15s.
20. Libellus de Vita et Miraculis S. GODRICI, Heremitæ de FINCHALE, auctore REGINALDO Monacho Dunelmensi. 15s.
21. DEPOSITIONS respecting the REBELLION of 1569, WITCHCRAFT, and other ECCLESIASTICAL PROCEEDINGS, from the Court of Durham, extending from 1311 to the reign of Elizabeth. 15s.
22. The INJUNCTIONS and other ECCLESIASTICAL PROCEEDINGS of RICHARD BARNES, Bishop of Durham (1577-1587). 25s.
23. The ANGLO-SAXON HYMNARIUM, from MSS. of the Eleventh Century, in Durham, the British Museum, &c. 16s.
24. The MEMOIR of Mr. SURTEES, by the late George Taylor, Esq. Reprinted from the Fourth Vol. of the History of Durham, with additional Notes and Illustrations, together with an Appendix, comprising some of Mr. Surtees's Correspondence, Poetry, &c. 16s.
25. The BOLDON BOOK, or SURVEY of DURHAM in 1183. 10s. 6d.
26. WILLS and INVENTORIES, illustrative of the History, Manners, Language, Statistics, &c, of the Counties of York, Westmorland, and Lancaster, from the Fourteenth Century downwards. From the Registry at RICHMOND. 14s.
27. The PONTIFICAL of EGBERT, Archbishop of York (731—767), from a MS. of the Ninth or Tenth Century in the Imperial Library in Paris. 11s.
28. The GOSPEL of ST. MATTHEW, from the Northumbrian Interlinear Gloss to the Gospels, contained in the MS. Nero, D. IV., among the Cottonian MSS. in the British Museum, commonly known as the Lindisfarne Gospels, collated with the Rushworth MS. 14s.
29. The INVENTORIES and ACCOUNT ROLLS of the Monasteries of JARROW and MONKWEARMOUTH, from their commencement in 1303 till the Dissolution. 12s.
30. TESTAMENTA EBORACENSIA, or Wills illustrative of the History, Manners, Language, Statistics, &c., of the Province of York from 1429 to 1467. Vol. II. 25s.
31. The BEDE ROLL of JOHN BURNABY, Prior of Durham (1456—1464). With illustrative documents. 12s.
32. The SURVEY of the PALATINATE of DURHAM, compiled during the Episcopate of Thomas Hatfield (1345—1382). 15s.
33. The FARMING BOOK of HENRY BEST of ELMSWELL, E.R.Y. 12s.
34. The PROCEEDINGS of the HIGH COURT of COMMISSION for DURHAM and NORTHUMBERLAND. 14s.
35. The FABRIC ROLLS of YORK MINSTER. 25s.
36. The HERALDIC VISITATION of YORKSHIRE, by SIR WILLIAM DUGDALE, in 1665. 30s.

The Volumes in course of preparation are

1. A New Volume of MISCELLANEA, comprising, The Account of the SIEGE of PONTEFRACT, by NATHAN DRAKE, the LETTERS of DEAN GRENVILLE, and EXTRACTS from the ROKEBY CORRESPONDENCE.
2. DURHAM and NORTHUMBERLAND WILLS, Vol. II., a continuation of No. 2.

The Council propose to select their future volumes out of the following manuscripts or materials that have been suggested to them, or from others of a similar description :—

1. WILLS, &c., from the REGISTRY at CARLISLE.
2. A continuation of the TESTAMENTA EBORACENSIA (No. 4 and 30.)
3. A Volume of the HERALDIC VISITATIONS of NORTHUMBERLAND.
4. The LETTERS of ALCUIN of YORK, from Contemporary MSS. containing many Epistles unknown to Froben, and not included in his Edition, nor in that by Dr. Giles.
5. The MEDITATIONS of UGHTRED, a Monk of Durham, during his solitary life upon Farne Island, in the 14th Century.
6. The Prose and Poetical WORKS of LAWRENCE, PRIOR of DURHAM, who died in 1153.
7. The HISTORICAL WORKS of AILRED, Abbot of Rievaulx.
8. LIVES of ENGLISH and SCOTTISH SAINTS, many from MSS. hitherto uncollated.
9. The NORTHUMBRIAN INTERLINEAR GLOSS to the GOSPELS of ST. MARK, ST. LUKE, and ST. JOHN, commonly known as the LINDISFARNE GOSPELS. (The Gospel of St. Matthew has been already published by the Society. See above, No. 28.)
10. The CENSOR MUNDI ; a Religious Poem in English verse, written about 1380.
11. EARLY ENGLISH METRICAL ROMANCES from the Public Library at Cambridge.
12. A VOLUME of NORTH COUNTRY POETRY, from the Cottonian Library and other sources.
13. FEODARIUM THOMÆ de MELSONBY. A Survey made by Prior Melsonby (1233—1244) of the Estates belonging in his time to the Prior and Convent of Durham, of the same nature as the Boldon Book and Bishop Hatfield's Survey.
14. CARDINAL LANGLEY'S SURVEY of the PALATINATE of DURHAM, together with Extracts from contemporaneous Bailiff's Rolls.
15. Two early SURVEYS of the ESTATES of the great Houses of PERCY and NEVILLE.
16. The HISTORIANS of the CHURCH of YORK, comprising the Lives of St. Wilfrid, St. John of Beverley, St. William, &c., the Poem of Alcuin de Pontificibus eccles. Ebor., the History of Hugh the Chantor, the Life of Archbishop Geoffrey, by Gerald Cambrensis, Stubb's Account of the Archbishops, &c., with an Appendix of Illustrative Documents; in several volumes.
17. The ACCOUNT BOOK of BOLTON ABBEY, ending in 1325.
18. Selections from the yearly ROLLS of the BURSAR of the Monastery of DURHAM, beginning in 1270.
19. The CHARTERS and ACCOUNT ROLLS of the College of the VICARS CHORAL at YORK, from 1250 downwards.
20. The CHARTERS and ACCOUNT ROLLS of the Cells of LYTHAM and STAMFORD, and the Compoti of DURHAM COLLEGE, OXFORD.
21. The CHRONICLES of the Religious Houses of KIRKSTALL and NOSTELL.
22. The LIFE of ST. BEGA, and Extracts from the CHARTULARY of HOLM CULTRAM.
23. A MONASTICON of the COUNTY of NORTHUMBERLAND.

24. FOUNTAINS ABBEY. The HISTORY of its FOUNDATION by HUGH de KIRKSTALL, and the CHARTERS and ACCOUNT ROLLS of that famous House.
25. ST. MARY'S ABBEY, YORK, its ANNALS by ABBOT SIMON de WARWICK with Extracts from the CHARTULARIES.
26. The CHARTER BOOK of ST. LEONARD'S HOSPITAL at YORK, with several of the early Account Rolls, Wills of Benefactors, &c.
27. The EVIDENCES of the ANCIENT FAMILY of CALVERLEY.
28. SIMEON of DURHAM: a new edition of his Works.
29. Extracts from the WARDROBE ACCOUNTS of EDWARD I., II., and III., illustrative of their expeditions into Scotland, and other matters connected with that kingdom and the North of England.
30. The REGISTER of the GUILD of CORPUS CHRISTI at YORK, with other documents of similar character.
31. Extracts from the GUILD BOOKS of the CORPORATIONS of BERWICK, NEWCASTLE-ON-TYNE, &c.
32. LETTERS from the British Museum and State Paper Office, RELATING to the DISSOLUTION of the NORTHERN MONASTERIES.
33. The ANNALS of the PILGRIMAGE of GRACE.
34. A VOLUME of EXTRACTS from the Proceedings of the COURT of CHANCERY at DURHAM.
35. LETTERS, hitherto inedited, RELATING to the OUTRAGES, FEUDS, &c., on the BORDERS of ENGLAND and SCOTLAND.
36. A VOLUME of EARLY DIARIES.
37. MISCELLANIES, containing documents too short for separate publication, to include (*inter alia*),
    1. The Iter Boreale.
    2. Documents relating to the University established at Durham by Cromwell.
    3. The Expenses of the Scottish Fortresses in the hands of the English during the Wars of Edward I., II., and III.
38. PRESENTMENTS at Episcopal and Archidiaconal Courts.
39. A Volume of EXTRACTS from the DEPOSITIONS, &c., in the Ecclesiastical COURT of YORK, beginning in the 14th century.
40. The INJUNCTIONS of the NORTHERN BISHOPS, together with the Proceedings at the Diocesan Synods and other Meetings of the Clergy.
41. An ECCLESIASTICAL SURVEY of RICHMONDSHIRE made by BISHOP GASTRELL.
42. The CORRESPONDENCE of JOHN COSIN BISHOP of DURHAM.
43. The AUTOBIOGRAPHY of ANNE COUNTESS OF PEMBROKE, DORSET, and MONTGOMERY, with other documents relating to the House of Clifford.
44. The CORRESPONDENCE of THOMAS BAKER, (the "Coll. Jo. socius ejectus,") with the Literary Men of his day.
45. The CORRESPONDENCE of Dr. GEORGE HICKES and HILKIAH BEDFORD, the celebrated non-jurors and antiquaries.
46. The LETTERS of THOMAS, 5th LORD WHARTON, and other documents connected with his family and the County of Cumberland.
47. A VOLUME RELATING to the CAVALIERS—their Compositions and their Troubles, from the State Paper Office and the Library of the Dean and Chapter of Durham.
48. EXTRACTS from ROGER DODSWORTH'S COLLECTIONS in the Bodleian Library at Oxford.
49. The Diary of ABRAHAM DE LA PRYME, the Yorkshire Antiquary.
50. A GLOSSARY of Ancient North Country Words.

LIST OF OFFICERS & MEMBERS, JUNE, 1859.

PATRON.

The Right Reverend Bishop Maltby.

PRESIDENT.

The Venerable the Warden of the University of Durham.

VICE-PRESIDENTS.

Robert Henry Allan, Esq., F.S.A., Blackwell Grange, Darlington.
John Burrell, Esq., Durham.
The Rev. Professor Chevallier, B.D., Durham.
Rev. John Dixon Clarke, M.A., Belford Hall.
Rev. John Cundill, B.D., Durham.
Rev. Henry Douglas, M.A., Canon of Durham.
John F. Elliot, Esq., Elvet Hill, Durham.
John Fawcett, Esq., Durham.
Rev. William Greenwell, M.A., Bishop Cosin's Hall, Durham.
Edwin Guest, Esq., LL.D., Master of Caius College, Cambridge.
William Henderson, Esq., Durham.
John Hodgson Hinde, Esq., Acton House, Felton.
Sir William Lawson, Bart., F.S.A., Brough Hall, Catterick.
W. H. D. Longstaffe, Esq., Gateshead.
Francis Mewburn, Esq., Darlington.
Richard Lawrence Pemberton, Esq., Barnes, Sunderland.
Rev. Daniel Rock, D.D., 8 Clarendon Villas, Brook Green, Hammersmith.
Henry John Spearman, Esq., Burn Hall, Durham.
Rev. Joseph Stevenson, M.A., Leighton Buzzard.
Sir Walter Calverley Trevelyan, Bart., Wallington, Newcastle-on-Tyne.
The Very Rev. George Waddington, D.D., Dean of Durham.
Albert Way, Esq., F.S.A., Wonham Manor, Reigate.
Rev. C. T. Whitley, M.A., Bedlington, Morpeth.
Sir C. G. Young, Knt., F.S.A., Garter King at Arms.

SECRETARY.

The Rev. James Raine, M.A., York.

TREASURERS.

John Gough Nichols, Esq., 25 Parliament Street, Westminster.
Samuel Rowlandson, Esq., Durham.

MEMBERS.

John Addison, Esq., Preston, Lancashire. Elected 15th Dec., 1852.
The Advocate's Library, Edinburgh. 13th March, 1851.
E. N. Alexander, Esq., Halifax. 16th June, 1852.
Robert Henry Allan, Esq., F.S.A., Blackwell Grange, Darlington. (*Treasurer*, 1834—1844. *Vice-President*, 1844—1859.)†
H. P. Allison, Esq., 1 Regent Terrace, Newcastle-on-Tyne. 13th March, 1857.
Mr. George Andrews, Bookseller, Durham. 26th Sept., 1839.
The Society of Antiquaries, Newcastle-on-Tyne. 24th Sept. 1853.
Richard Atkinson, Esq., Richmond, Yorkshire. 25th Feb. 1859.*
John H. Aylmer, Esq., Low Walworth, Darlington. 12th July, 1836.
Rev. Bulkeley Bandinel, D.D., Bodley's Librarian, Oxford. 13th March, 1851.
William Beamont, Esq., Warrington. 28th Sept. 1843.
Alfred Bell, Esq., 59 Lincoln's Inn Fields, London. 31st Mar., 1849.
William Henry Blaauw, Esq., M.A., F.S.A., Secretary to the Sussex Archæological Society, Beechfield, Uckfield. 15th Dec., 1852.
R. W. Blencoe, Esq., The Hooke, near Lewes. 13th March, 1851.
Rev. J. R. Bloxam, D.D., Fellow and Bursar of Magdalen College, Oxford. 13th March, 1851.
Beriah Botfield, Esq., M.P., F.R.S., etc., Norton Hall, Daventry.†
John Bowes, Esq., Streatlam Castle, Durham.†
The Viscount Boyne, Brancepeth Castle, Durham. 15th Dec., 1852.
William Henry Brockett, Esq., Gateshead. 15th Dec., 1852.
Douglas Brown, Esq., 6 Pump Court, Temple, London. 11th March, 1858.*
Rev. John Collingwood Bruce, LL.D., etc., Secretary of the Society of Antiquaries, Newcastle-on-Tyne. 6th June, 1856.
His Grace the Duke of Buccleugh and Queensberry, Dalkeith. The first President of the Society, 1834-1837.†
Rev. W. E. Buckley, M.A., Middleton Cheney, Banbury. 13th March, 1851.
John Burrell, Esq., Durham. (*Vice-President*, 1853-59.)†
Thomas Burton, Esq., Turnham Hall, Selby. December, 1857.*
His Excellency the Earl of Carlisle, K.G., Lord Lieutenant of Ireland. 11th December, 1856.
Ralph Carr, Esq., Hedgeley, Alnwick. 26th September, 1844.
Edward Charlton, Esq., M.D., Secretary of the Society of Antiquaries, Newcastle-on-Tyne. 6th June, 1856.
Rev. J. A. Charlton, M.A., Gosforth, Newcastle-on-Tyne. 8th December, 1853.
William Henry Charlton, Esq., Hesleyside, Hexham. 31st May, 1849.
The Chetham Library, Manchester. December, 1857.*
Rev. Temple Chevallier, B.D., Professor of Mathematics and Astronomy in the University of Durham. 12th July, 1836. (*Vice-President from* 1836.)

† Those gentlemen to whose names this is appended have been members of the Society since its foundation.

* Those gentlemen to whose names an asterisk is attached, have been elected members since 1857.

Rev. J. D. Clarke, M.A., Belford Hall. 1st June, 1853. (*Vice-President*, 1855-9.)

J. W. Clarke, Esq., Fellow of Trinity College, Cambridge. December, 1857.* (*Local-Secretary*, 1858-9.)

John Clayton, Esq., Town Clerk, Newcastle-on-Tyne. 8th Dec., 1853.

Alexander Cockburn, Esq., 60 Mark Lane, London. 6th June, 1854.

E. D. Conyers, Esq., Driffield, Yorkshire. 11th December, 1856.

William Henry Cooke, Esq., 4 Elm Court, Temple, London. 6th June, 1855.

John Cookson, Esq., Meldon Park, Morpeth. 15th December, 1852.

Rev. G. E. Corrie, D.D., Master of Jesus College, Cambridge. 28th December, 1837.

Rev. Thomas Corser, Rector of Stand, Manchester. 28th Sept., 1837.

The Venerable R. C. Coxe, Archdeacon of Lindisfarne, the College, Durham. 11th March, 1858.*

Christopher Croft, Esq., Richmond, Yorkshire. 8th December, 1853.

Rev. J. G. Cromwell, M.A., Principal of the Training School, Durham. 6th June, 1856.

James Crosby, Esq., 8 Church Court, Old Jewry, London. 31st May, 1849.

James Crossley, Esq., President of the Chetham Society, Manchester. 11th March, 1858.*

Rev. John Cundill, B.D., Perpetual Curate of St. Margaret's, Durham. 31st May, 1849. (*Vice-President*, 1849-59.)

John Dangerfield, Esq., 68 Chancery Lane, London. May, 1846.

Rev. W. N. Darnell, B.D., Rector of Stanhope, Durham. 15th March, 1856.

The Right Rev. The Lord Bishop of St. David's, Abeigwili Palace, Caermarthen. 13th March, 1851.

Robert Davies, Esq., F.S.A., The Mount, York. 13th March, 1851.

James Dearden, Esq., The Manor House, Rochdale. 13th March, 1851.

Mr. M. A. Denham, Piersbridge, Darlington. 15th December, 1852.

Rev. S. P. Denning, M.A., Worcester. 14th March, 1850.

William Dickson, Esq., Alnwick. 12th July, 1836.

John Dobson, Esq., Newcastle-on-Tyne. 6th June, 1856.

Rev. Henry Douglas, M.A., Canon of Durham. 28th September, 1837. (*Vice-President*, 1853-9.)

The Right Hon. Sir David Dundas, Inner Temple, London. 30th December, 1858.*

The Viscount Dungannon, Brynkinnalt, Chirk, North Wales. 12th July, 1836.

The Right Rev. The Lord Bishop of Durham, Auckland Castle. 13th March, 1857.

The University Library, Durham. 16th June, 1858.*

W. H. Dykes, Esq., York, Secretary to the Yorkshire Architectural Society. December, 1857.* (*Local-Secretary*, 1858-9.)

Rev. John Earle, M.A., Oxford. 13th June, 1850.

Rev. John Edwards, M.A., Canon of Durham and Professor of Greek in the University of Durham. 13th March, 1851.

John F. Elliot, Esq., Elvet Hill, Durham. 12th July, 1836. (*Vice-President*, 1849-59.)

William Ellis, Esq., Gloucester. 30th December, 1858.*

C. H. Elsley, Esq., Recorder of York, Mill Mount, York. 11th March, 1858.*

The Right Rev. The Lord Bishop of Exeter. 5th December, 1853.

The Very Rev. Monsignor Eyre, Newcastle on-Tyne. 11th Dec., 1856.

James Farrer, Esq., M.P., Inglebro', near Settle, Yorkshire. 31st May, 1849.

John Fawcett, Esq., Durham. 29th September, 1842. (*Vice-President*, 1843-59.)

John Fenwick, Esq., F.S.A., Newcastle-on-Tyre. 12th Dec., 1851.

The Lord Feversham, Duncombe Park, Helmsley. 24th June, 1859.*

The Earl Fitzwilliam, Wentworth, Rotherham. December, 1857.*

William Sidney Gibson, Esq., Tynemouth. 26th September, 1844.

Mr. W. Grainge, Minskip, Boro'bridge. 25th February, 1859.*

Rev. William Greenwell, M.A., Bishop Cosin's Hall, Durham. 28th Sept., 1843. (*Treasurer*, 1843-49. *Vice-President*, 1849-59.)

Edwin Guest, Esq., LL.D., Master of Caius College, Cambridge.† (*Vice-President*, 1856-9.)

Edward Hailstone, Esq., Horton Hall, Bradford. May, 1846.

The Venerable W. A. Hale, M.A., Archdeacon of London, Canon Residentiary of St. Paul's, and Master of the Charter House. 26th September, 1839.

Robert Hall, Esq., 8 Dean's Yard, Westminster. 13th March, 1851.

Rev. George Hans Hamilton, M.A., Vicar of Berwick-upon-Tweed. 31st May, 1849.

Philip Charles Hardwick, Esq., F.S.A., 21, Cavendish Square, London. 14th March, 1850.

Mr. W. Harrison, Market Place, Ripon. 30th December, 1858*

John Harward, Esq., Stourbridge, Worcestershire. 6th June, 1854.

The Right Hon. T. E. Headlam, M.P., Judge Advocate General, and Chancellor of the Dioceses of Durham and Ripon, 20 Ashley Place, Victoria Street, London. 13th December, 1855.

William Henderson, Esq., Durham. May, 1847. (*Treasurer*, 1847-58. *Vice-President*, 1858-9.)

Rev. W. G. Henderson, D.C.L., Principal of Victoria College, Jersey. 31st May, 1849. (*Secretary*, 1849-52.)

John Hodgson Hinde, Esq., Acton House, Felton.† (*Vice-President*, 1843-59.)

R. W. Hodgson, Esq., North Dene, Gateshead. 11th Dec., 1856.

Rev. Henry Holden, D.D., Head Master of Durham Grammar School. 16th June, 1858.*

Rev. Henry Humble, M.A., Canon of St. Ninian's, Perth. 31st May, 1849.

Richard Charles Hussey, Esq., F.S.A., 16 King William Street, Strand, London. 12th July, 1836.

Alan William Hutchinson, Esq., Durham. September, 1841.

Timothy Hutton, Esq., Marske Hall, Richmond, Yorkshire. 28th September, 1843.

Rev. Dr. Hymers, Brandsburton, Beverley. 30th December, 1858.*

Robert H. Ingham, Esq., M.P., Westoe, South Shields.†

C. J. D. Ingledew, Esq., LL.D., Northallerton. 13th Dec., 1855.

Rev. Henry Jenkyns, D.D., Canon of Durham, and Professor of Divinity in the University of Durham. September, 1838.
Rev. J. F. Johnson, Sherburn, Durham. 11th December, 1856.
William Kell, Esq., F.S.A., Gateshead. 19th December, 1854.
Rev. J. W. Kempe, B.A., West Harnham, Salisbury. 8th Dec., 1853.
John Bailey Langhorne, Esq., Wakefield. 31st May, 1849. (*Local-Secretary,* 1858-9.)
Sir William Lawson, Bart., F.S.A., Brough Hall, Catterick. (*Vice-President,* 1836-59.)†
George Lawton, Esq., Nunthorpe, York. 12th July, 1836.
The Leeds Library. 11th December, 1856.
Rev. H. G. Liddell, M.A., Rector of Easington, Durham. 28th September, 1837.
Lincoln's Inn Library, London. 13th March, 1851.
Ralph Lindsay, M.A., F.S.A., Biggin Lodge, Norwood. 26th September, 1839.
William Linskill, Esq., Morwick Hall, Alnwick. 13th Dec., 1855.
The Liverpool Athenæum. 6th June, 1855.
The London Library, 12 St. James' Square, London. 13th Mar., 1851.
William Hylton Dyer Longstaffe, Esq., F.S.A., Gateshead. 17th Mar., 1855. (*Vice-President,* 1859. *Local-Secretary,* 1858-9.)
Rev. J. L. Low, The Forest, Middleton-in-Teesdale, Durham. 16th June, 1858.*
Rev. H. R. Luard, Fellow of Trinity College, Cambridge. 24th June, 1859.*
John Whitefoord Mackenzie, Esq., W.S., Vice-President S.A. Scotland, and M.R.S.N.A. Cop., 16 Royal Circus, Edinbro'. 14th July, 1835.
The Right Rev. the Lord Bishop of Manchester. 11th Dec., 1856.
Thomas Mason, Esq., Copt Hewick, Ripon.†
F. C. Matthews, Esq., Driffield, Yorkshire. 11th December, 1856.
Francis Mewburn, Esq., Darlington.† (*Vice-President,* 1849-59.)
Richard Monckton Milnes, Esq., M.P., Fryston Hall, Pontefract. 30th December, 1858.*
Mr. John Mitchell, 24 Wardour Street, London. 24th June, 1859.*
C. T. J. Moore, Esq., Frampton Hall, Boston. 25th Feb., 1859*
Rev. James Morton, B.D., Prebendary of Lincoln, and Vicar of Holbeach. 12th July, 1836.
G. G. Mounsey, Esq., Carlisle. 17th March, 1855. (*Local-Secretary,* 1858-9.)
The Right Honorable J. R. Mowbray, M.P., Cambridge Square, Hyde Park, London. 8th December, 1853.
The Literary and Philosophical Society, Newcastle-on-Tyne. 17th March, 1855.
John Bowyer Nichols, Esq., F.S.A., 25 Parliament Street, Westminster.†
John Gough Nichols, Esq., F.S.A., 25 Parliament Street, Westminster.† (*Treasurer from the foundation of the Society.*)
His Grace the Duke of Northumberland, K.G., F.S.A., &c., Alnwick Castle. 13th March, 1851.
John Ord, Esq., Darlington. 30th December, 1858.*

Rev. George Ornsby, Fishlake, Doncaster. 24th June, 1859.*

Rev. Sir Frederick G. Ouseley, Bart., M.A., Precentor of Hereford, and Professor of Music in the University of Oxford. 11th December, 1856.

John Henry Parker, Esq., Oxford. 24th September, 1840.

Edward Peacock, Esq., The Manor Farm, Bottesford, Brigg, Lincolnshire. 10th June, 1857.

Joseph Pease, Esq., Darlington. 19th December, 1854.

Rev. John Pedder, M.A., Rector of Meldon, Morpeth. 14th March, 1850. (*Secretary*, 1852—1854.)

Richard Lawrence Pemberton, Esq., Barnes, Sunderland. 13th December, 1855. (*Vice-President*, 1857-9.)

James Stovin Pennyman, Esq., Ormesby Hall, Middlesbro'. 8th December, 1853.

Rev. G. H. Philips, M.A., Dringhouses, York. 30th Dec., 1858.*

Rev. Ralph Platt, Durham. 30th December, 1858.*

Mr. Thomas Pigg, Newcastle-on-Tyne. 6th June, 1856.

Mr. Bernard Quarritch, 16 Castle Street, Leicester Square, London. 24th February, 1853.

Rev. James Raine, M.A., York. 12th Dec., 1851. (*Secretary*, 1854-9)

Stephen Ram, Esq., Ramsfort, Gory, Ireland. 6th June, 1856.

The Lord Ravensworth, Ravensworth Castle, Gateshead. 6th June, 1856.

Charles H. Rickards, Esq., Manchester. 13th March, 1851.

Joseph Robertson, Esq., 23 Buccleugh Place, Edinbro'. 13th March, 1851.

Rev. C. B. Robinson, M.A., Fellow of the University of Durham, York. 12th December, 1851. (*Local-Secretary*, 1858-9.)

Rev. Daniel Rock, D.D., 8 Clarendon Villas, Brook Green, Hammersmith. 14th March, 1850. (*Vice-President*, 1851-9. *Local-Secretary*, 1858-9.)

Samuel Rowlandson, Esq., Durham. September, 1841. (*Treasurer*, 1858-9.)

J. B. Rudd, Esq., Gisbro', Yorkshire. 13th March, 1857.

Mr. John Sampson, Bookseller, York. December, 1857.*

Simon Thomas Scrope, Esq., Jun., Danby Hall, Bedale. 16th June, 1858.*

Rev. E. H. Shipperdson, The Hermitage, Chester-le-Street. 6th June, 1856.

Henry Silvertop, Esq., Minsteracres, Gateshead. 21st May, 1849.

The Library of Sion College, London. December, 1857.*

Rev. Richard Skipsey, M.A., Bishopwearmouth.†

Henry Smales, Esq., Durham. 16th June, 1852.

Rev. Henry Soames, Esq., M.A., Chancellor of St. Paul's and Rector of Stapleford Tawney, Romford. 13th March, 1851.

Henry John Spearman, Esq., Burn Hall, Durham.† (*Vice-President*, 1853-9.)

The Statistical Society, 12 St. James' Square, London. 30th Dec., 1858.*

George Stephens, Esq., Professor of English Literature in the University of Copenhagen. 24th September, 1853.

Mr. W. F. Stephenson, Kirkgate, Ripon. 30th December, 1858.*
Rev. Joseph Stevenson, M.A., Vicar of Leighton Buzzard.† (*Vice-President*, 1836-59.)
John Stuart, Esq., Secretary of the Spalding Club, and of the Society of Antiquaries of Scotland, Register Office, Edinburgh. 24th February, 1853. (*Local-Secretary*, 1858-9.)
Rev. W. Stubbs, Vicar of Navestock, Romford. 13th March, 1851
Mr. Robert Sunter, Bookseller, York. December, 1857.*
Henry Edward Surtees, Esq., Daue End, Ware, Herts. 10th June, 1857.
Robert Lambton Surtees, Esq., Redworth, Darlington.†
Robert S. Surtees, Esq., Hamsterley Hall, Gateshead. 28th September, 1843.
Sir S. V. Surtees, Chief Justice of the Island of Mauritius. 8th December, 1853.
Clement Tudway Swanston, Esq., Q.C., F.R.S., F.S.A., 51 Chancery Lane, London. September, 1841.
John Sykes, Esq., M.D., Doncaster. 24th June, 1859.*
The Lord Talbot de Malahide, M.R.I.A., President of the Archæological Institute, Malahide Castle, Dublin. 15th Dec., 1852.
Henry Taylor, Esq., Colonial Office, London. 6th June, 1852.
Thomas Greenwood Teale, Esq., Leeds. 8th December, 1853.
Lord Adolphus Vane Tempest, M.P. 15th December, 1852.
Joseph Francis Tempest, Esq., Nether Hall, Doncaster. 12th June, 1836.
Christopher Temple, Esq., Q.C., Temporal Chancellor of the Diocese of Durham, Temple, London. 6th June, 1856.
Stephen Temple, Esq., 15 Upper Gower Street, London. 11th Dec., 1856.
Ven. Archdeacon Thorp, D.D., F.R.S., Warden of the University of Durham. September, 1838. (*Vice-President,* 1844—1849. *President,* 1849—1859.)
John Tiplady, Esq., Town Clerk, Durham. 14th March, 1850.
Sir Walter Calverley Trevelyan, Bart., F.S.A., etc., Wallington, Newcastle-on Tyne.† (*Vice-President from the foundation of the Society.*)
Mr. William Trueman, Durham.†
Charles Tucker, Esq., F.S.A., Secretary of the Archæological Institute, 26 Suffolk Street, Pall Mall. 15th December, 1852.
Anselm Turner, Esq., 23 Park Crescent (N.W.), London. 8th Dec., 1853.
Henry Turner, Esq., Low Heaton Haugh, Newcastle on-Tyne. 12th July, 1836.
Rev. James F. Turner, North Tidcombe, Wilts. 14th March, 1850.
The Earl Vane. 17th March, 1855.
Lord Harry Vane, M.P. September, 1841.
The Very Rev. George Waddington, D,D., etc., Dean of Durham. September, 1841. (*Vice-President*, 1843—1859.)
Rev. Joseph Waite, M.A., Tutor in the University of Durham. June, 1852.

Rev. John Ward, M.A., Rector of Wath, Ripon. 6th June, 1856. (*Local-Secretary,* 1858-9.)

Edmund Waterton, Esq., F.S.A., Walton Hall, Wakefield. 10th March, 1856

Albert Way, Esq., F.S A., etc., Secretary to the Archæological Institute, Wonham Manor, Reigate. 15th December, 1852. (*Vice-President,* 1859.)

George Wetwan, Esq., Bridlington. December, 1857.*

His Excellency Monsr. Van de Weyer, Belgian Ambassador, 50 Portland Place, London. September, 1841.

Gerard Wharton, Esq., Lincoln's Inn Fields, London. 26th September, 1844.

Rev. William Whewell, D.D., etc., Master of Trinity College, Cambridge. 12th July, 1836.

Robert White, Esq., Claremont Place, Newcastle-on-Tyne. 12th December, 1851.

Rev. C. T. Whitley, M.A., Vicar of Bedlington, Morpeth.† (*Vice-President,* 1836—1859.)

William Woodman, Esq., Town Clerk, Morpeth. 31st May, 1849.

John Francis Wright, Esq., Kelvedon Hall, Essex. 10th June, 1857.

The Library of the Dean and Chapter of York. 13th March, 1857.

Sir Charles George Young, Knt., F.S.A., etc., Garter King at Arms, London.† (*Vice-President,* 1836—1859.)

Joseph Young, Esq., Hartford House, Morpeth. 11th Dec., 1856.

The Earl of Zetland, Aske Hall, Richmond, Yorkshire. 13th March, 1851.

MEMBERS ELECTED DEC. 1859.

Edward Akroyd, Esq., Bankfield, Halifax.

Mr. J. R. Appleton, Western Hills, Durham.

Sir Edward Blackett, Bart., Matfen, Newcastle-on-Tyne.

Rev. Wm. Collins, Knaresbro'.

R. R. Dees, Esq., Newcastle-on-Tyne.

The Hon. and Very Rev. Augustus Duncombe, DD., Dean of York.

Viscount Galway, M.P., Serlby Hall, Bawtry.

H. H. Gibbs, Esq., St. Dunstan's, Regent's Park, London.

Earl de Grey and Ripon, Studley Park, Ripon.

The Lord Herries, Everingham Park, Hayton, Yorkshire.

A. J. B. Hope, Esq., Connaught Place, Hyde Park.

Rev. H. D. Ingilby, Fellow of Magd. Coll., Oxon., Ripley Castle, Yorkshire.

Henry Jackson, Esq., St. James' Row, Sheffield.

Rev. John Kenrick, York.

C. Scott Murray, Esq., Danesfield, Great Marlow.

Wm. Rivington, Esq., Hampstead Heath, London.

Charles Freville Surtees, Esq., Chobham Park, Chobham, Surrey.

Christopher Sykes, Esq., Sledmere, Yorkshire.

J. R. Walbran, Esq., F.S.A., Fall-croft, Ripon.

Christopher M. Webster, Esq., Pallion, Bishopwearmouth.

ACCOUNT OF SAMUEL ROWLANDSON, ESQ., AS TREASURER OF THE SURTEES SOCIETY,

FROM JANUARY 1ST, 1857, TO DECEMBER 31ST, 1858.

Dr.	£	s.	d.
To balance in the hands of the Treasurer on last account	176	12	1
To amount of Subscriptions received by Samuel Rowlandson, Esq., and J. G. Nichols, Esq., from 1 January, 1857, to 31 December, 1858	405	11	0
To additional Donations received towards defraying the cost of publishing Bishop Hatfield's Survey	21	5	0
To amount received of Mr. George Andrews, for balance of Sale of Books, after paying expences	37	6	4
	£640	14	5

Cr.	£	s.	d.
By paid Dr. Raine, for editing the Durham Obituary Rolls	22	10	0
By paid Messrs. J. B. Nichols and Sons, printing the Durham Obituary Rolls, and binding 300 copies, &c. &c.	59	13	6
By paid for binding 50 copies Ebchester Roll	1	13	4
By paid Messrs. Mitchell and Son, printing Bishop Hatfield's Survey, Glossary, Index, &c. &c.	69	19	3
By paid for printing, &c., 750 copies of Report of the Society	5	19	9
By paid Rev. Wm. Greenwell, for editing Bishop Hatfield's Survey.	42	0	0
By paid Rev. C. Best Robinson, editing Rural Economy of Yorkshire	12	12	0
By paid Messrs. T. and J. Pigg, printing Rural Economy of Yorkshire, and binding 300 copies	54	12	10
By paid Mr. Wm. Monkhouse, for lithograph drawing, and printing 350 copies of the same, for Rural Economy of Yorkshire	5	0	0
By paid Rev. James Raine, for editing, &c., York Wills, Vol. II.	60	8	0
By paid Messrs. Duncan and Son, printing	1	13	0
By paid Messrs. T. and J. Pigg, for printing 350 and binding 300 copies of the Court of High Commission, Durham	78	18	11
By paid W. H. D. Longstaffe, Esq., for editing and preparing Index of the Court of High Commission, Durham	47	4	0
By paid Messrs. Duncan and Son, for printing circulars	1	18	6
By paid Rev. James Raine, for editing York Fabric Rolls, 24 sheets £2 2s. per sheet, and for preparing Index for the same	55	8	0
By paid Messrs. Mitchell and Son, for printing 350 copies of York Fabric Rolls, Glossary, Index, &c	98	17	6
By paid Messrs. Leighton, Son, and Hodge, for binding 300 copies of the same	9	17	8
By paid Mr. William Monkhouse, for engraving 350 copies of five historical plans of York Cathedral	2	10	0
By paid Assistant Treasurer 2 years' salary	2	2	0
By postage paid by Treasurer in 2 years	3	0	0
By Balance in hands of Saml. Rowlandson, Esq., Treasurer	4	16	2
	£640	14	5

We, the Auditors appointed to credit the Accounts of the Surtees Society, report to the Society that the Treasurers have exhibited to us their Accounts, from the 1st of January, 1857, to the 31st of December, 1858, and that we have examined the said Accounts, and find the same to be correct; and we further report that the above is an accurate Abstract of the Receipts and Expenditure of the Society during the period to which we have referred. As witness our hands

JOHN CUNDILL.

www.ingramcontent.com/pod-product-compliance
Lightning Source LLC
LaVergne TN
LVHW021147110826
845150LV00005B/1143

* 9 7 8 1 4 2 5 5 4 7 4 0 0 *